# ALBERT CAMUS

# ALBERT CAMUS

a biography

Herbert R. Lottman

DOUBLEDAY & COMPANY, INC.
GARDEN CITY, NEW YORK
1979

ISBN: 0-385-11664-0
Library of Congress Catalog Card Number 78–8199
Copyright © 1979 by Herbert R. Lottman
Printed in the United States of America

*To all those who helped me
for truth's sake
and to those who helped me
for love of their friend Camus.*

A première vue la vie de l'homme est plus intéressante que ses oeuvres. Elle fait un tout obstiné et tendu. L'unité d'esprit y règne. Il y a un souffle unique à travers toutes ces années. Le roman, c'est lui. A revoir évidemment.

*Carnets,* II


Pour l'acteur comme pour l'homme absurde, une mort prématurée est irréparable. Rien ne peut compenser la somme des visages et des siècles qu'il eût, sans cela, parcourus. Mais, de toute façon, il s'agit de mourir. Car l'acteur est sans doute partout, mais le temps l'entraîne aussi et fait avec lui son effet.

*Le Mythe de Sisyphe*

# CONTENTS

## Part II   Exile

## Part III   Fame

## Part IV   Forty

Part V    The Road Back

# PERSONAL FOREWORD

I had imagined biography to be written in an atmosphere of pipe smoke, in a wood-paneled study, perhaps even with a quill pen. Instead my chief activity during the preparation of this book would be field investigation, tracking down eyewitnesses, convincing some of them to break what they had felt to be honorable silence, urging even sworn enemies or those indifferent to offer, at least this once, full and objective witness. I was obliged to uncover original documents, often lovingly preserved, but also innocuous-seeming scraps, tracts, clippings. Often my greatest joy would be to locate a lost but capital source, or to confront a reluctant witness with information prompting his own fuller confession. My constant concern was how to deal with the mountain of previously published, widely disseminated, and totally erroneous data: confused chronologies, inaccurately dated manuscripts and letters. A whole shelf of books about Camus had been based on such materials, and I winced each time I saw a pile of them in a bookshop near a university. Clearly everyone interested in Albert Camus was getting his serving of error.

An incidental effect of Algerian independence (1962) is the gradual effacement of evidence of the 130-year presence of the French in that territory. The biographer of a man who was born and who spent all his formative years in French Algeria is confronted with the destruction or disappearance of vital records, not to speak of the dispersion of surviving witnesses. Finally the best records of Camus' childhood are the impressionistic, only slightly fictionalized evocations by the author himself, whose natural reserve (the *pudeur* endemic to the French which exasperates many visitors—or commands their respect) otherwise made the biographer's task a formidable one.

And if the Camus heirs allowed me access to documents and manuscripts, it was nevertheless on the understanding that they take no responsibility for the manner in which I have utilized or interpreted this material. They did not see or approve the book; this is no "authorized" biography. But I am grateful for the patient help of Madame Albert Camus and of her sister Christiane Faure. This book is my thanks. Camus himself was afraid of *"biophages,"* but I'd like to think that if he could read the present work he would understand the author's intentions.

For one of the risks of literary biography is that the reader may be lulled into thinking that all the essential is here, one need read no further, when in fact the essence of the life of the writer is his expression. Sometimes the biography of an author can seem like a banquet from which the guest of honor is absent. So what the biographer must do is to draw attention to the work without pretending to substitute his book for the collected works of his subject.

# ALBERT CAMUS

# Introduction

◆

# ALBERT CAMUS 1913–1960

Camus seemed to have everything: youth, good looks, early success (sufficient to evoke jealousy, even bitter jealousy, among some famous contemporaries). He had first come to the attention of his country with a short novel, *L'Etranger* (The Stranger), and this stranger obtained even greater fame, and an international reputation, with *La Peste* (The Plague). Sharing the mystical aura of the underground resistance, he had come out of the Second World War a young hero. In the early postwar years his daily newspaper *Combat* was a moral guide to a generation demanding change. A longtime friend (and then an enemy), Jean-Paul Sartre, recalled the magic of that time in an often-quoted description of Camus: "the admirable coming together of a person, an action, and a work." No one seemed to bear more of the hope of young France and of the world.

He shirked no battle then, became a friend in need of Spanish anti-Fascist exiles, victims of Stalinism, young radicals and conscientious objectors, after having been among the first to protest unequal treatment of North Africa's Moslems. When he received the Nobel Prize for Literature, the Swedish Academy cited him as one of the world's foremost literary antagonists of totalitarianism.

For at a remarkably early age—only Rudyard Kipling had been younger—he was given that prize. "His is one of the few literary voices that has emerged from the chaos of the post-war world with the balanced, sober outlook of humanism," a New York *Times* editorial greeted the award.

But by then Albert Camus was in trouble, and he knew that he was in trouble. The controversy provoked by his outspoken support of unfashionable causes, private stress brought on by the Algerian war, family illness and his own, had in incalculable proportions led to writing block—years of it (even if screened from public view by an abundance of ancillary activity). His worst critics of right and left had known how to make use of that, mocking him as on the decline, a self-satisfied impostor. On his side, the young man raised in poverty and humility who had always kept away from literary salons and literary glories, awards and decorations, refused to become reconciled to being a statue labeled "Albert Camus." "If they only knew who I really was," he lamented to his secretary, one of his few confidantes.

And then at last he thought that he had found a way to climb out of the morass: in a new house, a new routine. A return to important literary work (a major novel) and to his favorite kind of work (the theater) was now to become possible.

It was then that he was killed in an automobile accident.

# PART I

———◆———

# Mediterraneans

# 1

---◆---

# THE FIRST MAN

> He sees in outline the image of his father. Then all is
> erased. Finally there is nothing. It was always like that
> on this earth.
>
> Note for *Le Premier Homme**

When Albert Camus died in an automobile accident on the road back
to Paris on January 4, 1960, he was carrying with him a bulging black
leather briefcase, the expanding accordion type, with reinforced corners
and a three-position lock he never used. Caked in mud, it was found on
the road near the tree against which the car had smashed. Inside the
briefcase, along with personal effects such as a journal, some letters,
and a passport, was the manuscript of the novel he had been working
on in his recently acquired Provençal retreat at Lourmarin. The book
would have been called *Le Premier Homme* (The First Man). Camus
had written only part of the first draft—145 closely written manuscript
pages, some eighty thousand words. According to the schedule he had
mapped out for the project and for himself in the new year just beginning, he would not have completed the final version before 1961.

It would be difficult to overestimate the importance he attached to
this work in progress. In the last decade he had published two major
books, *L'Homme révolté* (The Rebel), a political essay, and the short,
curious monologue of *La Chute* (The Fall), considered his most personal book by those who had the keys to it, composed as it had been in
the wake of the storm which had crashed over his shoulders with the
appearance of *L'Homme révolté,* leading to the shock of his break with
Jean-Paul Sartre. It also coincided with a personal crisis, illness in the
family. Then in October 1957 came the announcement of his Nobel

---

* Quoted in Roger Quilliot, *La Mer et les prisons.*

Prize, which if it brought joy to his friends and admirers seemed one more affliction to its beneficiary, implying as he thought it did that all his important work was behind him. His enemies in the literary and political worlds, in any case, had been quick to make that point.

But Albert Camus was just as certain that his work was only beginning. In a state of psychological stress bordering on depression, increasingly alarmed by the nationalist insurrection in his native Algeria, harassed by those who wished him to play a role in that drama which he himself felt unable to assume, he believed that he was functioning at only half-speed. Of course he could pursue his theatrical activity, adapting and producing other people's work, of course he was publishing occasional essays and articles for the press. Yet he was clearly dissatisfied with his incapacity to undertake the significant work which he felt he had in him.

Now he was beginning to write again. With the money received from the Nobel prize he had purchased the house in Lourmarin, a village off main roads in the southern French Vaucluse region he loved. He was determined to live an increasing proportion of his time here. In what was to be the final year of his life, 1959, he spent part of the spring in Lourmarin, returned in midsummer, and then settled down in November to work through the end-of-year holidays.

So that *Le Premier Homme* would be the return to creation he had been promising his friends and himself (through his journal). But he wanted it to be considerably more than that. He was hoping to write what he called to friends, not jokingly, his *War and Peace*. In his journal he reminded himself: "He was born in 1828. He wrote War and Peace between 1863 and 1869. Between the ages of 35 and 41." Camus, born in November 1913, was forty-five in the year he began to work seriously on *Le Premier Homme,* although he had been planning it for a dozen years. Among personal papers found after his death was an elaborately prepared astrological prediction which contained the phrase: "The work bringing immortality takes place between 1960 and 1965." In any case it would be, as he told reporters in Stockholm the day before he received the Nobel Prize from the hands of the King of Sweden, "the novel of my maturity."

Leo Tolstoy had taken as his stage the great and declining empire of the Czars and the Napoleonic invasion of Russia. Camus would write the epic novel of Algeria, then still a French territory. He had lived there over half of his life, all of his formative years, so that the book would also be a growing-up novel.

Settlers, most of them penniless, had come to Algeria from all parts of France, but also from Spain, Italy, and other European nations, to build what they saw as a new country with limitless possibilities. Algeria was a melting pot, its pioneers winning if not the wealth they hoped for then the right to live under French protection alongside the large indigenous majority. The parallel with the colonization of the New World was not lost on the settlers. Camus himself would say (in *L'Eté*): "The French of Algeria are a bastard race, composed of unexpected mixtures. Spaniards and Alsatians, Italians, Maltese, Jews, Greeks, finally met here. These brutal cross-breedings produced, as in America, happy results."

He was one of these unexpected mixtures. Of Spanish ancestry on his mother's side, he believed (without foundation, as will shortly be seen) that his father's family migrated from Alsace, that eternal battleground between France and Germany. Europeans who migrated to Algeria virtually waived their ancestry. Like soldiers of the Foreign Legion who abandon their identities when they enlist, like former prisoners and other rejects of society who assume a new life in a far-off colony, these settlers who found a place in the countryside or in an old or a new town among the Berbers and Arabs of North Africa were given an opportunity to start afresh. They could be what they made of themselves. It was happening at the same time and in the same way in the United States of America but was then no longer possible in old Europe.

The First Man, then, was the first-generation French Algerian. It was Albert Camus' father, who was killed in World War I before Albert was a year old. But it was also Albert Camus himself, growing up in a cultural and historical vacuum accentuated by his family's illiteracy, symbolized by a home without books. "Thus I imagine a first man who starts at zero," he told an interviewer as early as 1954, "who can neither read nor write, who has neither morality nor religion. It will be, if you like, an education, but without an educator."[1]* He also informed his former teacher and lifelong mentor, Jean Grenier, that at age forty he was ready to write his *éducation* (à la Rousseau), and indeed he was beginning to outline its contents at that time, six years before his death.[2] Camus did not live long enough to see his First Man as the last man. For the Moslem Algerians, who had acquired a sense of nationhood in the mid-twentieth-century thrust of nationalism, would take possession of this territory only two years after Albert Camus' fatal accident.

*Le Premier Homme* in its present form (the family has not authorized its publication) is a painstakingly detailed description of the sor-

* Footnote numbers that are repeated in a chapter refer to the same source as the footnote with that number.

rows and the joys of growing up in French Algeria, in the shadow of a mythical father.[3] Camus had thought of calling his book *Adam*.[4]

The *first* First Man had to be the father of Albert Camus, for the son could not trace the paternal line much beyond him. Nearly everything he would learn about his father and his father's parents would come to young Albert from his mother and his mother's mother, neither of whom could read or write. Written records were virtually nonexistent. It has often been said and written that the Camus family migrated from Alsace; Albert Camus himself was convinced that his paternal grandparents, Alsatians, had opted for France in 1871, as he wrote in his preface to *Actuelles III*. The authorized edition of Camus' works accredits this version of the family's origin. And then in the autobiographical novel he was writing at the time of his death he would attempt to give an epic dimension to the arrival of the Alsatians; although he probably did not have the analogy in mind, his future readers may be reminded of the legendary ocean voyages of the Pilgrims, and their landing on the shores of the New World. If there has been any variation in the family legend, it is in the story that the Camus came not from Alsace but from the neighboring province of Lorraine. Albert's cousin Emile Camus, for example, was told this by his own mother. Albert's brother Lucien felt that both "Camus" and "Cormery" (maiden name of their paternal grandmother) are typical of Lorraine. He also recalled hearing his mother's sister, Aunt Marguerite, refer to his father's family as "those Germans." The epithet might be applied to natives either of Alsace or of Lorraine, since the Moselle district of Lorraine contains a German-speaking population.

Alsace? Lorraine? In the context of Algerian colonization the ensuing story would have been the same. When the Franco-Prussian War ended in January 1871 with the siege and fall of Paris, one result was the cession of the Alsace-Lorraine provinces to Germany. By the Treaty of Frankfurt the inhabitants of these provinces were offered the opportunity to elect French citizenship and the right to live in France. To help in the settlement of this new population, the French legislature voted to attribute nearly 250,000 acres of the best available land in Algeria to migrants from Alsace and Lorraine who opted for French nationality.

In the final decade of his life Albert Camus made a pilgrimage to Ouled Fayet, where he knew that his father's parents had lived, in an attempt to trace the origins of the family. Had he succeeded in his quest, his findings would have appeared in the early pages of *Le Premier Homme*. They do not. In the small book he wrote on his student Albert Camus, Jean Grenier revealed that when Camus had tried to trace his origins he discovered that Algerian municipal authorities do not possess this information, which in mainland France is a part of every Frenchman's birthright.

Family legend can seldom have been as misleading as it turns out to have been in the case of Albert Camus. The biographer begins with the discovery that the Camus name—see any genealogical dictionary—is present in widely separated parts of France: in Lorraine and points north and east certainly, but also as far west as Brittany, as far south as Provence. There exists for the historian (and any Frenchman can obtain this information about himself and his family) a public records office called the Etat Civil, which since the late eighteenth century has been recording the vital statistics of every citizen of France. Algeria was part of the French nation, and the same type of record was maintained for inhabitants of that territory. Then why didn't Camus, in the search for his father and his father's father, call upon the Etat Civil? We shall never know.

Whatever the reason, the fact is that Camus' biographer possesses information that neither Camus nor any member of his family ever had. And this information simply overturns the myth of Algerian ancestry. It places the Camus line in Algeria a full generation earlier than has been believed. And there is the irony that in his search for ancestors Camus could have found some of them in the region where he lived for over a year during World War II, when he was at times so desperately alone, and where he would return many times in pilgrimage or to rest.[5]

The first recorded Camus was named Claude, born in 1809 in Bordeaux, the large southwest French port and wine center. With his wife Marie-Thérèse (née Béléoud) he migrated to Algeria at the very dawn of French settlement of the colony.[6] They found a home in the agricultural village of Ouled Fayet (in Arabic "of the Fayet tribe or family"), on the outskirts of Dély Ibrahim, near Algiers. The villages of Dély Ibrahim and Ouled Fayet lie in a stretch of hill country known as the Sahel, a narrow ridge just inland from the Mediterranean Sea which runs a sinuous path parallel to the shore for about sixty miles (one hundred kilometers) between Algiers and Cherchel to the west.

We can imagine that the Claude Camus had been poor or at least landless back in France. Their son, we shall soon see, would never learn to read and write (but that had something to do with the absence of schools in the new colony). Whatever they hoped to find in French Algeria, it must have been a harsher life than they had been promised. The French had not yet completed the pacification of the Algerian territory. Their military conquest, which had been undertaken after a series of real and imaginary incidents culminating in the landing of troops in

1830, was to be pursued by an army of over 100,000 men under Marshal Thomas Bugeaud. From 1841 to 1847 the main effort would be directed against the legendary warrior Abd el-Kader. Although the French were more or less in control of the territory by the time of the Revolution of 1848, the final battles against the Berbers of Kabylie would be waged until 1857. All the while, colonization was being encouraged, and by 1848 the settlers numbered nearly 100,000. If life was rough in the colony for the newcomers, it was rougher still for the native Moslem population. Faced with a Wild West frontier mentality, the government in Paris often had to exercise as much effort to protect the Moslems and their lands as to encourage colonization by mainland Europeans.

The son of Claude and Marie-Thérèse, Baptiste Jules Marius Camus, was born not in Ouled Fayet but in Marseilles, on November 3, 1842. We can only guess that his mother journeyed there from Algiers (regular boat service connected the two ports) to obtain proper medical care as well as respite from the war then raging against Abd el-Kader. Baptiste Camus (and it is he who in Albert Camus' family legend migrated from Alsace after 1871) pursued his father's work as a farmer in Ouled Fayet.

He married Marie-Hortense Cormery, an Ouled Fayet girl, at the town hall of that village on December 30, 1873. "Town hall" is perhaps not the right term for it; an old blockhouse was utilized for official functions such as these. Ouled Fayet was not important enough to have a town administration of its own, so that the mayor of neighboring Dély Ibrahim and his deputies performed whatever public acts were necessary. The little pillbox fort was also symbolic of the colonial war which was only then drawing to an end. Later, and until Algerian independence in 1962, the pacification of the natives would be commemorated in Dély Ibrahim by a monument to a member of Napoleon's corps of engineers who had mapped out the area in preparation for the French landing, and a hilltop memorial to the soldiers of the 1830 expeditionary force, represented by a bust of their general, the Duc des Cars.

Another thing we know about this marriage, thanks to records of the Etat Civil, is that Albert Camus' grandfather did not sign his name to the marriage act, for he could not write.

If the Camus were from Bordeaux, what about the Cormerys? Are they the link to Alsace-Lorraine? Again no. Mathieu Just Cormery, father of the bride Marie-Hortense, migrated to Ouled Fayet from the Ardèche in south-central France, a mountainous district of forests and fertile valleys, although on balance the rural population is poorer than it is rich. Mathieu was born in 1826 in Silhac (son of Julien Cormery and Elisabeth Dumont), in a countryside of small farms on hilly slopes, whose inhabitants were occupied in cattle and goat-raising, raising wheat and tree fruit. In the nineteenth century the region was more densely populated than it is now. Today if the stranger passes through Silhac, it may be that he has lost his way to neighboring Vernoux-en-Vivarais, a popular vacation community offering pleasant walks or riding through wooded mountain scenery, views of the Rhône River valley, a visit to the ruins of an old castle-fort on the frontiers of the Languedoc region. But what is more significant is that Albert Camus lived not far from Silhac in virtual exile during what must have been the longest year of his life, during the grim Nazi occupation of France, when he was cut off from his family and his friends in Algeria. Le Chambon-sur-Lignon, where he resided then, is less than thirty miles (fifty kilometers) from his great-grandparents' ancestral home.

Marie-Hortense Cormery, Albert's paternal grandmother, was born in Ouled Fayet in 1852, the daughter of Mathieu Just Cormery and Marguerite (née Leonard). When Marie-Hortense married Baptiste Camus, her father was dead only a month, and although she just turned twenty-one it was recorded that her mother consented to the marriage.

Baptiste is listed in the marriage act as a farmer, although family legend has it that he was a blacksmith by trade; perhaps he was good at both jobs. He and Marie-Hortense would have five children. The first two were girls, then came three boys in a row, and Albert Camus' father Lucien Auguste was the last of the lot. Baptiste Camus was just forty-four when he died. His wife is believed by family legend to have died at the same time or soon after; in fact she survived him by seven years. Their two daughters Thérèse and Marie were placed as domestic servants, the two oldest sons were taken in by a maternal aunt, sister of Marie-Hortense, at Chéraga, less than two miles (three kilometers) north of Dély Ibrahim, where she and her husband were small landowners.

That left Albert's father Lucien Auguste Camus. (His middle name is used here to distinguish him from his son, Albert Camus' older brother Lucien.) We know that Lucien Auguste was born on November 28, 1885; he was just a year old when his father died. Too young to be of any use, he was left by his older brothers and sisters in a Protestant orphanage. The story goes that at some point in his adolescence he ran away from the orphanage, and was then placed as an apprentice laborer in a vineyard at Chéraga.

Although it should not have been easier to trace his mother's Spanish family than his father's purely French one, Albert Camus himself had been able to go as far back as his great-grandparents Miguel

Sintes Sottero and Margarita Cursach Doncella, who were married in Ciudadela at the westernmost tip of the Balearic island of Minorca, a Spanish territory. They had migrated to Algeria before the birth of Camus' maternal grandfather Etienne Sintes,* who was born in Algiers in 1850. Camus' maternal grandmother Catherine Marie Cardona (and not simply Marie Cardona, as some who found her named in *L'Etranger* have thought) was born in 1857 on the opposite coast of Minorca, in the village of San Luis on the outskirts of the capital, Mahón, where most of the island's population lives. Catherine Cardona was the daughter of José Cardona y Pons, who in Algeria would become Joseph Cardona, and Jeanne Fedelic.

The second largest of the Balearic islands, Minorca has a history of successive occupations, by the Moors, the British, the French, before final return to Spain in 1802. In legend the Minorcans descended from giants, and the island still abounds in megaliths recalling the primitive stone formations of Stonehenge and Brittany. More significant to our story, the centuries of occupation by Moors from North Africa is known to have left, with a heritage of Moorish architecture, traces of Moorish blood. We do not know whether Albert Camus was conscious of this further tie to Africa, a more deeply rooted one than the political occupation by the French of a colony.[7]

Then Etienne Sintes, a farm worker as his father before him, and Catherine Cardona (*sans profession*) were married in 1874 in Kouba, a town on the outskirts of Algiers. They had nine children, seven of whom lived to be adults: Jeanne, Marguerite, Catherine (mother of Albert Camus), Antoinette (who would marry Gustave Acault, Albert's first benefactor), Marie, Etienne (the barrelmaker who would be one of Albert's fictional characters after failing as a father substitute), Joseph. Catherine, born in Birkadem on November 5, 1882, was an unusually frail and delicate child.[8]

In Chéraga young Lucien Auguste Camus (Albert Camus' father) was brought back into his family's care, put to work by one of his brothers, a transporter of wine.[9] When he was drafted for military service, he listed his occupation as coach driver. Here at Chéraga he met young Catherine Sintes, three years his senior. Soon Lucien Auguste was virtually adopted by the large Sintes family. When father Etienne Sintes died in 1907, his widow moved from Chéraga with her sons and two of the daughters (Catherine included) to a working-class district of Algiers called Belcourt. On his return from military service Lucien Auguste decided that he himself did not want to go back to Chéraga,

* The Spanish spelling of Sintes was eventually changed to the preferred French spelling Sintès after the family became established in French Algeria.

and so one of the Sintes boys, Joseph, employed by the large wine shipper Jules Ricôme, got him a job with that company. The Sinteses also
took on the grudges of young Lucien Auguste. Because he smarted at
the memory of the orphanage, and what his sisters and brothers had
done to him by abandoning him to it, the Sintes never associated with
the other Camus.

—————— ◆ ——————

# 2

# FAMILY DRAMAS

The curious feeling the son feels for his mother constitutes *all* his sensibility.

*Carnets,* I

When Albert Camus spoke of his father it was necessarily at a remove, for no articulate witness, scarcely a document, survived to bridge the bottomless chasm separating a father who died after wounds received in the Battle of the Marne and an infant less than a year old when it happened. There would be respectful homage by the women of the household, grandmother Catherine Sintes, and Albert's own mother Catherine Camus, partly deaf and now (under the shock of her husband's death) with troubled speech. The growing child had little access to the Camus family, for reasons already mentioned. In his several attempts to conjure up memories of the forever absent father young Albert counted on the help of his mother. "Is it true that I resemble my father?" he would ask her. "The spitting image." (From *L'Envers et l'Endroit.*) At the end of his life, in writing *Le Premier Homme,* he would try again, but then he would create a father who was greater than life.

In fact Albert Camus hardly had more to go on, in recalling his father, than his biographer has.

Lucien Auguste Camus was drafted for a two-year tour of military service in 1906, an obligatory requirement which dates back to the nineteenth century in France, and which helped to keep the French Army in strength for decades of colonial war. He was just in time to serve in the expeditionary force which invaded Morocco in 1907. This era of North

African conquest is closely linked to Great Power rivalry on the European Continent. France was expanding its colonial holdings at the beginning of the twentieth century, but in Morocco it came up against Kaiser Wilhelm II, who supported the ruling sultan. At the Algeciras Conference of 1906, which brought together France, Germany, and other Europeans states with the United States of America, agreements were worked out to guarantee the internationalization of trade (thus protecting German interests) while placing police powers in the hands of the French and the Spanish. In fact the conference opened the door to domination by the French, who began their penetration of Morocco from Algeria with the occupation of Oujda by General Louis Lyautey. Then on the pretext that Europeans had been killed in Casablanca, the French landed a division there in August 1907, with 6,000 men under General Antoine Drude. France established a protectorate over Morocco five years later, which was to last until Moroccan independence was recognized in 1956.

Lucien Auguste Camus was a simple soldier, a *deuxième classe* in the French term, assigned to the 1st Regiment of Zouaves. After a period of basic training starting in August 1906 he was to serve in the Casablanca operation from December 1907 to August 1908—in what precise role we do not know, but he left the *corps de débarquement* with a certificate of good behavior. He was rated a "rather good marksman." These Zouaves were a particularly colorful arm of the French infantry, outfitted with baggy trousers and loose berets in an evocation of North African dress. Indeed the word "zouave" is of Arab origin, honoring a Berber tribe which furnished the first recruits for the corps (founded in Algeria in 1831). In a sense they were shock troops. "Brave as a Zouave" was a popular expression (although in later popular speech zouave was more likely to signify braggart or clown). After his service Lucien Auguste transferred to the reserves, and he would become a Zouave again when called up for duty at the outbreak of World War I.[1]

On his return from the Casablanca campaign two things changed in Lucien's life. He decided that he did not wish to go back to rural Chéraga, and through Catherine Sintes and her family he got the job at Ricôme already mentioned, joining the Sintes clan in Belcourt. Then he married Catherine Sintes, on November 13, 1909. At this time we know, thanks to his carefully conserved military papers (the only official records in family hands apart from the documents having to do with his death), that Lucien was five feet eleven in height, with chestnut-brown hair, blue eyes.[2] He had learned the rudiments of reading and writing in the orphanage, and his military papers attested to his literacy.

But according to his son Lucien it was thanks to the job at the Ricôme company that he became functionally literate. The reports he would send to his employers show stilted elegance, as well as evident pleasure in having the opportunity to express himself. His wife never learned to write; their marriage certificate attests that neither Catherine nor her mother could sign her name to it.

The French had discovered that one nonindigenous crop grew well in Algeria: grapes for pressing. The territory was soon covered with vineyards, often to the dismay of mainland French winegrowers, for the North African wine was both cheaper and stronger, and was of course exported to France. Jules Ricôme et Fils was a major dealer and shipper; its cellars, which have apparently survived in Algiers, could hold over two million gallons of wine, and quayside warehouses offered additional storage facilities. What Ricôme would do was to buy the produce of vineyards in various parts of the country for shipping to its customers. By 1912, Lucien Auguste Camus was being sent out to represent the firm during the pressing of the grapes by local suppliers, and then to supervise its shipping.[3]

That year he was in Sidi Moussa, not far from the capital in the canton of Alba. When living in Algiers the family would continue to reside in Belcourt. After a Rue Lamartine apartment, where Lucien Auguste's first son Lucien was born on January 20, 1910, they would live on the adjacent Rue de Lyon, the street to which he would return just before his death and his widow would never quit.

After the autumn grape harvest of 1913, Ricôme sent Lucien Auguste with his pregnant wife Catherine and infant son Lucien for a long-term assignment at a vineyard called Domaine du Chapeau de Gendarme (literally, Estate of the Gendarme's Hat) near Mondovi, in the richest growing country of the Bône region. Bône, now called 'Annaba, was French Algeria's principal port at the eastern extremity of the country, near the Tunisian border. Eight miles to the south, on the road running parallel to a railroad line along the Seybouse River valley, Mondovi was named for Bonaparte's victory over the Piedmontese at that Italian city in 1796. It was one of a number of Algerian townships bearing the names of Napoleonic victories, which the French created in 1848 simply by putting an "X" on the map, in order to settle convoys of unemployed urban workers from mainland France.[4]

It happened very quickly: Family legend[5] seems to be confirmed by family papers.[6] As soon as they reached their destination Catherine Camus gave birth, at 2 A.M. on November 7, 1913, to her second child.

The birth was declared in the town hall of Mondovi at ten the next morning by Albert's father, who gave his age as twenty-eight and his profession as cellarman. His wife, then thirty-one, was recorded as a housewife. The witnesses to the declaration were Salvator Frendo, an office employee, and Jean Piro, also a cellarman; Frendo would have been of Maltese origin according to his name, Piro a Neapolitan.[7] The place of birth was given as the Ferme Saint Paul; the village of Saint-Paul was some five miles north of Mondovi, and that much closer to Bône. Apparently the infant was delivered in a low whitewashed bungalow with a tile roof, part of a compound of similar houses. This is the way it appeared to a visitor in the 1960s.[8]

Since the augmented Camus family was booked for a long stay at the Ferme Saint Paul, Lucien Auguste registered the move as a permanent change of address (the same day he declared Albert's birth). Then he settled down to deal with the pressing and storing of the wine, processes the French call vinification, and arranging for its delivery to the port of Bône for shipment. His son Albert would keep, in a chest in the dining room of his Paris pied-à-terre apartment, some of the letters his father had composed in careful flourish for his employees back in Algiers.

On July 4, when Albert was not quite seven months old, Lucien Auguste reported to Ricôme that he had received notice for a seventeen-day training period in the Zouaves for September just at the time of the forthcoming harvest. It had been understood that he would stay on at the Chapeau de Gendarme estate through the harvest and pressing. Yet he didn't dare request a postponement, because he feared that the colonel would refuse it, and he asked for his director's advice.

But events were not going to allow Lucien Auguste or his director, or his colonel for that matter, to linger over a decision. The Great War was approaching, the great meat grinder of a generation of Frenchmen. On June 28, just a week before Lucien Auguste's letter to his director, Archduke Francis Ferdinand had been assassinated in Sarajevo. On July 28 Austria declared war on Serbia. Germany followed on August 3 with a declaration of war on France, after declaring war on Russia. The German invasion of Belgium and Northern France began in August. In fact the war might have come closer still to the Camus, for on August 4 the city of Bône was shelled by the off-lying German cruisers *Goeben* and *Breslau*.

But by that time Catherine Camus and her two young sons were back in Algiers, as Lucien Auguste reported to Ricôme on August 1. He had shipped back his furniture to the capital two days before.[9] And he himself was now called back into the Zouaves, assigned to the 1st

Regiment, 54th company. A souvenir postcard photograph often reproduced shows him to have been a handsome man in his embroidered dress uniform. Look closely, and the tassel dangling from his cap can be seen.

The regiment was badly needed in mainland France, where the German advance had taken on alarming proportions. Paris itself was threatened, and fresh troops were being sent to relieve it. The soldier was within commuting distance of Paris when he sent his wife a reassuring postcard dated September 4, 1914, postmarked from Montreuil-sous-Bois just east of the capital.

Late that evening Marshal Joseph Joffre, commander-in-chief of French forces, issued orders for a major counterattack the next morning against German forces advancing only a few miles north and east of Paris. Preparations for the Battle of the Marne had been under way since August 24 in the attempt to stem the German approach to the capital. Now the bulk of French forces was to be thrown into the attack; even the taxicabs of the city were mobilized in a legendary effort to move troops to the lines. Zouave Lucien Auguste Camus was struck by shell fragments, evacuated to a hospital removed from the battle lines. Catherine, in her mother's apartment on the Rue de Lyon, received a postcard from her husband sent from a hospital in the northern Brittany town of Saint-Brieuc, 227 miles west of Paris. This card, which Albert later took from his mother, depicted a prewar view of the hospital, when the building had served as a Catholic high school, Cours Secondaire de Jeunes Filles. Young girls, insouciant in their Belle Epoque dresses, are playing in the courtyard. Lucien Auguste marked his wardroom window with an "X." He wrote that he was getting better, and asked for news of the children. As far as we know this was Catherine's first news that her husband had been wounded, although it is likely that she first received an official telegram apprizing her of the fact.

Lucien Auguste Camus died on October 11, 1914, and this time Catherine did receive a telegram.[10] She also received, from well-meaning military hospital authorities, "a small shell fragment found in the flesh. The widow kept it," remembers the young boy in *L'Envers et l'Endroit*. He speaks of his father here "without conviction. . . . No memory, no emotion." He has heard that his father left for the war with great enthusiasm; he believes that after his wound he was "blind and on his deathbed for a whole week." As a matter of fact he had not been blinded, if his carefully penned postcard from the hospital can be invoked in evidence.[11]

The shock of the telegram, perhaps of the gift she received of bits of shell extracted from her husband's body, traumatized Catherine in a way her son never mentioned in the several descriptions he has left of his childhood.[12] Apparently she had an attack; the family called it meningitis. (Meningitis is a bacterial disease, but the term is often misused to describe the symptoms of shock.) Her sister Antoinette remarked that her speech was affected. Catherine could speak with more or less normal fluency, but she began to mispronounce words, and this in turn caused her to be shy with strangers.[13]

This handicap, the origins of which her son Albert may not have understood, together with her partial deafness, compensated by her ability to read lips (so that it was not necessary to raise the voice when speaking to her), and her inability to read and to write, made her a particularly passive member of the home in which her sons were to grow up.[14]

Catherine Camus placed her dead husband's Croix de Guerre and Médaille Militaire in a gilt frame in the Rue de Lyon apartment. She would never have an opportunity to visit his grave. It is in Saint-Brieuc, almost as far from Algiers as one can be on French territory, in the first row of the military compound of Saint-Michel Cemetery. And when Albert Camus received the Nobel Prize, a memorial association added a plaque to the tombstone, identifying the fallen soldier as the father of Albert Camus.[15]

Camus was to describe his early childhood several times. In the earliest attempts, the essays published in *L'Envers et l'Endroit* and the drafts of these essays, the mood is at once intimate and distant. As he grew older he would find it less necessary to protect himself or others, and his unfinished last novel would tell as much of the truth as he remembered. Over the years these recollections would oscillate between a desire to affirm that it had been a happy childhood ("The world was not an enemy at first.")[16] and the need, personal and occasionally tactical, to demonstrate that it was a very proletarian one.[17]

Poverty was only part of the story, the part he could most easily communicate, for it was a universal condition and he made no claims to originality. For the rest, he would attempt to deal with his family's specific dramas again and again, and he still hadn't finished the job at the time of his death. His last novel would have explored them more deeply, and art might then have given his Belcourt childhood a form which would have allowed the author to put it out of his mind.

The principal element of the drama was this: In returning with her two children to her mother's home in Algiers, without resources of her own, inarticulate and defenseless, Catherine Camus submitted to the domination of a stronger woman. Now the household consisted of Catherine's mother; and two of Catherine Camus' brothers, Etienne and Joseph. The apartment was composed of three rooms and a kitchen. One of these rooms, which served as the dining room, was also a bedroom for Etienne and Joseph; it had a small balcony which faced the Rue de Lyon. Catherine's mother had a room of her own. Catherine Camus shared the third room with her children, Albert and Lucien sleeping in a single bed. This room, and Catherine's mother's room, faced a small back yard.

For a while Catherine's niece Gabrielle, daughter of her sister, Jeanne, was also staying with them, sharing a room with Catherine's mother. Sometime around 1920 Joseph left to take up a life of his own, but Etienne, lame and inarticulate, stayed on, and he will show up in various flimsy disguises, at times without any disguise at all, in his nephew's books.

The apartment was one flight up (the top floor) of a house in the Belcourt district of Algiers. There were two other apartments on the floor, a toilet in the hall serving all three apartments; there was no bathroom. The ground floor was occupied by a wineshop (later a restaurant), a hairdresser, and a hat shop. Before 1930, when Albert moved out, there was no running water or electricity. An oil lamp above the table could be raised or lowered; they called it simply *la suspension*. The other room had table oil lamps.[18]

Used as material for a tale of hardship, the family drama came out this way:

Once there was a woman whose husband's death left her poor with two children. She lived with her mother, equally poor, and with a lame brother who was a worker. She had worked for a living, did housecleaning, and left the education of her children in her mother's hands. Rough, proud, dominating, the older woman raised them harshly. One married. We shall speak of the other one. Primary school, then high school, day-boarder, returning to a dirty and poor home, repelling, living with a grandmother without kindness and a good and kind mother who knew neither how to love nor to caress, and so was indifferent. . . .[19]

In its most idealized version—the preface Camus wrote for a new edition of his early essays in the year of his Nobel Prize—childhood becomes somewhat less painful:

Poverty, first of all, was never a misfortune for me. . . . To correct a natural indifference, I was placed halfway between misery and the sun. Misery prevented me from feeling that all is well under the sun and in history; the sun taught me that history is not everything.

It is thanks to the sun and sea that even a poor boy can grow up happy. And it is thanks to his family that he can grow up without feeling envy, to his family's "silence, its reserve, its natural and sober pride."[20]

Grandmother Catherine Sintes was a harsh woman, embittered by the early death of her husband, the dispersal of her daughters. Perhaps these events, and the return of Catherine Camus with two infants, exceeded her understanding. She ran the household with an iron fist, in fact with a ship known as a *nerf de boeuf,* literally the dried ligament of a bull's neck, applied regularly and effectively on young Lucien and Albert. They talked back to her, and she couldn't abide that. The children's mother was a passive witness to the brawling and the beating, restrained by fatigue, by fear of the old woman, and the inability to express herself sharply and effectively. "Don't hit him on the head," she will plead (in *L'Envers et l'Endroit*). Uncle Etienne also feared his mother but he loved her. It is less certain that Catherine Camus loved her mother.

Etienne worked at a neighborhood cooperage, his wages helping to maintain the household. He is portrayed in the early aborted novel *La Mort heureuse* under the name Cardona, which of course is the maiden name of Camus' maternal grandmother (Camus' fiction is filled with family names). In his nephew's early manuscript, *"Les Voix du quartier pauvre,"* Uncle Etienne is "deaf, mute, mean, and stupid." Note that this sketch was written only a short while after Albert moved out of the family apartment, his resentment still burning.

Later, with the passing years, Etienne Sintes will be idealized in the short story "Les Muets," written in 1955. Here he appears under the name Yvars, which in fact was the name of Etienne's brothers-in-law, the husbands of Jeanne and Marguerite Sintes. (Fernande, Yvars' wife in this story, was the name of the mother of Camus' second wife Francine, and also happens to be part of Francine's legal name.) The real Etienne Sintes had been entirely mute until the age of thirteen or fourteen, at which time he underwent a surgical operation.[21] He continued to speak with difficulty after that.

An event involving Etienne Sintes and his sister Catherine Camus, mother of Albert, recurs in the Camus oeuvre. When it actually took place, or with what consequences, we cannot know. At some point in the childhood or the young manhood of Albert and of Lucien, their mother had a lover. Etienne, furious, threw the man out of the house and then turned on Catherine. Albert's older brother Lucien moved to defend his mother.

As the story is told in "Les Voix du quartier pauvre" (dated December 1934), Etienne prevented his widowed sister from seeing the man she loved. Catherine's lover brought her flowers, oranges, and liqueurs which he won at carnivals. It was an adulterous relationship, but his wife was a drunkard. He was not handsome, but he was good. "She cared about him who cared about her. Is love anything else? She washed his laundry and tried to keep him clean. . . ."

Because of Etienne's objection to this liaison Catherine Camus had to meet her man secretly. But one day while he was visiting, her brother Etienne showed up, and there was a "frightful brawl." In this account the son is no longer living in the family's Belcourt apartment; his mother comes to see him to tell her story through tears. This would place the episode after 1930, when Albert's mother was forty-eight.[22] In a draft for *La Mort heureuse* Catherine herself moves out of the family apartment after the scene.[23]

On the whole, Albert's treatment of his uncle is balanced. He is both the man of sudden anger and the honest worker whose hands are covered with calluses. As for Etienne's opinion of his nephew, when reporters sought him out after Albert Camus got the Nobel Prize he seemed pleased enough. Retired, he was then dividing his time between bowling and cooking for himself, which he enjoyed. He recalled life at the family apartment in Belcourt: "I didn't earn much, but Albert always had everything he wanted, within our means."[24]

Albert's grandmother also received the benefit of vivid description. The same events, the same character traits recur, as if to signify not only the limited range of the relationship, but the strong impression made by these traits and these events on the child. In *L'Envers et l'Endroit* Grandmother Catherine Sintes is still ruling the household at seventy (she was seventy in December 1927, when Albert was fourteen). We are led to believe that this impossible person would wait until there were visitors present to ask her grandson: "Whom do you prefer, your mother or your grandmother?" And the child would have to reply, whether his mother was present or not: *"Ma grand-mère,"* while experiencing "an outburst of affection for that ever-silent mother." Should the visitor indicate surprise at his preference, Albert's mother would explain: "It's because she raised him." The grown-up Albert Camus explains it another way:

> It's also that the old woman believed that love is something one demands. She drew from the good conscience of a mother of a family a kind of rigidity and intolerance. She never cheated on her husband and gave him nine children.

Not only were Albert and Lucien intimidated by Grandmother Catherine, so were the children's mother and her brother Etienne.

We have the testimony of the older brother that tiny Albert did a better job than he in handling the old woman. She let it be known that Albert was the better of the two boys.[25] Albert and his inseparable primary school companion André Villeneuve would accompany Grandmother Catherine to the movies and even explain the action to her.[26]

Perhaps Grandmother Sintes had a good side, but her grandchildren were at the age of *"jugements absolus."* They saw her as a faker, appealing for sympathy and recognition, pretending (for example) to have been working when in fact she had been idling at a window. She could even become violently ill when it suited her. Then, when she fell genuinely ill, Albert simply refused to take her seriously until she died. "Only on the day of the funeral, because of the general explosion of tears, did he cry, but with the fear of not being sincere. . . ." (*L'Envers et l'Endroit*) After her death the house was run jointly by Albert's mother and Uncle Etienne, which changed the atmosphere.[27]

It may have been his grandmother Catherine Sintes née Cardona who told the child Albert Camus the only story of substance he would ever hear about his father, and which (perhaps in part because it was the only one) was to count in his life.

Speaking without a fictional screen in his essay "Réflexions sur la guillotine," Camus attributes the telling of the story to his mother. Shortly before World War I, the story went, the murderer of a farm family was sentenced to death by guillotine. Camus' father, who felt that beheading was too good for the killer of children, decided to attend the execution. He got up in the middle of the night so that he would be sure to reach the execution site in time.

What he saw there he would tell no one. His son only knew that he came home in a hurry, his expression one of distress. He said nothing, threw himself onto the bed, and suddenly began to vomit.

Camus utilized the story some forty years after it occurred to introduce his urgent appeal for abolition of the death penalty. For the ritual act of beheading must have been quite horrible, he observed, to overcome the indignation of the simple, honest man his father was; a punishment which he believed wholly justified had had no other effect than to make the man sick. One could question a punishment which provoked only vomiting in the honest man it was designed to protect.

In *L'Etranger,* his first published novel, Camus allows his hero Meursault to tell the story; he too had heard it from his mother. It was also the only precise information he had about his own father. But the child Meursault, who would become Meursault the killer of an Arab on the beach, is already too tough to be moved. His father's act had disgusted him a little when he first heard about it, although now, when he himself is waiting to be executed, he thinks that he understands. What could be more important than capital punishment!

Later in *La Peste* it will be the father of Tarrou, prosecuting attorney by profession, who rises early to attend executions by guillotine. In the end Tarrou leaves home because of it. All his life the account of his father's early rising, of his vomiting, will remain with the son. In his dreams he will be the executioner's victim. It didn't help that his grandmother would warn him that he'd wind up on the scaffold himself.[28]

As an adult Albert Camus would stand apart from his peers because of his refusal to accept the death penalty, opposing his resistance comrades' approval of the wartime execution of a Nazi collaborator, opposing postwar executions of convicted collaborators though detesting their actions; his abhorrence for the death penalty was a factor in his break with the Stalinists, and led him to refuse the use of terrorism in a just cause by Algeria's Moslem nationalists.

Once, at a time not specified, Albert's mother was attacked by an intruder in the Rue de Lyon apartment. As told in *L'Envers et l'Endroit* the aggression took place while she was sitting at her balcony at dusk. The intruder attacked her from behind, brutally dragged her back into the room, then fled on hearing noise. That was all. Already a young adult and living elsewhere, Albert was called in and on the doctor's advice spent the night lying beside his mother. His brother would later remark that everyone in the neighborhood believed that the aggressor had been an Arab.[29]

During the four years of World War I, war widow Catherine Camus was to receive no money from the government. Formal notification of her husband's death and her first pension checks would come only in the final months of hostilities. A neighborhood accountant helped her to apply for the pension, since no one at home could fill out a form. During the war Catherine went to work at a cartridge factory sorting shells, until she came down with rheumatism. From then on she would do house cleaning, washing, ironing. Later her children would be proclaimed *pupilles de la nation,* signifying that as children of a war victim they were entitled to small sums for purchase of an annual pair of shoes, a school smock, and school books, free medical examinations.[30]

Without general availability of Camus' unfinished novel, *Le Premier Homme,* readers will not know the full story of Camus' feelings for this silent, submissive figure who became a more marvelous woman to her son as he grew older. In his earlier books, one reader remarked, he seemed to blame his mother for his condition as *étranger*. Now she is seen to have been the *étrangère*.[31]

# 3

---◆---

# GROWING UP IN BELCOURT

My room faced the main street of the neighborhood. It
was a beautiful afternoon. Yet the pavement was damp,
passersby still rare and hurried. First came families taking
a stroll, two little boys in sailor suits, their shorts above the
knees, somewhat hampered by their stiff clothing. . . .

*L'Etranger*

The traveler arriving from the sea may decide that the port and city of
Algiers, capital of Algeria, resemble nothing so much as an ancient
Greek or Roman theater seen from the stage. The city seems to sweep
around its bay in a half-circle (actually a not very perfect half-circle).
Streets of white buildings rise in tiers to the enveloping hills, the thea-
ter's grandstand.

More than half the life of Albert Camus was played out in this theater. First, to the left as seen from the sea, in Belcourt, the lower-work-
ing-class and small-trades district where he grew up. To the right, beyond the densely populated Moslem Kasbah, is the mixed-nationalities
neighborhood of Bab el Oued, on the edge of which stood his high
school. Between the two extremes, in the center of the city, were the
seat of government (containing the auditorium so often used by amateur theater director Camus), the university, and his several temporary
homes on or near busy downtown Rue Michelet. Then, high above the
city center, rising to the crest, are the residential quarters where his professors and wealthier friends lived, where he himself would reside during his first marriage, and lived the community adventure of the Maison
Devant le Monde. It is further along these heights, on the last crest

above the horizon, that he would have liked to retire at the peak of his fame.[1]

But Belcourt made him. He lived there, in his grandmother's and his mother's apartment, from the time he was eight months old until he was seventeen. He would return again and again to visit, or for temporary shelter. Belcourt was the district of Algiers' deserving poor, those who worked hard for low wages in the small factories and harbor installations, or for themselves as independent craftsmen. It was also a dormitory for lower echelon civil servants, white collar employees, small tradesmen. Here, more than anywhere else, working-class Europeans were in contact with the native Moslem population. The Rue de Lyon separated Belcourt proper from a Moslem neighborhood known as Le Marabout, named for the eighteenth-century tomb of a holy man in the local Moslem cemetery.[2] It was said that the Europeans of Belcourt were largely of French origin, while the neighborhood of Bab el Oued, on the opposite side of the city center, had a high percentage of Spanish, Italian, and Jewish inhabitants. If this was true then the Sintes (of Spanish origin) were an exception to the Belcourt rule. But it will also be seen that Belcourt's school population was largely non-French.

"In Belcourt, as in Bab el Oued, one marries young," Camus will recall in *Noces*.

> One begins work early and in ten years one exhausts the experience of a lifetime. A thirty-year-old worker has already played all his cards. He waits for the end among wife and children. . . . One has one's morality, and a rather particular morality. You don't "fail" your mother. You make certain that your wife is respected in the street. . . . Two men don't jump on a single enemy. . . . But at the same time the shopkeeper's morality is unknown. I always saw expressions of pity around me when a man walked by surrounded by policemen. . . .

Belcourt ended at the waterfront. Its frontiers were the Jardin d'Essai botanical gardens at one extreme, a barracks and a playing field (once a parade ground and still known as Champ de Manoeuvres) at the other. One of the principal small industries of the district, barrel-making, would help keep the Camus-Sintes family alive. Albert's uncle Etienne worked in a large cooperage a few streets from the waterfront. The Rue de Lyon, where the Camus-Sintes apartment stood, was certainly Belcourt's main artery; indeed it was a national highway (route N8 on Michelin maps) leading out of the city. Along this street teenagers and young adults would stroll in groups in the early evening, boys together, girls in groups of their own. Here were the dusty movie houses where they would watch Tom Mix, Tarzan, Douglas Fairbanks, Greta Garbo. Camus' *étranger* lived on the Rue de Lyon.

Down at the waterfront near the slaughterhouse was the poor neighborhood's poor beach, known as Plage de l'Arsenal. Albert and his friends learned to swim here, kept afloat by belts made of cork. The narrow beach seemed marvelous to young children, who as they sunbathed could watch fishermen draw in nets filled with fish. The road along the beach was called the sheep trail because sheep were led along this street from the hinterland, to be shipped out from Algiers' harbor. When they were old enough, the youngsters of Belcourt would prefer to steal a ride on the back of a horse cart transporting Belcourt barrels to the docks, to go swimming in the harbor where deeper water allowed better swimming *and* diving. There were fewer fuel-burning vessels then, the water was clear. Belcourt's Plage de l'Arsenal no longer exists, having been swallowed up by an extension of Algiers' dock facilities.

Albert's Belcourt kindergarten, located in the Allée des Mûriers, was perhaps a charitable institution; in any case the family had paid no tuition. It was run by a Mademoiselle Marie, described as "a little woman hunchbacked and extremely devoted to her pupils."[3] Here Albert learned to read and write. He was apparently small for his age; when they played his comrades felt protective toward him. Later at the lycée if he got the position of goalkeeper in his favorite of all sports, *le football* (soccer or association football), it was to keep him away from the rougher action.

Of course the major Belcourt landmark for the child was his neighborhood primary school, the Ecole Communale on the Rue Aumerat (now called Tahar Boudoua), which in the same complex included separate schools for boys and girls. To reach it Albert could walk a couple of blocks along the Rue de Lyon, then a short block left. Home was a closed world, without a book, not even a newspaper or a magazine, as he would remark years later to a visiting friend. But in these early years he was not so willing to allow his peers to enter this household, and few if any of those who knew him as a schoolboy had ever gone beyond the corridor leading from the narrow street-front entrance to the stairs rising to the Camus-Sintes apartment. Was he ashamed of his home, of his family, of his cleaning woman, washerwoman mother? Evidence is conflicting. Louis Guilloux, another poor boy, believed that Camus never hid the fact that his mother had been a cleaning woman but *he* wanted to be the one to say it. Albert's brother Lucien insisted that they were poor but proud and, after all, the pleasures of Belcourt (sun and sea) were free. The boys always had shoes, they could always go to school.[4]

Not only were there no books at home, there was no desk Albert could use. All his school books and notebooks remained in his schoolbag. He would work on the dining-room table under the suspension lamp, and then put the books back into the schoolbag; nothing was left lying around. Once a week the boys could borrow books from the school's small library, and their grandmother enrolled Albert and his older brother in the municipal library. Elementary school teachers would lend their own books to pupils, so that a bright child would always have something to read. François Yvars, son of their aunt Marguerite, would lend the brothers popular adventure stories such as the tales of Nick Carter and Buffalo Bill, the detective novels of Gaston Leroux (whose hero Rouletabille was a newspaper reporter), or of Michel Zévaco, author of cloak and dagger novels. Albert would devour all of them. When they were a little older his brother noticed that Albert and his friend André Villeneuve were reading satirical papers like the Paris political weekly *Le Canard Enchaîné,* and understanding them faster than he could.[5]

Otherwise, home at this time may have been the home portrayed in *L'Envers et l'Endroit:* The mother returns from a day of exhausting housework to find the house empty, her own mother out shopping, the children still at school. She falls into a chair, stares at the floor, as the daylight disappears.

> If the child enters at this instant, he distinguishes the slender silhouette with bony shoulders and stops short: He is afraid. . . . He pities his mother, is that to love her? She had never caressed him because she would not know how. So he stares at her for long minutes. Feeling a stranger, he becomes conscience of her unhappiness.

Later, much later, when the young man returns to the Rue de Lyon to visit his mother, they will sit opposite one another in silence. When she asks whether it bores him that she speaks so little he replies: "Oh, you never talked much."

His reading, his contacts with the outside world, would necessarily have increased the distance between the child and the mother, even if he had not been Albert Camus. Every evocation of the childhood environment suggests this alienation. Home was also where Grandmother wielded a whip. And where one was put to use at household chores, such as fetching water from the fountain a hundred yards distant on Rue de Lyon, in wooden buckets which Uncle Etienne made at the cooperage.

Under such conditions the three-story Rue Aumerat school, well equipped and airy, with its recreation yard, must have seemed an escape to the child. Despite the discipline and the light corporal punishment, the long hours (from 8 to 11 A.M., then from 1 to 4 or 5 P.M., with an hour of study after that), it was here that Albert would begin to exercise his charm, a power over others based not on muscle but on intelligence.[6] Albert liked to have an audience, and others in the class would listen to him. But he could also go off by himself to nearby Arsenal Beach to declaim poetry with pebbles in his mouth, as he had been told that Demosthenes had done. Once the others followed him and discovered what he was up to. After the same thing happened a few times he realized that he was being watched, but chose not to notice the intrusion.

Few school records survive. The family kept none, teachers have disappeared, and so has the French school system from Algiers. On May 21, 1920, Camus was formally adopted as *pupille de la nation* as the son of a soldier killed in the Great War.[7] This lofty designation entitled him, as has been noted, to a modest annual allocation for school supplies and other necessities.

It was the era of black smocks and of sailor suits called Jean Barts. Teachers rapped on desks with wooden rulers to call classes to order; the rapping implied that identical means were available to enforce discipline when necessary. Outside the classroom windows the boys would hear the rhythmic hammering of the barrelmakers, the whistle of locomotives along the tracks which separated them from the beach a few hundred feet distant. These were the sounds made by the fathers, uncles, cousins of the children in the classroom, market cries, nailing and sawing of the cabinetmakers, the sounds of the furnaces, the railroad workshop, cement and match factories of Belcourt.

During recreation periods the children played with apricot pits, which were their currency as well as their game material. They used the pits to play *tchic-tchic,* a game in which a single die was tossed and covered quickly with a box; the player who guessed its number won the pits. Or *Oh! Lilo en gagne cinq,* Lilo being a cut-out face resembling Charlie Chaplin, which was placed some fifteen feet from the players, who tossed an apricot pit, winning it back plus another one if it went into the mouth, five if through an eye. On Thursdays the children would meet in a vacant lot to fly homemade kites made of codfish tails; nearly all their toys were homemade.

The empty lots were their dueling grounds, where they could fight with fists and heads. Fistfights to settle arguments were called *donnades,* with four schoolbags set on the ground to mark the ring. Alerted by "Arab telephone" (word of mouth) everyone came to watch, to the despair of teachers. In good weather they would sometimes play hooky, known as *macaoura* in Belcourt dialect, to go down to the harbor to swim or to watch the large masted sailing ships, while dreaming of islands and of far-off countries to discover (there were still such places). *Macaoura* often ended with spankings.[8]

When they were older they would go to the movies at the Cinéma Alcazar on Rue de l'Union, or to watch boxing matches at the Salle Piochelle. Opposite the Alcazar Theater was the Belcourt market, where they could play ball after shopping hours. They could also watch occasional performances of Guignol puppet theater in the school courtyard.[9]

Directly opposite the Ecole Communale was the entrance to the local Amer Picon aperitif factory, where the basic raw material was orange peel. The peeled oranges were piled up outside the building, so that the schoolchildren need only cross the street to pick them from the pile. But they usually did not, because the oranges were too easy to get. They preferred to flirt with the older girls at the neighborhood factories (Albert did not, presumably to maintain his distance). During summer vacations they might work at the ceramic factory on Boulevard Thiers halfway between the Rue de Lyon and the waterfront, painting Arabic patterns on decorative tiles before they were baked, to be paid a few centimes per tile. Albert probably also worked for a while as a helper at the cooperage where his uncle was employed, as an often-reproduced group photograph suggests, and the description of the cooperage in the short story "Les Muets" would seem to confirm.

One favorite pastime was to plunge into the fountain on the Place Jeanne d'Arc, cotton stuffed in ears and nostrils, to see who could stay under longest. Once Albert's schoolmate Louis Pagès brought cotton from home for all his friends. Later noses and ears began to swell, and their parents feared an epidemic of a mysterious disease. It turned out that what Louis had been distributing so generously was thermogenetic wool.

Albert seemed to his classmates to lack endurance. Was he undernourished? He did not participate in the rougher expeditions, as when some of the others would roam far from home for days at a time, or what later in reminiscence seemed like days. Some of the boys, not including Albert, once wandered into the middle of a Moslem religious festival and got "baptized" (circumcised) on the spot. No one thought to go to the police, no fuss was made by parents. Or they would walk into Arab huts in a nearby shantytown, elbow their way to the common pot, and share the community meal.

Belcourt did have some dangerous Europeans, and crime was a popular subject of discussion among small as well as big folk. Convicted killers were guillotined at Barberousse Prison beyond the Kasbah, out of doors at three in the morning. Children would walk there, instead of going home, to watch the executions. We already know that Albert's only knowledge of these beheadings came from his father's disastrous experience.

That he did not participate in his comrades' rougher expeditions seems to add credence to the aloofness which his classmates remember, or does it merely speak for the limited free time available to him between classes and a strict home? It was almost as if he already knew his place in society, or so his comrade Louis Pagès believed. Yes, Albert was a leader, but unlike the other leaders they knew this one preferred words to fists. He was a benevolent dictator. He could fight but he was not aggressive. When really annoyed he would know how to manifest his contempt, for schoolmates and teachers alike.

Everyone in school had a nickname, and sometimes a child would know his classmates only by that name. But Albert was always Albert. At worst someone would call him Bébert, a vulgar sobriquet he would not hear again after high school except from the friendlier prostitutes of Saint-Germain-des-Prés. He seemed to his admiring friends to be playing a role. At ten he was already displaying elegance in dress; later this would be the characteristic most often cited by those who shared his high school and college years.

At about this time he read Jules Verne's *L'Ile mystèrieuse,* in which the theorem of congruent triangles is used by the engineer hero to measure the height of a cliff. Struck by the notion, Albert sat his friends on the ground in a neighborhood park to explain Verne's application of geometry. Then he posed questions to each of his friends in turn.

He gave his friend Pagès books of poetry. They would read in the streets, on walks out of town, and when they had finished reading they would box. Pagès once picked up a notebook Camus had left behind in class. It contained the beginning of a description of landscape with metaphors he barely understood. Camus would later tell his friend Marguerite Dobrenn that he had wanted to be a writer from the age of seven.

The European inhabitants of Belcourt generally remember that relations between themselves and Moslems were good. They lived side by side, or in contiguous neighborhoods, they went to school together. Perhaps a third of a class, in the memory of Camus' schoolmates some fifty-five years later, had been of Moslem origin. A teacher might say, "Look at Tewfik's paper. He understood the subject better than any of you, and he's an Arab!" There was no segregation in the street either; Moslems and Europeans played together.

Yet the only classroom record available, the list of pupils in teacher Louis Germain's *cours moyen, 2e année* in 1923–24, equivalent to the U.S. fifth grade, contains only one or two Arabic-sounding names out of thirty-three, so that it is difficult to confirm the collective memory. Is it possible that young Moslems seldom reached the fifth grade? Certainly there were Moslems out of doors, including Arab storytellers, and many of the Belcourt kids acquired the elements of Arabic (Louis Pagès did).

The mortality rate was high even among Europeans, with typhus, typhoid, tuberculosis, snake and insect bites, and diseases brought to the city by desert nomads (or so it was thought). Each year a number of pupils would die, and the children to whom they had been closest would accompany their teacher to the funeral. Those who survived the eight grades received a *certificat d'études* and after that might be apprenticed to a trade. Few children went on from the Belcourt elementary school to the lycée. Louis Pagès knew of no pupil besides Camus who went on to a notable career. In fact almost none of the bright young people of Algiers whom Camus would meet later on had come from Belcourt.

If there is a moment in young Albert's life when his future can be said to have been determined, it is at the age of ten, and in the elementary school classroom of Louis Germain. Germain did not teach him everything he would ever learn, but the master was capable of recognizing an outstanding child and willing to make the effort (great in that time and place) to prepare him for a career. Albert Camus never forgot what he owed to Germain. When he published his Nobel Prize acceptance speech and lecture, he dedicated that small book to his teacher. Not to plain Louis Germain, as he had dedicated books to high school teacher Jean Grenier or to his poet friend René Char. But to M. (for *Monsieur*) Louis Germain.

Not that Monsieur Germain was overly indulgent to Albert Camus. A master of irony, a stern disciplinarian, he seemed mercilessly authoritarian to some of the others in his classes. For their pains his brightest pupils, such as Albert Camus and André Villeneuve, got extra assignments, worked longer hours. Germain struck recalcitrant pupils on the fingers with a ruler he called his peppermint stick. A perfectionist, Germain didn't think that his own children were up to the mark, as Albert's brother discovered, for the older of the teacher's sons was in Lucien's class. Louis Pagès even thought that Germain's commitment to Camus may have led to problems at home with his own children.

Yves Doyon, who attended classes with Albert Camus from kindergarten up to the beginning of the Germain year, remembered that Albert had always been the best in the class in literature, while Doyon was best in mathematics. Camus had unusual facility in speaking, reading, recitation, oral replies to questions; his behavior was exceptional everywhere except during recreation periods. Somewhere along the line a teacher of a lower grade who had been astonished at Albert's ability had shown some of his work to Germain, who had the reputation of being an unusual teacher, and a leader of his teaching colleagues, all of whom looked up to him. He was a tall man, light complexioned, with hard blue eyes. His specialty was French.[10]

Albert was a month short of ten when he entered Louis Germain's fifth grade class (*cours moyen, 2e année*) in October 1923. Germain kept a record of the grades he gave to his pupils for part of that school year (which at the end of his life he turned over to the Camus family). So that we know that in the very first month of that school year Albert was number two in the class (and he had two bad marks for misbehavior); Villeneuve was number three. By December, Camus was number one; in January he was number one again. The subjects included history, geography, science, recitation, civics. The names of the other students show the neighborhood mix: Cornillon and Fleury, yes, even Levêque and Pasquier, but also Almadovar, Graviero, Guardiola, Guida, Hamoud, Llobel, Madrid, Moscardo, Santiago, Vincensini.

At some point in that year Germain realized the exceptional caliber of the child he had in his class whether or not he had been forewarned by Albert's earlier teachers. But what could be done about it? Most Belcourt children were on a single track leading, at the end of compulsory schooling, to a job in a local trade. At the age of fifteen Albert's brother would be sent to work for 100 francs a month (worth some 220 francs now or about $45), for the family needed his contribution.

One day, a day without a date but worth noting all the same, Monsieur Germain accompanied Albert to 93 Rue de Lyon to talk to the boy's family. Albert, he insisted, must be allowed to stay in school as long as possible. He could try for a scholarship which would allow him to attend high school. This scholarship, which was designed for the needy, paid for books and lunches in the otherwise free public school system. Grandmother Sintes retorted that everyone in her family had to work, including Albert. But this time Albert's mother got a word in. Since her older son would be going to work, she believed that Albert could be allowed to stay in school.

The grandmother yielded. A period of intense study began, which he shared with classmate Villeneuve. Pupils had to be nominated by the principal of their school in order to be admitted to the examination, which was held at the Grand Lycée (Lycée Bugeaud) in June 1924. Both Albert and his friend André Villeneuve passed.[11]

Germain certainly gave Camus books to read during that school year. And he gave him his first experience of what a book could be. The teacher read aloud to the class from Roland Dorgelès' *Les Croix de Bois,* the popular novel about trench life during World War I, a bestseller since its publication in 1919. Young Camus couldn't fail to think about his father as he listened to this realistic account of the daily trials

# 4

## SUDDEN CHILL*

"Tuberculosis is the only disease they know how to cure.
It's just that it takes time."

Patient in "L'Hôpital du quartier pauvre"

A schoolmate of Albert Camus, sifting memories of a half century ago, recalls most vividly the daily tram ride from Belcourt, through the heart of Algiers, toward their high school, known as the Grand Lycée.[1] The half-hour tram ride on the old CFRA line (for Chemin de Fer sur Routes d'Algérie) was the boys' discovery of the greater city, and consequently of the rest of the world. Standing on front or rear platform (and sometimes they would even ride part of the way on the exterior running board, for the main section of the vehicle was always jammed), they would chatter (everything was a lark then) or simply gaze out at the passing cityscape. From the Rue de Lyon the tram would run along the Champ de Manoeuvres, their Thursday soccer field. After passing the barracks of local regiments the packed tram would take a nose dive down the Mustapha hill; the boys were excited each time by the speed of the vehicle hurtling down the hill. The conductor braked short for the Mustapha stop.

Leaving the Gare de l'Agha on the right, they came to the Marché Clauzel, a bustling intersection which was the last stop for many of the Belcourt workers, whose other main destination was the central post office, Grande Poste. Now they were at the foot of the Plateau des Glières, leading to the imposing complex of the Government General, a fourteen-story building then going up, to be completed for the 1930

* From *La Mort heureuse*.

of simple soldiers, of sudden death in battle. Germain himself had come out of the war alive, so that he felt he should replace their fathers, at least in the school. The teacher will also reconcile the child with his grandmother, will encourage his love for his mother, and provoke the adult Camus to a veritable exaltation of the public school system.[12]

For one was a Catholic or a non-believer in those days, and attending public school was already a choice. The child's family was more superstitious than religious, and no one ever attended Mass. "Baptism and extreme unction, nothing more," he would later explain. But his attitude to Catholicism was one of neutrality rather than hostility.[13] There is a touching photograph of a neatly dressed eleven-year-old Albert Camus in his first Communion outfit.

Yet all one can know about this experience is what happens in *Le Premier Homme*. And here Albert's stand-in, Jacques Cormery, is slapped by a priest, unjustifiably, he feels. At least one student of *Le Premier Homme* believes that Camus reacted to this aggression all his life long, certainly all through his writings.[14]

In fact all of Belcourt was Camus' first school. The neighborhood with its mix of races and trades allowed him to grow up in daily confrontation with a life which most of his Algiers' middle-class friends, to say nothing of the writers and other intellectuals he would encounter later on in France, had not shared. According to his friends he never lost the ability to talk to people of all levels, and with the same informality.[15] Much later, replying to a critic who observed that he had not learned about freedom in Marx, Camus would say: "It is true: I learned it in poverty."[16]

centennial of French conquest of the territory. Only the scaffolding of the highest floors could be seen from the tram. But all around them they were witnessing a changing city. From here, along the Rue Alfred Leulluch (previously Rue de Constantine), they would pass lots where the new City Hall and the Hotel Aletti were under construction. Each day the buildings got a little higher; the tram ran alongside these work sites until it approached the Boulevard Carnot, built along a terrace fifty feet above the harbor.

Now they had arrived at the nicest part of the route. Just below was the bay of Algiers: a riot of activity, different each day, with the arrivals and departures of steamships from the European Continent, the unloading of freight, the incessant movements of tugs to and fro across the harbor. Sometimes larger vessels arrived with cruise passengers, or a fleet of imposing warships moored offshore.

At the next tram stop, Place Bresson, birds sang in a forest of trees —palms, figs, magnolias. Now they would pass on the left the solid arcaded buildings which housed the major banks, then the run-down old City Hall, soon to be replaced. And finally the Place du Gouvernement, last stop for the tram, a large square bounded with arcades, dominated by the horseback statue of the Duc d'Orléans, eldest son of King Louis Philippe and a leader of the French forces in the conquest of Algeria.

The square teemed with Moslems from the nearby Kasbah. And here was the venerable Mosquée de la Pêcherie, Djamaa el Djedidd, built in 1660, with a minaret twenty-five yards high. But the boys would have their eyes on the far end of the square, where their favorite ice-cream vendor held forth. There they would sometimes stop at the end of the school day for a lemon sherbert called a *créponné;* to achieve its waffled texture the vendor would scrape it from the sides of a cylindrical container as it revolved in a bed of ice.

From here the young men still had a ten-minute walk to the lycée. They would take the Rue Bab el Oued under the arcades, flanking the Kasbah on the left, and on the right the old Marine district, a colorful sailors' haunt later torn down to make way for low-rental housing. Now they found it increasingly difficult to stride along, the crowd was so dense: Moslems from the Kasbah, Neapolitan fishing families from La Marine. Here and there they were held up by outdoor stands displaying Oriental goods, or *beignets* cooked in oil and honey-soaked *zlabias*— temptations for after school when there would be more time to linger.

Conscious of the little time left before school started, the boys moved out from the arcades to walk along the tram tracks. (Private automobiles also used the street, but there were not many of those at the time.) Moving back and forth between road and arcades to gain precious seconds, the boys were almost running now, fighting for space among people and vehicles.

Then, at the end of the arcades, they came out into another square, with military barracks to the right, the Grand Lycée on the left—the latter literally rubbing against the Kasbah.

The school itself, which had been inaugurated in 1868, had a white stone façade and a neo-Greek pediment. It was separated from colorful Bab el Oued by the Marengo gardens.[2] There was a second, more exclusive lycée, the Lycée Hoche, or Petit Lycée, up above on the middle-class heights of Mustapha. Le Petit was looked upon with condescension by students of Le Grand. The Grand was mocked by students of the Petit. But for the higher grades all had to switch to the Grand anyway.[3]

Bébert (still Bébert) was seen by his comrades as a relaxed student in those first high school years, average in most subjects, although he stood out in literature. He was lively, and a good buddy. If he had less pocket money than many of his friends, the difference didn't matter among lycée students. Perhaps he changed his suit less frequently. He had no overcoat, but a raincoat was quite adequate for the Algiers climate.[4] As a half boarder from the time he entered the lycée in October 1924, he would have his lunch at school. There were three "tracks"; he was in the A program, which emphasized French and Latin.

Classes in the Grand Lycée ran from the *sixième* (sixth) up to the *première* (first), this last the year of preparation for the *bac,* or *baccalauréat* degree, that all-important diploma which is required for entrance to a university or to any school of higher education in France. It was understood in the family (according to Albert's brother) that Albert would pursue his studies to become a schoolteacher, and indeed academic studies (the A track), particularly for a child from a family without means, were largely directed to that career.

Each class had thirty to forty pupils. The school day ran from 8 A.M. to 12 noon, then from 2 to 4 P.M.[5] The adult Camus would tell an interviewer that he had taken Latin in the lycée, had been bored by Cicero and Virgil ("What a nuisance!"), and that he had also studied English. Spanish he would learn, insufficiently, on his own.[6]

One of the few surviving documents of his early lycée years is a certificate of satisfaction dated November 16, 1928, attesting to good behavior and good work for the first weeks of that school year. At about this time he began working during summer holidays instead of joining his schoolmates at the beach. His grandmother had him lie about his age so that he could take a job in a hardware store, if we can accept as biography the experience of Jacques Cormery in *Le Premier Homme.* Later Camus recalled that his summer employment included work at a ship's broker's and at an auto parts shop. Meanwhile his brother Lucien was employed full time at Jules Ricôme et Fils, where his father had been before him.

Later on, when he was a famous writer, every evocation of the life of Albert Camus would call attention to his love for sports, usually introduced as an antidote to the presumed austerity of his writings. And there is no doubt that the playing field mattered to him, probably more than classwork in those early lycée years. Most of the friends he made prior to 1930 remember him best as a fellow athlete, and he himself would remember having only one friend whom he met elsewhere than in sports.

Yet he was small for his age. A schoolmate described, almost tenderly, his "roguish little triangular face with eyes curiously slit like almonds, two mischievous dimples, a mouth which seemed to mock."[7] During recreation they would choose sides to play soccer informally, kicking a large soft ball in the schoolyard. After school, between 4 and 5 P.M., they would divide into proper teams, eleven to a side. Albert was the goalkeeper, sometimes center-forward, often leading the team, distributing passes.

A fellow player, Ernest Diaz, recalls that Albert was particularly able at short kicks, dribbling. Later they would join the junior team of the Racing Universitaire Algérois (RUA), the sports division of the Association Générale des Etudiants d'Algérie. Here Albert was regular goalie. They played in a stadium at the far end of the Rue de Lyon adjacent to the Jardin d'Essai, which the RUA shared with a neighborhood team, Gallia Sports d'Alger. In addition to a soccer field, this sports complex included a training pool and a cement bicycle track which sometimes drew French champions.[8]

But it was le foot which captivated Bébert. He played well and with considerable courage. Throwing himself at the feet of opponents on the rough ground, he was often hurt. Without a doubt he was on his way to the main team.[4] In a reminiscence written a quarter century later for an alumni sports magazine Camus guessed that he had begun to play with a RUA junior team in 1928. Before that he had belonged to the Association Sportive Montpensier (ASM). "God knows why, because I lived in Belcourt, and Belcourt-Mustapha's team was the Gallia." But a close comrade with whom he went swimming in the harbor had gotten him to join ASM. "That's how lives are settled." ASM usually played at the Champ de Manoeuvres.

> I learned right away that a ball never arrives from the direction you expected it. That helped me in later life and especially in mainland France where nobody plays straight. But after a year of the ASM

and of bruises, they teased me at the lycée. A "college" boy had to be in the RUA.

They practiced on Thursdays (which at that time was the midweek school holiday), played matches on Sundays, and when there was neither practice nor match and weather allowed, they went swimming. Albert loved his team, "for the joy of victories, so wonderful when they are linked to the exhaustion which follows effort, but also for that stupid desire to weep on nights after a defeat." One of his teammates was Raymond Couard, later to become a professional player. You had to play by the rules but also "in a virile way, for after all a man is a man." Camus described a particularly rough match played in a stadium next to a cemetery, where they were warned without charity that the passage was direct from the one to the other. One of the opposing players "landed with all his weight, regularly, on my back, without counting the rest: a spike massage of my shin-bones, hanging on to my sweater, a knee in my crotch, squeezing me against the goal-post, etc. . . ." But he will conclude his homily:

> After many years during which I saw many things, what I know most surely about morality and the duty of man I owe to sport, and learned it in the RUA.[9]

When his friend Charles Poncet later asked him which activity he would have chosen had his health permitted it, soccer or theater, he replied: "Soccer, without hesitation." Poncet remembered watching his friend, after a political meeting one Sunday morning when Camus was dressed, as always, impeccably, dribbling an old can of shoe polish along the sidewalk.[10]

Clearly he would have joined the regular college team of RUA, which in the eyes of Camus and his lycée classmates was made up of heroes.

The classroom was also contributing to an expansion of horizons. At about this time (1928–29) he may have run into another lycéen six months his senior, who had switched over from the Petit Lycée. Max-Pol Fouchet, later to become known as an essayist and poet, editor and art historian (and in due course a television personality in France), was the only other member of that school and generation to acquire a national reputation. Fouchet had actually migrated to Algeria from his native Normandy. He was soon to become part of a circle of the most promising students of the lycée, then of the university, who would form a group with young artists and architects not of the university; together they would become the nucleus of the prewar cultural community of Algiers, joining forces with an older group of university professors imported from France. If Fouchet had not actually met Camus by 1930, he certainly had another significant encounter at that time.

To celebrate the centennial of the conquest of Algeria, the French settlers mounted a major commemoration that year. One day, watching a Fêtes du Centenaire parade from a friend's balcony, Fouchet discovered that he was sharing the view with a stunning girl. Four years later, when Camus took Simone Hié away from Fouchet and married her, the two most eminent members of the young Algerian cultural community parted forever.

Another near-encounter that year: Albert Camus was sixteen (November 1929) when he discovered the work of André Gide. His uncle Gustave Acault (married to Antoinette Sintes) had taken Camus under his wing then. A butcher who loved reading more than cutting meat, Uncle Gustave occasionally gave his nephew books to read. One day he handed him a small volume with the title *Nourritures terrestres,* remarking that it should interest his nephew.

But Albert was not ready for an artistic representation of the bounties of nature which he could see and touch all about him; in Algiers a sixteen-year-old was covered with this kind of wealth. He returned Gide's book to his uncle with the remark that it had indeed interested him. Then he returned to the beach, to his idle reading, "also to the difficult life I was leading. The rendezvous didn't take place." ("Rencontres avec André Gide.") It would require at least another year, a new professor, and perhaps also the scare of his life, for the lycée boy to be ready for belles lettres.

During the school year 1929–30 he was in the class of *première,* which concluded with the first part of the examination for the *baccalauréat* diploma. He continued to find time both for study and sports. In fact the only available documentation for this period of his life consists of copies of the university sports weekly *Le Rua,* published every Tuesday with reports of the previous Sunday's games. So that we know that Albert Camus played on the RUA junior team through most of the year 1930, and that his team lost nearly every game. ("The ball, very slippery, played tricks on Camus."—*Le Rua* of February 18.) But he was regularly cited as among the best on the team. On March 20 he played not for the RUA juniors but on his own lycée team, and his side won. "The best in the Lycée were Nim and Clément, Branca, Belaïd and Alla, without forgetting the goalie, Camus." (*Le Rua,* March 25.) *Le Rua*'s April 22 issue cites Camus among those in the Lycée who practiced a sport every Sunday. For unknown but surely good reasons he played one Sunday with the Ecole Pratique d'Industrie *against* his lycée (*Le Rua,* May 27). After the summer holidays his performance with the Rua junior team won him special mention in *Le Rua* of October

28: "The best of all was Camus, who was beaten only because of floundering, and handled himself well." Then at long last RUA won a game. The rival team, Union Sportive de l'Ouest Mitidja, got its single goal "by surprise because of a referee's error. Camus played well at other times." (*Le Rua*, December 2, 1930.)

If these banal student newspaper reports are cited at length, it is because they are not only the unique surviving souvenir of Camus' early high school years but also incontrovertible evidence of the date he fell ill, a date which has remained uncertain until now (cf. the authorized collection of Camus' work). And the precise date is important: Camus' attitudes as well as his activities will change after his first attack of tuberculosis. With the reports of weekly sports events from *Le Rua* in hand, we can say with certainty that Camus' first symptoms of tuberculosis were discovered in December 1930 or in the first half of January 1931. In *Le Rua* of January 20, again in the February 10 issue, there are reports of the young goalie's absence because of illness.[11]

Just before that, in the previous October, he had entered the class of *première supérieure* (also called *philosophie*), at the close of which comes the second and final examination for the *baccalauréat*. He would have as his teacher the thirty-two-year-old philosophy professor Jean Grenier, who had arrived in Algeria only at the end of September, after having taught the previous school year at the old fortress city of Albi in southwest France. Grenier had grown up in Brittany, in his mother's home near Saint-Brieuc. (His paternal grandfather had been jailed as an opponent of Napoleon III, and had taken his sons, one of whom would be the father of Jean Grenier, to the United States, where he scraped a living giving French lessons in New Orleans.) A teacher all his life long, Jean Grenier was also to carve out a modest career as a man of letters. He had worked briefly at the prestigious Paris publishing house of Gallimard in 1927, where he met his future wife Marie. From then on he was in regular touch with the editors of Gallimard's *Nouvelle Revue Française,* for which he would be writing regularly during the 1930s. Before reaching Algeria his publications were insignificant (e.g., a short contribution to a collection of essays, *Ecrits,* published by Bernard Grasset; André Malraux, another young writer, was a fellow contributor to this volume). But in 1930 he would be published four times in *La Nouvelle Revue Française* (his essay on Provence, "Cum Apparuerit . . ." in May, and a three-part essay on India beginning in July).

It was while he taught in Algiers that Grenier began to write and to publish the small books of personal philosophy defining his feeling for Mediterranean life which would make his name, and not incidentally to awaken and to inspire his favorite student, Albert Camus. For Camus and for his classmates, this low-ranking professor was their first and their sturdiest link to the world of books and ideas beyond French Algeria. Self-effacing but also artful, a lay Jesuit of a sort, he was undoubtedly the most outgoing teacher Camus would know.

When Grenier walked into the classroom that first morning, his glance caught one young man "with large shoulders, a lively eye, determined expression." Something told him that Camus was going to be an interesting specimen. He told Camus: "Sit up front in the first row, with the stubborn ones!"[12] Was it because the young man seemed "naturally undisciplined"? When Grenier went home after one of his first classes with Camus, he told his wife that he had encountered a most promising young man.[13]

Even before the symptoms of his illness became evident, Albert's family had noticed that something was amiss. The previous summer the Acaults had taken their nephew to the seaside, at Saint-Cloud-sur-Mer, some eight miles north along the coast. They remarked that Albert was coughing a lot. Once he fainted.

Then, at some point during the winter, Albert's grandmother Catherine Sintes rushed the boy over to the Acaults' apartment in central Algiers (at 3 Rue de Languedoc, not far from the butcher shop). She told them in frantic tones that Albert had been coughing blood, *vomiting* it; this had been going on for two days. The Acaults called in their doctor, who also happened to be the official doctor for *pupilles de la nation*. He pointed out that as a war orphan Albert had the right to free hospital care. He was taken to Mustapha Hospital, most of whose patients were Moslems. The experience frightened him, and he begged the Acaults to take him home. A specialist discovered that his right lung was affected. He told Gustave Acault: "You are the only one who can save the boy's life."

The implication was that the Acaults were well-to-do, and possessed a more comfortable home for a patient than the Rue de Lyon family apartment. But also that butcher Acault would be able to supply his nephew with lots of red meat, which was believed to be helpful for tuberculosis victims. Indeed, the family doctor recommended overeating. He also insisted on rest: Albert should not even read a book. The boy moaned: "What will I do, if I don't get better?"[14]

He had just turned seventeen. His world until then had been centered on the playing field, swimming, roaming the town with his friends. Life in the sense he knew it seemed to have come to an end, when it should just be beginning.

Some time later, in his sketch, "L'Hôpital du quartier pauvre," the young writer tried to make sense out of his stay at Mustapha Hospital.

His brief account mixes hope, or ironic comment on hope, and despair. "The sickness comes quickly," says one of the patients, "but for it to go away again takes time." The reply is: "Yes, it's a rich man's disease." Some of the same material is used again in the draft novel *La Mort heureuse,* whose hero, the first incarnation of the Etranger Meursault, will die of pleurisy at the close of the manuscript. In the very first chapter there is a sign of what is to come, when Mersault feels a chill and sneezes. "He was shaken by a third sneeze, and felt something like a fever chill."

It was a common enough idea that the infectious diseases of tuberculosis and pleurisy could come from a chill. Several of his friends felt Camus' disease was brought about by a soccer match played in a downpour, or that it resulted from a blow received while he was a goalkeeper. From a student's souvenirs: "One day, in a stadium of Algiers, Albert Camus received a ball in the chest kicked by an opposing player, and fainted between the goal posts he was guarding."[7] As a matter of fact tuberculosis cannot be contracted by exposure or violent exercise, but it might be triggered or aggravated by either, or by substandard living conditions and undernourishment.[15]

In 1930 no wonder drug was available to cure the disease. The patient would be treated by artificial pneumothorax (collapse therapy), consisting of the injection of air into the pleural cavity between lung and chest wall to collapse the lung, immobilizing the affected area and allowing it to heal. The first injection would be followed by further pneumothorax injections at regular intervals, possibly every twelve to fourteen days, for an indefinite period. At various times in his life there would be periods when Camus would have to submit to a new series of injections, and when in 1942 his other lung was infected he would begin periodic pneumothorax treatment of that lung too, for no medical cure was available even then. In 1940 there were 140 deaths per 100,000 inhabitants from tuberculosis in France. After Selman Waksman's discovery of streptomycine, used in conjunction with active medication against the bacilli, the death rate dropped quickly: to 27 per 100,000 in 1957, 22 in 1960, the year of Camus' death. For most of his life he would not benefit from these discoveries. In the last decade of his life, when he was recovering from still another attack, he would finally be treated by the new drugs, but by then his lungs were in distressing shape.

In 1931, all seemed lost.

His teacher Jean Grenier remarked the absence of his "stubborn one" in the front of the class. He inquired, learned that Camus was ill. Perhaps such things were not done by lycée professors at the time, but Grenier decided to track Camus down. He took a fellow student along, hailed a taxi for the ride across downtown Algiers to the Belcourt district. Camus was at the Rue de Lyon apartment (which contradicts accounts which have him living with the Acaults from the day of his release from the hospital). Grenier and the classmate felt that they were intruders, and in a sense they were: The boy hardly knew his teacher, after only a few weeks of classes. He barely said hello, replied in monosyllables to questions. Grenier would later chalk it up to adolescent pride, the unwillingness to trouble others with his problem; call it *pudeur,* that French word inadequately translated as "reserve."

Whatever the reasons, the teacher came away with the impression that the sick boy had refused an outstretched hand. Later, a full decade later, the student would write to Grenier to try to explain his silence of that time, the distance created by that silence. "Perhaps, to speak in absolute terms, you represented Society. But you did come, and that day I felt that I was not as poor as I had thought."

His hostility had not been directed against Grenier as a person. Still later, referring to the sickroom visit, Camus would explain that he had not been able to express his intimate feelings then; the difference in age between them had been too great.

The calmest person of them all, if we can believe an early manuscript version of "Entre Oui et Non," was Albert's mother:

> At the time of the first symptoms, abundant spitting of blood, she had not been frightened; she had certainly been worried, but no more than a person of normal sensitivity would worry about a headache of a member of the family.

She would visit him at the Acaults', sitting in silence; each struggled for words which never came. The boy was told that his mother had been seen to cry. She knew how serious the illness was, but maintained her "surprising indifference." In truth they shared this indifference; their attachment went deeper than that. Albert's brother remembered that their mother had been frightened by the first attack of coughing blood. There had been *buckets* of it. When Lucien returned from military service in 1931, he barely recognized his brother, who was seated in the Rue de Lyon dining room reading a book. And Albert scarcely spoke to Lucien; he seemed bitter. According to Lucien, Albert would stay at the family apartment until autumn, when Lucien moved out to get married, at which time Albert returned to the Acaults'.[16]

Could the tuberculosis attack have killed him? "I don't want to die," Camus announced flatly to his uncle Gustave.[16] And in the draft already cited for "Entre Oui et Non" he recorded, speaking of himself in the third person: "At the worst of his illness, the doctor showed no hope for him. He had had no doubts about it. Besides, the fear of death troubled him considerably." It was conceivable, before the introduction of the new drugs, for a patient to be dragged down by the disease in two or three years' time. With an artificial pneumothorax, the chances of coming out of it were estimated at 70 per cent.[17]

This all too personal confession was left out of the final version of "Entre Oui et Non." It lacked development and would never be reintegrated into Camus' work. Max-Pol Fouchet, who also had tuberculosis, once saw Camus coughing up blood while they were at the movies together. Afterward Camus remarked that he believed that tuberculosis was a metaphysical disease. "You can cure yourself if you want to." Fouchet agreed. Fouchet and his friends were discovering philosophical overtones in their affliction which they found confirmed in Thomas Mann's *The Magic Mountain,* where both the hero and the author betray morbid fascination with the disease. For it allowed its victim to become closer to life even as he approached death, and incidentally gave him the leisure to write.[18]

The fact of the matter was: All his life Albert Camus would be handicapped by his tuberculosis. He would miss out on an otherwise certain professorship, he would be exempted from World War II military service (two consequences which on balance were not all negative). And he would constantly be obliged to slow down, to cancel travel or other activity, because of a new attack and the long convalescence which necessarily followed. From now on, the bitterness he felt in those first months when he watched others kicking soccer balls and running in the sun would never be far below the surface; he had been as they were still. In his writings it would come through as irony.

# 5

◆

# AWAKENING

*Childhood of poverty.* Essential difference when I went to
my uncle's: at our house objects had no names; we said:
the soup dishes, the pitcher on the fireplace, etc. At my uncle's: the Vosges glazed earthenware, the Quimper plates,
etc.—I was awakened to choice.

*Carnets*

All of these things would happen now: time for reading and reflection,
forced on him by the exigencies of a long convalescence. The many
stimulations of a new environment in the company of his uncle, for all
his faults a thinking man. The slow beginnings of what would become a
regional literary movement, French Algerian, "Mediterranean" literature, on the periphery of the *Nouvelle Revue Française,* enhanced by
the interest in things North African demonstrated by influential men of
letters such as André Gide and Henry de Montherlant. Undoubtedly his
teacher Jean Grenier, who would follow Camus through his higher education, was the chief catalyst for this change, receiving as he did all the
new books, the latest issues of the literary journals, the new ideas from
Paris. For better or for worse, Grenier would also help the young man
take his first steps into the political arena, for in the ebullient 1930s
French Algerians were also coming to realize that what happened on
the European Continent might affect them too.

In 1931, Gustave Acault, then forty-six years old, was a prince of
a man. Indeed, all witnesses agree, he walked in measured steps as if on
parade. Tall and slender, with a thin nose and a handlebar mustache, he
was a character who did not escape notice in prewar Algiers. But if he

owned the city's best butcher shop, he was equally well know as a café
sitter. At a table of La Renaissance, a brasserie just opposite his shop
on the busy city-center Rue Michelet (the street has since been
renamed Didouche Morad), a glass of anisette within easy reach, he
would hold forth on politics and literature, which in between-the-wars
France could often be a single subject. Or he would play cards (*belote*)
with friends. Meanwhile his wife Antoinette, the sister of Albert Camus'
mother, would be tending the business, a knitted scarf thrown over her
shoulders, her hair drawn up in a bun. Acault refused to call his wife
Antoinette, so that she was known only as "Gaby."

In the café and on the street, as at his place of business, Gustave
Acault would be attired in a red scarf, white silk socks, and a well-
pressed butcher's blouse with fine blue stripes on which (so said his
nephew) he would sprinkle a few drops of beef blood as an affectation.
In a word, the word of one of Camus' close friends of the time, he was
a butcher out of a René Clair movie.[1] "He devoted his mornings to the
meat business," his nephew would later remember, "the rest of the day
to his library, to the papers, to interminable discussions in the cafés of
his neighborhood."[2] Among his tablemates, if we can believe one of his
admirers of the time, were the rector and distinguished professors of the
nearby University of Algiers.

Acault was born just outside of Lyons, at Saint-Genis-Laval, and
grew up in that no-nonsense industrial region where the chief vice is
gourmandise. (His own favorite food was the dry Lyons salami known
as *rosette*.) With his mother and stepfather (a butcher) he had settled
in Algiers, where he met Antoinette Sintes. When he decided to return
to Lyons to find a job, Antoinette followed him, and for a while she
would accompany him in his travels in a horse-drawn carriage, for he
had become a salesman. During World War I, Acault was kept out of
the uniformed forces for medical reasons. While performing auxiliary military service daytimes, he took a night job cutting meat in a
large Paris food store, professing experience he didn't have. But soon
he had won a prize for the best shelf display, called in French shopkeeper slang a "paradise." That got him out of the cellar and behind a
counter. He spent half of each day learning how to cut meat. Finally he
was put into uniform anyway, and when he married Antoinette in July
1917, it was a military wedding; they were one in a roomful of similar
couples. After the war they returned to Algiers and opened the butcher
shop on the Rue Michelet.[3]

Later, when he attempted to persuade his nephew Albert to learn
the butcher's trade, he pointed out that it was an easy way to earn
money without doing much, and so leave time for the pursuit of a writing career. "In a week's time I'll teach you how to be a butcher," he

said. "You'll earn lots of money and you'll be able to write as you like."[4]

Camus told Jean Grenier that Uncle Acault had been a militant anarchist, and he certainly seemed to be everybody's favorite non-conformist. His cherished writer was Anatole France, whose complete works he owned. He was reputedly familiar with the nineteenth-century social classics: Charles Fourier, Victor Hugo, Emile Zola. But Acault also quoted Paul Valéry, royalist Charles Maurras, and read the right-wing-royalist *L'Action Française*. If his customers enjoyed listening to him, so did the young men around Camus, many of whom came away with vivid memories.

The Acault apartment at 3 Rue de Languedoc, close to the Acaults' business, was on a raised ground floor. Although ensconced in a building it had the appearance of a villa with its large entrance hall, four bedrooms, a garden at the back. During his years at the Acaults', Albert Camus had a comfortably spacious room facing the street. Although the apartment was dark he could read in the back garden while seated under a lemon tree. And he got all of the thick steaks he required from the Boucherie Anglaise, a trade name chosen by his uncle to suggest that he sold only the best imported products, good meat being a scarce commodity in Algeria in those days. His nephew also probably received a generous allowance, money for the clothes and books he needed, and of course he participated in the Acault's outings on weekends and on longer holidays. Gustave Acault was proud of his nephew, and liked to talk about him to customers.

Certainly the young man was well treated, if not spoiled by the childless couple. Encouraged by the versatile butcher, cared for by the strong-willed aunt, his convalescence took place under the best possible conditions. Periodically he would go to the hospital for a pneumothorax treatment. From the Rue de Languedoc the daily trip to the lycée was cut in half; the University of Algiers would be virtually around the corner.

For now he could attend classes again. He would have to repeat the final lycée year *(première supérieure)*, which gave him further exposure to Jean Grenier. If participation in sports was no longer possible, he would be an assiduous spectator at RUA games. One of the few outlets for his fantasy now was dressing up. Inspired by his flamboyant uncle, certainly financed by him too, Albert, who had always been neat, now became a dandy. Max-Pol Fouchet, a Frenchman from France (a *francaoui* in the local dialect), saw his comrade Camus as *le type suprême de l'Algérois in his* accouterment.[5] When Fouchet introduced Camus to Jean de Maisonseul, the young poet from Normandy seemed to Maisonseul almost patronizing: "You know," Fouchet told him,

"he's the type that wins first prizes." Despite Fouchet's irony Maisonseul was immediately taken by Camus, who was indeed dressed elegantly in a white shirt and white socks (his uncle's influence), and with
a Borsalino felt hat. They were not quite nineteen, this was in 1932.[4]
Testimony varies as to Camus' manner of speaking. The Normandy import, Fouchet, of course remembered it as typically *pied noir,* an Ital-
ianate singsong, accompanied by a distortion of vowel sounds, a heavy
dose of local expressions. Maisonseul, descendant of one of the *grandes
familles* of the territory, was quite sure that Camus had no such accent,
although he knew how to assume one, for fun. In fact, as recordings of
his voice made in the final decade of his life demonstrate, Camus never
lost his French Algerian accent, however modulated it had become,
and he could imitate a *pied noir* when he wanted to.

Maisonseul also remarked that his new friend was exceptionally
polished in manner, with a touch of irony, natural ease, and elegance.
And tenderness of a sort, "with an astonishment in his expression which
would soon be nuanced by the slight irony of the mouth, the glint in his
eye, and at times a great melancholic lassitude, although he could also
be quite merry, with a sense of the comic. This seduction acted on anyone to whom he was introduced." Albert was also remembered for that
untranslatable *pudeur.* Alone with a good friend, he betrayed a humility
which moved the sensitive young man that his friend Maisonseul was,
because Maisonseul had also experienced Camus' pride.

But sometimes friendship had to be won. Louis Benisti, a jeweler
turned sculptor, at times found Camus ferocious. The artists in their
group lacked his intellectual polish and he let them know it. One day
Benisti, self-taught and older than the others in the group by a decade,
snapped at Camus: "We're all doing our best, so why be ironic?"
Camus blanched, and from that day on they were fast friends.

A snapshot out of the past: In September 1931 his Belcourt
schoolmate Louis Pagès ran into Albert Camus, saw him attired all in
white, with a white tie, in homage to Gabriele D'Annunzio. To Louis
Benisti, Camus was Lafcadio, a handsome young man with a casual tie,
the allusion being to the hero of Gide's *Les Caves du Vatican.*[6]

With Max-Pol Fouchet and Camus taking the lead, there would be
interminable discussions, often in the heart of the Kasbah, at a crossroads café called the Fromentin, where it was said that the nineteenth-
century painter Eugène Fromentin used to sit, and later, on his visits to
Algiers, their culture hero André Gide. Here they would sip mint tea
while a muezzin summoned the faithful to prayer from atop the minaret
of the small mosque just opposite. Fouchet noted that Camus was particularly moved by the prayer call, for he was then reading the mystics,

John Ruysbroeck (the Dutch Augustinian), St. Theresa of Avila, and, under Grenier's influence, the *Bhagavad-Gita.*

Or they would ride a bumpy bus on Sunday mornings to a village on the heights above the city, Bouzaréah, delighted to learn that the name signified "kissed by the air." Then they would return on foot along a road which snaked back and forth, hugging the hillside, as it descended toward the sea. They would pass an old cemetery which never failed to draw Camus to its tombs testifying to a century of Spanish, Maltese, and French settlement. One day Camus called attention to a swarm of ants filing out of one of the graves, and it became another subject for their irony. Further along, at a bistrot run by Maltese, they would eat the Mediterranean sausage *soubressade,* accompanied by heavy wine.

Once, descending from Bouzaréah, they were witnesses to an accident. A Moslem child had been hit by a bus and seemed to be in a coma. They watched the huddled crowd, listened to a wailed Arabic lament for as long as they could stand it. Walking away, Camus turned toward the landscape of blue sea and sky. Raising a finger toward the heavens he said: "You see, He says nothing." Fouchet was certain that Camus had no fundamental objection to religion, although he found the situation of man in the face of suffering and death, alone in the silence from the sky, unbearable.[5]

They were a group now, Camus, Fouchet, Maisonseul, Benisti, Louis Miquel. (A fifth-generation Algerian whose Spanish ancestors settled in Oran, an architectural student and later an architect who worked for Le Corbusier, Miquel was brought by fellow student Maisonseul to Fouchet's apartment and met Camus there.) The most thoughtful of them would take part in these long walks. They would go together to watch Westerns and horror films, sit in the small bars of Bab el Oued or just below the Kasbah, in the colorful sailors' bistrots of the Marine district. For about seven cents (thirty-five centimes) they would get a glass of anisette at the bar with small side dishes of chickpeas, peanuts, fried potatoes, small broiled fish, olives. They particularly liked Les Bas Fonds (The Lower Depths), a dimly lit bar decorated with a guillotine and a suspended skeleton whose trunk was covered with a cloth. When the cloth was pulled a spring released a giant phallus. Coco, a dwarf, the owner of Les Bas Fonds, sprayed customers with water from another phallic device. Camus got along famously with Coco, and suggested that the café be renamed Friends of Death and Sex (Aux Amis de la Mort et du Sexe).

On Sunday afternoons they would go to dance halls built on piles over the Bab el Oued beaches, the Bal Matarèse and the Bains Padovani (this last would be the site of amateur director Camus' first theatrical experiment). Here they would meet girls, mainly of Spanish origin, who worked in the nearby tobacco factories. Fouchet recalls, probably only partly in jest, that by hugging these creatures the students felt they were embracing the great proletarian goddess of the Mediterranean.

Camus listened to people in the streets, repeated their savory phrases to his friends.[5]

In the classroom he was receiving the standard education dispensed to all the lycée students of France, all of whom were subjected to the same examination at the conclusion of their obligatory school program. They used the then new *Manuel de philosophie,* by Professor Armand Cuvillier, which provided all one needed to know about the major philosophers; in it Camus discovered Schopenhauer and Nietzsche.[7] He was reading Dostoevsky, too, and the Bible. Max-Pol Fouchet remembers lending him James Joyce's *Ulysses,* which Camus enjoyed although he found it "disordered."[5] This version of how Camus read Joyce for the first time makes more sense than the notion that Gustave Acault, he of Anatole France and *L'Action Française,* read and admired *Ulysses,*[8] which would have meant that his nephew read *his* copy.

Certainly Grenier and all that he represented, the books and magazines he was getting from Paris, the contacts he maintained with the *Nouvelle Revue Française,* were the revelation of that last year of the lycée. It was only a step from Grenier to Gide. And much later, in his preface to a reprinting of Grenier's *Les Iles,* Camus would remember that this small volume, read for the first time when he was twenty, created a shock comparable to the shock he received when he read *Les Nourritures terrestres.* (Prior to their publication in book form, some of Grenier's essays appeared in *Nouvelle Revue Française.*) But this second revelation was different in an important way. Jean Grenier's notion of happiness seemed more reasonable to the young man that Camus was. Both Gide and Grenier sang the virtues of the Mediterranean, virtues which southerners not only understood but utilized daily. What Camus and his fellow sun worshipers needed was something else. It was rather to be "turned away a bit from our avidity . . . our happy barbarity." Not by somber warnings by solemn preachers. "We needed more subtle masters," Camus explained,

> and for a man, for example, born on other shores, he too in love with light and with the splendor of bodies, to come to tell us, in a matchless language, that these appearances were beautiful, but they were to die, and so one had to love them desperately.

> (Preface to *Les Iles*)

Camus was particularly struck by one phrase from Grenier's book, introducing a theme which would have frequent echos in his own work. in "Les Iles Kergulen" Grenier had written: "I have often dreamed of arriving alone in a strange city, alone and stripped of everything. I should have lived humbly, even miserably. Above all I should have kept the *secret.*"

But his student must also have been drawn to another remark thrown out almost gratuitously, or as if its author had Camus in mind when he wrote it:

> People are astonished by the great number of diseases and accidents which strike us. It's because humanity, tired of its daily work, finds nothing better than this miserable escape into illness to preserve what remains of the soul. Disease for a poor man is the equivalent of a journey, and life in a hospital the life of a palace.

It was during this period that Albert Camus discovered that he wanted to write. *Les Iles* confirmed his determination. He would later recall that Grenier had lent him another book, a novel by André de Richaud, *La Douleur,* whose author was the first to speak to him of things he knew: "a mother, poverty, lovely nights under the sky." The book had a liberating effect. He read it in the space of a night, woke to a revelation. He had learned that books were not only for escape and distraction. They could speak of "My stubborn silences, these vague and sovereign sufferings, the singular world which surrounded me, the nobility of my family, their misery, and then my secrets. . . ." At last he could penetrate "the world of creation." ("Rencontres avec André Gide.")

Perhaps. But a reading of *La Douleur* shows it to be a somewhat conventional tale of the brief unhappy infatuation of the widow of a French officer, during World War I, with a German war prisoner billeted in the village, her young son as an unwilling witness. Like Albert the boy is a *pupille de la nation,* but the resemblance ends there. The widow Delombre is not poor, she and her son do not live in anything resembling Belcourt.[9] The pain *(douleur)* in this book, with its overtones of *The Scarlet Letter,* derives from jealousy and shame. No, there is not much in this little novel which will leave traces in Camus' own writing.

Grenier's essays, on the other hand, provided a terrain for reflection, even a format. Grenier himself would say in his memoir on his dead friend (*Albert Camus,* 1968) that his influence had not been deliberate. For if he was teaching Camus, he was also busy writing his own work, and if he happened to communicate his dreams to the impressionable young man it had not been intentional. Of course he invited the most serious of his students to his home, talked with them, lent or gave them books. Yet Grenier would confess to Camus, after the latter had become a famous writer, that he felt he had been overly severe to him as a young man, grading him as a failed philosopher rather than as the brilliant maverick he was.

While no evidence of it survives, Camus apparently did his first gratuitous (that is, non-school) creative writing at this time. A fellow student, Georges Didier, started a magazine which he called *Le Monde Vu de Ma Chambre;* in Camus' recollection it was handwritten. Camus contributed an essay in praise of airplane pilots, now lost.[7] Jean Grenier believed that the small magazine was published during the *classe de seconde* and perhaps the *première,* which would be from 1929 to 1931 or later, when Camus was between sixteen and eighteen. And that is all we know. Grenier fixes the moment of Camus' desire to become a writer at the time he passed the *baccalauréat,* which would be in June 1932. Student and teacher met on the street one day near the main post office of Algiers. Camus asked Grenier if he thought that he was capable of writing for publication.[10]

Jean Grenier lost no time in putting his student to the test.

Then Camus' formidable grandmother died. Her last days are described with power and economy of means in *L'Envers et l'Endroit,* where the young man first sees her illness as only another piece of histrionics. The child had too many bad memories; he would not allow himself to become tender. "But if one plays at illness, one can actually feel it: the grandmother pushed simulation until she was dead." The death scene had no effect on the grandson. But he broke down at the graveside service, because of the weeping going on around him, even as he feared that he was not being sincere.

In this essay Albert and Lucien are children at the moment of their grandmother's death, and they are apparently still living at home with their mother. But it seems that we are not to take this literary transformation of the material of his life as autobiography, no more here than elsewhere. The best evidence is that the children were not children anymore when their grandmother died. Albert was living at home at the time, after the first attack of tuberculosis. His brother had returned from compulsory military service and was also living at home before leaving definitively to be married. That places the event between May and November 1931.[11]

During this last year of lycée work leading up to the second and final *baccalauréat* examination, Albert Camus became a "published" writer. He had been reading *Nouvelle Revue Française* from the age of seventeen, or so he recalled much later;[7] now he would be able to write

. *NRF*-type essays of his own. The outlet for them was ready-made: a small literary and art monthly called *Sud,* encouraged if not actually published by Jean Grenier, who felt that print was a necessary stimulant for beginning writers. In three issues of *Sud* during that school year, in March, May, and June, essays appeared over the signature of Albert Camus. They were clearly the product of the classroom, or derived from class discussion. "These are drafts," warned Grenier in presenting them. The only one of these texts which survives in manuscript form, "Essai sur la musique," originally included an outline and a bibliography, as befits a class paper.[12]

The first of these essays, "Un Nouveau Verlaine," appeared in the March 1932 *Sud*. It is a touching attempt to demonstrate that the poet deserved more than his reputation as an innocent dreamer. "He suffered in his sick body, in his painful heart." Verlaine sinned, repented, knew when he was doing wrong. Of more intrinsic interest is the contribution to the May *Sud,* "Jehan Rictus, le poète de la misère," dedicated to the rehabilitation of a minor cabaret poet, author of *Les Soliloques du pauvre* (1897), whose penniless hero seeks to escape his lamentable state through dreams. "What is especially seductive in the book," young Camus concludes, "is the contrast between the muddy, filthy life of the Pauper and the naive azure of his soul . . . He kept his childhood beliefs . . . Let us not correct his illusions."

Camus appeared in *Sud* again in June. In "La Philosophie du siècle," he expresses disappointment with Henri Bergson's then new (1932) book, *Les Deux sources de la morale et de la religion,* which should have crowned the philosopher's work but in the reviewer's opinion failed to go beyond Bergson's previous preoccupation with method. The more ambitious effort by Camus in the same issue, "Essai sur la musique," is a tribute to the spiritual values of music, reinforced by Schopenhauer and Nietzsche. Rejecting music which tells a story or conveys a message, young Camus insists: "In general and to conclude, really fertile Music, the only kind which will move us and which we shall really relish, will be a Music of Dream which will banish all reason and all analysis."

Several things are worth remarking here. One is the topicality of the Bergson article, which in fact is the review of a new book rather than the study of a classic (the usual lot of lycée students). The choice of Jehan Rictus is unorthodox in another way, for Rictus (who wrote in street slang) was simply not classroom material in pre-World War II France. The final point that might be made is that Grenier was taking his students (certainly taking Camus) seriously. Further evidence of this is found in Grenier's correspondence with Max Jacob, that remarkable combination of poet and painter, Breton-born Jew and devout

Catholic. Jacob was born on July 12, 1876, but apparently insisted that it had really been on July 11, for as a clairvoyant and amateur astrologist he believed that the number 12 signified prison and death. He lived much of his life in meditation and prayer at Saint-Benoît-sur-Loire. The Gestapo would find him there in 1944 and send him to a concentration camp, where he fulfilled the original prophecy by dying. (When his body was transferred to Saint-Benoît for burial after the liberation of France, the military truck lost its way, following the plot of one of his poems: "The burial had already taken place on the previous day, but it had to be done over because of an error in the itinerary.")

A prolific writer, Jacob was already famous when Jean Grenier was a young lycée teacher in Algiers. And Grenier, a longtime correspondent of Jacob, was telling him about *Sud,* for which he hoped Jacob would write, and even about his young student Camus. By the summer of 1932 Albert Camus and Max Jacob had become correspondents too. Jacob wrote to Grenier on September 28, 1932: "Mr. Camus seemed to me a young man with a future; he demonstrates a faith in art which could well transform itself into other faiths."[13] Not yet nineteen years of age, a full decade away from the publication of his first book in France, Camus was already engaged in a dialogue on literature with a famous poet. From then on, the distance between himself and the makers of contemporary literature in France would never seem as great.

He had read, thanks to his "happy disease," Gide's *Traités.* Whole passages of *La Tentative amoureuse* he knew by heart. To Jean Grenier he remarked that he found Gide's *Journal* "human." Soon he had read all of Gide, and Grenier gave him Proust's *A la recherche du temps perdu.*[14]

Sometime during his lycée years, perhaps during this final term, the young student had joined the group that was publishing a weekly newspaper called *Ikdam,* founded in 1919 to raise Moslem consciousness by Emir Khaled, grandson of legendary nationalist fighter-hero Abd el-Kader. By this time Khaled, author of an early exposé of the condition of Algeria's Moslems (*La Situation des Musulmans d'Algérie*), was living in exile. His follower Sadek Denden was running *Ikdam* and the movement Fraternité Algérienne. The paper's line was quite radical for that time, demanding equality of Moslem and French-European settlers, an end to special and discriminatory legislation for the indigenous majority, freedom of speech, of travel, the right to organize. Nothing more is known of Camus' work on *Ikdam* or of his relationship with Sadek Denden, but this encounter, however brief, must have been a significant one, representing as it did Camus' first experience of Algeria's Moslems and of their aspirations.[15]

The school year 1932–33 was a curious no-man's-land for Camus. It followed the lycée, but it was not yet the university. In mainland France the two years of preparation for entrance to Paris' prestigious school for professors, Ecole Normale Supérieure, are called respectively *hypokhâgne* and *khâgne*. But only the *hypokhâgne* year was available in Algiers, and as a consequence it was something of a dead end. For the students it seemed an easy year, heavily concentrated on philosophy, with frequent dissertations, but the final examination was superfluous. Two of the bright young men Camus met that year, André Belamich and Claude de Fréminville, returned to their homes in Oran without even bothering to take the year-end examinations in June.

Fréminville (his full name was Claude de la Poix de Fréminville, of an eminent family some of whose members had been officers of the royal court) had been born in Perpignan, the son of an army officer. Although he went to Paris after the *hypokhâgne* year to pursue his university studies, he remained in close touch with Camus, and on his return to Algeria they would become associated in literary and political adventures. As the first of the group to join the Communist Party, Fréminville was more than a negligible political influence on his stay-at-home friend. After World War II he worked as a journalist in Paris, where under the name Claude Terrien he became a news editor and commentator on the French station Radio Europe No. 1. He died in January 1966. Belamich settled in France after the war as a literary translator (e.g., of Jane Austen and D. H. Lawrence). Later, thanks to Camus, he would do translations for Gallimard.[16]

At about the time Camus began that school year, he was composing a series of prose poems which he grouped under the heading "Intuitions" (published posthumously in *Cahiers Albert Camus 2*). He called them reveries. A brief introduction, probably written in October 1932, hints at resistance to their message: "If they are sometimes discouraged, it's because no one wanted their enthusiasm. If they are sometimes negative, it's because no one wanted their affirmations." We are left in the dark as to the source of this resistance; probably it had been expressed by the friends to whom he began to show his writing. Whatever the case, "Intuitions" is the first free-flying work that we have from Camus. Romantic in tone, it is *fin de siècle* in style; *Bonheur* and *Unité* are capitalized. "I know only one thing," it concludes, "my mystic soul which burns to give itself with enthusiasm, with faith, with fervor."

With Max-Pol Fouchet, now with Fréminville, Belamich, readers, writers, dreamers, literary discussion could become more formal, car-

ried on during those walks through old Algiers, hikes along the
enveloping slopes, or in the old student cafés. Presumably there was a
certain amount of trading back and forth of manuscripts. Thus when
Camus wrote an essay called "Beriha ou le rêveur," not a line of which
has survived, Fouchet reproached him for having portrayed not a
dreamer but a logician. Camus replied with a ten-point memorandum
defending "Beriha," and the memorandum has survived. In it he explained to Fouchet that, if his personage Beriha seems to express himself logically, it is because much pleasure can be derived from expressing deep feeling in an unorthodox form. Gide, he points out, uses
commonplace words for philosophical speculation. Beyond that, he
says, "I place above logic both Dream and Action." Camus concludes
by wondering how Fouchet can say that he likes the essay while at the
same time claiming that it is logical, since he also says that he doesn't
appreciate logic. Camus is willing to concede that the essay requires
more than one reading.[5]

These exchanges, the *hypokhâgne* program, the growing intimacy
with Grenier (whom he would visit at home), were rapidly expanding
his universe. He was apparently sitting in on classes at the University of
Algiers as well.

In a series of notes on his reading ("Notes de lecture") dated
April 1933, reproduced in *Cahiers Albert Camus 2,* he refers to
Stendhal, Aeschylus' *Prometheus Bound,* Léon Chestov, Dostoevsky,
Nietzsche, Grenier, and especially Gide. These notes are the first journal known to have been kept by Camus, whose more formal journal
later published in book form was begun in May 1935. In these April
1933 notes he will commit his first introspection to paper:

> I must learn to tame my sensibility, too ready to overflow. For
> hiding it under irony and coolness I thought I was the master. Now
> I must sing a different tune.

He notes that he has completed another essay, "La Maison mauresque," in which he has managed to conceal his *"souffrances présentes";*
only in the final lines do they show through. "La Maison mauresque"
represented considerable effort; he is at once proud of it and unwilling
to reread it before Jean Grenier does.

He delivers himself of a personal note, of the kind we are not often
to find in the later journal:

> When walked through the city with S.C. humored myself by re-
> citing verses and banalities to conceal a too natural exaltation. The
> sun smelled good on the waterfront.[17]

He has read Jean Grenier's book [this would be *Les Iles*]:
The unity of his book is the constant presence of death. This is how

I explain that the very sight of G., while changing nothing in my way of being, renders me graver, more fully penetrated with the gravity of life.

I know no other man who can affect me in this way. Two hours spent with him always enrich me. Will I ever know all that I owe to him?

"La Maison mauresque" survives only as a manuscript written in a school notebook, published posthumously. The subject is an Algerian-style house in the Jardin d'Essai near Belcourt, built in 1930 as part of the celebration of the centennial of French conquest. Camus uses the house as a launching platform for a flow of reflections, creating a *"maison d'émotions."* There is interplay between this house and other landmarks noted in passing, and the writer's own feelings. The essay is composed in the poetic style he will employ for all of his early exercises, for he is now consciously training himself to use words. In the same notebook the final pages contain a fragment entitled "Courage," which for the first time makes use of the real stuff of the young man's world. "The five lived together: the grandmother, her younger son, her oldest daughter and the daughter's two children," it begins, and concludes with the formidable grandmother's anticlimactic death. It is a draft for what will become a section of Camus' first published book, *L'Envers et l'Endroit.* And it is accompanied by one of the most revealing of all Camus' texts, expressing not only the intentions of *L'Envers et l'Endroit* but the world view of the young man. "It bothers people when you are lucid and ironic," he begins. And concludes:

These essays [which were not yet written as far as we know] were born of circumstances. . . . It is true that I can only live in the countries of the Mediterranean, where I like the life and the light; but it is also true that the tragedy of existence obsesses man and that this place is associated with the deepest silence. Between this wrong side and this right side of the world and of myself, I refuse to choose . . .

Recall that he has just read *Les Iles,* about which he wrote in his "Notes de Lecture" . . . "G. [Jean Grenier] . . . renders me graver, more fully penetrated with the gravity of life."

But on reflection, and with maturity, Camus was going to discover that Grenier's *Iles* were deserted islands, leaving men stranded, with no earthly recourse. He himself thought that salvation was possible, salvation not through the unfathomable, the mystical, but through man's own will. Camus was going to stay on solid ground.[18]

# 6

## SIMONE

> I shall take my little girl by the hand and have her sit be-
> side me. There she will look at me steadily and in the eyes
> of one another we shall follow the slow sea journeys to-
> ward unknown waters. . . .
>
> Note left beside his sleeping wife

At the beginning she was by all accounts a ravishing girl, even-featured, healthy-seeming, with a firm jaw and high cheekbones. All of young Algiers recognized her when she passed along the street, admired her lithe dancer's build, her reddish-blond hair, her high-fashion clothing, extravagant for that time and place, and in broad daylight, too. A flirt, worse, a vamp. If she was seldom caught wearing the same dress twice, she never wore anything under her dress, and *that* was rather exceptional at the time. "We were all a little in love with her," one of the young men around Camus would later confess. The pin-up of the student generation, she was also their "Nadja," a reference to the mysterious, capricious heroine of André Breton's tale, and the retreat into darkness of Breton's heroine anticipated Simone's.[1]

Her mother, Marthe Sogler, was a successful ophthalmologist with a reputation (not necessarily deserved) for loose living; of her father, Achille, nothing more would be heard. Madame Sogler's brother-in-law, Amédée Laffont, was a noted surgeon and professor of obstetrics, who would later become dean of Algiers' Faculty of Medicine. Simone Hié was born in Algiers on September 10, 1914. So that she was not yet sixteen when she met Max-Pol Fouchet as they watched the conquest centennial parade on the balcony of a mutual friend's apartment.

From then on Fouchet and Simone Hié, whom he refers to only as

"S." in *Un Jour, je m'en souviens* . . . , a memoir of his youth, were together nearly all the time. According to Fouchet their liaison infuriated Simone's stepfather, Marthe Sogler's second husband, who seemed intensely and even suspiciously jealous. Fouchet recalls having been struck by the man, who would follow and then corner the young couple. Yet Fouchet thought that Marthe Sogler herself approved his relationship with her daughter. Max-Pol and Simone were unofficially engaged, and it was understood that they would marry on Fouchet's return from military service.

But Fouchet was also quite busy. With his studies, presumably, but above all with his political activity. He had set up the Fédération des Jeunesses Socialistes in Algeria, and as its leader he often had to travel out of the capital to help establish branches of the movement in smaller towns. Sometimes they would confront hostile European settlers, or Moslems who had been incited by the hostile settlers to attack the young organizers, in total ignorance of their political program. During these absences from town, Fouchet believes, his friend Albert Camus would see Simone. Camus was attracted to her as a fellow romantic; together they would act out the characters in the books they were reading. For Camus (to hear Fouchet tell it), she also played a seduction scene.

One day, when Fouchet thought that he had an appointment with Simone Hié, she did not appear. Nor did she come to the meeting place on any of the following days. Finally Camus let Fouchet know that he wished to speak to him. The young men met in the Jardin d'Essai and walked down to the beach (the beach of Camus' Belcourt childhood), from which they could look back to see the sweep of the city around its bay.

Fouchet opened with the subject of Simone, confessing that he was unhappy. Camus stopped and turned to face him. "She won't come back," he said. "She has chosen." Fouchet knew immediately whom it was that she had chosen. He recalls that he felt both pain and joy, in a sense that he was glad that his successful rival was a member of their group, someone he liked and admired. He said as much to Camus, who replied: "I was wondering if you had genius, and you're proving that you do." It was part of their game to act like that, or so Fouchet would later believe.

But it meant a break in their friendship all the same. The wound was deeper than Fouchet then realized. Their estrangement worsened, and others contributed to making it worse. The two men would never again be friends. Still, in 1934, after Camus' marriage to Simone Hié, when Fouchet was sent to the student sanatorium at Saint-Hilaire-du-Touvet in mainland France following an attack of tuberculosis, Camus could write to him:

. . . . the only value of our little personalities resides in the witness that we are able to bear about life. We say it and we fade away: It's what one calls simplicity, and as the hotel owner in Tipasa says: You can die and they won't talk about you.

Yet it would be wrong to be pessimistic, Camus concluded. Love, art, religion still existed. "What more can I say to you? I do believe that you are for me one of the beings who make up my circle of experience."[2]

Becoming involved with Simone Hié was not the way to a happy end. For Albert Camus this captivating girl (he would have been not quite nineteen, she not quite eighteen, when they met) would serve as an object of his reveries, an audience for his prose poems, so that the more ethereal she was, the better. But some of this other-worldliness turned out to have a more down-to-earth explanation. She sought a "disordering of all the senses," in Fouchet's phrase, and she found it in drugs.[2]

The story accepted by her family and friends was that at the age of fourteen or so she had been given morphine as treatment for menstrual pain and then had become addicted. The less charitable would see her as naturally wild, a driven creature, mythomaniac. Everyone agreed that she was well in advance of her time not only in taking drugs but in her daily life style. It was rumored that she cast a spell on the young doctors of the city to obtain the drugs she needed, after exhausting her mother's pharmaceutical cabinet and her access to blank prescription forms. Her later life would be spent in and out of private hospitals and rest homes.

Camus believed at the time that he could rescue her. He may have thought that by marrying her he would have a better chance of success. Certainly Marthe Sogler must have believed so, for she encouraged the marriage between her daughter and this jobless, sickly young man, helped set up the newlyweds' household, and would never cease to be grateful to her son-in-law. For until the final instants of his life Camus would be asked to help Simone Hié, and his help would be forthcoming.

The Acaults, who continued to provide room and board for their nephew, took another view. They felt that Albert had too much promise, faced too long and hard a climb, to be burdened at that moment with marriage, and with *that* marriage. Already Simone was being seen all over town with their nephew. Although not enrolled as a student, for she had never received her *baccalauréat,* Simone had a lively intelligence, assimilated quickly. She would sometimes attend classes with Camus, but unlike the girl students who wore practical school clothes, she would walk into the classroom wrapped in a fox stole. Of course this elegance met an elegance already being cultivated by her fiancé. It also represented the achievement of a goal of sorts, for Simone was the exaggerated symbol of the upper middle class, with her extra-wide-brimmed hat, her extra-high heels, her extra-long cigarette holder, all of which attributes were out of place in their group.[3]

But for Gustave Acault she was worse than that. She was a *gour-gandine* (read chippy), who was gradually taking possession of his nephew. For Acault, a good woman was a woman who worked, worked in silence, and who knew how to be self-effacing while her man held forth in public places. Simone was definitely not that kind of woman, and consequently she was not a wife for his Albert. Albert was too young, his health too frail; he had his studies to pursue, and no independent means of livelihood. It was also wrong, Gustave Acault believed, for a boy from Belcourt to become involved with a girl from another social and economic milieu.[4]

And it was likely, as at least one of Camus' friends believed, that Gustave Acault was jealous of the hold Simone had on his nephew.

Simone, who was then living with her mother on downtown Rue d'Isly, where Dr. Sogler also had her office, was seeing Albert in his room at the Acaults'. Uncle Gustave put a stop to that.

Jean de Maisonseul, the School of Architecture student, dropped in to see his friend one evening and discovered him in the depths of despair. Camus turned an expressionless face up to Maisonseul and said simply: "She won't come back." It was not much of an explanation, but Maisonseul made it a point not to ask questions. He limited his response to a reassuring hand on his friend's head. "Let's go out to eat something," he suggested.

While Camus was getting ready Maisonseul noticed a book lying open on the mantelpiece and read these lines:

> When with the sun in your hair, in the street
> And in the night, you came to me laughing
> And I thought I saw the fairy whose hat was brightness

He turned the book over and discovered that it was a collection of Mallarmé's poetry. The poem was "Apparition."

"Lend it to me."

Years later he would discover the book on his shelf, with the inscription "Albert Camus 1932" inside the cover. He had never remembered to return it.

The dinner in a run-down Arab restaurant on Rue de la Marine in the old fishermen's district seemed unending, the indifferent food was eaten in gloom.[5]

Life at the Acaults' was now coming to an end. The young man was increasingly irritated by what he felt was authoritarian behavior on his uncle's part, by the older man's need to dominate. In a sense it was a clash of two strong wills. Camus felt hemmed in. Even Gustave Acault's mingling with university professors at the Brasserie de la Renaissance annoyed him, reinforcing Acault's "uncle knows best" image.[6]

The year of *hypokhâgne* was over. If all went well, there would be summer holidays, followed by the first year of college, when he would be attending classes practically next door to his Rue de Languedoc room.

But it was not to be that way. It was Simone Hié or nothing, his own way of life or nothing. In July he moved in with his brother Lucien at 117 bis Rue Michelet. He told his teacher Jean Grenier, in a letter dated July 13, that he was no longer sure that he would be able to pursue his studies toward a college degree. Yet, he insisted, "I regret nothing . . . I acted according to my heart and my feelings." He suggested to Grenier that the break resulted from conflicting ideals as well as from personal differences. But he did not ask Grenier, who had also come under the spell of Acault's primitive intelligence and attractive personality, to choose sides. In a second letter to Grenier (like the first, quoted in Grenier's preface to Camus' works but with no explanation of their context), he concluded:

> What is important is that I have set myself a goal, a work . . . I see without any self-satisfaction that I am capable of resistance, of energy, of will. My physical state, it is true, leaves much to be desired. But I want to be cured.

He did not add that he had chosen to be accompanied in the pursuit of his oeuvre, and of his cure, by one of the most talked-about young creatures in town.

In the fall of 1933 Camus entered his first university year. He could no longer count on his uncle's backing. Soon he would be getting help from his future mother-in-law. He was also determined to earn money for his daily needs as he could, for example by giving private lessons to lycée students working for the *baccalauréat*. In his letter to Max-Pol Fouchet at Saint-Hilaire-du-Touvet he asked if his unhappy rival could help him find private lessons, or a job writing articles or even handling someone's correspondence.[7]

The University of Algiers was housed in a neoclassical pastiche of a building in the center of Algiers, just above the Rue Michelet. At the time it held only a few hundred students, all of them Europeans, for Moslems in a position to attend college usually preferred to study in an atmosphere of greater equality in mainland France. When Camus entered the university, the chair of philosophy had only recently been established. The regular program of studies lasted three years. During the first two, students would work for four certificates, leading to the *licence;* in the third year (and no more than a third of the student body got this far) they could work for a *diplôme d'études supérieures,* which required the writing of a dissertation. After that one would have to go to Paris to take exams for the *agrégation,* gateway to a teaching career in higher education, or for a doctorate.

Depending on the year the student enrolled, his program would consist of work toward the first two or the last two certificates; there was no necessary order. As it happened, Camus would begin by taking the examination for the *certificat de morale et sociologie,* which required no further study. Apparently his *hypokhâgne* year and his reading got him through it, and he received the certificate on November 6, 1933. During that first college year he worked for the *certificat de psychologie,* which he passed in June 1934. After that he would obtain his *certificat des études littéraires classiques* on November 8 of the same year, and the *certificat de logique et philosophie générale* on June 4, 1935.

Within this system there was total freedom of subject matter. The professor would choose the material he wished to impart to his students during that particular term. Classes were small, more on the scale of seminars. Students were expected to prepare oral reports, to be followed by discussion. In a sense, in the words of Camus' professor René Poirier, the Université d'Alger was a gathering place of the self-taught, who carried out their own education under the guidance of their professors.[8]

It helped that these professors were René Poirier, somewhat austere, intellectually sure of himself, and Jean Grenier, more fanciful, tempering intellectual severity with some knowledge of the needs of the creative man (of his own needs first of all). Born in 1900, Poirier had been a lycée teacher in Chartres, then received an appointment to the University of Montpellier in Southern France, before being transferred to Algiers at the age of thirty-three. His students, who tended to be left-wing, saw him at once as a reactionary. Most of Camus' friends, in any case, didn't like him, and felt that he graded their examination papers too harshly.

Privately they accused him of discrimination against students who practiced their politics openly, such as Yves Dechezelles, who wore a lapel button consisting of three silver arrows, the insignia of the Socialist (Third) International. Camus was aware of Poirier's views, but he had made up his mind to be a good student and not to allow political differences to interfere with the acquisition of a university education.

He did all of his preparatory work on time, so that he was irreproachable and invulnerable. This did not mean that he would kowtow to his
professors. If he refrained from open rebellion, he kept his distance all
the same.[9]

Not everyone received the cold, brilliant teaching of Poirier with
the same suspicion. An Algerian Jew, reminiscing about these college
years, felt that Poirier "incarnated this French intelligence, this intellectual elegance to which our generations [of Algerian Jews] had
aspired . . . Poirier spoke to [Camus]; we, the other students, felt like
little boys."[10]

For if Poirier found Camus' politics distasteful, to the extent that
they mattered to him, if he found Camus' manner slightly overdone
(given his record of accomplishment to date), he could also recognize a
mind in the making. Poirier remembered that his own professor had
given him a grade of 14 (out of 20) and added the comment: "very
good." He himself would admire Camus' dissertation—and give him a
15, which upset Camus. Seen from the professor's side of the room, the
university year had its pressures. Poirier, who taught four hours a week,
preparing the course material as he went along, would recall that during
his years in Algiers he had been able to do no work of his own.[8]

And then Camus' lycée teacher and intellectual guide, Jean Grenier, was on hand as Poirier's assistant. Grenier had gotten his *agrégation* alongside Poirier in 1922, but they had never been close. (Poirier
felt that it was Grenier who lacked warmth, but he could also observe
that as a writer Grenier would necessarily be closer to Camus than he
would ever be.) Grenier's teaching introduced fantasy into the curricu-
lum. He invented his own program, would talk of marginal subjects
such as Taoism.[11] Camus later recalled reading Hindu philosophy, and
Grenier also introduced Camus to Plato and to Chestov. They read
Spinoza, Descartes, Kierkegaard.[12]

Now, for the first time, the young man was going to be judged not
only by his teachers, who obviously represented a class and a milieu far
removed from his own, but by his peers. In those days the French university was accessible principally to the middle class, sons and daughters of the liberal professions. The sifting process was such that one was
likely to encounter students of more than usual gifts, more than common intellectual curiosity. So that it was going to be harder for Camus
to maintain his distance now, even if he wanted to. He couldn't be a
leader, for example, as he had been in elementary school, even in the
lycée, without imparting something in return. Yet his college classmates
considered him a natural leader, so convinced did he seem of his place
in the world. He himself never made the slightest effort to plead for
their affection, never used a trick to get someone to like him. He was

as independent as a shying horse. It was as if he bore a sign reading *"Noli me tangere."*

He never let his poverty (past or present) show, and this contributed to his mystery. His *pudeur* might have made him seem what he may not have been at all: pretentious.[13]

Two weeks after meeting Albert Camus, Yves Dechezelles, himself of a more comfortable family environment (he had cultivated his diction in Normandy and Brittany, and would later become a nationally known attorney, defending Algerian militants during the insurrection), addressed his new friend using the familiar *tu* form. Camus replied coolly: "I like you, but I prefer *vous* to *tu*." Dechezelles was shocked, and attributed Camus' behavior to his association with a group of self-avowed aesthetes outside the university (Jean de Maisonseul, Louis Miquel, and their friends). And it was true that Camus and his "aesthete" friends used the *vous* form to each other. Later Camus would be more relaxed about such matters, but Dechezelles (and others) would never feel that he was totally relaxed, certainly not about being addressed in the *tu* form.[14]

He did not appear to be without funds; probably he was still wearing the clothing bought for him by the Acaults. Some new friends even saw him as a dandy. Dechezelles, then preoccupied with his Socialist youth movement activities, felt that there was a contrast between Camus' appearance and his expressed opinions. A radical, in Dechezelles opinion, should not be taking such good care of his clothing. Dechezelles' wife-to-be, Myriam Salama, was perhaps more observant when she noted that he possessed only a single suit, light gray in color. But he wore golden-yellow shoes. Once he raised his foot to show her that the sole of his shoe was so thin that it was peeling. He joked: "Better total poverty than counting pennies."

It was during this period that he let on to his new college friends that his mother lived in another town (Oran) and that she was mentally ill. That put an end to any likelihood that they would ever meet her. He didn't bother to say, at least to his college circle, that his mother was of Spanish origin. Friends normally visited each other's homes but one simply didn't go to Camus'. At least not to his real home. Some of them visited him at his brother's, or his uncle's or at the small top-floor room which he rented as soon as he could afford to, where they would listen to Ravel and Debussy on the phonograph. In his behavior he seemed quite aristocratic, as if his *game* was to play that he grew up in Belcourt.[9]

Among his artist friends he was far from seeming poor and humble. He had more pocket money than they did, at least while he was living at the Acaults'; *he* was the one who bought books and records to lend to the others (or Simone bought them).[15]

His response to things that might go wrong was characteristically stoical. Once, when they were to take a psychology examination, Yves Dechezelles told Camus in error that it would be given in the afternoon. When they arrived together at the designated room they learned that the examination had already been held that morning. Camus was patently upset, the examination was obviously of importance to him, but he didn't let on that it was. In a gracious way he said: "We'll take it the next time." The next time was six months away.

There was constant tension between leftist and rightist students at the university. Dechezelles as a Socialist militant was right in the middle of it. But Camus never participated. Dechezelles felt that Camus' uncle might have disapproved, or that his health did not allow him to risk the violent form the clashes sometimes assumed.[16]

What was certain was that, despite the extracurricular activities which would soon make him a local celebrity, Camus in the immediate university environment was a serious student. In turn his teachers began to treat him differently from the polite and somewhat condescending way they usually dealt with good students. "Camus was something else," remembered Jacques Heurgon, then a young professor of Latin.

> Of a maturity which abolished the separation of age, of a seriousness without heaviness which discouraged small talk, of a ceremonial politeness which protected an acute sensitivity, he inspired our friendship based on respect. He had simply loomed up among us as someone whose life was going to be important, who was going to begin, starting at zero and without complacency, the great enterprise of being a man.[17]

He seemed to be living several public and private lives now. He had his university career, he had his "aesthete" circle outside the university, he had Simone Hié. He was also testing himself further as a writer.

Just about now, at the beginning of his first college year, he wrote a poem called "Méditerranée" (and gave the manuscript to Jean de Maisonseul, to whom he had lent the Mallarmé poems). In four stanzas, totalling fifty-five lines, the novice poet attempts for the first time to define in his own words the Mediterranean ideology that would permeate his work, a quality that necessarily distinguished it from that of mainland French writers. It would be the first version of the final truth contained in his philosophical testament, *L'Homme révolté*.

He was being pumped full of this Mediterranean ideology by everyone around him, and notably by non-Mediterraneans, émigrés or tem-

porarily transplanted mainlanders like Grenier, by favorite writers like
Gide, who with Montherlant and earlier visitors such as Pierre Louÿs
and even Oscar Wilde had invented a North Africa which Camus and
his friends thought they could recognize, and with which they certainly
wished to identify. Surely this theme was a subject of their long talks
during hikes along the roads and paths dominating the Mediterranean
coastline.

The conceit of Mediterranean man (and of his allies) is that these
sun-blessed shores breed men who know their limits and the just measure of things. If for the Northern European the voluble, easily excitable
Mediterranean seems anything but evenhanded and serene (at times
he is even a figure of fun), the literate Mediterranean is imbued with
the certainty that he has inherited from the classics, has been tamed
along with nature. Camus would soon find a symbol of his Mediterranean in Tipasa, a romantic excavation site whose Roman ruins contrast with the runaway vegetation, the adjacent sea. A friend he made in
Poirier's class, Philippe Coulombel, took him on weekends to his parents' home, one of the houses with "white walls and roses and green ve-
randas" which dominated the village.[18] "In the springtime, Tipasa is inhabited by gods and the gods speak in the sun and the odor of
wormwood," begins the often-quoted "Noces à Tipasa" (*Noces*).

Camus' early poem "Méditerranée" is truffled with this doctrinal
content:

> Mediterranean! Your world is on our scale
> . . . . . . . . . . . . . . . . . . . . . . . . . . .
> Blond blue cradle where certainties balance
> . . . . . . . . . . . . . . . . . . . . . . . . . . .
> The Latin land does not tremble.
> . . . . . . . . . . . . . . . . . . .
> In you the worlds are polished and made human,

to quote *only* doctrinal content. The young poet concludes:

> Mediterranean, oh! Mediterranean sea!
> Alone, naked, without secrets, your sons await death.
> Death will give them back to you, pure, pure at last.

The poem would be published posthumously, along with other
manuscripts dating from this period. Among these are more prose
poems, or prose highly charged with poetic rhythm and emotion. A
short piece, "Devant la morte," describes the successive states of feeling
of one confronted by the inert body of his beloved, despair rapidly
transformed into cruel lucidity and cynicism—but then the observer is a
very young man. Another exercise, "Perte de l'être aimé," is undated
but could serve as philosophical gloss to the dramatic "Devant la

morte." For the death of the beloved, one might also read the frustration of desiring the unattainable, or of not being able to possess it wholly, once attained. But: "So many things are capable of being loved that without doubt no discouragement can be definitive." In the absence of information as to the beneficiary of these lines, we can guess that they were addressed to the writer himself, as a warning in his present circumstances. Everyone who knew the couple agreed that he had not chosen facility by falling in love with Simone Hié.

Several other manuscripts bear the date of 1933 or are believed to have been completed by that year (before or during the first semester of college). A brief "Dialogue de Dieu avec son âme" is a witty reflection on the nature of hope. "Contradictions" is an argument that accepting one's fate or revolting against it is each an aspect of a "sinister comedy," for life remains as it is no matter how we react to it. The chief interest of these pages is the practice they give the young writer in using words. Invariably he uses too many of them, and the texts are flowery, cerebral, self-centered; but that is how writers begin; their education is to learn how usefully the overflow can be eliminated. On the basis of this evidence Camus was learning fast; his art-for-art period developed and died almost simultaneously with the need to express palpable things convincingly.

For in addition to these speculations there was to be another attempt this year to capture and to refine his adolescent trauma. "L'Hôpital du quartier pauvre" undoubtedly draws on his brief stay at the Mustapha Hospital at the outbreak of his tuberculosis, and on follow-up visits to the outpatient clinic for pneumothorax treatments. In this sketch a group of tuberculosis patients is taking the sun on the hospital grounds. It is the month of May (a detail which has contributed to the confusion about the date of inception of Camus' own illness). The patients exchange gossip, joke about the misfortunes of fellow patients: about a hairdresser who tried to kill himself by throwing himself in front of an automobile and came out of it with a kick in the pants from the driver; about another who continued to make love to a demanding wife (tuberculosis had made him exceptionally virile) until abuse of this exercise killed him. They also talk about the likelihood of getting well again. "Tuberculosis is the only disease they know how to cure. It's just that it takes time."

A final piece dated 1933, "L'Art dans la Communion," betrays the formality of a class paper, and it is equipped with a conclusion labeled as such. But as such things go it is quite personal, and in a sense may be taken as a declaration of intentions of a young man "on the threshold of life" who doubts all received ideas while fully aware that an unmoored existence is vain. He chooses, as his means to transcend the quotidian, Art. Or rather the Arts, and here the author proceeds to describe architecture, painting, literature, music, this last the most perfect. Together they represent a communion which ignores life; but to turn away from life toward art underscores the importance of life, and art can't ignore that.

He had found an audience for his inchoate attempts to reconcile art and life, belief in something or someone better or higher than himself, and freedom. If Simone Hié was not attending classes regularly, she was getting the benefit of the young philosophy student's findings at a remove. And she was shrewd enough, as her former suitor Max-Pol Fouchet had observed, to read the books her friends were reading, sufficiently intelligent to understand them. A letter of Camus to Simone which has been dated at about this time (the end of 1933 or early 1934, in any case before their marriage) has Camus writing to her as he was writing class papers for Grenier. From the text as published in the Pléiade edition of his work:

> Our table bends under the mayflowers which remind us that the springtime we dreamed has no equal save in the death which frightens us. . . . Thus do we march toward Unity or toward plurality in our admiration or our pantheism.
>
> . . . Is there something behind the wet skies and the morning prairies, behind the perfumes and the flowers? And who am I to speak of all that, of all this absorbing mystery, who am I other than he who believes? But it is not in what is behind the perfumes and the flowers that I believe, it's in the perfumes and in the flowers. . . .

Courting Simone, seeing her more regularly, had been the most notable activity of this first college term. But in addition to his private exercises in expression and his class papers, he was ready to take on another kind of writing. Association with Jean de Maisonseul, Louis Miquel, and their artist comrades had expanded his interest in the plastic arts; at least he was the member of their group who had the talent to write about what he was seeing.

Algiers had become a minor capital of painting, as a kind of vacation retreat of the Ecole de Paris at its most sensuous. The sun and the sea, which were also Camus' themes, indigenous architecture and dress, African vegetation were compelling subjects. Just as young French artists were going to Rome to work at the French Academy's Villa Medici there, others from the mainland were receiving two-year resident fellowships to Algiers' Villa Abd el-Tif, an attractive Moorish house on the wooded slopes of the Jardin d'Essai, so that the Mediterranean port city could consider itself something of an artistic crossroads. Camus would later betray a weakness for these French painters who themselves betrayed a weakness for the pastel-pale landscapes of North Africa, and he would favor them (e.g., Edy-Legrand, P.-E. Clairin) as illustrators of his books.

He arranged to review art exhibitions for the university newspaper *Alger-Etudiant*. The first one might have been devoted to the Salon des Orientalistes, a show on Mediterranean themes, if Camus had not chosen to focus this review on his sculptor friend Louis Benisti, who had sent three pieces to the show. A note at the bottom of the column promised a more general report on the salon in the following issue.

This first review, published in *Alger-Etudiant* on January 25, 1934,[19] opens with an evocation of Benisti's studio: "a long damp room, an angry fire, two armchairs nearby." On the walls, works of Despiau and Maillol. An unfinished sculpture in a corner. Silence.

But now some of these works, "nourished in silence," have been tossed to the multitude, in an excessively lit exhibition space. Only three works, but Benisti is one of the rare young artists who believe art comes slowly. "His art is only beginning, his conceptions are almost ripe." Beginnings indeed. This was Benisti's first public appearance. A jeweler by trade, he had found himself in financial straits after a robbery, at which time he decided to throw over his business to do what he had always wanted to do. He began attending life classes at the studio of an older painter, and there met Jean de Maisonseul.[20] Born in 1903, Benisti was thirty years old, ten years Camus' senior, when Camus wrote about this "rare young artist."

The review is pure praise, although it concludes with a reservation: If painting can consist of silences or bursts of laughter, sculpture must assert itself. But Benisti's affirmations are timid; a strong work, which he can and must create, is lacking here.

The neophyte critic followed up with the promised article on the salon proper. He began by deriding the very idea of a large show. Paintings need to be lived with, require "long and silent waiting, almost a love affair." He will write only of the paintings he has examined attentively. He will also refrain from discussing acknowledged talents. Each of the painters he considers worthy of attention receives a few lines, and then there is a long paragraph for another local artist, René-Jean Clot, whose work he felt was among the most remarkable in the salon. He lingers over Clot's painting of one of his own favorite haunts: ". . . It pleases me to recognize in it the delicately resonant poetry of Bouzaréah, its Virgilian softness and the indolence of the air. . . ."

This critic does not claim to possess absolute truth, but he feels that he is offering sincere opinion. He only regrets that "so little good wheat is mixed with so many tares." For him the Salon des Orientalistes is monotonous, gracelessly triste. His friend Maisonseul would never forget Camus' concluding remark about the hall in which the exhibition was held:[21]

> At the back of the room, large windows opened on to the harbor on a half-awakened morning, filled with indistinct masts, mists into which sirens enter as knives. . . . That was the best picture of all.

He would write two more reviews for *Alger-Etudiant,* one on the painter Pierre Boucherle,[22] another on the resident fellows of the Villa Abd el-Tif. Here he focused on the work of Richard Maguet, paintings of the Jardin d'Essai which surrounded the villa, of "the landscape of Tipasa in the spattering of the summer sun." He is equally moved by the sculpture of Damboise, for he is *affirmatif,* producing work with "lovely shoulders of flesh, protective and masculine." And in a postscript he explains that he has not spoken of André Hambourg, another exhibitor, for he is not sure what to make of this painter. "I should like to speak only of things of which I am more or less certain. This is not the case here. And to remain silent is better than to be wrong."

Young Hambourg, not much older than Camus himself, took this badly. He was a newcomer to Algeria, and he was aware that he did not fit into the provincial atmosphere, or he hadn't been allowed to fit. Some of the other young painters made him suffer for his being different. After the publication of this article Hambourg heard that one of them had let it be known that Hambourg was going to "sock Camus in the face" for his article. Then the same painter turned up to tell Hambourg that he must not hit Camus because of his tuberculosis. All of this seemed ridiculous to Hambourg, who had not intended to hit anybody, and certainly not Camus, who he felt was a victim of the manipulations of some of his friends who did not like the bohemian and free-wheeling Jewish bachelor from mainland France that Hambourg was at the time.[23]

Albert Camus married Simone Hié in a simple civil ceremony on June 16, 1934, just twelve days after he passed his *certificat de psychologie.* If Aunt Antoinette showed up, alerted by Albert's brother (she felt it was a way to face down Simone's parents),[4] none of her nephew's closest friends attended the wedding. The official marriage certificate indicates his mother's consent, for Camus was not quite twenty-one. (When his mother asked him what he would like to have as a wedding gift, he replied: a dozen pairs of white socks, the only kind he wore at the time.)[5] Later the couple told a friend how they had indulged in the humorous gesture of spending the wedding night apart, she at her mother's, he at his. Like their use of *vous* to each other, he supposed that this flaunting of conventions was meant to suggest that for free spirits marriage did not imply overfamiliarity.[24] Indeed, they would always use the *vous* form to each other, and she may not even have called him Albert, a name he disliked. He was "Camus" to his friends, and they all continued to use the formal *vous* to him.[5]

Jean de Maisonseul, who was perhaps Camus' best friend at the time, accompanying Simone on a shopping tour, discovered that she did not even know what a casserole was. In her usual disconcerting way she confided to shopkeepers that he, Maisonseul, was the groom. Her trousseau included sixteen bedsheets, four bolsters, six pillow cases, a set of tableware, and for her personal use two pairs of pajamas, a dishabille, a bed jacket, six slips, six nightgowns. The generous Dr. Sogler helped the couple set up their home in a villa in a pleasant resident neighborhood on the heights of Algiers called Parc d'Hydra. A rent receipt for 1935 survives, in the amount of 450 francs (some 535 current francs, or over $100), considered high for the time and place. Yet their new home was modest enough in appearance. Its chief attraction was a large living room opening onto a covered terrace which faced the hills (not the sea). Maisonseul designed their bedroom, all in horizontals, which had an unconscious Japanese effect with its simple wood furniture and shelving. A window desk board would hold a plaster Khmer Buddha which Camus had acquired in Maisonseul's company.[25]

The Jean Greniers lived nearby, in a box of a house with white stucco finish, also facing the hills and not the sea. There would be frequent evenings together.[26] The couple also re-established relations with the Acaults, and they would return to the Rue de Languedoc holding their heads high. After lunch, Aunt Gaby would fill up their market baskets with red meat to take back to Hydra.

There would also be a more conspicuous token of the Acaults' kindly feelings for the newlyweds, in the form of a 14-chevaux Citroën. The Acaults had acquired the automobile, a large vehicle for the time, back in 1930. Like other French Algerians they had been led to expect big things of the hundredth anniversary of the French conquest of the territory. While continuing to operate their Boucherie Anglaise they bought a hotel, expecting to share in the prosperity that was predicted for the centennial, and the revitalization of Algeria that would follow.

The centennial boom was a bust. But while they owned the hotel Antoinette had to work double time, dividing her day between the meat business and the tourist business. As a reward, Gustave gave her a choice between a mink coat and a Citroën motorcar and she chose the latter. Now they had offered the automobile as a gift to Albert and

Simone, with the understanding that Aunt Gaby would have the use of it one day a week.

But Simone Camus apparently didn't like the idea very much, this sharing of a car. One day the Citroën didn't show up at the Acaults' when it should have been there. They sent a complaint to their nephew. There was no reply, except for a message from the local police station: An automobile had been parked in front of the station and the Acaults' papers had been found inside.

And that would be that. While Gustave and Antoinette felt that Simone was the evil influence, they could only take this as a final break in their relations with the young Camus couple. Meanwhile André Villeneuve, Albert's schoolmate from Belcourt days, from whom he had been inseparable in the past, continued to visit the Acaults. They had all but adopted him, and their nephew was visibly irritated if not jealous. Meeting Villeneuve on the street, he jibed, "So, you've been to see your uncle." Although Albert Camus continued to have a deep affection for his uncle, and probably even understood his attitude, he and Villeneuve had a falling out and would never see each other again. No one has ever furnished a better reason for the ending of their friendship than this one.[27]

Living with "Nadja," living alone with her now, far from Dr. Sogler and her husband, far even from his friends (for few would share their home life), Camus set about making use of this captive audience for his creative urge. As an audience, but not as a subject, for he never achieved sufficient distance to be able to recall Simone in tranquillity. But that is for later.

At first it was pure bliss. Camus, who had a summer job, would rise early each morning and leave a note for the sleeping girl, perhaps to remind her of their lunch meeting that day, or simply to say: "You are sleeping. I don't dare wake you. You are lovely. That's enough for me." In one of these notes which Simone was to preserve, her new husband explains that he is leaving the house early to save 1.50 francs in tram fare (about 1.80 of today's francs, or some 37 cents). He would walk down the hill to the center of the city five kilometers away.[28] Possibly it was at this time—for no records exist, no infallible recollections of friends—that he was working for a ship's broker, one of four such in Algiers authorized to handle customs clearances, all of whom had offices in the same building on Boulevard Carnot dominating the port. (His brother remembered that he had worked for a ship's chandler, and guessed that it may have been the Amartini company, which was both a ship's broker and ship's chandler; in any case the job required that he cover the waterfront, carrying papers or handling other errands. The opening of *L'Etranger* makes use of this colorful but brief experience.)[29]

In another early-morning note left at Simone's pillow there is a suggestion of complicity in the construction of a private universe for the couple:

> We want to break the narrow bounds of thought and of human things, above Time, beyond Space. And because we wish it, it is done. I shall take my little girl by the hand and have her sit beside me. There she will look at me for a long time and in the eyes of one another we shall follow the slow sea journeys toward unknown waters which Sinbad's vessel sailed. Look; we are there.[30]

If she slept so much, one friend decided, it was because of drugs. Did her husband have any illusions about that? Very likely not. His friends watched with pain his ineffectual efforts (and those of Simone's mother) to arrest the girl's slow decline. Camus acted like a "saint," one of them thought, noticing that he had even given up cigarettes so that she would stop her obsessive chain-smoking.

She seemed more extravagant in manner, in dress, each time their friends ran into her. Max-Pol Fouchet, not an objective witness, it is true (certainly not at that time), remembered passing her on the street a few months later. Her beauty was fading. She held a bouquet of flowers, wide-eyed and distracted, singing to herself oblivious of passers-by, a sad Ophelia. He wondered whether Camus really wanted to cure her, or simply watched her as one observed an experiment.[31]

Another friend recalled getting up from the table in a restaurant to use the toilet which Simone had visited shortly before, and finding an empty glass tube there. It almost didn't matter whether any single one of these stories was true, since they were all accepted as true. Camus' friends were a little afraid of her and of her provocative attitude. She could have driven any one of them to suicide, is the way one of them put it. When Claude de Fréminville visited the Camus one evening for dinner and was confronted with Simone naked under an all-but-transparent veil, he refused the provocation, lowered his eyes, seized the first excuse to leave. In North Africa you respect the wife of a friend.[32]

"You don't belong to the daytime," one of their friends would later say to Simone Camus. "You are a creature of the night." And she exclaimed: "That's funny, Camus said exactly the same thing." What the friend meant was that she came straight out of *Les Fleurs du mal*. He wondered if Camus meant the same thing.[33]

◆
_____

# 7

# ENGAGEMENT

I have such a strong desire to help reduce the sum of
unhappiness and of bitterness which empoisons mankind.

Letter to Jean Grenier on joining the Communist Party

It is difficult to perceive any immediate effect on Albert Camus' creative
and public life of this uncommon existence with Simone Hié. His writing at that time and later appeared to make it a point to omit any character who could be identified with his wife. She seems to be absent even
from the draft novel *La Mort heureuse*, where so many characters can
be paired with real-life models. There is little direct reference to his
unsettling home life in his correspondence, and very little in his conversations with friends. Reticence of the sort was quite the expected behavior of a French Algerian, a Mediterranean man. Home life was home
life; married or not, men frequented other men in public places, where
they spoke of public things.

As it happened, there was plenty to talk about in public places
now. France, and with only a little delay French Algeria, would soon be
entering another turbulent political period, perhaps the only time since
the Dreyfus years that politics could be passionate. With the rest of the
world France had slipped into economic crisis, leading to reinforcement
of traditional divisions of the French polity, indeed to their aggrava-
tion: the right moving toward the extreme of Fascism, the left toward
Communism, each drawn to its respective model, Hitler Germany, the
Stalinist Soviet Union.

On February 6, 1934, in the second half of Camus' first university
year, the French center and left were shocked by the size and intensity
of the right-wing demonstrations at Paris' Place de la Concorde, just

across the Seine River from the Chamber of Deputies. The lower house of the French Parliament was preparing to vote confidence in the Radical Socialist government of Edouard Daladier, and the demonstrators were out to block the vote or to impose an authoritarian government on France, for the rallying cries had overtones of Fascism. The ensuing riot left 17 dead, 2,329 wounded, and brought down the government. The scar was eternal; "6 Février" still means something to Frenchmen. Some days later Communists and Socialists, traditional rivals, joined forces in a general protest strike. It would take another eighteen months for the movement toward unity of action of moderate and left-wing forces to take concrete form, but the wheels had begun to turn.

To those who were not privy to his daily movements, Camus seemed not to budge. In the university he continued to behave, even with Socialist friends, as an apolitical student—likable enough, but not to be counted on. Camus' college friends simply didn't know the whole story. His influences were coming from elsewhere, and he was increasingly attentive to them. One of his non-college friends was an easygoing, handsome young man who was studying architecture, knew the same young artists Camus knew. Robert Namia was born in the Aurès, where his Jewish parents were settlers. After his school years in Blida, he left his family to work in a bindery, threw himself into politics. Later he would be a hero to the Camus crowd, for when the Spanish Civil War broke out they were all deeply concerned, but it was Namia who enlisted in the International Brigade.

Another early convert to militant politics was Claude de Fréminville, a rebel against his bourgeois upbringing, who after the year of *hypokhâgne* with Camus went on to Paris to pursue his university education. He fell easily into the spirit of time and place. For the young students of Paris, militancy signified engagement with the Communists. "Did I tell you that I am a Communist?" Fréminville wrote his former classmate André Belamich in January 1934. "In Oran or in Algiers you can believe in the SFIO [Socialist Party]; here it's impossible. All of my boarding house is Communist except two idiots and some old maids."[1]

In July 1934, French Socialists and Communists signed a pact for unity of action, hammered out a common program. Indeed, the heretofore isolated Communist Party was prepared to go beyond class action, beyond unity with the Socialists alone. Stalin and the Soviet party were alarmed by the rise of Hitler, the potential threat of European Fascism, which had made Communism the principal target. As a consequence, the call was out for unity of action with all acceptable forces, and that included the more conservative Radical Socialists. In the new tactic of "Front Populaire," all center and left movements would be fused into a front against domestic and foreign Fascism.

The Popular Front soon had its press and quickly developed an organizational framework for political activity on the provincial level, even the Algerian level. An anti-Fascist congress had been held in Amsterdam in August 1932, called Congrès contre la Guerre et le Fascisme, organized by leftist writers Henri Barbusse and Romain Rolland. A year later a Congrès Antifasciste Européen met in Paris at the Salle Pleyel concert hall. Out of these two meetings developed an "Amsterdam-Pleyel" movement. In 1933 an Association des Ecrivains et Artistes Révolutionnaires (AEAR) began to sponsor the magazine *Commune*, advertised as "La Grande Revue pour la Défense de la Culture," in which the activities of France's intellectual Communists and their fellow-travelers were faithfully reported from issue to issue. The manifestos, the newspapers and magazines quickly made their way across the sea to Algeria. Jean Daniel, later to become a journalist in France, was then a student (younger than Camus) in the provincial town of Blida. He describes in his memoirs the effect of the Popular Front's activity on the youth of his town. "The table of contents of *Commune*," he wrote,

> filled us with enthusiasm even before we read the articles. Each name was burdened with a prestige which guaranteed the "line" for us. Besides, how could we have hoped for a clearer situation? Could anyone doubt that Nazism, Fascism, and their French accomplices incarnated Evil? As for Good, it sufficed to look toward Moscow.

The fact that their culture hero André Gide had thrown himself head-first into the anti-Fascist and pro-Soviet movement was no small factor in their enthusiasm.[2]

Characteristically, Camus entered the political arena with sober determination, after considerable deliberation, and without letting it affect his classwork—his rapport with Professor Poirier, for example, who was to supervise the writing of his dissertation. Through a mutual friend, André Thomas-Rouault, he had met a Communist militant, Emile Padula, who was deputy secretary-general of Paix et Liberté, the formal name of the Amsterdam-Pleyel movement. This was to be one of the first Communist fronts set up to carry out strategy mapped at Paris headquarters. The secretary-general of the Algiers chapter, Charles Escoute, was not a Party member; the Communists then and later preferred to have their fronts presided over by non-Communists.

It was agreed, in an organizational plan for Algiers that Camus worked out with Padula, that the young recruit would be responsible for a district committee in his own working-class neighborhood of Belcourt. He dived into the job. Running into his old friend Louis Pagès, a classmate at the Belcourt elementary school who had recently left the French Navy and was now a merchant seaman, he insisted that Pagès join him immediately. Though Pagès later confessed that he never knew what "Amsterdam-Pleyel" signified, he agreed and attended meetings in a basement room of the Café des Sports in Belcourt, at which Camus presided.[3]

And Camus soon had the help of another Belcourt man, Charles Poncet, who would become a lifelong friend. Camus confided his preoccupations to Poncet: "The Belcourt guys, I know them quite well. For bowling, card-playing and drinking anisette they're champions. Getting them interested in politics is another matter." Poncet stared at his new comrade, wondering how such an elegantly dressed young gentleman could possibly know anything about the little people of Belcourt. For Poncet, Camus at this time was

> Tall, very much at ease in a well-cut suit; a bow tie gave a slight touch of careful dressing to the ensemble. . . . Green-brown eyes, small ears stuck out from his head, a large fleshy mouth, the whole making a winning impression.

But nothing about him suggested the Algiers that Poncet knew. His speech was too precise; if he allowed a little banter into his discourse on occasion, it was within the limits of a proper education. "After some minutes of conversation," remembered Poncet, "one was struck by the serious expression . . . but in which there would often be a fleeting flash of amusement. The man was seductive. An intellectual, of course, but of an unusual quality."[4]

At the University of Algiers, Camus was also remarked for the elegance, the precision of his speech. In one class he delivered an explication of a text of the Roman historian Sallust, but rather than limit himself to a grammatical and literary analysis he surprised his professor by a philosophical interpretation. "We can see, Mr. Camus, that you are a philosopher," the professor commented.[5] In René Poirier's class he presented a paper on Jules de Gaultier, the philosopher (still alive at the time) who was best known for his definition of Bovarysme: man's proclivity to see himself other than he is, to lie to himself.[6] By doing all his preparatory work on time, Camus remained invulnerable and irreproachable, whatever his activity might be outside the university building. As for his elegance, it is striking in a classroom photograph taken in May 1935 in Professor Poirier's philosophy class, where neatly combed, impeccably attired Albert Camus is seated alongside Liliane Choucroun, Yves Dechezelles, and Dechezelles' future wife Myriam Salama.

Political directives continued to come from Paris, publicly from the front organizations and their press, privately from Claude de Fréminville, who was sopping up all of the excitement, releasing it in the form of projects certain to appeal to Camus. Tying up in one parcel their political, intellectual, and literary concerns, Fréminville made plans for a literary-political magazine for Algiers, as capital of North Africa, which would serve to bring together Europeans and Moslems. Such a magazine, he felt, would make them all better Communists, while helping to draw others to the movement. But it would not be parochial, for it would be open to perpetual discussion. It would be a dialogue first of all between Fréminville in Paris and his friends in Algeria. He wanted the magazine to be published under the responsibility of Camus, feeling that both he and Camus had sufficient experience to handle their share of the job.

The title of the publication, as suggested by Belamich, third corner of the triangle, would be *La Nouvelle Journée*. Among the first articles to be published were (by Camus) an essay on Honegger and Stravinsky, a review of Gide's *Journal,* a discussion of Louis Aragon's *Hourra l'Oural,* a study of Eugène Dabit (novelist of working-class life who had written the popular *Hôtel du Nord*). There would also be a regular survey of current periodical literature, Camus to cover *Nouvelle Revue Francaise* and the left-wing intellectuals' magazine *Europe,* Fréminville the rest. Fréminville wrote Belamich: "A. Camus, although overworked, will be in charge of the sincerity of the self-criticism inside the magazine and will suggest major subjects for discussion." He also announced that Jean Giono, already a famous novelist, had agreed to support and to write for their magazine. It would be printed in Algiers, where Fréminville knew a printer, writers, even readers; but Camus would handle the fund-raising. Fréminville then had an afterthought (in a letter to Belamich of September 7, 1934): "Would you believe in the usefulness of the magazine if you saw Camus and so many others join not only in theory but in practice the C.P. [Communist Party]?"[1]

But the least expected advice was coming from Jean Grenier, Camus' acknowledged mentor, whom all his life he would refer to as his *maître*. For if one is to doubt that Camus and Grenier were communicating, one is confronted with the accumulated testimony of all Salama who knew either of them, with the evidence of their discussions in classroom and out, in their evenings at Hydra, and with the assiduous correspondence which had begun a couple of years earlier and would not cease until one of them was dead. And yet . . .

It was at the very moment when Camus was discovering political action, learning that efficacity might mean to work with the best organized, learning, in other words, how to work alongside (and later inside)

the Communist Party, that Grenier was to undertake a series of reflections on political orthodoxy which led him to reject the intellectual
prison which the Communist Party represented. To take this position,
and at this time, when the young men's culture hero Gide had pledged
his art to Communism (until, in 1936, he discovered in a journey to the
Soviet Union how Communism worked), when their other culture hero
André Malraux was rallying intellectuals to unity of action with Communism national and international, was to stand alone.

And yet that is what Jean Grenier was doing. In his essay "L'Intellectuel dans la société," published in that threshold year 1935, he
warned against involvement with the Party, warned specifically, in a
phrase which his student Camus would remember, at least uncon-
sciously (for he would adopt it as his own rule of behavior after World
War II), against the temptation of the intellectual to join a movement
which claims to be moving in the direction of history.

> There is an advantage, in any case [so he wrote Grenier], in not
> rushing into a party without being pushed by all one's mind and
> heart. It happens that the artist, having suddenly become conscious
> of his own misery and of human solidarity, suddenly joins a party,
> simply to get outside himself, just as girls used to decide hastily to
> marry in order to escape their families. But that makes for unhappy
> households. It is very possible, therefore, that Gide's marriage with
> Communism will turn out badly.[7]

Grenier was not only writing these reasonable things, he was
declaiming them from public platforms. Young Jean Daniel heard him
analyze "the spirit of orthodoxy," criticizing Marxist dogma, Stalinist
infallibility, the Moscow "Vatican," the bureaucratic hierarchy, dictatorship not of the proletariat but of a new class of inquisitors. Grenier
was saying these things before Arthur Koestler did, before Raymond
Aron or Isaac Deutscher. But what could he do, wondered Daniel,
against the influence of Malraux?[2]

The question might also have been put this way: What did Grenier
really want to do? Not, at least in the case of his favorite student, to
discourage him from pursuing the Communist experiment. For in this
one instance where Grenier might have been able to put his own arguments to practical application, might have been able to convince one
young man, there and then, and in the comfort of his own living room,
that "the spirit of orthodoxy" led to cruel deceptions, he chose to desist.
Chose, rather, to help his favorite student to play with fire.

Probably at this time (the summer of 1934, unless it was the following
summer, for no official or private records are available to pinpoint the

date), Camus got a job at the Algiers Prefecture, the central administration responsible for government operations for the *département* of Algiers, under the authority of the Government General (which controlled similiar prefectures in Oran and Constantine, and a military district for the southern desert territories). He had begun the summer with a job in a private company, he told Jean Grenier, but then the manager of the firm absconded with the company's funds. Penniless, Camus sought a civil service job and began asking friends for help. At his request, an old friend, Marcelle Bonnet-Blanchet, who frequented Maisonseul and other young artists, found him employment at the Algiers Prefecture, where he was put to work in an office just below the roof, to roast under the North African sun seven hours a day. When the wife of a friend dropped in to see how he was doing, she discovered Camus sweating profusely, visibly attenuated.

He rapidly acquired an office reputation as a non-talker. Certainly the atmosphere could not have been stimulating. At the end of the working day, at least some days, his new wife Simone would be waiting for him at the front entrance.

He worked as an auxiliary clerk in the section which issued drivers' permits and automobile registrations.[8] The story, quite possibly true, is that he was fired because "he did not know how to write." Camus confirmed this comical version of the event.[9] Indeed, he could be quite funny about the episode of relaxed pen-pushing at the prefecture;[10] he told another friend that he had been fired after he gave the same license number to two motorcars.[11] But the immediate result of the episode was that he required two months' rest because his doctor feared that his second lung had been affected by the strain. From then on he would have to limit his breadwinning to giving private lessons.

His doctor, Stacha Cviklinski, was a sympathetic eccentric, described by one of their circle as "a noble, large, magnificent specimen of a man," and the possible inspiration for the character called Zagreus in *La Mort heureuse*. A dedicated leftist, he had been a Communist or was then a Communist. His wife would play in Camus' first theatrical production, the adaptation of Malraux's *Le Temps du mépris*. He treated his patients with herbs and chicken embryos, wrote treatises on mysticism that were never published. As a friend as much as a doctor, Cviklinski told Camus to live his life fully, not to fear either sun or sea. Camus considered him more of a friend and philosophical adviser than a doctor, but he did go on swimming, and in the summer sun.[12]

Now would have been the time for him, along with every Frenchman of his age, to enter the Army for compulsory military service (which was then a twelve-month obligation). He went in for the physical examination in October 1934, but of course the state of his lungs won him an exemption.[13] Back at the university, he took and passed the examinations for the *certificat d'études littéraires classiques,* the third of the four that he would require for his *licence* (college degree), and began reading for the final certificate in logic and general philosophy.

As early as the lycée year of *première supérieure,* his teacher Jean Grenier had been referring to Suetonius' *Lives of the Caesars;* he recalls in his memoir of Camus how in his classes, with Camus present, he had underscored Emperor Caligula's ringing cry, "They are all guilty!" Now Camus had an opportunity to attend the lectures of Jacques Heurgon, professor of Latin, on the Augustus family. Heurgon, who had arrived in Algeria in 1931, was widely known as a friend of André Gide, and willingly discussed Gide with his students. Later, when Gide came to Algiers, he would stay with the Heurgons. Heurgon's father-in-law had founded the famous annual seminar at Pontigny, near Paris, gathering place of the *Nouvelle Revue Française* intellectuals, so that in a sense Heurgon offered another bridge between literary Paris and Algiers. Like Grenier, Heurgon made himself available to his students, participated in their extracurricular activities (as French professors generally did not do at that time or later).[14]

The only surviving writing by Camus of this time consists of an exercise in belles lettres lovingly presented to his wife Simone in the form in which it was written, a school notebook, with the title "Le Livre de Mélusine," and the draft essays grouped as "Les Voix du quartier pauvre," an early version of the material to be published as *L'Envers et l'Endroit.*

The first text, given to Simone in the course of December 1934, is a group of three brief tales. "It is time to speak of fairies," begins the first, "Conte pour des enfants trop tristes," and its author does just that in charming, occasionally ironic, more often precious prose, the chief purpose of which seems to be to pay reverence to the beloved: ". . . She's a child, this fairy. She doesn't think of the future, nor of meals. She lives in her moment and laughs with her flowers. . . ." (Note that André Breton's otherworldly "Nadja" thought of herself as Mélusine, the legendary water sprite who married a mortal man.)

"Les Voix du quartier pauvre" is signed and dated December 25, 1934, dedicated to his wife. But this work is of another caliber. If these "voices" are also presented in polished style, avoiding realism, political argument, or even a direct exposé of life as it is lived in Belcourt, they have clearly been carved out of the Camus-Sintes family dramas. Here, only partly submerged in artistry, can be read for the first time the story of the Rue de Lyon household. The author tries to come to terms with his mother's silences; he has moved far enough away from Belcourt to be able to do that now. He narrates the tale of his mother's lover, and how the liaison was thwarted by her brother. Camus never published these essays, choosing to make use of the material in another form.

He continued to be attentive to the minor ironies of life which might also be major tragedies. In January 1935, when the Algerian newspapers published an Associated Press report of a misunderstanding which led to the death of a son returning to visit his mother in Yugoslavia, Camus clipped the story and put it away for future use, first as an anecdote in *L'Etranger,* later as the plot of his play *Le Malentendu:*

> A man, returning home after an absence of twenty years is murdered and robbed by his mother and his sister who had not recognized him

> *(La Dépêche Algérienne)*

> Aided by her daughter, a hotelkeeper kills a traveler who happened to be her son in order to rob him.
> In realizing their mistake, the mother hangs herself, the daughter throws herself into a well.

> *(l'Echo d'Alger)*[15]

That spring he opened a small (6¾"×8½") notebook, in the format that every student in France was using then and is still using, to begin his writer's journal. From the inception it would take literary jottings, ideas and outlines for stories, novels, plays, notes on reading. There would also be introspective notations, descriptions of people and landscapes, particularly during his travels. Sections would be utilized later on in works to be published. Until the 1950s this journal would contain little intimate detail, so that it has been possible to publish, almost intact, the volumes covering the period from May 1935 to March 1951.[16]

May 1935 also happened to be the month that the Franco-Soviet pact was signed, after which French Foreign Minister Pierre Laval traveled to Moscow to meet Joseph Stalin. The Soviet leader gratified him with a statement designed to please French moderates, and hence to remove another barrier to unity of action between middle-of-the-road Frenchmen and the Moscow-oriented French Communist Party. "Stalin understands and fully approves the national defense policy of France designed to maintain its armed forces at a level appropriate to its security," read the communiqué.[17] It was too early for anyone to realize that the French Communist Party would now have to revise some of its basic rallying cries—to silence its anti-colonial idealists, for example. For the moment some of these anti-colonial idealists were getting ready to *join* the Party.

In June 1935, Albert Camus obtained the fourth and last of the certificates needed for his degree, the *certificat de logique et philosophie générale*. Now he was free to concentrate on the *diplôme d'études supérieures,* which required the writing of a dissertation. In July, there was stimulation of a more immediate sort. A Comité de Vigilance des Intellectuels Antifascistes (CVIA) had been founded in Paris. Marcel Bataillon, a Spanish professor at the University of Algiers, became secretary of CVIA's Algiers section. In this capacity he invited André Malraux, now the brightest star on the intellectual left, to come to Algiers to speak at a public meeting.

Fresh from the Congrès International des Ecrivains, where he had joined his peers of the European left, Gide, Julien Benda, Julian Huxley, E. M. Forster, Heinrich Mann, Ilya Ehrenburg, Max Brod, in a new writers' front against fascism, Malraux decided to make his speech a reply to the right-wing extremist Colonel François de La Rocque, who shortly before had assembled his Croix de Feu followers in the region. Malraux made one of his dramatic entrances, arriving in Algiers by seaplane, and was greeted at the waterfront by Bataillon and his friends. The Bataillons had Malraux sleep at their home, since the Fascists had been known to kidnap opposition speakers before a rally. The guest speaker had scribbled notes for his speech during the flight; his "Réponse à La Rocque" was remembered as a Jacobinic evocation of the French Revolution. The meeting was held in a small Belcourt movie theater near the Champ de Manoeuvres, since the owners of larger and more centrally located halls had been terrified at the idea of renting to militant anti-Fascists. But the Bataillon forces took their revenge by setting up loudspeakers so that passers-by as well as sympathizers for whom there was no room inside the cinema could hear the speech.[18]

If the meeting went forward without incident, Malraux himself would later recall that it was the one occasion on which he faced, or so he believed, a hostile audience.[19] In fact the theater was protected by hefty men recruited by CVIA. Malraux spoke in shirt-sleeves, a cigarette in his mouth, pacing back and forth across the stage. And when he left, the young anti-Fascists of Algiers saw him off at the docks with raised fists.[20]

At least one participant also remembered that after Malraux's speech in the Belcourt movie theater, Albert Camus went forward to greet him; they may even have exchanged a few words.[21] Malraux himself could recall no such meeting then or at any time in Algeria.[22] Whatever happened, Camus now possessed something more tangible than a remembered handshake. For Malraux had just published *Le Temps du mépris* (Days of Wrath), a novelized tract in which art was sacrificed to a good cause, the glorification of virile camaraderie in the fight against Nazism. Malraux's hero, Kassner, and the young militant who assumes his identity to take his place in a Nazi jail, are both Communists with whom it was possible to identify. Indeed, Kassner was the son of a worker, a scholarship student, and a writer. (The Malraux novel appeared in installments in *Nouvelle Revue Française* in March, April, and May 1935.)

The same month, in Paris, at the suggestion of the Amsterdam-Pleyel movement, all the left-wing forces of France—parties, unions, political groupings—joined on France's national holiday, July 14, to parade through the city behind a banner of "Rassemblement Populaire." The organizers claimed the participation of a half million marchers.

Jean Grenier, who was aware of Camus' growing interest in politics, his active participation in Popular Front activities, knew also that the Communist Party was furnishing the shock troops of the Popular Front. He thought that the Party might provide a worthwhile career to a new Julien Sorel. In saying as much to his favorite student, in writing it down later on, had Grenier thought of all the implications of what he was suggesting? Hadn't Stendhal's young hero Julien Sorel *cynically* opted for the church as a platform for his ambitions? Surely Grenier did not mean that he wished to encourage Camus to act hypocritically. Or if he expected Camus to be sincere, was Grenier being the cynic? The book that comes to mind, in observing what was about to happen, is not so much *Le Rouge et le Noir* as *Les Liaisons dangereuses.* "I began from this general maxim," Grenier would later recall, "that men have the right to happiness, and not necessarily to the truth."

Whatever Grenier really meant, he was aware that the Communist Party needed leadership. Despite what he was writing and saying about the dangers of Communist orthodoxy, he advised his student to join the Party. Grenier could see no serious objections to such a move, for Camus had not embraced any particular belief to the exclusion of all others; on the contrary, he was seeking first truths. Camus also had the appropriate fraternal spirit, he supported equality between European settlers and Moslems, he was prepared (in his teacher's view) to undertake a career whose advantages and whose dangers would not betray his convictions. A career in which he could prove himself, could take those risks without which life would not be conceivable. So said Grenier as he walked with his student one evening from his Hydra home to the tram stop.[23]

Meanwhile at home things were not going well with Simone. Her behavior, real or rumored, must have been upsetting to a young man who liked his affairs to be orderly and discreet. If he didn't know what was being said about her, that she was giving herself to young doctors for drugs, for instance, he had to deal with more quotidian problems, such as her unwillingness to share his life. Some of Camus' friends who happened not to be "creatures of the night" never met her at all.

The scenes between them were discreet; no friend could say with certainty why they seemed on the verge of breaking up. It was agreed that she would go away; temporary separation might help, might at least remove her from the temptations of Algiers, or at least from its facilities. She decided to try a retreat. It wasn't the same thing as being confined to a clinic in Algiers. She would go to the Balearics, and he could join her later; they apparently set a date. She sailed, and he walked back alone to the house on the heights, which now seemed very big.

It was probably now that he decided that he was too must flee. He called on Edmond Brua, then editor in chief of a public works journal, *Travaux Nord-Africains,* to introduce himself on the recommendation of Jean Grenier (who had been Brua's classmate at the Sorbonne). Brua's magazine had special connections with the steamship lines; could Brua get him a free berth to Greece? Brua could not, but the two men became fast friends from that time.[24]

He had been seeing a good deal of the Raffis, a leading family of the intellectual bourgeoisie, who occupied a house on a hill called La Redoute separated by a ravine from the Hydra villa. He would pass the Raffi home on his way to and from town, and sometimes in the evening he and Simone would visit them.

André Raffi, a former ship's captain, was *chef d'armement,* in charge of fitting out ships, at the Société Algérienne de Navigation pour l'Afrique du Nord Ch. Schiaffino et Cie. The Schiaffino company had a virtual monopoly of shipping between Algeria and mainland France. André Raffi's own father-in-law, Ernest Mallebay, was the dean of Algeria's journalists, founder of a cultural magazine, *La Revue Algérienne,* in 1888, which would later be published by his daughter, André's wife. Patrons of the arts, the Mallebays and the Raffis would soon be providing help and encouragement to young Camus; the Raffi children would become his friends, the youngest, Jean, virtually his disciple. Paul, the oldest, would participate in Camus' political and cultural adventures.

Now his visits to the Raffis became more frequent, and his distress was apparent to this kindly family group. André Raffi came home one day to say that he had berths for Camus and his son Paul on a freighter that would sail along the North African coast east and south from Algiers, past Bône, Bizerte, and Tunis, as far as Gabès, the last Tunisian port before the Libyan frontier. It would be a fine way for a lonely husband to spend the time he would have to wait for Simone. He agreed to go along.

But soon after they left the port of Algiers, Camus became ill. He began to cough, spitting up blood. Alarmed, the friends decided that they would have to leave the ship at the next port of call, Bougie, only 145 land miles from where they had begun. They returned to Algiers by bus, a long day's ride in torrid heat. Camus would spend the next few weeks in convalescence.[25]

From Tipasa, where he was resting, he wrote to Jean Grenier on August 21, 1935:

> You are right when you advise me to join the Communist Party. I shall do it on my return from the Balearics. I confess that everything draws me to them and that I had made up my mind to undertake this experiment. The objections I have to Communism, it seems to me it would be better to live them.

He regretted that Communism lacked religious meaning, allowed man to suffice unto himself. But perhaps Communism could prepare him for more spiritual concerns.

> I don't say that this is orthodox. But in the experiment (sincere) that I shall attempt, I shall always refuse to place a volume of *Capital* between life and mankind.

He would join the Party to see its doctrine evolve. He knew already that Communist philosophy contained error, such as the false rationalism tied to the illusion of progress, the concepts of class struggle and historical materialism benefitting the working class alone. But:

> It seems to me that, more than ideas, life itself often leads to Communism. . . . I have such a strong desire to help reduce the sum of unhappiness and of bitterness which empoisons mankind.[26]

Such motivations could not fail to move this professor who favored intellectual experiment, for whom life was speculation. Indeed, one can almost say that Grenier had dictated the letter that Camus was writing to him now.

Whether the letter represented the proper attitude for a candidate member of the French Communist Party, whether such an attitude could help him or even keep him inside the Party, are matters which will have to be judged on the evidence.

# 8

◆

## ENLISTMENT

Seek out contacts. All contacts. If I want to write about
men, how separate myself from the landscape?

*Carnets*

The time had come for him to join Simone in her island retreat. He left
Algeria in virtual secrecy, managed not to tell any of his friends what
he was up to. However badly he may have felt about the separation, we
are not going to find out about it from his journal. It is conceivable that
he did confide in his *cahier* at this time, and that the nature of his
confidences led him to expurge his notes later, to save only the literature. For what remains is a set of traveler's impressions which he would
draw upon for his essay on the Balearics in *L'Envers et l'Endroit*.

Nor is there any evidence that he took the time to visit the Balearic
island of his maternal ancestors (Minorca). His attention would be
concentrated elsewhere. Yet he did have the leisure to observe his own
reactions to this first trip out of his country. Now, as later, travel would
inspire a "vague fear . . . an instinctive desire to return to the shelter of
old habits. . . ." Parenthetically he records the need of the disoriented
traveler in a strange land to find a newspaper in his own language, a
café where he can approach other people. These are the reflections of a
solitary, perhaps on the eve of his reunion with Simone (or a solitary
*with* Simone). We do not know how he found her. Rumors later circulated that he discovered that a "convent" she had pretended to have
selected for her retreat had in fact not been open for many years, perhaps for centuries.[1]

The couple returned to Algiers together, but Simone remained distant, invisible to friends. Soon she would enter a private clinic to attempt another cure.

And he set about to fulfill his political commitments. He joined the Communist Party with great discretion, but so would he do most of the significant things in his life. Apart from those few friends with whom he chose to share this adventure, he would inform no one. His college classmates, his teachers (except Grenier) would remain unaware of the engagement. Even his old comrade Louis Pagès, although of working-class origin and consequently (one imagines) the right kind of person for the Party—and he was of unquestioned loyalty in the bargain—would never find out that Camus had become a Communist. Yet for six months they would work side by side in political activities, and another friend of Camus who was also Pagès' friend (and relative), Paul Raffi, was brought into the Party by Camus.[2]

But there were other activities that could take place out in the open, for everyone to see and to join. The first was artistic, certainly inspired by that brief exposure to André Malraux, by admiration for Malraux's engagement and the way he was utilizing art in the service of his beliefs. Malraux himself would later dismiss his political novel *Le Temps du mépris* as a failure, and would not allow it to be reprinted during his lifetime.[3] Certainly its chief value was its political message, made even more telling by a preface (not published in the *Nouvelle Revue Française* serialization). In this preface Malraux had written: "It is difficult to be a man. But not more difficult to become one in reinforcing one's communion than in cultivating one's differences. . . ."

So Camus began "reinforcing one's communion" by bringing his friends together in a theater group which would also be a form of political action. They would call it Théâtre du Travail, and the first play would be an adaptation by Camus himself of *Le Temps du mépris*.

He would also be a leader of another of the Communist Party's fronts, an adult education program for workers carried out under the sponsorship of left-wing unions, a "people's university" whose formal name was then Collège du Travail.[4] These movements, Théâtre du Travail and Collège du Travail, would have a counterpart in Ciné-Travail, a movie club originally founded by the Socialist Max-Pol Fouchet, which acquired this name when it was taken over by the Communists.

To complete the picture, the young activist was about to enter his third and final year at the University of Algiers, during which he would work for his *diplôme d'études supérieures*. In meetings with Professor Poirier a subject for his dissertation was chosen, requiring that he treat both Hellenic thought and early Christianity, with the Egyptian-born philosopher of neoplatonism Plotinus, and that North African Christian, St. Augustine.[5] He had been doing extensive reading for this paper, the bibliography for which covers nearly four pages of the Pléiade text.[6] Meanwhile, to meet at least some of the household expenses, he was earning money in one of the ways a fragile young man could, by giving private lessons. To make it pay, these private lessons would have to be virtually public lessons. One lycée student, who had received tutoring from Camus the previous year, now found herself in a class of seven, all girls, in the living room of the Camus' Hydra home. They were all studying for the second and final half of their *baccalauréat* of philosophy. The lessons were carried out as informally as one could wish: Camus served tea, handed cigarettes around. All of the young ladies passed their bac "seven out of seven," the highest possible grade.[7]

An effort of imagination will have to be made to understand the position of the French Communist Party in Algeria in the mid-1930s. To understand, first of all, its relative insignificance. In all it hardly controlled a hundred active members in the capital; it was a tour de force for its leaders to make up a list of thirty-five candidates at election time.[8]

To understand, too, the particular climate which reigned in Algeria, so different from that of mainland France. Algeria was in the hands of a proconsul, under pressure from a hard core of unreconstructed colonial settlers. Public life was not to be compared to that of Paris, with the free play of democratic forces which sometimes made the Third Republic's politics seem irresponsible. Algeria was governed like a frontier post, with frontier law. If one could be a Communist openly in Paris, it was hard to be a Communist in Algiers. By encouraging Algerian nationalism (for in the 1930s the Moslem majority lacked even minimal rights), by contributing to the development of progressive organizations among Moslems not only in North Africa but (among migrant workers) in mainland France, the Communists were sure to be feared and despised. They were soon also to be prosecuted, and their local leader would have to flee Algiers for the more reasonable climate of wartime Spain to escape a prison term.

At the time Camus joined the Party, the Algerian branch had not yet been given its autonomy. It was still only a regional division of the French Party, whose headquarters were in Paris. Locally it was organized into geographical "sections," each section into small cells. Camus was assigned to a cell more or less specifically created for the young intellectuals who had begun to join up now, in the university and upper middle class neighborhoods; it bore the name of this district, Plateau Saulière. The cell fell under the responsibility of the secretary of the

Alger-Belcourt section, Emile Padula, Camus' friend in the Amster-dam-Pleyel movement. Padula had been one of those involved in bring-ing Camus into the Party (feeling that there was no good reason why he should *not* be a member). A youthful veteran of the Communist move-ment, Padula had privately decided that Camus would have been ill at ease in a strictly working-class cell, where he would not have been able to communicate with rank and file members.[9] Elie Mignot, himself a young craftsman who became a permanent official of the local party only on September 1, 1935, felt that Camus and his young friends were enlisting in the Party out of emotional feeling, revolt against coloni-alism; he and his worker comrades tended to think of them as "boy scouts."[10] But the boy scouts were welcome in the Party all the same. "The Party needs us at this time," the ever-enthusiastic Claude de Fréminville explained to his reticent friend André Belamich. "In the past Camus, myself, we should have had a rather cool reception. They would have asked us to change."[11]

The Plateau Saulière cell rapidly filled up with like-minded boy and girl scouts. One was Maurice Girard, a painter, brother-in-law of Pierre-André Emery, an architect for whom Jean de Maisonseul was working. Another was Paul Raffi. Through Raffi's wife-to-be, Colette, Camus had already met (the previous May) two inseparable Oran stu-dents, Jeanne-Paule Sicard and Marguerite Dobrenn, who joined him now in the Plateau Saulière cell. Jeanne Sicard belonged to one of the great Oran planting families; her mother was a Bastos (the cigarette manufacturer). After getting her college degree she would go on to a *diplôme d'études supérieures* in literature, but the war would draw her to Charles de Gaulle's resistance government, where she would meet René Pleven and become his chief aide in his successive cabinet posts, so that she was one of the most powerful women in France in the im-mediate postwar years. She died in an automobile accident in Septem-ber 1962. Marguerite Dobrenn was also of a comfortable Oran milieu (her father was a dental surgeon there), but was studying in Algiers for a *diplôme d'études supérieures* in ancient history. She joined Jeanne Sicard in the Algiers provisional government, also followed Pleven to Paris, where she pursued a civil service career. Henceforth Sicard and Dobrenn would be associated with all of Camus' political and cultural activities, would join him in renting the "House Above the World," the hillside Maison Fichu; later some of their Party cell meetings would be held in the Maison Fichu.[12]

When Camus' architect friend Louis Miquel returned from Paris, fresh from his apprenticeship to Le Corbusier in the latter's celebrated Rue de Sèvres studio, Camus recruited him into the Party as well. (Miquel had previously been a member of Max-Pol Fouchet's

Jeunesses Socialistes.) Camus led the discussions, calling his cell the Marx-Engels group, and told Miquel its purpose was to train leaders.[13]

Out in the open, Camus was busily opening classrooms for the Collège du Travail. One of the classrooms was—expectedly—the Parc d'Hydra villa. Once again he would recruit Louis Pagès. Pagès found himself in the villa's living room with twenty-two other students, some merchant seamen like himself, laborers. Camus was teaching them the elements of Freud, and Pagès felt that the level of discourse was over his head, but he came out of it convinced that the students were different men after the course.[14]

Now the Camus circle would be augmented by the arrival of a brilliant young lycée teacher, a political maverick who would never join the Communist Party but nevertheless would throw himself into the turbulent political activities of the young French Algerians. Born in 1909, Yves Bourgeois had attended the prestigious Paris teachers' college, Ecole Normale Supérieure, where he received his *agrégation*. He had been an assistant teacher of French at King's College in London, and had spent another year as Jusserand Scholar at St. John's College in Annapolis, Maryland, before entering the French educational system as a teacher in Lyons, and (from autumn 1935) at the Lycée Bugeaud in Algiers. By that time he had visited twenty countries and was more or less fluent in four foreign languages.

At the first meeting of the Comité de Vigilance des Intellectuels Antifascistes (CVIA) at the beginning of that school year in October 1935, Bourgeois made the point that young leftist intellectuals should be taking part in cultural activities, amateur theater for example. He was immediately advised by teachers and students alike to get in touch with a young college student who was planning to set up just such a company. Yves Bourgeois sent a note to Albert Camus closing with the slogan *"Front rouge!"* Bourgeois included a description of himself: He'd be wearing a loden topcoat, so that Camus would recognize him at their appointment at the Bar Automatique. They took to each other at once, plunged into a discussion of contemporary theater, of which Bourgeois had firsthand experience and of course Camus did not. Camus saw the slight, blond, handsome young man as an unquestionably attractive personality; Bourgeois saw Camus as personable and courteous, mature and well educated, quite dashing despite his history of illness, and he also knew that Jean Grenier thought the world of him. Later Bourgeois would think back on this period of intense political-cultural activity as Camus' "Camelot" period.

Bourgeois was rapidly co-opted into the Collège du Travail, where

he taught English and later Spanish, while others taught French, mathematics. . . . They would find a roster of students assigned to them by
the unions, and then go out to scrounge rooms which could be used for
classes. Usually they were shabby rooms in run-down neighborhoods.
Camus would come in during classes to give pep talks, clearly enjoying
what he was doing. But he could also bewilder working-class students
by telling them that true revolution was not a matter of wearing better
shoes but of dignity. In joining the Collège, Bourgeois brought with him
another lycée teacher, Alfred Poignant, and Poignant's future wife
Elise. Bourgeois' own second wife, Yvonne Jarnias, would later also
join the volunteer faculty, and once told Bourgeois how thrilled she was
after teaching a class for illiterates, to see young Moslem workers sitting
on the curb outside the building trying to memorize the alphabet.[15]

In organizing an amateur theatrical group limited in intention, did
Camus know that he was also taking his first steps into what would
be lifelong involvement with the theater, which would lead to the writing of plays performed on the professional stage as well as to a secondary career as a director? No evidence has been found that Camus began
his Théâtre du Travail after sketching out even a tentative plan for his
own career, let alone a philosophy of the theater; all the evidence seems
to suggest that it was after adapting and casting, directing and acting in
his first plays that he discovered how essential the theater was to his
life.

Camus took André Malraux's short (186-page) novel, *Le Temps
du mépris,* cut it into a play suitable for staging, using off-stage narration, brief scenes, rapid shifting of scenes through use of spotlights
placed on- or off-stage. He recruited a company of his friends to play in
it, among them Louis Miquel, Robert Namia, Louis Pagès, Paul Raffi,
Jeanne Sicard, Marguerite Dobrenn, Yves Bourgeois (who brought
along fellow-teacher Alfred Poignant). But he also had to obtain permission from the novelist whose play he was adapting. The story is that
he received a one-word telegram in reply: *"Joue"* (Play), and that he
was delighted that Malraux had used the familiar *tu* form.[16] Camus'
dramatic version retained the essence of the original, in which a German Communist leader, arrested by the Nazis, is released because an
unknown comrade assumes his identity. Kassner flies off to Prague in a
plane piloted by a member of the underground organization, attends an
anti-Nazi political rally there, is reunited with his wife. Malraux had
written it as a contribution to the campaign for the liberation of imprisoned German anti-Nazis, and it was praised by Communists as far away
as Moscow. In a manifesto-tract surely written by Camus it was announced:

> A Labor Theater is being organized in Algiers thanks to collective
> and benevolent efforts. This theater is aware of the artistic value in-
> herent in all mass literature, wishes to demonstrate that it is some-
> times advantageous to art to descend from its ivory tower, and be-
> lieves that the sense of beauty is inseparable from a certain sense of
> humanity. These ideas are hardly original. . . . Its effort is to re-
> store some human values and not to present new subjects of reflec-
> tion.
>
> It has been necessary to adapt means of production to theoreti-
> cal aims. Thus some innovations in the staging and the scenery,
> through the application of conceptions until now unknown to Al-
> giers.

They were beginning, the tract went on, with a play produced and acted
by themselves. "The Labor Theater is nevertheless conscious of its
limits and its weaknesses. It asks to be judged on its acts and not on its
intentions." The manifesto concluded with the promise that all the
profits would be turned over to the unemployed through an organization called Secours Ouvrier International.

This first play of the Théâtre du Travail, the first performance of
*Le Temps du mépris,* Albert Camus' first contribution to the theater,
was an event for all these reasons and more. Somehow, because of the
lack of means (they all chipped in for whatever materials had to be
acquired with hard cash), the young organizers had heightened the dramatic effect by the choice of a theater, which choice would never be forgotten by anyone who attended it. On the beach at Bab el Oued, among
the bathhouses and the café-dance halls built over the sand on stilts, the
Bains Padovani was a vast ballroom about fifteen yards wide and forty
yards long, with a board floor and windows facing the Mediterranean
Sea. Since most of the acting troupe—some neighborhood workers
among them, even what a cynic described as a "token Moslem"—were
busy during the working day, they rehearsed in the half-light of late afternoon, and the unattached intellectuals among them would continue
the evening with shish kebab at an Arab-style restaurant on Rue de la
Lyre, after which they would walk the girls back to their hostel.[17]

Architect Louis Miquel designed the scenery, and also had a small
role as a participant in the political meeting. The faithful Louis Pagès
played a German officer, and allowed his head to be shaved for authenticity. He took his role of a Nazi so seriously that he gave another actor
a wallop which sent him flying, and the others had to warn him not to
live his part so intensely. André Belamich played the chairman of the
meeting, whose role consisted only of saying, "[Name of actor] has the
floor." He himself was impressed that Camus had succeeded in making
the audience participate in the action regardless of their political opin-

ions. Marguerite Dobrenn had one line to recite from the audience as Lenin's widow: "Vladimir Ilich loved the people deeply." The wife of Camus' doctor, Stacha Cviklinski, played Kassner's wife.[18]

From Hitler Germany the peripatetic Yves Bourgeois had brought back Nazi military marches which provided a thumping overture, and his reserve officer uniforms and boots were ideal for the costumes of the storm troopers. Bourgeois himself played a young concentration camp inmate, and also sang *"Ich hatt' einen Kameraden"* off-stage. Camus himself didn't play on-stage, but spoke Kassner's monologue from the wings through a megaphone. In the scene of the revolutionary meeting, the real audience became the imaginary public for the meeting, and it shook the rafters with a ringing "Arise ye prisoners of starvation . . ."[17]

How many *Algérois* attended this first performance of *Le Temps du mépris* on January 25, 1936? One closely associated with the project said two thousand; another, an architect familiar with the hall, felt that no more than three hundred persons could fit into it.[19] But it is true that many stood, or sat on the window ledges. *La Lutte Sociale,* the local Communist Party biweekly organ, claimed "1500 persons of all classes . . . workers, office clerks, students, professors, doctors, women, youth. . . ." (Two performances of fifteen hundred spectators would mean that three thousand persons saw it at that time.) What everybody was certain to remember even forty years later, was the interaction of the play and the environment. The actors had to speak their lines between the waves breaking onto the beach just yards away, which (in the opinion of Pierre Emery) gave their speech an added nobility. "For a try-out effort," the Communist organ reported, "this was a master effort." Even the conservative *Echo d'Alger,* in a story preceding the first performance, hailed the adapter as "a student whose youthful literary talents have already manifested themselves with great authority." The same critic, René Janon, in the April 15 *Echo d'Alger* (after a spring performance of the play) would cite the troupe's "surprising sense of drama, and atmospheric qualities that we have seldom had the opportunity to discover in Algiers," remarking the "success achieved . . . from a public belonging to all classes of society."[20]

This first play, as theatrical sophisticates would have realized, had echos of the epic theater of Erwin Piscator (Poncet remarked it in his account of the Bains Padovani performance). If Camus had not begun reading the theory and history of the theater at that time, he would do so later, and specifically acknowledge the influence of the twentieth-century theatrical movement: Jacques Copeau, inventor of spartan stages (which were being invented elsewhere by the Piscators); Antonin Artaud; Edward Gordon Craig (author of *The Art of the Theatre,* who had begun shaking up the European stage from London and Berlin), Adolphe Appia, another innovator reacting against the previously dominant realistic movement. Later Camus would dedicate his Théâtre de l'Equipe (1937) to Copeau's work at the Théâtre du Vieux Colombier in Paris. He had not seen anything of that, either, but he could read about Copeau and the other new theater men in *Nouvelle Revue Française* and other magazines.

He also had the benefit of some firsthand reports from a Swiss architect who had been Le Corbusier's disciple, and who had settled in Algeria in 1926 at the age of twenty-three. Pierre-André Emery worked in a local architectural studio; its staff included the young draftsman Jean de Maisonseul. When Maisonseul introduced him to Camus, Emery was already twenty-eight years old, Camus eighteen. The older man had become friendly with the celebrated between-the-wars acting couple, Georges and Ludmilla Pitoëff, and had been given a part in one of their plays. Later they would take over the Théâtre des Mathurins in Paris, where they reigned from 1924 until Georges's death in 1939, introducing many of the modern masters, Chekhov, Shaw, Pirandello, O'Neill, and Frenchmen Claudel and Anouilh. Emery was not only the most experienced theater man around the Théâtre du Travail, he also had the appropriate political sympathies. One brother-in-law was secretary-general of the leading Popular Front organization in Algiers, another was a cellmate of Camus in the Communist Party. As a Swiss, Emery himself could not join the Party. Although his age prevented him from being fully integrated into the group of young people who roamed the old town's cafés and restaurants after rehearsals, or who would later camp, commune-style, at the Maison Fichu, he was called on for advice, for example in the choice of plays, and he gave it. He began designing scenery for the Théâtre du Travail with the performance of *Les Bas Fonds* (The Lower Depths) by Maxim Gorky, and from then on was involved in all their productions.

But Camus was the boss. He had "natural authority," Miquel observed. He always had the last word, but without a fight. The choice of new plays to perform was debated freely, the proposals coming from Camus, the political line undoubtedly reinforced by his Communist friends, but this one young man led the company. "Above all he had the inestimable gift," Poncet would later say, "to create around him, by the extraordinary density of his presence, by saying the right word at just the right moment, a marvelous atmosphere of friendship and of confidence . . . Camus was persuasive, cheerful, and his jesting was friendly."[21]

Now there was no holding him down. Almost as soon as *Le Temps du mépris* was under way, he and his friends began to plan further pro-

ductions. A lecture was scheduled on "Les possibilités du théâtre revo-
lutionnaire," under the sponsorship of Amis de la Revue *Commune,*
organ of the Association des Ecrivains et Artistes Revolutionnaires, and
it can be assumed that the unidentified speaker was Camus.[22] The more
one does, the more one can do. Suddenly his private journal fairly
sprouted new ideas—for a group of stories, a first novel. He may have
begun drafting the essays that would become *L'Envers et l'Endroit.*[23]
Claude de Fréminville, himself a ball of fire, eternal inventor of new
publications and organizations, was frankly admirative, in a letter from
Paris to dear André Belamich:

> Camus says that he is a Communist out of despair and as an
> adventure. . . . We'll see about that. Because in the end acts will
> scare off adventure and despair. . . .
> In addition to that I have noted a disparity between Camus and
> his acts. Camus continues to *think* despair, even to write it; but he
> *lives* hope. You can tell him that without fearing that in a spirit of
> contradiction he'll become even more hooked on his line. He is al-
> ready cured and you know that better than I do. And you know that
> his convalescence will be rapid. . . . He is not always his own de-
> famer and sometimes I hear a Camus I know well, who wasn't born
> in the Communist Party but who is growing there. . . . [January
> 9, 1936][24]

Camus' own journal entry of February 13 seemed to be an appeal
for help, a recognition that he could not do everything alone:

> I ask more from people than they can give me. Vanity to pre-
> tend the contrary. But what a mistake and what a despair.

He told himself that he would have to:

> Seek out contacts. All contacts. If I want to write about men, how
> separate myself from the landscape?

But his reaching out failed to elicit a response, or at least he felt that he
was not being listened to:

> You go to see a friend older than yourself to tell him everything
> . . . But he is in a hurry . . . And then I'm more alone, more in a
> vacuum.

If the Camus who went home to write these things was the real Camus,
his friends who shared his Camelot years did not know it.

At last Fréminville had burst onto the Algiers scene, transferred to the
local Party organization, determined that his mission would be to bring
about a reconciliation between the European population of Algeria and

its Moslems. He became secretary-general of a new Union Franco-Musulmane, drew up its program and bylaws, obtained the support of Marcel Bataillon of CVIA and the moderate Moslem leader Sheikh El Okbi, mapped out a strategy to set up branches throughout the capital and elsewhere in the country. Soon he had set up a meeting with the support of the Ministry of Labor (and why not? for he had the Moslem participants singing the French national anthem in Arabic. But perhaps it needs saying that in pre-World War II Algeria it was a radical thing to do to suggest that Moslems were like Frenchmen and therefore were equal to Frenchmen. At that time the colonial territory's indigenous majority lacked the basic civil rights which all European settlers enjoyed).

With a legacy from his father which came to him at age twenty-one, Claude de Fréminville purchased a small printing press and began to publish tracts and periodicals for his Communist comrades, for the nationalist Moslems as well. Among his contacts were organizers of the Etoile Nord-Africaine (ENA) movement of Messali Hadj, and the moderate businessman Ferhat Abbas (who much later turned from moderation to become nominal leader of the Algerian insurrection).[24] In addition to everything else he was doing, Camus was probably now helping Fréminville print the propaganda of his Moslem friends. Robert Namia accompanied Camus to a printing plant during this period, where the French edition of Messali's newspaper *Etoile Nord-Africaine* was being published. Camus had some editing and proofreading to do, and Namia pitched in, figuring that if Frenchmen were doing the job it was because any Moslem caught working on such material would be pulled in for questioning.[25]

Fréminville had probably been accurate in his analysis of his friend's mind, of the contradiction which would never be fully resolved between his thought and his action. Camus' difficulties with the Communist Party line would come out later on, but meanwhile he was reminding himself, for private reflection in his journal, of what Jean Grenier was saying about Communism: "For an ideal of justice, must one subscribe to stupidities?" To answer "yes" would be noble; "no" would be more honest. It was no different from the problem faced by intelligent Christians. Need the believer worry about the contradictions in the Bible, the fable of Noah's Ark, need he defend the Inquisition or the court which found Galileo guilty? "But, besides that, how reconcile Communism and disgust?"

His only answer was to throw himself even more deeply into political action. He and his comrades of the Théâtre du Travail would follow up the triumph of *Le Temps du mépris* with another politically oriented production. This time he insisted that it be a collective effort, the subject to be the revolt of the miners of the Asturias province of Spain in October 1934, their proclamation of a Workers and Peasants Republic, and their surrender to the Spanish Government's counterattack with Moroccan and Foreign Legion troops, followed by cruel repression. Yves Bourgeois suggested that the mood be that of Lope de Vega's *Fuenteovejuna,* which dramatizes a poor community's silent resistance to oppression. There would be four authors: Camus of course, his friend Jeanne Sicard, and the lycée teachers Bourgeois and Poignant. They would meet at the Maison Fichu, which was then not being lived in and served chiefly as a place to work for Camus and his friends. Sections of the play were assigned to each of the writers, who were to turn in their contributions to Camus, and he would tie them together.

Camus admired Bourgeois's gift for rapid dialogue, and it was Bourgeois who wrote the interrogation at the beginning of Act 4. Jeanne Sicard wrote the scene of the meeting of the government ministers; the radio announcements were probably all written by Poignant. At first they intended to do without love interest, but they ended by establishing a sentimental tie between Pepe and Pilar. Camus wrote the final spoken chorus, and most of the other scenes. The characters of Père éternel and Pepe were his suggestions, and so was the finely chiseled irony of lines such as *"I* voted for him, because he isn't proud." They had considered giving the play an evocative title such as *La neige* or *La vie brève,* but finally rallied around *Révolte dans les Asturies* on the advice of Jacques Heurgon, their Latin professor, who thought this title would have a "Claudelian" ring.[26]

Camus also wrote the main stage directions, and notably the opening description, in which the stage is to "surround" the spectator "to prevent him from defending himself." On each side of the audience are the streets of Oviedo, the miners' capital, with the central square up front. The conference table of the government ministers is placed in the center of the auditorium, a loudspeaker represents Radio Barcelona. "And the action takes place on these varying levels around the spectator forced to see and to participate according to his personal geometry," Camus' directions go on. "The ideal is that seat number 156 sees things differently from seat 157."

The young man writing this had never seen epic theater, but he was producing it. After it was over he would confide to a friend[27] that *Révolte dans les Asturies* was not a good play, he would never have written anything like it alone, but for him it was less a work of art than an act.

They rehearsed in a large shed in Belcourt which belonged to an amateur band. Bourgeois opened with his own (admittedly poor) rendering of a genuine Asturian song, found in his collection of folk song records. Vincent Solera, an anarchist comrade, played a concertina. An elderly schoolmaster from Picardy played the Prime Minister of Spain. Bourgeois was a philosophical old miner, Camus the juvenile lead. But the "Spanish" atmosphere, the colorful speech, and the humor in the play came not from Spain but from the streets of Algiers.[17]

In the middle of March the Communists' biweekly *La Lutte sociale* published the Théâtre du Travail's announcement of the forthcoming production of *Révolte dans les Asturies*. "We found in the revolution of October 1934 in Oviedo an example of human force and nobility." The next issue of *La Lutte Sociale* announced that the first performance would be on April 2.[28]

Now the long period of preparation was coming to an end. "It seems to me that I'm coming up for air," Camus told his journal, adding, as if in explanation: "The soft and reserved friendship of women." For he had discovered that marriage had not deprived him of his freedom of association, and that despite the Mediterranean myth that women were there to be courted, he found that a female could be a good comrade beyond any consideration of sexual attraction. Jeanne Sicard and Marguerite Dobrenn were such friends, and he was so close to Jeanne that some of their friends thought that they were lovers, but they were not.

With public performance of *Révolte dans les Asturies,* he decided, he would have done his duty. Then he would devote himself to his personal work, such as the book that was now taking shape. "Reconstruct once again after this long period of agitated and desperate living," he promised himself. "At last the sun and my panting body."

But events were not to follow this timetable. Camus got a summons to City Hall. Although the young producers had gone ahead with their project on what they thought was verbal approval from the prefecture, the city's mayor, Augustin Rozis, had given orders that the play was not to be performed, and without explanation. (A Communist publication, *L'Algérie Ouvrière,* reported on May 7 that the mayor had banned the play because "The subject is dangerous during an election campaign.")

There was nothing to do now but to turn the ban to political advantage. Abandoning personal projects, Camus got to work organizing a campaign of letters to the editors of the Algerian press, planned to print posters and tracts, if possible to hold a protest meeting. He thought, too, of establishing a club to give ostensibly private performances if they were not to be allowed to give public ones, or to hold a third performance of *Le Temps du mépris* and include a public reading of *Révolte dans les Asturies*. The bombshell had exploded during school (Easter) holidays, his best comrades were home in Oran or elsewhere, so that he was alone not only in planning but in executing the campaign, which would finally have to be limited to sending out some letters.[29]

On April 13, Camus sent out an open letter protesting the mayor's ban. Their play, he wrote, had been intended to show "artistic conceptions still new to Algiers. Thus did we hope to continue our efforts in favor of theater, this form of art which has been so neglected in our city." He pointed out that with 300 francs (321 francs today, some 65 dollars) collected from workers and students they had done what the city theater had not done with their official subsidy of 800,000 francs. They would not pretend to be surprised that the mayor refused an authorization already granted by the Prefect, the protest went on, but the Prefecture's approval suggests that there is nothing subversive in the play. The proceeds, furthermore, would have gone to needy Algerian children whether of European or indigenous origin.

Their meager funds were irretrievably lost. Three months of effort had been reduced to nothing by the city's action. "For too long have the interests of art and good works been sacrificed to the benefit of stupidity," Camus concluded. "And we are young enough to believe it is possible to remedy this."[30]

Once again the conservative press lent a sympathetic ear. On April 15 in *L'Echo d'Alger* critic René Janon signed an article which paraphrased the letter (changing Camus' term about the play having been *brutalement* banned to *brusquement*). Janon insisted on the "artistic interest, the unselfish work" of the troupe, which (he added) intended to protest the ban in every way it could.

The best way they found was to publish the play. Camus and Bourgeois met in a café and in ten minutes, under Bourgeois's admiring eyes, the younger man had added to the script what he called "the poetry," such as the broken reminiscences and fantasies of Alonso in the second act. Bourgeois assumed that Camus had been inspired by the Balearic Islands, birthplace of his mother's family, just as Bourgeois himself had contributed the name Porcuna, which was not in the Asturias at all; it happened to be an Andalusian town which had struck him, with its Calle Carlos Marx and its inhabitants wearing white linen trousers and large hats.[31] Camus also added a brief foreword warning that theater wasn't meant to be presented in such a form, but since the play couldn't be acted it would at least be read. Its authors offered it as an "Essai de création collective," and its only interest came from that. But his conclusion might have been written by Malraux:

. . . It is a trial effort to introduce action into a framework unsuited to it: the theater. It is sufficient that this action, furthermore,
leads to death, as happens here, for it to achieve a certain form of
nobility peculiar to men: absurdity.

The book was published almost immediately, and in quasi-clandes-
tinity, by twenty-one-year-old Edmond Charlot, who was not yet even
open for business as a publisher. The cover bears only his initials,
"E.C.," which were taken by some in their circle to signify "Editions
Camus."

"It's enough to read ten lines to recognize your style, even your
manner of speaking," Fréminville told Camus. "Why this coyness of
anonymity?"

"After all," Camus protested, "it is perhaps time to return to the
superiority of the work over the artisan."[32]

A printer sympathetic to the young man, Emmanuel Andréo,
owner of the Imprimerie Victor Heintz, ran off 500 copies, and charged
Charlot 500 francs (535 francs; U.S. 110 dollars). The young publisher
put a five-franc retail price on it and sold out the edition in a fortnight.

One of Edmond Charlot's antecedents on his father's side had been
a ship's baker, who got off his ship when it moored in Algiers in 1830,
and stayed on. His father broke the family's baking tradition and went
into the book trade. Born in 1915, Edmond Charlot was raised by his
mother's father, of Maltese origin, a peddler in the southern desert. He
lived in the Hydra neighborhood, and had been a philosophy student in
Jean Grenier's class; the first time he met Albert Camus was at
Grenier's Hydra home. When Grenier asked Charlot what he planned
to do with his life, the student said he wished to open a bookshop.
Grenier gave him two pieces of advice: concentrate on Mediterranean
subjects; don't just sell books, publish them. His father, who ran the
Hachette book distribution service in Algiers, arranged for him to do
his apprenticeship at a large downtown bookshop. He began to make
plans to open his own store, but before he was ready he published a
friend's book (the story of a local aviation club), for sale to mutual
friends. *Révolte dans les Asturies* was the second book he would publish, in May 1936. The third, *Rondeur des jours,* by Jean Giono, was
printed for free distribution to the first 350 customers of his new shop.
Later the shop would be given the name Les Vraies Richesses, using
(with permission) the title of another book by Giono. And it was probably because he published *Révolte dans les Asturies* when he did that
Charlot would later become the publisher of Camus' first literary work.
Jean Grenier gave Charlot the manuscript of his own essay, *Santa Cruz,*
and of Camus' first book, *L'Envers et l'Endroit.*[33]

The cover of the slim, sober volume read as follows:

---

Essai de Création Collective

Révolte
dans
les Asturies

Pièce en 4 actes
e.c.

A Alger

Pour les Amis
du Théâtre du Travail

---

After *Révolte dans les Asturies* was printed, Yves Bourgeois got hold of a manuscript that included most of it and had been written all in one hand (probably Camus'). But during World War II, when Bourgeois was away from home and an anti-subversive campaign was raging in Algeria, his wife thought it would be prudent to burn a lot of her husband's papers, and the original manuscript of *Révolte dans les Asturies* was one of them.[31]

# 9

## DEATH IN THE SOUL

Not to be separated from the world. One doesn't waste his
life when one places it in the light. All my effort, in all situations, misfortunes, disappointments, is to reestablish
contacts. And even in this sadness, what a desire to love,
and what intoxication at the very view of a hill in the evening air.

*Carnets*

"The tender and reserved friendship of women." At least one of his
new women friends was indeed a friend before she was a woman, and if
there was a romantic attachment as well it was not to endure. Marie
Viton, who painted under that name, was actually Baronne Marguerite
d'Estournelles de Constant, a distinguished member of what sophisticated Frenchmen call the "HSP," for Haute Société Protestante. A
*grande bourgeoise*—"her aristocratic appearance accentuated by a
touch of masculine rigor," noted Charles Poncet, she was also a good
comrade, who would fall in with the young group around Camus, most
of whose members were ten to fifteen years her junior. She was intrigued by Camus in particular, and quickly recognized his talents. She
lent her own with generosity, and became a designer for his theater, in
charge of costumes, working with her friend Pierre-André Emery and
Louis Miquel on the scenery.[1]

Marie Viton was also an amateur pilot. Although her daughter had
died in a plane crash she continued to fly. It may have been on the very
day that Camus was summoned to the City Hall to be informed that
*Révolte dans les Asturies* was banned that Camus flew with her for the
first time, accompanied by his friend Jean de Maisonseul, who would

later recall strolling along the boulevard with the smartly dressed
*baronne,* who dropped them off at the door of the City Hall with an
ironic smile.

Shortly after that Viton took her new friend on a two-hundred-mile
flight to Djémila, where in a rugged site three thousand feet above sea
level they visited the ruins of the colony founded by the Roman emperor Trajan, with vestiges of the theater and temples, forum and baths,
contiguous to later Byzantine constructions, set below a backdrop of
hills. This visit was probably the basis for an essay which he would
work on the following year, and publish as "Le Vent à Djémila" in
*Noces.* But there is more than scenery in the essay: Djémila helps to
prepare a man for death, he will write, while illness, which attenuates
the certainty of death by creating an "apprenticeship," is a delusion.
For he wishes to face death with lucidity.

The other girl-comrades in his life would be that couple from
Oran, Jeanne Sicard and Marguerite Dobrenn, daughters of families
who could afford to send them to the university in Algiers, where both
were studying for higher degrees. Jeanne, who was "plain, slight, bony,
tense, intense, and outwardly cold," was accepted by Camus as his
equal whom he could understand and who understood him; Marguerite
was faithful to Jeanne and to the team. And both were quite capable of
joining their friend in his cultural and even in his political adventures.

One day in that spring of 1936 the three friends were walking
along the Chemin Sidi Brahim high above central Algiers when they
came upon a "For Rent" sign on a house which—they realized it at
once—must have a sweeping view of the bay, the harbor, the distant
mountains. They knocked on the door and talked to the landlord,
Georges Fichu, who told them that he was renting the upper floor,
while he lived with his family on the ground floor. They could have it
for 300 francs a month (about 321 francs today, some $65). The three
young people looked at each other. The girls were living in a Foyer des
Jeunes Filles, a student hostel, and Camus was ostensibly living with
unpredictable Simone. This villa wasn't furnished, but it hardly mattered, for they would use it as a day camp, or so they thought at the
time. They began to furnish it as they could, with a secondhand bed
they picked up at an auction, an old table. "The house was suspended
from the summit of a hill from which one saw the bay," begins the
description—a faithful one, according to surviving witnesses—in
Camus' draft novel *La Mort heureuse,* published posthumously, and
whose most convincing passages concern this house. "You climbed to it
by a difficult path which began in olive groves and ended in olive
groves." At the top at last, in "a great distress of sweat and deep
breathing," one found a small blue gate after which one mounted, while

trying to avoid getting scratched by bougainvillaeas, a staircase steep and narrow.

The floor plan was roughly a square. In the rear, facing the Rue des Amandiers, there were a bedroom and the kitchen. In the front, a second bedroom opened onto a large outdoor terrace, facing the city and the harbor, and adjoining it was a living room with the same view through windowpanes. "Completely opened to the landscape, it was like a cockpit suspended in the exploding sky above the many-colored dance of the world." A view through trees, clotheslines, red roofs down to the bay, to violet mountains beyond.

This was the House Above the World (*la Maison Devant le Monde*), as the gang would call it. From the first it had an almost inexplicable appeal for Camus; even unfurnished, before he began to work there or to live in it alone or with a girl friend, it represented what a secret place was for a child, and indeed his evocations of it would betray a longing for a childhood and an adolescence he never had. He would write a poem to this secret place, and to friendship, to the tune of the German marching song "I Had a Comrade," which Yves Bourgeois had sung in *Le Temps du mépris*. As published in Camus' works, the essence of it runs:

> I had some comrades,
> A house above the world.
>
> . . . .
>
> There where the world stops,
> Friendship is born,
> Stubborn desire for openness
> Which defines freedom,
> Our house progresses (repeat)
>
> . . . .

When his friends packed up to return to their respective families in Oran for summer vacation, Camus promised to send them a regular chronicle of events at the Maison Fichu, where he expected to live a great deal. And he kept his promise, his playful letters enhanced by his own illustrations, e.g., a self-portrait with halo. By now he and his volatile wife had given up the Hydra villa and were living at Simone's mother's villa, on the heights of Algiers above the Boulevard du Telemly (now called Boulevard Salah Bouakouir), with a sweeping view of the city and its bay. It was an original structure with abundant terraces, tastefully furnished, built by Dr. Sogler to her specifications.[2] Camus was alone there much of the time, with Simone in her clinic undergoing one cure or another. Even when she was living at home she seldom made an appearance; either she was in another part of the house or she was out, but none of Camus' friends dared ask. All the more reason for his own retreat, even to the childhood fantasy of a houseload of good friends. He had even agreed with Jeanne Sicard and Marguerite Dobrenn that their experiment in community living would be extended. Later they'd buy a farm together, to be called the Farm of Another Day (*Ferme du Lendemain*); they were drawing up bylaws for it.[3] Camus noted in his journal (when mapping out an essay on the House Above the World, perhaps for *Noces*) that the Maison Fichu was already being called in the neighborhood "the house of the 3 Students."

His notebook at this time was being filled with jottings and outlines for the novel that would become *La Mort heureuse*. If we are to accept the order in which the notes appear in his journal (and generally we should not, for reasons that have already been explained), the plan to utilize the idyll of the Maison Fichu preceded the more commonplace plot, in which a young man kills an invalid and uses his money to create a fugitive happiness. "Catherine," says Patrice (in one of the earliest of these notes), "I know now that I am going to write." Catherine is Christiane Galindo, who will move into the Maison Fichu in autumn 1936, Patrice is Albert Camus. In fact Patrice-Albert will soon begin making journal entries which will serve for essays in *Noces,* for his play *Caligula,* and for *Le Mythe de Sisyphe.*

He also warned himself in his journal that he must pay attention to his body, to fight against fragility and a relapse of illness. He made the first of a number of lists which were to group his future work into categories:

> Philosophic work: absurdity.
> Literary work: strength, love and death under the sign of conquest.

But first he had to finish his dissertation for Professor Poirier. In "Neoplatonisme et pensée chrétienne" the student will of course contrast the Greek system in which man is the measure of all things with the Christian supernatural. Not accidentally, the protagonists in this spiritual combat are both North Africans, Plotinus (whose neoplatonism had a major influence on the early Christians) and St. Augustine (who would use the methods of the Greeks but reject their serenity). Christianity, Camus concludes, "has kept its deep truth in dealing with all difficulties on the level of Incarnation."

Poirier scribbled on the dissertation: "More a writer than a philosopher." He took note of the errors, the misspellings of Latin, but he also knew that you didn't argue philosophy with an artist. The jury sitting in judgment on Camus' paper consisted of Poirier, Dean Louis

Gernet, historian of Greek law, and Jean Grenier. They jointly signed the certificate, on May 25, 1936, which bestowed the *diplôme d'études supérieures* on Albert Camus. Now, if he had been able to, he would have gone on to the *agrégation* entitling him to enter the higher teaching profession. But that meant being taken in tow by the state for his life long, and the state expected a candidate to be in good health. While tuberculosis was still an incurable disease, Camus could not claim to possess the good health that was demanded of teachers.[4]

But he intended to live, and to live fully. After a walk he noted in his journal the sensations he had experienced in admiring sea, sun, flowers. But also the "tender friendship of women. . . . Smiles, jokes and plans"—with his Maison Fichu comrades, of course. And then this sudden cry: "I hold on to the world by all my acts, to men by all my gratitude."

Now his journal will deal more frequently with specific writing projects. And to his friends he confided other preoccupations. He was disturbed by the increasing disorders in Spain, which suggested that a Popular Front government would fail in its attempt to cope with the threat of Fascist extremism. (It would be difficult for a Communist to care about what happened in Paris and not what was happening in Spain; and Camus was not only a secret Communist, he was also something of a secret Spaniard.) He decided to read and see everything he could about Spain. At that time Franco had not yet begun his insurrection. Spain's prime minister was Santiago Casarès Quiroga, who challenged the Fascists openly but could not fully cope with the disintegration of public order. (In less than a decade the prime minister's daughter, the actress Maria Casarès, would be the heroine in Camus' first performed play.) In France the Socialists had come out of the national elections of May 3 victorious, and were now the largest party in the Chamber of Deputies. On June 4 their leader, Léon Blum, put together his first Popular Front government, supported by the Communist Party in parliamentary votes, though the Communists refused direct participation in the cabinet.

School was over. With dispersion of his friends for the summer holidays, no organized activities would be possible until autumn. Camus was spending his lonely days and nights reading, some of it unlikely reading: the Count de Gobineau, Céline. (But when he picked up Céline's *Mort à crédit* [Death on the Installment Plan], he put it down again after reading the opening pages, telling his friends that as far as he was concerned the most pessimistic sentence he knew contained no scatalogical word. It was Stendhal's remark that man isn't even capable of being entirely bad.) He was enthusiastic about Kierkegaard's *Diary of the Seducer,* in the first volume of *Either/Or,* a confession of young

Søren Kierkegaard's love—and rejection—of Regine Olsen (whom Kierkegaard felt too young and innocent for all his guilt). Presumably looking over his daughter's shoulder to read Camus' letters, Jeanne Sicard's father warned her that Camus' behavior betrayed lack of ambition. Camus assured his Oran friends that in his case it was a demonstration of an *excess* of ambition.[3]

He was seeing more of Yves Bourgeois now. They would go out together with some of the girls to movies, concerts, or simply to wander through the Kasbah, to sit at the Café Fromentin, to visit local sights such as the Cemetery of the Princesses, a small Moslem graveyard where three ancient fig trees shaded the tombs of Fatma Bent Hassane Bey and Nfissa Bent Hassane Pacha. They even played tennis with some of Camus' affluent friends.

Camus suggested that Bourgeois meet his wife Simone, who was undergoing a cure in a clinic at Ben Akroun on the heights above the city. Bourgeois went up to pay his respects, and got along well with her, took her on a short walk through the nearby countryside. Then Bourgeois joined the Camus for the Whitsun holidays at Teniet el Had, a town 125 miles southwest of the city. They didn't even bother to go to the famous cedar forest there, but walked in the fields, played chess, rested. Back in town, Simone was out of her clinic now, living with Camus at Dr. Sogler's (on the floor above her mother's living quarters). Camus showed Bourgeois what he called his favorite work of sculpture, the cast of a beautiful girl drowning in the Seine. Bourgeois was less enthusiastic about listening to the entire album of Bach's "Goldberg Variations." Camus lent him books—on China (including a classic, *La Musique chinoise,* by the composer Louis Laloy), another by the nineteenth-century anarchist theoretician Max Stirner, but also an Erskine Caldwell novel. (It had to be *God's Little Acre,* the only work of Caldwell then available in French, published that year by Gallimard in a translation by Maurice-Edgar Coindreau, with a preface by André Maurois.)

Bourgeois remarked that the couple's favorite books were *The Magic Mountain* by Thomas Mann, Jakob Wassermann's *The Mauritius Case,* and quotations from the early Spanish poet Luis de Góngora remembered from a lecture. He also learned about Simone's dancing, heard from her that she intended to train to be a professional. It was also understood that she would join the Théâtre du Travail when it resumed activities in October, playing Natasha to her husband's Pepel in Maxim Gorky's *The Lower Depths,* which was to be the next play on their program.

At that time, Bourgeois's definition of paradise was to canoe through Central Europe. He suggested that they make a trip together.

Apparently the scheme struck the young couple as a splendid opportunity to put their marriage back on the rails. They went down to the harbor together to try out Bourgeois's old kayak, which he had given to Marthe Sogler.

Before leaving, Camus went off to Tizi-Ouzou, the chief township of Upper Kabylie west of Algiers, where he was sent by the Amsterdam-Pleyel movement to speak at a rally. He later recalled that he had addressed a sea of fezzes, the soft red caps worn by rural Moslems.

In early July the couple, with Bourgeois, sailed to Marseilles, steerage class. From Marseilles they traveled by train to Lyons, where Bourgeois borrowed a double-seater kayak for himself from friends, and rented another for his companions. He took them around the grim old city, which at the time seemed a perfect setting for a mystery story, with its mist and its secret alleys.[5] They also visited nearby Villeurbanne. Camus found it all very middle-class—the standard of living, the cooking, the manners—even the prostitutes. He was tired, and looked forward to the adventure which was about to begin. But without enthusiasm: Once again, as in the Balearics the previous summer, he discovered that travel aroused an indefinable fear in him. Bourgeois assumed that he was bored or exhausted, but that was not the whole story.[3] It was almost as if the unpredictability of his health heightened his anxiety, as if he were afraid that he would have another attack of his disease in a strange and far-off land.

On July 15 they boarded a train again, this time for Austria, and after a fatiguing journey arrived at the Tyrolean capital, Innsbruck, where they rode grandly in a hackney in the dusk from the station to a famous old (1390) inn, the Golden Eagle, which had hosted nobility, and also Goethe. The following day Bourgeois took the Camus on a sightseeing tour of the city. Camus decided that Innsbruck was a comic opera set, with its burghers attired in short pants, feathers in their hats. The friends did some shopping connected with canoeing.

And they picked up newspapers. The headlines concerned Spain. An uprising of the Army in Spanish Morocco, led by General Francisco Franco against the Popular Front government in Madrid, had spread to the mainland.

Bourgeois had reckoned that the most appropriate stretch of river for the couple's initiation would be the forty miles to Kufstein (near the German border), along the lovely Inn River valley. On the afternoon of July 19 he assembled the two folding kayaks and they moved off on the strong current, Camus and Simone in one boat, Bourgeois (with their baggage) in the other. Everything went well that day. They pulled to the bank to set up Bourgeois's tent for the night, but slept uncomfortably because one tent proved insufficient for the three campers.

Next morning, as they were walking, Camus suddenly stopped, paralyzed with pain. Only then did he remember that he had been warned against violent exercise involving use of his shoulders. He remembered too, with bitterness, that he was not like the others, was not able to do everything he wanted to. All that morning they debated about what to do. Finally Camus suggested that he take the train to Kufstein to wait for them, to allow his friend and Simone to pursue the river journey. He stood on the shore watching as they flashed by like "a lightning bolt." Bourgeois and Simone Camus were in the front kayak, he at the stern; the second kayak was in tow.

But the trouble with this arrangement was that the head canoe had to maintain sufficient momentum to draw the one behind faster than the current. Now a contrary wind rose and, however hard they paddled, slowed them down. Bourgeois found that he couldn't prevent the boat in tow from revolving on the painter and coming to a forty-five degree angle, which would have made passing under pier bridges difficult. So they stopped to camp until the wind dropped, reaching Kufstein twenty-four hours late. It was drizzling, and they spotted the lone figure of Camus on the bank waiting for them. ("The chapel and the fields under the rain along the Inn," he noted in his journal. "Solitude which implants itself.") He told them that he had been alarmed at their failure to show up when they were expected, and had alerted the police. It all ended in a bar, with a police inspector obliging Bourgeois, as entertainment for his companions, to translate bawdy stories from Italian.

The next stop was a place that Bourgeois was anxious to visit because of its famed beauty; at the time he was not aware that Berchtesgaden was now Adolf Hitler's cherished domain, after having served as his retreat following the aborted 1923 *Putsch,* and that Hitler's old chalet had received palatial transformation since. A former ecclesiastical principality, Berchtesgaden had breathtaking mountain scenery, most conspicuously the 8,900-foot peak of the Watzmann; even without Hitler it was a favorite of tourists in the Bavarian Alps. They found rooms in a local inn only after much searching, and were soon listening to a concert of folk songs which turned into a Nazi rally. Bourgeois was irritated with what he felt was Camus' intolerant attitude to Germans, not only to their ideology but, he felt, to Germans as human beings. He decided that there were great differences in mentality between himself and the younger man, began to remember examples of Camus' unwillingness to accept political views different from his own. There had been a similar situation in Lyons, when a former student of Bourgeois saw them sitting in a café and came over to greet him. The student happened to be a right-wing activist, and after his departure Camus expressed his horror at the young man's opinions. Later, while they were visiting a Lyons church, Bourgeois found himself telling the Camus that he himself was a Catholic (which was only half true at the time and soon became quite untrue). But he noted that Camus winced then, as he had when Bourgeois made an anti-Communist remark. Now Bourgeois's basic admiration for Germany and Camus' clear dislike for everything he saw here proved irreconcilable. And Bourgeois began to feel that Simone's *femme fatale* elegance and make-up contrasted a bit too much with the reigning dirndl culture; people were always staring. Camus himself never mentioned the disastrous visit to Berchtesgaden, neither to his friends nor to his journal.

But they spent a good day on the Königssee, the great Bavarian lake just three miles south of Berchtesgaden, each going his separate way. Bourgeois and Simone, early at the agreed meeting place, had their first serious talk. He found her to be less affected than she had seemed to him up till then.

Camus was making notes of things observed in trains and in the streets. And he began to dream of traveling with people he really cared for, his Maison Fichu comrades for instance. He took time out to apply by mail for a job teaching in a private school, the Cours Fenelon in Oran; he was determined to get out of Algiers if he could; perhaps he could change his life with Simone, and Simone's life, by changing cities.

They proceeded to Salzburg, fifteen miles north of Berchtesgaden, where there was much to see, much walking to do. Camus seemed interested in the roomful of model stages at the Mozart birthplace house. He was stirred by an outdoor performance of Hugo von Hofmannsthal's mysteries on the cathedral square; *now* he was sharing in the excitement of the trip. It was the first time since they began that he felt in tune with his surroundings. The music was the catalyst.

Salzburg and its music were not a setting for comic opera but for grand opera. For here Camus was going to suffer one of the great shocks of his life, and when he least expected it.

All along the way, the Camus and Bourgeois had been receiving mail: letters from friends, but also money orders (Bourgeois's salary, additional funds from Marthe Sogler), and of course the correspondence related to job possibilities (Claude de Fréminville was writing to him about a likely opening in journalism). They had left instructions back in Algeria for mail to be sent to them at key stops on their itinerary, addressed to general delivery. In Salzburg, on July 26, Camus went alone to pick up the mail at the post office. He found several letters. Two of them were from his Maison Fichu comrades. Apparently there was also a letter for Simone, which he was able to pick up in her absence. It looked important, or suspicious—it had a doctor's return

address. He opened it. He read in it an offer of more help—drugs—and
a clear indication that the relationship between the writer and Simone
Camus was more than that of doctor and patient.

No one alive has read the letter Camus discovered that day, and
the contents which struck Camus as a great tragedy can be reconstructed only from confidences made to a friend who shared his life
subsequently.[6] Bourgeois could only sense that a stormy confrontation
was taking place in the couple's hotel room. But Camus was determined
to continue the trip as if nothing had happened, mainly because of
Bourgeois, and because he felt that Bourgeois had noticed nothing.
Then one morning he confronted Bourgeois with a set face and
confessed: "I have decided to separate from my wife," adding, to the
other's surprise, because it seemed a superfluous remark, "You had
nothing to do with it." To his comrades back in Algeria he would never
say more than that his life would henceforth be different, for henceforth
he would live alone.[3]

Right now, the Camus and Bourgeois would continue their trip as
before, separating only when canoeing was involved, joining up to pursue the journey overland to Dresden, Silesia, Moravia, and into Northern Italy, then home to Algiers. It would be assumed by friends, baffled
or inspired by Camus' silence, that something *else* happened; it is now
recorded in literary history, for example, that Camus' wife ran off with
Bourgeois, leaving him alone in Prague.

Of course a new source of tension had been added to the tension
between Camus and his wife: that of Bourgeois as the unlucky by-
stander. The lycée teacher made up his mind to remain non-committal
but chivalrous to Simone, convinced that Camus realized that she
needed more comfort than Camus himself did.

They crossed the lakes and mountains of the Salzkammergut, the
*White Horse Inn* country, partly on foot, partly by lake steamer, at
times forced to call a halt because of rain. Camus managed to be natural and even humorous. When they reached Linz he went off to have a
pneumothorax injection, while Bourgeois arranged to have one of the
kayaks returned to France. Since all the practical problems fell on
Bourgeois's shoulders (he was the guide, the interpreter, the boat expert, as well as their treasurer), he sometimes acted in an authoritarian
manner, and Camus snapped back. At the Czechoslovakian border
there was an anxious twenty minutes for the couple when Bourgeois left
the train to disappear inside the customs office, the train was about to
start, and they suddenly realized that they had no money or tickets and
knew not a word of any language spoken within five hundred miles.

Bourgeois was determined to canoe across Bohemia, and it was decided quite simply that Simone Camus would accompany him. Obvi-

ously he would not have suggested it outright, not after Camus' declaration at Salzburg. Only Camus could have had the idea, or perhaps it had been Simone, and Camus would have made it a point of honor not to object. Bourgeois was pleased, in any case, especially when the going got rough on the Upper Moldau and she proved tougher than he had expected her to be; he attributed it to her Austrian blood. They glided on northward, camping out, or stopping in towns such as Krummau (Cesky Krumlov) and Budweis (Ceske Budejovice), where Camus might be waiting for them. (Indeed, Camus himself may well have gotten off the train in this latter town before going on to Prague, for the first title he would give to *Le Malentendu* was "Budejovice.") When the rain delayed them, they folded the remaining kayak and got on a train, stopping on the way to visit Tabor, the old Hussite center, just an hour from Prague.

Camus had indeed been alone in Prague. He fell into a depression which made it difficult for him to enjoy what he was seeing. Decidedly it was time for his traveling companions to show up. He had sufficient funds to live without them for another week, but he was nervous about the situation anyway. He found it hard to make his way around this strange city, couldn't find the old Jewish cemetery, for example, one of the sights on his list; he discovered that the main museum was closed. He detected a worsening of his health. Thinking about the teaching opportunity in Oran, he realized that he would not like to leave Algiers after all, despite the new reasons he had for not staying there.[3] In lieu of a diary, there is Camus' essay "La Mort dans l'âme" (Death in the Soul), recording his arrival in Prague with just enough money to survive six days until his companions joined him, reliving his anxieties—the price of his room, of his meals, the fear of falling ill among unsympathizing strangers, his failure even to visit the old city the way he should have liked to; in passing, the sight and odor of cucumbers in vinegar—which would be his madeleines-of-Proust whenever he thought of Prague.

He tried culture, finally got to some churches and museums, but: "As soon as I was out again, I was a stranger." His own condition became desperate; he hadn't spoken for days. Then there was a knock on the door and his "friends" (Simone and Bourgeois actually) entered. He probably said: "I'm glad to see you," and they would have perceived nothing strange in his behavior. Camus' essay contains an accurate account of the pursuit of their journey through Silesia and Moravia and into Northern Italy, but it is written in an intense first person, reinforcing the notion that Camus continued his journey alone, abandoned by his companions. He would use the self-pitying description of the young man's arrival in Prague, alone and without sufficient funds, as a

chapter in *La Mort heureuse,* the material hardly transformed; there too
would be retold the pursuit of the journey through Czechoslovakia and
down to Italy.

In truth, when his friends arrived in Prague, he could begin to take
advantage of his stay in that marvelous old city. They did get to the
principal museum now, as well as to the Jewish Museum. They also saw
a play by Maxim Gorky, the author they were to bring to their own
stage that fall. The play, *Les Petits bourgeois,* was being staged in
Prague by an amateur company (Camus called it a local Théâtre du
Travail)—and staged badly, with vulgar scenery and poor lighting.
They were sure that they would do better in Algiers.[7]

On August 15, Camus and his estranged wife took the train together to Dresden. Bourgeois wanted to try the Elbe, so after assembling the kayak he began his sail. Joined up again, the travelers du-
tifully visited the Dresden museums, admired Raphael's *Sistine
Madonna.* At last Bourgeois got rid of his boat, booking it through to
France. They continued east to medieval Bautzen in Upper Lusatia,
where Camus remarked the Gothic cemetery: "Geraniums and
sunflowers in the brick arches." At Görlitz in Silesia, Camus teamed up
with Bourgeois for some strenuous sightseeing. They wanted to visit the
grave, mentioned in Bourgeois's Baedeker guide, of the mystic Jakob
Boehme, but the hike was too much for Camus. Then "tragic" Breslau
(Wroclaw), where Camus saw churches and factory smokestacks
through a fine drizzle. As conscientious tourists they were exhausted
now, and their funds were low. So they decided to skip Cracow, the old
Polish capital, to go straight to Vienna. On the way they were
impressed with the plains of Silesia, "pitiless and ungrateful."

But in Olmütz (Olomouc), in bleak Moravia—they were in the
heart of Czechoslovakia now—they had to stop, short of funds, for
Bourgeois's salary hadn't arrived. The couple had already wired Marthe
Sogler for money and it was received at once; she had offered still more
but they thought that they could get along without it. They were now in
the third week of August, planning to stay abroad another three weeks.
Above all, Camus was more relaxed now, his morale improved considerably. He would record his impression of "Tender and indolent
plains," and would remember this place when it came time for a setting
for *Le Malentendu.* Moravia, then a region whose population was 75
per cent Czech and 25 per cent German, had long ago been an independent principality. Merged with neighboring Bohemia, it became the
possession of the King of Hungary under the Treaty of Olomouc in
1478.

After Olmütz, they stopped off at the ancient manufacturing center

of Brno, where Camus would remember to mention "poor neighborhoods," in his journal.

Then Vienna, where Camus' notation seemed a sigh of relief:
"Civilization." He saw both the luxury and the "distress," but they
would do what they could to enjoy their stay. An evening was spent
pleasantly at Grinzing, the city's Montmartre, with its rustic cafés serving white wine and hearty food on outdoor tables. But there was a genuine money problem now. And they were tired; too much togetherness
for too long proved a strain. Camus and Bourgeois walked for an hour
through St. Stephen's Cathedral and along the Ringstrasse without saying a word to each other. Finally they decided they would take advantage of the special tourist rate on Mussolini's Italian railways, requiring
a minimum stay in Italy. Bourgeois suggested his favorite city, Vicenza,
and they got back on the train.

The descent from the Alps to the Adriatic on a late summer afternoon was a delight. At moments Camus would point out details in the
landscape through the train window for Simone, and Bourgeois was
reminded of their happier days. "Nevertheless, in the train which took
me from Vienna to Venice," Camus would recall in "La Mort dans
l'âme":

> I was waiting for something. I was like a convalescent who had
> been nourished on broth and who wondered what the first crust of
> bread would taste like. A light was about to appear. I know it now:
> I was ready for happiness.

On the train Camus whispered to Bourgeois that a middle-aged
traveler in a corner of their compartment seemed to be the French-
Swiss writer C. F. Ramuz, and Bourgeois thought that he very likely
was.

At Venice they had nearly two hours to wait between trains. Bourgeois walked them briskly from the station through the narrow passages, up and down the small bridges, to Piazza San Marco, and back
again to the station. It was festival time (the annual historical regatta
surely), and, crossing the Rialto Bridge, they found palaces and boats
strung with lanterns: the setting for an opera. The Piazza dei Signori at
Vicenza had a similar effect on them when they arrived that night. On
the following day they would do some of their last sightseeing together.
Camus admired the jewel of the Teatro Olimpico with its *trompe l'oeil*
effects, designed by Palladio. At the tourist office they found exactly
what they needed: the address of a pensione at Monte Berico, a village
a mile and a half south on a ridge dominating the plain, near the Villa
Valmarana, decorated by Tiepolo. Here they spent a week, wandering

separately, meeting for meals at the boardinghouse. Once the two men went bowling and Camus won.

Although Camus betrayed none of this emotion to Bourgeois, he was clearly at home in this "Terre faite à mon âme." He recollected as much in "La Mort dans l'âme" but he must also have noted this in his journal, on a page perhaps later torn out of the first notebook. For if he was careful to record his feelings in Austria, Germany, and Czechoslovakia, even during brief stops, he had more leisure to do so now, and more reason, as his essay proves (written in his hilltop room, windows open to the plain below).

He walked through Vicenza, or in the other direction further into the country. "Every being encountered, every odor of that street, everything is a pretext for loving without bounds." He was once more aware of what the sun and the countries of the sun could mean to him. The noonday sun stripped him of everything except himself, confronted him with his anguish, the anguish meeting the indifference of the beautiful earth. At times the odor of cucumbers and vinegar stirred up his anxiety, but he would only have to think of Vicenza to appease it.

The return sea voyage from Marseilles to Algiers, where they arrived on September 9, was again in third class steerage accommodations, heavily overcrowded, for the summer holidays were coming to an end. Camus moved into his brother's small apartment in the center of town; the Maison Fichu, with its transportation problem and lack of convenience, was a luxury he couldn't then afford. Simone went back to her mother's. He would continue to try to help her in her ups and downs, mainly through consultations with Marthe Sogler, for whom Simone would be a dead weight for the rest of her life, in clinics and out. Although the couple would not even bother to divorce for another four years (when Camus was preparing to remarry), they would never live together again. Simone died after a second marriage and divorce, in 1970.

# 10

♦

## HOUSE ABOVE THE WORLD

The House Above the World, they said among themselves, is not a house where one has fun but a house where one is happy.

*La Mort heureuse*

Salzburg (not Prague) had been a turning point. From now on Albert Camus would wear the stigma of his burnt marriage, face the full impact of his essential solitude. There was no longer a Marthe Sogler to replace a Gustave Acault, no comfortable home in which to take refuge, and student days (when a bohemian existence was in the nature of things) were behind him. He told his aunt Gaby with bitterness that Simone Camus had been his guinea pig.[1] Henceforth he would assume the character that close friends would recognize all his adult life: a more than usual pride, a more than necessary susceptibility, an "African temperament" in Jean Grenier's phrase.[2] His life held more secrets than ever; various groups of friends were compartmented as in the occult chambers of an espionage network. His "Spanish" side also came out, or was cultivated; one of his fellow French-Spanish Algerians, Emmanuel Roblès, called it an *alma torera,* bullfighter's soul, a mixture of modest courage and pride. He also cultivated his "Mediterranean" character, whose most obvious manifestation was his attitude toward women: respect, keen regard, for the mother, and for the wife as mother, but with a sharp eye for new conquests. Almost as if taking revenge for the wounds inflicted by Simone, he was also punishing himself by refusing the comfort and the reassurance of a single, enduring liaison. Some saw his behavior as intense misogyny, and he cultivated *this* notion, too. Grenier thought that Camus recognized himself in Mozart's

Don Juan, "eternal pursuer of beauty but also as solitary and dominating man, 'living on the high seas, threatened, in a regal happiness.' "² A Don Juan who despised the women he seduced, a deliberate breaker of hearts.

But that would be too easy. Some of his best friends were and would always be women; they could also be lovers.

Jeanne Sicard and Marguerite Dobrenn would not be his lovers, but they were close enough, often enough, for some of Camus' other friends to refer to them as his "bodyguard." Their presence made of the villa on the hill, the House Above the World, a refuge from the world, where he could put aside Spanish pride, Mediterranean gamesmanship, to play children's games. While he was away in Central Europe the girls had been putting the Maison Fichu in order. After that they returned to their parents' homes in Oran for the balance of the school holidays. Camus began to find it pleasant to sleep at his brother's (or wherever sleeping quarters were available), and to use the Maison Fichu daytimes, writing on the open terrace facing the sea. He realized that he couldn't afford to rent an apartment of his own just then, for he hadn't yet found a job; he could barely buy postage stamps. But in his last summer month before his friends returned, before anyone was available to do anything, whether it was political action or amateur theater, it was nice not doing anything at all. In ten years, he thought, he would call such a state bliss.³

Then, as his friends began to return to jobs, to school, he joined the most militant of them in setting up an organization which could carry out the political and cultural activities they thought necessary, and which for Camus himself would represent an extension of his Communist Party commitment. He and Charles Poncet, with their comrade Emile Scotto-Lavina and his Maison Fichu friends, were already participating in the embryonic activities of Amis de la Revue *Commune*. Soon they would give their efforts a still more tangible form, with the foundation of the Maison de la Culture, literally House of Culture, the Algerian counterpart of a national movement directed from Paris by the Communists and their sympathizers.⁴

By now the Popular Front had conquered all reticences, had become the prevailing ideology of thinking people; in its largest sense it encompassed the Radical Socialists, whose ranks included many of Algeria's most reactionary settlers and businessmen. Yves Bourgeois noted with glee that he and his friends were now the Establishment.⁵ They were convinced that it was a beautiful time for creative young people: They could give something of themselves, take responsibility for the cultural development of rank and file citizens. It was a kind of explosion, one of them would remember later. The "Arabs" didn't participate? But these young people were no ordinary colonials; they worked as hard as "Arabs" did. Sons of the middle class for the most part, in the sense that all Europeans in Algeria were bourgeois vis-à-vis Moslems, they were making a revolution of their own, and doing it together, eating, sleeping, working, writing together. And of the whole group Camus appeared the least undisciplined, the most concentrated in purpose; his health and his lack of means were responsible for that.[6]

On September 29, 1936, rehearsals got under way for Maxim Gorky's *The Lower Depths,* which was to be the next play in the repertory of the Théâtre du Travail, to be followed (at least in the original plan) by Machiavelli's *Mandragola,* revival of *Le Temps du mépris,* Balzac's *Vautrin,* and *La Celestina* (La Célestine), by Fernando de Rojas. But the separation from Simone had created a crisis of sorts, for Camus had to find a replacement for her in the feminine lead of the Gorky play, tentatively set aside for Simone in the happier time when it seemed that she might be ready to share his universe. Now he offered the role to Jeanne Sicard, but she did not want it. In fact she and Marguerite Dobrenn were taking their time about returning from Oran to Algiers, and rehearsals had to begin without them. New actors were recruited, and Camus began to discover that an unending supply of attractive young ladies was prepared to play the heroines under his direction. Otherwise he felt that this time his actors were inadequate (or he was becoming more demanding); he had soon grown tired of the text and wished it were time to get on to something new.[3]

New tensions were developing, notably between Camus and Yves Bourgeois. The lycée teacher and his friends felt that Camus was taking himself too seriously as a producer-director, seeing himself as a Meyerhold or a Stanislavsky, while behaving as an amateur. They pointed out that he had dropped a young man from the cast for missing rehearsals, while he was prepared to wait weeks for the return of his friends Jeanne Sicard and Marguerite Dobrenn. There developed a tacit division between those of the company who were personally devoted to Camus and all the others. Bourgeois was among the others. He continued to be friendly to Simone Camus, and was seen in public with her.[5]

For his part, and although he went ahead with rehearsals, Camus wasn't at all sure that he himself would be in Algiers for the performances, scheduled now for the end of November, for he was earnest about his job-hunting. He had even applied for a position as a teacher of young patients in a sanatorium in the Alps. In his heart he hoped that that job would not come through, but then he would have to look for local office work, for no money was coming in at all now. He kept reading help-wanted advertisements, even the most outlandish ones, but

they couldn't be outlandish enough for him. He confessed that his secret hope was that an Indian prince would advertise for a Western-
educated secretary.

He watched with interest the development of his new friend Edmond Charlot's publishing program, agreed to be editor of a series of
works, called "Méditerranéennes," by Mediterranean writers and poets.
He promised Charlot that he'd find a dozen subscribers for the series in
Oran, and then passed the job on to Jeanne Sicard, well connected with
the Oran bourgeoisie.[3] For Charlot had at last opened his bookshop,
and at once this matchbox-sized bookstore became the gathering place
for all their reading friends. Here they could leaf through the new
books and the political and literary magazines, and if they couldn't
afford to buy books they could borrow them. The lending department
charged the equivalent of the price of a new book as a membership fee,
after which a borrowed book could be exchanged for another one as
often as desired at no additional cost. For a higher fee, the borrower
could take two books at a time, and so on. As an informal associate,
and then as a house author, Camus was in the shop all the time, reading
while seated on the narrow stairway which led to the upstairs office,
taking books home. Soon he would be advising Charlot on what new
books to buy, on what manuscripts to publish.[7]

A newcomer joined the Maison Fichu's boy and girl scouts. Jeanne
Sicard and Marguerite Dobrenn knew a girl in Oran, Christiane
Galindo, who sought a job in Algiers, and Camus was asked to help
her. This sort of assignment was certain to appeal to him, and he invited Christiane to come at once, even to camp at the Maison Fichu;
he'd have her at home but he had no home.[3]

This time the new Establishment was able to obtain one of Algeria's most attractive auditoriums for the two scheduled performances
of *The Lower Depths* on Saturday evening (November 28) and Sunday
matinee. The Salle Pierre Bordes (today called Salle Ibn Khaldoun)
was part of the high-rise administrative complex of the Government
General, designed by the architect Jacques Guiauchain with the Perret
brothers, these last a famous family of builders who innovated with
reinforced concrete. A vast rotunda, its dome spanned a hundred feet;
it would make for grandiose productions, enhancing the rigorously
spare décor of epic theater, but alas, the acoustics were more appropriate to musical events than to spoken drama.

The action of the play was simple, centered on a hostelry for the
down and out, one of whom will murder the owner of the establishment. After a period of turbulence, the group will return to the miserable existence they had momentarily shaken. Jean Renoir had just
made a film of the Gorky play (which received the new Delluc prize as

the best motion picture of the year), starring Louis Jouvet and Jean Gabin, the latter playing the thief Pepel, the role Camus would take in Algiers.

For this Théâtre du Travail production the décor was designed by Camus' architect friend Pierre-André Emery, who from now on would be associated with all the stagings of the young company. Emery made use of what was available, above all the wooden cubes used to build up varying levels for the musicians who were meant to use the auditorium. There was also effective use of plywood panels. Maks Wigdorczyk, a Polish cabinetmaker, contributed his carpentry skills. Costumes were no problem for actors playing paupers. Bourgeois, who played the wise old tramp Luka, lent the set an Austrian earthenware plate showing the Virgin and Child, which from a distance could pass for an icon.[8] However improvised it may have appeared in the days immediately preceding the first performance, the result was gratifying. "For the second time," reported *L'Echo d'Alger,* "the young and courageous troupe of the Labor Theater was on stage. . . . A dense crowd filled the vast hall. . . ." The critic pointed out: "An increasingly large audience is tired of the sophisticated theater of the boulevards." It took courage to choose this desperate subject. But the effort succeeded: décor, acting, lighting . . . "the beauty of certain scenes to which the play of shadows in silhouettes, in the background, lent an air of fantasy." He noted that the troupe wished to remain anonymous, refused the customary applause at the end of each act. "But what a beautiful lesson in modesty!" The Communists' *Lutte Sociale* added that the troupe was attempting to do with a few hundred francs what Pitoëff and Lugné-Poe were doing thanks to the facilities of the Paris stage.

Rule of anonymity or not, it was clear that Albert Camus was the unquestioned leader here, his fellow trouper and lifelong friend Charles Poncet observed.

He was also becoming a competent actor. Never a great one; not even the most fervent of his admirers would say that. Some would feel that he was the least bad of the amateur company, with his athletic build the one with most stage presence: an American-style young leading man. Others of the troupe never could overcome the impression of regional comedy, could not shed their heavy *pied noir* accents, Mediterranean gesticulations; Camus at least could control his.[9]

Now the happy community days would begin, the idyll described in adolescent rhetoric in *La Mort heureuse,* giving that work, which Camus never intended to publish, an ineffaceable stamp of immaturity. Jeanne Sicard and Marguerite Dobrenn had finally arrived, this time to settle in as permanent residents of the Maison Fichu. Jeanne came as a rebel, for her upper-class family had learned about what they could only consider her life of dissipation in Algiers: the stage acting, perhaps even the Party membership. They had refused to allow her to return to Algiers, so she simply gave up the student hostel (Foyer des Jeunes Filles) altogether and moved in with Marguerite Dobrenn and their Oran friend Christiane Galindo. Christiane, who had gotten her *baccalauréat* from an Oran lycée, had found a job in Algiers as a secretary, working for an automobile sales company, so she would contribute her share to Maison Fichu rent.[10] Camus lived there on and off—mostly on, now that Christiane was there; his flirtation with this girl who liked to sunbathe in the nude is one of the least heavy motifs of *La Mort heureuse*.

And Yves Bourgeois was so far from feeling inimical toward Camus, even if he had become testy with Camus' unconditional admirers, that he carried up on his shoulder a large shelf he wasn't using, as his contribution to the furnishing of the Maison Fichu.[5]

Jeanne and Marguerite shared a bedroom facing the Rue des Amandiers. Christiane got the room with large bay windows facing the terrace "above the world." Camus set up his writing table—actually a plain wooden kitchen table—in front of her window (she was out at her job all day). In the framework of the contrived plot of *La Mort heureuse,* the chapters on the Maison Fichu are a faithful record of life as they were living it from the end of 1936 through the following year. Claire is Jeanne Sicard, Rose is Marguerite Dobrenn, Catherine is Christiane Galindo, and their friends have new names too. Only the pets have kept their real names: Cali and Gula, the cats (cats would henceforth be a necessary element in the life of Camus). One of the principal products of that little writing table before the window would be the first draft of *Caligula,* a play that Camus was beginning to compose about the capricious tyrant, and that would go through many versions before its first public performance in 1945. There was also a stray dog, which Camus baptized Kirk, "the dog of anguish," whose anguish may have derived from his ticks, which spread through the house until the exterminators were summoned. All the pets belonged to the community, and would remain when the friends passed on the villa to other friends—the Fréminvilles,[11] who in turn left it to Robert Namia.

One day, when Yves Bourgeois was teaching a class, he was called down to the public parlor, and urgently. A large, well-attired older woman who had obviously rushed to the school straight from the railway station demanded to hear what Bourgeois could tell her about the whereabouts of her daughter Jeanne Sicard. Bourgeois realized at once that Camus' friend must have mentioned his name as an acquaintance because he held a respectable position in the community. He employed his built-in talents for acting dumb. When Madame Sicard asked for the names of the other young men in the group, he invented some names for her. She apparently realized what he was doing for she stalked out, after digging her nails into his hand in the guise of a handshake.[5]

For their theater group, Camus had been working from the time of his return from mainland Europe on the production of Aeschylus' *Prometheus Bound*. Having decided that all existing translations were laborious, he began to rewrite it from start to finish. He counted on Jeanne Sicard's intelligent counsel, for she was now his best collaborator, capable of understanding his intentions, for the staging and musical accompaniment. Meanwhile they undertook a rapid production of Ramon J. Sender's *The Secret* (about the interrogation of a worker by the police), a command performance for a workers' festival, Fête de *l'Algérie Ouvrière,* on December 6. Produced in six days, it was hailed by *L'Algérie Ouvrière* as an artistic tour de force.[12]

Still without a job, Camus made a quick trip to Oran to see about the newspaper work that Fréminville was trying to get for him. Popular Front forces in that city had put together funds and talents to launch a daily newspaper of their own to counter the only available press, controlled by conservative settlers. Marcel Chouraqui, a law student, was helping to recruit a staff for the paper. He interviewed Camus and told him that they would be able to pay only 1,200 francs a month (972 francs today, not quite $200), for it had been decided that all editorial staff members would receive the same low salary, while the printers would get 2,000 francs. Camus told Chouraqui that for the miserable salary being offered he preferred to stay in Algiers. Apparently at the same time he dropped in at the Cours Fenelon, with which he had been in correspondence about a teaching appointment, but decided that he did not like the high-society, royalist atmosphere he found there, even had he wanted to live in Oran.[13]

When a job came through at last, it was from a totally unexpected quarter, and yet it had a certain logic to it. He was hired by Radio Alger on a year's contract with that station's acting company, led by an old trouper. The job would require some local radio performances, but above all periodic travel through smaller towns and villages of Algeria's provinces—Orléansville, Mascara, Sétif. He was even given a stage name, or he took it: Albert Farnèse. (When Liliane Choucroun, his college friend, was working in Mascara, he told her that he had stayed three times in that town, where he had become friendly with the *patronne* of a local hotel, who knew him as Albert Farnèse.)[14] He was paid 80 francs (about 65 francs in the 1970s, under $14) for each performance. The repertory on the two-week tours included Molière and

Beaumarchais.[15] *L'Echo d'Alger* on February 25, 1937, reviewed a performance of *Gringoire* by the popular nineteenth-century romantic poet Théodore de Banville, in which Camus played the role of Olivier le Daim: He is mentioned here under his own name. Later he would tell funny stories about his train journeys in third class railway carriages in the company of Moslem agricultural workers. Once someone had entered a compartment and spread his suitcases over all the seats so that no Moslem could share the compartment with him. When the man left the compartment for a moment, Camus and another actor tossed the valises onto the station platform shouting to passers-by that they had been forgotten on the train.[16] A note made during one of these tours in his journal betrays another tone: "In the morning, tenderness and fragility of an Oranie better known for the harshness and violence of the midday sun . . ."

Meanwhile Christiane was working as a secretary at 700 francs a month, while Jeanne Sicard, for whom work was something new, proudly reported earnings of 180 francs.[14] She was giving lessons in French and mathematics to all comers, all levels. One day Camus brought her the nephew of his grade-school teacher Louis Germain; the child needed help in studying for the *baccalauréat* in geography, history, and French. When his nephew passed, Germain invited the lot of them for a party in his house in Belcourt.

Camus was also giving lessons when he could, mainly at the homes of his pupils. And he was sharing domestic chores at the Maison Fichu. Each of the cohabitants in turn was responsible for cooking meals for a week's time, taking the money out of the kitty. The food was simple enough—broiled meats, supplemented by the food parcels that Marguerite Dobrenn was receiving weekly from her parents back in Oran (the parcels included cooked meals).[3]

But all this was apparently too much for a young man in Camus' physical condition. "I'm furiously angry with Camus," Claude de Fréminville wrote to his comrade André Belamich back in Oran. "He is betraying me completely. He is too much in love with a false existence which leaves him no time, exhausts and isolates him." He was losing weight, coughing blood again.[17] Still, the relapse of his tuberculosis would not seem serious for another few months, and he would not stop until he had to.

In the idealism that was to characterize much of the activity of the Popular Front, but also in the strategy of Communist officials who had learned how to channel idealism toward goals consistent with their political line, one of the most efficient organs for propaganda among thinking persons was the House of Culture, Maison de la Culture, a multiart, multimedia approach which was designed to appeal to intelligent people of all professions, who could feel that they were contributing to the raising of cultural and political awareness in the larger society which surrounded them. A House of Culture could promote lecture tours on science as well as politics, on literature too, could offer film and even theater programs. There was no requirement that its activists be Communist Party members or totally committed to the Communist line; they were certain to be partisans of the Popular Front. Certainly the audiences did not consist solely of card-holding Communists or even Socialists, although they were supposed to come out of the lectures and the performances feeling better disposed to the slogans and the programs of the militant left. All existing cultural and political movements could join their talents in a House of Culture, and when such an institution was created in Algiers it could be presented as the emanation of thirteen such organizations.

Camus and his friends, bursting with projects, anxious to make them socially useful, were ripe for the House of Culture concept. No cumbersome, expensive infrastructure was necessary, not even a "House." Later, in the Gaullist 1960s, André Malraux would create a network of architecturally bold, costly Houses of Culture in the provinces of France, Houses which combined proper theaters, conference halls, art galleries, and libraries, which Malraux referred to as the cathedrals of the twentieth century. But that was when Malraux was Charles de Gaulle's Minister of Culture. Back in the 1930s the Houses of Culture were make-do affairs. The Algiers branch operated from a dingy room in an old building alongside other dingy offices serving as headquarters for left-wing causes, while its public activities would be put on in local halls such as the impressive Salle Pierre Bordes. Little more than that was needed, for the structure, the program, even many of the speakers were furnished by House of Culture headquarters in Paris; it was for the Algerian group to add their particular talents—amateur theater, for example, and a regional point of view—the unity of Mediterranean culture.

All of Camus' friends who were committed to the left joined him in this adventure. They selected a board of directors consisting of Camus as secretary-general, Jeanne Sicard, their Belcourt comrade Charles Poncet (who was in charge of the small office at 8 Rue Charras, practically next door to Charlot's bookshop). The speakers' bureau included an old lycée comrade who had gone to Paris for his higher education, Robert Jaussaud, whose friendship would become a lifelong attachment to Camus, during which he would share not only Camus' public life but his private one, and Camus' Maison Fichu comrade Marguerite Dobrenn. Emile Scotto-Lavina was in the press office, Jeanne Sicard on the theater committee; Camus, an art critic friend Marcelle Bonnet-Blanchet, and sculptor Louis Benisti were responsible for exhibitions, while Camus' doctor and friend Stacha Cviklinski was a member of the scientific committee.

Immediately a broad and ambitious program was agreed upon. The speakers' bureau would organize fortnightly talks on Mediterranean culture, on North African folkore, i.e., native Moslem art, literature, philosophy, music, architecture, theater, the minor arts. The press office, according to the organizational plan drawn up at the outset, was to perform normal publicity tasks and publish a bulletin, but it would also organize talks on Radio Alger. The performance committee would be concerned with theater and film programs, arrange entertainment at local festivals, set up concerts of indigenous music. The exhibition committee would also be concerned with indigenous art as well as "local" art (not the same thing—this last referring to the work of European Algerians), and shows of architecture and urbanism. The science committee was to raise funds for a research laboratory.

Not all of these things would come about, but more of them than might be imagined, considering that the young men and women involved were students or working for a living (or trying to) and that funds were always scarce. A printed Manifeste-Programme was nevertheless distributed, announcing the founding of Algiers' House of Culture, an affiliate of the Association des Maisons de la Culture in Paris. The Algiers section would be sponsored by Ciné-Travail, the Théâtre du Travail, Médecine et Travail, Amis de *Commune,* Les Amis de l'U.R.S.S. (Friends of the U.S.S.R.), and other organizations including the Le Corbusier-oriented Congrès Internationaux d'Architecture Moderne, and local associations of revolutionary painters, sculptors, writers, and architects. The purposes of the House of Culture, as set forth in the manifesto, were as follows:

1. To co-ordinate and unify cultural activities which would otherwise be spread out or conflicting;

2. To provide smaller groups with the support of a better equipped one;

3. To organize an intellectual and artistic campaign in which writers and artists would participate;

4. To serve Mediterranean and indigenous culture.

For 1937, the manifesto announced, the House of Culture would sponsor performances of the Théâtre du Travail and of Ciné-Travail, and would organize lectures on "Can we base the hope for a new culture on the working class?" It would attempt to bring Gide, Malraux, and Jean Giono to Algeria, to arrange concerts by Darius Milhaud and Arthur Honegger, art shows from Paris. Scientific talks would be given

on subjects such as "Biology and Marxism." Indigenous customs would
be studied, a Théâtre Populaire Arabe would be organized. Memberships were solicited from groups and individuals who would have the
right to reduced-price tickets to all events organized by the parent
House of Culture, "in France as well as in the colonies."

The conclusion, representing the profession of faith of the House
of Culture's young organizers, bore the stamp of Camus' preoccupations of that time:

> The House of Culture appeals urgently to all to understand and
> support its activity. The intellectuals of this country have a unique
> task to carry out on behalf of Mediterranean culture. Those who
> have come together in the House of Culture feel strongly about this
> and shall seek to make their contribution to Culture, threatened in
> our time by mediocrity and by violence. *To that end we must make
> Algiers the intellectual capital that it has the right and the duty to
> be in the Mediterranean world.*[18]

If the scope and the program of the Algiers House of Culture were
ambitious, the early achievements were no less so. The very first,
heralded by a story in the Communist *Lutte Sociale* on February 6,
1937, was a talk on the subject "Can a Mediterranean culture be
achieved?" to take place at the Salle de l'Entr'aide Féminine Laïque et
Sociale, on Monday, February 8. The name of the speaker was not
given, but the newspaper urged workers to attend and to join the House
of Culture. "For it is a matter of nothing less than to create a Cultural
Front, counterpart of the Popular Front."

Workers may not have furnished a sizable contingent to the audience at this first meeting, but attendance (by students and professors,
intellectuals in all fields) was heartening. "Rejuvenated and quite sympathetic atmosphere," reported conservative (but Radical Socialist)
*Echo d'Alger*. The audience faced a stage on which speaker Albert
Camus, "one of the most fervent and most remarkably talented organizers of the House of Culture," was flanked by fellow-officers. Two of
them were women, it was reported, indicative of "a new spirit" (the reporter who wrote the story was also a woman).[19]

Camus' talk, printed in essence in the bulletin of the House of Culture, *Jeune Méditerranée* (and collected with his *Essais*), probably reveals more about his own conceptions, and those of his intellectual
guides (notably Grenier), than it does about the Popular Front spirit in
Algiers. But he was careful to fit his Mediterranean ideology into the
general framework of House of Culture preoccupations. He acknowledged that regionalism was sometimes taken over by the extreme right
(e.g., Charles Maurras' "Latinity"), to be twisted into a kind of Fas-

cism. The error, he felt, was to confuse Mediterranean and Latin, Athens and Rome. It was not a matter of dead tradition, decadent nationalism, Mediterranean superiority. It was rather a matter of helping a nation to express itself. Camus' Mediterranean was a "certain taste for life" shared throughout the Mediterranean basin, so that one felt closer to an inhabitant of Majorca or of Genoa than to a Norman or an Alsatian. There is a shared history. There is a bridge between Occident and Orient. The speaker drew on his own travel experience: He had felt repelled by a Central Europe buttoned up to the neck. Even Italian Fascism was tempered by the affable and merry Italians. So that Mediterranean collectivism would necessarily be different from the Russian example. "Our task here is to rehabilitate the Mediterranean," he insisted, "to take it back from those who lay claim to it unjustly, and to prepare it to receive the economic order which is ready for it." Their work must support those aspects of Mediterranean culture which would favor man rather than crush him. Camus did not think that there was room for hope in the present world of violence and death, but there was probably a place for civilization.

Flushed with the success of this first public event, Camus and his friends threw themselves into other new activities. He himself remained on call for Radio Alger road company tours. Meanwhile he continued to supervise rehearsals of the next Théâtre du Travail program, which would be a double bill, *Prometheus Bound* (Prométhée enchaîné) and Ben Jonson's *Epicene, or the Silent Woman* (La Femme silencieuse).

He made preparations for the reception of the House of Culture's first invited speaker from mainland France, Claude Aveline, a popular leftist novelist and contributor both to *Commune* and to *L'Humanité,* who was to talk about "Anatole France révolutionnaire." Aveline had been touring the French provinces with the same lecture, under the sponsorship of the Paris headquarters of the House of Culture, his stops including Lyons, Saint-Etienne, Nice, and other mainland cities, and in North Africa, Sousse, Sfax, and Tunis. On February 19 Camus was able to make a brief presentation of his guest speaker on Radio Alger. Noting that Aveline's work was directed "toward the world's misery," he borrowed a description of the guest from *Vendredi,* a Popular Front-inspired weekly: "a tall and slender young man, slightly bent, of a mild and somewhat shy disposition, speaking without violence . . . but persuasive and charming." Aveline's lecture at the Salle Bordes would focus on the political side of Anatole France, citing that author's tribute to the Soviet Union published in *L'Humanité* on the fifth anniversary of the October Revolution: "They scattered the seeds which, if destiny favors them, will spread over Russia and perhaps one day will fertilize Europe."[20]

Possibly it was during this visit by Aveline that he spoke to a group of pacifist students on a Sunday morning in the basement of a café called Le Quartier Latin. Camus, who was already something of a celebrity to these younger people, had been invited to attend the meeting (which did not draw a crowd on that sunny day). Camus was pointed out to one of the organizers, who detected a slight smile on his face, and felt embarrassed that Camus was present during a particularly naïve diatribe against military service delivered by the chairman of the meeting. Camus stopped smiling when Aveline spoke. Then at the end of the meeting he joined Aveline at the speakers' table. Addressing the young man who had spoken so vividly about the horrors of military service, Camus asked him his age; the young man said he was seventeen. "Good," said Camus. "If I understand correctly, you haven't done your military duty. Then I admire even more your vehemence and your talent in describing barracks life. But I think that it's still better to speak of what one has experienced, don't you agree? That being said, I find you likeable and I'm with you." And with that they went in a group to the Brasserie des Facultés, where Camus was again seen to be a local celebrity, greeted by all.[21]

From then on activities exploded in all directions. On March 10 the House of Culture inaugurated its Cercle Culturel du Plateau, in the neighborhood in which Camus had his Communist Party cell, with a debate on "People and Culture," perhaps conducted by Camus. On April 26 the Cercle du Plateau held a meeting on the Blum-Viollette bill, then before the French Parliament in Paris, which would provide for the enfranchisement of a certain number of Algerian Moslems; Camus' talk was entitled "Intellectuals and the Viollette Bill." A cospeaker was the secretary of the Union Franco-Musulmane, possibly Claude de Fréminville. Camus again represented his House of Culture at a rally organized by the Ligue Internationale contre l'Antisémitisme (LICA), together with the Moslem religious leader, Sheikh El Okbi, and in the presence of LICA's founder, Bernard Lecache. Soon the activities of Algiers' House of Culture were being reported back in Paris by *Commune,* which in its May issue said: "The prestige of Algiers is growing. The House of Culture sponsored a talk by scientist [Irène] Joliot-Curie . . . and held . . . a remarkable Pushkin gala. . . . Algiers has an excellent theatrical company, the Théâtre du Travail. . . ."[22] (Frédéric Joliot-Curie was on the stage alongside his wife as she spoke.)[23] In July *Commune* would again praise the Algerians: "Algiers has quite understood the necessity of setting up cultural circles on a regional basis and in a form peculiar to the region."[22] The House of

Culture used a specially printed letterhead for its department called Bureau des Etudes Scientifiques; on this letterhead Camus invited a cousin of his friend Liliane Choucroun to speak to a meeting on the present state of atomic theory.[24]

The May 1937 issue of the House of Culture organ, *Jeune Méditerranée*, leads off with a lecture by Professor Jacques Heurgon on Pushkin, delivered at the special Pushkin evening on March 24. The same issue indicates the broad scope of the House of Culture's uplifting mission. Under the heading "La Culture indigène" there is a poem translated from Arabic. An article signed by Frédéric Joliot-Curie deals with "Transmutation de la matière et radioactivité artificielle." A manifesto of the Painters and Sculptors Section of the House of Culture is signed by Camus' friend Marie Viton, aristocrat, painter, amateur pilot. After a report on the evolution of Soviet cinema contributed by Ciné-Travail (which defended current Soviet films against the charge of conformity), there is a listing of House of Culture activities. On April 4 the House had been responsible for the musical and theatrical program at a Socialist Party local festival; there the Théâtre du Travail had staged Georges Courteline's *L'Article 330*. An April 10, during a Ciné-Travail film showing, the Théâtre du Travail had performed *Espagne 34*, an abbreviated version of the previously banned *Révolte dans les Asturies*. On April 9 during a Popular Front film program including *The Lower Depths*, the House had furnished a speaker on Gorky and his play of that title. On April 18 the Théâtre du Travail had again performed *L'Article 330*, *Espagne 34*, and *Le Temps du mépris* at a Popular Front festival in Blida, and the same day gave a repeat performance of *L'Article 330* at the inauguration of the Belcourt section of Fréminville's Union Franco-Musulmane. It was decided that a co-ordinating committee would be responsible for joint activities of the House of Culture and the Union. Finally, *Jeune Méditerranée* finished off with a manifesto of Algeria's intellectuals in favor of the Blum-Viollette electoral reform:

> One can't . . . speak of culture in a country where 900,000 inhabitants are deprived of schools and civilization, handicapped by poverty without precedent, and repressed by special laws and inhuman regulations . . .

Providing as it did for expanded Moslem suffrage, the Viollette bill was considered by the fifty petitioners (whose names are not given) as a "step in the total parliamentary emancipation of the Moslems. . . ."

In all of the foregoing it can be imagined that Camus was never far from the center of things, director of the theater programs, an actor in the plays, lecturer, co-ordinator, petitioner. And that was not all. The season was to conclude with a talk by Communist intellectual André Wurmser (June 6), an art show by young Algerian painters and sculptors (June 12–13), an exhibition of young Moslem illuminators at Les Vraies Richesses (June 24–July 12), and an end-of-season festival (July 31).[22] By this time, as Charles Poncet was able to report to René Blech, secretary-general of the parent House of Culture in Paris, responsible for the nationwide program, the Algerian branch had a couple of hundred dues-paying members. But by this time, too, the atmosphere had changed, partly due to André Gide's pessimistic report on the Soviet Union in his *Retour de l'U.R.S.S.;* Poncet for his part was shocked by the sophisticated atmosphere which he discovered at the top echelons at Paris headquarters. Algiers' House of Culture decided to sponsor a public discussion of Gide's book (which was under attack in *Commune* by André Wurmser and by Communists in every other possible medium). Blech asked Algiers to give up the idea of talking about Gide and his criticism of Moscow, but by joint decision the young men and women who ran the Algiers' branch went ahead anyway.[23]

And Albert Camus, although he didn't say a thing about it to his friends, was now fighting a personal battle within his Communist Party cell which would lead to his expulsion from the Party. His indictment, trial, and sentence (for the procedure amounted to that) would be the dramatic dénouement to his frenetic activity in the House of Culture and its many chambers.

The Théâtre du Travail had achieved a certain organizational regularity of its own. Each new production would be performed at least twice, on a Saturday evening at 9 P.M., and the next afternoon at 1, with further performances depending on demand. Aeschylus' *Prometheus Bound* and Jonson's *Epicene* were first given as a double bill on March 6 and 7, 1937, at the Salle Pierre Bordes, for the benefit of Soutien de l'Enfance Malheureuse and Secours Populaire, the latter a kind of Communist Red Cross. Camus directed the plays, Louis Miquel designed the scenery and Marie Viton the costumes. Louis Benisti designed masks for all the actors except Prometheus, an idea of Camus'.[3] (Camus had first asked Benisti to do the costumes too, which for the Greek play he hoped would be "Algerian" in inspiration, emphasizing vineyard activities. But with the appearance in his life of Marie Viton the costumes were assigned to her, and executed in quite another spirit.)[25] An English friend of Viton, Frank Turner, wrote special music based on Bach for the Aeschylus play. Camus played the lead in *Epicene,* where the prologue was to be recited in front of the stage by André Thomas-Rouault, nephew of the painter. Suddenly, the story goes, Thomas-

Rouault fell silent, for he had forgotten his lines. The audience applauded, thinking that the gag was part of the play.[26]

These were efforts which were to be remembered all their lives long by the participants, but which apparently did not reach the audience hoped for by the young idealists who mounted these plays. *L'Algérie Ouvrière* remarked that while the plays were produced for workers few of them attended, seemingly because they preferred uncomfortable seats at the municipal opera theater to the comfort and low prices (free for the unemployed) at the Bordes auditorium. Another performance was scheduled for the following Sunday.

The Pushkin evening on March 24, on the centennial of the poet's death (actually on February 19, 1837), featured the talk by Professor Heurgon reprinted in *Jeune Méditerranée,* a piano recital by Frank Turner, and then Pushkin's *Don Juan.* Camus played Don Juan, of course, a character who would forever fascinate him, one of the models of human behavior described later in *Le Mythe de Sisyphe.* He would conceive projects for further stagings of Don Juan by other authors several times in the course of his life, even if circumstances did not allow him to carry them out. Pushkin's play was given again for Les Amis de l'U.R.S.S. on May Day, then again under joint sponsorship of the House of Culture and the Union Franco-Musulmane on May 5. At the end of the performance a huge portrait of Pushkin painted by Maurice Girard was carried onto the stage.[27]

As for Georges Courteline's *L'Article 330,* first produced in Paris in 1900, this perfect little satire of official pomposity was an easy favorite of local left-wing festivals, with Camus in the lead as La Brige, the harassed defendant whose response to bureaucratic procrastination during the play's single courtroom scene is to drop his pants.

But *Espagne 34* was theater of a different sort. As has been noted, it was a short version of the play banned by the city of Algiers, *Révolte dans les Asturies.* In fact it consisted of the final chorus of that play, beginning *"Moi, je suis le vieux Santiago,"* performed against a background of a Bach chorale (which Louis Miquel remembered because at one point Camus directed all the others to stop singing and he was left alone with his voice). Robert and Madeleine Jaussaud also played parts, reciting:

> "Soon the snow will come,"
> "And who will remember?"[28]

Camus may have had a private reason for presenting this particular extract from *Révolte dans les Asturies.* For he was now no longer on speaking terms with Yves Bourgeois, and this section of the play was indisputably his own work.

Whatever the effect of Fréminville's remonstrances, his comrade continued to live his exhausting life. He found the time to pursue his writing, making notes for future work. Perhaps the notation on the theme of *L'Etranger* published in his journal under April 1937 is correctly dated:

> Narrative—the man who does not want to explain himself. He dies, alone in being conscious of his truth—Vanity of this consolation.

Another note, dated June, is a first sketch of the dialogue with the priest at the climax of that novel.

It is preceded by notes for the essay on Djémila, which will be published in *Noces,* a note on "La Mort dans l'âme," soon to be published in *L'Envers et l'Endroit,* a note on his favorite House Above the World theme, and a reminder to work on his novel, an essay on Malraux (never written), his thesis. (If this last is a reference to his dissertation, the note should be dated April 1936 and not April 1937, but possibly it refers to a plan to revise his paper for publication.) Then a note dated May is a draft preface for *L'Envers et l'Endroit* in which the writer confesses to an "insufficient maturity" to explain the lack of form of these essays. But justification seemed vain; he knew that one always preferred to a man the idea that one has of him.

Bitterness aside, *L'Envers et l'Endroit* would be published now.

# 11

---

## HINGE

> I hold on to the world by all my acts, to men by all my gratitude. Between this right side and this wrong side of the world, I refuse to choose. . . .
>
> *L'Envers et l'Endroit*

On May 10, 1937—the date can be found at the back of that slender volume—Camus' first book, *L'Envers et l'Endroit,* was published by Edmond Charlot as the second title in a series called "Mediterranéennes." The edition of 350 copies, in a format roughly 6½" by 8", was printed on the presses of Emmanuel Andréo's Imprimerie Victor Heintz. It was dedicated to Jean Grenier, and represented the first public recognition of the teacher's influence on the young writer. Despite the many copies given to the author's friends, and the copies purchased by less intimate friends, it took two years to sell out the edition (all of it in Algeria, for Charlot did not then possess distribution facilities in mainland France).

Charlot was now publishing a book every two months. He calculated that a book cost 750 francs to print (less than 610 francs in the mid-1970s, the equivalent of some $125). That was just about a month's decent salary. And so he decided to live for two months on a single month's salary drawn from his bookshop, and to spend the second month's 750 francs to publish a new book. During the first year and a half of his business career he published at this pace and never reprinted. Indeed, until *Noces* appeared in 1939 Charlot never ordered more than 500 copies of any book he published. *L'Envers et l'Endroit* was placed on sale at 20 francs a copy (about 16 present-day francs, some $3.30).[1]

So that this highly personal book of essays would exist in the body of Camus' work without existing, and its republication in a form, a time, and a place for a wider readership would not come until the last years of his life, after he had received the Nobel Prize, and only because "this book already exists, but in a small number of copies, sold dearly by the booksellers. Why should only wealthy readers have the right to it?" (Preface to 1958 reprinting.) It is difficult at this remove, and in the absence of the critical response such a work might have commanded in Paris, to imagine what the contemporary reader would have found in these evocations of a Belcourt childhood, of a very lonely trip to Central Europe and Italy, to the Balearics. In the title essay the young man tells the story of an old woman who invests her money in the purchase and decoration of her tomb, while he has turned *his* face toward life.

He was disappointed to learn that the local press had nevertheless found his book bitter and pessimistic. Yet if he had not affirmed his taste for life, for biting it whole, then he had said nothing. In a letter to his friend Jean de Maisonseul, the only person to whom he would speak of the book, he wrote that he agreed with the criticism that he might have been less personal. Later, he promised, he would write a book which would be a work of art, although the only progress would be in the form, which would be more objective even if it said the same things.

He reminded Maisonseul that he had often said to Camus that he feared sudden death, say a street accident, which would not allow him the time to say what he wanted to say. Camus himself had always been indifferent to the state of his own health. But now he did have something to say, and he wanted to live for that. "Isn't it marvelous, Jean, that life can be such a passionate and a painful thing?"[2]

Health was indeed a problem he had to face now. Too much had been too much. The combination of public activity and, perhaps, the strain of his private battle with the Communist Party apparatus had worn him down. His friends worried about what effect this activity and these occult events would have on him. Sometime after the performances of *Prometheus* and *Epicene,* Charles Poncet discussed Camus with a doctor friend, Paul Legendre, who had treated Camus at the onset of his tuberculosis. Dr. Legendre now expressed concern for his former patient. "He's burning the candle at both ends, and that is likely to end badly."

Poncet waited for the right moment to talk to Camus.

It was summer now, and they were going swimming on the north jetty. The little boat they had boarded to cross the harbor was sailing past the old town, where the Kasbah was visible just behind office buildings on the seafront boulevard. Poncet knew that it was difficult to talk to his friend about his health, but he also felt that Camus might be ready to listen to advice that day. "Be reasonable, a stay in a sanitarium will help you; we'll make an arrangement, probably get you free treatment."

Camus thanked him, seemingly moved by his comrade's words. He replied that Poncet was probably right, but that he could not live in an atmosphere of the sick, among strangers. "I need the warmth of the friendship that I find among you," he added with a slight smile, as if to mock himself.[3]

For the time being he was scaling down his activities, concentrating on his own writing to the exclusion of everything else. Exhaustion? Doctor's advice? Political disappointments? It was also Algerian summer, when all public activity was put on a side burner. He assured another friend that he was no longer involved in useless activity, which allowed him to do his own work for a change.[4]

He did leave the hot city occasionally. His July letter to Maisonseul speaks of a planned camping trip to Kabylie in the middle of the month. He was visiting Tipasa when he could, that favorite site of his some forty miles west of Algiers, beyond the Sahel and at the foot of imposing Chenoua Mountain, with its excavated Roman ruins, including an ancient theater in a good state of preservation, an amphitheater, a forum, all in a naturally wild setting whose description is best left to Camus himself (in "Noces à Tipasa," much later in "Retour à Tipasa"). In the first essay he explains that he never spent more than a full day at a time in Tipasa; there comes a moment when one has seen too much of a landscape. On one exalting day Camus visited Tipasa with Christiane Galindo (whom he called La Terre, The Earth, for the sensuous, palpable qualities he discovered in her), and in the company of their sculptor friend Benisti. During all that day Camus declaimed his feelings in phrases Benisti later found in "Noces à Tipasa," which led Benisti to conclude that Christiane had inspired it.[5] And after reciting this paean to his earth goddess he began to write it; in July he sent the manuscript to his professor and friend Jacques Heurgon, to Marguerite Dobrenn,[6] quite likely to Jean Grenier, too.

He allowed himself to be convinced to take a real rest now, together with Claude de Fréminville, who was in the process of divorcing. The Degueurces, personal and Popular Front friends, had lent the young men an empty chalet at Lucinges in the French Savoy mountains, near Mont Blanc and Geneva, where they were assured that they could even do their own cooking. Camus calculated that he could live there for 7 francs a day (less than 6 of 1970s francs, or about $1.25). He also hoped to make a first trip to Paris, see a bit of Provence, and then (as the real treat) to journey through Italy to Florence, Siena, Rome, Naples, and from Palermo in Sicily to sail to Tunisia. He urged his friends Jeanne Sicard and Marguerite Dobrenn, who were in Paris to visit the 1937 World's Fair (Exposition Universelle), to join him for the Italian portion of the trip.

He sailed with Fréminville on July 29 for Marseilles, from there stopping off at Arles, site of a famous Roman arena and theater; Avignon, with its ramparts and massive papal palace; and Orange, with one of the most striking and well-preserved theaters remaining from Roman times. From there they were to go to Paris. On the way Camus took up his journal to record his anguish: "This fever which strikes my temples, the singular and sudden abandonment of the world and of men." He admonished himself: "Struggle against my body."

For by the time they reached Lyons he was feeling ill. And all the anxieties he experienced whenever he traveled flared up again. The friends gave up the idea of going north to Paris; it seemed wiser to flee to the chalet in Haute Savoie. "What is waiting for me in the Alps," he added in his journal, "is, with solitude and the idea that I shall be there to cure myself, the *consciousness* of my disease."

They arrived to find the Degueurce property a ruin—absolutely uninhabitable. In addition to that it lacked even basic necessities, which had to be hauled up from the village by Fréminville on a steep path. (The name of the chalet, Château des Affamés (Castle of the Starved), had been well deserved.) On the first evening Camus had a coughing fit, spat blood, and his companion sat up all night with him, terrified. Next morning one was as pale as the other. Fréminville kept careful watch over his friend and patient in the days that followed.

Fortunately there were other friends in the village. The Cviklinskis (he was Camus' philosopher-doctor and friend) also had a chalet at Lucinges. Morella Cviklinski, the doctor's wife (who had played Kassner's wife in *Le Temps du mépris*) took them in. It was a tight squeeze, and they began to look for another chalet they could rent. But there seemed to be nothing available in midsummer, at least nothing they could afford. And Camus wasn't doing any work. He began to wish that he could return to Algiers, which he would have done if he hadn't so looked forward to Florence.

They walked in the mountains, Camus in the hope of taming this hostile landscape, but there was nothing to do: All his life he would detest the anti-Mediterranean prospect of forbidding peaks. At best he could conclude a truce with them, the truce of hard and savage enemies. They crossed the frontier to visit Geneva, toured Lake Leman in a boat. While walking Camus would suddenly have to stop to rest on a bench. "It's nothing. It will pass. Excuse me."

Finding nothing to rent in Lucinges, he decided to visit Paris after all.[7]

Camus had often thought that he would move to Paris to find or take a job, to make a career. For a writer, for a teacher-to-be, it was the *only* city in France. He had considered it, and then he had realized that for a penniless young man Paris could only be an inferno. Now, in early August, he was on a train bound for his nation's capital, all his forebodings for baggage. And then, in Paris, he discovered a city quite different from the hell he had imagined. His journal notices "Tenderness and emotion . . . Gray colors, the sky, a great show of stone and of waters." For a young Algerian who lived in the booming, building Algiers of the 1930s, Paris (which had not yet caught its speculation fever) could actually seem tender.

He walked the city up and down, began to feel after a few days that he knew it as well as if he had been born there. Probably, he thought, his old childhood experience helped him, for in Paris he found many Belcourts: on lively, vulgar Rue Mouffetard, in the old neighborhood behind Notre Dame cathedral on the Ile de la Cité. He fell in love with Paris, but he knew that he had fallen in love with a woman who could cheat. He could not be happy with her, but he did think that he could write in this city.

Before leaving, did he pay his respects to the national seat of the House of Culture, and to its Communist director René Blech? Apparently he so confided to fellow-Communist cellmate Maurice Girard. He added that while in the House of Culture he ran into Louis Aragon, then and later the Party's number one recruit among French men of letters. They had an altercation, the young man from the Algiers Maison de la Culture and the already famous Aragon. About Gide's *Retour de l'U.R.S.S.* perhaps? We cannot know.

From Paris, Camus returned to the mountains, this time to Embrun, a picture postcard site, a medieval village built on a terrace 2,800 feet high over a river valley, the village itself dominated by a mountain peak. Here he would stay from the middle of August until the second week of September, when Jeanne and Marguerite—for his pleas had won them over—would join him for the journey to Italy. At Embrun he took a room with full board at 33 francs a day (27 francs in the mid-1970s, or some $5.50), far from the 7-francs-a-day budget he had started out with. Worse, he found the furnishings depressing and the people around him stupid. But he was conscious of the fact that he was in these mountains for his health, and he promised himself that he would stick it out.

Enforced idleness—for now there was really nothing to do—did not make him particularly happy, but it gave him more time for reflection. Walking in Embrun one evening—it was the evening, the night, of August 20—he realized that his retreat in Embrun was precisely what he had desired all that year: an opportunity to be alone to think about a certain number of things he had to work out for himself. He was quite aware of the fact that in Algiers, with the feverish political and cultural environment in which he lived now, he would never have the time or even the desire to make plans; it was all he could do to keep up with the daily round of activities imposed on him or which he imposed on himself.

He also began to think about his writing. Not as an occasional activity, not in terms of short essays expressing a mood, reporting an experience; this time it would be a longer work. He began to outline what would become his first novel, *La Mort heureuse,* and to invent his characters. He had already begun to discuss his hero, Patrice Mersault, with Fréminville in their walks around Lucinges. He was tentatively calling the book *Le Joueur* (The Player), a title he would also consider for the play which became *Caligula.* He recorded scraps of dialogue in his journal.[8]

His intentions are clear enough from these outlines: He would attempt to assemble materials from his various lives, the Belcourt childhood, the absurdity of his first marriage (particularly in its disastrous dénouement), the idealism of the Maison Fichu. He would have a place in the planned novel for every significant activity, every trade, every important encounter: The outline mentions "The mute," "The grandmother," "Illness. . . ." his theatrical road company job, the prefecture, even conversations with Grenier and his recent walks around Paris. One of his notes would be the theme not so much of the aborted *La Mort heureuse* as of the genuine novel to follow almost immediately, *L'Etranger:* "A man who sought life where it is usually found (marriage, job, etc.) and who discovers all at once . . . how much he had been a stranger to his life. . . ."

A revelatory journal entry at this time indicates his discouragement with politics, with the statements of France's political leaders, in which he found no "human sound."

He also reveals, in these journal entries, the importance he wished to give to the theme of sexual jealousy, associated with the voyage to Salzburg and Prague; the notes suggest that the young husband was genuinely surprised at his wife's betrayal (despite the assumption of the couple's friends that they had decided to live a modern marriage, unconcerned by the other's adventures). The notes include this outline:

1. Liaison with Marthe . . .
2. Marthe tells of her infidelities.
3. Innsbruck and Salzburg   the comic opera
                           the letter and the room
                           departure in a fever

But the theme of "sexual jealousy" will not be significant in the text of *La Mort heureuse,* as we know it, nor will Simone (if it was she who was troubling him still) remain as a notable character. If she is the inspiration for Marthe or one or more of the other women who wander through these pages, she is hardly the unforgettable character we already know better as Nadja.

At the conclusion of his long retreat—long for this particularly active young man—he took up his schoolboy's notebook again to write:

> This month of August has been something of a hinge, a deep breath before spreading out everything in a delirious effort . . .
> I must live and create. Live to the verge of tears—as before this house with round tiles and blue shutters on a slope covered with cypress trees.

He will write this in Provence, on the way to Marseilles to catch the train for Italy. It is not clear from the recollections of his friends, from his own notes and correspondence, precisely what part of Provence he was visiting now. His only traveling companion, Claude de Fréminville, is dead. It is conceivable that on the way from Embrun to Marseilles Camus took the trouble—it would have been trouble then, it isn't so easy even now without a private automobile—to seek out Jean Grenier's favorite village of Lourmarin, where Grenier had spent a season as fellow in residence at the Château de Lourmarin just prior to teaching his first class in Algiers to lycée student Albert Camus. Grenier had published an essay on Lourmarin, perhaps the first writing of Grenier's that Camus had read, and Grenier had certainly talked about Lourmarin; perhaps he had also made his student promise to visit the village as soon as he could. Jean Grenier is no longer alive to confirm this. Years later, when Camus visited Lourmarin with a group of writers, ostensibly for the first time, he would mention the trip in his journal as a return visit "after so many years . . ." And at least one witness recalls having met Camus in Lourmarin in this summer of 1937.[9]

Lourmarin or no, this summer was indeed a "hinge." Henceforth Camus' inner life would take precedence over his public one. He would not abandon public life; he was only now beginning to participate in it seriously. But henceforth he knew that his real work was to create books out of the life he was living. He had to save his time, above all he had to save his strength, for that. In this sense the summer of 1937 was a watershed (which may in fact be the best way to translate the word he used, *charnière*).

In Algiers his teacher and friend Jacques Heurgon had urged him, while he was in France, to attend the annual seminar in the ancient Cistercian monastery at Pontigny, where Heurgon's father-in-law, the philosopher Paul Desjardins, regularly brought together the cream of France's intellectual life, notably the *Nouvelle Revue Française* group with Heurgon's friend André Gide, Roger Martin du Gard, Jacques Rivière. Camus would have liked to experience Pontigny, to meet its participants in the company of Heurgon. But the Pontigny seminar took place each year at the end of September, and he knew that he couldn't hang on in France that long.

Now it was the girls from Oran, Jeanne and Marguerite, who were strapped for funds. They didn't see how they could join him in Italy. They needed 1,000 francs (810 francs of the mid-1970s, some $165), but he of course had none to give them; already he'd had to borrow hundreds of francs from Fréminville. Finally he borrowed some more from Fréminville, who was himself quite broke by now. Fréminville parted company with him when the girls joined Camus for the trip to Italy.

They stayed overnight in Marseilles (on September 8), dining in a restaurant at the old port, which still looked then as it did in the Marcel Pagnol movies, before the heavy destruction of World War II. Next morning they were up at five for breakfast in a bistrot, where Camus admired the workers drinking coffee and rum in equal doses. And then the train to Italy.

But even in that brief moment in Marseilles—which he seemed to be enjoying—he had time to experience "this bitter taste of solitude," a sentiment he confided to his journal.

The train trip was another delight, through the glorious landscapes of the French and Italian Rivieras, past the oleanders of Monaco and the flower gardens of Genoa. But again he was writing in his journal: "My exhaustion and this desire to weep. This solitude and this thirst for love." Was it a soulmate he needed, one to make love to as well as to walk with, to talk to? It would be a while before he would find her.

But he had found himself, at least, by the time they got off the train at Pisa. Leaving his friends to go off by himself through the deserted streets of the town, he gave in to the urge to cry. Now the wound could begin to heal, he decided.

When you want desperately to fall in love you do. He fell in love with the Italy he discovered in Pisa and in Florence. Here was another facet of his Mediterranean: Mediterranean civilization. He was ready to forget his private unhappiness. "Things, beings are waiting for me and without doubt I'm waiting for them too and desire them with all my strength and my sadness," he confessed to his journal. "But here I am earning my living through silence and secrets."

Certainly there is more in this journal about his week's stay here (from September 9 to 15) than about any other single place he visited. He will repeat this confession of happiness in "Le Désert," published in *L'Eté*. Nowhere else in Camus' work is the interaction of landscape, of man-made things, and of individual needs explored so deeply, so ardently, as in this essay. Even if he had not confessed later to his Maison Fichu friends that in Florence he had found himself, the reader would know it. What Camus had discovered in Grenier's *Les Iles:* the ephemerality of beautiful things under the sun, or of man contemplating beauty—he found for himself in Florence.

On September 16 it was all over. Although they had been living in a pensione at thirty lire a day, none of them had any money left, and even with Italy's reduced railway fare for tourists there was no question of proceeding as originally planned to Rome, Naples, and Sicily, but would he have wished to now? They stopped in Arles on the way back to Marseilles, where he discovered that he had just enough money for a third class ticket entitling him to deck space across the Mediterranean to Algiers.[6]

Back in Algiers he was soon deep into the writing of *La Mort heureuse,* long passages of which he tried out first in his journal, admonishing himself (on September 30) that he must not hesitate to rewrite. But he also knew that in the autumn of 1937 he was going on to his twenty-fifth birthday. It was time to do what everybody else did: to take a job, make a career. Perhaps the right place for him was in teaching. An appointment came through as an instructor of grammar at Sidi-bel-Abbès, once a frontier town with walls and gates, the first outpost of the French Foreign Legion, where new recruits were trained. Named for a descendant of the Prophet who was born there, Sidi-bel-Abbès was now a medium-sized agricultural center with rigorously rectangular streets. Far from Algiers, the town was fifty miles due south of Oran.

The teacher-appointee arrived in Sidi-bel-Abbès on a Saturday evening, and immediately called on the school's principal. He checked into a hotel. Then all at once he realized that he would be *stuck* in this place, and in a way of life he detested, for the next nine months. On one hand he would have the security he needed, time to write. And he did not mind the job he would have to do here; he had always worked harder than others around him. Surely it was a good thing for his writing, to take a quiet job as this one was certain to be. He remembered that when he had that full-time job at the prefecture he had not been able to do his own work at all; he had been too exhausted mentally for that.

Next morning he continued to contemplate, from his hotel room, nine months in this city. And realized that he couldn't live them through. Ten minutes before the departure of the train for Algiers he tossed his things together in his valise, checked out of the hotel, and ran for the station. He needed a job and in a place which would leave him . . . intact.

He couldn't explain it easily to friends, this fear of being muzzled in a provincial teaching post; he was afraid that they would think him lazy. On the contrary, he was prepared to work longer hours than would have been demanded of him in Sidi-bel-Abbès.[10] "I refused that," he explains in his journal (in an entry dated October 4, 1937), in what seems like a draft for the letters of explanation he would be writing to his friends and former professors in the coming days, "certainly dismissing concern for security in favor of my chances for a real life. I retreated before the dullness and the numbness of such an existence." Soon he would be accepting a job involving still more drudgery than teaching a class; it wasn't that. It was "fear of solitude and of the definitive." Of settling into "something ugly."[11] He didn't know whether it was strength or weakness to have refused a future, to return to the uncertainties of his present situation. He couldn't decide, but indecision was a form of deciding.

> October 10.
> To have or not to have value. To create or not to create. In the first case, all is justified. Everything, without exception. In the second case, it is total Absurdity. It remains to choose the most esthetic suicide: marriage+the forty-hour week or a revolver.

But there was to be a last escape before he settled down to life in Algiers. His journal reports his hiking expedition in the Atlas Mountains above Blida, Algeria's garden city, famous for citrus fruits, olives, mimosa, yet only thirty miles from Algiers by train. This time he was testing his body. "The body, culture's true road, shows us its limits." His philosophical doctor Stacha Cviklinski told him not to force things, to take life as it comes. That might sound cynical, he added, but it also happened to be the point of view of the prettiest girl in the world. (*Carnets,* November 13.)

He wasn't sure about that. Despite the violence of his reaction to Sidi-bel-Abbès, he did believe that it was normal to sacrifice a bit of one's life so as not to lose all of it. Six or eight hours a day so as not to die of starvation. "And then all is profit to one who wishes to profit from it." (*Carnets,* November 22.)

# 12

## THE PARTY

Politics and the fate of men are shaped by men without ideals or nobility. Those who possess nobility are not in politics.

*Carnets* (December 1937)

The paradox is that Albert Camus, who never attained any prominence or rank within the Communist Party, was perhaps the most active, the best-known Communist (although a secret member) in the political and cultural life of Algeria. But Camus' party work, strictly speaking, which means the meetings of his cell, the tasks he would carry out at the behest of his immediate superiors, was never as significant as his public life. The Théâtre du Travail could reach all social and cultural milieus, could even command favorable notices in the conservative press. The House of Culture in its brief life performed myriad political as well as cultural functions. Camus as public speaker, as itinerant actor, now as aspiring writer, played roles more visible, perhaps more rewarding, than any the Party could demand of him. And it is not to be forgotten that the Théâtre du Travail was a Popular Front creation fully acceptable to the Party hierarchy; the House of Culture was a scarcely disguised Communist front.

There is every reason to believe that Camus was a lucid Communist, aware of all the good reasons to be cautious of the apparatus. If only because his former teacher, present friend, and spiritual adviser Jean Grenier was so openly skeptical of Communist Party orthodoxy, he owed it to himself (and to Grenier) to take constant measure of his own position vis-à-vis the Communists. He told Grenier that he had been obliged to become a Communist in order to remain close to the people with whom he identified, the working class of Algiers, whose cause the Communists had annexed. But if he had thrown himself into the movement, applying all his energies in behalf of Communist goals, he remained wary of the ultimate aims and practices of the Communists. One could "accept activity in favor of Communism while remaining pessimistic with respect to it."[1]

Perhaps at the beginning a very young Camus seemed to some of his friends to be aping Communist terminology, swallowing Communist dogma whole. Max-Pol Fouchet remembers being reproached by Camus as a social traitor, a derogatory term Communists applied to Socialists. "In any case," he quotes Camus, "you belong to a reformist party, and reformism makes the bed of Fascism."[2] But Camus was never a Marxist and had doubts about the Marxist analysis of history;[3] before joining the Party he had not read Marx, Engels, or any other Communist philosopher.[4] This might explain his flexibility in discussions (with others besides Max-Pol Fouchet, at any rate). At least one friend was struck by the softness of his answers turning away wrath: When he disapproved an outrageous remark he would say simply: "That wasn't necessary." Shocked by someone's behavior, he would observe: "They don't know how to live."[5] Not the language of a dogmatist. Even his surface irony, well known to his adversaries, hid a "shy and tender" comrade.[6]

Now for the first time Camus would have genuine contacts with Moslems of a social and intellectual level corresponding to his own. For if he had always possessed the faculty of communicating with what he and his friends called "Arabs," in truth Moslems, whether Berber or Arab, shared no significant division of the universe of Camus and his friends, who met Moslems neither in school nor at play, nor later at work (not as equals). The wide gap in living standards created a de facto social segregation. Religion, ethnic mores were contributing factors. There could hardly be any intimacy between Europeans and Moslems, for even if a French Algerian became friendly with a Moslem, he would never meet him with his wife.[7] Interest in "Arabs" was, even on the part of French Algerian liberals, interest in The Other; it was hard not to be paternalistic.[8] To have the good rapport he had with Moslems despite his poor-white upbringing, Camus and his comrades in the theater group, House of Culture, the Union Franco-Musulmane were taking giant steps into the future (and incidentally increasing their distance from the majority of French Algerian settlers).

No one will now claim that there was significant Moslem participation in the Popular Front. It wasn't their Front; they didn't even have the right to vote. Yet the Communist Party focused its attention on the Moslems, who made up the vast majority of the population of Algeria.

They were the real proletariat. This explains why even a Camus would be given the task of "Recruitment in Arab circles," which he later said represented half of his Party activity.[4]

Secret Communist Amar Ouzegane would one day be arrested as a secret leader of the Algerian Moslem insurrection against France, would be kept in prison until a grateful independent Algeria made him a cabinet minister. Then he would travel to the United States of America to request aid to restore Algeria's abandoned vineyards, and he would return to the United States as a member of Algeria's official delegation to the funeral of President John F. Kennedy. An admiring French friend once called Ouzegane "the 1,001 nights of Algerian politics."

When Albert Camus met him, Ouzegane had just returned from Moscow, where he had been the leader of the Algerian delegation to the seventh congress of the Communist International, known as the Comintern. He spoke at the congress under the name "Arthur Doden," an indication of the risk a Moslem was taking in being a Communist in Algeria. Ouzegane was born in Algiers in 1910, eleventh child of a family of fourteen, most of whom had died young. His grandfather had been a rebel against French authority whose land had been confiscated as punishment; his father worked in a hotel restaurant. Pious parents had sent him to Koranic school priority to elementary school. Later Ouzegane sold newspapers, worked as a messenger, then as a postal telegraph clerk. In 1926 he was co-founder of the post office labor youth movement Jeunesse Syndicalistes, in 1930 co-founder of Friends of the U.S.S.R.

He rose in the ranks of the pro-Communist Confédération Générale du Travail Unitaire (CGTU), a leftist fractional split from the more moderate Socialist CGT trade union central of Léon Jouhaux. Ouzegane was put to work setting up sections for Moslem workers, which Jouhaux's CGT was apparently not doing. (The CGTU would rejoin the CGT in the euphoria of the Popular Front in March 1936.)

In 1934, Ouzegane had become secretary of the Algiers Communist Party and clandestine editor of its organ La Lutte Sociale. After the exclusion of one Moslem secretary of the Political Bureau of the Algerian regional federation and the arrest of his successor, Ouzegane got that job. The Communists of Algeria were not then organized as a separate party, but were a branch of the French Communist Party whose Central Committee was in Paris. At the Comintern meeting in 1935, Ouzegane had demanded—and eventually he obtained —the establishment of a separate Algerian Communist Party (PCA). As secretary of the regional federation, then propaganda secretary of the PCA, Ouzegane attempted to create a united front of anti-colonialists grouping French Algerian sympathizers and Moslem religious leaders (the ulemas), Moslem civil servants, and trade unionists. He gave up his activity in the then reunited CGT, devoting his energy to the organization of dockers, farm laborers, miners. In 1936 he helped in the founding of the Congrès Musulman Algérien, becoming secretary of its executive committee, and worked to bring the new movement into the Popular Front. He was elected a city councilman in July 1937.[9]

Ouzegane lent a friendly ear to the Plateau Saulière cell, known as the "intellectuals' cell." But if it was composed principally of the young student and artist comrades—Camus, Jeanne Sicard and Marguerite Dobrenn, Claude de Fréminville, Louis Miquel, Maurice Girard, a salesman and his pharmacist wife, there were some indigenous members as well, a few of them genuine working-class. Ouzegane remarked that Camus was interested in the Moslems and their social conditions. The strange thing was that Camus seemed to understand them without having taken the trouble, as other Europeans (known as Arabists) had, to learn their language. So Ouzegane encouraged Camus to pursue contacts with young Moslem intellectuals who because of their French language and culture were more easily reached by "national-reformist" ideology, the objective being to lead them to a "national-revolutionary" orientation close to the Communist line and if possible, for the most advanced of them, to bring them into the Party. On a personal level, Camus began to associate with Moslem writers and with the ulemas, particularly with their president, Sheikh Ben Badis, and their vice-president, Sheikh Taïeb El Okbi.

Camus in turn elicited lively interest from his new Party friends, who were charmed by his culture, devotion, simplicity. When he fell ill at one point during his Party career, Ouzegane joined the delegation of the section which visited him and along with pastry and flowers gave him an envelope containing money contributed by Belcourt militants.[10]

Under the impulsion of Camus, the "intellectuals' cell" had begun to deal with the Moslem problem in a way not usual among the *pieds noirs,* even the best disposed ones. It was more in line with the ideology of Arabists such as Emile Padula, an accountant who was the Party's Belcourt Section secretary. Padula was both a veteran Communist and one of the few non-Moslems in the Party who understood and cared about the day-to-day problems of native Algerians irrespective of tactical and ideological considerations. When in 1924 the French Communist Party had asked its Algerian cells to set up Algerian nationalist organizations, Padula had opposed this strategy on the grounds that Moslems were highly vulnerable in Algeria, risked arbitrary imprisonment by French colonial authorites and deportation to the southern desert territories. Padula was summoned to the Party's colonial section in Paris, whose chairman at the time was Jacques Doriot (later to turn to Fascism and collaboration with the Nazis). After explaining why such a Moslem movement could not be organized in Algiers, Padula requested that it be set up on the less dangerous territory of mainland France. The result was the founding in 1926 of the Party's Moslem front, Etoile Nord-Africaine (ENA), sponsored by Emir Khaled, with a newspaper of the same name (under Padula's direction). Moslem workers in France could join ENA, and its activity and press could have an influence in the more tightly controlled Algerian situation, yet without subjecting the colony's Moslems to unnecessary risk.[11]

Now a third element would appear in the equation, in the form of maverick nationalist Messali Hadj, born in Tlemcen in 1898, the son of a shoemaker. After primary school he had migrated to France to find work, as so many of his fellow-Moslems would do then and later. As a factory worker he involved himself with political activities, joining both the French Communist Party and the Etoile Nord-Africaine on its founding. But by 1926 he had quit the Party (accusing it of paternalism with respect to migrant laborers), and a year later he took over ENA. Under his leadership (and until 1934), nevertheless, ENA remained closely allied with the Communists, participated in the Popular Front. Then and later, the Messali movement identified with rank-and-file workers, many of them still imbued with religious tradition, and this characteristic would always distinguish ENA from the more ideological, less religious movement which would become the insurrectionary Front de Libération Nationale (FLN), essentially an emanation of the middle class.[12]

During Camus' membership in the Communist Party, which ran from autumn 1935 until November 1937, the political picture in France, and necessarily—if more subtly—in settler-dominated Algeria, was changing fast. Popular Front ideology had gripped Paris, a Popular Front embracing not only the Communists and the Socialists but the more moderate Radical Socialists as well. But in May 1936 the chief victors in the national legislative elections were the Socialists, and so it was Socialist leader Léon Blum who was called on to head a government which was to last until June 1937, when it fell, victim of France's deteriorating economic situation and the inability, or lack of powers, of the Socialist Prime Minister to cope with it. In all its trials the Popular Front government was assisted in a singular way by the French Communist Party, which had been a key instigator of unity of action between all democratic forces. Indeed, the Communists would have liked the Popular

Front to encompass a wider range of parties and movements than it in fact did.

For in those days, when Nazism and Fascism were beginning to display their strength, the Soviet Union (then firmly in control of the world's Communist Parties) enforced a general line of union with all democratic forces, and at whatever sacrifice to local objectives that might signify. It meant that Communists were asked to join their historic enemies in labor movements (as in the CGT-CGTU merger), in political action, even to work alongside the conservative Radical Socialists. "Social Fascist" was no longer to be employed as a taunt to the more moderate Socialists.[13]

In Algeria, the new Communist line was to require an even more violent adjustment, leading to the trial and expulsion of Albert Camus.

One of the twenty-one conditions for membership in the Communist (Third) International was that each Communist Party promote the liberation of colonies, while demanding the expulsion of "imperialists" to their countries of origin. Despite this unambiguous platform, the Communists of Algeria had never succeeded in making a deep penetration of Moslem nationalism, for educated Moslems were more likely to favor integration with the French community rather than independence. The result was that Algeria's Communists were considered dangerous outlaws by French colonial authorities, but for all their pains they had failed to win over the Moslems. They were "more Arab than the Arabs," in the words of one of their leaders of that time, and it was in this spirit that they had created the Etoile Nord-Africaine movement. The seventh congress of the Communist International in Moscow in 1935 (at which Amar Ouzegane spoke) reiterated its anti-colonial position, but privately the Communists were concerned with the Algerian situation, fearing that the real victors in any confrontation were likely to be the rightists, who would organize the Moslems of Algeria as General Franco was to do in Spanish Morocco.

It was then that French Communist Jean Chaintron, under the name "Jean Barthel," a pseudonym he acquired when he was a factory organizer and had to keep his Party activity secret, was sent by Paris headquarters to advise—in effect to lead—the Party's Algerian regional federation. He had previously been organizational secretary of the Party's City of Paris section. His mission, which he was to assume at the very moment that Albert Camus joined the Party, was to find and train leaders for a separate Algerian Communist Party, using Moslems whenever possible. Actually he had two goals: to promote the organization of a mass (and Moslem) movement, while stimulating anti-Fascist activity against the increasingly powerful reactionary right.

The two goals, Chaintron-Barthel was to discover, were largely contradictory. On the one hand Moslems were simply not interested in anti-Fascism, which seemed to them a strictly European problem. On the other hand, rank-and-file French Algerians were hardly enthusiastic about all-out anti-colonialism, which risked pitting Moslem nationalists against French settlers of all classes.

There was also an internal Party problem. In Paris, Chaintron had been briefed by the head of the colonial affairs section, André Ferrat, who placed heavy emphasis on the anti-colonial campaign. But before leaving for Algiers, Chaintron was summoned to a meeting with Party chief Maurice Thorez, who knew that Ferrat's briefing was likely to minimize the anti-Fascist campaign. Thorez warned Chaintron: "If Fascism takes over the world, the Moslems will hardly be better off."

Chaintron arrived in Algiers to find himself virtually the leader of the local Communist Party, working alongside Secretary Ouzegane and young Elie Mignot. Abandoning the idea of trying to combine the anti-colonial and anti-Fascist lines, he tried each in turn, predictably losing one of his audiences while he was trying to reach the other one. He told French Algerians that only by supporting Algerian independence could they hope to get the Moslems to accept anti-Fascist solidarity.

He also drew up a table of organization for a separate Algerian Communist Party (PCA), which in theory would no longer be an offshoot of the French Party in Paris. And so the PCA was founded at a First Congress in Algiers on July 4, 1936.[14] At last the more radical and militant Communists of Algeria, Europeans as well as Moslems, felt that they were getting what they had fought for: autonomy, and perhaps Moslem leadership as well.[15]

For the world had not been standing still while Algerians attempted to work out the problems which were peculiar to Algeria. Something that had happened far away was soon to have its first repercussions in North Africa. Joseph Stalin had decided that the interests of the Soviet Union would best be served (in the face of the growing threat of Adolf Hitler) by a strong France, a France favorable to Moscow, of course. As a consequence, in May 1935 the French Foreign Minister, who was then Pierre Laval, traveled to Moscow to talk to Stalin. In the official communiqué issued at the close of their meeting, Stalin stated that he fully approved France's defense policies, a not very subtle invitation to French Communists to abandon anti-militarism and other positions that might weaken France or irritate potential allies of the Communists.

One of the policies that might weaken France was anti-colonialism; henceforth *that* policy would have to be put on a shelf.

It took time for the new line to filter down to the working level;

Chaintron-Barthel was not to stay in Algiers long enough to see it through. For his aggressive activities—anti-colonial activities, of course —had triggered a local campaign against him, culminating in front-page attacks in *La Dépêche Algérienne* accusing Jean Barthel of seditious intent for his suggestion that "Algeria is not France." He was duly tried and sentenced, for one could be jailed in Algeria for statements that were permissible in mainland France, but he escaped the three one-year jail sentences handed down by slipping out of the territory. During the period of his mission in Algeria he would cross the path of Albert Camus only once, when he attended a Théâtre du Travail performance of Maxim Gorky's *The Lower Depths*. He certainly never exchanged more than a few words with young Party member Camus.[16]

When Barthel slipped out of Algeria, junior Party official Elie Mignot held the fort until the arrival of a new "adviser" from Paris, for the ostensibly autonomous PCA in fact remained under the guardianship of Paris headquarters. By the time the new envoy, Robert Deloche, had arrived, the new Party line had been communicated to all echelons: Tone down anti-colonialism, emphasize the struggle against Fascism. In the opinion of young Mignot the new line was wholly justified, for Algeria in particular was a hotbed of French Fascism. Local supporters of right-wing extremist movements, like that of Colonel de La Rocque, often used airplanes as well as tractors in their political demonstrations.[17]

The trouble was that Deloche lacked the reasonable behavior, the diplomacy, of Barthel; he applied the new directives from Paris brutally, without regard for the special Algerian situation.[10] One of the principal victims of the new Communist line was the Etoile Nord-Africaine movement of Messali Hadj. Messali's followers were well aware of this scaling down of anti-colonial activity, but they were not going to be part of what they considered a sellout. Messali and his ENA members soon found themselves in a crossfire: from the moderates, with the banning of ENA by Blum's Popular Front cabinet in early 1937; from the Communists, who were increasingly hostile to what now seemed a troublesome rabble on the fringes of the united struggle against Fascism. A battler against left, right, and center all his life long, eventually a prisoner of the French and then a target of the anti-colonialist, anti-French Front de Libération Nationale, Messali retaliated to the banning of ENA by setting up a Parti du Peuple Algérien in March 1937, which advocated "Neither assimilation nor separation, but emancipation." Until then Messali had been operating from mainland France; now he transferred his headquarters to Algeria and campaigned in the municipal elections of June 1937 in opposition to the Communist ticket.[12] The Communist Party had not reacted when the

French Government banned ENA and jailed some of its militants; now Messali's new PPA would circulate tracts attacking the Communists. Messali's men called Communist leaders government agents and provocateurs; the Communists called PPA Fascist and provocateur.[18] In the Communist press the campaign against the "pseudo-nationalists" of PPA became outright psychological warfare: Amar Ouzegane published the names of alleged agents of the French police inside PPA.[19]

Ouzegane himself was soon in difficulty, for anti-colonialism dies hard, particularly if one has been born a Moslem victim of colonialism. As editor of *La Lutte Sociale,* Ouzegane had played up three reports of attacks on Moslems in separate incidents in Algeria and France, placing them under a single front-page headline, for to his mind they all represented aspects of the same problem. But Robert Deloche and Elie Mignot, looking over the layout of that issue, removed the banner headline and redistributed the stories in three different places, which of course reduced their impact. Ouzegane took up the matter with the Political Bureau, which dismissed it as a technical problem. He then resigned (in July 1937) both as editor of *La Lutte Sociale* and from his Political Bureau position. He traveled to Paris in a vain and drawn-out attempt to talk to Party chief Thorez, only to find himself blackballed as a deserter on his return. He demanded that the matter be cleared up, carried his case all the way up to the Central Committee, objecting to French Communist Party interference in Algerian Communist Party affairs. Finally he was heard; Deloche would soon be recalled.

The split between Communists and Moslem nationalists could only puzzle and distress Albert Camus. At the beginning of his Communist adventure, he had been asked to recruit young Arab militants in order to convince them to join Messali's ENA. Now the same young Arab militants were being tracked down by police and thrown into jail, and to the applause of Camus' chosen party. Moslems who had managed to avoid arrest came to him and asked if he would continue to tolerate such practices. He trembled with rage, made no attempt to conceal his indignation.[20] And his heresy would be to continue to associate with the Messalistes now considered fascistic by his fellow Communists.[14]

Camus was well aware of the explosion of anger that even the most reasonable proposal for reform could provoke among diehard colonialists, for he was campaigning actively for the Blum-Viollette bill then before the French Parliament. Introduced in the Chamber of Deputies (France's lower house) by Blum's Minister of State, Maurice Viollette, this bill would have given voting rights to an estimated 21,000 Moslems —war veterans, grammar school graduates—at a time when there were nearly six million Moslems (and 890,000 French Algerians) in the territory. It was a first step toward assimilation with French Algerians, and moderate Moslems then aspired to such assimilation. The Communist Party considered the Blum-Viollette bill "progressive and useful," and the moderate Moslem religious leaders, the ulemas, also supported it.

Indeed, this bill was so moderate that Messali Hadj rejected it as just another "instrument of colonialism." But the resistance of conservative French Algerians was more dangerous. The debates in the French Parliament detonated violent reactions in Algeria, inspired rallies at which slogans included "Death to Blum" and "Death to the Jews." When the bill was amended to extend voting rights to a total of 200,000 Moslems, protest became tumult. The Popular Front was never strong enough to override the threat from reactionary settlers; the bill never got a full airing in the French Parliament. But the controversy surrounding it left in its wake new bitterness, of settlers against Moslems, of Moslems against a colonial regime from which it no longer expected justice. Henceforth those favoring assimilation would lose ground to those favoring separation from France, a goal they would attain a generation later.[21]

It was certainly in terms of moderation—insisting on the need for unity now more than ever—that Camus' superiors in the Communist Party attempted to appease the young man. Robert Deloche and Amar Ouzegane attended meetings of the Plateau Saulière cell, listened to the discussions, and even tried to pursue the dialogue with Camus privately. Ouzegane was well aware of the Moslem-nationalist orientation of this boy from Belcourt, for that neighborhood had been a pilot zone of "Arabization." He had also remarked that Camus was veering from the Communist line in his opposition to an essential element of Popular Front strategy, for Camus objected to the Party's association (in the Popular Front movements) with the Radical Socialist Party, which was so clearly a "bastion of colonialism."[10] Even though the Radical Socialist Party was a member of the Comité du Front Populaire d'Alger, for example, it opposed the Blum-Viollette reforms. And privately Camus was certainly unhappy about the Communists' sudden love for the French Army and defense of the fatherland; to close friends he could be ironical about that.[22]

Ouzegane decided that Camus was a clever dialectician rather than a man of action. Within the Political Bureau, Deloche dismissed Camus out of hand as a Trotskyist. Ouzegane demurred, arguing that Camus' position might be erroneous but that it was less dangerous than the opposite extreme—colonialism. Ouzegane knew quite well that Deloche also felt that Ouzegane himself was suspiciously partial to Moslem nationalism, notably in promoting a PCA alliance with the ulemas. By harping on Camus' dissidence, Ouzegane decided, Deloche was really delivering a message to Ouzegane to mend his ways.[10]

Another problem for local Communists was the attitude of Emile Padula, for he was both a loyal Communist and an honest man. Though a disciplined Party worker, Padula had always favored Moslem nationalism, and could not be happy with the new anti-nationalist line. He could only sympathize with the "leftist" heresy of Albert Camus.[10]

In fact Padula was discussing the changed line in his own cell. He argued that oppressed Moslems could not be compared to Fascists. Both he and Camus had been stung by Ouzegane's attacks in the Party weekly on the Messalistes as "Fascist." But while Padula had felt bound by Party discipline, Camus no longer confined his protests to his own cell. So as secretary of the Belcourt Section, which included Camus' Plateau Saulière cell, Padula had given Camus a friendly warning.

Now the matter of Camus' dissidence was formally put on the agenda of the Plateau Saulière cell. At first the majority of his comrades supported him. Then they began, one by one, to yield, convinced of the logic of the Party line, or choosing discipline over logic. Only Maurice Girard stood beside Camus when the votes were counted.[10] At some point during the procedure Camus was summoned to Party headquarters and asked to revise his position. Instead he reconfirmed it, observing that the Party had been right to support Moslem nationalists earlier and it did not have the right to discredit them now, thereby playing into the hands of the colonialists.[23]

For the new Party line was having serious consequences. Messali and his nationalists were now fair game both for the Party and the Government General. In July 1937, Messali's Parti du Peuple Algérien (PPA) was excluded from the Second Moslem Congress because it rejected assimilation. A month later Messali and his co-leaders were indicted for provoking disorders against state sovereignty, and Messali received a two-year prison sentence. (Immediately after his release in 1939 he would be arrested again, drawing a sixteen-year sentence at hard labor in 1941. Amnestied after World War II, he would be exiled to France after another nationalist campaign and would die in France.)

Under the procedures of the Party's "democratic centralism," it was now up to the Belcourt Section, grouping all of the cells of the district, to settle the matter of dissidence in the presence of all the members of the Plateau cell, and the Bureau of the Algiers region ordered it to do so.[10] This meeting was held in the basement of a café on the Rue de Lyon, not far from Camus' childhood home, still his mother's home. One participant thought that the site might have shocked purists in the Party, who disapproved of holding meetings in such places. Robert Deloche, the eye of Paris, was in the chair, assisted by Ouzegane, Mignot, Ben Ali Boukhort (nominally the "autonomous" PCA's secretary general). In this far from merry atmosphere Camus rose to defend himself and to defend the dissident position. He criticized the lack of comprehension on the part of the Party's leadership of the social evolution of the Algerian people oppressed by colonialism, an evolution which he felt lacked cohesion and risked developing into radical nationalism. But there were peaceful alternatives to violence, he said, and by insisting on its own program the Party failed to take these alternatives into consideration. No one replied.[24]

Padula himself was not put on trial, because of his long service to the Party (and his cell, after all, had endorsed his position). While he was defending Camus in the Comité de Section, privately he advised Camus to resign before he was expelled, but Camus chose not to heed this advice. Others of Camus' friends had long since drifted away; Paul Raffi, for example, had simply sent a letter to the effect that he would no longer participate in Party work.[25]

The Party then called a meeting of the heads of all the Comités de Section, i.e., the districts comprising the Algiers region (or, in Party jargon, the *rayon*). Here Section Secretary Padula was confronted with Party Secretary Ouzegane. Neither Camus nor Girard was invited to this discussion. Padula reviewed the evolution of the Party's position on nationalism, his theme being: How can you put a "Fascist" label on organizations which you helped to set up? Padula lost; Camus and Girard were expelled by vote. The Comité Régional, the Party's highest organ in Algiers, was then called on to ratify the expulsion, and did so.[23] When Camus returned from Party headquarters after being informed of the decision, he ran into Girard, who remarked that Camus' only reaction was a "gentle smile." Girard himself had not waited for the expulsion notice, but had handed his Party card back to Deloche on the day following the Rue de Lyon meeting.[24]

And as neither Camus nor Girard appealed the decision, the Political Bureau did not have to intervene.[26] Henceforth no good Communist could as much as say hello to Camus.[10] The only Algiers official of that time who remains in the Party today concedes privately that the Party was probably not flexible enough with young Albert Camus, while Camus, although of good faith, simply didn't understand the nature of the class struggle.

But Camus did understand the nature of Moslem nationalism. He would never forget Messali Hadj, and when he was in a position to do so, he would use his influence time and again on behalf of indicted or convicted Messalistes (often through his old college classmate Yves Dechezelles, who became Messali's attorney).

Although few of his friends, even the closest ones, would ever know what had happened within the Communist Party—and this helps to explain the conflicting accounts of his Party membership in those books and articles in which it has been mentioned—the effects of his disillusionment, of his dissidence and expulsion, were to be evident in Camus' more public activities all through the year 1937. In fact one of the few friends who did know what had taken place in those cell and section meetings was Claude de Fréminville, who had joined the Party before Camus did, and had been confronted with a similar challenge to his principles when the Party line turned against Moslem nationalism. Since he continued to print the propaganda materials of the Moslem nationalists on his press, he was accused of having purchased his printing equipment with funds obtained from moderate nationalist Ferhat Abbas, a Sétif pharmacist who would later become figurehead president of the insurrectionary government of the Front de Libération Nationale (FLN). Fréminville replied by quitting the Party, as he reported to André Belamich on December 28, 1937. "As for me I'm proud not to be treated as a Trotskyist as Camus and Girard, who were expelled, instead of having left as I, humble Ferhatist, did."[27]

At one point in the tumultuous life of the House of Culture, Camus himself had been involved in an expulsion, but no one alive today seems to know what the circumstances were. One Gabriel Prédhumeau, a sometime anarchist, heavy-set and a fighter by nature, had been spreading nasty stories about Camus and his friends. What kind of stories? The incident took place in the spring of 1937, perhaps too early to be connected with the internal discussions in the Communist Party. More likely the theater group was involved, for Prédhumeau had participated in the Théâtre du Travail and would remain in what was left of that troupe when Camus abandoned it after his fight with the Party.

On June 9, then, the executive committee of the House of Culture met to hear Prédhumeau's explanation of the "scandalous rumors" he had been spreading against the House of Culture's secretary-general and top officers. He admitted having made such remarks, and was expelled from the House "immediately and definitively," while it was decided to give the sanction the widest possible publicity. That meant communiqués in La Lutte Sociale and L'Algérie Ouvrière.[28]

Whatever importance should be attached to the events of June, by autumn the House of Culture had collapsed, all of its vital components having left the Communist Party, even as the line of the House of Culture stiffened. Camus' non-Communist friends would probably have kept away from House of Culture meetings at which hard-line Commu-

nists denounced André Gide as a renegade for having written his confession of disillusionment with the Soviet Union, *Retour de l'U.R.S.S.*
Even as Camus was organizing a new and non-political theater group to
replace the Théâtre du Travail, a rival company which included some of
the anti-Camus forces, Théâtre des Artistes Associés, had begun rehearsing *Julius Caesar* (inspired by Shakespeare, Suetonius, and Plu-
tarch).[29] On a different plane, Yves Bourgeois had become something
of a magnet for those who disapproved of the Party loyalty of Camus
and his friends, or who for reasons of personal incompatibility rejected
Camus' leadership. Following the Camus couple's trip to Central
Europe with Bourgeois, there had never been a public or even a private
quarrel, simply a drifting apart, which subsequent events would turn
into quarrels.

Bourgeois's faction, for example, had inherited the Collège du
Travail. He organized a homage to Federico García Lorca, an evening
of speechmaking, songs, and poetry reading. Apart from theater, which
they left to the rival Camus forces, the Bourgeois group did everything
else. They worked in co-operation with the undergraduate student associations, for Bourgeois and fellow-teacher Poignant were both working
for degrees at the university. Among their activities were lectures on literary and historical subjects, an exhibition of indigenous arts and crafts,
an evening of cartoon drawing (featuring a star artist from France,
Jean Effel), a concert of Oriental music (for which Camus' estranged
wife Simone lent a piano). Sometimes emulation became open confrontation: a Bourgeois man excelled at bland letters informing the Camus
side that the Bourgeois group had booked the only available hall in
town (knowing that the Camusians had planned to use it that very
day).

Sometime during that winter Bourgeois received a note from
Camus, complaining of some unspecified wrong, and concluding with
the remark that if there was one thing he (Camus) could not tolerate it
was "baseness." Since Bourgeois did not want to leave Camus feeling
superior, he suggested a meeting in a café to discuss the matter. The ensuing conversation was relaxed, so that the motivation could not have
been important. Camus and Bourgeois concluded that one's supporters
could sometimes be an embarrassment. During their talk one of Camus'
friends turned up, possibly Claude de Fréminville, and appeared astonished when Camus introduced him to Bourgeois. Bourgeois decided
that Camus' friends must think that he wore horns and a tail.

It was the last time he ever saw Camus. Years later, a decade after
World War II, he learned from his best friend in a prisoner-of-war
camp, whose younger brother had married Camus' niece, that Camus
still thought highly of him.[30]

# 13

## THEATRE DE L'EQUIPE

It is normal to give part of your life so as not to lose it entirely. Six or eight hours a day so as not to die of hunger.
And then everything is profit to those who know how to
profit from it.

*Carnets*

It is futile to seek evidence that the months of internal debate in the
Communist Party, the polemics in public places, the brutality and the
finality of the expulsion had undone the young militant or even
distressed him unduly. The ensuing period saw no new plunge into feverish activity of the kind one undertakes in order to forget; rather was
there a continuation of his social and cultural life through other means,
with a different orientation.

The reader of Camus' journal, for example, will find no telltale
remark of despair, not even a betraying slip of the pen. The young man
was still unwilling to confide to his journal.[1]

And this new round of activity, the new theatrical adventure with
all the structuring and programming it implied—rehearsal schedules
and getting the amateur actors to the rehearsals; booking or borrowing
halls, promotion—would once more be accompanied by uncertainties
as to his personal future. We know from his journal that he was now
well into his draft novel, *La Mort heureuse,* that he was collecting ideas
which would furnish his second book of essays, *Noces,* while looking
beyond both of these projects to a more ambitious scheme of work. But
Camus was now twenty-four years old, and it was time to be like other
men of his age: to be launched on a career.

Perhaps he might look for it in Paris. In his top-floor room on the

Rue Michelet, which at one time was decorated with a single poster advertising the Gallimard Pléiade series of ancient and modern classics, one of several small bachelor flats he occupied during this period (for he was constantly moving, often to the apartments of absent friends), he talked to Louis Miquel about the possibility of artistic expression in Algeria. "You find a resonance only in Paris," Camus told his friend. Miquel didn't reply. Camus pursued: "Obviously, you're going to ask me, do you need to have resonance?" Miquel saw this as a play on words, *résonner* for *raisonner*, "to reason."[2]

There was a man in Paris to whom a young Algerian with literary aspirations could appeal. To the would-be writers of North Africa, Gabriel Audisio was something of a father figure. From Algiers his works had gone to France to be published, and by their idol among publishers, Gallimard (which brought out his *Jeunesse de la Méditerranée* in 1935). He had exported the notion of the peculiar genius of Mediterranean man to the very heart of literary and intellectual France. "He was the first to give a literary consciousness to the country of his youth," Max-Pol Fouchet would remember. "For his Algeria, he wanted writers." He was the originator, senior adviser, and benefactor of the North African school that would include Camus, Jules Roy, Emmanuel Roblès.[3] Actually this "Algerian" was born in Marseilles (in 1900) and first landed on North African soil at the age of ten, when his father was appointed director of the Algiers Opera theater.[4] In the Office Algérien d'Action Economique et Touristique (OFALAC) with headquarters on Avenue de l'Opéra in Paris, he was virtually the cultural attaché in France for Algeria's Government General.

When Camus wrote to Audisio from the Maison Fichu on November 9, 1937, the two men had never met, although Audisio knew Camus by reputation, and his OFALAC information bulletin had been the first publication on mainland France to announce (on the previous May 25) the appearance of *L'Envers et l'Endroit*.[5]

> At present without a job [Camus wrote him], I have a great need to live in Paris. Do you believe that at the age of twenty-four with a literary degree, a diploma in advanced philosophy, a year of practical journalism (writing and make-up) and two of theater as an actor and director, I can find a job in Paris which will allow me to live and to work for myself? . . . It's very important for me to be able to live there as soon as possible.[6]

Audisio replied gently, honestly, that he had no job to suggest. It was not easy for a young provincial, as well equipped as he might be, to find work in that depression year. But if Camus would come up to Paris to spend some time there, Audisio might be of more help to him.[5]

It was not what Camus had hoped to hear from Audisio. He was prepared to struggle, but at this time struggle signified holding a bread-winning job which would enable him to do the writing he was ready to do. The unsettling experience of a transfer to Paris would have been justified if he could be sure to find security at the end of the journey. He did not necessarily wish to leave Algeria, despite the sentimental and political disappointments he had been experiencing. An eight-hour-a-day job in Algeria, other things being equal, was better than the uncertainties of Paris. But first he had to find that eight-hour job.

In May 1937, Jean Coulomb, a young meteorologist who had been born and raised in Algeria but who was making his career in France, was appointed director of the Institut de Météorologie et de Physique du Globe, attached to the University of Algiers. He discovered that his institute had inherited some 355 observation posts scattered over Algerian territory, and decided that with data available through these posts he could establish a record of Algeria's climate. Coulomb had also been asked by one of his university colleagues, perhaps by Jean Grenier, whether he could employ Camus, who was desperately in need of work. Coulomb indeed thought that he could use Camus—for the weather record project. But the first problem was to find the funds to pay a new employee. The solution was a government grant which allowed him to pay a modest 1,000 francs a month (710 present-day francs, or some $145), for a technical assistant. His offer to Camus included a friendly warning: "Would you be willing to undertake a job that has nothing literary about it, and isn't even interesting?" The young man replied that he had no choice.[7] "It is normal to give part of your life so as not to live it entirely," he told his journal on November 22.

He began working at the institute early in December 1937. The office day ended at four, allowing him to spend his afternoons and evenings on other things.[8] He got off another letter to Gabriel Audisio (on December 3), thanking him for having been so frank about his chances.

> Without doubt the risk you offer me is quite attractive. But I have been playing that game for over two years now and I feel the need to regain my calm and my health. To tell the truth, when I wrote you, I had only enough money to buy deck space on the ship to Marseilles. . . . Perhaps it's a matter of physical exhaustion, but I tell myself that it is useless to run after a poverty with which I'm already familiar and which is never productive. . . .
>
> I've found an office job here which takes my daytime hours and leaves evenings free for work. It is not always easy, but it gives me time to reflect and to plan my life. . . .[9]

His first assignment at the Institut de Météorologie was to make an inventory of data recorded in 355 weather stations over a period of twenty-five years, not the weather itself, but an indication of which months and years the particular station had reported on. Each of the stations measured rain, for example, but some made further observations, noting temperature, humidity, atmospheric pressure. Camus was to note, on large-format cards each of which dealt with a single station, the type of information available for each of the three-hundred months (twenty-five years times twelve) included in the survey. These cards came to be known as *les fiches Camus,* and at last reports they were still on file at the institute. They helped provide the data for a book called *Le Climat de l'Algérie,* by Paul Seltzer, published in Algiers in 1946, in whose introduction "A. Camus" is duly thanked for his work as technical assistant on the project.[10]

Coulomb's aide Paul Seltzer found himself admiring the way Camus threw himself into the job, despite the fact that the subject matter was so far removed from his usual concerns. In the case of rainfall, for example, if a weather reporting station had been closed a whole year, and if that year had been an exceptionally rainy one, the average rainfall calculated on the basis of the twenty-four remaining years would be too low. So Camus would have to look for one or more neighboring stations which did operate during the missing year, to be able to estimate the annual rainfall of the missing station. (In fact the averages had to be calculated for each of the twelve months of the missing year.) When Camus had completed the inventory of the 355 weather stations, he was assigned to a study of atmospheric pressure.[11] In his journal he remarked that, since temperature varies from one minute to the next, the record had to represent "an arbitrary slice out of reality." Later he recalled with humor how he had been calculating in millibars from basic data which he found filled with errors.[12]

When he arrived at the institute each morning, the young technical assistant donned a white smock which fell below his knees. Soon he would be perched on a ladder, consulting dusty file boxes on high shelves. Coulomb felt embarrassed at having put Camus to this sort of work, and asked him if he didn't find it too boring. But his new employee did the job gently and efficiently, and when Camus finally left (on September 30, 1938) he would thank Coulomb for having helped him through a difficult period.[7]

Meanwhile he could think about his real work again. He could also reorganize his home life. Until then he had been writing at the Maison Fichu, sleeping wherever he could find a bed, keeping his papers at still another place. Now he rented a small room of his own on the Rue Michelet, in a new if modest building.

An amusing side effect of the job at the Institut de Météorologie would be the increasing attention he would pay to weather. The first journal entries for December 1937 were jottings for *La Mort heureuse* (and eventually for *L'Etranger*). The first describes winter rain, the second a man "who seemed destined for a brilliant career," but who now has an office job; on Sunday he gets up late and looks out the window at the rain or the sun. "And so on all year long. He waits. He waits to die. What good are promises, since in any event . . . ?"

And after hours he lost no time setting up, with his faithful followers, a Théâtre de l'Equipe—literally Theater of the Team—to replace the Popular Front-bound Théâtre du Travail, as if his expulsion from the Party had diminished his desire to carry on a theater of political commitment. Here the inspiration would be the best contemporary theater, a new look at old works, a theater of ideas instead of ideology. In mainland France such theater was exemplified in the labors of Jacques Copeau, one of the founders of the *Nouvelle Revue Française,* whose famous Parisian playhouse, the diminutive Théâtre du Vieux Colombier, was already a landmark. Camus would imitate and sometimes borrow Copeau's repertory, notably Charles Vildrac's *Le Paquebot "Tenacity"* and Dostoevsky's *The Brothers Karamazov,* which Copeau himself adapted from the novel for the Vieux Colombier. The Camus team began rehearsing almost as soon as the 1937 summer vacations were over. Camus announced the founding of the new company in a manifesto, "For a Young Theater," leading off with a quotation from his master Copeau:

> Of theaters whose watchwords are work, research, boldness, one can say that they were not founded to prosper but to endure without compromising their principles.

At a moment when all France was experiencing an "explosive rebirth" of theater, characterized by decentralization, the Théâtre de l'Equipe promised to provide young Algiers with a drama season worthy of it. The members of the new team shared certain ideas they would put into practice.

> Theater is an art of the flesh in which living bodies teach its lessons, an art both rough and subtle, an exceptional combination of movements, of the voice and of lights. But it is also the most conventional of arts, entirely framed within that complicity of the actor and his audience, who together give mutual and tacit consent to the same illusion.

The theater thus served both to communicate deepest feelings: love, desire, ambition, religion, and to satisfy the "need to construct" natural to the artist. The new theater, Camus went on—for who doubts that Camus wrote this manifesto?—would ask of its plays "truth and simplicity, violence in feeling and cruelty in action," a bow to Antonin Artaud. It would dig into the classic repertory—Aeschylus, Aristophanes, the Elizabethan drama, Spanish classics (Fernando de Rojas, Calderón, Cervantes), the Americans (Faulkner, Caldwell), contemporary France (Claudel, Malraux). But the staging would be young and free.

The Equipe proclaimed itself without political or religious tendency, wished to make friends of its audience, and offered membership in Friends of the Equipe (Les Amis de l'Equipe) at twenty francs per year; membership allowed a 25 per cent reduction on theater tickets and provided regular information on new productions. Fréminville printed the manifesto; the Equipe's address was given as care of Charlot's bookshop, Les Vraies Richesses.[13]

For their first production, Camus had not chosen an easy play. Rojas' *La Celestina,* or, in French, *La Célestine,* was an early Spanish Renaissance masterpiece, the first notable achievement of Spain's Golden Age, an influence on all European theater of its time. Yet it had not been designed to be acted; it was rather a novel in dialogue, divided into twenty-one acts. Yves Bourgeois had originally called it to Camus' attention, suggesting it for the repertory of the Théâtre du Travail. Camus utilized a French adaptation by Paul Achard, who had attempted to make it into a playable four-act play.[14] He himself took the part of the young hero Calixte, while Jeanne Sicard was Célestine, the go-between. Pierre-André Emery and Louis Miquel designed the scenery, which consisted largely of pieces of equipment found in the theater, Marie Viton the costumes. But the tradition of anonymity would be carried over from Théâtre du Travail to Théâtre de l'Equipe; none of the programs or advertising mentioned the names of the actors. The new play was announced for December 3, a Friday, and December 5, a Sunday.

Now another bright young girl would be co-opted into the Camus group. For while Camus was perfectly happy to recruit agreeable and admiring young women for one or another of his activities, it was always more pleasant when the recruit showed evidence of understanding what she was doing, and an extra dividend when she was capable of understanding him. He may have thought at one time that Simone Hié was such a person, and perhaps she had been, at first. Jeanne Sicard considered herself his intellectual equal, and perhaps she was, but they could only be comrades. Many of the young persons who were chosen as actresses for Théâtre du Travail-Théâtre de l'Equipe plays stayed on, for a while, as *petites amies.* But they were not built to endure.

On Sundays, Blanche Balain would go to Maison Blanche Airport near Algiers to fly with a cousin, an amateur pilot, in his small Aiglon plane. She had begun to notice the presence, week after week, of a striking woman: tall, aristocratic Marie Viton, who was completing her own apprenticeship as a pilot—an act of courage, Blanche decided, when she learned that the twice-divorced woman's own daughter had been killed in a plane crash. She learned also that Marie Viton was a painter, and frequented artists and writers; Blanche Balain was writing poetry. One day she tendered some of her poems to her new friend. Handing them back another Sunday, Madame Viton said that she found them interesting. "You must join our group," she added. "I'll introduce you to sympathetic people, you'll see how exciting it is!" She invited Blanche to give her more poems. "I'll have them read by Albert Camus, a young writer." Marie Viton invited her to visit her at home, and at last suggested that she attend a rehearsal of *La Célestine*.

Blanche Balain arrived while a rehearsal was under way. She was introduced to Claude de Fréminville, "a poet like yourself." Their expressions were composed of both irony and pleasure, as if they were each a little ashamed to wear such a title. But Blanche Balain also saw that she could relax here; camaraderie quickly won out over vanity.

Observing the stage, she noted that the actors were reciting without costumes. In the middle of the group a tall and slender, pale young man seemed to be in charge of everything. She guessed that he was Albert Camus. And in an instant he had left the stage to greet petite Blanche. He invited her to join the cast at once. She was horrified at the idea, and he laughed. "You'll come back, I hope."

And she continued to attend rehearsals. At the beginning she felt that these amateur actors and actresses were working hard for no apparent result; she had to wait for the first performance to see that it all fitted into place. The rehearsals were often held in the homes of members of the company who happened to have room, sometimes at Benisti's sculpture studio. Suddenly a group of young men and women, ranging in age from sixteen to thirty, would begin to show up from school, from jobs, and just as quickly they began to work in harmony, voluntarily accepting the necessary discipline.[15] Every actor was also involved in moving scenery, doing whatever other chores were necessary. Young women in the cast applied themselves to cutting and sewing the costumes Marie Viton had designed. Maks Wigdorczyk, the carpenter who had already helped out on Théâtre du Travail productions, was in charge of building the sets, but he wasn't the only one to use hammer and nails; anyone available and capable was put to work. Wigdorczyk himself had met Camus in 1935 at a showing of Benisti's sculpture, and had fascinated Camus with his knowledge of the literature and music of Eastern Europe's Jews; Camus was often a guest at his home.

During early rehearsals Camus would make notes on the staging, which was what interested him most, as he confessed one day. After rehearsals they would go for sandwiches to the Brasserie des Facultés, sitting on the outdoor terrace. A flower vendor would put necklaces of jasmin around the necks of the female members of the cast, an Arab custom. They might go on from there to the Marine district, perhaps to eat couscous, more often to the popular, working-class Restaurant Marseillais, where every dish cost exactly one franc; the waiters would tote up the bill, which Camus always tried to pay, by counting the number of plates stacked in front of each diner.[16]

They would again be using the Government General's Salle Pierre Bordes—vast, extravagant but not in rent, for the administration was trying to encourage use of this white elephant. (Architect Emery felt that the rent was low because of the poor acoustics: Only one-hundred or two-hundred persons in the 1,200-seat hall could really hear what was going on; it was true that the Théâtre de l'Equipe never drew more than four hundred.) A sympathetic critic, G. S. Mercier in *L'Echo d'Alger,* suggested that the hall rendered a disservice to the company. As for the play itself, Mercier felt that, while the troupe had had a noble try at resurrecting an unknown work, some cutting was advisable. "It doesn't matter, it is a fine achievement to have obtained such results with extremely limited material means. There is something generous and even heroic in their endeavor which moves us very much." He had kind words for the bravura of Sicard's Célestine, "the passionate ardor" of Camus' Calixte.

Blanche Balain remembered best the costumes designed by Marie Viton: long gowns for the young women of a violent acid pink which, like Rojas' cruel story, "set our teeth on edge."

After the public performances of *La Célestine* they all met again at Benisti's studio. The choice of the next play was debated. One possibility was Machiavelli's *Mandragola,* and Camus read out passages from it. But after discussion they set it aside. Camus said that he had also thought of *L'Annonce faite à Marie,* by Claudel. Finally there was agreement for a double bill, André Gide's "treatise" *Le Retour de l'enfant prodigue,* which Camus planned to adapt for the stage, and Vildrac's *Le Paquebot "Tenacity,"* two works which were quite unlike. They needed more actors and actresses, and this time Blanche Balain agreed to try out for the role of Thérèse in the Vildrac play, for which she had the physique but not, she realized, the temperament. She wasn't a good enough actress to overcome what she felt was her lack of compatibility with the role. But she acquitted herself, according to a local critic, "quite honorably," thanks, she believed, to Camus' direction and the support of the other players—among them Jeanne Sicard as the café owner, Emile Scotto-Lavina, a dark and handsome young man to whom Blanche found it difficult to direct a convincing "darling," Célestin

Recagno, whose *pied noir* accent was impenetrable.[15] Camus asked his teacher and friend Jacques Heurgon to read his adaptation of Gide's treatise—he had made a twenty-minute curtain-raiser of it—and also enlisted his help in obtaining Gide's authorization to play it. He had changed nothing, added only a line, introduced a narrator to reinforce the ambiguity of the text. Heurgon soon had obtained both an authorization and the good wishes of Gide.[17] Meanwhile—such was the order of things—Camus also made sure he could have the theater on the dates he needed it—the evening of Saturday, February 26, the matinee of Sunday, February 27. (Writing to Monsieur le Directeur of the Théâtre de l'Equipe, the secretary-general of the Salle Pierre Bordes confirmed these dates, noting that the only other use of the auditorium that week was for a February 22 matinee concert by the cellist Pablo Casals.)[18]

They rehearsed at the Salle Pierre Bordes, starting in January, every Monday, Wednesday, and Friday from 6:30 to 9 P.M.[17] They were paying the administration a modest twenty francs for each use of the hall, which was cheap even for them. Although their total budget per play was limited to five hundred francs, and they earned additional revenue from memberships in Les Amis de l'Equipe, they were often in debt after their two performances, and had to pass the hat to make it up.[16]

For *Le Retour de l'enfant prodigue,* Marie Viton and Louis Miquel designed the costumes, Frank Turner composed the music. Camus played the prodigal son and a young student at the Algiers actors' academy, Jean Negroni, the second son. (Negroni would go on to become a professional actor and director in France; his teacher at the academy, Jeanne Marodon, played the mother.)[16] In the unsigned program notes Camus spelled out his intentions: "The action will not be natural, and the family drama will borrow the style of its divine personages from the biblical parable." Since Gide himself in a brief preface had said that he had been thinking of ancient triptych panels, the adaptation used appropriate costumes and scenery. "While the narrator . . . recalls that the very personality of Gide, torn in the beginning between flesh and spirit, then accepting the painful alternance of the two, gives the tone to the play."

The choice of a play written by Gide at a time when that veteran of French letters was being reviled by the Communists for treason against Stalin might have been considered a political statement by Camus, but no one said so. On the other hand, the main play on the bill, *Le Paquebot "Tenacity,"* had been written in 1920 by a favorite writer of the Communists and the Popular Front, Charles Vildrac. Hence the boost given to the play by *L'Algérie Ouvrière*, which might have been considered a political enemy of Camus now, on February 19:

> Go in crowds to see Charles Vildrac's *Le Paquebot Tenacity*. The famous play by the great French writer on the condition of workers after the war, shown for the first time on an Algiers stage. . . .

The performances would be hailed by conservative *Echo d'Alger*, whose G. S. Mercier began a long review with the comment: "The persevering efforts of the young troupe of the Théâtre de l'Equipe have found their reward in a success which we are happy to applaud." This double bill, the critic went on, would have represented a better beginning for the company than its experiment with *La Célestine*. Mercier praised the adaptation of the Gide play, and the décor "symbolizing with its high and narrow door the attraction of departure." Although the troupe continued to insist on anonymity, the critic pierced the curtain to identify Camus' "great progress as an actor. He was the tortured and badly informed prodigal son with a staggering accent." He cited Charles Poncet, who played the father with "a sober attitude and a moving voice," Raymond Sigaudès in the role of the older brother; the critic regretted that he didn't know the name of the young man who played the younger brother, and whose "precise understanding suggests remarkable gifts and an innate sense of the theater." Indeed. The unidentified young man was future actor-director Negroni.

Critic Mercier found that he had no room to do justice to the main feature, Vildrac's play, but he had praise again for Camus, who played the worker Ségard, for Blanche Balain, a "charming Thérèse in her feminine naiveté," Jeanne Sicard, "who is not afraid to become old and ugly to portray the café owner with an astonishing display of true and human character." Miquel's scenery was cited for "striking suggestiveness in its simplicity."[19]

Camus had been seeing more of Blanche Balain. One of his notes to her bore this invitation:

> If you were free Wednesday [December 29, 1937] at 2:30, we could walk around the Kasbah. I could show you what I like in Algiers, a city in which one can gain time (some call it wasting time —if you're sure you'd like to).

In the Kasbah they sat at the Café Fromentin watching the passing scene while sipping mint tea. "Look," he said of the Moslem crowd, "how they are, how they go, so noble, indifferent." He added: "They are more civilized than we are." He confessed that he would like to be in Spain, fighting with the Republicans. "To possess everything, to accomplish everything, in an instant, and die!" They speculated about suicide—to them a fascinating conception.

"I feel like walking around the city," he said to her one day. "Would you like to?" They crossed the city, went down to the harbor. The sight of successive tiers of houses descending to the docks, the illuminated boats at twilight, led him to say: "Isn't this the loveliest city, the loveliest bay in the world?" They followed lonely streets which rose to the heights of Algiers, taking the same route again and again. He confessed his exhaustion after the days at his job, the afternoons and evenings of amateur theater. He took her to Edmond Charlot's bookshop; soon her own poems, *La Sève des jours,* would be published there.

For the first time Camus had a friend who was also an attractive girl and a writer, and he appreciated each of these qualities in turn. Their *amitié amoureuse* would continue as long as he lived, and certainly for Blanche Balain it was the single most important event of her life.

During an evening walk in January 1938 he told her about the novel he was writing. He explained the theme of *La Mort heureuse:* "Can one be happy after an evil deed?" And he warned her: "It's a hard book." He gave her part of the manuscript to look at and she noted in her journal:

> It is a strange book, a subject terrible, curious, cruel and heavy with meaning . . . admirably written, and filled with energy by an atmosphere which grips you. . . . Reading some passages was at times painful for me—there is anguish in this hard and cynical narrative.[20]

He would also show the manuscript to Jacques Heurgon, who saw what was the matter with this young man's book: the brutal realism, the hero's criminal act, were inadequately integrated with the literary passages; it seemed badly assimilated Montherlant.[21] Christiane Galindo, who had typed the first draft of the manuscript, apparently in April 1938, met Camus immediately after his talk with Heurgon and found him discouraged.[22] No date can be put on this meeting, but Camus' own journal in June lists the rewriting of the novel as a summer project.

He did in fact work on a revision of *La Mort heureuse* that summer. But at some point, perhaps because of the advice of his mentors, and a voluntary renunciation of the beginner's tendency to put everything into a first novel at the risk of letting the puppet strings show, the contrivances and the Montherlant would be discarded. But then the novel would no longer be *La Mort heureuse*.[23]

That Camus realized he did not have an acceptable manuscript is suggested by his failure even to mention it to his publisher, Edmond Charlot.[24]

Until now there had been an unbridgeable chasm between the brilliant organizer and developing novelist, on one side, and the silent young man on the other who worked at a dull job for a meager living. "How much is sordid and miserable in the condition of a working man and in a civilization founded on working men," he had noted in his journal in April 1938. Then he replied to this proposition himself:

> But it's a matter of holding on and not letting go. The natural reaction is always to disperse oneself outside of work, to create around oneself facile admirations, a public, a pretext for cowardliness and falsehoods. . . . Another facile reaction is to make phrases. . . .
>
> It's a matter of remaining silent first of all—of getting rid of the public and knowing how to judge oneself. To balance a careful development of the body with a careful awareness of life. To abandon all pretense and to devote oneself to a double labor of liberation—with respect to money and to one's own vanities and cowardliness.

He told himself—and he was both laying the groundwork for his writing of *L'Etranger* and making what turned out to be an accurate estimate of the time it would take to complete it: "Two years are not too many in a life to reflect on a single point." So he would start from scratch, and give himself a chance to escape from that most miserable of conditions, "that of the man who labors."

Immediately after this journal entry he records, in April 1938, other projects and preoccupations: *Caligula,* which was not yet "ripe enough"; an essay on culture. He seems to be planning to pursue his studies toward the *agrégation* degree, which would open the doors to a career in higher education; he had not yet been told definitively that with his medical history the authorities would never accept him into the teaching corps. An alternative he lists is "Indochina." Did he actually plan to follow the footsteps of the young Malraux by making his fortune, or at least a reputation, in that far-off French colony? (In a journal entry only a couple of pages previous he had cited Malraux in a reflection beginning: "The revolutionary spirit is contained wholly in a protest by man against the condition of man.")

Musings of a frustrated technical assistant in a white smock climbing ladders in a weather research bureau. Only the final reiterated promises he makes to himself in this April 1938 journal entry need be remembered: "In two years to write *une oeuvre.*"

There could be still another way out for a would-be writer who had to earn his daily bread: a job which would not merely furnish a livelihood but allow further development, broader experience. Such a job was about to be created, although it would take a good part of that year 1938 before it was ready for him.

In Oran, the momentum of the Popular Front had brought about the founding of a left-wing daily to combat the press of the conservative, often reactionary majority (we know that Camus had been offered a job on this paper by Marcel Chouraqui). Visiting that region with his wife, an Algiers builder named Jean-Pierre Faure remarked posters on the walls advertising the new *Oran Républicain.* He happened to be the son of Elie Faure, the philosopher and art historian, who himself had been active recently in a Comité pour la Défense des Mineurs des Asturies, and who as president of Amis d'Espagne had visited the Loyalist fronts in Madrid and Barcelona. Then thirty-six, son Jean-Pierre had made a speaking tour for the Algiers Section of the Comité de Vigilance des Intellectuels Antifascistes, and he had participated in a July 14 parade of Popular Front supporters in Algiers which had troubled conservative forces by the turnout.

Faure realized how useful it would be to publish in Algiers a Popular Front daily similar to *Oran Républicain,* at a time when there were only two newspapers there, right-wing *La Dépêche Algérienne* and the so-called Radical Socialist (but actually quite conservative) *Echo d'Alger* (sympathetic, for example, to General Franco). Back in Algiers, he discussed his notion with friends such as Marcel Bataillon of the Comité de Vigilance, Louis Bureau, a left-wing engineer, and others in the legal and teaching professions. Faure was certainly a member in good standing of the Algiers establishment. His grandfather, the father of Elie Faure, had been a winegrower, and he himself had a degree as an agronomist. In fact he had originally migrated to Algiers to establish a vineyard in partnership with a distant cousin, Jacques Régnier, grandson of the nineteenth-century geographer Elisee Reclus (whose brother Elie Reclus participated in the Paris Commune). But after five years as a planter Jean-Pierre Faure went into real estate and was active in the construction of large co-operative buildings. He had written a book on the urbanization of Algiers. Faure moved among architects (his brother had been a co-disciple of Le Corbusier with Pierre-André Emery) and artists as well as planters; he had even been a regular luncheon guest at the Villa Abd el-Tif, and so knew Maguet, Damboise, and other members of that community. He was also a friend of Frank Turner, the English musician who composed music for Camus' theater.

Now Faure and friends who shared his views began to seek financial support for the launching of their newspaper. They created a committee which was to become a governing board consisting of representatives of leftist parties and unions, of the Moslem and the Jewish communities, professors, teachers, scientists, businessmen. The idea was to make *Alger Républicain* a truly non-capitalistic effort, so they formed a co-operative, selling shares at 100 francs each (71 francs, or about $15 in the mid-1970s), both in Algiers and through the *département;* in all they collected close to 1.5 million francs (1,065,000 francs or well over $200,000 in 1975). If two or three wealthy but Socialist planters contributed 30,000 or 40,000 francs each, not expecting to reap any returns, the majority of shareholders would buy only one or a few 100-franc shares; some bought a share a month or every two months. The majority of the smaller shareholders were Jewish, with Spaniards from Bab el Oued, Kabylie functionaries and teachers, middle-class Moslems. Faure and an associate, Paul Schmidt, were the largest shareholders, with over 100,000 francs each in stock. They had begun to sell shares in the final weeks of 1937, continued through the summer of 1938, meanwhile proceeding to set up editorial and business offices, to acquire a plant. Later they would rent a building in Bab el Oued, purchase secondhand printing equipment, with the technical assistance of *Oran Républicain* (which lent the head of its printing plant, while its editor in chief provided editorial advice).

As general manager of *Alger Républicain,* Faure went to Paris to interview candidates for the job of editor in chief. He had several in mind. But the man he finally selected may have seemed a surprising choice. Pascal Pia preferred the background to the foreground; his shyness sometimes took on the appearance of wildness; one would not have guessed that he had been a companion of André Malraux, a literary adventurer like the young Malraux, a poet. The son of a soldier killed in combat during World War I, Pia had begun to work for a living at an early age. He was to become one of the best editors of his day.[25]

In Algiers, Camus had lost no time in contacting the organizers of *Alger Républicain* and getting what he at least thought was a commitment for a job. (Faure's partner, Schmidt, had set up temporary offices in a Rue Charras building which also housed the House of Culture and other political movements, but Schmidt did not meet Camus at this time.)[26] Although most accounts place Camus' hiring in late summer or early autumn, the fact is that Camus considered himself hired as early as March 1938, for that is when he told Christiane Galindo about it, asking her if she would want to replace him at the Institut de Météorologie.[27] But *Alger Républicain* was far from ready; Pascal Pia himself had not yet been interviewed, and many months would pass before the newspaper was able to employ anybody at all. (It was only that fall, for example, that Camus' newspaper salary would enable him to move to a larger apartment with a terrace on a more convenient part of the Rue Michelet.)[28]

The drudgery of sorting out weather reports would continue for many months. More stimulating things were happening after working hours at the Salle Pierre Bordes. Another theatrical event was in preparation: the ambitious staging of *The Brothers Karamazov* in the adaptation of Copeau. Performances were scheduled for May 28 and 29, 1938. Camus chose to play Ivan, one of the Karamazov brothers. He wanted Blanche Balain to play Grouchenka, a loose lady; she accepted although the role seemed unsuited to her (she would have had to sit on the lap of Alioucha, played by Jean Negroni). But this time her family called her to order, and she was obliged to withdraw. She herself should have preferred to play Katherina Ivanovna, but Jeanne Sicard got that part. Instead, after Marie Viton had designed the costumes without being able to follow through on their execution, Blanche pitched in to see that the men's costumes were completed by a local dressmaker, who showed up just before the dress rehearsal with a collection of outfits in bright satinet which made the actors seem to be wearing slickers. So everyone had to scrounge through family trunks to find suitable old clothing; Blanche Balain herself brought in some old redingotes and capes. Camus floated in his borrowed burgher's suit. Evoking the original possessor of this hand-me-down clothing, he exclaimed: "You can see that he never went hungry!" Another young man, later to become a professional actor, Paul Chevallier, played Smerdiakov, while the third Karamazov brother was played by Raymond Sigaudès.[15]

"The play that the Théâtre de l'Equipe presents to its public today has nothing seductive about it and everything to repel," warned the unsigned program note. "Its function is not to please but to carry along." If the theater companies that usually visited Algiers seemed to prefer to stage plays without soul although executed by admirable actors, the program note explained, the job of the Equipe was to begin where theirs ended, with good plays presented by young actors whose anonymous teamwork served the authors' intentions as best they could.

In the event, the intentions of the young cast were rewarded. Both Algiers dailies praised the performances. Faithful G. S. Mercier in *L'Echo d'Alger* began his review:

> After the performance of the "Retour de l'enfant prodigue" by the Théâtre de l'Equipe last March, with "Paquebot *Tenacity*," and,

last night, of "Brothers Karamazov," there is no longer any doubt:
Henceforth we have in Algiers a young theater comparable to those
that Paris, with two or three provincial cities, has the luck to possess. They have been called "avant-garde", but in reality they are
only what every theater worthy of the name should be.

As pleased as the critic was by the performance, so was he saddened by
the lack of audience response. He congratulated the small group of
faithful patrons of the outsized Salle Pierre Bordes. The actors had gotten the tone right, Emery's stylized scenery helped create the proper atmosphere. This scenery had been built at a minimum of expense,
proving that you didn't need large sums of money to compose a work of
art—"for, in summary, we take away from this memorable creation an
impression of pure and true dramatic art. . . ." In *La Dépêche Algérienne,* Charles Delp focused attention on Copeau's adaptation, written in 1911, but he also found the performance excellent, regretted the
cast's anonymity, for they "compose a homogeneous group, play with
intelligence, and apply their energies with skill to the task of moving
us."

One of the group, Charles Poncet, had decided that Célestin
Recagno, playing the father, Feodov, was by far the most talented of
the company. Certainly Recagno had strained for authenticity: He had
demanded real food and drink on the stage, and got a *pâté en croute*
and wine, adding mouth-filled realism to his rendering of the line:
"Ivan, does God exist?" To Camus' "No," Recagno replied: "Then everything is lawful?" Camus later told Poncet that Recagno's metaphysical reflection had hit him with a blast of garlic full in the face.
"That puts you in the mood for talking about spiritual nourishment!"[16]

# 14

---

## ENCOUNTERS

The true work of art is the one which says less.

*Carnets*

That spring a group of young Mediterraneans and some older men—
their teachers and their spiritual advisers—joined forces to produce a
literary magazine which might serve as a showcase for the Mediterranean spirit in literature. They decided to call it *Rivages,* "Shores."
The cover designed by Pierre-André Emery was decorated by a drawing
of the Mediterranean Sea, or rather of the coasts which define it, the
blue of the sea clearly dominant. The editorial board of *Rivages* included Camus, René-Jean Clot, Claude de Fréminville, with Gabriel
Audisio, then living in Paris as representative of the Algerian Government; Latin professor Jacques Heurgon; and Jean Hytier, a thirty-nine-
year-old professor who had served in the Army with Audisio, had been a
student of Jules Romains in Paris, later the publisher of a literary magazine of his own. He had just arrived in Algiers. (Hytier would later be a
professor at Columbia University in New York, where he published
*Romanic Review.*)

The subtitle of the magazine described its program: "Revue de
Culture Méditerranéenne." It was to be published six times yearly from
Edmond Charlot's bookshop, or so was the hope. Fréminville would
print it. The idea for the magazine, Charlot recalled later, was his own.
The plan was to obtain material from all the nations bordering the
Mediterranean Sea. Later they would have published cultural docu-
ments as well, such as ancient Cretan texts. Camus liked the idea at
once, and Charlot set about to map out the first issues.[1]

On a spring visit to Algiers, Audisio met Camus for the first time.

The occasion was a meeting of the editorial committee of *Rivages* held in the rear of Charlot's tiny bookshop on May 4, 1938. Alongside the older Mediterraneans, Heurgon and Hytier, Audisio saw a young man who seemed silent and serious, modestly holding back, "but with a lively expression, an attentive forehead, an intelligence so obviously alert." Camus would say almost nothing during the gathering, but he was asked to write a declaration of intentions for the new magazine.[2]

Now Mediterraneanism was in the air. Young Frenchmen and others of French language and culture were beginning to be heard from not only in Algeria but in Morocco to the west, Tunisia to the east, and soon Max-Pol Fouchet would be publishing his own poetry review (although it would not be turned exclusively toward Mediterranean culture as *Rivages* was to be.)[3]

Usually, Camus would write in his presentation of *Rivages,* a new magazine has a reason for existence. But this magazine fills no need. Rather will it attempt to define itself, and to define a culture which exists. "It will escape no one that a movement of youth and of passion for man and his works has been born on our shores." This movement was finding expression in diverse areas—theater, music, and plastic arts, literature.

> At a time when the fashion for doctrines would like to separate us from the world, it is not a bad thing that young men, in a young land, proclaim their attachment to these few perishable and essential qualities which provide meaning to our life: sea, sun, and women in the light. . . .

*Rivages* represented no school. Yet the sensibilities of its members were shaped by the same vista, from Florence to Barcelona, from Marseilles to Algiers. They had their differences, too. The only criterion would be quality, freedom would be the watchword.

Indeed, it was this eclectic approach which saved the young and older Mediterraneans of Algiers from the narrow racism which is an occasional by-product, and therefore the risk, of regionalism. (Camus himself had considered this risk in his February 1937 House of Culture talk.) The material in *Rivages,* from this point of view, was harmless enough. The first issue, to appear just before Christmas 1938, contained contributions by Audisio, Blanche Balain (a poem), Jeanne Sicard (a translation from Cervantes' *Los Baños de Argel*), Fréminville (part of a novel), along with texts by Jules Supervielle and (from the Spanish) Antonio Machado and Federico García Lorca among others. Of course there was space for the manifesto of the Théâtre de L'Equipe, identified as "the Théâtre d'Etudes de la Revue *Rivages.*"

Issue number two, which would also be the last issue, contained a three-page essay on Eugenio Montale, three poems by Montale in the original Italian with French translations on facing pages; some Andalusian folk poems, called *coplas,* later to appear in book form; another installment of Fréminville's novel; an essay by Emmanuel Roblès on Andalusian healers (*curanderos*). But this issue also presented a five-page extract from Camus' "L'Eté à Alger" dedicated to Heurgon, to be published in May 1939 in *Noces.* Facing the title page there was an advertisement for the spring 1939 performances of *The Playboy of the Western World,* by John Wellington (*sic*) Synge. At the back of the magazine there were ads for the books of Charlot. The offerings include *André Gide* by Jean Hytier, *Santa-Cruz* by Jean Grenier, *Des Bagnes d'Alger* by Cervantes in the French translation of Jeanne Sicard (actually never to be published), the anonymous translation of *333 Coplas Populaires Andalouses,* in fact translated by an Algiers tax inspector named Louis-Léo Barbès (and in fact not published by Charlot at all but by Editions Cafre, the short-lived publishing venture of Camus and Fréminville). Inside the back cover of *Rivages* number two was an advertisement for *Noces,* to be published (the advertisement promised) in an edition of 1,000 copies at 18 francs, 100 copies on Alfa paper at 25 francs, 14 on Hollande at 40 francs, 6 on Japon at 60 francs, entirely composed by hand.

Events would prevent *Rivages* from publishing a third issue. It was ready and in type, but it contained a tribute to García Lorca. The poet was considered an opponent of Franco Spain, so the type was confiscated and ordered destroyed after the coming to power of the Vichy regime in 1940.[1] For her part, Jeanne Sicard decided not to publish the full text of Cervantes' *Baños* because of its anti-Jewish content, which in 1940 would have signified running with the hounds.[4] (As will be seen later, the difficulties Charlot was having with his publishing activity in the spring of 1939 were responsible for the long interruption in the publication of *Rivages;* when it might have been possible for the third issue of *Rivages* to be published, war and then Vichy ruled that out.)

Camus was spending more time at the Charlot bookshop. He had of course been dropping in from the time Charlot opened it, thumbing through the new literary magazines (*Nouvelle Revue Française, Commerce, Europe*), the new books, including translations into French of Faulkner, Hemingway, Dos Passos, Kafka, Silone. At first he had signed up as a member of Charlot's rental library, but later he was able to get all the books he wanted free, when he became a reader for Charlot's publishing enterprise. For Editions Charlot was also based in the narrow confines of the Rue Charras bookshop. The ground floor, virtually a corridor fifteen feet wide and thirty deep, was the bookshop proper, Les Vraies Richesses. Over half this space was roofed over for a loggia. Upstairs, over the balustrade, Charlot, his secretary—and sometimes his adviser, Camus—seated at one of the two desks at balcony edge, could observe the bookshop down below. Open from dawn (which Edmond Charlot found was the best time to get his paperwork done) until 10 P.M. or even later, Les Vraies Richesses was not only unique in Algiers but one of the few stores of its kind anywhere; in Paris, Adrienne Monnier ran a similar bookshop cum literary salon on Rue de l'Odéon, as did her American friend Sylvia Beach (whose Shakespeare and Company was an English-language equivalent). Charlot's Les Vraies Richesses also promoted cultural events such as concerts, and served as subscription and ticket office for the Théâtre de l'Equipe.[1] "Towards six in the evening," Max-Pol Fouchet remembered, "we would go to see the latest books published, that we could not always buy, for we were all very broke. Then we'd go off together to drink the traditional anisette in a nearby bistrot. Charlot polarized the intellectual life of Algiers, and he first brought to public attention certain writers such as Emmanuel Roblès, and others."[3]

Camus had soon become Charlot's chief editor, reading manuscripts submitted for publication (for a fee), often at a desk in the loggia. Later, when he became the director of a book series at Charlot's publishing house, he also received a percentage of the royalty on the sale of books in the series. He would go through manuscripts rapidly, dash off reading notes for his *patron* Charlot. These were sharp, uncompromising judgments, but if Camus thought that a book was commercially viable despite its lack of literary value he would not necessarily dismiss it, knowing that Charlot had a balance sheet to worry about.[1] By early 1938, when the first issue of *Rivages* was being planned, Charlot had published, in addition to Camus' *L'Envers et l'Endroit,* works of Audisio, Grenier, Clot, Fouchet, and Fréminville.

It was here, in Charlot's bookshop-publishing office, that Camus met Emmanuel Roblès, six months his junior, born into an Oran working-class family of Spanish origin (his father had been a mason). Roblès' mother, like Camus', was illiterate, and a laundress.[5] From Blida, where he was serving out his two-year military draft obligation beginning in September 1937, Roblès had submitted a first novel entitled *L'Action* to Charlot, who gave it to Camus for advice. Roblès knew Camus by name only, although he had attended performances of the Equipe; a specialist in Spanish history and culture, he had been fascinated by Camus' production of Rojas' *La Celestina*. He arrived early for an appointment with Camus at the Rue Charras shop. Climbing to the loggia floor to wait, he looked over the balcony as Camus entered the shop, to discover "a thin young man with a bony face, with a grave air attenuated by a certain irony in his expression." Camus asked him a few questions about army life. Then he led Roblès to a corner table at the Brasserie des Facultés on nearby Rue Michelet for a discussion of Roblès' manuscript.

Camus directed the conversation immediately to a particular passage of the novel in which the author evoked the attitude toward death of one of his characters. He had marked the passage with a cross. Roblès had been describing a sort of anxiety which could empty life of all meaning, and which each person attempted to exorcise in his own way. "Men pass like the waters of a river," he had written, "and because men are always there one forgets that they are not always the same. . . ." Roblès decided that Camus' curiosity about death, like his own, was a function of a Spanish heritage.[6]

In the end *L'Action* was too big an undertaking for Charlot, whose catalogue was limited to slim volumes in small printings, so Roblès took it to another Algerian publisher-bookseller, Soubiran, which brought it out in 1938.[5] But in the process Roblès and Camus had become friends, henceforth associated in all things Algerian, as Roblès went on to write a body of work, popular novels of Mediterranean life but whose themes were universal, which would see him translated all over the world. In France he would later be elected to the Goncourt Academy prize jury, and Luis Buñuel would make a major film of his *Cela s'appelle l'aurore.*

In the company of this little band of writers, all of them competent and sympathetic critics too, young Camus' own work would now move forward. There would be no more distracting theater work after the May performances of *The Brothers Karamazov,* not before *The Playboy of the Western World* the following spring. From now until the end of September 1938, while its organizers were financing and preparing the ground for the first issue of *Alger Républicain,* Camus would remain at the Institut de Météorologie, which left him many splendid daylight hours to live, and unspent energies for his writing. In these circumstances he could set fires burning under several projects at once.

In June 1938 he listed his summer projects in his journal. Not only would he rewrite his novel but he would work on his first play, *Caligula,* on a book-length essay "L'Absurde" (to become *Le Mythe de Sisyphe*). He would write the "Mediterranean" essays on Florence and Algiers to appear in book form next spring as *Noces,* as well as essays on theater, on the 40-hour work week. This last, which he completed in the fall for submission without success to Jean Giono's *Cahiers de Contadour,* was a socially oriented argument for humane working hours, dedicated to Nietzsche's principle that anyone who does not have two thirds of his day for himself is a slave.[7] "In my family: ten hours of work," he would tell his journal.

There was also to be a light "Impromptu d'été," probably never completed, which, judging from the few lines of it tried out in his journal, would have been a comedy about theatrical art in the tradition of Molière. His notes on *La Mort heureuse* continue to emphasize the artificial construction of that book, e.g., in the character of Zagreus, the wealthy invalid. (For this character Camus had found a model in a retired naval doctor who had lost both legs. He had become fascinated by the invalid's passion for life, his curiosity about art, books, objects, and above all by his intelligence. The real-life Zagreus, who was married, finally died one day when his tropical disease began to spread again; there had been no more to cut off.[8])

Camus was seeing a great deal of a young lady from Oran who was to become his second wife. Actually his first meeting with Francine Faure had been the briefest of encounters, and that years earlier. Francine was then attending a special class in mathematics, her strongest subject, at the Lycée Bugeaud, which was otherwise for boys only. Her friend Liliane Choucroun told her about the extraordinary philosophy course she was following, extraordinary for its professor, René Poirier, but also for one of Poirier's students. So one day Francine walked into Poirier's classroom, remarked Camus seated in the first row alongside a young woman definitely not of the university, if clothes were any indication. Liliane Choucroun introduced Francine to Camus (but probably not to Simone). Later Francine Faure would remember Albert Camus as having light hair and blue eyes, neither of which was true (his eyes were gray-green).

Francine then went to Paris to study math at the Lycée Fénelon, which was considered a reliable steppingstone to the Ecole Normale at Sèvres, the equivalent for women of the prestigious Rue d'Ulm school for male teachers. She would be hearing more about Camus, notably from Marguerite Dobrenn, another girl from Oran (who had been a classmate there of Francine's sister Suzy). In September or October 1937, Francine was in Algiers, after a summer vacation in Oran, to spend ten days at the Maison Fichu. She was immediately taken by that delightful house and above all by the casual life style of the talented people who lived there or passed through, Albert Camus among them. But then she had to return to her school in France.

Not without leaving some of her heart at the Maison Fichu. Camus was also interested in this bright, picture-pretty girl, whom he discovered to be an accomplished pianist as well. They began to write to each other during the school year. In June 1938, at the urging of her friends

(Marguerite, Liliane, but also Albert now), she was back in Algiers. She couldn't stay very long. Her schoolwork in France, preparing for Sèvres, had been too much of a strain. So she went off with her sister Christiane, then teaching French at the Oran lycée, to the French Pyrenees. That fall she made an effort to resume her studies closer to home, at the University of Algiers. But she spent more of that year in Oran than in Algiers, and by April 1939 had taken a job as a substitute teacher of mathematics in her home town.

Snapshot out of the past: One day Camus bursts into Louis Benisti's studio to exclaim: "Today I'm having the adventure of my life. Lend me a shirt and your sandals." (Benisti had made the sandals himself.) Camus disguised himself as a Prince Charming, curled his hair, tinted his toenails in the sandals. A few days later he introduced Francine Faure as his fiancée. But to indicate the particular respect in which he held this young lady from Oran, he would refer to her in speaking to another old friend as *"ma femme."*[9]

This comely girl, now here, now there, was bound to appeal to a Camus who had been taking his women for granted. He had a steady friend at the Maison Fichu, and many less steady ones. Now here was a girl of impeccable (and strict) upbringing, one he'd have to court. Courting was a step toward marriage. Did he want to take that step? Soon he began to speak to close friends of the kind of life described by the writer Eugène Dabit, in which a man could be in love simultaneously with two women, one of them his wife.[10]

Francine Faure's father, Fernand, had been a soldier in a Zouave regiment, like the father of Albert and Lucien Camus. And like Camus' father, Francine's was killed on the Marne, on December 17, 1914. She was born (as Marguerite Fernande Francine Faure) just one week earlier. Fernand's father, Jean Faure, had been a constructor of public works. (They were not related to the Faures of Algiers previously referred to.) In Oran he had built part of the harbor, and he had also put up four successive blocks of arcaded buildings which were collectively known as "Les Arcades"; the building on the Rue d'Arzew where Francine lived with her mother and two sisters was one of these. Francine's mother Fernande (née Albert) had a maternal grandfather who was a Berber Jew, and who married a Turkish Jew. (Later Madame Albert Camus would be able to point out that her Berber-Jewish blood put her among the oldest indigenous inhabitants of Algeria, for the Berbers preceded Arabs on that soil; although the conquering Arabs had tried to convert Berber Christians and Jews to Islam, some continued to exist —even in independent Algeria.)

When Francine Faure's father died in World War I, the Faure women were virtually penniless (Grandfather Jean had declared bankruptcy before his death, son Fernand had been in the process of starting over from scratch when he was caught in the Great War). So that Francine's mother was working in the post office, and she had to put her daughters Christiane, Suzy, and Francine to work as soon as they got out of school (where they had been *pupilles de la nation*).[11]

During one of her trips home to Oran, Francine announced brightly to her mother and older sisters that she wanted to marry a young man whom she had been seeing in Algiers. He was tubercular, she explained, and he had no serious breadwinning occupation. Furthermore, he was not yet divorced from a previous marriage; in fact he believed in a kind of marriage in which husband and wife would each keep his freedom.

The reply was an explosion of laughter. Of the three daughters, petite Francine was by far the most eligible for marriage. With all the suitors who were hovering about, it was hard for her mother and sisters to believe that she had chosen this particular *Algérois* as a fiancé. Examining a photograph of Camus which Francine had produced, sister Christiane observed that with his ears stuck out from his head he resembled a monkey. Francine replied sweetly: "The monkey is the animal closest to man." Later the girls' mother would use another animal metaphor: This lithe and wiry young man, so desperate for his freedom, reminded her of a fennec, the small Algerian desert fox, also with large, pointed ears. (Massive and white-topped Madame Faure made *him* think of Moby Dick.)[12]

Another significant non-literary encounter occurred at this time. In July 1938, Christiane Galindo, Camus' Maison Fichu mate, had him read a letter she had received from her brother Pierre, who was a partner in a grain export business in her home town of Oran. The letter revealed a remarkable personality, someone Camus thought he would like to know. The opportunity would not be long in coming, possibly in Oran, but more likely (for Camus then had no reason to travel to that city) in Algiers, when Galindo visited there with his daughter for medical treatment: She had been scratched by a cat which might have had rabies.[13]

Galindo was a heavy-set man with a large head, a dark complexion, "Spanish black eyes." He never seemed thoroughly shaved. He could remain silent for a quarter of an hour during a conversation. Laconic, phlegmatic, were terms used to describe him. He was built like a fighter, he swam like a fish. Intelligent, he was without culture or the social graces; he had something of the aura of a bad hombre, and he himself enjoyed a tough-guy photograph showing him with a cigar planted in the center of his round face. There were rumors of a mean incident on a beach involving Arabs, the anecdote which was to furnish his new friend Albert with an element of the plot of *L'Etranger*. But he would soon be serving Camus in another way, as a matchmaker, helping to put down the reluctance the Faure women might be entertaining concerning Francine's unlikely suitor. The Galindos knew the Faures, and Pierre Galindo would be able to vouch for Camus as something more than a starving actor whose wife was likely to face a lifetime of traveling theater companies.

Galindo's later activities might be mentioned here out of chronological order in a further effort to define the man: When the Vichy Government controlled Algeria during World War II he threw himself into underground resistance. An officer in the Foreign Legion, where his soldiers were in the main Jewish and Spanish Republican refugees benefiting from the Legion's policy of anonymity, he organized local liaison activities with American forces, took a carload of men with him to capture Oran's La Sénia Airport to facilitate the American landing on Algeria's coast in November 1942. Thereafter he served as a liaison officer with the Americans.[14]

It was said that Camus would have wished to be a fighter like Galindo, instead of the pallid young man he was, who seldom stood sufficiently erect to show his true height. Henceforth he would always be close to Galindo. He would dedicate his long essay "Le Minotaure ou la Halte d'Oran" to him, and at the end of the war he would invite Galindo to share the adventure of *Combat*.

The job at the weather institute continued to provide the technical assistant with time for his own work. Now he completed *La Mort heureuse* as we know it, and although his friends admired the manuscript,[4] he himself was not sure enough about it, in the face of the adverse opinions of the men he had chosen as his masters, to seek to have it published.

In December 1937, then again in May 1938, Camus opened his journal to enter some early notes for what would really be his first novel. "The type who showed so much promise and who now works in an office. . . ." Then "The old woman in the old age home, who dies. . . ." But these beginnings by no means marked the death of *La Mort heureuse* and its replacement by the new project. Further journal entries containing suggestions or new material for *La Mort heureuse* would appear at least until the late summer of 1938. What was actually taking place at this time was the coexistence in the writer's mind of romantic notions distilled in *La Mort heureuse* with material recorded in a new, disabused tone. The Camus of the House Above the World was rapidly giving ground to an adult surer of himself but less sure of the world. It would be pleasant to be able to demonstrate that the change coincided with his change of job, from the weather institute to *Alger Républicain*. The evidence is contradictory. Disillusion with *La Mort heureuse* had certainly taken place before that. Yet it was probably in the first weeks at his newspaper job that he decided that "The true work of art is the one which says less." The relationship between an artist and the work which reflects his experience is bad when the work offers all of this experience surrounded by a coating of literature. It is good when the work of art is carved out of that experience.

Just before a journal entry which is dated December 1938, a brief undated text appears which will become the opening lines of *L'Etranger;* its first paragraph will appear in the book as published:

> Today mother died. Or perhaps yesterday, I don't know. I received a telegram from the old age home. . . .

In June 1938 he had also promised himself to begin a major essay that summer on the Absurd. Notes for it will begin to be jotted down now. One thing that was *not* taking up his time was the Théâtre de l'Equipe, whose volunteer actors had dispersed for the holidays and did not seem eager to reassemble for another season. In August, Camus confided to Jeanne Sicard that he did not have the strength to start over again; despite the happiness the amateur company had given him, he was prepared to give up that luxury.[4]

He did put the final touches to the essays for *Noces* that summer, and turned them over to Charlot, who (again because of personal difficulties) could not publish them until the following spring (on May 23, 1939). Even in August, Camus knew that this little collection of essays on Tipasa, Djémila, Algiers, and Florence was well behind him, closing an earlier and a youthful era, in a sense helping to purge him of that era. He knew, too, that on publication there would be people ready to believe that it marked the *beginning* of a new period.[4]

And, soon enough, with the intensity of experience of his new life in the office of a combative daily newspaper, the world of *Noces* would indeed seem very far behind him.[15]

As if the year 1938 was fated to be a year of significant encounters, Camus was now to be brought face to face with the man who might be the most significant to the adult Camus. Certainly the new friend was to assume the role that Jean Grenier had played in Camus' adolescence and young adulthood; Grenier's departure for France that July was almost a symbol of this change. Pascal Pia, who would be Camus' best friend and worst enemy, characteristically began his association with Camus with an ambiguity. He understood that, as director of the projected Popular Front daily, he was being asked to examine the candidacies of Camus and others,[16] when in fact Camus had already been offered a job, or thought that he had, and had given notice at the Institut de Météorologie prior to Pia's arrival in Algiers in late summer.[17] Camus was to be a reporter, rewriting dispatches, responsible for cultural and art news, working each day from 5 P.M. to 1 A.M. During the summer of 1938 he even planned to visit *Oran Républicain* to inspect its operations, for *Alger Républicain* was to be modeled on the older publication.[4] His new job also allowed him to rent a larger studio apartment, with a terrace.[18]

When Jean-Pierre Faure interviewed Pia in Paris, probably at the suggestion of veteran left-wing journalists Georges Boris and Georges Altman, both then associated with the anti-fascist weekly *La Lumière,* for which Pia had worked, Pia was general news editor on the evening daily *Ce Soir,* disguised as an organ of the Popular Front, but in fact a Communist front, directed by Louis Aragon and Jean-Richard Bloch. (Pia dealt only with non-political news.) Prior to that Pia had spent a couple of years in Lyons working for the important regional daily *Le Progrès,* but his wife had not liked Lyons, so they had moved to Paris. And prior to that, he had worked on the news desk of a number of Parisian newspapers and press agencies, breaking away every time the opportunity arose, for he never had liked newspaper work.

It just happened that from the point of view of the newspapers concerned Pia was probably as good as one could find in France, a newspaperman's newspaperman. He had been born in Paris on August 15, 1901. His grandparents had come from Southern France—Provence or Languedoc, he wasn't sure; they were poor, and poor people like the Pias and the Camus don't have family histories. Like Camus, Pia was a war orphan, his father having been killed in September 1915 on the front just northeast of Paris, for the French and the Germans were still locked in there a year after Camus' father was killed. Pia had begun to work at an early age, and never stopped.[16]

But this is hardly a complete description of this remarkable man. During an adventurous youth he wrote poetry, moved in Parisian literary circles. In the offices of a literary journal in 1920 he met another would-be writer, André Malraux; one of the latter's biographers observed that Malraux's two most important encounters at that period were Pia and Clara Goldschmidt, who would become Malraux's wife. With Pia's "ironic lucidity, his absolute independence of spirit, and a clear taste for mystifying," his broad culture, his astonishing memory, he enchanted Malraux, stimulated his literary curiosity. He published a pastiche journal of Baudelaire (*Années de Bruxelles*), to which Malraux contributed. Years later, he would produce a pastiche of Rimbaud (*La Chasse spirituelle*), which he introduced as a newly discovered manuscript. When he published erotic books in the familiar pink covers of a famous series of children's books, Malraux attended the ensuing trial in the company of their mutual friend Francis Ponge. With Pia, to an extent thanks to Pia, Malraux had become the multifaceted personality we know.[19]

On his return from military service Pia had written a violent text, *P.P.C.* (signifying *"pour prendre congé,"* to take leave), which no one dared publish. He moved from minor job to minor job, living most fully at night, on coffee and cigarettes. With his talent and his erudition he might have done significant things; instead he chose to devote himself to the work of others—Malraux and Aragon, for example, always ready for the minor but necessary tasks bringing no glory.[20] This is the biography of Pascal Pia before he met Albert Camus, but it throws some light on all of their subsequent joint history.

When Pia arrived in Algiers in late August 1938, less than two months from the date of the first issue of *Algier Républicain,* he found a makeshift plant, a dozen linotype machines, an old rotary press which Faure had purchased in France and literally reassembled with his own hands, and some candidate journalists whom Faure rounded up. Had he known how bad it would be, he would never have accepted a job in Algeria.

"See if he can be of any use," Faure said of Camus, introducing him to Pascal Pia. "Among the people I know he seems the most likely to make a newspaperman." Camus indeed seemed a splendid recruit, but Pia didn't have much of a choice. They could not afford to hire anyone away from one of the existing Algiers dailies, and the motley crew the *Alger Républicain* board had managed to round up was discouraging to the professional journalist Pia was. (One old reporter from France arrived smelling of liquor, and they sent him home.)[16]

They had rented a large building in Bab el Oued, on Rue Koechlin, near the main gateway to that working-class neighborhood in central Algiers. Faure got Maurice Girard to design a poster of a shoeshine boy, barefoot and in rags, wearing a fez, running along the street hawking copies of *Alger Républicain.*[21]

All during the summer they had been collecting money, buying equipment, recruiting staff. Now they were ready, and the first issue was scheduled on October 1. But then the director of the *Oran Républicain* printing plant, lent by that sister paper to help set up *Alger Républicain's* presses, and who traveled back and forth between Oran and Algiers twice a week—250 miles each way, working nights in Oran and days in Algiers—died on the road when his automobile hit a tree; the accident was attributed to his fatigue. So the first issue did not appear until October 6.[22]

# 15

♦

## ALGER REPUBLICAIN

> . . . if colonial conquest could ever find an excuse, it
> would be in the extent to which it helps the conquered
> peoples to keep their personalities.
>
> <div align="right">"Misère de la Kabylie" (<i>Actuelles</i>)</div>

Now, alongside the two existing daily newspapers, *La Dépêche Algérienne* (right-wing) and *L'Echo d'Alger* (Radical Socialist, but actually quite conservative, reflecting colonial interests), came a third morning newspaper frankly dedicated to the ideology of the left, its columns
open to the Socialist (even to the Communist) outlook on French and
international affairs. It remained for the staff, consisting largely of ama-
teurs apart from *rédacteur en chef* Pascal Pia, to introduce a specifically
Algerian element, to apply Popular Front ideology to colonial affairs.

The newspaper offices in Bab el Oued were in a rather commonplace building. In the basement with the presses and the composing
room, there was a table for the editor who made up the pages. Administrative and delivery services were on the ground floor. Upstairs were the
offices of the editorial staff.

As a morning paper, *Alger Républicain* was of course printed during the night. Typesetting began between 8 and 9 P.M. Pia had assigned
city news to his young recruit Albert Camus and to another neophyte, a
former Protestant minister in his fifties. They would make the usual
rounds of neighborhood police stations, the security police, law courts,
city council, the legislature when it was in session. This was routine
work, although it could require further and deeper investigation when
there was a news event such as a major crime or trial, even a fire caus-
ing extensive damage. Some days were busier than others. As a full-

time staffer, Camus might begin at four or five in the afternoon, working till about eleven, with breaks for meals. But he would be on call at other times, as when it was necessary to attend a trial or to visit the scene of a crime, accident, or demonstration. Then he returned to his desk, wrote his stories rapidly, turned in his copy around 7 P.M. He would come back to the office an hour or two later to read proofs and to assist Pia with make-up.

Pia observed that the young man was patently not in good health. He often seemed feverish, racked by coughing; sometimes he had boils, and Pia guessed that he ate poorly. Clearly the young man should have been out in the sun rather than be confined to the unhealthy atmosphere of a newspaper office. Camus dressed simply—one could not be a dandy at *Alger Républicain*—in cheap ready-to-wear. And one didn't need a jacket at all in hot weather.[1] Publisher Faure also saw a "casually dressed" Camus, remarked his lively talk, his irony, and comic effects Faure would not later find in his writing.[2]

Camus was paid according to the union scale, but from the low end of the scale.[1] Faure recalled that the figure was some 1,800 to 2,000 francs per month (in mid-1970s francs, equivalent to hardly more than 1,200 to 1,340, or not quite $250 to $270).[2] A staff member not necessarily privy to company secrets guessed that the figure was 3,000 to 4,000 francs—that is, 2,010 to 2,680 1975 francs, or between $400 and $450).[3] Pia estimated that Camus' salary was equivalent to that of a modest white-collar worker or a shopkeeper's assistant. Yet as a mainland Frenchman, Pia found that life was not so cheap as all that in Algiers, except for vegetables, fruit, wine, poor quality lamb. Everything else was more expensive because it had to be shipped from France. Salaries were low because of the availability of cheap indigenous labor.[1]

As on other newspapers, writers for *Alger Républicain* received a byline on stories of significance, representing investigative reporting or other special effort, as well as for reviews in which personal opinion was expressed. Certainly the paper was generous with its bylines; Camus began to see his name in print almost immediately. Pia had told Camus that he could review books if he wished to, but that literary reviewing was not expected of him.[1] The first article signed by Camus, on October 9, in the fourth issue of the daily, was a book review under the heading "Salon de lecture." Camus led off with a statement of principles: His reviews would not be concerned with political dogma, would be faithful to the "living work." His "Salon de lecture" would deal with Aldous Huxley, Sartre (*La Nausée, Le Mur*), Gide's *Les Faux-Monnayeurs* (The Counterfeiters), Jorge Amado, Jean Giraudoux. He would praise Montherlant (for *L'Equinoxe de septembre*) as "one of the three or four great French writers who offer a system of life, which

will appear ridiculous to impotents. . . ." But he would also be able to
give space to friends and fellow Mediterraneans: to Blanche Balain's
book of poetry published by Charlot (*La Sève des jours*), Jean Hytier's
*André Gide,* Edmond Brua's *Les Fables bônoises,* Armand Guibert's
*Oiseau privé.* In these articles Camus had an opportunity, if he wanted
it, to hammer out a doctrine of his own. Writing about Gide, for example, he might say:

> It is through an error of judgment that so much has been said
> about Gide's partisanship. For on the social level his opinion has
> *no* more importance than that of any cultivated, generous, and
> reasonably idealistic Frenchman.[4]

From the beginning there would be the less glamorous aspects of
quotidian journalism. Pia himself spent ten to fifteen hours a day at the
newspaper plant, reread every line of copy including the classified ads
in the composing room, having little confidence in amateur proofreaders. Jean-Pierre Faure was in constant conflict with the printers,
who made no concessions to this dedicated left-wing enterprise, insisting on strict union conditions. The lower-ranking employees in handling
and shipping—Spaniards, Jews, Moslems—were more likely to be co-
operative.[5]

For major news, *Alger Républicain* received dispatches and articles
from *Oran Républicain* and from its correspondents in Paris, since
there was no competition for readership between the two left-wing
dailies. Meanwhile Camus might be assigned to cover an accident such
as the following:

Mortal accident
on Rue Michelet

———

An old woman
is run over
by an auto and dragged
some one hundred
yards

———

She dies in arriving
at the hospital

Of course the story was unsigned. But Camus' friend Marguerite
Dobrenn thought she recognized something of Camus in the last sentence:

> On the scene, several minutes afterwards, only some scattered vege-
> tables, a bunch of grapes on the hood of the car, remained as
> derisory witnesses of this sorrowful accident.

When she asked him about it, he acknowledged that he had written it.[6]

Had Albert Camus done no more than this kind of work for *Alger Républicain,* the experience would hardly have been considered a step up or forward from his previous jobs. For he had written literary criticism before; he had worked for newspapers. But all his previous activity had been voluntary. His theater company, the House of Culture, *Rivages,* his writing could almost be considered the normal production of a university undergraduate, while his breadwinning jobs had been clerical. Camus was just turning twenty-five. For the first time he was engaged in an adult's work. Certainly Pia was treating him as an adult, and by signing his newspaper writings Camus was assuming responsibility he had not known until now.

His first signed news story was headlined "La Spéculation contre les lois sociales" (on October 12), which attempted to demonstrate that the rise in salaries granted by the Popular Front government hadn't created more buying power because prices were rising faster still. He pursued these social and economic themes in subsequent stories. His "Dialogue entre un Président du Conseil et un employé à 1200 F par mois" (on December 3) constituted an indictment of the government's policy on salaries. For now the era of Popular Front rule had ended. Edouard Daladier was in power, Paul Reynaud his Minister of Finance, and the government was dealing with serious social issues by decree. On November 30, 1938, a general strike was called to protest the government's turn to the right, but the government was not moved.[7] For all intents and purposes the right was now in power in France, and left-leaning *Alger Républicain,* created in the hopeful atmosphere of the Popular Front, became an organ of the opposition (and of a much-divided opposition). On the municipal level Camus had an opportunity to settle scores with Augustin Rozis, the mayor who had banned *Révolte dans les Asturies.* In article after article he hammered at the right-wing city administration, took up the cause of municipal employees. In one story, under the headline:

> Pursuing organized workers with his hatred, Mr. Rozis suspends
> and wishes to fire 7 municipal employees

Camus wrote: "I should have summed up my feeling weakly in saying that he is grotesque, illegal, and odious."

Of course Camus was particularly sensitive to the lot of the workingman and his family; the word *misère* appears frequently in his stories, where it is clear that it is not an abstraction. When the mayor fired city employees because of trade union activity, Camus described the consequences to families, adding: "But Mr. Rozis, who has never experienced it, did not know that poverty has no party." And if French Algerian workers could suffer, conditions of the Moslems were worse still, as Camus was able to see during the annual New Year's distribution of couscous to the indigenous poor:

> I don't think that we shall do away with poverty in a day. But I must say that I have never seen a European population as impoverished as this Arab population. . . We must dedicate ourselves to eliminating this disproportion and this excess of poverty. . . .

If Camus was at last coming to grips with the real world, he was also being given an opportunity to work on his own writing. He had been dreaming of this kind of life for so long that he had begun to doubt that he would ever achieve it. But of course in the first weeks of this new job he found it impossible to make good use of his time.[6] Finally he got to work on an essay on Kafka, probably inspired by *The Castle,* which had been published in French only that fall; he would also deal with *The Trial.* He intended to submit the essay, called "L'Espoir et l'Absurde dans Kafka," to the *Nouvelle Revue Française.*[8] When he completed it in early 1939 (probably in February), he gave it to Jacques Heurgon, informing him that although it seemed to him complete in itself he intended it to be part of a longer essay on "Philosophie et roman," which would be an appendix to a still longer work on "L'Absurde," which of course was the early title of *Le Mythe de Sisyphe.*

Heurgon promptly sent the essay on to Bernard Groethuysen, the *NRF*'s acknowledged authority on German (and on Russian) literature and philosophy, a major influence on Malraux, Gide, and the *NRF*'s remarkable editor Jean Paulhan; Groethuysen was also the man primarily responsible for introducing Kafka into France.[9] Groethuysen's reaction was a surprise: He found that Camus took too Christian a view of Kafka, whereas an Old Testament point of view would have been more appropriate. Groethuysen wished that Camus had dealt more with Kafka's symbols, less with philosophy à la Kierkegaard or recently deceased Léon Chestov. Nevertheless he promised to try to place the essay in a magazine (but he did not mention the *Nouvelle Revue Française*). When Heurgon passed on Groethuysen's reactions to Camus, the young writer agreed that they were unexpected and amusing, and he could understand them; Groethuysen had been fair. At last (Camus might have added) he was being judged by those he admired, those who were well established in Paris, at the summit of French letters.[10]

On Christmas Day, 1938, Camus told Christiane Galindo that he had begun to work on "L'Absurde."[8] An entry in his journal at this time seems to concern both *Mythe de Sisyphe* and the novel which was also on his mind now, *L'Etranger*. It begins: "There is only one case in which despair is pure. It is that of a man sentenced to die. . . ." He was also making notes for the third panel of his triptych on the Absurd: the play *Caligula*.

Now, although apparently he had not yet spelled this out to friends (or even to himself in his journal), Camus had developed the strategy which would serve him for all his future writing. On a given theme—for the moment it was the Absurd—he would write, simultaneously, three works in three different genres: a philosophical essay, a novel, a play. *Le Mythe de Sisyphe, L'Etranger,* and *Caligula* were started at approximately the same time, the writing would be carried on simultaneously, and if possible they were even to be published together. He knew that in outlining such a program he was in for years of effort, but this was the way it was going to be.[8] His journal at the end of 1938 lists at the top of his priorities: "Mersault" (presumably not *La Mort heureuse* but the new novel *L'Etranger,* although he would be writing passages of the former in his journal as late as March 1939); *Caligula;* and a special issue of *Rivages* on the theater which would make use of the stagings of Camus' own theater groups. In early 1939 he lists among his projects in order of priority:

> Lecture on the Theater
> Reading about Absurd
> Caligula
> Mersault . . . .

And on May 23, *Noces* was published by Charlot, as a slender volume 4⅜″ by 6⅝″. Perhaps the only review it received in mainland France was the notice in Audisio's OFALAC bulletin (*Nouvelles et Informations d'Algérie*), where it was greeted as "of a quite remarkable density . . . does the greatest honor to Algerian literature and publishing. In it one finds a sensibility and a spirit of meditation which lend a new accent to North African writing." But Camus confessed to Heurgon that he was aware of the book's deficiencies. He had sought to "conclude," something one doesn't do at the age of twenty-five. He would avoid trying to do that the next time. Rereading these essays, which were actually written two years earlier, he was ready to recognize that he had been engaging in combat with shadows, forcing doors that were already open, but in another sense he had written them against himself. One thing he knew now: He *had* to write. And as soon as his newspaper job gave him more time he would attack his major projects.[10]

Meanwhile he was giving a hand to his old friend Fréminville, who was realizing an ambition of his own by becoming a book publisher. During a temporary eclipse of Edmond Charlot's business Camus joined Fréminville in activating a short-lived venture they christened Editions Cafre, taking the first syllable of each of their names, using Fréminville's press set up in an old garage. They printed the books that Charlot himself would have published if he could. They might have published *Noces* as well, but Camus had promised his book to Charlot, even though Charlot would have to delay publication for six months. When he was able to publish again, he simply took over distribution of the Camus-Fréminville books. It was probably during this troubled period in Charlot's business life that the *Rivages* editorial board was dissolved and an alternative publication was planned, which would have been called *Cahiers de l'Equipe.* But before Camus had taken any concrete steps to produce such a magazine, the war crisis, not to speak of the crisis of *Alger Républicain,* made any such venture impossible.[11]

Soon after the beginning of his professional career in journalism, the size and quality of *Alger Républicain*'s staff being what it was, Camus would be doing the kind of reporting that is usually assigned to veteran newsmen: the coverage of major criminal trials, the investigation of political and social problems. These were often, but not always, bylined articles.[12] That Camus was already aware of his rapidly acquired expertise is suggested by his comment after a meeting of the shareholders of *Alger Républicain,* during which a woman reporter mentioned in passing that she and one other reporter in the room were "the only professional journalists present." Afterwards Camus said to a friend in a loud sotto voice: "She has a lot of nerve. What am I supposed to be?"[3]

The first important trial which Camus was to cover with signed articles was the complicated Hodent affair, made even more complicated by the capability of local colonial authorities not only to enforce frontier justice but to suppress news of it. In this particular case Camus was dealing with a matter which even the newspaper located in the town where the trial was held had failed to report. Michel Hodent, attached to a public food distribution agency, had been arrested on the complaint of a wealthy planter in the region of Tiaret, charged with the theft of wheat, with another French Algerian and six Moslems as his alleged accomplices. The charge was immediately seen by progressive forces as a frame-up, an attempt by colonial authorities, planters, and even local Moslem leaders to discredit an agency born of the Popular

Front. Hodent had written to *Alger Républicain:* "I've been abandoned in a jail for months." But by the time Camus had published an open letter to the Governor of Algeria in *Alger Républicain* on January 10, 1939, Hodent had been released pending trial. Camus began his investigation from Algiers, exposing the nature of colonial justice in a series of pretrial articles. Pia sent Camus to Tiaret, an agricultural center perched on a mountain slope, 135 miles southeast of Oran, where he began an investigation on the scene prior to the trial, which opened on March 20. In the preliminary articles, then in his courtroom reporting, Camus exposed methods used to obtain false testimony, the bias of the judge, making it clear that he and his newspaper felt Hodent to be entirely innocent. In the process *Alger Républicain* created a *cause célèbre,* and a verdict was rendered which might not have been possible otherwise. On March 23, Camus was able to report it under a headline: "The innocence of Hodent and of the warehouse clerk Mas finally triumphed."[13]

Apparently the reporter had been able to take some time off while in Tiaret, for his journal at this time contains vivid impressions of the region of Oran and the bay of Mers-el-Kébir. In Tiaret, Camus found himself in the company of some bored schoolteachers who explained to him their remedy for boredom: to get drunk and to go to the bordel. So he describes a visit in their company to the bordel. "Outside again, still snow. Through a clearing you could see the countryside. Still the same desolate stretch, but white this time."

The El Okbi affair was more complicated still. On August 2, 1926, the Grand Mufti of Algiers, the principal religious leader of the city, was assassinated near the Kasbah. The killing took place in the context of Popular Front effervescence, the growing progressive movement among Moslem intellectuals led by the ulemas, the religious chiefs. The Grand Mufti was on the side of the colonial administration and the conservative settlers, as he proved by a telegram he sent to the French Government denouncing Moslem reformists and specifically Sheikh Taïeb El Okbi. Both reformists and conservatives called rallies for the same day, August 2, to issue conflicting demands—Popular Front-inspired reforms for the former, maintenance of the status quo for the latter. The Grand Mufti was killed at the very hour set for the meetings. Two leaders of the reformist Cercle du Progrès, Sheikh El Okbi and Abbas Turqui, were arrested and brought to trial nearly three years later.[13] By this time *Alger Républicain* had been founded, investigative reporter Camus was available. His reports in *Alger Républicain* highlighted the weakness of the prosecution case. The headlines tell part of the story:

In three years Inspector CHENNOUF
has not learned much
about the killing of the MUPHTI
but in revenge he forgot a great deal

———

Several European and Moslem personalities appeared yesterday to
express with warm their conviction as to the innocence of Sheikh
El Okbi and Mr. Abbas Turqui
(June 25, 1939)

The prosecutor gives up the unreasonable accusation against Sheikh
EL OKBI and Abbas Turqui.
(June 27)

The criminal court, recognizing the innocence of Sheikh el OKBI
and Abbas Turqui, has acquitted them
(June 29)

Summarizing the testimony in his June 25 story, Camus wrote:

> None of his witnesses heard the Sheikh pronounce a word of
> hatred or insult toward anybody. His doctrine repudiated the use of
> violence, in which he saw an element of weakness. Could it be oth-
> erwise on the part of a man who has always preached love and
> brotherhood? The French idea, further, has always found in him
> the most intelligent and most ardent of supporters.

Good liberal that he was, Camus could only believe that El Okbi
was innocent of this terrorist act. Although he identified himself with
the plight of Algeria's Moslems, he did not know, he could not know,
the true nature of the nationalist struggle of that time; he did not have
sufficient entry into the Moslem community for that. For truth may
be that El Okbi was guilty after all, that he had recruited an assassin to
kill the Grand Mufti. According to this theory the authorities, convinced that El Okbi was behind the killing but lacking proof, had simply arrested an innocent man and had him testify that El Okbi had in-
stigated the killing; when this accuser's story was dismantled, El Okbi
was acquitted.

This turn-about version of the El Okbi affair was first brought to
public attention in 1970 by Mohamed Lebjaoui, former head of the
French Section of the Algerian insurrectionary movement FLN (for
Front de Libération Nationale). Lebjaoui observed that El Okbi's triumphal court victory paradoxically marked the end of his career as a
national leader, since the assassination of the Grand Mufti had not led
to a general uprising, while El Okbi's supporters were frightened into
inactivity by his arrest.[14] Fellow FLN nationalist Amar Ouzegane, in his
own revelations about the affair, did not agree that El Okbi had the

Grand Mufti killed in order to provoke hostility and an uprising among Moslems, for El Okbi was reformist and pro-French, an instrument (if an unwitting one) of French policy. And he also felt that, by obliging the government to back down by releasing El Okbi, Camus participated in a just anti-colonialist combat, and was therefore not a dupe.[15]

The affair of the incendiaries of Auribeau was a lost cause. In September 1937 ten agricultural workers were arrested for having set fire to straw huts—called "edifices" in the accusation—and were sentenced to five to seven years at hard labor; *Alger Républicain* took up the case on appeal in July 1939. Reporter Camus insisted on their innocence, revealed the use of torture to obtain confessions. "No free man is assured of his dignity faced with such procedures," he warned.

> And when abject methods succeed in leading to the penal colony unhappy men whose life had already been only a series of miseries, then it represents for each of us a kind of personal injury that it is impossible to accept.

Camus demanded that those responsible for the torturing be prosecuted, that a spotlight be played on the agricultural wage system. And when the appeals court sent the case back for a new trial, Camus retorted that the conventional phrase which preceded the decision, "In the name of the French people," was a lie.[13]

However useful frank reporting may have been in the Algerian context —and it did help free some innocent men—surely Camus' inquiry into economic and social conditions in the mountainous Berber territories was of even greater significance.

In *L'Echo d'Alger,* a correspondent had described the delights of Kabylie.[16] Only a couple of days after Charlot's publication of *Noces* in May, Pia dispatched Camus to bring back a more realistic account of the situation in that deprived region. Camus' illustrated reports, published under the banner headline "Misère de la Kabylie," began to appear in *Alger Républicain* on June 5. The first was headed: "Greece in Rags," with this subtitle: "Let war come. They'll give us enough to eat . . ." Camus' articles continued to appear over the following ten days, providing a graphic description of a degree of poverty which was unknown to most urban readers of the newspaper. (A partial text of his report was reprinted nearly two decades later in *Actuelles III,* subtitled *Chroniques algériennes,* representing his response to critics who felt that he had not spoken out on contemporary Algeria.)

Here was an overpopulated region which had to import wheat but had no way to pay for it; its best lands had long ago been taken over by French settlers. Only charity allowed Kabylie to survive. Camus piled

up facts and figures, described the nature and quantity of food available, the nature and inadequacy of the school system. His survey was
clearly the product of legwork, of talking to rank-and-file victims of the
colonial system. As in his courtroom reporting, he used the first person,
expressed his personal indignation; for the first time he had a major
subject worthy of him. As when, with a Kabylie friend, he climbed a hill
dominating Tizi-Ouzou:

> There, we watched night fall. And at that hour when the shadow
> which descends from the mountains to this splendid earth brings
> rest to the heart of the most hardened man, I knew nevertheless
> that there was no peace for those who, on the other side of the val-
> ley, were gathered around a biscuit of inferior barley. I also knew
> how sweet it would have been to abandon oneself to an evening so
> surprising and so magnificent, but that the misery represented by
> the fires on the opposite hill placed a kind of ban on the beauty of
> the world.
> "Let's go down, shall we?" my companion said.

Is it to be a bad Frenchman to expose poverty in a French territory? he
asks in his final article. France cannot be better represented than by
acts of justice, he replies.

> For if colonial conquest could ever find an excuse, it would be in
> the extent to which it helps the conquered peoples to keep their
> personalities.

If the bellicose campaigns of *Alger Républicain* were clearly upsetting to the Government General, they did not help to increase its circulation; for most *Algérois, Alger Républicain* remained a complementary
newspaper, which they might buy in addition to one of the two major
dailies. Even the paper's shareholders, at least the rank-and-file of
them, must have been alarmed by their paper's iconoclasm. Did the
paper's strong stand in favor of Moslem freedoms win it the custom of
that population? Clearly not; Pia decided that Moslems felt they were
being made fun of by *Alger Républicain*'s use of "Monsieur," which
was not usually applied to a native. Those Moslems who did buy a daily
preferred the more conservative of the two competitors, *La Dépêche
Algérienne*. Advertisers were reluctant to associate their names with
the left-wing daily; even movie houses advertised only when the nature
of the film prevented it from being mentioned in the virtuous
*Dépêche*.[17]

Of course there was space in *Alger Républicain* to report the cultural activity of Camus and his friends. He did not deprive himself of
the opportunity to publicize the first issue of *Rivages,* and he would also
reprint the manifesto of the Théâtre de l'Equipe. New issues of his
friends the Raffis' magazine *La Revue Algérienne* were announced in its

columns. Indeed, two issues of that magazine, which was largely devoted to the arts, contained contributions by Camus in 1939. In January, *La Revue Algérienne* published Camus' "Historie vraie," a little-known prose poem less than four hundred words in length, a touching observation on the changing of the seasons; it begins: "In January, the almond trees blossom." The same issue led off with an article on Goya by José Bergamín, the Spanish philosopher-essayist, translated by Jeanne Sicard, and also contained an article by Pierre-André Emery on local farmhouses called, presumably because of the origins of their builder-owners, Maisons Mahonnaises (i.e., of Mahón in Minorca). For the February issue Camus contributed "Chronique du Jeune Alger," which appeared with only slight changes as an appendix to "L'Eté à Alger," published in *Noces* later that year; one reader was reminded of the "Chronique du Vieil Alger," which appeared regularly in *La Dépêche Algérienne*.[18] The same issue of *La Revue Algérienne* announced the forthcoming production of the Equipe's *Playboy of the Western World*.

For the Théâtre de l'Equipe was back in business with what was to be (although its ever-eager organizers did not know it) the last production; the political uncertainty of those last prewar months, then the outbreak of war, would be its final curtain despite sporadic attempts to revive it. Even to bring the cast together for this last effort proved difficult, and Camus appealed for volunteers both in *Alger Républicain* and in *Rivages*. In the days preceding the two performances on March 31 and April 2, 1939, readers of *Alger Républicain* (at least) were not permitted to ignore the forthcoming event. For those who did not read the newspaper there was a poster in bold red and black type:

Théâtre de l'Equipe
Théâtre d'Etude
de la Revue "RIVAGES"
Vendredi 31 Mars, à 21 heures
Dimanche 2 Avril, à 16 heures

Salle Pierre Bordes

Le Baladin
du Monde
Occidental

Farce cynique en 3 actes
de John Millington Synge
Le chef-d'oeuvre de la littérature dramatique Irlandaise

Places à 8 Francs, 12.50 et 15.50
Location   Aux Vraies Richesses, 2 bis, Rue Charras
A l'Oeuvre Moderne, Place Bugeaud
Réduction de 15% aux Amis de l'Equipe

Rehearsals were held on Sunday mornings in the studio of the painter Armand Assus, two of whose children were in the troupe. The apartment, on the top floor of a building on Place Bresson, possessed a terrace facing the boulevard, the harbor, the bay beyond. Here Camus introduced a young lady from Oran to his friends; she had a smile for everybody. And of course Francine was trying out for a part in their company. When the time came for her to speak her part, Camus fixed his gaze on her, a gaze in which a friend noted both tenderness and a "gently condescending recognition of the beginning actress."[19]

Naturally Camus himself played Christy Mahon, the young man who claims to have killed his father. (The first performance took place only a week after his final article on the Hodent trial and just before the publication of a series of reports on discrimination against North Africans in France in social security benefits.) As usual, Emery and Miquel designed the scenery. The review in *La Revue Algérienne* was mildly critical: "An occasionally defective diction, and the acoustics of an auditorium designed to discourage the best wills did not allow the spectators to appreciate the rare quality of the translation." Yet if the Equipe had done nothing more than to reveal this masterpiece in French it would have the right to our entire gratitude, the critic went on: "But the attentive presence of a faithful public proved that the experiment of a young, vital and independent theater was worth trying."[20] This article was followed by a listing of future productions, all scheduled for the period following the outbreak of World War II:

November 3: *Le Coup de Trafalgar,* by Roger Vitrac;
December 29: *La Condition humaine,* an adaptation [that Camus would have done] of Malraux's novel; or *La Locandiera* by Goldoni;
Early March 1940: *Hamlet,* in the Jacques Copeau translation;
Early May: A play by Aristophanes [no title given], in a new translation making use of familiar speech.

To avoid an overly eulogistic review in *Alger Républicain,* Camus asked Jacques Heurgon if he would be willing to write it. In theory Camus himself was supposed to review plays in the newspaper, but decency forbade it this time, and Pia had asked him to find a friend to do it. Naturally, Camus told Heurgon, he could say whatever he liked—as long as he got the article in Saturday night. Heurgon declined.[10]

Camus was able to exercise his theatrical experience some weeks later in a review of the efforts of another amateur theater company, the Groupe Théâtral Universitaire, which on May 20 put on Jean Cocteau's *La Machine infernale* at the Salle Pierre Bordes. The critic had an opportunity to remind fellow-*Algérois* that there was more than boulevard comedy to the theater. But his favorable disposition did not inhibit him from examining this amateur production with a theater man's eye. He regretted the absence of direction; after further technical advice he reminded his readers that the hall was unfair to the young actors because of its acoustics and extravagant dimensions.

> In any case these criticisms must be taken for what they are, a manifestation of esteem. And one must congratulate the Group for proving that neither money nor fame is necessary to love and to serve the Theater.

In the same issue of *Alger Républicain* (May 23, 1939), Camus was to review the French translation of *Bread and Wine,* by his future friend, the Italian anti-Fascist Ignazio Silone. In this book Camus saw a true revolutionary work, which he defined as one which brings to the surface the most anguishing of the revolutionary's doubts: Silone's hero had wondered "if the theories through which he had travestied the love that he felt for this people did not in fact separate him from this people," which Camus could take as justification for the distance he had taken from the Communists. And there was no revolutionary work without artistic quality, no middle ground between what Malraux called "the will to prove" and Malraux's *La Condition humaine.*

One day Camus called on Emmanuel Roblès in the small furnished room—once the hotel's bathroom—which he rented in downtown Algiers to do his writing when he was on leave from the Army. He asked Roblés to write a twice-weekly column in which he would report his experiences in working-class neighborhoods. Camus also asked Roblès to write a novel to be serialized in *Le Soir Républicain,* the afternoon edition of *Alger Républicain,* which would eventually replace it, and, sitting in his converted bathroom, the indefatigable Roblès produced *Place Mahon* (it would later be published in book form as *La Vallée du Paradis*). For his contributions to *Alger Républicain*—as a soldier he could not use his own name—Roblès signed Emmanuel Chênes (French for oak trees; his real name meant oak trees in Spanish). He also used the pen name Pétrone, which would later be attributed to Camus.[16]

Roblès also remembered having joined a group of *Alger Républicain* editors in composing a crime serial, "Le Mystère de la rue Michelet," each writer in turn to produce an installment. One of the writers killed off a character named Gilberte, but the others didn't pay attention to her disappearance, and Gilberte was put back in to the story in subsequent installments. Protest letters arrived at the newspaper office. Roblès, then a secretary at the General Staff, was not loved by his superiors. Camus phoned his office and spoke to a sergeant:

"*Alger Républicain* here. Would you kindly ask Private Roblès if he read the paper and if he has anything to say about the murder of Madame Gilberte?" Roblès took the phone to swear that "he hadn't done it," that he had a clear conscience. When he hung up he faced the stares of all the officers in what he described as the silence of a court-martial.[21]

On his return from the Spanish Civil War, where he had been wounded, Robert Namia went to work for *Alger Républicain,* joining Camus, after all the copy was in, to meet old friends at the Brasserie des Facultés, then to return to the paper until press time. One day Camus gave him the manuscript of *Caligula* to read. Another time, Namia was sent to cover a fishermen's strike. He spent five days aboard trawling vessels and turned in what would be his first major series of articles. When Camus read them he said that he'd try to publish them not in *Alger Républicain* but in *Rivages.*[22]

Other candid snapshots of Camus at the paper come from staff members who had even briefer encounters with him. Thus Laurent Preziosi, an Algiers elementary school teacher who had been suspended from his job for taking part in a strike, was hired by *Alger Républicain* and worked there for six months until he was reintegrated into the school system. Preziosi was responsible for rewriting press agency dispatches. But he had other duties as well. Each night, publisher Faure would leave him a sealed envelope containing an order for the number of copies to be printed. Preziosi would take the envelope to the basement and hand it to the printers. Then he was responsible for supervising the loading of copies of the paper on waiting trucks.

Although he observed that the workers admired Camus, he also knew that most of them were Communists. Preziosi himself belonged to the left-revolutionary party founded by Marceau Pivert called the Parti Socialiste Ouvrier et Paysan (PSOP), which was a *bête noire* of the Communists. Pivert, a friend of Preziosi, would send him copies of the party organ to distribute. One evening Preziosi walked into the composing room and started to hand out copies of the PSOP newspaper. He gave one to a member of the Socialist Party (SFIO), a secretary of the CGT, who was making up the special page of union news which *Alger Républicain* published regularly. The man threw the copy to the floor ostentatiously.

Camus, who was working at his make-up table in the same room, asked for a copy of Preziosi's paper. After looking it over he said in a loud voice that he would like to subscribe to it. Preziosi gave him a form to fill out and Camus completed it then and there. Preziosi attributed the gesture to Camus' absolute respect for free expression.[3]

# 16

---◆---

## SEPTEMBER 1939

War has broken out. Where is the war? Aside from the
news reports one must believe and the posters one must
read, where find signs of the absurd event? It is not in this
blue sky on the blue sea, in the crisp song of the cicadas,
in the cypress trees on the hills. . . .

*Carnets*

At times the world—which then meant Europe—could seem even further away from the North African coast than it really was. Necessarily
the causes taken up by *Alger Républicain* were local causes, and the
terrifying events then occurring in Europe were received here as
through a muffler.

The true state of affairs was something else again. Algeria belonged
to France, France was one of the front-line European nations, soon to
be a battlefield again. If nothing else Algeria would supply a considerable number of foot soldiers for the next war. Colonial government
being what it was, sacrifices not only of material but of personal freedom were often greater here than in mainland France. In July 1939, for
example, weeks before the outbreak of war, the Government General
had already banned both Messali Hadj's Parti du Peuple Algérien and
the Algerian Communist Party, while in France the Communist Party
would be banned only after war was declared. Algeria was being run
more as a military district than as a part of democratic France. In *Alger
Républicain,* Albert Camus would protest prosecution of the PPA in
these prophetic terms (August 18, 1939):

It is surprising to see the blindness of those who prosecute these
men, for every time that the PPA has been attacked, its prestige has

grown a little more. The rise of Algerian nationalism is accomplished by the persecutions carried out against it. And I can say without paradox that the immense and deep credit that this party obtains from the masses today is entirely the work of high officials of this country. The only way to stop Algerian nationalism is to get rid of the injustice which gives birth to it.

Even France's Popular Front lost something in traveling south. But to many socially concerned Frenchmen on both sides of the Mediterranean, the Popular Front had by now lost much of its significance. Perhaps it had never really existed, if by that term is meant a genuine Socialist-Communist alliance. For the Communists had never participated in the Blum government, although the Party might support it in Parliament. And then the Blum cabinet, however worthy of praise for its social reforms, a French "New Deal" including social security, the forty-hour week, paid vacations, representing the first humane approach to the working class since the Industrial Revolution, had lost all credit in international affairs, at least as far as a considerable part of its electorate was concerned, by its refusal to come to the aid of Spain's besieged but legitimate Republican government—its natural ally—even when that government appealed to Blum for aid.

But Blum was out of power, Daladier was in, when the Frontist *Alger Républicain* was founded in October 1938. Only the week before the first issue was published, Prime Minister Daladier had been in Munich to sign, with Chamberlain, Hitler, and Mussolini, but not with the Czechs, the pact which allowed Hitler to enter Czechoslovakia and in fact justified all ensuing seizures of territory.

Following Albert Camus and his friends through this period may seem like a bad movie: insouciant romantics living on the edge of a volcano, or party-going on the eve of an earthquake. For despite the evident brutality of the Government General, Algeria was far from the firing lines.

In July 1939, for example, Camus was still convinced that there was a future. With Francine Faure he had begun to plan what was to have been his first voyage to Greece. Fatigued by his relentless round of court and police reporting, his long nights at the newspaper office, he was looking forward to the three-day sea journey from Algeria to Greece, to the days and nights of silence.[1] On his return from a visit to Francine in Oran, still excited by planning for the trip, he telephoned to urge her to buy a knapsack; the realistic side of him remembered that they would be roughing it in Greece.[2] The unrealistic side was deep in a rereading of the Greek classics, chiefly of its myths and legends; all but one of his notebook entries for August dealt with ancient Greece.

He also realized that going to Greece with this proper girl meant that marriage was in the cards, so he set about negotiating the divorce that he had not yet obtained from Simone Hié.

While he continued to work whenever he could at a plain wood kitchen table at the Maison Fichu, in the company (at least) of the cats Cali and Gula, it hardly seemed to matter where he slept at night. There was a succession of small bachelor flats, but every time the opportunity presented itself he would accept the loan of a friend's more comfortable apartment. In August he gave up the last of his studio apartments to return to live in his mother's on Rue de Lyon prior to his departure for Greece,[3] and when he didn't go to Greece he got the keys to a small flat furnished by Edmond Charlot, but which Charlot was giving up to go into the Army at the outbreak of war. (When Charlot was drafted in September, the bookshop was carried on by his wife, and Camus would come into the bookshop to give advice on ordering new books. On Charlot's return Camus began to read manuscripts for him again, and received reading fees which were paid to Camus' mother or to Francine when Camus was in France.[4])

What he was doing at the Maison Fichu table, in the succession of bachelor flats and loaned apartments, perhaps too in Charlot's bookshop loggia and in one or two of the quieter cafés, was to work virtually simultaneously on the three "absurds," L'Etranger, Mythe de Sisyphe, and Caligula. Deep into the manuscript of the novel now, he told Christiane Galindo at the end of July 1939 that the three books together would constitute the first stage of what he was not afraid to call his oeuvre. At that moment he was devoting himself entirely to Caligula, presumably during a fortnight's vacation from his newspaper job, swimming the rest of the time. By July 25, 1939, he was able to report that he had completed the first draft of the play. (Camus would later remember that he wrote the play in 1938.) As unsatisfactory as he felt it to be—for he attached great importance to its success—he set about to recopy it by hand so that Christiane could retype it. But then he reread it and decided that he was not quite ready to hand it over to this faithful volunteer typist. He continued to work on it in August, simplifying, reinforcing what he called its transparency—but also its bitterness. He felt that it was a rather faithful reflection of himself. Then the war caught him in Algiers, and he hesitated to send it to Christiane by mail, fearing that the censors would not be able to decipher his handwriting and would decide that it was a letter from Stalin to Hitler; by now the Caligula manuscript seemed too precious to be risked that way.[5]

In fact the play would be rewritten again, and retyped, by Christiane in 1942. It would be revised again and again for successive editions and performances, each time reflecting the author's present profile, the events of his life but also of his country and the world. The "definitive" *Caligula* might be that of 1958, but perhaps only premature death prevented the appearance of a final version.

The absurd in *Caligula* could be exaggerated, travestied. The raw materials of the story, the story of Gaius Caesar (A.D. 12–41) and the legends reported by Suetonius, of this capricious, arbitrary emperor who played cat and mouse with his courtesans, could be shaped by a modern author to fit his conception of the absurd here and now. But the novel that was to be the second panel of the triptych (the second, at least, in order of writing) was to use the materials of the here and now, and the style would have to be a contemporary style. In fact it would come from the modern American novel, the tough-guy school of Hemingway, Steinbeck, Caldwell, James M. Cain. In choosing this form Camus was also settling the fate of the aborted draft novel *La Mort heureuse* more finally than any of his friendly mentors had done.

But how much of *L'Etranger* is simply the hot beaches of Algiers and of Oran of that summer? The contact with rough-talking, plain-speaking, tough-acting little Pierre Galindo, at once a Meursault and a Raymond? Surely a novel that was at one time to be called *L'Indifférent,* as Camus informed Roblès, could apply to a Galindo. (It was sometime during the 1938–39 winter that Roblès walked into Charlot's Vraies Richesses to borrow books from the lending library and saw Camus upstairs, writing at the balcony desk; they went out for a drink at the Brasserie des Facultés and it was then that Camus told him about the novel he was writing.[6])

It is said that while Camus was seated in a café one day with Louis Benisti, the painter Sauveur Galliero, a somewhat nonchalant minor artist of bohemian habits, came up to say hello. Knowing that Galliero's mother had just died, they commiserated with him. Galliero told them that after he had buried his mother he had gone to the movies with his woman. Camus told Benisti: "Now I have the second panel for *L'Etranger.*"[7]

If Camus really said that, then he may have considered an episode involving Galindo as the first panel. The Galindos had rented a villa with another couple on the beach at Bouisseville, some six miles from Oran. The friend's wife had been accosted by an Arab; the friend interposed himself; in the ensuing fight he received a knife wound on the mouth. He returned to the villa to pick up Galindo and his revolver and they went back to look for the Arab. They found him, but apparently no shot was fired.[8] A frequent enough incident on the beaches in those times, a resident at that time and place has said.

Of course *L'Etranger* would not be "about" Galindo or "about" Galliero, and not entirely "about" the death sentence Meursault will receive for killing an Arab, for that (in the social and political climate of Algeria) was hardly the book's most realistic element. (Camus' stranger, tried for the inadequately motivated shooting of the Arab after a minor incident on a beach, is really sentenced to death because he seems indifferent to things that are supposed to matter, but he will not pretend that they matter.) Camus himself noted in his journal that there are three people in *L'Etranger:* Pierre Galindo, Pierre's sister Christiane, and himself. The novel is "about" absurdity. When Camus sent the manuscript to Jean Grenier, Grenier found Kafka in it, but Camus replied that he hadn't needed Kafka; at *Alger Républicain* he'd been having plenty of experience with the courts. Camus' hero seemed undefined, hardly more than a shadow, but the author made it a point to put a higher value on this character than his readers tended to do; he wrote in a preface to an American edition of the novel, evoking an earlier summary of the book he had attempted: "In our society any man who doesn't cry at his mother's funeral risks being sentenced to death."

Meursault refuses to play the game, refuses to lie. Far from being deprived of all sensibility, he is animated by deep passion for the absolute and for truth. On the whole, Grenier had been more negative about this book than he had been about any of Camus' more conventional efforts. He would have had to work alongside Camus at the newspaper office, to share his fight with the public powers, and the world, to understand Camus' hero—or even to understand the Camus of 1939–40. For the first time Grenier had been distanced by his student. This time the young man did not put the manuscript in a drawer as he had done with *La Mort heureuse.* He was confident enough now to go it alone.[9]

But this is to anticipate. Camus would be writing *L'Etranger* in Algiers through that summer, fall, and winter, and in Paris during early spring 1940, where at last it was completed. The third panel of this triptych, *Le Mythe de Sisyphe,* would take a little while longer.

All of the contradictions of Camus' position seemed to come to the surface with the declaration of war on September 3, 1939. The Communist Party was then opposed to the war, for the Soviet Union had just agreed to a division of Poland with Hitler Germany, which Stalin thought would keep the U.S.S.R. out of the war while his new ally Hitler was free to attack the Western states. But of course Camus' attitude was not inspired by the Party. And if he was non-violent, he was not really a doctrinaire pacifist either, so when his brother and all his friends were called up for military duty, he tried to enlist despite his health deferment. He returned from the recruiting office totally depressed, having been rejected once more.[10] The incident is dramatized in his journal: "But this little one is very sick," the lieutenant said. "We can't take him." And Camus added to that: "I'm 26, alive, and I know what I want."

He had sought to enlist, he told Grenier, not because he accepted the war, but so as not to use illness as a shield, and also to express solidarity with those who were being called up to fight. Far from having accepted the war, he broke with his friends (such as the Dechezelles) over what they felt was his pro-Munich Pact attitude. On the day of the declaration of war he had lunch with Jaussaud and Emery at a Rue Michelet bistrot. Camus and Jaussaud argued heatedly about the meaning of the event. Camus opposed what he considered an absurd war which would be fought for the wrong reasons, while Jaussaud countered that it was clearly an anti-Fascist war. For a long time after that Jaussaud and Camus would not speak to each other.[11] Camus' bitterness can be surmised from an entry in his journal that might have been written after an argument like that:

> All have betrayed, those who urged resistance and those who spoke of peace. They are there, as docile and guiltier than the others. And never has the individual been more alone in the face of the lie-making machine. He can still scorn, and use scorn as a weapon. If he doesn't have the right to scorn from afar, he does retain the right to judge. . . .

"The reign of the beasts has begun," he would conclude a journal entry on September 7. And the next one begins: "This hate and this violence that one already begins to feel rising in everyone. No longer anything pure in them. . . . One meets only beasts, bestial faces of Europeans. . . ."

The war was also to signify the beginning of the end for *Alger Républicain*. As early as July strict military censorship had been decreed, prompting the expected reaction from those individualistic editors Pia and Camus. Indeed, their anarchistic tendencies were similar, which is certainly why they worked so well together at the time. Both agreed that the Munich Pact was absurd, just as the *casus belli* had been absurd (why go to war for Poland when we didn't do it for Czechoslovakia, or for Spain?). Their skepticism, their outspoken dissent, had to cause difficulties with the censors. But also with a considerable part of their readership, and apparently with their own board of directors—or what the war had left of it.[12]

For the man who had held that shaky enterprise together—who had been largely responsible for putting it together in the first place—was himself off to war. At the time of the general call-up Jean-Pierre Faure could have obtained an exemption to stay on at *Alger Républi-*

*cain,* but he felt that his place was at the front, and in any case he realized that a newspaper with *Alger Républicain*'s political orientation
would no longer be able to hold onto its freedom. As a reserve officer
he joined his corps, was sent to Tunisia.[13]

Things had been bad for the newspaper; now they became disastrous. Advertising was down, contributions were no longer coming in
from shareholders. Salaries were paid, but late, and employees who left
for the Army were not replaced. Pia himself was seldom paid from then
on.

Not only was the censorship stricter than in mainland France, but
there was less recourse against it than a newspaperman would have had
in Paris, for against the Government General there was no appeal. An
Army officer came in daily to read proofs, and he might even censor stories based on news heard on the radio—the paper was using such news
when its cable dispatches were held up. The censors did not want the
paper to be published with blank space, so readers would not realize
that the newspaper had been censored, but Pia refused to comply with
that. One day when a censor complained that the paper was going to
contain almost nothing but blank space, Pia and Camus offered to let
the officer write and sign an article to fill it, but of course that offer was
declined. It was then that Pia and Camus decided to play tricks on the
censors, provoking them with unidentified classical quotations actually
written by Pascal, Corneille, Diderot, Hugo.

Meanwhile the war was making printing and distribution more
costly, and *Alger Républicain* lost readership beyond the city limits. Pia
decided to publish a two-page afternoon paper which could be sold by
street hawkers.[12] Thus was founded *Le Soir Republicain,* on September
15, which would coexist with *Alger Républicain* until October 28, when
the latter was shut down because of the scarcity of newsprint. Requiring
less of a staff—Camus would be editor in chief—consuming less paper,
it would be a pure journal of opinion, and Pia and Camus, twin
mischief-makers, had soon turned it into an anarchist organ.[14]

Indeed, both *Alger Républicain* and *Le Soir Républicain* had become, at least for the editors' sympathizers, more of a daily entertainment than a source of information, and there is an abundance of entertaining anecdotes about those desperate weeks. Baiting the censor:
"When a man is on a horse, the horse is always the more intelligent of
the two" was one of the thoughts for the day (attributed to André
Maurois). Or "Men are judged by the use they make of their power. It
is remarkable that inferior souls always have a tendency to abuse the
morsels of power that chance or stupidity has given them." (This one
was signed "Caligula.") Emmanuel Roblès, still a simple private in the
Army, escaped to the newspaper office in civilian dress every time he

could to enjoy the spectacle. *"Messieurs,"* Camus would say to the military censors, whom he had confined to a corner of the office, "it's by Montaigne. The name was omitted. Shall we strike it out?" Once the slogan *"Le Soir Républicain* is not a newspaper like the others; it always gives you something to read" remained all alone in the middle of a blank page when the censor had gotten through with it.[15]

Another time the Pia-Camus team tossed a ringer at the censor: Their slogan of the day, attributed to Ravachol, the nineteenth-century anarchist who was beheaded, read: "Suppress the scombroids" (in fact, a kind of fish). The censor asked for a dictionary and they told him they had none, and there was another blank in the newspaper.[12]

Each of Camus' friends had his own favorite story. According to Pierre-André Emery, one censor was a reserve officer, actually an architect of little culture. The struggle between this officer and Camus was an epic one, but the censor was no match for the editor. Once Camus tried to publish one of Pascal's *Provinciales* but it was cut out. He submitted the speech of Hector from Jean Giraudoux's *La Guerre de Troie n'aura pas lieu* and was again censored. Camus told the officer in angry tones that he could censor neither Pascal nor his own chief (for Giraudoux was Commissaire à l'Information in the French Government). He added that *he* didn't interfere in military matters, while French literature was his affair. Camus concluded that he did not know whether the architect-officer ever finished a house without putting in a staircase, but that *he* knew what *he* was doing. The officer flushed and ordered Camus out of his office. Emery later told Camus that as a matter of fact the officer had forgotten to put a staircase in a house he was building, but Camus had not known that.[16]

For Camus the daily job became an exercise in creative expression. More and more pseudonyms were to be used—"Vincent Capable," "Jean Mersault," "Demos," "Irénée"; one researcher believes that these names were employed not to escape prosecution but to suggest to readers and adversaries that the staff was larger than it was. The same writer analyzed the weapons used by Camus in *Alger Républicain* and *Le Soir Républicain* and found they included parody, satire. . . .[17]

In a more serious vein Camus could sign his own name to an editorial in *Le Soir Républicain* on September 17, 1939, which began: "Never perhaps have left-wing militants had so many reasons to despair." If many of us had not understood the men of 1914 before, we do now, he wrote, because we know that one can make war without consenting to it. "We know that at a certain critical limit of despair, indifference appears and with it the sense and the taste of fatality . . ." In the final sentence a word or a phrase had been censored (the space was marked: "[*censuré*].") He signed another editorial entitled "Notre

Position," on November 6, in which he worried that the many blanks left by the censor may have caused the paper's position to be misinterpreted. It was wrong, he insisted, that a nation's morale required the disappearance of its freedom; look at the example of England, where a pacifist can run for office and conscientious objection is authorized. Camus counted himself among those who protested the errors of the Versailles Treaty following World War I, convinced that the harsh terms to Germany, the splitting up of Europe spelled out in it, would lead to war. He asked that even in the middle of war the means of concluding a peace be considered. He was placing his hopes in international agreement, on total disarmament—not on Hitler's word. The German leader's demands were a curious mixture of legitimate claims and unjustified pretensions, while international politics had been refusing the former and according the latter. Although opposing Hitlerism he asked that the German people not be humiliated, that they be granted what was justified while being refused what was not. He demanded the right to defend truth, not to despair, to maintain values which would prevent collective suicide.

Then, in a reply to attacks from the conservative press, a "Profession of Faith" signed jointly by Pia and Camus (but which was censored and never published) included the declaration: "We are deeply pacifistic. We do not approve the prosecutions and the dictatorial measures taken by the government, even against the Communists. . . ." They noted that one of the articles attacking *Le Soir Républicain* alleged that civil and military authorities wished to close down the paper, and found it significant that this allegation had not been censored. The editors of *Le Soir Républicain* had already proved their resolution; they didn't need to be insulted to declare themselves ready to answer for their acts and their writings.

Published or not, these articles were strong medicine. Certainly their authors had now lost most of their supporters. Charles Poncet, one of Camus' faithful friends, heard others express regret that Camus' attitude represented the scuttling of a newspaper which had been founded with so much difficulty and enthusiasm. Had Camus been more flexible, perhaps the paper could have been saved (and not become the Communist Party organ it would be in its revived form later on). But Camus refused to compromise with principles. Poncet attributed this to Camus' Spanish origins, and was reminded of Don Quixote by Camus' behavior at a local police station when complaints against his activity were read to him. As his friend heard the story, Camus replied coolly by adding a number of charges not contained in the police file.[18]

On December 28, 1939, Général de Corps d'Armée Goudot wrote to the director of *Le Soir Républicain* to complain that the newspaper had published an article which had been censored by the officer in charge, and that on December 23 the director of *Le Soir Républicain* had written a letter "in impolite and threatening terms." Therefore, concluded the general, "I hereby pronounce a reprimand and this without prejudice to the more serious sanctions that may be taken against you."[19]

Gabriel Audisio, who had been brought back from Paris to serve in Algeria, was himself in the Army's Service des Informations. He heard the officers grumbling about the seditious paper. The director of his department would say of Camus: "We're going to take care of that fellow." Wearing a uniform, Audisio couldn't approach Camus directly but let him know through mutual friends that he'd do well to watch his step.[20]

The crucial blow would come from higher up. After Faure's departure for military service his cousin and associate, Jacques Régnier, continued to represent the shareholders (most of whom had gone off to the war themselves or were unwilling to be associated with the subversive sheet their daily newspaper had become). The Governor General called a "friendly" meeting of those of the board who remained, and convinced them that the paper had to be shut down. "We're at war, *que diable!*" he exclaimed. "I'm counting on your patriotism."

But the editors were not prepared to relinquish their freedom as easily as that. Even the censors seemed less intimidating as Pia and Camus saw the day approach when there would be no more paper. They had been living on newsprint obtained from their sister paper *Oran Républicain,* and a local printer had given them some more. But one day there was no more paper at all. Had the Government General and the military authorities realized this, they would have spared themselves the trouble of closing the paper, but with the reduced staff the Government General no longer had an informer on the newspaper's payroll to tell them what was really going on. If Pia and Camus published one final issue without the approval of the censor, it was because they knew that it was the last one they could publish anyway.[12]

Then, on January 10, 1940, a notice was delivered to Camus at the offices of *Le Soir Républicain:* At the request of the Prefect of Algiers, the Commissaire Divisionnaire of the Police Spéciale Départementale informed him, as editor in chief, that the newspaper was suspended as of that moment. At the policeman's demand Camus countersigned the notice.[19]

Soon after that the skeleton board of the paper drafted—but may not have sent—a formal act of censure of Camus. He had been engaged as an editor from the time of launching of *Alger Républicain,* the text began, and there did his apprenticeship as a newsman. When the paper

ceased to appear he had been kept on to work with the reduced staff of
*Le Soir Républicain.* Thus Camus had always benefited from constant
sympathy. Yet he had not ceased, from the inception of the enterprise,
to pursue his private policies, policies in contradiction with the original
purpose of uniting republicans of all tendencies. The board had become
aware of the paper's internal difficulties by the drop in sales, the nature
of the polemic, the daily fight with the censors—evidenced by the larger
and larger blanks in its pages. The board (the statement continued)
had then remonstrated with Camus through Pia, but instead of heeding
this plea Camus aggravated the situation. Twice an official reprimand
and confiscation of the paper had been ordered, to which measures Pia
and Camus had replied by letter that in future they would pay no attention at all to censorship. The board was never informed of these facts.
Worse, when the government banned *Le Soir Républicain,* Camus, although without authority to do so, simply countersigned the notification
himself, as if the paper belonged to him. When the board protested the
suspension, it was informed by the authorities that the paper could not
be revived as long as Pia and Camus remained on the staff.

The board discovered (so said the unpublished statement), by examining articles that had not appeared in the paper because of censorship, that Camus had tried to give the afternoon daily an orientation absolutely contrary to the opinions of the paper's backers. The draft
"Profession of Faith," for example, signed by Camus and Pia, with its
anarchistic position that "all the parties have betrayed us," must have
been known by Camus to be contrary to the views of the board and
harmful to the war effort. It appeared, as one reader had suggested, that
*Le Soir Républicain wanted* to disappear.

> Quite to the contrary [the statement went on], during all of this
> difficult period, the newspaper's board, attempting to deal with the
> worst difficulties, was occupied only with the concern to keep the
> enterprise going. One may say that instead of helping them Mr.
> Camus did all he could to give the coup de grâce to a work which
> had survived through the sacrifice of devoted citizens with whom he
> had the duty to be a faithful collaborator, and who, besides, guar-
> anteed his personal situation. It is true that Mr. Camus now indi-
> cates his intention to move to Paris, which explains why the future
> of *Le Soir Républicain* no longer interests him at all.

While the board would not go so far as to say that Camus had willfully
scuttled the newspaper, it felt that he was responsible for the present
situation. Despite this *faute grave*—a French legalism invoked to dismiss an employee—the administrators were prepared to pay Camus, as
well as Pia (who accepted), wages due up to the date of closing of *Le*

*Soir Républicain*. But Camus, the statement alleged, was demanding an indemnity besides. The matter would go to court.[19]

In fact it never did go to court. Pia, who assumed that this reprimand was drawn up after his departure for France in February 1940, guessed that it was written by three or four surviving board members, perhaps civil servants unwilling to compromise their careers. (Pia himself had begun to look for a way to return to Paris even before the official closing of *Le Soir Républicain,* for he could no longer carry on without a regular salary. Among those he wrote to ask for a job was his old friend Jean Paulhan.)[21]

The original publisher of the newspaper, Jean-Pierre Faure, absent during all of these troubled final days, would later speculate that opposition to Camus might have come from Socialist board members who felt that their young editor was indifferent to the material survival of a newspaper which had represented so much effort for all of them. The newspaper's accountant, for example, who would later participate in the anti-Vichy resistance, and who had been one of the devoted staff who kept the papers afloat as long as he could, would have been opposed to scuttling. Faure himself regretted that his press had been closed down before taking a strong stand against Fascism, in recognition of the position of its founders. But he was prepared to believe that anarchistic scuttling was preferable to carrying on a newspaper without character, as *Oran Républicain* had been carried on. Later Faure would meet former shareholders who felt that they had been cheated, but *they* were referring to the later take-over of revived *Alger Républicain* by the Communists.

For the title was resuscitated at the initiative of the Gouvernement Provisoire installed in Algiers in 1943. Faure preferred to take part in the war and left its administration to an associate, and eventually it fell into the hands of the Communist Party.[22]

Stormy as these events had been, they did not seem to have traumatized Camus, nor did they keep him from his personal work. The simultaneous preparation of three important books did not even prevent him from giving some of his attention to less ambitious projects. For example, his frequent trips to Oran to see Francine Faure (and Pierre Galindo and other friends) had led him, probably in November 1939, in the middle of his fight with the censors at *Le Soir Républicain,* to see the material for an essay in that city so different from his own Algiers. Here was a familiar landscape, but without the aspirations (and the talents) of Algiers; here was a Chicago, Europe's Chicago.

This is not to say that he was oblivious, once at his writing table, to the larger world outside. The proliferation of projects mentioned in his journal had a constant accompaniment: the horror of the war which he was taking almost as a personal insult. He pursued his reading of Nietzsche, finding rules of behavior which he would like to follow. On November 29, for example, he saw merit in total chastity (sexual and of thought), and steady working habits. More often his journal yielded to pessimism. But in a "Lettre à un désespéré," which he recorded in the notebook at this time and which reads like an elaboration of his editorials for *Le Soir Républicain,* he told the unidentified *désespéré* that there was something he could do: "You can persuade ten, twenty, thirty men that this war was not and is not fatal, that means to stop it can be atempted. . . ." Say these things, write them when you can, cry them out when necessary. And each of these ten to thirty men will tell ten others, who will repeat it. . . .

In the last days of *Le Soir Républicain,* Camus was living in a large house dominating the sea in the district called Notre Dame d'Afrique, named for its church, the center of Catholic missionary activities.[23] The neighborhood was an attractive residential area known as the Vallée des Consuls. The house itself was surrounded by almond trees; here he would begin the brief essay "Les Amandiers," which offered, to himself first of all, a way toward inner peace in a time of troubles, making ample use of the lessons he was learning from Nietzsche. And from Napoleon. "In the end the sword is always conquered by the spirit." Completed in France during the course of 1940, the essay was seen as an appeal to moral resistance against Vichy (it was first published in *La Tunisie Française* in January 1941). Read in the context of Camus' mood when he entered Napoleon's remark in his notebook in November 1939, and when he was living among the almond trees of the Vallée des Consuls, it is more of a piece with Camus' general condemnation of the use of force, by his own country as well as by an enemy.[24] It is too soon to see Camus as an anti-Fascist fighter.

With the newspaper closed, both Pascal Pia and Camus began looking for other jobs. By February, Pia had found one in Paris as a *secrétaire de rédaction,* or editorial assistant, at the popular daily *Paris-Soir.* All sorts of stories have been told about Camus' own situation at this time. That he had to hide out in Oran, that he was expelled to France—as if a man considered subversive would be expelled toward the battlefront. (Really dangerous people, such as active Communists, were sent to detention camps in the southern desert.) What seems to have happened is that Camus found it difficult to obtain a job (although with so many eligible males away at war that should have been easy), and when he did find one, the government stepped in deftly and took it away from him.

The bits of evidence available vary in minor detail, but what essentially happened was that an old benefactor, the printer Emmanuel Andréo, took Camus on at the princely salary of 3,000 francs per month (worth 1,620 francs in the mid-1970s, or some $330). Urged by his daughter Gilberte to do something for the young man, Andréo had devised the expedient of a magazine he was prepared to publish, and asked Camus to plan a pilot issue in the spirit of an American magazine. Camus worked up a dummy. But despite Andréo's good intentions, it happened that his enterprise, the Imprimerie Heintz, did a good deal of work for the Government General (printing the national lottery tickets, for example, and other official publications). Either government pressure or an offer by the government to buy out the projected magazine squeezed Camus out of his job.[25] So by mid-February 1940 he was in Oran again, where Francine had been trying to find work for him, and for herself. "They had better decide to let me work," he had complained to her bitterly.[2] In Paris, Pia was also looking for employment for Camus, and reporting to him regularly on his progress. Camus told Christiane Galindo that he would go anywhere to work, now that he could no longer choose. By the third week in February he had begun to do private tutoring again, which gave him enough income to allow him to wait, for Pia had promised that a job in Paris would be opening up soon.[5]

On February 20 there was more good news: A divorce court had dissolved his marriage to Simone Hié, a decision to become effective in September, after which he would be free to remarry. When Louis Miquel met Francine for the first time, he found her most attractive. If she lacked Simone's glamour, she (like her fiancé) manifested a *pudeur* which Miquel found very appealing.[19]

In early March, perhaps in unconscious homage to Jean Grenier ("I have often dreamed of arriving alone in a strange city"), Camus wrote in his journal:

> What is the meaning of this sudden awakening—in this dark room—with the sounds of a suddenly strange city? And everything is strange to me. . . .
> Strange, confess that everything is strange to me.
> Now that all is clear, wait and spare nothing. Work at least in order to perfect both the silence and the creation. Everything else, everything else, whatever happens, is indifferent to me.

# 17

## PARIS-SOIR

To feel at *Paris-Soir* the very heart of Paris and its abject
shopgirl mentality. . . . The sentimentality, the picturesque, the complacency, all these slimy shelters in which
men defend themselves in a city so harsh to man.

*Carnets*

The contrast is striking between the impressions of Paris recorded by
the young tourist of 1937, poor and sickly, and the working newsman's
Paris of 1940. The text to read in this connection is Camus' first Paris
journal entry, dated "Mars 1940." For the young Camus, social lion,
leader of a generation in Algiers, Paris could only be a shock of solitude. Yet he was convinced that "to know how to remain alone for a
year in a poor room teaches a man more than a hundred literary salons
and forty years of experience of 'Parisian life.'" Perhaps it would be
hard, harsh, a form of torture—"and always so close to madness." But
in Paris the quality of a man would affirm itself—or perish.

It could not have seemed a gay city to him, even if the sky had not
been a March gray, the rain interminable. This was the period of
"phony war," the calm before the storm, when France had snuggled
behind its Maginot Line, while Germany was free to pursue its advance
elsewhere, completing the occupation of Poland, the invasion of Nor-
way (April 1940); only in May would the Germans launch their western attack via the Low Countries, and then into France, confounding
the French defense system. By early June they had smashed all resistance, to parade into Paris on the fourteenth.

As soon as there was an opening at *Paris-Soir,* because of the drafting
of many of the staff, Pascal Pia approached editor Pierre Lazareff to tell
him about Camus. Pia knew that Camus could handle the work, and he
felt that he would not mind the kind of work it was. For Pia himself
had received something of a demotion, at least in rank, in moving from
Algiers back to France; the director of an Algiers daily had to take a
subordinate position on a large Paris newspaper (but then it sometimes
seemed that Pia was predestined to fill thankless jobs behind the
scenes). Lazareff told Pia that he would not pay Camus' fare to Paris,
but if Camus managed to get there quickly he'd have a job.[1] Camus received the message in Oran on March 14, packed and left the same day.
By March 23 he was in Paris, and at work.[2] Apparently his passage was
paid by friendly members of the *Alger Républicain* board, as Pia's had
been.[3]

Nothing in Algeria could have prepared the young newspaper veteran
for the phenomenon known as *Paris-Soir.* Even seasoned French journalists had to adjust to it. Scion of a wealthy textile dynasty of Northern
France, Jean Prouvost, publisher of *Paris-Soir,* was one of France's
twentieth-century press lords, one of the inventors of the mass-circulation daily newspaper offering entertainment in lieu of serious editorial
content, "entertainment" which included crime and accident stories. It
was the kind of journalism that Camus, like Pia, detested, but it sold
some two million copies every day in the pre-World War II years.
Prouvost also published *Match* (the postwar *Paris-Match*) and a popular women's magazine, *Marie-Claire.* Minister of Information in the
Reynaud war cabinet in 1940, he would stay on in Pétain's Vichy regime.

In the monstrous machine that *Paris-Soir* was, a newcomer like Albert Camus could only be a tiny cog. In fact he need not have worried
about soiling his hands producing copy for the newspaper, for he was
never asked to do so. Prouvost journalism had devised the job of *secrétaire de rédaction,* a halfway house between the editorial staff and the
composing room, responsible essentially for layout, making up the
paper on the composing-room floor, galley proofs in hand, on the instructions of the editors. Although the *secrétaire de rédaction* did no
writing—at most he would have to reduce or revise headlines—it was
better paid than such technical jobs had been in the past, for daily
papers of the *Paris-Soir* sort were importantly what they appeared to
the eye, and the *secrétaire de rédaction* saw to the paper's eye appeal.
There were two shifts, one beginning at 6 A.M. or thereabouts, ending
in the early afternoon, the other starting then and ending at 6 P.M.; edi-

torial secretaries would sometimes be assigned to one shift, sometimes to the other.

Prouvost had found, for the job of editor in chief, one of the most versatile between-the-war (and then postwar) journalists, Pierre Lazareff. Son of a diamond merchant, he began working for newspapers at the age of fifteen (he was turning thirty-three when Camus began to work for him). Lazareff had been a reporter on *Paris-Midi,* in charge of city news for that paper in 1927 (at the age of twenty), chief editor of *Paris-Soir* in 1937. His technical editor, Raymond Manevy, later a historian of the French press, dealt with the editorial secretaries, who included Daniel Lenief and a half-dozen others, among them Pia and Camus. They all worked in a vast city room, American style. The job of an editorial secretary being what it was, Camus was to make most of his friends in the composing room, among typesetters and proofreaders, rank-and-file trade unionists. To them he seemed better than his job (but none suspected *what* he might do better). He seemed to thrive in the atmosphere of the printing plant, spent most of his working time there. They noticed with gratitude that he listened to the advice of veteran printers.[4]

Pia had found Camus a room in a more than modest Montmartre hotel on Rue Ravignan, set on a small square which served as a staircase landing between streets immediately above and below. Just opposite was the *Bateau-Lavoir,* a shapeless wooden structure containing a maze of small studios resembling ship's cabins, where painters such as Picasso, Modigliani, and even Camus' mail friend Max Jacob had worked. As for the hotel itself, his room had neither a bath nor a toilet, and the stairway leading up to it was dark and dirty.[5] After five or six weeks of that he moved to a more comfortable—and more expensive—room at the Madison Hotel, just opposite Saint-Germain-des-Prés church.[1]

Paris repelled him, he would tell Jean Grenier. But for the moment it served his purpose; he would leave it when he'd had enough. His journal entries are filled with his moody Paris: "Black trees in the gray sky and the pigeons colored like the sky. Statues in the grass and that melancholic elegance."

But he found familiar faces: the Enrico Terracinis. He was an Italian anti-Fascist émigré of Jewish origin, journalist and writer; she from the Algerian Jewish bourgeoisie, a longtime friend of Camus. She would later translate a book of her husband's for Charlot; her other translations included works by Alberto Moravia from the Italian, Arthur Koestler ("The Yogi and the Commissar") from English. They were living on the downtown Rue Condorcet, in an apartment which they had turned into a way station for fellow Italian émigrés. It was also a halfway point between Camus' office and his hotel, and he was a frequent visitor that spring. He would walk straight through the apartment to the kitchen, calling out, "There's nothing for me tonight?" and then proceed to cook whatever he found. The Terracinis accompanied him to the theater—the small playhouses of Montmartre (they saw, among other things, Charles Vildrac's *Le Loup Garou*). He would comment amply on sets and directing. In fact he would comment on almost everything except the things that mattered to most people, and his friends never knew when he was only being ironic. He did begin to draft the preface for a book Terracini was writing, the opening of which it was now easy for him to write: "This taste of exile, many among us also feel its nostalgia. . . ." (Only the passage from his journal survives.) Terracini returned to Italy after the war to find that his family had been sent to camps and murdered by the Nazis. Until his retirement he was a member of the Italian diplomatic service, with the rank of Minister Plenipotentiary.[6]

Another editorial secretary, Henri Cauquelin, two years Camus' junior, found himself in an embarrassing situation with the new staff member. During a break when they were sitting around talking Cauquelin happened to remark—their subject was diseases—that he wouldn't work or eat alongside a man with tuberculosis. He felt a kick under the desk (from Lenief), who later took him aside to explain the *faux pas*. An hour later, realizing that he would have to take the bull by the horns, Cauquelin went up to Camus to apologize. Camus told him: "You're the first person in Paris I understand." In this cold city of subways, so different from his native Algeria, he had discovered someone who seemed genuine, who might be a friend. From then on they would often go out together, or to Cauquelin's home for spaghetti. Camus never mentioned his personal writing or indicated that he was in a hurry to get back to it.[7]

One time Pia took him to a movie theater for a private screening of the film Malraux had made in wartime Barcelona of his novel *L'Espoir* (Man's Hope), and afterwards Pia introduced Camus to his old comrade Malraux (but Malraux scarcely paid attention to the young unknown).

Camus wrote two articles for Pia's friends at the anti-Fascist weekly *La Lumière,* the first a new look at the reputation of Maurice Barrès in the light of then current attempts by the right-wing intelligentsia to annex him, the second, taking off as a critique of a revival of Jean Giraudoux's *Ondine,* being Camus' first opportunity to write about the modern stage after having seen examples of it in Paris.

He was also finishing *L'Etranger* now, working at it steadily in his hotel room; in early April he was ready to send the first half to Christiane Galindo for typing, and in May he told his journal that he had completed it. More or less simultaneously he worked at the manuscript of *Le Mythe de Sisyphe*. One of the themes of *Mythe*—one of the subjects that would haunt him all of his life—Don Juan as symbol and rule of behavior, was emerging now, and he began sketching out a play that he would never finish:

> The Franciscan father—Then you believe in nothing, Don Juan?
> Don Juan—I do believe in three things, father.
> The father—May one know what they are?
> Don Juan—I believe in courage, in intelligence, and in women.

Just now he would make the acquaintance of a young woman who would be a solace to him during these last weeks of war, the débacle, and the exodus from Paris, and who would later become, with her future husband, Michel Gallimard, one of his closest friends in Paris. (She was in the automobile when it crashed into a tree, killing Camus and her husband.) But for the moment he saw her as that ravishing girl who passed him in the corridors at *Paris-Soir*.

Her mother had brought Janine Thomasset and her sister to Paris when she separated from their father in Bayonne near the Basque coast of southwest France. Janine was then seventeen. She found work on a daily newspaper called *L'Ordre,* then at the publishing house of Fernand Nathan, for whom her father wrote children's books, including a collection of folk tales from the Basque region. Then her father wanted to take her with him to Indochina, where he was going to make a film, and she resigned from the job at Nathan. But the film didn't work out, and she was left without work.

In January 1939, Janine was spending an afternoon at the popular Grands Boulevards dance palace Le Coliseum, a favorite of Parisian socialites, and there met a number of the publishing Gallimards, Gaston (patriarch of the book firm), his wife Jeanne, his nephews Pierre and Michel, Michel's sister Nicole. When she found herself without employment, she asked the Gallimards for help, but they could only give her a temporary job as a replacement. Finally her father sent her to see his friend Pierre Lazareff, who put her to work as his number three secretary at *Paris-Soir*. That was in February 1939, thirteen months before Camus arrived.

A year later, while making the rounds of the newspaper offices to collect cash to buy a gift for a secretary who was getting married, she approached Camus, whom she knew as the young man who always wore a tweed jacket and smoked brown cigarettes. He said to her, "You never say hello to me, but now you ask me for money."[8]

The German offensive which had put an end to the stagnating war broke through near Sedan in northeast France; by May 28 tiny Belgium had surrendered. Then, suddenly, the Germans seemed to be everywhere, in eastern Normandy, in Champagne—a familiar battlefield. Paul Reynaud, who had replaced Daladier as prime minister on March 21, was soon to learn that he had no army, or what was left of it possessed no arms. The need for national unity brought old Marshal Philippe Pétain into the government as his deputy on May 18. The government was operating from Tours, south of Paris on the Loire River, when the Germans marched through the capital on June 14. The cabinet then shifted to Bordeaux in the extreme southwest of the country, whose large port was also a potential escape route. There, on June 16, the war cabinet became a peace cabinet under Pétain.

The evacuation of Paris, however much it must have hurt, was better prepared than the short war had been. Several weeks before the débacle publisher Jean Prouvost had sent aides to key provincial cities to study the possibilities of transferring the national institution that *Paris-Soir* was to a site allowing uninterrupted publication. Nantes, on Brittany's Atlantic coast, was an early choice, and so was Clermont-Ferrand, where arrangements were made to print the paper in the plant of *Le Moniteur,* which happened to belong to Pierre Laval.

The last issue of Prouvost's *Paris-Soir* would appear in Paris on June 11. But by then the key people were already on the road. Rooms had been reserved for essential staff in Clermont-Ferrand. *Paris-Soir*'s chauffeured fleet of specially decorated cars was dispatched to pick up employees at their homes. Henri Cauquelin, for instance, was swimming at his club when a phone call came in: He would be picked up in front of his house in an hour's time. He rushed home to pack, and the chauffeured car arrived at the promised time. The editorial secretariat was obviously an essential element in the Prouvost universe, and the publisher made sure that these people got out of the doomed city in time. But Pascal Pia would not join the exodus, for in April he had been called up for military duty and sent to a camp not far from Paris; he would not return to *Paris-Soir* until the paper had set up headquarters in Lyons in October. Janine Thomasset drove off with a friend in a tiny Fiat.

Camus was assigned to drive a car with a fellow staff member, proofreader Rirette Maîtrejean, but with one of *Paris-Soir*'s chief executives in the rear seat. They traveled all night on "sinister" roads, Camus' boss talking to him continually to make sure he stayed awake. When they got to tree-lined Place de Jaude in the center of old Clermont-Ferrand, 230 miles south of Paris in the capital of the mountainous Auvergne province, the radiator was smoking, the car out of gas

and oil as well as water. Camus leaped out and rushed to open the
trunk; he had suddenly realized that he might have forgotten to pack
the manuscript of *L'Etranger*. He hadn't, but in his haste to evacuate
Paris he had left other papers and personal effects at the Madison
Hotel. Later in the summer, when Pia contacted him and told him that
he was going to Paris, Camus asked him to stop in at the hotel to pick
them up. Pia discovered that the Madison had been taken over by German troops, and decided that it would be imprudent to walk in to ask
for papers in the name of Albert Camus.[1]

Camus made only one note in his journal on the "Exode":

> Clermont. The insane asylum and its curious clock. The dirty
> early mornings at five o'clock. The blind—the building's madman
> who shouts all day—this land on a small scale. The whole body
> turned toward two poles, the sea or Paris. It's in Clermont that
> you can get to know Paris.

It did not seem very promising, this provincial town, although the
exiles learned to make the most of what entertainment they could find,
mainly of their own devising. A camaraderie developed which hadn't
been possible—or necessary—in Paris, and also a certain promiscuity.
Camus lived in a twin-bedded hotel room with his colleague Daniel
Lenief. He would go out walking with Janine, they would eat and drink
together—especially drink—and then stroll on the large Place de Jaude.
One image stayed with her: Camus wearing a tweed jacket, looking into
shopwindows at other tweed jackets he wished he owned.

With Jean Prouvost in the government, which was then still in Bordeaux attempting to negotiate an honorable peace, the staff packed
again and moved in convoys to Bordeaux. Here in mid-June, along the
waterfront, one could almost imagine oneself in Algiers; perhaps Camus
did, as he walked along the quays with Janine. But the bustle of Bordeaux in June 1940 was unfamiliar, even to the Bordelais, with the
panic buying in the shops, jammed restaurants and hotels. The prefect
had not even been able to house the totality of government personnel
who had suddenly descended on that graceful old city.[9]

Marshal Pétain, the new chief of government, led the way back to
Clermont-Ferrand, setting up his armistice cabinet there on June 29,
the ministries divided between this capital of the Puy-de-Dôme *dépar-*
*tement* and nearby hillside watering places with good hotel and private
accommodations. Here Pierre Laval, master in his own city, convinced
France's President Albert Lebrun to resign, to allow Pétain to preside
over a new regime to be created in Vichy. For on July 1 the government moved to that other watering place barely thirty-five miles to the
north. Prouvost would become a member of the government there, as

Haut Commissaire à la Propagande Française, while his newspaper remained in Clermont-Ferrand. The first issue appeared there on July 1. From then on, and until the middle of 1943, Prouvost's *Paris-Soir* would be published in various parts of central and Southern France (called the free zone until November 1942, when the Germans took over this half of France too). But back in Paris, in recognition of the importance of mass-circulation *Paris-Soir* as a national symbol, the Germans began to produce an ersatz *Paris-Soir,* which they maintained throughout the war, with ragtag staff recruited among Nazi sympathizers and political neuters; in fact they managed to get the first issue onto the newsstands on June 21, ten days before Prouvost's own first issue was ready in Clermont-Ferrand. Both papers collaborated each in its own way, the Nazi-sponsored Paris version without restraint, Prouvost's in the free zone following the Vichy government line (which meant supporting Franco-German "co-operation").

With the completed manuscript of *L'Etranger* safe in a drawer, Camus would spend that half of each day when he wasn't on duty at *Paris-Soir* working on *Le Mythe de Sisyphe;* he had finished the first section of it by the time the staff left Clermont-Ferrand in September. Otherwise, Clermont-Ferrand was an opportunity for Camus to become better acquainted with his fellows. ("It's in Clermont that you can get to know Paris.") Perhaps he had been a solitary in Paris. But in this city of less than 90,000 souls, the crowded *Paris-Soir* team would not only live together, they would play together. By now Janine had left them. (She had gone directly back to Paris from Bordeaux, where she joined Pierre Gallimard, to accompany him to his parents' home near Carcassonne, for soon she would marry Pierre.)

There was only one edition of the paper in Clermont-Ferrand, so the staff was free in the early afternoons for excursions, dining out in groups.[10] They had automobiles and sufficient gas to drive into the Auvergne countryside for a change of air and diet. Once Camus joined the composing-room staff for an outing at a country inn near the Puy-de-Dôme mountain, which they proceeded to climb (it is 4,800 feet to the summit). Here Camus was master of ceremonies, buffoon, charmer, at times melancholic. He entertained with ribald songs. One of the songs he sang to the company—and to their choral accompaniment— he had discovered or may even have invented himself: A parody of turn-of-the-century realism, its subject was a waif:

> She was born on the Day of the Dead,
> What a fateful destiny.
> She was seduced on the Trinity,
> What a calamity.[11]

Georges Altschuler, veteran French journalist, then diplomatic correspondent at *Paris-Soir,* would remark Camus along the downtown Rue Blatin shopping for food, which he would bring back to the house he shared with other employees of the paper. He would cook the evening meal for everyone, then return to his room to write. Altschuler recalled that he was working on *L'Etranger,* so perhaps he was revising it then, concurrently with his work on *Mythe.* In any event Altschuler heard Camus read parts of *L'Etranger,* "in that somewhat muted voice," to other staff members.[12]

During this period Camus had a young visitor from his home town. Pierre Salama, brother of his college classmate Myriam (who became Yves Dechezelles's wife), was a soldier stationed in Clermont-Ferrand from mid-June to mid-August of that year. When Salama called on Camus in his furnished rooms in an old house in a seedy neighborhood, it seemed to him that all of Clermont-Ferrand was there—all of the female population, anyway. (Here, Salama remarked, the girls were doing the cooking.) He (and others) recalled one particular young lady, heavy, with prominent breasts. It was she who opened the door for Salama, introducing herself: "I'm of the nobility of the ass!" (She had a *de* in her name.) Camus confided to another friend that when he had showed up in town the same young lady suggested he take a nap at her place and when he started to fall asleep he felt that huge body climbing into bed alongside him.[13]

During these evenings the talk might also turn to politics. Camus confided to Salama that he expected to be fired at any moment because of his views, and hoped that he would not be arrested in the bargain.[14]

Certainly there was a new irony in Camus' position. A recent graduate of a wildly anarchistic newspaper largely of his own invention, here he was writing to old friends and using as his return address *Le Moniteur,* the newspaper of Pierre Laval, proponent of peace abroad but a target of the French left, now a collaborator of growing influence, later to be the symbol of Vichy's pro-Hitler policies; he would be executed as a traitor after the war. For Camus it was a humiliating period, and he didn't wish it to be spent in Clermont-Ferrand. He tried to get out—tried to get a job in Algiers (through benefactor Emmanuel Andréo), but there was nothing for him.[15]

In September the *Paris-Soir* offices were moved to Lyons, 110 miles due east of Clermont-Ferrand. No one has ever described Lyons as cheery, but it was surely a lively metropolis compared to Auvergne's little capital; with over a half million population it was France's third city after Paris and Marseilles. The paper was set up in a warehouse at 65 Cours de la Liberté, only a block from the Rhône River in the center of town, but the best thing that could be found to lodge its bachelor

Camus' mother, Catherine Camus (née Sintes). Courtesy of Madame Albert Camus.

Camus' father, Lucien Auguste Camus, in zouave uniform circa 1914. Courtesy of Madame Albert Camus.

Workshop of Camus' uncle in Algeria in 1920. Camus is in the front, center, in a black smock. Courtesy of Roger-Viollet.

Albert Camus, age 11, at Communion. Courtesy of Madame Antoinette Acault.

The Camus house at Lourmarin. Courtesy of Madame Albert Camus.

Simone Hié, Camus' first wife, in 1934. Courtesy of Dr. Léon Cottenceau.

Design by Jean de Maisonseul for the bedroom of Albert and Simone Camus at
Parc d'Hydra, 1934. Courtesy of Jean de Maisonseul.

Blanche Balain in Algiers in 1937.
Courtesy of Blanche Balain.

Francine Camus, in Oran, 1941.
Courtesy of Madame Albert Camus.

Students in a class preparing *"Normale"* in Algiers. In the second row, in the center, Claude de Fréminville (his newspaper pen name: Claude Terrien). Last row, second from right, Camus. Courtesy of Roger-Viollet.

In the offices of *Combat* in 1944 — from left, Camus, Jacques Baumel, André Malraux, and (facing back) Albert Ollivier. René Saint-Paul.

Francine and Albert Camus, winter 1945–46. The twins Catherine, at left, and Jean, at right. Courtesy of Madame Albert Camus.

staff was a small hotel across the river, off famous Place Bellecour with its Louis XVI elegance; the hotel had formerly been a bordel. By this time Prouvost had sent part of his staff to Toulouse and to Marseilles, so that the free-zone *Paris-Soir* could publish three regional editions, with local pages added for each region.[10]

Camus had arrived in Lyons in time for autumn, and this autumn was to be a severe one. The sparse journal entries at this time are mainly devoted to his reading, but he did memorialize a visit to a small village overlooking the Rhône, deserted and cold, under a gray sky and icy wind. He records his talk with local people about the war. He meets a schoolteacher, a refugee from Alsace, who has not heard from her parents. "Do you think it will stop soon, monsieur?" Her son had been wounded in 1914, and she had gone to the Marne to fetch him, finding herself in the vicinity of the French retreat. She had brought her son home, where he died. "I'll never forget what I saw." At the station he has an hour to kill, with the distant sound of trains, and the evening wind in the valley.

> So isolated and so near. Here one can touch his freedom, and how frightful it is! In unity, in unity with this world where the flowers and the wind will never excuse all the other things.

For the Camus who was so alone was not the merrymaker, the master of ceremonies everybody loved. In the gloom of Lyons' wintry autumn the war got to him at last. He began to think of its other victims. His college mate, Liliane Choucroun, for example, who had been suspended from her teaching post, for under the Pétain government a Jew could not teach French children in a public school. (He offered her whatever support he could give her from so far away.)[16] There was the story that Malraux had been captured, or had vanished. (In fact Malraux and others of his tank corps had been captured on June 16, confined to a camp at Sens, but he had escaped, and by this time was en route to the Riviera villa where he would spend part of the occupation period.) Camus learned of the death at the front of an old Algiers comrade, Max Béral, who had been in the Jeunesses Communistes movement.

A fellow-worker on *Paris-Soir*, Adalbert de Segonzac (later chief correspondent in North America for *France-Soir*), expressed the wish to get out of occupied France, and to join the Free French. On Camus' recommendation he went to Oran to seek a way to travel from there to England across the Moroccan border. But without Camus on the scene, Segonzac never was able to get out of Algeria, and so abandoned the plan.[17]

Pascal Pia turned up in Lyons now, and took up his job as editorial secretary. He had a war story to tell: When the Germans arrived in the

Paris region, his little unit stationed in the woods had been forgotten, and no one remembered to order its evacuation. Pia managed to avoid being taken prisoner, got to Avignon, where he was discharged from the service, then went up to Paris to gather his personal belongings. (That was when he tried to get Camus' own things out of the Madison Hotel at Saint-Germain-des-Prés.)[1]

One of the familiars of the communal gatherings in Clermont-Ferrand was a prewar film star, Gilbert Gil, known for his roles as a young man with problems.[14] Gil told Camus of his plans to produce playable versions of early classics on the Paris stage. An adaptation was required of a sixteenth-century *commedia dell'arte* by one Pierre de Larivey, son of a Florentine merchant who was a canon in France. On November 12, 1940, Camus wrote a long description of the project to his friends of the Théâtre de l'Equipe, who at the time were planning to revive the amateur troupe, notably with Luigi Pirandello's *Six Characters in Search of an Author*. Camus set about translating the Larivey text into modern French, turned the five short acts into three longer ones. He sent his friends, presumably with the adaptation, suggestions for casting, acting, even a sketch for the single stage set that would be required.[18]

At last the divorce decree had become final (as of September 27, 1940), and he could marry again. (So could his former wife, Simone Hié, who wedded a young doctor, Léon Cottenceau, almost immediately thereafter—on October 22. Simone had met the doctor in Paris in 1938, but when the Germans invaded France she had returned to Algiers. In August 1940, Cottenceau himself was posted to Algiers as a soldier.[19])

Francine Faure arrived in Lyons at the beginning of December. Camus had gotten the train schedules mixed up, so he wasn't at the station to meet her. The weather was not only grim, it was fearfully cold for France, five degrees Fahrenheit for the first days of her stay, and twenty-three degrees on the day of their wedding. Camus was working nights, returning at 3 or 4 A.M.; he would walk on snow packed hard and never removed from the sidewalks. The wind was icy; he had to cross a bridge over the Rhône to reach their hotel, and by the time he got there his skin was violet. Francine would be waiting up for him, reading with gloves on. There was no heating system at all in their room.

Not only had the hotel been a bordel, there hadn't been much of a renovation, for paintings of naked ladies still decorated the ground-floor parlor, and the madam still seemed to be in charge. And the *Paris-Soir* offices across the Rhône were in the middle of a red light district. One

day when pert and proper little Francine was waiting for Albert outside
the building, a man rode up to her on a bicycle and asked: *"Combien?"*
Daytimes, she would join Camus for lunch at the employees' restaurant
in the newspaper plant.

Francine and Albert were married on December 3, a week just before the bride's twenty-sixth birthday. They had purchased brass wedding rings because they couldn't afford gold. The marriage was the
usual civil ceremony in the town hall, enacted in the presence of Pia
and Lenief. Four members of the composing-room staff arrived, thrilled
at the invitation. "What a proof of friendship for us!" one of them later
recalled, remembering the bride's *simplicité* and *gentillesse*. They had
brought along a bouquet of Parma violets and a homely quatrain (since
lost). After the ceremony they all went off for a drink together.[20]

Although the city seemed sinister to Francine, there was her husband's job to consider, so they began to look for an apartment, assuming that they would be staying awhile. Camus was being paid on Thursdays, but by the following Wednesday there was no money left to buy
food; the bride found prices—even for their comfortless room—outrageous. She had her own work to do: to copy *Le Mythe de Sisyphe* by
hand, so that there would be a second copy available; no one had a
typewriter.[21]

At the end of December, *Paris-Soir* carried out its third reduction
in staff since the evacuation from Paris. The paper was being printed on
four pages now; it was overstaffed, and expenses had to be reduced. In
addition to that, employees who had been called up for military service
in 1939 were now being discharged and were drifting back to the office.
Being without children, Camus was one of those dismissed.[1]

Jean Prouvost's *Paris-Soir* lasted until the spring of 1943 (its Lyons
plant shut down on May 25 of that year). Following the Liberation,
Prouvost rushed to Paris in an attempt to revive the paper, and was
apparently surprised to learn that his publication was considered collaborationist and would not be allowed to reappear. An ordinance of September 30, 1944, established the cut-off date of November 26, 1942,
shortly after the Germans had completed their take-over of the so-
called free zone. Any newspaper which had failed to scuttle itself by
that date was considered to have collaborated with the enemy and could
not be revived after the war. Prouvost himself received a *non-lieu*
(finding of no grounds for prosecution), and he would soon be one of
postwar France's press tycoons again. His prewar editor in chief Pierre
Lazareff, who had been stripped of French nationality by Vichy, his
property confiscated, when he escaped to the United States to continue

the war in the Office of War Information and the Voice of America, returned after the war to become editor of the resistance daily *Défense de la France,* which became *France-Soir,* a postwar imitation of *Paris-Soir.*[22]

# 18

♦

# ORAN

Why is it that we become attached to and interested in something that has nothing to offer us? This emptiness, this ugliness, this boredom under a sky implacable and magnificent, what are their seductions? I can reply: the creature. For a certain kind of men, the creature, wherever it is beautiful, is a country of a thousand capitals. Oran is one of these.

*Carnets*

Albert Camus and his new wife Francine left Lyons at the beginning of January 1941 in an unheated railway coach bound for Marseilles, their port for Algeria. But the harsh winter pursued them, and in Orange the train was blocked by a snowbank (not a usual occurrence in Provence). The passengers had to leave the train in an icy wind to wait in the station—no one knew for how long. Most passengers slept there. Francine knew a professor who lived in Orange, and through him they were able to get a room for the night (the hotel's proprietor gave up his). Then when they could travel again they got to Marseilles and boarded a steamer sailing directly to Oran, thereby avoiding a land journey from Algiers to Francine's home; at the time such a journey meant an all-night train ride.

Oran at once fascinated Camus—and repelled him. There was a traditional rivalry between the two coastal cities some 250 miles apart, Algiers and Oran. The latter seemed to have all the attributes of a city without even the incipient cultural environment Algiers could boast. He had thought of Oran as Europe's Chicago, but it could have been any tributary city against any metropolis, a Lyons against Paris, for example. The university and every other significant cultural institution were in Algiers, while the Oranais were left with material things. Oran was the product of speculation, every potentially beautiful site marred by ugly constructions; this city had even managed to turn its back to the sea. And yet, as he would tell his journal in that first month of residence in January 1941—the rich land was there, and Oran couldn't hide or deny that land; thanks to the soil one could dominate ennui. "Oran offers proof that there is something in men stronger than their works." In fact the region was the orchard and the wine cellar of Algeria, because of this rich soil and an ample water supply.

Camus' attraction-repulsion toward this city is spelled out at length in one of the most transparent essays of his Algerian period, dedicated to that Oranais par excellence Pierre Galindo. For Camus, the Oranais were being devoured by a Minotaur; the Minotaur was ennui.

Although he would spend a good deal of time in Algiers in the next eighteen months—to see his mother and the rest of his family, to visit friends, above all to find meaningful work to support himself and Francine—his home from January 1941 until August 1942 was Oran. Oran meant the Faure family apartment on colonnaded Rue d'Arzew, now called Rue Larbi Ben M'hidi, then and later a fine place to live. (Arzew was the name of a nearby coastal town and harbor; Larbi Ben M'hidi that of a nationalist fighter who had been arrested by the French and who died under torture.)

The Faures had contiguous apartments at 65 and 67 Rue d'Arzew, one floor over the street arcades, connected in the rear by terraces, a special arrangement designed by builder Jean Faure for his family (for the other apartments in these buildings possessed walled-in terraces for privacy). When the Camus couple returned from France, Francine's sister Christiane gave up one of the apartments (at number 67) to move in with her mother (at number 65), leaving her flat to Albert and Francine. At the time Francine's mother was working at the post office, Christiane was a teacher in an Oran lycée, and now Francine (who had already taught in the Oran elementary school system during the 1939–40 school year) found a job as a substitute teacher in elementary school. They had little money, they ate badly, for black market food was dear.

There seemed to be no job for Albert Camus in Algiers, although he asked everyone he knew. He even tried to sell antiques and bric-a-brac in association with a friend.[1] The prospects in Oran seemed no better. When his *Alger Républicain* comrade Laurent Preziosi met him on the street near the post office, Camus asked Preziosi to help him find a job; he'd do *anything*. Preziosi was himself then employed as a salesman, and could give his friend no encouragement.[2]

Of course there were things he could do to occupy his time, but these things brought in little or no income. On Edmond Charlot's discharge from the service in the previous July, he had taken up publishing again, with which he associated Camus immediately (at first through correspondence to Clermont-Ferrand and Lyons). Now, with Camus back in Algeria, and until his total isolation in France after the Allied landings in North Africa in November 1942, Camus would be an editor (meaning a regular reader and adviser) for Editions Charlot. Then in February 1942, Charlot was arrested by Vichy authorities in a general crackdown on leftist intellectuals, was sent to an isolated post near Orléansville under house arrest, to be released after a month thanks to the intervention of a friend, and then he was back in the book business. When the Free French took power in Algiers, Charlot joined the provisional government there, running the publications department; when he moved to Paris at the end of the war, it would be on assignment to the Ministry of Information in Paris.[3]

What Camus could do for Charlot was essentially to help choose books for the series called Poésie et Théâtre. The first five titles advertised were *333 Coplas Populaires Andalouses* (previously published under the imprint of Editions Cafre); a translation by Felix Gattegno of García Lorca's *Romancero gitan*—this was one of the best-sold titles; *Liberté des Mers* by a poet employed by a local shipper, Louis Brauquier; William Shakespeare's *Sonnets,* translated by Giraud d'Uccle; García Lorca's *Romances historiques* translated by Roblès. Among books announced as "in preparation"—but actually not to be published until 1953, and by Gallimard in Paris—was Camus' adaptation of Larivey's *Les Esprits.* The first title published expressly for the Poésie et Théâtre series, in September 1941, was *Romancero gitan,* García Lorca's masterpiece, and Camus' journal at that time showed evidence of energetic readings in the theater.

He was also involved with books not directly connected with the Poetry and Theater series. When his friend Roblès submitted his novel *La Vallée du Paradis* for publication, Camus took charge of seeing the manuscript through the presses and into the bookshops; he was the editor as the term is used today. When a short text of presentation was needed for the book (called in French the *prière d'insérer,* used in advertising and promotion and often as a jacket blurb), Camus wrote it for Roblès' book:

> A Mediterranean city, magnificent and unbuttoned, serves as a turntable for all the miserable convoys of hope. . . .

The notice was published without Camus' name attached to it, as was

the wrapper text, that strip of paper used to envelop French books as
an additional promotional device:

> For the true paradises are those that have been lost.

To announce Roblès, next novel, the widely hailed *Travail
d'homme,* published the following year, Camus signed his name to the
*prière d'insérer:*

> Departures, revolts, friendship free and fierce, truth on the
> mountainside. . . . They make of this novel an exceptional success
> in the literature of today and link Emmanuel Roblès to some of
> the great American novelists.[4]

Concerning a possible revival of the Théâtre de l'Equipe in Algiers,
there are at least as many stories as there are surviving witnesses. It
seems clear that Camus' old team was planning to pursue the amateur
company's activity with his encouragement, even while he was still
working in Lyons and expecting to stay there. But on his return to Algeria he found a new context. Algeria was being governed by sympathizers (and delegates) of France's Vichy regime, who in some ways
were more flexible than their chiefs in mainland France (because they
were so far away from Pétain's capital in Vichy, and even further from
the Germans in Paris). In other ways they were as bad when not worse,
for Algeria's extreme-rightist and racist activists now benefited from
official sanction.

What is certain is that Camus and his friends began to plan the
staging of Molière's *Dom Juan*—Don Juan of course being that favorite
and persistent theme of his, soon to be presented in *Le Mythe de
Sisyphe* as a model for behavior. Molière's play could also be considered a challenge to authority, with its hero who rises above conventional ideas about crime and punishment. It is a remarkably provocative
play, and all of the Equipe agreed that it would be banned if they
tried to do it.[5] They did read through the play together, with Francine
Camus reciting the role of Elvira. Without Camus the Equipe attempted to stage Chekhov's first play, *Ivanov,* whose hero, a ruined
landowner who indulges in gratuitous anti-Semitism, shoots himself
in the realization of the futility of his existence.[6]

Another old friend had a different recollection of what the Equipe
actors were doing. Apparently two young ladies were attempting to re-
activate the Théâtre de l'Equipe as a pretext for the setting up of a resistance group. Most of the old hands voted against the revival of the
company, unaware of this occult motivation.[7]

Camus' own role in the resistance against the German occupation and
the collaborationist government may or may not have its place in this

chapter. Camus was not then an active participant in a resistance movement, if by movement is meant a formal organization of the kind that
sprang up throughout occupied France. In the autumn of 1943 Camus
would indeed join the movement which was publishing the clandestine
newspaper *Combat* in mainland France. Before that, Camus would
never be more than an occasional participant, helper, or sympathizer, in
the groups of his friends or of others with which he happened to come
into contact. Despite his initial pacifism, his reluctance to accept the
war as his, it seems clear from this time that Camus was sympathetic to
resistance, that in a way he was involved in intellectual resistance. It
was said later that his friends wished to spare Camus, for if arrested he
might not have survived interrogation. In fact the resistance movement
became a serious affair in Algeria only after his departure for France in
the summer of 1942. But even if he had stayed, he would not have been
a convenient recruit; among other things he was an obvious suspect to
the Vichy regime because of his past connection with the Popular Front
press.[8]

Naturally many of his friends were or would become active resistance agents. Pierre Galindo was involved in passing information gathered by Oran port workers (on the transport of German supplies to the
Tunisian battlefront) to the American consul who opened an office in
Oran after the June 1940 armistice. Galindo also helped hide American
agents until they could be picked up by submarine off the Algerian
coast. Claude de Fréminville and another friend, the future poet Jean-
Paul de Dadelsen, were also active in Oran. Certainly Camus discussed
or attended discussions of resistance activity; some friends in Algiers
even believed that he was organizing such a movement in Oran.[9] What
he could do, and often did, was to facilitate the travel of those who
wished to leave Vichy-controlled Algeria for Morocco, from where the
escapee could join the Free French in London or sail elsewhere—to the
United States for example.

Many of the old Algiers group took part in this informal escape
route. The escapee might begin at Charlot's bookshop, then stay at a
sympathizer's apartment in town. He would travel by rail from Algiers
to Oran, and from there on to Casablanca, a port to freedom. Robert
Namia, who had taken over the Maison Fichu, housed some of the
refugees at that villa. At various times he had in tow Randolfo Pacciardi,
head of the Garibaldi Battalion in the International Brigade during
the Spanish Civil War; French journalist Adalbert de Segonzac (whom
Camus had sent on from Lyons), and the Italian anti-Fascist writer
and critic Nicola Chiaromonte.[10]

Chiaromonte had turned up first at the doorstep of Enrico and
Jeanne Terracini (Camus' friends in Paris in early 1940), who were
now living in a villa at El Biar in the Algiers hills. Chiaromonte, who

was then forty years old, had false papers in the name of "Albert
Maillot," and like other Italian émigrés who called on the Terracinis he
had a letter of recommendation from Jeanne Modigliani, daughter of
the painter. The Terracinis first put up Chiaromonte in the back of their
house. Then, when they needed his room, they asked Camus to find another place for him, and he saw that the Italian found temporary shelter
at the Maison Fichu.[11]

When Chiaromonte arrived at the Maison Fichu, he walked in on a
group of young people reading *Hamlet,* Camus in the title role, Francine as Ophelia. For they were still considering a revival of the Théâtre
de l'Equipe at the time, and whenever the Camus found themselves in
Algiers, they would join the old team to plan forthcoming productions.
Later they learned Chiaromonte's story. An émigré in Paris since 1934,
he had fought in Spain with Malraux, breaking with Malraux when he
found him too servile to the Stalinists. When the Germans reached Paris
the parents of his Austrian Jewish wife committed suicide, and she herself had died of tuberculosis in Toulouse during the difficult exodus toward the south. Francine Camus confessed to Chiaromonte that she
was ashamed that a man who had been through so much suffering had
to watch young people play-acting. Chiaromonte asked the Camus to
put him up in Oran, so that he could proceed from there to Casablanca,
then across the Atlantic to America.[12]

As for Chiaromonte, he observed that he was in the presence of a
rather famous young man, clearly the leader of a group of interesting
young people. To the extent that he could, he began to participate in
their discussions.[13] Then, when Chiaromonte arrived in Oran, he was
put up at the Camus apartment on Rue d'Arzew. (When he wished to
go from there to the adjoining apartment of Francine's mother and
sister, he would get down on his hands and knees to crawl along the terrace separating the two apartments, protected by the wall from prying
eyes.)[14]

Soon, however, they all felt more relaxed. The men would ride bicycles to a deserted beach beyond Mers-el-Kébir, where Chiaromonte
discovered that he and Camus shared a love for the sea. Then, probably
after checking his valise through to Casablanca, the Italian émigré took
a train in the direction of the Algerian-Moroccan frontier, perhaps
switching trains or walking across the boundary line. However he did it,
he managed to reach Casablanca and there board a ship for the United
States. He lived in New York through the war years, remarried, wrote
for liberal intellectual periodicals such as *Partisan Review, The New
Republic, The Nation, Politics.* From then until Camus' death they
would always be friends (Chiaromonte himself died in 1972).

Once Chiaromonte wrote to the Camus' from New York, and shortly after that time the police called in Camus for questioning. They insisted that he had known that "Maillot" was really Chiaromonte and he denied it. (At this time he had already had his relapse and was coughing up blood.)[12]

And then Camus' daredevil friend Namia—there was no hiding *his* affiliations, after his return from combat alongside the Spanish Republicans in the International Brigade—was arrested at 4 A.M. one morning at the Maison Fichu, simply as an anti-Vichy suspect. But there was a note on his desk which he was about to mail to Camus in Oran, announcing that he was sending someone through on the escape route. Namia tried to conceal the letter but one of the inspectors saw it and opened it, put it in his pocket. Namia was sent to detention in South Algeria from January 1942 until January 1943; that would certainly be another reason for Camus' interrogation in Oran shortly thereafter.[15]

Once, when Charles de Gaulle, speaking on the radio from London, asked all patriots to stop work for five minutes as a symbol of their support for Free France, Francine's mother put her pencil down in the post office, and began to freshen her make-up. In that very special atmosphere of occupied France she was promptly denounced by fellow-employees, and suspended without pay for two months.[1]

A project which if it had succeeded might have had broader and lasting impact was the national literary magazine which Pascal Pia was planning from Lyons. For Pia, however complex a personality he may have seemed, never left any ambiguity as to where he stood in the war. From the start he was a deliberate if discreet conspirator. Later he would be entrusted with secret and dangerous work in the organized anti-Nazi resistance. Characteristically, Pia would gain no glory from any of this, nor would he seek any. He is probably unique in the importance of his activity and the little fuss that was made over it later on.

Pascal Pia was one of those Frenchmen who early understood the nature of "intellectual collaboration." For an author, a dramatist, critic, poet, for artists and writers in all media, to contribute to an atmosphere of business-as-usual when in fact things were not usual, was to provide moral assistance to the Nazi occupying forces in Paris, to the Pétain regime in Vichy; by keeping open dissension in check, France would be a more reliable base and supply center for Germany. By writing for a magazine, for example, from which left-wing writers and Jews were barred, one could seem to be reinforcing the legitimacy of Nazi-Vichy discriminatory policies. So that anti-Nazi intellectuals very soon had begun to refuse to write not only for publications expressing Nazi ideology, but for any medium published in Paris or elsewhere which accepted the regime's ground rules, guidelines, and censorship. A rule of thumb for some Frenchmen, at least in the period running from June 1940 to November 1942, during which France was divided into a northern German-occupied zone and a southern Vichy-controlled free zone, was that it might sometimes be possible to publish in the so-called free zone but never in Paris, which was under the direct control of the Nazis.

For reasons which will become apparent in subsequent examination of *La Nouvelle Revue Française* (or *NRF*), which began to reappear in December 1940, six months after the fall of Paris, under the editorship of intellectual Fascist Pierre Drieu La Rochelle, Pascal Pia desired to publish a high-quality magazine in the free zone, which would publish writers whose work could not appear in *NRF* or who did not choose it to be. (Banned writers included Jews such as Julien Benda, author of *La Trahison des clercs* [The Treason of the Intellectuals], and philosopher Jean Wahl, as well as outspoken anti-Nazis such as Georges Bernanos and Jules Romains, while a number of equally famous writers chose to collaborate.)

Prior to Camus' return to Algeria he and Pia had talked about the magazine project in Lyons. Quietly Pia began to gather manuscripts and commitments. Soon he had promises of support from former *NRF* regulars Bernard Groethuysen (the Kafka authority), Jean Wahl, Raymond Queneau, Malraux, and he was expecting favorable responses from Gide, Montherlant, and Paul Valéry (but so was Drieu La Rochelle, and more or less at the same period). At the same time Pia was engaged in an effort, presumably encouraged by Jean Paulhan, to convince fence-sitting authors such as Gide *not* to write for Drieu's *NRF*.

But the most surprising source of support for Pia's project was coming from former *NRF* director Jean Paulhan. For Paulhan, the *éminence grise* of French letters as chief editorial adviser for Gallimard, Paris' major literary publisher since the 1920s, and certainly through the 1940s (and well into the 1950s), was playing a subtle game, continuing to work for the *NRF* and Drieu, and for Gallimard, while participating in a considerable number of other (and less public) activities on the side. For example, Paulhan was helping Pia gather manuscripts for *his* magazine.

They had chosen a title, during Camus' discussion with Pia in Lyons during the *Paris-Soir* days, a title that was certain to appeal to the younger man (perhaps he even suggested it): *Prométhée* (Prometheus), later to be Camus' chief symbol of revolt, the unofficial title of his series of books on this theme. It had first seemed advisable to utilize the name of an existing or of an inactive periodical, for in that case permission to publish (from the Vichy government) would be easier to obtain. Pia wanted to called it *Mesures,* the title of a prewar magazine published by Paulhan's American friend Henry Church, but that required a complicated correspondence with Church via Switzerland. They also considered borrowing the title *Rivages. Prométhée* itself proved impossible; after a two-month wait they discovered that they could not use this title because it belonged to a pharmaceutical magazine. Then, when a friend of Pia from his days on *La Lumière* applied to the Vichy government for authorization to publish the new literary magazine, the only concrete result was to have Pia placed under surveillance by the security police, after a grilling in Sûreté headquarters in Lyons.

Although this project would never be carried out (the Germans would invade the southern zone, and Pia would go on to more urgent clandestine activities), it did help sort out some of the moral and political questions of collaboration in more than one writer's mind, probably strengthened Paulhan's own resolve to resist, weakened Drieu's position (for he would have increasing difficulty in obtaining suitable contributions to the *Nouvelle Revue Française*). And had Pia's magazine appeared, it would certainly have contained two contributions that were ready to hand. One, as Pia informed Paulhan in April 1941, was the manuscript of an excellent novel which Pia was certain Paulhan would soon be reading, *L'Etranger;* the other was the same author's *Caligula.*[16]

Finally Camus had settled into a routine in Oran. He found work of a familiar kind. There was now a rather special need for private teachers. Under the Vichy regime, not only were Jewish teachers dismissed from the public school system, but there was a quota on Jewish students: Only one in seven pupils in a school could be Jewish. If this was seldom a serious problem in mainland France, in Oran with its large Jewish population some classes were practically wiped out. André Benichou, a high school teacher of philosophy, was one of those who were no longer allowed to teach. His students had asked him to continue his course, and he did what he could. The law did not allow him to teach more than five students at a time, and since he was under surveillance—including house visits—he didn't try to evade the ban. Instead he taught the same course five times, to twenty-five students in all. He recruited other teachers to handle other subjects. The Benichous and the Faures were old friends; Francine Faure and Madeleine Benichou (André's wife) were childhood companions, and their mothers had been friends. Benichou asked Camus to teach French. The classes were held at

Benichou's apartment, at the office of an architect, or wherever else around the city they could find adequate facilities. Camus probably taught each class of five for four hours weekly, for twenty hours in all. He showed himself to be an inventive teacher; to teach Molière, for example, he had the students act out a play.[17]

During the same period Camus began teaching at another private school. It was not run by Jews but could take in Jewish pupils because it was not a state institution, and quite possibly the majority of its student body was Jewish during the Vichy period. At Les Etudes Françaises, Camus would be responsible for a number of subjects, including French history and geography, perhaps in a class of *première*—the highest grade in a lycée, just prior to the bac. There is a photograph showing Camus with the school's football team.[18]

Working in a regular school program meant that there could be no more escapades to Algiers outside of regular school holidays; and that meant a steady diet of Oran. "The days are long and weigh on me," he complained to Emmanuel Roblès.[19] He felt very much alone. When Edmond Brua sent him his new book, a parody of *Le Cid* in the street language of Algiers, he couldn't even find a place to review it; he lived far from the circles over which he had any influence.[20]

But when he could he would escape to Algiers. His journal in March 1941 records impressions of a visit there: "The heights above Algiers are overrun with flowers in springtime. . . ." He admired the "blossoming of the girls on the beaches," too. On March 21 he even tried out "The icy waters of springtime." He had time for a bitter reflection on love:

> One can know the pain of love, one can't know what love is. Here it is privation, regret, empty hands. I won't have had the excitement; what remains to me is the anguish. . . . Departure, constraint, breaking up, this heart without warmth fragments inside me, the salty taste of tears and of love.

In July of that year he spent a week living in a tent on the dunes near Oran. "Dunes before the sea—the little tepid dawn and the naked bodies before the first waves still black and bitter." At noon the heat was oppressive: "This sun will kill." Then it is night again: "Nights of happiness without measure under a showering of stars. . . . To be able to write: I was happy eight full days."

The very first journal entry Camus made on his arrival in Oran in January 1941 reads as follows:

> Story of P. [presumably Pierre Galindo]. The little old man who throws bits of paper from the second floor to attract cats. Then he spits. When one of the cats is hit, the old man laughs.

The anecdote would be used in *La Peste*. For Oran, in 1941 and 1942, provided the launching platform for that book. Henceforth *La Peste* would be his chief concern. By April he had promised himself, in his journal, that this project and a new play he was planning, *Le Malentendu* (under the tentative title "Budejovice," the name of a town he had passed through during his journey through Czechoslovakia), were to represent what he was already calling his "second series," to which would soon be added "my essay on revolt."

He could begin working on a second series because the three works of the first were behind him now. *L'Etranger* was probably now almost in the form we know it, and so was the first incarnation of *Caligula*. *Mythe* was completed shortly after his arrival in Oran, on February 21, 1941, on which date he proclaimed to his journal: "The three Absurds are finished." He added just below that: "Beginnings of freedom," a sigh of relief that would be heard again over a decade later after the long period of self-imposed discipline required by the writing of *L'Homme révolté*.

These things bear saying because it has often been written that *L'Etranger,* as well as one or both of the other works of this "first series," were products of Camus' Oran period.

One old friend who turned up now was Emmanuel Roblès, who with his wife was teaching school in Turenne, a largely Moslem settlement near Tlemcen. Roblès would make a fortnightly visit to Oran, some eighty miles distant, to visit his mother, and of course he would call on Camus.

Typhus broke out in Turenne, and Roblès' wife came down with it in April 1941. Roblès was vaccinated and got a medical certificate allowing him to travel. Naturally Camus questioned Roblès in detail about the quarantine, the zones of epidemic where neither entry nor exit was permitted. In Roblès' village, Senegalese riflemen guarded the tents, but families of the ill would try to sneak water to the patients—which in fact could kill them. There was insufficient vaccine, because it had to be imported all the way from Toulouse, and many of the stricken died.

Camus accompanied his friend back to the railroad station and pursued his questioning. Finally he confessed that he himself was working on a story about an epidemic.[21]

He said nothing more. He would never even discuss his writing with Francine.[12] The Faures were impressed with his working habits, his sense of order. When the newlyweds took over sister Christiane's apartment, they had found it in academic disorder, books spilling over everywhere. In a jiffy, under Camus' hand, everything had soon found its place. Christiane Faure never once saw Camus making notes or working on a book, although he was definitely writing at that time.[22]

Another old friend from Algiers turned up now and then. Marcelle Bonnet-Blanchet would join Camus and Francine and their friends (remarking that most of them were Jews) on outings to Canastel, or to a restaurant with a fierce-looking clientele but the best food one could get during the war. Back at Rue d'Arzew she also saw how Camus could share with friends—even share a single egg that Francine had managed to find for him, or the meat that his uncle Gustave Acault had sent from Algiers. She was amused, too, to see how little Camus' charming wife knew about kitchens.[23]

# 19

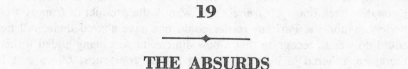

## THE ABSURDS

To Pascal Pia

(Dedication of *Le Mythe de Sisyphe*)

To understand the effect of *L'Etranger* on its first readers, it is certainly necessary to know something about the situation of French letters in the 1930s, largely in the hands of the *Nouvelle Revue Française* clan, consisting in the main of graduates of good schools whose best efforts represented forays out of the narrow confines of the French bourgeoisie. The case of Céline, not of that class but capable of forcing his way into it with a rhetoric of his own, was almost unique in France— and not always understood (not even by Albert Camus, as we have seen, in his belletristic university days). André Malraux, a product of literary Paris, had sought to break through these confines by re-creating revolutions in an exotic milieu. But for genuine exoticism, the thrill of the journey, Malraux and his peers had to turn to the between-the-war Americans (to Faulkner, for example, whose *Sanctuary* appeared in France as early as 1933 with a preface by Malraux, and who had six books in print with Gallimard before the outbreak of World War II; to Steinbeck, whose *Of Mice and Men* was translated in 1939; to Caldwell, whose *God's Little Acre* appeared in France in 1936, *Tobacco Road* in 1937; even to James M. Cain, whose *The Postman Always Rings Twice* was in French by 1936).

No one expected an American novel to come from a Frenchman. A pastiche perhaps, but *L'Etranger* was not a pastiche. In a postwar interview Camus would confess to having used American techniques in the book because it served his intention to describe a man "without apparent consciousness"; but to generalize this procedure, he feared, would lead to a "universe of robots and of instincts" impoverishing the novel. He would give one hundred Hemingways for a Stendhal or a Benjamin Constant, he said in 1945.[1]

The secret, of course, was French Algeria, that frontier post melting pot, where a working-class boy could enter the world of letters through a back door. *L'Etranger* was wholly the product of Camus' experiences, and the Parisian reader could not have shared them. All he could do was to recognize that a new dimension was being added to his literature, ushered in by a frightening gong: "four short blows that I struck at the gate of misfortune." In the first major review of *L'Etranger,* Sartre would recognize its existential quality, a historian would see it as the symbol of the Algerian Frenchman isolated in his Moslem milieu. Much later, a hostile Algerian would decide that in killing the Arab, Camus (or his hero) subconsciously acted out the dream of the *pied noir* who loved Algeria but without [Moslem] Algerians. A Finnish economic geographer would tell the author of this book that he saw in the beach scene, when sunstruck Meursault pulled the trigger, a textbook example of the effect of climate on population.

Perhaps *Caligula,* with its sharp dialogue, its paradoxes, could be assimilated more easily into the French experience; the Parisian public was certainly used to hearing outrageous propositions on its stages, and one need not know what *Caligula* signified to its author, nor care. But what to make of *Le Mythe de Sisyphe,* third panel of Camus' "absurd" triptych? Here the reader was at once more at ease and less informed. Frenchmen of the 1940s would see in it a tour de force, an attempt to make sense of a world they knew. But the reader familiar with Camus' own life to this point is certain to read *Mythe* differently. At times it seems veritable autobiography, a portrait of the artist as a young man. When the book opens with the now familiar proposition that "There is only one philosophical problem which is really serious: suicide. To decide whether life is or is not worth living," one can imagine that one is reading Camus' journal. Remarkably, the section of the book which describes models of behavior limits these to three: Don Juanism, the actor, the conqueror. Each description contains concepts which will make most sense to the reader who has gone this far in Camus' biography. "It isn't for lack of affection that Don Juan goes from woman to woman," he will write:

> But it is rather because he loves them with equal enthusiasm and each time with all of himself, that he must repeat this gift and this exploration . . . Why must one love rarely to love well?

In this book the author is asking the reader and himself whether, in the face of the silence of the world, life is worth living. It is worth living if it is lived in lucidity; the creator (the writer) is well placed to go forth with his eyes open. The labor of Sisyphus, condemned to push a rock up a hill only to see it roll down again, is absurd man's plight, which he surmounts by consciousness. "The struggle toward the summits itself suffices to fill a man's heart," is his conclusion. "One must imagine Sisyphus happy."

One man who knew as much of Camus' biography as anyone was instrumental in seeing these books through to publication: Pascal Pia. Another man was capable of understanding this product of lived experience if only because he had traveled the same path through intuition and invention: André Malraux. Both men participated in the adventure of getting the manuscripts of a lonely young man in Oran to the seat of literary life in Paris, even if it was an enemy-occupied Paris.

Which came first, Librairie Gallimard or *La Nouvelle Revue Française?* Historically there was the literary review created by André Gide with essayist-novelist Jean Schlumberger (founder of the Vieux Colombier with Jacques Copeau), and the enterprising young businessman Gaston Gallimard. Gallimard's first books were published under the imprint Editions de la Nouvelle Revue Française in the years immediately preceding World War I; it became the Librairie Gallimard in 1919, under the ownership of Gaston and his brothers Raymond and Jacques. Henceforth the names "Gallimard" and *NRF* would be indistinguishable, either or both representing nearly all that mattered in French letters in the first half of this century; one could grow up on the *NRF* and be an informed reader; one could be aware of the principal trends in foreign literature, or of the contemporary French theater (without ever having seen a performance in Paris).

The monthly *NRF* served as launching pad for the writers whose books would then appear in the sober (and soft) white covers of the soon-to-be prestigious Gallimard *Collection Blanche*. One could be a young hothead like Malraux and expect consecration from the *NRF,* one could be a surrealist like André Breton, a Communist like Louis Aragon, a conservative like Montherlant, an outright reactionary like Marcel Jouhandeau, a Fascist like Pierre Drieu La Rochelle: If one's work had a certain style, one would find a home in the shrine on the Rue de Beaune (later renamed Rue Sébastien Bottin), a short three streets from the Seine River at its most elegant, opposite the Louvre palace-museum, on the fringe of Marcel Proust's Faubourg St. Germain.

The situation of the house of Gallimard during World War II reflected the ambiguities not only of the men and women of letters of that time, but of all Frenchmen. The reader who was raised in the fiercely contrasted blacks and whites of the World War II movies, where good people were resisting the Nazis and bad ones were collaborating, may have considerable difficulty in understanding what really happened in wartime France. Few of the good were all good, or all of the time; not all of the bad failed to have some concealed virtues, even some small act of resistance to their credit. A Malraux was not untypical, he who began the war living idly in a Riviera villa with a terrace view of the Mediterranean, until he decided that something could be done in the form of armed action in the maquis. Or a Sartre, who began with a scheme for ideological resistance and settled down to writing and publishing—even writing plays produced in occupied Paris which were hailed by German critics (while Simone de Beauvoir was working for the official radio station).[2]

When the Germans approached Paris the first concern of Gaston Gallimard was to keep his publishing family intact. A convoy of five automobiles moved the Gallimards and their files, the *NRF* treasury, to a villa in Normandy surrounded by cow pasture. After the German occupation of Northern France the Gallimards retreated to the south.

And if the Gallimards were interested in the survival of their house, the occupying forces were no less interested. If it had been necessary to invent a *Paris-Soir* in order to show the man in the street that business-as-usual was possible, it was no less necessary to convince cultivated Frenchmen that the *NRF* lived on. The story quickly made the rounds that the German ambassador had said: "There are three forces in France: Communism, the banks, and the *NRF*."[3] Another version of the story was that the first governor sent by the Germans to run Paris had a letter in his pocket giving him two non-military priorities: the City Hall and the *NRF*.[4] Whichever version is true and even if neither is true, it was clear that the continued activity of the magazine, the collaboration of familiar and prestigious names, would be a great force for stability; even the Nazis understood the use of intellectuals.

What happened then requires more knowledge of the inner workings of the mind of the late Jean Paulhan, then director of *Nouvelle Revue Française,* than we possess. For the bargain was a simple one, and loyal Paulhan undoubtedly had a hand in its realization. If the Gallimards would revive *NRF* and allow it to be published under a director approved by the German occupying forces, then *they* would be allowed to pursue their book publishing, and even keep on the staff such independent spirits as Paulhan, Queneau, and Groethuysen; if they did not, the Germans might take over the publishing house and do with it what they would.

It then became vital for all concerned to convince the literary elite

—save Jews, Communists, and others unlikely to accept any such compromise—that they should continue to write for the magazine. The hope was to retain the historic figures—Gide, Valéry, Jacques Audiberti, Jouhandeau, and there would be the addition of some willing collaborators.

Part of the bargain was to take on a new director of *Nouvelle Revue Française* acceptable to the Germans, to replace Jean Paulhan. Such a man was already available in the person of a regular contributor to the magazine, a veteran Gallimard author and an avowed Fascist, Pierre Drieu La Rochelle, who would soon be using *NRF* to hail "the genius of Hitler and of Hitlerism." Drieu would have at his right hand —and this was not the least remarkable aspect of the arrangement—the same Jean Paulhan who was chief editorial adviser to the Gallimards on the book publishing side of the house. Anti-Nazi, roundly resistance-minded, refusing to write for *NRF* while his Jewish and anti-Fascist friends were banned from it, Paulhan was at the same time pro-*NRF* and anti-*NRF*. He wrote to the magazine's regular contributors to obtain their collaboration while privately telling them that he hoped they wouldn't, and he even helped Pascal Pia try to give concrete form to an anti-*NRF*.

Paulhan found perverse pleasure in turning over a manuscript by a Jew such as Julien Benda and waiting for Drieu to say that he couldn't publish it. "And why not?" Paulhan would ask ingenuously, so that Drieu would have to reply: "Because he is a Jew."

When Drieu told Paulhan that together they could publish a magazine serving to link the occupied and "free" zones—north and south France—Paulhan replied: "Better still if we added the forbidden zone —I mean Jews."

Yet when Paulhan was arrested in May 1941 because of his association with a resistance movement (the Musée de l'Homme network, seven of whose leaders were executed), Drieu got him out of jail quickly, and Drieu was also certainly responsible for the immunity that his old friend André Malraux enjoyed on his forays into occupied Paris (even as a resistance leader); during Malraux's visits the two old friends would take the time to discuss current events.

The bargain was kept on both sides. Gaston Gallimard could reopen his publishing house under German censorship. An intelligent German official was assigned to keep the house in line. He was clement, although he couldn't do much to help Jewish authors, and even the chapter concerning the Czech Jew Kafka had to be eliminated from Camus' *Le Mythe de Sisyphe* before Gallimard could publish it. Meanwhile the collaborationist *Nouvelle Revue Française* would appear as long as Drieu could find writers willing to contribute to it, and when he no longer could, and neither Gallimard nor Paulhan could come up with an acceptable alternative, the magazine was shut down with the June 1943 issue, and to Paulhan's relief. In March 1945, after having failed in two previous attempts, Drieu committed suicide; and as punishment for having appeared in occupied Paris, *NRF* was not authorized to be published in liberated France.[5]

And so it was that Gallimard could publish, under the Nazi occupation, a Communist Louis Aragon, a libertine Georges Bataille, could advertise Jean Grenier's *Essai sur l'esprit d'orthodoxie* in the same catalogue with Drieu La Rochelle's *L'Europe contre les patries*. And publish Sartre's *L'Etre et le Néant,* Camus' *L'Etranger, Le Mythe de Sisyphe.* The confusion was such that an early issue of *NRF* published under Drieu—that of February 1941—would contain a poem of Paul Eluard dedicated to Paulhan (but that was the last contribution of Eluard, later to be better known as a Communist and resistance activist) and a section of Gide's journal, while the back cover announced future contributions not only by Alain, Marcel Arland, Abel Bonnard, Alfred Fabre-Luce, and Gide, but by André Malraux—who of course never sent in a manuscript.

Could Edmond Charlot have published Camus' first major books? What would have been the effect of their appearance in provincial Algiers? Could the books have achieved national attention from a small publisher practically unknown in Paris? According to Charlot himself, Camus came to him in 1941 and asked whether he could publish all three "absurds," i.e., *L'Etranger, Le Mythe,* and *Caligula,* in a single volume; in this way would he wrap up the absurdity question. Charlot replied that this was impossible, he didn't have the money to produce such a big book, and that in any case the works should appear in France for maximum effect.[6] But not long after that, Charlot was to prove himself to be a desirable alternative to publication in occupied Paris, and during the war he would have in his growing catalogue prestigious names such as Jean Giono and Pierre Emmanuel, Pierre Jean Jouve, Gertrude Stein, even Gide. When he transferred operations to Paris in 1945, he would issue as many new books each month as Gallimard, among them important new authors such as Arthur Koestler and Alberto Moravia, would win important literary prizes for works of Jules Roy and Henri Bosco, for Roblès. At the suggestion of Gide, Charlot then sponsored a magazine (*L'Arche*) to fill the vacuum left by the disappearance of *NRF,* and if Gallimard had not survived the war Charlot might have become the leading literary publisher of France.[7]

But with Pascal Pia (still based in Lyons) in regular contact with Paulhan and Malraux, the "absurd" books were assured of the best possible treatment. Pia had received the manuscript of *L'Etranger,* sent to him by Camus in Oran, in April 1941. Soon after that he had a manuscript of *Caligula* (but not the one that would be published, for an announced delay in publication allowed time for at least one more revision).[8] Pia showed the books to his friend Francis Ponge, whose own ground-breaking work, *Le Parti pris des choses,* would soon be published by Gallimard; Ponge found the manuscripts extraordinary. Then in early June, Pia dispatched both works to Malraux, at that time living in a villa at Cap-d'Ail, near Saint-Jean-Cap-Ferrat and halfway between Nice and Monte Carlo. When the manuscript of *Le Mythe de Sisyphe* was ready, Camus sent that to Pia as well, and he passed it on to Malraux.

At the time both the southern half of France (including Lyons and of course the Riviera) and Algeria were under Vichy's authority, so letters and even packages moved freely between the two. To correspond from Lyons or from the Riviera with Paris, in the German-occupied north, was something else again, and special interzone cards were used. Pia could send longer letters to Paris via a *Paris-Soir* messenger, but for the sending of manuscripts between the two zones the Gallimards had a system of their own: Packages would go to a Gallimard address in Cannes (the hotel of Raymond Gallimard, Gaston's brother and partner), and a courier would take them to Paris. Thus were the three "absurds" submitted to Gallimard (at the end of September 1941).

Meanwhile other intermediaries were turning up. Jean Grenier, despite his reservations concerning *L'Etranger,* offered to give the manuscript to his friend Marcel Arland, an old *NRF* hand, but Camus feared that this might cross wires with the Pia-Malraux exchange. So instead Grenier recommended Camus and his work warmly to Gaston Gallimard's adviser Paulhan. Malraux sent the Camus manuscripts directly to Gaston Gallimard with his own enthusiastic recommendation (he apparently also showed them to Roger Martin du Gard, a fellow-resident of Southern France).

At the weekly reading committee meeting presided over by Paulhan in the Gallimard building (Janine Gallimard taking notes), Paulhan told the assembled literary advisers: "I've just read a manuscript sent in by Malraux written by a young man living in Algeria. I'll read you the first lines." And he did, in the flat tone for which he was known. Then he put the manuscript on top of a pile, saying: "Recommendation one, naturally." "Recommendation one" meant that the book would be published. Among the members of the reading committee at that time were Raymond Queneau, Brice Parain, Jacques Lemarchand, Ramon Fernandez, Albert Ollivier, Bernard Groethuysen.

Gaston Gallimard agreed with Paulhan without reservations. Galli-

mard's secretary took the manuscript to Gerhard Heller, then working
for the Propaganda-Staffel, on the German side the chief adviser on
French publishing during the occupation. (Heller worked at the Propaganda-Staffel from November 1940 to July 1942, then carried out the
same functions at the German Embassy in Paris.) The secretary explained to Heller that Gallimard was curious to know what he thought
of the book and whether it was liable to represent a violation of self-
censorship. Heller got the book in the afternoon, and began to read it at
once, didn't put it down until he had finished it—at 4 A.M. He was
enthralled, saw it as a great step forward in literature. Early that morning he phoned Gallimard's secretary to indicate his accord and to offer
help in the event of difficulties—a procedure that had worked several
times (although not in the case of Saint-Exupéry's *Flight to Arras*).

Gaston Gallimard was ready to publish *L'Etranger* immediately,
and he so informed Camus through Malraux in November—Gaston
personally had found it remarkable. Paulhan confessed that he too liked
the book very much, but he would be less enthusiastic about *Le Mythe
de Sisyphe*.

Still, Camus had not submitted *L'Etranger* as a single work, but as
part of a "series," something Pia had made clear to Paulhan. But in
Paris they were less sure that such a publishing program was advisable.
Indeed, because of the paper shortage, it was practically impossible. In
December 1941, Gallimard offered to publish *L'Etranger* immediately,
with a 5,000-franc advance (2,000 francs in the mid-1970s, or just
over $400), a royalty of 10 per cent to 10,000 copies, 12 per cent
thereafter. (Like other French publishers, Gallimard gave a 5 per cent
royalty on reprint editions.) Meanwhile Malraux promised to try to see
that *Mythe* was published simultaneously with *L'Etranger*. Finally, the
next March, there was agreement for subsequent release of *Mythe,* but
without the chapter on Jewish Franz Kafka. (That would be published
separately in a free-zone magazine.) Of *Caligula* nothing would be said
immediately; later Gallimard would offer to publish it after *Mythe,* but
by then (September 1942) its author felt that more work needed to be
done on it, and he preferred to wait. *Caligula* finally appeared in book
form in 1944.

Following these complicated movements of his manuscripts from
remote Oran was well-nigh impossible. At one point Camus lost complete control of events, and so did Pia, for apparently Paulhan accepted
*L'Etranger* on the basis of the manuscript received from Malraux after
another copy of the same manuscript sent by Pia via Raymond
Gallimard in Cannes had gone astray. Camus worried that an early
manuscript of the novel might have reached Gallimard, and waited for
reassurance (which came from another Gallimard editor, Raymond

Queneau) that the proper text was to be published. And with Camus so far from occupied Paris, Paulhan read the proofs in his place.

But if Camus was unable to control the movements of his manuscripts from Oran, he nevertheless had a firm grasp of what was happening in France. In March 1942, apparently discouraged by the falling off in quality of his *NRF,* Drieu La Rochelle considered withdrawing, leaving the magazine in the hands of a non-political editorial committee, which he and Gallimard hoped would be headed by Paul Valéry, André Gide, and Léon-Paul Fargue, to guarantee the literary quality of the magazine, with a subcommittee to operate it, composed of Drieu, Paulhan, Arland, and Jean Giono—if the Germans would swallow Paulhan. In a discussion with Gerhard Heller, Valéry apparently agreed to take part if Gide would, but Gide hesitated. Then the whole reorganization appeared to be a scheme by the Germans to blackmail Gallimard into reinforcing the credibility of the magazine, and Drieu himself was no longer certain that he wished to go along with a change which would be a recognition of his own failure.

But while the reorganization was considered possible—from March to at least May 1942—Paulhan again acted as loyal servitor. He didn't feel that he had the right to refuse to carry on the magazine, with Gallimard convinced that his refusal would automatically lead to the closing of the publishing house. (Some of Paulhan's negotiating went on in the form of coded letters—the code being to replace the name of an author by the name of one of his works: "Eupalinos" was Valéry, "Desqueyroux" was Mauriac, "Salavin" was Georges Duhamel.) Paulhan wrote to Camus on March 12, 1942, asking if he could have *L'Etranger* for *Nouvelle Revue Française* (a rather flattering proposal, after all, since Malraux's early work had also been published in the magazine, including *Man's Fate*). Paulhan also hoped Camus would contribute to a special issue on Stendhal.

And all by himself in Oran, Camus had to make the decision— whether or not to receive consecration in the magazine of his culture heroes, even if it was now a magazine published with Nazi approval. In fact he had already decided he would not be published in the wartime *NRF,* and had rejected a similar overture from Drieu La Rochelle. He had confidence, certainly, in Paulhan but hoped that Paulhan would understand his problem of conscience.

It is not known what Camus would have done, or what Paulhan would have done, in the event of the total reorganization of the magazine. What is certain is that Camus was prepared to pass up the opportunity to be published in the holy of holies, unknown as he may have been at the time. A number of his peers, a considerable number of his elders, were less categorical.

All these events took place after Camus' new attack of tuberculosis in Oran, when he felt unable to handle his personal affairs, and while he was recovering in bed.[9]

Gallimard put *L'Etranger* into production in early February 1942; Paulhan read the second proofs in mid-March. Camus was sent an advance on royalties for both *L'Etranger* and *Mythe* on April 30, and at last *L'Etranger* was published, in a printing of 4,400 copies, on June 15. By July 26, Malraux was able to inform Camus that he had seen the novel in bookshop windows along the Riviera. *Mythe,* for which Gallimard had offered the same terms as for the novel, was released on October 16, 1942, in a printing of 2,750 copies.[10]

What did it mean for a book to be published in the capital of enemy-occupied France? Aside from the moral problems, what did it do for the book's audience?

For all of the history of French publishing, Paris had been the center of things. All the publishers were there, and so were the principal literary journals. Writers might live far from Paris, but what counted was what was said in Parisian salons and cafés.

But now the best people were out of Paris, or silent. If newspapers and magazines had not been totally under the control of the Nazi propaganda apparatus, they would have been of little help anyway because of the lack of space available for non-essentials such as culture. Paper shortages kept newspapers slender. In the so-called free zone, censorship was more lax for the smaller literary reviews dispersed around the provinces, but their audience was negligible.

There was the convenient fiction that a non-political paper could exist in occupied Paris. In 1941 such a publication was launched, under the guise of reviving a prewar publication: the weekly *Comoedia,* published in large-newspaper format. The tactic was to play up celebrities of the literary world, the theater, music, and the other arts, as if life was proceeding as usual. The very first issue led off with a text by Henry de Montherlant, Jean-Paul Sartre on Herman Melville, an interview with Paul Valéry, contributions by Jean-Louis Barrault, Arthur Honegger. Over the years of German occupation *Comoedia* managed to obtain the contributions of Jean Giraudoux, Jean Cocteau, Jacques Copeau, Charles Dullin, Colette—even of Jean Paulhan. Each issue also served up a generous portion of "European" (read German) culture, the constant theme being the essential brotherhood of the German and French heritage.[11] (Sartre soon realized that the weekly was less independent than its director claimed, and ceased to write for it, reminding himself that the first rule for an intellectual was not to write for any periodical published in the occupied zone.)[12]

But *Comoedia* was the best one could hope for in Paris. On the publication of *L'Etranger,* the July 11, 1942, issue of the Paris weekly would welcome it in a headline covering two of the large front page's six columns:

**A Coming Writer . . .**
**ALBERT CAMUS**

The author of the article was Marcel Arland, a regular contributor to *Comoedia.* A noted novelist who would one day be elected to the French Academy, he not only worked for *NRF* (he would be co-editor with Paulhan of *La Nouvelle Nouvelle Revue Française* in its postwar reincarnation, then on Paulhan's withdrawal because of illness would be editor in chief until his own retirement in 1977), but he happened to be the editor at Gallimard to whom Jean Grenier had intended to submit Camus' novel. Arland's review, like Paulhan's original presentation of the manuscript to Gallimard's reading committee, led off with the opening paragraph of *L'Etranger.* He referred to a recent reprinting of *Noces* by Charlot, evoked Jean Grenier and the work of Sartre, before concluding:

> Perhaps this conception of purity and disdain for "ideal" truths contains many illusions, and literary illusions. But the thought and the attitude of Mr. Camus are at once those of a man and those of a country or climate: the morality and the song of the sun, the desperate exaltation of mortal life. . . . And despite reservations one may have concerning this thought . . . the important thing is that Mr. Camus' position is sincere, his tone moves us. Already in [*Noces*] one found the qualities that one recognizes with greater force today in *L'Etranger:* those of a true writer.

In the Vichy-controlled free zone, one publication whose independence was uncontested was *Cahiers du Sud,* published in Marseilles. (Paradoxically, this magazine was openly dispatched to Paris all during the German occupation, where it was distributed by the bookseller-publisher José Corti, who never lost any copies to the censors.)[12] The February 1943 issue contained a long essay by a frequent contributor to that periodical, Jean-Paul Sartre (with twenty-nine footnotes), "Explication de *l'Etranger.*" Had Sartre then been the influential figure he would become, had the magazine a broader audience, such an article by itself could have assured the success of Camus' work. Sartre had understood the connection, in any case, between *L'Etranger* and *Le Mythe de Sisyphe;* he realized that the theory of the absurd novel in *Mythe* would help the reader understand Camus' own novel. "*L'Etranger* is a classic work, a work of order," he wrote, "written about the absurd and against the absurd." He called it "a short moralist's novel," and it reminded him of a tale by Voltaire. He dismissed the notion that the novel represented "Kafka written by Hemingway," because "The views of Mr. Camus are quite down-to-earth." If Camus used the tools of American fiction he was not influenced by that fiction, Sartre decided, astutely predicting: "I doubt that he will use them again in his future work."

In the same issue of *Cahiers du Sud* there is a shorter review of *L'Etranger* by Jean Grenier, emphasizing again the author's background, Algeria. "Here are united people of all conditions and origins, without beliefs, without regrets, without traditions, and who in summer dream only of enjoying, vulgarly without doubt, but clearly and without ulterior motives, the sun, the sea, and everything that can intoxicate the senses." And in Max-Pol Fouchet's *Fontaine,* Henri Hell would write: "With *L'Etranger* Camus ranks at the apex of the contemporary novel, in that path which from Malraux, passing by Céline, ends with Jean-Paul Sartre, and which has endowed the French novel with a new content and style." Yet Hell felt that Camus' contribution was too consciously literary, found it to be in the line of Sartre's *La Nausée,* remarked the influence not only of Kafka but of Chestov and of Kierkegaard; the book was the sign of Kierkegaard's arrival in France. In style Hell discovered the mark of Americans such as John Dos Passos, which he felt well suited to Camus' work.

Neither then nor later could one be assured of an objective literary review in France. Arland worked for Camus' publisher and was Grenier's friend; Sartre was a Gallimard writer; Grenier was both a Gallimard writer and a friend of the author; and so was Hell a friend. Camus had certainly made an impression on the French literary establishment, kind reviews notwithstanding. He would not become a best selling author during the war, but who could, with the chronic paper scarcity? During a railway journey not so long after that Simone de Beauvoir overheard fellow passengers discussing *L'Etranger,* comparing it to *La Nausée.*[13]

# 20

---◆---

## LA PESTE

The headlands of the coast have the air of a fleet ready to
sail. . . . All of Oranie is ready for departure, and each
day at noon a rustle of excitement runs through it. One
morning perhaps we shall leave together.

*Carnets*

If fame traveled by train in those times, trains ran slowly, and days and
nights were long. People were reading then, for there were few alternative sources of entertainment. Had more paper been available, more
copies of *L'Etranger* and other books would certainly have been published. By printing good literature, even in small editions, publishers
were adding to their catalogues; an author like Albert Camus was
money in the bank. And did Camus realize that he had already
achieved all the notoriety that mattered in France? In and around the
house of Gallimard were the readers who made literary history. They
were the French literary establishment.

Camus received a copy of his book from Gallimard—only one, for
his author's complimentary copies didn't get through—but the reviews
took longer to reach him. Grenier told him about Arland's review in
*Comoedia,* but he was not to see that or any of the other Parisian notices for a while. What he did see, the reviews published in the "free-
zone" press, did not please him; he was being attacked from the point
of view of morality, what he called *la moraline*. "Imbeciles who think
that negation is a surrender when it is a choice." He expressed his bitterness in his journal: "Three years to write a book, five lines to ridi-
cule it—and false quotations." He drafted a letter to one of his critics,
"destined not to be sent." The unknown reviewer had failed to see the

importance of what was essential to the understanding of *L'Etranger:*
the last chapter in which the protagonist reveals something of himself.
Because Camus had wished to "say less," the reviewer had dismissed
the book as negative, the hero as vegetable. The author refused to the
critic the right to say that a book served or harmed the country at this
time.

He concluded the unsent letter: Let's not have another misunderstanding; I am not an unhappy author, and I don't want this letter to
be published. You don't often see my name in the magazines, although
it's easy enough to be published today.

> It's that having nothing to say to them I don't like to sacrifice my-
> self to promotion. At the moment I am publishing books which
> took me years of work, for the sole reason that they are finished
> and that I'm working on those which are to follow. . . .

As for what was to follow, he would be working on his next novel,
*La Peste,* during all the time he lived in Oran. What he had been looking for was a strong symbol to carry his theme, and he had read deeply
and carefully in *Moby Dick,* noting in his journal the pages where symbol was used effectively: "The feelings, the images multiply the philosophy by ten." (Gallimard had published *Moby Dick* in a translation by a
group of three, including Jean Giono, only the previous year.)

But one would like to know more about the origins of the notion of
using a city stricken by plague, cut off from the world and its citizens
quarantined, as a model of the situation of the world as he knew it: war
and occupation, the infection of Nazi ideology. In April 1941, at the
time of the epidemic of typhus in the Tlemcen region and Roblès' report on this epidemic to Camus, his journal provides the first specific
reference to a novel about plague: *Peste ou aventure.* In this first outline, the story is presented much as it will be published six years later.
But there is a curious subtitle for this journal notation: *La Peste libératrice.* This suggest that from the beginning there was a conflict in intention in the author's mind, for *La Peste libératrice* may be a reference to
Antonin Artaud, whose plague is purgative and beneficial. Camus would
have read Artaud's remarkable comparison of theater and plague published first in *Nouvelle Revue Française* (in October 1934) and then as
a section of *Le Théâtre et son double* (published by Gallimard in
1938). Later on, as we shall see, when Jean-Louis Barrault produced
Camus' dramatic version of the plague story, *L'Etat de siège,* this play
would fail because Barrault would look for Artaud in it (purgative,
beneficial plague), while for Camus the disease was all bad, like totalitarianism.

That Camus saw plague as unmitigated evil from the very inception of his project is suggested by his reading notes in October 1941: In 1342, he discovered, at the time of the Black Death, Jews were executed. In 1481, when the plague ravaged southern Spain, the Inquisition blamed the Jews.

But before harboring plague Oran had already harbored ennui, and now something was tearing at Camus, who felt a prisoner of this materialistic city. Standing on the beach, he dreamed of his own departure. "Separate myself from this empty heart—refuse everything that dries me up," he confided his hopes to his journal. If the spring tides are elsewhere, why insist?" He confessed: "At a certain time one can no longer feel the emotion of love. Only the tragic side remains." Through the Oran winter his mood was gloomy, now resigned, now intentionally ascetic. "Rid oneself of everything. Lacking a desert, the plague or the little station of Tolstoy." And his journal in the beginning of 1942 contains his first comment on Nazi collaboration. He accuses the Vichy government of "the fury and the low desire to see the downfall of the one [England] who dares resist the force which crushed you yourself."

Camus was at home at their Rue d'Arzew apartment one evening at the end of January 1942 when a coughing fit broke out. It grew worse, he began spitting blood. Alarmed, Francine rushed out—they had no telephone then—to find their doctor, Henri Cohen, brother-in-law of Camus' college classmate Liliane Choucroun. Dr. Cohen was called out of the movies to examine Camus. When the first long night was over Francine crossed the terrace to tell her mother and her sisters what had happened. Christiane Faure rushed in to find Camus stretched out in bed. "I thought it was all over for me this time," he told her in a weak voice.

For this time—for the first time—Camus' left lung was affected, as badly as the right one had been when he had his first attack at the age of seventeen. He would have to undergo another lung collapse and suffer periodic pneumothorax injections, indefinitely. The hemoptysis was stopped soon enough, but the doctor prescribed a long period of rest, and that also meant no swimming, which had been Camus' chief distraction in Oran.

Dr. Cohen was himself about to become the victim of a form of plague: the Vichy government's anti-Jewish decrees. A quota had been set on the number of Jewish doctors who would be allowed to practice; they could represent no more than 2 per cent of the medical profession. A similar quota applied to lawyers and others in state-controlled professions, and of course pupils and their teachers had already been expelled from the school system. During a spring vacation at a beach resort near

Oran, Canastel, the Camus and the Benichous decided to invite Dr. Cohen and his wife to join them, hoping to cheer him up, for the ban was now being applied in Oran, and he was required to give up his practice.

Even in good times Dr. Cohen was known as a serious man. He had prescribed an austere convalescence not only for Camus but for André Benichou, who suffered from heart trouble. But out at Canastel in the glorious May weather the good doctor forgot his own medical advice; with patients Camus and Benichou he was soon engaged in an exhausting tournament of *pétanque,* the southern French bowling game. The others enjoyed the spectacle of Dr. Cohen's no-holds-barred tossing, and perhaps for a moment he did forget the racial laws.

Back in the city, however, the local delegates of Vichy—always zealous about applying Nazi legislation—put official seals on Dr. Cohen's office. In order to treat his patient and friend, the doctor received Camus at the office of his brother-in-law, Dr. Maurice Pariente, who as a World War I veteran had been given a priority and was still allowed to practice.[1]

It was while in bed that Camus found himself keeping track of the movement of his manuscripts between Pascal Pia and the Gallimards, and it was also while he was in bed, far from the literary world (even of Algiers, such as it was) that he made his decision not to allow his work to be published in *Nouvelle Revue Française.* For a long while his activity would be limited to reading and note-taking; for the first three weeks he couldn't even leave his bed. It was now that he began hearing from the critics of *L'Etranger.* He was pleased, when at last he could read it, by the front-page welcome that Marcel Arland had given his book in *Comoedia.* Otherwise he discovered a failure to comprehend both in the reviewers who praised and those who attacked the book.

The question was, what to do with his life now? For the first time in a long time the word "sanatorium" was mentioned—and not dismissed. At the very least it was considered desirable that he escape the damp climate of North Africa before summer. In May the Camus applied for a pass which would allow them to travel to the French mountains at the end of Francine's teaching year on July 1. The application was backed up by an urgent medical recommendation.[2] While waiting, they spent two weeks away from city heat on the seacoast, near Aïn-el-Turk, nine miles west of Oran, in an old Spanish farmhouse belonging to Marguerite Dobrenn's family, surrounded by friends. Since Camus wasn't allowed to swim, Francine stayed out of the water too. But Camus was allowed to cook, and one day he made a grandiose bouillabaisse for the household, employing all the spices he could find in the kitchen.

When the travel pass was at last granted in August, the couple packed hurriedly and grabbed a train for Algiers, where they boarded a steamer for Marseilles. Emmanuel Roblès, among a group of friends who lunched with the Camus in Algiers, noted that Camus was perspiring profusely all during the meal; he could barely speak.[3]

The choice of a mountain retreat for Camus' convalescence was determined by their limited means. Luckily, the Faure family had in reserve just what was needed: an isolated rural site which was practically their private vacation resort. The sister of Francine Camus' father, her aunt Marguerite, had married the actor Paul-Emile (called Paul) Oettly. Oettly's mother ran a boardinghouse at Le Panelier, a hamlet— actually no more than a patch of farmhouses—just outside the town of Le Chambon-sur-Lignon, lying at 3150 feet in the Vivarais range of what is known as the Massif Central, a landscape of splintery schist rock summits and benign tree-covered slopes, some thirty-five miles south of the industrial center of Saint-Etienne, itself about thirty-five miles west and south of Lyons. Camus of course was never to know that this was the land of his maternal grandmother's family (Silhac is only a few miles southeast of Chambon). The Faures had been going to Le Panelier in the summertime since they were children. Another occasional boarder at Madame Oettly's was the poet Francis Ponge, soon to become Camus' friend, who had watched little Francine playing in the back yard while he discussed serious literature with Francine's older sister Christiane. One day Ponge would meet a young lady in Chambon who would become his wife.

Their hostess, Sarah Oettly, a strong, kind woman, was widely admired. She would go by foot from Le Panelier into the town of Chambon two and a half miles away to do her shopping, and haul the supplies two and a half miles back again.[4]

Isolated Chambon, which had fewer than one thousand inhabitants before World War II, less than a third of its present population, was a stronghold of French Protestantism. From the time of the sixteenth-century Reformation the population of Chambon and its sister village, Mazet-Saint-Voy, had been doing battle with France's Catholic majority, and was frequently a target of persecutions and forced conversions. But the only access to the towns was through mountain passes, and the people of Chambon and of Mazet resisted. The region remained a Protestant enclave down to the present day, and with the development of tourism a preferred summer retreat of the country's Protestant families (who before the war included the Gides and the Ponges). The house that Sarah Oettly ran as a *pension* at Le Panelier was part of a cluster of massive stone buildings grouped as a fortified farm, the eighteenth-

century domain of a family of Protestant notaries. Its crenellated gate
and its tower, later converted into living quarters, were local tourist
attractions.[5]

The steamer to Marseilles took the long way around, following the
Spanish coast to avoid storms, for the poor quality of wartime coal
would not have permitted them to withstand a storm at sea. The cabins
were jammed, but fine weather made it possible to sleep out on deck.
The Camus couple had something to keep them occupied from the time
of boarding, for Jacques Heurgon had told them that a friend was to be
a passenger on the same ship. Louis Joxe, an *agrégé* in history, son-in-
law of the historian Daniel Halévy, had gotten an appointment to a lycée
in Algiers after the fall of France, and was also giving courses at the
university. But he was not the sort of man to stay put for long; a number of his friends had joined the active resistance to the occupying
forces and to Vichy, and he wished to make contact with them. The
friends included Pierre Brossolette, another *agrégé* in history, who
would participate in the Musée de l'Homme resistance group whose dis-
mantlement had led to Paulhan's arrest, would be de Gaulle's adviser
on resistance matters and a key figure in setting up a Conseil National
de la Résistance; arrested by the Gestapo, he killed himself rather than
reveal secrets. Another friend was Jean Moulin, sent into France by de
Gaulle to unify the underground movements; arrested and tortured, he
died on the train taking him to a German camp. A third was Georges
Bidault, president of the Conseil National de la Résistance after the
death of Moulin.

Joxe looked for Camus but couldn't identify him because he understood that he was traveling alone. He did wonder about one young man
reading a brand-new white-cover Gallimard novel by Louis Guilloux,
*Le Pain des rêves.* Meanwhile Albert and Francine decided that their
man was that scholarly-looking little gentleman holding a volume by
Théophile Gautier, and they pounced on him. From then on the Camus
and Joxe were inseparable, sharing the hardships of wartime travel. For
example, each traveler had to strip to be examined for lice, after which
he received a certificate to the effect that "the following ———— has
been found free of ————." At Marseilles they boarded the train to
ride to Lyons together, separated only after ardent promises to see each
other again, even to stage plays together—and in any case to meet six
months after hostilities ended at the Pyramide Restaurant (Chez Point)
in Vienne, south of Lyons, already at that time the possessor of three
stars in the Michelin Guide as one of the great kitchens of the country.

What Joxe did in France was to see resistance leaders who could
put him in touch with those back in Algeria who were preparing the
Allied landing there. When de Gaulle and his Free French arrived in

Algiers, Joxe became secretary-general of the provisional government, a job he would carry on in post-Liberation Paris. Later he would be appointed French Ambassador to Moscow, then to Bonn, and as a close confidant of de Gaulle he was significantly responsible for the negotiations leading to the independence of Algeria.[6]

To reach Le Panelier one took a train to Saint-Etienne, a grim industrial town with no apparent saving graces, whose population was then about 170,000. Another train, with a change to a narrow-gauge track, served Le Chambon-sur-Lignon. From Chambon a country lane crossed a stream, often becoming a torrent as it rushed along its narrow bed of fallen rock, then in ups and downs joined a straight ribbon of road shielded on either side by tall plane trees; just beyond was the farm-fortress of Le Panelier. The surroundings are hilly, pine-covered slopes often shrouded by mist. The evergreen hills contribute to a melancholy atmosphere, and local inhabitants willingly speak of their landscape as *triste*. Camus' own first description was written into his journal shortly after his arrival.

> This sound of springs all along my days. They flow around me, through sunny meadows, then closer to me and soon I shall have this sound inside me, this spring at the heart and this sound of fountains will accompany all my thoughts. This is oblivion.

He recorded a view from his window at dawn:

> Before sunrise, above the high hills, the pine trees cannot be distinguished from the rolling ground which supports them—

an observation which every visitor to this mountain country will ratify.

> As the sun gets higher and the sky lighter, the pine trees grow larger and the barbaric army seems to advance. . . . And it seems a savage race toward the valley, the beginning of a brief and tragic struggle in which the barbarians of the day will rout the thoughts of the night.

By the third week of August 1942 the Camus were settled in at Le Panelier. One thing they soon discovered: They could eat better in Chambon than in Algeria (which depended on the mainland not only for manufactured products but for meat and vegetables, even fats). Camus quickly arranged for regular visits to Saint-Etienne for pneumothorax injections, which were administered every twelve days. On his return to Chambon in the evening Francine would meet him at the station and they would walk back to the fortified farm. At least once, he rode thirty-five miles of roads winding up and down the mountains on a bicycle, but that could not have been recommended by his doctor.

In a long passage in his journal he summed up occupied France and its tribulations as seen from the little train taking him to Saint-Etienne: "Hopeless and silent life that all of France accepts in expectation. . . ." Then "The filthy landscape of an industrial valley," the gloom aggravated by rain. But back in Le Panelier, isolated from civilization, isolated even from the burg of Chambon, with only the sound of rushing water to distract him, in the healthy air, and with the best chance a Frenchman of modest means could have of a proper diet in 1942, he began to feel that he might get better here, and after that anything was possible. "Anything" meant returning to Algeria, of course. But not to Oran; both Francine and he agreed about that. His dream was to find a house at Bouzaréah on top of the crest overlooking the bay of Algiers, far from the central city, where he had biked with Max-Pol Fouchet and their friends in lycée days. (Yet it had to be on a bus line, too, for he hoped to resume active duties at Edmond Charlot's publishing house.) He asked Emmanuel Roblès, who lived in Bouzaréah, to try to find him a house with a view of the sea.[7]

Meanwhile he had lost no time returning to his writing, principally to *La Peste,* which he now realized was not going to be an easy book to finish. "I must stick closely to the idea," he warned himself. "*L'Etranger* describes the nakedness of man faced with the absurd. *La Peste,* the deep identity of individual points of view faced with the same absurd. It is a progression which will become clearer in other works." He wondered if the title should not be something other than *La Peste*— like "Les Prisonniers" for example. After another glance at the reviews of *L'Etranger,* whose critics saw "Impassiveness" rather than what they might have seen, "Benevolence," he reminded himself that he must make his intentions clear in *La Peste.*

He was now also deep into the play "Budejovice" (to become *Le Malentendu*), based on the archetypal story that had first come to him in the form of a news dispatch: the son who returns to the inn run by his mother and sister, concealing his identity, only to be assassinated by them, for in his absence mother and sister have adopted this means of earning their livelihood.

And he began making notes for the third book in his "second series," a book, that would one day become *L'Homme révolté.*

During the long evenings he was reading Joyce. He decided that what moved him wasn't the work; it was the fact that Joyce had undertaken it. And Proust; he found *A la recherche du temps perdu* heroic and virile "1) by the persistency of the creative will; 2) by the effort it demands from an ill person."

He learned from Algiers that Charlot's planned publication of *"Le Minotaure,"* an essay he had written about Oran which was to have ap-

peared as a slim book, had not received the necessary approval of the
censor, and Camus had been counting on income from sales to keep
him alive until spring. Jean Grenier had arranged with *Cahiers du Sud*
for publication of an essay-review by Camus of *Le Portrait de M.
Pouget,* by Jean Guitton, a devout account of the life of a traditionalist
Catholic priest (whose good sense, Camus decided, could be accepted
even by someone not of the Church). Camus had written the review in
Oran and faithful Christiane Galindo had typed it for him. He would
send it on to Grenier, but not before adding a footnote to indicate the
distance he intended to take from Guitton's wartime attitudes: *"Le Portrait de M. Pouget* was written before the war. Since the armistice, on
the contrary, Mr. Guitton has published writings and articles to which I
would not give the same approval." The article was to appear, with
what was then a courageous footnote, in *Cahiers du Sud* of April 1943,
after the Germans had invaded the previously unoccupied south to control all of France including Marseilles, where the magazine was published.[8]

Now it was time for Francine to leave her husband and to return to Algeria. In accordance with their plan, she was to see if she could find
teaching jobs for both of them in Algiers, and of course a place to live,
while he stayed on as long as possible at Le Panelier, getting all the
mountain air he could. His wife stopped en route at Lyons to see the
Pias, and to bring them a pâté from Le Panelier, for in the cities one
didn't eat as one did in the country; and then she stayed a week with an
old friend in the Drôme valley; by the middle of October she was back
in Algiers.

And her husband settled down to watch autumn come to the Haute
Loire: "Red beauty." He was resigned to the need for a long convalescence, a more ascetic existence, smoking no more than four cigarettes a day, abstaining from wine.[3] He made one of several entries in
his journal on the value of chastity: "Sexual life was given to man perhaps to divert him from his true road," he wrote. "It's his opium. . . .
Without it, things come back to life." Deprived of an opportunity to
talk about himself and his work, he talked to his notebook, admonished
himself: "A writer should not speak of his doubts in confrontation with
his creation. . . . Never speak of his doubts—*no matter what they may
be."*

Again, after a journal entry dated October 23 marked "Début,"
perhaps signifying the commencement of actual writing of *La Peste,* he
reminded himself: "Sexuality leads nowhere. It is not immoral but it
isn't productive."

He made a brief trip to Lyons, probably now booking passage to

Algiers on a steamer that was to sail on November 21,[9] and he met
Grenier there. He thought that he might be able to obtain a pass for the
occupied zone, to allow him to do some library research on plagues in
Paris; in that city Gallimard was just now publishing *Le Mythe de
Sisyphe*. To his journal he complained:

> It isn't I who give up beings and things (I could not), it's the things
> and the beings who have given me up. My youth escapes me; that is
> being ill.

The note was probably written on November 7, 1942, Camus' twenty-
ninth birthday.

That night, off the Algerian coast, Operation Torch began. At 1
A.M. President Franklin D. Roosevelt spoke by radio to the French
people, promising that the Allies had no interest in their territory, as
American and British troops landed to the east and west of Algiers. Simultaneously, in the Bay of Arzew east of Oran, more troops were
landed. This, the first such Allied offensive of World War II, would in
seventy-six hours control 1,300 miles of North African coastline, the
objectives being to drive the enemy from North Africa and to prepare a
base for the invasion of Southern Europe. Planned in total secrecy, the
landing took the Axis powers by surprise; some 60,000 men in 600
ships turned the war around; from then on the western Allies would
move from victory to victory until France, Italy, and all of Western
Europe were liberated.

Not unexpectedly, in view of the ambiguities of Vichy, and of
divided loyalties both in North Africa and on the mainland, the political
problems faced by the Allies seemed at least as difficult as the military
ones. The invasion had been prepared by a small group of trusted
French resistance leaders; negotiations had been carried out by the
American diplomat Robert Murphy, under cover of an embassy still
accredited to Vichy, then by General Mark W. Clark arriving by night
in a submarine to meet French Algerians in a house on a Mediterranean beach. But on North Africa's D-Day, Vichy loyalists fought
back, sank Allied ships in an intensive artillery barrage in the Algiers
bay, while Vichy-French opposition to American ground troops continued until November 11. In Algiers the Allied objective was to obtain a
formal cease-fire from Vichy representative Admiral Jean Darlan (soon
to be assassinated) while imposing General Henri Giraud's authority
(which de Gaulle suspected was a way to freeze him out as leader of
the resistance). On the French mainland, meanwhile, German forces
began to move south in the early hours of November 11, that day effectively putting an end to the Vichy-controlled southern zone of France.
Henceforth the whole country was under the authority of German

troops, so that liberated North Africa was totally cut off from mainland France.

*"Like rats!"* Camus scribbled into his journal on November 11. The notation has been taken to refer to the trap that had been laid for him by the Allied landings three days earlier. More likely he was reacting to the day's news of the German invasion of the Vichy zone in which he lived. The consequences were that Camus could not use the steamer passage he had booked in Lyons; he could not join Francine (or even get in touch with her), now that mainland France and Algeria were on opposite sides of the war.

He had been warned to come back sooner, but in veiled language he hadn't quite understood.[9] For back in Algiers, where Francine had gone directly from Le Panelier, she had been put up at the Acaults'. And soon she had more than an inkling of what was in store for North Africa; it was clear that an Allied beachhead was in preparation, and that her husband was not going to be able to return. But how to tell him that? Knowing that he listened to Emmanuel Roblès, she went up to Bouzaréah and found him teaching at the Ecole Normale there. A telegram was sent to Camus urging him to come home, but by that time it was too late. Later they discovered that the ship Camus would have taken to return to Algiers was stopped en route by Vichy patrols and escorted back to Marseilles.[7]

Without money, facing the approaching winter, Camus' feelings could have been predicted. His disappointment was augmented by anxiety for his family, for he assumed that the Germans would be bombing Algiers as a legitimate target. And he would now, for the first time, indicate intense concern for his country; the German occupation had seen to that.[9]

Already the ground at Le Panelier was covered with frost in the early mornings. Seated on a spur of land at the confluent of two streams, the spur like the prow of a ship:

> I pursue this immobile navigation in the land of indifference. Nothing less than all nature and this white peace that winter brings to hearts too warm—to appease this heart devoured by a bitter love. . . . Be silent, lung! Gorge yourself with this pale and icy air which is your food. Stay quiet. Let me no longer be forced to hear your slow decaying—and let me turn finally toward . . . [text ends here]

# PART II

# Exile

# 21

◆

# "WHO IS THIS STRANGER . . . ?"

> And one must not forget those for whom . . . the sadness
> of separation was amplified by the fact that, travelers sur-
> prised by the plague and retained in the city, they found
> themselves removed at once from the person they could
> not rejoin and from their country. . . . In the general
> exile, they were the most exiled, for if time created in
> them as in everyone the anguish appropriate to it, they
> were also attached to a space, and threw themselves with-
> out cease against the walls which separated their contami-
> nated refuge from their lost country.
>
> "Les Exilés dans la peste"

As soon as he could Camus made the journey to Lyons (not a very
long one by private automobile, but it meant changing trains, long waits
in stations, in occupied France). His benefactor Pascal Pia was still
there. At the time of the German invasion of what had been the "unoccupied" southern half of France, Pia had left *Paris-Soir* to join the active resistance, becoming deputy to Marcel Peck, chief of "R. 1," the
Rhône-Alpes region of the underground movement called Combat, responsible for the departments of Jura, Saône-et-Loire, Ain, Rhône,
Loire, Haute-Loire, Ardèche, Drôme, Isère, Savoie, and Haute-Savoie.
Pia's pseudonym was "Renoir."[1]

Camus had no income at all now; he had counted on the small
sums he had been receiving from Charlot. And if he might have been
able to find a job before, the German occupation of Southern France
made it impossible for him to work on a newspaper. So the good Pia
decided to take charge of Camus' material needs. Knowing that Camus

would die before asking for anything, Pia wrote to his friends Malraux and Paulhan to describe Camus' straits. Could Gallimard help with a monthly stipend, say 2,000 francs (in the mid-1970s worth a little more than 600 francs, or about $125)? Perhaps as an advance against his next novel? Malraux quickly endorsed the suggestion. The house of Gallimard put Camus on the payroll as a reader.

The arrangement embarrassed Camus. He confessed to not liking the idea of writing for money, but events had made it impossible for him to refuse. What he really hoped was to find a job in Paris, and he asked Paulhan if there was any chance of that.[2]

Pia also concerned himself with Camus' spiritual needs. Christmas was approaching; he gave Camus several volumes of Kierkegaard in a limited edition published by the translator Paul-Henri Tusseau. (These books were later republished in Kierkegaard's complete works.) Not that Camus admired Kierkegaard that much, but he had said that he wanted a deeper understanding of the existentialists, inspired by Sartre's writing on Heidegger.

Possibly it was now, or if not it was on a subsequent visit to Lyons, that Camus met some of Pia's friends. One was a quiet, conscientious poet, a lesser figure on the fringes of the *NRF* and the surrealist movement since the early 1920s, a secret Communist Party member, who had just published (at Gallimard of course) the work that would assure his survival in French letters, *Le Parti pris des choses,* a small volume of concise, ironic, or pathetic prose poems to the glory of the materiality of objects, which would inspire a postwar generation of "new novelists." But Francis Ponge, then forty-three, was anything but a famous author. He had been working as an insurance salesman in Roanne, a town some fifty miles from Lyons, when Pia had written to him to say that he wanted to publish a "free *NRF*" called *Prométhée,* and wished Ponge, as a former contributor to *NRF,* to write for it. Ponge told Pia that he had no texts available but could help in practical ways (he thought of addressing envelopes). The two men had then met at Tarare, a town almost exactly halfway between Roanne and Lyons, at which time the irrepressible Pia asked Ponge if he would like to work for Lyons' daily newspaper *Le Progrès,* where Pia knew everyone. After submitting some sample articles Ponge was hired as the newspaper's regional chief stationed at Bourg-en-Bresse.

On visits to Lyons, Ponge would stay at an apartment belonging to the sister of René Leynaud, who also worked for *Le Progrès.* The apartment served as occasional shelter for Leynaud himself and for visitors on resistance missions; Camus would also stay there when in Lyons. Ponge had read Camus' three "absurds," shown to him in manuscript by Pia in August 1941, long before he met Camus, and their mutual association with the Oettlys and Le Panelier cemented the relationship. Meanwhile Ponge, who in Roanne had been serving as an intermediary between Communist resistance agents (with formal instructions not to talk like a Communist, for it was important that he appear apolitical in order to assure the security of his liaison function), now asked the Party to give him a more active assignment. Henceforth he would work as a recruiting agent among journalists; as an emissary of the Communists' Front National, his mission was to contact newspaper staff members in the towns he visited, and to arrange to keep them informed, to help them prepare to take over their newspapers on the day of national insurrection.[3]

Camus was also to meet Leynaud. Then thirty-three years old, Leynaud was also a poet, although an unpublished one. There was immediate and reciprocal sympathy, an exchange of books and manuscripts. After the war in a preface to the posthumous publication of Leynaud's poems Camus would tell the rest of the story: how during Camus' visits to Lyons Leynaud would put him up in a small room on the Rue Vieille-Monnaie (now called Rue René Leynaud); how before going out to find a bed elsewhere Leynaud would smoke a pipe, and they would talk until curfew time. "The heavy silence of occupation nights settled around us. This large and somber city of conspiracy which Lyons was emptied little by little. . . ." But they did not speak of conspiracies: Leynaud seldom talked about what he was doing, unless it was absolutely necessary. They spoke rather of mutual friends, of sports and swimming, sometimes of books. The room was filled with volumes of poetry.

Leynaud had stopped writing. He told Camus that he would do that *afterwards*. Following his service in the French Army at the outbreak of war, during which he participated in the retreat at Dunkirk and across the Channel to the English coast, he had returned to join the active resistance as head of an intelligence group under Combat's regional chief Peck. Arrested in May 1944 on Lyons' Place Bellecour, he was shot in the legs as he tried to escape. Taken prisoner, he was executed by the Germans as they prepared to withdraw from that city.

But before that, on visits to Saint-Etienne for his pneumothorax treatment, Camus would arrange to meet Leynaud. They would spend a few hours together in that "hopeless city." Camus had warned Leynaud that it would be difficult to undertake any resistance activity in Saint-Etienne, a place which for Camus would have been hell if hell existed, with "these interminable and gray streets, where everyone was dressed in black." And Camus was convinced that he himself would be useless as a member of the resistance, "never having felt anything but the most unreasonable of torpors." Leynaud told him that he was exaggerating.

They made an appointment in Saint-Etienne (this was in September 1943) so that Camus could introduce Leynaud to a friend. "He is an energetic and irreverent Dominican, who said he detested Christian Democrats and dreamed of a Nietschean Christianity." (He was Father Raymond-Léopold Bruckberger, bad boy of the French Church, certainly everything Camus said he was.) Bruckberger and Camus waited for Leynaud at the railroad station restaurant, but Leynaud arrived only in time for dessert, ill and unable to speak; five minutes later Bruckberger had to catch a train. Leynaud and Camus, whose own trains left late in the afternoon, wandered about, "deadened by heat and boredom, collapsing, at regular intervals, in front of a saccharine-sweetened soda, in cafés deserted and filled with flies." Seeing Leynaud off, as they were both seized with fits of laughter, Camus said, "As you see, nothing can succeed here." Another time Camus walked with Leynaud in Lyons, strolling along the Place Bellecour among the children and the pigeons which had not yet been caught for food. They walked for a full half hour without speaking, but, Camus felt, thinking the same things.

They would meet a final time, in the spring of 1944, in Paris, so fully in accord that they decided that they would work together after the liberation of France.

There is at least a minor irony in the fact that resistance activity was taking place in Le Chambon-sur-Lignon of which Camus was not aware, or was only partially aware, perhaps because of the impermanence of his association with the region. In its isolation, Chambon and the surrounding country were an ideal refuge for those having to flee the Nazis or from Vichy. Most of the refugees were Jews. Leaders of the movement were the Protestant pastors Edouard Theis and André Trocmé, the mayor of Chambon, and the director of the town's Protestant school, called Ecole Nouvelle Cévenole, which grew from 18 pupils in 1938 and 40 in 1939 to 150 in 1940, 250 in 1941, 300 in 1943, 350 in 1944; today it is the nationally known Collège Cévenol, with a student body of some 500. The teachers included Pastor Trocmé and well-known Protestant laymen such as the philosopher Paul Ricoeur and André Philip, who would become Commissaire à l'Intérieur in de Gaulle's London government. There were also Jewish teachers such as Daniel Isaac, professor of letters at the Paris Lycée Henri IV, who had been dismissed under the racial laws.

From the pulpit, the pastors belabored the Vichy authorities. Non-violent activities of Chambon's residents included the refusal to take an oath to the chief of state, Marshal Pétain. On August 15, 1942, when the Vichy Youth Minister visited the town with the prefect and subprefect, there were no flags flying to greet them. Theological students from the Cévenol school handed the minister a petition protesting Vichy's treatment of Jews. When the Directeur de Police Départemental showed up to demand a list of Jewish residents, accompanied by buses to take them away, he found none at all. Pastors Trocmé and Theis, and Roger Darcissac, director of the Ecole Publique, were arrested and sent to a detention camp. On their return, constantly harassed by the Gestapo, the pastors went into hiding.

Outsider that he was, Camus didn't know these good people and they had little opportunity to get to know him. He did meet one old friend from Algeria here, André Chouraqui, who had been expelled from the University of Clermont-Ferrand under the racial quota, and had been taken in by a Protestant doctor who had a house in a village not far from Chambon. Camus visited Chouraqui regularly and they would dine on couscous, talk about Camus' work; it helped relieve Camus' anxiety to be with someone from his own country. As a biblical student (who would later translate the Bible into French, after writing an authoritative history of the Jews of North Africa), Chouraqui pointed out passages of the Bible having to do with plagues, and Camus took careful notes.

But he knew nothing of Chouraqui's role in the resistance, in a movement whose cover name was Oeuvres de Secours d'Enfants (he actually did find homes for refugee children), whose real work involved providing temporary hideouts for underground activists as well as refugees en route to Spain. Such activity entailed constant risk, and twenty-nine of the first thirty-three members of Chouraqui's group were killed. At one time Chouraqui had to hide when the French police began a search for him, returning to Chambon only when the informer had been killed by a resistance fighter. It was expected by Chouraqui that the Germans would clear the region of resistance movements after they had wiped out the maquis of the Vercors.

But one didn't talk about resistance work then, even to old friends. Chouraqui himself once learned that a neighbor he was seeing all the time was in fact the head of his own underground movement, whom he knew only by a code name.[4]

Winter augmented his sadness, the nostalgia for Algeria. The journal reflects his desire to forge a way of life in isolation. A morality: "Women, outside of love, are boring," he assured himself. "You have to live with some and be silent. Or sleep with them all, and act. The important things are elsewhere." It was the North African Frenchman, Mediterranean man, talking—or trying to make the best of Le Panelier. Once again he turned for solace to his writing desk. Before he left it and Le Panelier, "Budejovice," now also called "L'Exilé" (early titles for *Le Malentendu*), would be completed. An exile he certainly felt he was, and there could be no better place than lonely Chambon to take him back to central Europe, to the long week spent in Olmütz in bleak Moravia, for example, where he and Simone and Yves Bourgeois waited for the arrival of money from home. The unrelieved monotony of the setting all in monochrome, which so disconcerted the first audiences for *Le Malentendu,* owed as much to wartime Chambon as to Olmütz.

He was also working on the new essay on revolt, and on what he was calling the second version of *La Peste,* the first having been completed the previous winter—containing a key figure, the teacher Philippe Stephan, who will be eliminated entirely before the final version of the novel. A resident of Chambon later noted that Camus had borrowed local names for several of the characters in the book: Father Paneloux from Le Panelier, Dr. Rieux from Chambon's local Dr. Riou, Joseph Grand from the Grands, Camus' neighbors.[5] In his detailed notes for the second version of *La Peste,* Camus planned a chapter on illness. His quarantined Oranais "remarked one more time that the physical illness never came alone but was always accompanied by moral suffering (families—frustrated loves) which gave it its depth. . . ." He also noted the "moral" of the plague: It had no moral at all, serving nobody and nothing.

At last in mid-January 1943 he went to Paris on a visit. He had been there twice before, in 1937 as a convalescent counting his pennies, for nearly three months in 1940 as a junior staff member of *Paris-Soir,* author of minor works published in a distant province. Now, although he would stay only a fortnight, in a sad Paris decorated with swastika flags, and although he was still counting his pennies, he was a celebrity of sorts, a promising young author published to the acclaim of his elders, on terms of near-friendship with the lions of the *NRF* (except, perhaps, with its Fascist director), a man for whom André Malraux had spoken. He met Jean Paulhan at last, and they got along. He met another *NRF* regular about whom he was writing an essay, the philosopher Brice Parain. Quite possibly it was during this visit that a third Gallimard man, Jean Blanzat, encountered Camus in the company of Bernard Groethuysen and Paulhan and provided this candid snapshot: "Young, thin, in a rather rumpled raincoat. . . . He had that somewhat ambiguous air, a bit weary, that we were so ready to recognize in 'underground' people, although he was probably not one of them at that time." Blanzat had been hearing about the young writer for months, and now experienced his regard: "Direct, penetrating, intensely attentive to you, and also amused, malicious, full of an irony which was perhaps wicked, but which seemed indulgent and distracted."[6]

And at the Gallimard building on Rue Sébastien-Bottin, he fell into the arms of Janine Thomasset, now Janine Gallimard, for she was now married to Gaston's nephew Pierre. Janine found him a hotel just off the Rue de Rennes near Montparnasse, the very modest Hôtel Aviatic on Rue Vaugirard. He also met Michel Gallimard, son of Gaston's other brother, cousin and inseparable friend of Pierre. One evening Janine took Camus to the theater to see a play that all Paris was talking about, *Deirdre of the Sorrows,* by John Millington Synge, at the Théâtre des Mathurins. The play had opened in November, to reveal (alongside actors Jean Marchat and Michel Auclair) a slender, emotive young actress, daughter of an exiled Spanish prime minister, and still a student at Paris' acting school, Maria Casarès. Based on an Irish legend about doomed young lovers, ending with the boy slain and the girl a suicide, the play left the critics unmoved, but Casarès fascinated them. "She seemed like a surrounded doe," one of them reported. "A surprising conductor of dramatic energy," said *Cahiers du Sud.* Janine, who had already seen the play on the opening night with the Gallimard party, knew the Mathurins' actor-director Marcel Herrand and Herrand's associate Jean Marchat, and took Camus backstage after the performance to meet them, and of course to congratulate Maria Casarès. In little more than a year the Mathurins would take on his *Malentendu,* and Casarès would play in it.[7]

Through Michel Gallimard, Camus now met that singular Dominican, Father Bruckberger, writer, editor, film maker (as co-author of *Dialogues des Carmélites*), self-styled Chaplain of the Resistance, who would receive Charles de Gaulle at the Liberation of Paris in Notre Dame Cathedral. Then thirty-five, Bruckberger seemed a real-life version of the hearty monk of fables, enjoying his brandy and the company of attractive women. He divided his time between Paris, the Dominican convent at Saint-Maximin-la-Sainte-Baume in the South of France, and the cities and towns in between. It was he who had to rush off after the briefest of meetings with René Leynaud at the station restaurant at Saint-Etienne, and there would be other brief—and longer meetings with Camus later in the same year, first in Chambon, then at Saint-Maximin. At some point Camus and "Bruck," as his friends knew him, rode a train together, for Camus described such a trip with the odd Dominican making anti-Nazi and anti-Pétain statements in a compartment filled with passengers they didn't know. Once Bruck pushed into his hand a copy of *La Dernière à l'échafaud* (Die Letzte am Schafott), written in 1934 by Gertrud von Le Fort, from which Georges Bernanos had taken the story for *Dialogues des Carmélites*. Camus liked the book.[8] That Paris meeting would be followed by regular correspondence between Bruckberger and Camus, just as Camus would continue his relationship with Paulhan by letter.

In Le Panelier he found that he not only had more letters to write to new friends, but he was writing labels for food packages to send to those in the big cities who could not get the fresh products and fats that were available in the Chambon region. But if food was available, paper and string were not. So he asked Jean Grenier, who was sending him money orders for his food packages, to save all the wrapping paper and string he could, and to leave it in Paris with Paul Oettly, then living on the Rue du Dragon, who would carry down these vital materials on visits to Le Panelier. Letters he would write on whatever scraps of paper he could find, usually the rough notepaper he used for his manuscripts.

Jean Grenier in turn asked Camus for something: the exact date of his birth, for a horoscope that his friend Max Jacob wanted to make for him. Jacob took his time about it, or found it hard to turn it over to Camus, for it was nearly a year before he told Camus that he feared he would die a tragic death.[9]

The dialogue with Francis Ponge, by letter chiefly, would be a major activity in Le Panelier. Not only did Ponge take words and their meanings seriously, but he took his new friend (nearly fourteen years his junior) seriously. Ponge, Leynaud, and a third friend, Michel Pontremoli, a Jew later killed by the Nazis, listened to a reading of *Le Malentendu* in Leynaud's room. On January 27, 1943, Camus sat down to write Ponge a long letter after a rereading of *Le Parti pris des choses,* which Camus recognized to be "an absurd work in the pure state" in that it demonstrated the "non-signification of the world." (The letter appears in part in the Pléiade edition of Camus' work.) What he admired above all was Ponge's mastery of expression, which made his confession of failure to find meaning all the more convincing.

But their dialogue also concerned Ponge's reading of *Le Mythe de Sisyphe,* which Ponge had entered into a journal of his own in August 1941, and which betrays Ponge's down to earth view of things in observations such as this one:

> Sisyphus happy, yes, not only because he takes stock of his destiny, but because his efforts lead to very important relative results.
>
> Of course he won't manage to *wedge* his rock at the top of its track, he will not attain the absolute (inaccessible by definition) but he will achieve positive results in the various sciences, and in particular in political science (organization of the human world, of

human society, mastery of human history, and of the individual-society paradox).[10]

Camus insisted on the temporary nature of the position defined in his essay. He would have liked to go beyond that to undertake "an immense revision of values, total and clear-sighted," but did he have the talent or the strength? "You can probably claim that Sisyphus is lazy," he concluded his January 27 letter. "But it's the lazy who move the earth. The others don't have the time."

Soon after that Ponge decided to begin his secret recruiting mission for the Front National with a stopover in Le Chambon-sur-Lignon, highlighted of course by a visit to his new friend at Le Panelier. Drafting a reply to Camus' letter on the train ride, on February 1, a reply which was perhaps meant to be delivered orally, Ponge wondered:

> If you had read *Parti Pris naïvely,* without knowing me *at all,* do you think that you would have attached any importance to it, or even that you would have *read* it . . . If your reply is affirmative, then there is no longer any *duty* that I explain myself otherwise. . . .

Then in another vote, perhaps written after his visit to Le Panelier:

> Only literature (and in literature only description—in opposition to explanation—: the bias of things, phenomenological dictionary, cosmogony) allow playing the big game: to remake the world, in every meaning of the word *remake,* thanks to the character at once concrete and abstract, interior and exterior of the VERB, thanks to its semantic destiny.
> Here Camus and myself join Paulhan.[10]

Ponge arrived at Le Panelier to see Madame Oettly's boardinghouse all but deserted, when he had known it packed with vacationers during prewar summer holidays. Sarah Oettly would usually shut it down entirely in the winter. This year she had kept her establishment open because of Camus, but moved him into a small house in the same compound which was easier to heat.[9] To Ponge, Camus seemed depressed in his solitude, although he had a fox terrier named Cigarette who followed him everywhere.[3]

With Paulhan the dialogue was less heady, although Paulhan was also a perfectionist. He had just published *Les Fleurs de Tarbes,* on which he had been working for a decade. In a letter to Artaud in 1931 Paulhan had written:

> I'm working, and I hope that those *Fleurs de Tarbes,* once completed, will satisfy you. The happiness they give me make me think that they are certainly true and define—with a precision I see as mathematical—this other world, where we live in reality.

In 1936 he wrote Marcel Jouhandeau that he had to begin his book all over again. So that when it finally appeared, in 1941, one imagines easily the importance it had for Paulhan, and Camus was well advised to comment with circumspection on its contents.[11]

This back and forth correspondence with Paris, Lyons, and other points of France suggests that mail moved quickly in occupied France, and indeed it did; it has been said that the postal service worked better then than it does today. But if all of France was now a single zone, Algeria remained out of bounds. Camus found a way to write to his wife by a roundabout method. The French teacher Armand Guibert, formerly a resident of Tunisia (and whose poetry Camus had reviewed in *Alger Républicain*), was now living in Portugal. Camus wrote to ask him if he would be willing to forward letters from that neutral nation on to Algeria, and for the next year Camus would be writing to Francine that way, the letters acquiring a swastika-decorated Nazi censor's stamp somewhere en route. Yet in one of his covering notes to Guibert, Camus wrote: "We must hold on until the time comes to show ourselves."[12]

Camus received a first reply from Francine via Lisbon at the end of March. After living at the Acaults' for a while she had moved into an apartment above the Boulevard du Telemly which the Louis Miquels had left to Jeanne Sicard and Marguerite Dobrenn. She found a job teaching mathematics in a private school, and it was her naïve hope that by staying in Algiers she had a better chance of rejoining her husband than if she returned to Oran. Once she actually thought that she might try to enter France from Spain—reversing the refugee route—but she feared that any false move would call attention to her husband, who she felt was in danger. Francine also thought that she had found a way of getting money to him: She turned over part of her salary to someone whose family in France was to remit a corresponding amount to Camus regularly. But Camus would see none of these funds until the Liberation. Finally Francine returned to Oran after all, and after teaching for a while she joined the Allied forces, first playing piano to entertain troops in the camps along the coast, then working at Psychological Warfare Branch headquarters in Oran, helping to produce propaganda materials in behalf of the war effort, for local consumption. At home, her sister Christiane helped her invent anti-Vichy slogans. But she became increasingly uncomfortable about what she felt was unhealthy American interest in France's Moslem population, and so she was relieved when Louis Joxe, their shipboard companion, was able to give her a job in de Gaulle's provisional government.[9]

Camus got some help from Gabriel Audisio. As director of a North

African aid committee in Paris, Comité d'Assistance aux Nord-Africains, Audisi was able to obtain a loan for Camus, which he had Marie Viton send so as not to offend Camus, who would not have accepted official charity.[13]

"Four months of ascetic and solitary life," Camus wrote in his journal on February 10. "The will, the spirit profit. But the heart?" He found that he was letting himself be taken over by his imagination, an unbridled imagination which he had only now discovered, and which was interfering with the exercise of thought and the discipline necessary to his work. Sometimes in a train, or on a bus, he let himself drift along, tired of setting himself back on the track.

At this time the manuscript of *La Peste* might have been a personal notebook, for he was writing about *les séparés,* those separated from loved ones by the quarantine, who read the news looking for reasons to believe in a rapid end to the epidemic, conceiving hopes without basis, picking apart words a journalist may have dashed off at random. "Thus make the theme of separation the major theme of the novel," he concluded one day, while he was confiding to Ponge: "Exile weighs on me." A function of his solitude, the increasing personalization of *La Peste* nevertheless went hand in hand with the impersonal formulations on the subject of revolt. It was clear that "Essai sur la révolte," as he was calling his non-fiction project, would be a summing up of the subject, although when the time came to write the final drafts, as will be seen, he again found the need to make his philosophy autobiography.

In early March he received the February issue of *Cahiers du Sud* containing Sartre's essay on *L'Etranger,* which he decided gave too much place to conscious intent, not enough to the intuitive element in creation. He noted in passing that Sartre hadn't really appreciated *Le Mythe de Sisyphe.*

As an interlude, he sketched out an introduction to an anthology of insignificance, which seemed to have grown out of his discussions with Ponge. Why such an anthology? Because it would "practically describe not only the most considerable part of life, that of small gestures, small thoughts, and small moods, but also our common future" (since even great thoughts and actions end up in becoming insignificant). The text would be rewritten and finally published in the late 1950s in a literary review, *Cahier des Saisons.*

In March it was still snowing, and yet the first periwinkle flowers appeared on March 9—worthy of mention in his journal. Tuberculosis, he also noted, is not always accompanied by pain. Pain keeps one in the present, requires a struggle which distracts the patient. "But to feel death on the simple view of a handkerchief filled with blood, is to be

thrown back into time in a dizzying fashion: it is the horror of becoming." Thus he kept watch on his health and on the seasons.

Through Ponge and Leynaud he was in touch with René Tavernier,
publisher of a literary review in Lyons, which continued to be able to
appear because it was not a political publication, although in fact the
contributions, and the contributors, clearly indicated that it was committed. At one point, after publication of a poem by Aragon, Tavernier's magazine was banned for a period of several issues. He managed
to print and distribute ten-thousand copies of *Confluences,* mostly in
Southern France, but also via selected booksellers in Paris.

At Aragon's invitation, Camus was to contribute to a special issue
of *Confluences* on the novel, and his journal showed that he was working on it this spring. "L'Intelligence et l'Echafaud" would be an attempt
to define the classic spirit in the French novel, its chief illustration being
Madame de Lafayette's *La Princesse de Clèves.* Camus began his essay
with a story of the beheading of Louis XVI, who when he asked one of
the guards taking him to the scaffold to give a message to the queen was
told: "I'm not here to do your errands, I'm here to lead you to the
scaffold." He would seek to demonstrate that the classical novelist refuses errands, keeping to the point. But he also found a way to introduce Ponge's *Le Parti pris des choses,* which he calls "one of the few
contemporary classics." The essay was published in the July 1943 issue
of Tavernier's magazine.

At that time, Tavernier's home and office in an eastern suburb of
Lyons—an isolated country house on a slope, reached by a long flight
of narrow steps, and with several side entrances by alternate routes,
facilitating the holding of clandestine meetings—served as temporary
residence and refuge for France's best-known Communist writer, Louis
Aragon, and his Russian-born wife Elsa Triolet. An early surrealist,
dadaist, Aragon had joined the French party in 1927 and ever since
had been an outspoken apologist for Stalin's U.S.S.R.; he would remain
an orthodox Communist until the Soviet invasion of Czechoslovakia in
1968, and even after that. In Tavernier's home, where Aragon lived for
over a year during the German occupation, he held meetings of the intellectual resistance group, Comité National des Ecrivains (CNE), of
which he was head of the southern French section. (In Paris the CNE
numbered among its members leading writers both Communist and
non-Communist, among them the Catholic novelist François Mauriac,
*NRF* men Paulhan and Blanzat. Indeed, it was sometimes said that
"everybody" belonged to the CNE, and that it was a terrain of incessant
internecine warfare. If during the occupation years it could seem to be
a genuine meeting ground for Communists and non-Communists, its role

as a screen for Communist Party intellectual activity would become apparent soon after the liberation of France.)

To one of Aragon's CNE meetings at Tavernier's house, Camus brought Father Bruckberger, who promptly signed up as a member; presumably Camus himself had joined on a previous occasion.[14] Aragon had little contact with Camus during these visits, but his wife Elsa was intrigued by Camus and talked to him several times. A brief essay of hers was published as a booklet sufficiently quixotic to pass whatever censorship it may have been subjected to: *Qui est cet étranger qui n'est pas d'ici?*

> "Who is this stranger who is not from here?" wondered the inhabitants of the hamlet where Albert Camus, of Algiers, had taken refuge, caught in France by the American landing. Perhaps they felt, these people of lively vital instincts, that the Stranger was a magnificent myth, a philosophical contribution, a stimulant for the intelligence.

That an Aragon could live in Lyons, receiving well-known or at least conspicuous visitors, and could be published in Paris by Gallimard, that Tavernier could go from Lyons to Paris on CNE business, Malraux could move about as he did, Sartre could be at once a public figure and a participant in CNE meetings in Paris, all this may be difficult to comprehend by non-Frenchmen brought up on the war movies. In fact the Gestapo generally left major personalities alone; in a sense that was part of the *NRF* bargain. The German officer Gerhard Heller, who knew all the French writers from Mauriac to Jouhandeau, and Ribbentrop's ambassador Otto Abetz, soft spokesman in Paris for Nazi collaborationist ideology, were both said to be moderating influences. Had the Germans been as severe with prestigious French writers as they were to unknown citizens, there could have been no CNE, the relative freedom of the literary magazines would not have been possible, and a Malraux would not have survived to join the fighting.[15] While some Frenchmen—Jews for example—were crossing the north-south demarcation line to escape the Nazis, a Sartre and a Beauvoir could slip over for a holiday, and then slip back again.[16]

Similar ambiguity exists with respect to Camus as an active participant in the resistance. Much has been written about his role during the German occupation, published in the most authorized books (the gist being that he was a member of the underground Combat network in Le Chambon-sur-Lignon, later assigned by that movement to Paris). In fact Camus took part in no resistance group's activities, neither in intelligence gathering, sabotage, nor propaganda, all the while he lived in Le Panelier. At the end of 1943, when he became a permanent resident of

Paris, he was taken on by the team which was publishing Combat's underground newspaper, also called *Combat,* and helped prepare the aboveground newspaper which was to be published after the liberation of Paris.

Still, from Le Panelier Camus contributed essays to underground periodicals, such as his first two essays in *Lettres à un ami allemand* (Letters to a German Friend), and he was in touch with active resistance agents like Pia, Ponge, and Leynaud.

What is significant is that the negative view which Camus had taken of the war against the Axis powers, manifested principally in the editorial content of *Alger Républicain* and *Le Soir Républicain,* had disappeared now. Perhaps he remained a pacifist and a non-killer, neither of which was always consistent with participation in the active resistance against the German occupation and the Vichy collaborationist government. It was also true that secret resistance activity required that the agent work in his milieu as a fish in water, while in France Camus had no milieu.

He did try to build one. Janine brought some of the Gallimards to visit him in Le Panelier. Father Bruckberger was trying to find a way to bring him to the more clement skies of Provence. He discovered that his Algiers companion Blanche Balain was in Nice, and at his request she tried to find a mountain resort for him just behind the Riviera coast. He would not follow up on that, but Blanche came north to her home town of Anneyron, close by in the Drôme département, and they met near there at a convenient train stop, Valence, and later again at Saint-Etienne. (The only souvenir of the Valence interlude is the melodramatic dialogue he overheard in the next room at their hotel, an hour and a half of it, as he noted in his journal. During their Saint-Etienne meeting he was amused by a remark Blanche made, and recorded it in his journal: "Nobody realizes that some people make Herculean efforts just to be normal.")

Blanche Balain was shocked at how thin he had become, and as soon as she returned home she began to send him eggs and cheese, for not everything was available at Chambon. But at Saint-Etienne she noticed that he seemed to know all of the right places, such as black market restaurants, unmarked, on upper floors of buildings; they splurged there with money he had just received from Gallimard.[17] Money was for spending: "Any life directed toward money is death," he was writing in his journal. And about Saint-Etienne and its surroundings:

> Such a spectacle is the condemnation of the civilization which gave birth to it. A world where there is no more room for human beings, for joy, for active leisure, is a world which must die.

He began to feel the onset of a writing block, the evaporation of his confidence that he had something to say. At the end of April he could write to Ponge: "Everything would go better if I didn't blame myself for not being able to return home."[18]

Now he was going to lose a friend he could rely on in Lyons, for "Renoir," running the underground Combat movement, was being hunted by the Vichy police and the Gestapo, and he had to flee to Switzerland. (Pia managed to get across the frontier, but when he was ready to return to France again clandestinely in August, he had trouble with the Swiss, who didn't allow him to leave. By that time, under the urging of de Gaulle's emissary Jean Moulin, the Combat movement had merged with Libération-Sud and the Franc-Tireur group to form Mouvements Unis de Résistance (MUR), one of whose missions was to maintain contact with the French railways for intelligence and sabotage. Headquarters of MUR were moved to Paris, and Pia was sent there as secretary-general.)[19]

Camus went to see Francis Ponge at Coligny, a village near Bourg-en-Bresse, where the friends discussed *La Peste* at length; Camus' mood changed. A journal entry for May 20, 1943, makes no attempt to conceal elation:

> For the first time: curious feeling of satisfaction and of fullness. Question that I asked myself, lying in the grass, in the heavy and hot evening: "If these days were the last . . ." Reply: a tranquil smile in myself. Yet nothing of which I can be proud: Nothing is resolved, my behavior is not so decided. Is it the hardening which ends an experience, or the softness of the evening, or on the contrary the beginning of a wisdom which no longer denies anything?

The weather, surely; the economic geographer would insist on that. And there was something else: He was about to go to Paris again.

# 22

## OCCUPIED PARIS

> Most certainly what one seeks in European cities is this solitude. . . . Centuries of history and of beauty, the ardent testimony of a thousand lives accompany them along the Seine and speak to them at once of traditions and of conquests. But their youth incited them to evoke this company. The time comes when it is not so welcome. "Just the two of us!" cried Rastignac, before the heap of mouldiness of the city of Paris. Two, yes, but that's still too many!
>
> "Le Minotaure"

Camus arrived in Paris for another visit on June 1, this time more convinced that Paris was partly his. A number of people knew he was coming, such as Jean Grenier, to whom he had continued to send food parcels from Le Panelier, and kindly Gabriel Audisio, and he would see them both.

Thanks to the Gallimards a capital event occurred at once. At the opening of Jean-Paul Sartre's play *Les Mouches* he met its author, who was henceforth to play a significant role in his life, both by the dominating, almost cumbersome presence of the little man, and later by the equally cumbersome vacuum he would create. At this time Sartre was already almost famous. Although never a member of the *NRF* group of esthetes, Sartre was of course a Gallimard author (who was not?). Actually he was closer to Camus, at least in ultimate intention, than a Paulhan, a Parain, a Queneau could ever be, for his philosophy was active, his essential positions political; he was at once a teacher and a man of the street; he demanded relevance. If Paulhan was difficult to seize because he was elusive, Sartre would present another kind of difficulty, for he was always in motion. Even when he was dead wrong (as he would usually confess in the next stage of his thought), he was always doing or saying something, and one knew where he stood.

Of course he shared the ambiguities of his time. Sartre's new play was being performed at the Sarah Bernhardt Theater, even though the theater had been renamed (because Bernhardt was Jewish) "Théâtre de la Cité"; neither director Charles Dullin nor Sartre seemed to mind that, nor did they desire anything but good reviews from the collaborationist press. Simone de Beauvoir believed that it was impossible to mistake the real meaning of the play, containing Orestes' cry for freedom, but she reported in her memoirs that the critic in the German occupying army's *Pariser Zeitung* made it a point to review the play favorably. Such was public life under the occupation. Beauvoir, who didn't meet Camus just then, remembered that the first performance of *Les Mouches* took place (on June 2) in the afternoon, because there were often electricity cuts in the evening. It was while Sartre was standing in the lobby near the box office that a young man walked over to introduce himself as Albert Camus.[1] The next encounter would have to wait until Camus' permanent establishment in Paris that autumn.

Camus was on the best possible terms with Jean Paulhan. They decided that they shared a love of animals, and Camus told Paulhan about the dogs and a Siamese cat that were waiting for him at Le Panelier. On the other hand, there is no indication that they talked about the matter that was tearing apart the Gallimard building at that very moment, and with Paulhan right in the middle: At long last Pierre Drieu La Rochelle had resigned as director of *La Nouvelle Revue Française,* and although another Gallimard man had been selected to run the magazine, the Germans decided to put an end to this enterprise which had not served them. The June 1943 issue would be the last one.

Paulhan showed himself to be a loyal supporter of Camus, and not only to Camus' face. In a discussion with François Mauriac concerning the award of the Grand Prix de Littérature of the French Academy (Mauriac had been a member of that illustrious fraternity since 1933), Paulhan came out flatly for *L'Etranger,* the only novel published in the past two years which he felt showed both craft and scope. He assured Mauriac that Camus was courageous and reliable. But Mauriac would have none of that. Later on he would be the bête noire of crusading *Combat* editor Albert Camus, in constant opposition to him, often with no discernible motive (for Camus could not have been as far from Mauriac's views—his political views—as Mauriac enjoyed thinking he was). As if by instinct the Catholic novelist of Bordeaux did not like the young writer from Algiers; what would he have thought about Camus had he known that the Camus family came from Bordeaux?

Paulhan had assured Mauriac that *L'Etranger* was well within the bounds of Mauriac's Catholicism, for its subject was "How can I love my mother (or my wife) if I don't love God?" Mauriac rebutted that what bothered him was the book's artifice, its borrowings from the American novel. Paulhan pointed out that it was closer to Voltaire's *Candide* than to any American work. Finally the Academy prize went to a left-wing novelist-philosopher, Jean Prévost, killed the following year (at age forty-three) while fighting the Germans in the Vercors Mountains.

While in Paris, Camus showed Paulhan a section of his novel in progress, *La Peste,* which Paulhan thought should be submitted to his friend Jean Lescure, who had begun publishing his own anti-*NRF* called *Messages* (taking over a prewar title) in 1941, and of course with *NRF* man Paulhan's blessing. It is clear that Paulhan was encouraging Lescure's *Messages* as he had encouraged the early aborted project of Pascal Pia's *Prométhée* and probably encouraged other anti-*NRF* schemes as well, all the while seated in the Gallimard building near Drieu La Rochelle. There is the story that Paulhan asked his friends to submit texts as if for publication in *NRF* but which he would put in a trunk, to be published only after the war. This was considered a joke, but wasn't Paulhan really using his adventurous friends' wartime magazine projects as the trunk? After the final issue of Drieu's *NRF,* Paulhan wrote to a friend to say that if it had continued to appear "from the moment that I took charge of the magazine, either it would be done away with, or else it would become from the first issue *different* enough so that the difference becomes obvious to everyone."[2]

At first the Germans allowed Jean Lescure and his friends to publish *Messages* in Paris, although this was partly because of Lescure's subterfuge: Once he got the censor's approval for an innocuous text bearing a particular title, he published a *different* text under that title. (He published Picasso's play, *Le Désir attrapé par la queue,* after the Germans had approved the title over a text by the Fascist Robert Brasillach.) Then, when the Germans caught up with him, Lescure published another issue (called *Silences*) in occupied Brussels. After that he decided to collect material for a larger issue to be printed in neutral Switzerland by his friend François Lachenal, who had a publishing venture called Editions des Trois Collines there. Lescure smuggled the manuscripts to Switzerland via Lachenal himself, who was then serving as an attaché at the Swiss Legation in Vichy, responsible for foreign interests (including those of the United States). Contributors to Lescure's anthology were warned that the preface would compromise them. Indeed Lescure's text, signed with his initials and dated

Paris, August 1943, emphasized the subversive intent of the book-sized volume, which was entitled *Domaine Français:*

> For months it must have seemed that all the Frenchmen of France were condemned to silence. Yet it was not long before we were to discover a bold refusal to surrender, a refusal to forgo the affirmation of the dignity of a conception of man which a military and political event, however crushing it had been, could not put down.

The present anthology, he went on, was an attempt to "bring together that sudden fraternity concerned with man and freedom," and in which the "very fact of their encounter manifested the deep commitment to freedom in man."

The first page of *Domaine Français* contained a poem on France by Walt Whitman, the last a poem by the surrealist Saint-Pol-Roux, "murdered in 1940." The contributors included Louis Aragon and Elsa Triolet, Paul Eluard, Charles Vildrac, Claude Morgan—all prominently of the left—as well as Sartre, Mauriac, Paul Valéry, Paul Claudel, Henri Michaux, Raymond Queneau, Francis Ponge, Paulhan, and Lescure. The books—three thousand copies were printed—were imported clandestinely into France, handed out or mailed in plain wrappers (not sold).[3]

Camus had hesitated before giving Lescure a chapter of *La Peste* because he wasn't quite sure that it would make sense out of context; Queneau had told him that he found it disconcerting, and suggested that it not be published in that form. He let Paulhan decide, and Paulhan wisely decided that it should be published.[4] For not only did "Les Exilés dans la peste" (an early version of Chapter 1, Part II, of the novel) reflect the isolation of Camus in that unhappy period, it is a metaphor that he himself had chosen for the separation caused by the present situation of his country. "In summary," begins the text as published in *Domaine Français,* "the time of the epidemic was above all a time of exile." It is his own "temporary" separation from his family and his country, which so quickly became an interminable separation. And it closes with the extraordinary discovery that separation was a distraction, preserving the exiles from the general distress which surrounded them, and from panic. Even when one of the separated was stricken by the dreaded disease, this distraction could prevent him from thinking that he was going to die.

Camus agreed to edit a volume of selected writings of Nietzsche, and to write a preface for it, in a series called Classiques de la Liberté, which Lachenal wanted to publish at his Editions des Trois Collines in Switzerland. But there was too much else to do, and when Lachenal reminded him of his promise in 1945 Camus replied: "The war is over; it's no longer necessary."[3]

During one of his absences from Le Panelier, a visitor showed up at Madame Oettly's boardinghouse: "Renoir"—Pascal Pia. He had remembered Camus' desire to return to Algeria by a clandestine crossing of the Pyrenees into Spain, so Pia was bringing him some foreign money he would find useful—American and Swiss currency (which he left with Madame Oettly) in case Camus still intended to try the escape route.[5]

Back at Le Panelier himself, Camus recorded a meeting with "Bruck" (probably at the end of July). Of "G," possibly Gaston Gallimard, Bruckberger remarked: "G. has the air of a priest, a sort of episcopal unctuousness. And already I have trouble standing that in bishops."

Camus said to him: "When I was young I thought that all priests were happy."

Bruck: "Fear of losing their faith makes their sensibility shrink. Now it's only a negative vocation. They don't look life in the face." His dream, Camus added, was "the great conquering clergy, but splendidly poor and brave." They pursued their dialogue with a "Conversation on Nietzsche damned."[6]

Camus sent a letter to Ponge complaining once more of boredom. But he was writing: He revised an act of *Caligula.* "No, my last word is not despair . . . For the moment it is patience." He also told Ponge that he had been obliged to carry his sick dog on his back to the veterinarian.[7]

Now he undertook another piece of writing that he would not mention in his correspondence, even to a friend as trustworthy as Ponge. He wrote a "Lettre à un Allemand qui fût mon ami," which would appear without a signature in the February 1944 issue of the underground organ of the Franc-Tireur movement, *La Revue Libre,* printed (cheaply) "somewhere in France." In this first of four letters later collected as *Lettres à un ami allemand,* Camus at last spoke without ambiguity about resistance. Without renouncing deeply pacifistic feelings: "It's a considerable thing on the contrary to advance towards torture and death when one is certain that hate and violence are in themselves vain things. It is considerable to fight while despising war. . . ." This pamphlet in the guise of a letter to a former comrade is written in a mode of reasoned reflection, as if the author were really attempting to convince him. But in the end the reasoning man is justifying the resistance struggle, predicting its triumph. One more such letter would be published by the underground press, in *Cahiers de Libération* (where it is signed "Louis Neuville"), while the last two were not published until after the liberation of France. In a postwar preface to the Italian trans-lation of the small volume containing all four letters Camus explained that "They had a purpose, which was to clarify to some extent the blind combat in which we were engaged and thus to render this combat more efficacious."

The second letter, dated December 1943 but published in 1944, continues in the same vein ("our struggle contains as much bitterness as confidence"), again fodder for the thinking man, but unlikely to arouse the masses. The last letter, written in July 1944, begins: "The time has come for your defeat. I am writing to you from a city famous the world over and which is readying itself for a new day of freedom at your expense." For by then Camus was living in Paris, part of a team putting together the daily *Combat* that would appear with the first shots fired in the insurrection of Paris.

Finally *Le Malentendu* was ready, at least in its first version, for he planned to attack it again when he finished revising *Caligula*. He sent it, as always, to his maître, Jean Grenier, who, as always, made com-ments in the margins. (He would take exception, in particular, to the way Camus ended the play.) Now it could be submitted to Gallimard together with *Caligula* (the two unplayed plays would be published to-gether). Grenier, who was preparing an anthology on *L'Existence,* which would contain contributions by Grenier himself, Brice Parain, Etienne Gilson, a specialist in medieval philosophy, and others, also asked Camus if he would contribute to this volume, so Camus suggested that he send a section of his work in progress, the essay on revolt. "Remarque sur la révolte" would appear in Grenier's anthology, pub-lished by Gallimard in October 1945.

In midsummer he made an excursion from Le Panelier to volcanic Mount Mézenc. "On the plateaus of Mézenc, the wind whistled in vio-lent sword swipes." Wind sufficient to send him to bed with flu, he re-ported to Ponge on August 11. But on August 15 he was able to ride a bicycle all the way to Saint-Etienne with his old Algiers comrade Louis Miquel, who was stunned to see frost on the ground in the morning—a wondrous sight for a *pied noir*. Also wondrous was the serving of two pats of butter at breakfast, and on the day they biked to Saint-Etienne, Madame Oettly put an enormous chunk of it on their table.[8]

Then Bruckberger, who had been trying to find a more pleasant place for Camus—he was thinking, among other possibilities, of a sana-torium near Lourdes, France's miracle shrine—invited him to the Saint-Maximin Dominican monastery. Camus explained to Ponge on August 30: "I have Catholic friends, and for those among them who are really so, I have more than sympathy, I feel a bond. It's because in fact they are interested in the same things I am. In their opinion the solution is obvious; it isn't for me. . . ." Camus suggested that Catholics and Communists, Ponge being one of the latter, both believe in an absolute, in this world or in the next, but Ponge vigorously denied that. On September 1, Camus wrote in his journal: "He who despairs because of the news is a coward, but he who sees hope in the human condition is mad."

Saint-Maximin, where he arrived at the beginning of September, was a delight. Gentle Provence was more like the world he knew. The old Dominican monastery, with buildings dating back to the fourteenth and fifteenth centuries, the large basilica, nearby Sainte-Baume mountain, were all observed in a sun-baked setting of vineyards and olive trees. Camus stayed at the monastery's guesthouse. Priests looked better to him than pastors, at least in that heavenly Provençal light. He found "the interior silence" he needed, or so he told Ponge. Back in Le Panelier on September 20, he was not necessarily converted to Christianity but he was prepared to do battle with Ponge's rationalism. "I see no advantage in replacing the reign of the eternal by that of abstract idols. . . . Man is sometimes as heavy a burden as the world itself." If Christianity was not his religion, he would nevertheless refuse to accuse it of evil intent. Perhaps it was being misused, but it had not been conceived to be misused. "One should not judge a doctrine through its by-products but through its peaks." He concluded: "The objection to Christianity is that earth-shaking human creation which is called justice." As for himself, he would stay clear of Bruck's Christianity and of Ponge's Marxism, refusing all forms of messianism, contenting himself with "giving a form to the relative."[7]

All of his professional life Camus would be invited, cajoled, into a commitment on Christianity, which he never made. After his death, believers often left crosses on his grave (which is otherwise singularly undecorated). Essays and even books have been written about a Christian Camus, and they could not have been difficult to write, for Camus seeded the ambiguities. He usually refrained from attacking Christianity and the Church, although criticizing Church policy—in Franco Spain, for example. Despite the almost natural enmity which developed early between Camus and the man who otherwise might have been his political ally, François Mauriac, Camus coexisted easily with Catholicism, the religion of the overwhelming majority of churchgoing Frenchmen.

The "misunderstanding," if that is what it was, was created by Camus first of all in fiction which suggested a void Christians were anxious to fill, or left ambiguities they were prepared to clarify. But it is also interesting to observe that La Peste, written during the years he was seeing a good deal of Father Bruckberger, paints the portrait of a Father Paneloux who has the wrong answers.

Summer travel had left Camus exhausted; he was no closer to a cure for his tuberculosis. "I don't have all my faculties," he informed Ponge on September 29. "I am extremely tired. . . . I've been struggling with the angel for over a year." This time he was definitely going to leave Le Panelier before the onset of winter, either for a proper mountain resort, such as Briançon in the Hautes-Alpes, or (if at last the hoped-for job came through) Paris. Even an enemy-occupied, food-rationed, fuel-short Paris.[7]

In any event—goodbye to Le Panelier, and to absolute solitude. The year had marked him, he would later remember. It had been another "hinge," separating the brilliant young playboy cultivating his cynicism from the mature Camus, clearing away both the baggage and the attitudes of what had been, despite all, a spoiled youth, and rendering him sensitive to what was to come.[9]

The decision was made for him by his friends at Gallimard, for as of November 1, 1943, he had a job there. When he moved into the beehive on the Rue Sébastien-Bottin, he was placed in a cell alongside the cells of nearly all those who mattered in French letters. His own turned out to be not bad at all, one of the few offices in the old building possessing a terrace; it had previously been occupied by Malraux and by Paulhan. At the outset Camus shared his office with Jacques Lemarchand, author and critic; he was the man who had been tapped to take over the *NRF* from Drieu, had the magazine survived.

Then and later the Gallimards eschewed any semblance of hierarchy. Under patriarch Gaston Gallimard there was no editor in chief, no director of this or that. One was a reader, and the most experienced were members of the Reading Committee, which elite group certainly had more influence on the situation of French letters than the French Academy or any other institution, and here Paulhan was the first among equals. Naturally the house was also heavily seasoned with Gallimards. Gaston, who was already sixty-two years old in 1943, was responsible for the editorial side of the company, his partner and brother Raymond for financial control. (A third brother, Jacques, was not associated with the company.) Gaston and Raymond were seconded by their respective sons, Claude and Michel; later the two fathers and the two sons would share a large oval office on an interior garden, Gaston and Claude at one desk, Raymond and Michel at the other. Michel's sister Nicole would also work for the house, with her husband. So would Pierre, Robert, and Marie, children of Gaston's non-participating brother

Jacques. Pierre Gallimard of course was married to Camus' friend of
*Paris-Soir* days, Janine; Janine's sister Renée married Robert Gallimard.

A year after Camus' arrival the Gallimards acquired a large town
house on the Rue de l'Université and connected at the rear to the Rue
Sébastien-Bottin building around the corner, an acquisition that at once
gave them space for expansion of their beehive (it became a maze) and
some convenient apartments for the Gallimard children on a splendid
formal garden. The new annex had been built in the early seventeenth
century, occupied by a poet, then by a minor essayist (Gédéon
Tallemant des Réaux); the Gallimards took it over from the publisher
Léon Bailby. For the building was (and remains) in the heart of smart
Paris, on the edge of Proust's Faubourg Saint-Germain, for centuries a
preferred in-town residential district, also the center of arts and letters.
Most of France's publishers are within walking distance, and most of its
writers have tried to be.

Camus found a hotel room on the Rue de la Chaise near the corner
of the Boulevard Raspail, an easy ten-minute stroll to his office. (He
would never live more than a twenty-minute walk from the Gallimard
building.) It was more of a rooming house than a proper hotel, this
Hôtel de la Minerve, run by an eccentric elderly woman who be-
friended resistance activists. A number of Camus' friends would stay
here, including Claude de Fréminville, and when Edmond Charlot arrived in Paris, he took over its unused ground-floor restaurant as the
first headquarters of his Paris publishing house. It was of course a hotel
of minimal comfort; Camus had a sink in his room but no bath or toilet. When Gabriel Audisio visited that winter, he and Camus spent the
evening, after a frugal supper, in overcoats pulled up to their ears as
Camus read him passages of his writing.[10] Indeed, he returned to work
immediately on his arrival: Gallimard had handed him the proofs of
*Caligula* as soon as he showed up in the office.

On November 7 he was thirty years old, which was the occasion
for a serious reflection in his journal: "Man's first faculty is forgetting.
But it is correct to say that he forgets even the good he has done." He
wondered whether he should include a "Journal du séparé" in *La Peste*
(the book was moving forward, or he was trying to drive it forward).
To Ponge he complained: "I feel curiously sterile, full of doubts and
sad."[7] He began to make notes for what he thought would be his final
work, "La Création corrigée," which from the surviving notes sounds
like a series of horror stories of man's inhumanity to man.

For despite the distraction of the stimulating new job, he had probably arrived in Paris at its least happy time in the present century. In
this last winter of German occupation, everything was worse than be-

fore. The Germans were now feeling the full effect of the Allied offensive in Italy, where French troops had joined the Americans and British in the advance northward. In the east Red armies were on the offensive everywhere, driving the Germans out of Soviet territory. For occupied France, food and fuel could only be scarcer; repression grew more savage, Vichy became more pliant to the Germans, endeavored to convince the French that German victory was inevitable.

Yet not only did life go on in grim, rationed, Nazi-patrolled Paris, but writing and publishing went on, plays were rehearsed, and there were opening nights. Movies were shown. One traveled to work or to the theater on bicycles or on foot, but one got there. Close to the offices of Gallimard and of the Hôtel de la Minerve, the small restaurants were jammed with the writers and artists, actors and singers and directors who were to make the reputation of the Saint-Germain-des-Prés of the immediate postwar years. In coal-short Paris, with its frequent electricity blackouts, cafés such as the Flore, with their wood-burning stoves, warmed the writing hands of a generation of French men and women. In her memoirs Simone de Beauvoir paints a group portrait at the Flore, where resistance agents and collaborators mingled, Pablo Picasso might be at one table, a film director at another, as Sartre and Beauvoir sat writing the books that would stamp their times. (More modestly, Camus received his Algiers comrade Louis Miquel in his room at the Minerve, and made him a cup of hot chocolate, pouring hot water from the tap on the precious powdered chocolate.[8])

At Gallimard, Camus was at once part of the scene and not a part of it. As a very junior member of the firm he could only be a polite and admiring acolyte of the Paulhan priesthood. He was also by training and temperament a world away from the literary cliques or movements that existed within the *NRF:* the surrealists and former surrealists (with Georges Bataille, Michel Leiris, Maurice Blanchot, Raymond Queneau)—disabused intellectuals with whom Camus had little in common; or his elders of the so-called Pontigny group (Paul Valéry, Paul Claudel, André Gide, Jean Schlumberger, and their junior members Paulhan, Groethuysen, Malraux). Born under other skies, educated not at the Sorbonne or the Ecole Normale Supérieure or the Paris lycées where one had to have been educated, stranger to the salons and the cafés of the French capital, Camus also brought a new kind of literature to Gallimard, one of moral commitment, and esthetes of all categories tended to mock such pretenses.[3] For a Paulhan or a Groethuysen or even a Parain, a Camus could never be a member of their group. Hence the stories that would circulate of the scorn in which the *NRF* esthetes held him. Did Paulhan, in his comment on the manuscript of

*L'Etranger,* say that Camus' novel reminded him of Ponson du Terrail, author of extravagant adventure stories? Did Paulhan say at another time, speaking of Camus, "He's our Anatole France"?—words still more perfidious coming from a Paulhan?

But then Paulhan was known for having something to say, something witty to say, about or against everyone, friend and foe alike. Of this elusive man André Pieyre de Mandiargues would write that "one was never certain that something didn't escape you in what Jean Paulhan had said, or that Paulhan hadn't said slightly less than what you thought you had heard. . . ." It was part of his *coquetterie* to be an eccentric. Perhaps his sophistication was too rich for Camus' blood, but in the house of Gallimard were many mansions, a Camus could work down the hall from a Paulhan, and one could even provide momentary entertainment for the other.

On his side, Camus had his youth, and the sensation he had created with his first books, not only in the face of the minor gods of the *NRF,* but within their godhood, with their help and support. And in these first days he did all that he could to stay in his place, and not to attempt to outshine. Was it his fault if in the eyes of the Gallimards, who had been nurturing successive generations of literary giants, he represented the future? From 1925 until the war Paulhan had been Gaston Gallimard's eminence grise, closer to Gaston's heart than his two other favorites, Drieu La Rochelle and Léon-Paul Fargue. Now young Camus arrived with books that were already more important than the books of all the Paulhans, the Drieus, and the Fargues, and with sound literary judgment as well. The mocking or the disdain of the Paulhan generation, if it really existed, might have contained an element of jealousy.[11]

Almost from the first days Camus was invited to participate in the Reading Committee. He teamed up with office-mate Jacques Lemarchand and chose as his spiritual guide Brice Parain, author of works of philosophy published by Gallimard.[12] Born in 1897, Parain was an agrégé of philosophy, but he had also studied Russian and had been a cultural attaché in the French Embassy in Moscow before joining Gallimard in 1927. His philosophy of language fascinated Camus. ("He considers the problem of language as metaphysical and not social and psychological," Camus had noted in his journal in Le Panelier after a reading of *Essai sur le logos platonicien.*) Now Camus would expand his reading of Parain into a long essay, published during that winter in *Poésie 44.* That magazine had been founded at the beginning of the war in Villeneuve-lès-Avignon by Pierre Seghers, who had soon made of the successive *Poésie 40, Poésie 41,* etc., a rallying point for resistance intellectuals—Aragon and Eluard, but also Gide, Malraux,

Mauriac. By publishing in Southern France, where the German presence was less evident, Camus was sticking to the principle he would not abandon until the departure of the occupying forces. And when a young man about Gallimard, Guy Dumur, showed Camus the manuscript of an article he had written about Camus for the Paris *Comoedia,* Camus advised him not to publish it there. (Dumur gave it to René Tavernier, who used it in *Confluences.*)[13]

Camus had another immediate trump at Gallimard: his friendship with the youngest generation of that family, through Janine. In that last year of the war Camus made a capital friend of Michel Gallimard, Gaston's nephew. Born in February 1918, Michel had been given an elite education at Paris's private Ecole Alsacienne. Then he had a brilliant professor and Gallimard author, René Etiemble, as his private tutor. Through another Gallimard author, Antoine de Saint-Exupéry, Michel and his cousin Pierre both became interested in flying. Michel was given an open-cockpit Aiglon plane by his grandmother (Gaston's mother), and after the Liberation he would fly a closed-cockpit four-seater Nord 1100. Michel's wife had been killed when they were riding bicycles together and she had been run down by a truck just ahead of him.

Michel was fascinated by Gaston and by everything he represented; he knew that the world of books was the one in which he wished to live. A likable young man, with a "roguish face of a little redheaded boy who never grows old," as Etiemble would recall, Michel quickly developed a relationship with his authors that French publishers didn't usually have (and seldom sought). He was fascinated by literary people, although he had no literary pretensions of his own. "There are several ways to have genius, the most difficult one being to introduce into one's love life, or one's friendship, the qualities that so many place in science or the arts, even if it means living as they can, often badly. Michel Gallimard had the genius of friendship."[14] He also learned the business side of publishing, taking ledgers home to study. Later his tuberculosis would reduce his activity, all but putting him on a side track in the family company. And then he would die at forty-two in the automobile accident with his friend Albert.

Thanks to Michel, to Janine, to others of their generation, Camus was more than an author-editor at the Librairie Gallimard from the time of his entry into that house.

In her memoirs Simone de Beauvoir describes her first meeting with Camus at the Café de Flore. Sartre was also present, but he had already talked briefly with Camus at the opening performance of *Les Mouches.* Now the three of them had the first of a long series of encounters which would bring them so close that strangers to their circles would pair them up (outside of France they would be considered of the same school). At this first meeting the conversation began slowly, with talk of books. Sartre shared Camus' admiration of Ponge's *Le Parti pris des choses*. And when Sartre spoke of his new play the ice was broken.

Sartre had written the brief *Huis clos* (No Exit) at the request of a pharmaceutical manufacturer who published an elegant magazine at his own expense, operating the handpress himself (this was *Arbalète,* which published the essay on Kafka that censorship had kept out of the Gallimard edition of *Le Mythe de Sisyphe*). The manufacturer wanted a play for his new wife, a friend of Sartre and Beauvoir, who was studying acting; he would finance the production of a low-budget work which would tour France and thus provide an airing of her talents. At their Café de Flore meeting Sartre suggested that Camus direct *Huis clos* and even play the leading man; Camus hesitated, then accepted. Soon they were rehearsing in Simone de Beauvoir's room at the Hôtel Louisiane on the Rue de Seine, with its view over the rooftops. But the road-show project was suspended when the manufacturer's wife was arrested after having called on friends active in the resistance. When the Vieux-Colombier theater expressed interest in Sartre's play, Camus bowed out, judging that he was not qualified to direct professional actors, nor to mount a play on a Paris stage.

But from now on the Sartre-Beauvoir couple and their inner circle were seen everywhere with Camus: at local bistrots, often at entertainments at the apartment of Michel Leiris. Or Beauvoir would invite them all to dinner—the Leiris, the Queneaus, Camus—at her room at the Louisiane. She could seat eight at her table. Zette, the wife of Leiris, might bring the meat, she would find the wine. She would make pot roast (*boeuf mode*) or a pot of beans, aided by Jacques-Laurent Bost, Sartre's former student, who liked to cook. "It's not very impressive by its quality, but there is the quantity," Camus would remark. Simone de Beauvoir enjoyed receiving guests; she had never done it before.

In her memoir published long after the momentous break between Sartre and Camus, she remembered Camus of that time in this way:

> His youth, his independence, joined him to us: We had all developed without a tie to any school, as solitaries; we had no home, nor what one calls a milieu . . . He accepted success, fame, with a good appetite, and didn't hide the fact . . . He sometimes betrayed a Rastignac side, but he didn't seem to take himself seriously. He was simple and merry. His good humor didn't turn up its nose at facile jokes: He called the waiter named Pascal at the Flore "Descartes"; but he could afford to do this; his charm, due to a happy mix of nonchalance and enthusiasm, guaranteed him against vulgarity.

Their common plight, Beauvoir was convinced, developed the solidarity between Camus and their group that tastes and opinions alone would not have been able to explain. They all listened to the BBC broadcasts from England, exchanged news of the war, shared feelings about what was happening. They promised each other to be forever united against systems, ideas, the men they opposed. They would do things together. For example, they planned as a group (including not only Camus and Sartre-Beauvoir but Sartre's philosopher friend Maurice Merleau-Ponty) to take over the ethics section of the volume on philosophy which Gallimard was to publish in the *Encyclopédie de la Pléiade*. And Sartre was going to found a magazine that they would publish together. Camus was soon reading Sartre's weighty philosophic treatise, *L'Etre et le Néant* (Being and Nothingness), recently published by Gallimard.

Sartre and Camus were both members of a new literary prize jury established by Gallimard, Prix de la Pléiade. Others members of the jury included Paulhan, Malraux (then presumably fighting the Germans in the hills of south-central France), Paul Eluard, and the *NRF* regulars Queneau, Blanchot, and Arland; Lemarchand was secretary of the jury. Their first prize was voted in February 1944 to *Enrico,* by the actor and singer of Berber descent Marcel Mouloudji; both Sartre and Camus had voted for him.[1] (One of Camus' jobs at Gallimard was to sift manuscripts for the prize.) Camus suggested that fellow North Africans host a couscous lunch at the Hoggar restaurant on the Rue Monsieur-le-Prince, and Gabriel Audisio agreed to handle arrangements.[15] Simone de Beauvoir, who was invited with Sartre to join the nostalgics, remembered that lamb chops were served, and how disappointed she was to see that hers was only a bone enveloped in a little fat.

Soon after that Michel Leiris invited the group to give a public reading of Picasso's *Le Désir attrapé par la queue,* written in the 1920s surrealistic style. Camus was put in charge. He held a large cane with which he struck the floor, French-stage fashion, to indicate a change of scene, and also served as narrator to describe the scenes and to introduce the actors, while directing the cast chosen by Leiris (which included Sartre and Beauvoir). The performance took place in the Leiris' living room, but there was standing room only and some of the audience had to watch from an adjoining room. According to Beauvoir, she, Sartre, and Camus were taking as a lark what others in this crowd of old surrealists took seriously. Picasso was present, and so were Georges Braque, Georges Bataille, and Jean-Louis Barrault. The reading began at seven; by eleven most of the guests had gone, but the Leiris urged the cast and some close friends to stay beyond the midnight curfew. They drank wine, played jazz records, but didn't dance because of the neigh-

bors. Mouloudji sang; Leiris and Camus read a scene from a melo-
drama. Outdoors, Beauvoir felt, Paris was a vast prison camp, but they
were conjuring that Paris. They broke up at 5 A.M., when the curfew
was lifted.[16]

This was the first of several such events which Leiris baptized
fiestas. Another would be held at the home of Georges Bataille in the
Cour de Rohan, where the musician René Leibowitz was in hiding with
his wife. At these evenings they would disrupt the normal economy of
the time by an orgy of consumption, after having carefully hoarded the
food and wine. If friendship was evident, sex was absent; the catalyst
was alcohol and lots of it. And then each of them would employ his
drunkard's talents as he could: Sartre in a closet, conducting an imaginary orchestra; Camus and Lemarchand playing military marches with
pots and pans. Camus was also a good dancer.[1]

# 23

## COMBAT

Act; you don't risk more, and at least you'll have the clear
conscience that the best of our people take with them even
into prison. . . .

Article in clandestine *Combat,* March 1944

Before it was an underground newspaper or a famous Paris daily, Combat was a clandestine resistance movement, founded in 1942 to gather
intelligence on German occupation forces, to sabotage their installations, when possible to fight the enemy with arms. In 1943, Henri
Frenay, one of the movement's founders, left France in an attempt to
convince the Free French leader Charles de Gaulle to co-operate with
American intelligence operatives, specifically with the Office of Strategic
Services and its Switzerland-based chief Allen Dulles. Frenay's place in
France was taken by Claude Bourdet, formerly in charge of Combat's
propaganda activities, which included the publishing of resistance peri-
odicals and tracts. The son of a popular between-the-wars playwright,
Edouard Bourdet, Claude would go on to a postwar career in politics
and journalism. In the last months of 1943, the preparation of news-
papers and other propaganda materials was the specific responsibility of
René Cerf-Ferrière and a young woman named Jacqueline Bernard,
sister of one of Combat's chiefs, Jean-Guy Bernard, head of Résistance-
Fer, the railway sabotage group; he would be arrested and confined to
Auschwitz concentration camp, where he died. The Bernards were a
Jewish family of Alsatian origin; the father of Jacqueline and of Jean-
Guy was a career officer in the French Army; an uncle had been a
major figure in the defense of Dreyfus.

André Bollier (whose code names were "Vélin" and "Carton")

was in charge of printing and distribution. The first issue of their under-ground newspaper, entitled *Combat,* was printed in ten thousand cop-ies; by May 1944, on the eve of the Allied landing on Normandy beachheads, the printing was up to 250,000. In addition to using a Lyons printing plant, Bollier supervised the operation of fourteen presses in as many cities of what was then called the free zone of France, the southern half of the country. Bollier would send a matrix of the newspaper to each of these printing plants, which made local pro-duction and distribution possible, thus decreasing the risks. To obtain official paper allocations, he had set up a mythical company; the paper came from Germany, and was delivered to Lyons in railway car loads.

Bollier also produced false identity cards and police credentials to help resistance fighters and refugees, forged official rubber stamps to authenticate them. He was twice arrested by the French police and released. In March 1944 the Gestapo found him in Lyons, tortured him over a period of two months, but he didn't talk (none of his resistance comrades was arrested). He escaped and went back to work, under the cover of a Bureau de Recherches Géodésiques et Géophysiques, with a photogravure workshop as well as a press. On June 17, 1944, the police appeared with guns drawn at his window. Bollier slammed the shutters and the police fired, killing one of his men. Bollier replied with pistol fire, got out to the courtyard with a woman assistant, but they were sur-rounded. He was wounded by machine-gun bullets and used his own pistol to kill himself, saying, "They won't get me alive." His assistant was also wounded, but friends helped her escape from the hospital sev-eral weeks later.[1]

When Pascal Pia got to Paris in August 1943, after having served as deputy to the Lyons-based regional chief of the Combat movement, Marcel Peck (Peck was arrested and never heard of again), Pia was a natural choice as editor of the underground newspaper. It was also felt that someone should be on hand as a replacement for Cerf-Ferrière, who had joined the Gaullists in Algiers, since the printer Bollier didn't get along with Jacqueline Bernard, *Combat*'s editorial secretary. But Pia had other responsibilities in the resistance movement, as secretary-general of the new Mouvements Unis de Résistance, a merger of the Combat, Libération, and Franc-Tireur movements.

Once more, Pia thought of Albert Camus. He was seeing Camus, but prudently, for Pia knew that he was still being sought by the Ge-stapo, so that he had to avoid Saint-Germain-des-Prés and the Galli-mard building.[2]

Jacqueline Bernard had found a concierge who allowed the secret group to use the back of her small ground-floor apartment for meetings. It was not the best possible arrangement—for tenants entering the concierge's room for their mail could see them—but it was an indication that safe meeting places were hard to come by. At one such meeting, which took place soon after Camus' arrival in Paris at the beginning of November, Pia brought along Camus. The others present were Jacqueline Bernard and André Bollier. The young woman decided immediately that the young man in a worn raincoat was undernourished, but so many people were undernourished—and poorly clothed—at the time. She also noticed that he had a quizzical, observant air, but she was willing to believe that he was a kind man. Pia said: "He'll be able to help you because I'm leaving next week." She asked Camus: "What do they call you?" "Beauchard." Beauchard said he could do make-up and write articles for the paper.

They were just writing their first Paris issues; perhaps the first published in the capital was number 49, dated October 15, 1943 (but printed sometime before that, since clandestine printing and distribution required so much time). That issue contains a letter from Charles de Gaulle and a story about the liberation of Corsica. For each issue, the layout had to be perfect before it was sent to press; words had to be counted, for example, for no editor would be available at the underground printing plant. The method employed at the time was to set the type and make up the newspaper pages, then to reproduce them by photogravure in reduced format, after which zinc plates were sent to printers scattered around the country. Jacqueline Bernard was then working out of a tiny servant's room with the aid of a secretary who typed and delivered copy (it helped that the secretary looked fifteen years old, so she was allowed to slip through surprise police roundups and searches). Copy for the newspaper was compiled by correspondents who listened to the British radio (the BBC) and other short-wave broadcasts, or who received information from Switzerland or other foreign sources. Funds were parachuted from London earmarked for the Combat movement, sent from Free French headquarters. (It was when they took money from the United States via Dulles—a move that Frenay favored—that de Gaulle became angry.) They recruited helpers to carry supplies, distribute finished copies. Eventually they acquired bicycles for everybody because the Paris subway was so unreliable in those days. (Once, thanks to the good connections of a liaison agent, Jacqueline Bernard was able to procure tires for Camus' bicycle.)

In all their trials, she discovered Camus to be most un-Mediterranean, except when he was being lyrical and enthusiastic, when he indulged in Mediterranean gesticulating. He seemed rather "English"— the opposite type—in that he avoided speaking of what really troubled him. One day he remarked that he couldn't attend a meeting because he had to have a pneumothorax injection; otherwise he would not talk about his health. He refused to be invited to lunch on Combat movement funds or ration tickets.

Although they all used pseudonyms to each other, after a while those in the inner circle found it necessary to know one another's true names, so that they could be reached at home or at their place of work in an emergency. Jacqueline Bernard would phone Camus at Gallimard but when asked who was calling by the switchboard operator she would give a pseudonym. Once Camus asked her: "What shall I do? They want me to talk over Radio Paris." She was startled that he would even consider speaking on the collaborationist station. "You understand," he explained, "it's the only way to let my wife and mother know that I'm still alive." This was the first time he had mentioned his family, the first time Jacqueline Bernard realized he had a wife and a mother. She offered instead to have a letter sent via the underground.

Camus expressed curiosity about each new recruit, wondering what had made him want to join the movement. One time, Camus himself brought a new couple to their meeting, under pseudonyms. The small man offered to do anything, including writing crime stories. And he did anything he was asked. Then Jacqueline Bernard went to see *Huis clos* and discovered that her volunteer couple were Jean-Paul Sartre and Simone de Beauvoir.[3] Soon Camus had recruited another friend, Henri Cauquelin, who had written to his fellow *Paris-Soir* staffer at Gallimard to say that he was looking for a job. Camus found work for him, work which would keep him alive and also serve as cover while he helped Camus and his friends on the underground *Combat*. At one meeting Cauquelin attended at the home of Marcel Paute he listened impatiently to the suggestions of a small man they called "Miro" (French slang for blind or weak-eyed); then Cauquelin broke in to say that Miro wasn't very logical. Camus told Cauquelin: "All right, you write the article." And later he took Cauquelin aside to explain: "Do you know who you were calling illogical? Jean-Paul Sartre."[4]

When Pascal Pia introduced Camus to the Combat movement, he certainly took him to meet Combat's leader, Claude Bourdet. This fact, and the inevitability of memory failure after so many years, and memories of a very special, secret kind in dangerous and confused times, have led to conflicting accounts of how Camus was brought to Combat. Camus' friend Father Bruckberger remembers having suggested Camus to Bourdet, and why not? Bourdet could well have heard of Camus from several sources. It now seems that Camus was already working on the newspaper *Combat* before Bourdet was introduced to him, such is

the nature of clandestine operations, especially when run by a true secret agent like Pascal Pia. When Bourdet met Camus for the first time
—he placed the event in January or February 1944—this was his impression: "I had read *L'Etranger,* and I rediscovered, in the half-smile
slightly sad and ironical, the lowered eyes, but at the same time the
firmness of his expression, that heart-rending and winning contrast that
had caused me to admire Camus' first book."

Bourdet later remembered that Camus was put to work on a project for a magazine that was to be published by the Combat movement.
The magazine would have longer and more reflective articles than the
underground newspaper could use; Bourdet wanted to call it *La Revue
Noire.*[5] He had even chosen an editor for the projected magazine, Maximilien Vox (whose real name was Monod); the intention was to reach
a wider audience than was usually attained by the underground press.

Camus was indeed tapped to take part in the effort, but his connection with *La Revue Noire* would be brief and pathetic.

The co-ordination between writers, editors, and the printer was
being handled by Maximilien Vox's son Flavien Monod, with the familiar title of editorial secretary. The son lived just opposite his father's
apartment on the narrow Rue Visconti (which connects the Rues
Bonaparte and Seine a few blocks from the Gallimard building). Camus
agreed to serve as liaison between the editors of *La Revue Noire* and
the printer.

And one day—it was sometime between March 10 and 20, 1944—
Maximilien Vox advised his son that "one of ours" would call on him
in the afternoon to pick up a package of manuscripts, which included
unsigned texts by Vox, Flavien Monod, Maurice Clavel, Yves Gandon,
and other writers. The caller would use a password. At the expected
hour there was a knock on the door. Flavien Monod opened to a character he thought rather miserable in appearance, with a waxen complexion he found displeasing; the caller was wearing an old raincoat which
to Flavien Monod spelled cop. And this suspicious-looking character
asked for the manuscripts but couldn't supply the password. In return
Monod himself pretended not to know anything about anything. The
suspicious man on the landing turned around, descended the two flights
of stairs empty-handed. Monod quickly alerted his father, burned everything he could, and both he and his father hid everything else they
thought compromising in a cellar.

The suspicious character, Camus, therefore had nothing more to
do with *La Revue Noire.* Its single issue, numbered issue 0, was dated
March 1944, but it was printed only after the liberation of Paris. Maximilien Vox referred to the event in an editorial in that issue:

La Revue Noire was put together, from December 1943 to March 1944, by a group of fighters and writers most of whom were in contact with the Combat group. The very moment when, after many difficulties not entirely overcome, we were going to go to press, was the moment of the breaking up of the group because of one of those accidents which are never unexpected in wartime.

Deprived of their liaisons, isolated from their friends, the editor-in-chief and the editorial secretary were unable—and they regret it —to carry out the task assigned to them. . . .[6]

Camus' contribution to clandestine Combat may have consisted only of the two articles that have been positively identified as his, the first published in March 1944, entitled "A guerre totale résistance totale," which was a warning against inertia, lack of involvement. ("Because you will be killed, taken away to a camp, or tortured just as well as a sympathizer as an activist.") The other article, published in May, was headed: "Pendant trois heures, ils ont fusillé des Français," a story about the German reprisal killing of eighty-six men in a village after the derailing of a train (which had caused no casualties). Two other articles have been attributed to Camus, one published in April 1944 on the French Milice, which served as an auxiliary force to German occupation troops, and which contains the line: "Sganarelle wants to do better than Don Juan, the servant outbids his master." The other, in July, also concerned Milice activities and quotes Malraux to the effect that it is impossible to aim a flame-thrower at an enemy who is looking at you.[7]

One day Camus called on Jacqueline Bernard to say that he had been told that "Renoir" (Pascal Pia) had been arrested in Lyons. She had already heard the report but didn't believe it. He insisted that she check it out, "because you can't replace a man like that." If the arrest was confirmed, he intended to go to Lyons to stage an escape; she agreed to go with him. Actually Pia had not been arrested, although someone with a similar pseudonym had been.[3] Combat's chief Claude Bourdet was himself arrested on March 25, 1944, sent to the Buchenwald camp, from which he was released in April 1945.

A major problem for the Combat group was the movement of printed copies of the small-format, single-sheet newspaper from printshop to reader. Even to buy large valises with locks was difficult during the war years. The usual procedure was to check baggage through from Lyons by railroad—the baggage of course containing copies of Combat. Then the valises would be picked up in Paris at the station, as if by the passenger who had traveled up from Lyons. But as the shipments got bulkier, the Combat team began to use crates, shipping companies, fake company labels. They might mark the crates "cleaning supplies," for example, and address them to an imaginary hardware store. But one time they used the name of an existing hardware store, since in any case the crates were to be picked up at the railroad station by a *Combat* agent holding the receipt. Normally the railway express services didn't deliver during the war, but that one time they did; the crates went to the hardware store. The innocent dealer opened them, discovered the stacks of copies of *Combat,* and at once notified the police. He was arrested for his pains. Jacqueline Bernard learned of the arrest through agents in the police department, and told Camus what had happened. She spoke with a certain amount of anxiety, fearing his anger; like everyone else around she had succumbed to his charm and she hated the idea that he might bawl her out.

But Camus only laughed. "You see, it can be as dangerous not to be in the resistance as to participate." Later she would read something like that in *La Peste*. Plague is everybody's business. It was also the theme of those two articles attributed to Camus with some certainty, published in clandestine *Combat*.[3]

At best the newspaper was a drop in the bucket. Produced in danger, with the risk of arrest, torture, and imprisonment or execution, it could only serve to lift morale a mite; it could not change the course of the war. Could it change the postwar world? For active resistance workers, such as those of the Combat movement, were laboring not only to rid their country of enemy troops and of a collaborationist government; if they were making sacrifices to free France, it was because they also hoped to make a better France after the liberation. All the resistance organizations had programs for that postwar world, and Combat was no exception. By the spring of 1944, and although the end of the war still seemed far away, the clandestine team responsible for the underground edition of *Combat* began to make plans for the publication of an aboveground newspaper, a daily, when France was liberated from enemy occupation.

On a visit to the *Combat* staff while on a brief trip to Paris, Pascal Pia warned them that in order to publish a Paris daily professional journalists would be needed. Camus and Jacqueline Bernard began to look for some. Pia himself brought in Georges Altschuler, the diplomatic correspondent of *Paris-Soir,* who in the early part of the war had worked with a resistance intelligence network in Southern France before joining the Combat movement. Altschuler sat in at an early meeting of the planning committee for the postwar daily with Camus, Jacqueline Bernard, and Pia at the apartment of Suzanne and Marcel Paute (known as "Gimont"), facing the heights of Buttes-Chaumont in northeast Paris. Maurice Leroy, a printer, lent his apartment on the Rue d'Aboukir for another planning meeting, attended by the same group plus Henri Cauquelin and Albert Ollivier; his concierge was the lookout.[8] Camus brought in Sartre, Sartre's friend Bost, and Dionys Mascolo. Each of the recruits was told that he was not needed at the moment but that he should be ready to begin working when called. A special committee of the clandestine press, representing the resistance as a whole, worked out a sharing arrangement of existing newspaper plants. It was agreed that *Combat* and two other resistance papers would get the large Rue Réaumur plant, then a production center for the collaborationist press, including the German Army's own daily *Pariser Zeitung,* printed in the German language. But what if the Germans defended the plants? Jacqueline Bernard was given the task of contacting resistance action groups to secure their help in protecting the Rue Réaumur building, but she was told that on the day of liberation they'd have more urgent missions.

She received a bundle of 200,000 francs through the underground courier service, earmarked for salaries of the staff of daily *Combat* (worth no more than 54,000 francs of the mid-1970s, or some $11,000 in U.S. currency). They asked Michel Gallimard to hide the money in his safe. Then they forgot about the cash for a long time (and paid salaries out of proceeds from sales).[3]

In these early Paris months, Camus was transformed from an interested but casual contact of the underground—hardly more than a camp follower—into a committed activist, taking risks. He couldn't have known it, but the mission he had undertaken was designed to catapult him into instant postwar stardom, he more than anyone else connected with *Combat*. For the moment it involved danger, but also dreary meetings in remote, unlikely places, an expense of energies he could scarcely afford. Surely his double life—the Gallimard office, the underground— served one purpose: to fill up his days and nights; they were insurance against solitude during the Parisian exile.

He acquired a set of false identity documents in the name of "Albert Mathé," editor by profession, born in May 1911 at Choisy-le-Roy in the vicinity of Paris. His residence was listed as Epinay-sur-Orge, in a neighboring district. This card, ostensibly issued in May 1943, contained his photograph, fingerprint, false signature, but also a tax stamp, the local town hall's official seal and the signature of the mayor. In the name of "Mathé" he also had ration tickets and a German Army document certifying that he was a *französisches Soldat* released from a German prison camp.[9] Possibly the fake identification was printed in

Lyons; the man who did the work there for the Combat movement was
known as "Pierre Faux-Papiers"—Peter False-Papers.[3]

Sometime in the early months of 1944, André Malraux came to
Paris on temporary leave from the Dordogne redoubt from which he
was directing an interallied command of his own making. Pierre and
Janine Gallimard invited him for dinner at their apartment on the Rue
Saint Lazare, and arranged for Camus to be there. It was the first meeting of any duration between the two men, who seemed to take to each
other at once. They left the Gallimards together, one to walk the other
home. Then they changed direction to accompany the other, all the
while talking, and so on until near curfew time. Next day the Gallimards asked Camus if he had been able to get a word in and he said
yes, they had had a good talk.[10]

All the while, Camus was performing his job at the Librairie
Gallimard, among young men and some older ones who thought and
acted as he was doing, and some who were in the other camp: the intellectual collaborators. He was partying with the Sartres and the Leiris,
drinking at the Flore with the litterateurs of Saint-Germain-des-Prés.
And in his hotel room, later in borrowed quarters, he was writing. *La
Peste* was being completed—or so he thought. He was deep in the
"Essai sur la révolte," making notes for new works (e.g., a novel about
a man who sets a date for his suicide one year ahead, and the superiority it gives him in that he becomes indifferent to dying).

Even inside the Gallimard house there was a place for resistance
activity. Some of Camus' recruits came from there. At least once he had
Janine Gallimard type out some information which seemed to concern
German military strength—and hide the papers for him.[10]

Once he walked into the office and looked around, as if seeking
somebody. He noticed Jean Lescure, the editor of *Messages* (and of
*Domaine Français*). He asked Lescure in sotto voce whether he could
hide someone in his apartment. Lescure, who was living with his wife
and new baby in a single room, said that didn't seem possible to him.
Camus walked around some more, apparently to ask the same question
of others; Lescure noticed that he was getting nowhere and seemed
downcast. Lescure asked him: "Is it very important?" Camus: "Very."
Lescure said he would do what he could. Camus took him downstairs
and out into the street, where Lescure recognized André Malraux, in
the company of a blond giant of a man with a very red face. (As it happened, Malraux's regular liaison in Paris was the absent Pascal Pia;
running into Camus on the street, he had asked his intervention rather
than take the risk of entering the Gallimard building himself.)[11]

Lescure took the blond giant to his small room. He shared his bed
with the man, his wife sleeping on the mattress but on the floor, beside

the baby's cradle. It did not take him long to discover that his guest was a British officer.

That night the officer slept through the Allied bombing of the key railway junction at Villeneuve-Saint-Georges south of Paris, which meant that he would not be able to leave for the Dordogne maquis as had been planned. So the officer had to remain with the Lescures for a while. One day he walked in with a huge dog; he had passed a pet shop and couldn't resist buying it; the Lescures' room seemed smaller than ever. When Malraux showed up he exploded, took the dog back to the shop. Later Lescure learned from Malraux that his officer guest was Major George Hiller.[12] In the Dordogne, at Malraux's interallied command, Hiller—"George l'Anglais"—was one of those with whom Malraux organized what was called the most important arms drop carried out over enemy-occupied territory during the war. That was in July 1944. Later the same month Malraux, Hiller, and others of their group, driving imprudently along a national highway, were attacked by a German motor patrol. Hiller was seriously wounded, Malraux was captured.[13]

Another of the young men about Gallimard was Dionys Mascolo, who had been a classmate of Michel Gallimard at the Ecole Alsacienne. He was invited to join Camus in editing the clandestine *Combat,* but he told Camus that he was more interested in action; he asked to be put in touch with the Combat movement's military groups. The contact was never arranged; after the war Camus confessed that he hadn't felt that Mascolo was cut out for fighting. Mascolo nevertheless found his own way into an armed group, François Mitterrand's Mouvement National des Prisonniers de Guerre et Déportés (MNPGD). At one point he kept a revolver in the Gallimard building without anyone else knowing it. (After the war Mascolo joined the Communist Party, and on his departure from it wrote a well-received analysis of French Communism.)

If Camus didn't see Mascolo as an armed fighter, Camus' friends were also anxious to preserve *him* from dangerous activities, fearing that arrest and interrogation might kill him. But twice Mascolo was associated with Camus in specific acts which might have become dangerous. The first time, in the early spring of 1944, Mascolo was in charge of moving a clandestine printing press. Camus stationed himself (with the actress Maria Casarès, who was then rehearsing *Le Malentendu*) at a café terrace near the subway station Barbès-Rochechouart to observe Mascolo's activity, prepared to alert others in Mascolo's group if Mascolo was intercepted or if he noticed anything suspicious.

When another Gallimard man, Robert Anthelme, was arrested in June, Mascolo and his companion, Marguerite Duras, then at the beginning of her career as an avant-garde novelist, had to remove possibly incriminating papers from Anthelme's apartment on the Rue Saint-Benoit, around the corner from the Café de Flore. Camus again stood guard, this time at the corner of the Rues Jacob and Saint-Benoit, to be ready to warn his friends of suspicious movements.[14]

Francis Ponge, on his arrival in Paris, found himself drawn into the ambiguous cat-and-mouse game, with resistance fighters and pro-Nazis all but cohabiting in the publishing world as on the street. He walked with Camus down to Montparnasse to call on an old *NRF* friend, the anti-Nazi Bernard Groethuysen, but when they approached the Rue Campagne-Première, where Groethuysen lived, Camus stopped short, remarked that the area was dangerous for him; there was a Gestapo headquarters in the vicinity.

Another time, when Ponge was talking to Camus in the Gallimard office he shared with Jacques Lemarchand, then jammed with visitors, Camus asked him to stay on when the others left. Then Michel Gallimard walked in. Ponge accompanied Camus and Gallimard to the office of Pierre Drieu La Rochelle on the same landing. It was late; everyone else including Drieu had gone home. They opened a closet in Drieu's office, and under some files found what they were looking for: large cans containing the movie Malraux made in Spain of his propaganda novel *L'Espoir* (Man's Hope). They took the reels with them to Neuilly just west of the city, where in a large house facing the Bois de Boulogne owned by a onetime business associate of Gallimard they found Malraux's sons and their mother Josette Clotis; Malraux had sent them here to safety while he led his resistance group in the south. Ponge had one awkward moment when he observed Camus drawing up an elegant chair, sitting down on it, putting his feet on an elegant table. "It's not bad here," Camus observed. The ascetic Ponge felt that Camus was behaving like an arriviste, a Rastignac in Paris.[15]

It is of course equally interesting to speculate on what the motion picture of *L'Espoir* was doing in Drieu's office. Was it actually the only copy of the film? (The Germans had tried to destroy it, found what they thought was this film in a can labeled with the name of its producer Edouard Corniglion-Molinier, but what they actually destroyed was only a copy—and not the only copy—of another film of the same producer, Marcel Carné's *Drôle de drame,* starring Louis Jouvet.)[13] Did Drieu know that the reels were in his office? Wasn't he, the pampered collaborationist, protecting his old anti-Fascist friend's property? In that strange atmosphere of wartime France, such a possibility is more than likely. Although Drieu had written in 1942 that if he encountered Malraux in battle he would have to shoot at him, and in certain circumstances he would have to let Malraux be executed ("If I don't believe that, I don't take M. seriously. . . ."), the two old friends were meeting regularly during the German occupation, and Drieu was to be the godfather of his second son born to Josette Clotis, this while Malraux was a resistance fighter.[13]

Nearly all of France's patriotic writers belonged to the clandestine Comité National des Ecrivains. That the most militant leaders of this organization were also identified with the Communist Party or its fronts did not prevent leading non-Communists, including Jean Paulhan and François Mauriac (and of course Father Bruckberger) from belonging to it in the last somber days of German occupation. The Communist Party's control of CNE, its increasing exploitation of the movement for its own political goals, would be apparent only later. During this final year of the war it seemed more of a summit group of the best and worthiest of French letters, an underground Academy, even their court of appeals. It was the CNE which informed Simone de Beauvoir, for example, that she could accept the Goncourt Academy's prize if it were voted to her for her first novel, *L'Invitée*.[16] The CNE's underground periodical was *Lettres Françaises,* which by January 1944 included on its board of directors not only Camus but Jean Paulhan, Jean Lescure, and Paul Eluard.[12] *Lettres Françaises* was edited by the CNE's Claude Morgan, a prolific left-wing writer of the period, son of a member of the French Academy. Morgan (whose real name was Lecomte) actually put the clandestine monthly together in his office in the Louvre Museum.

It was now that Camus would have the first serious controversy of his French career, and with a familiar opponent. In Algeria the provisional government of Free France had just executed a leading Nazi collaborator and member of the Vichy government. Pierre Pucheu had been a prewar Fascist, and during his service as Vichy's Minister of the Interior he had collaborated in the execution of hostages taken by the Germans. But after the Allied landing in North Africa, Pucheu had gone there intending to change sides, to take up arms against his former German friends. The Gaullists thought otherwise, tried him for treason, and sentenced him to death.

Albert Camus was now a committed resistance worker, but his lifelong opposition to the death penalty created a barrier between himself and his anti-Nazi comrades. He set about to write what he must have felt was a thoughtful dissenting opinion. In this unsigned article, in which Camus' hand is all too apparent, he began:

> There isn't a writer who ignores the value of a human life and
> I suppose that this is one of the honorable definitions of that pro-
> fession. It is perhaps for that reason that I have always detested
> the justice of men in power.

The author expressed his "disgust" and his "revolt" at executions, yet he saw Pucheu's crime as one of "lack of imagination," for having allowed men to die in the name of abstract principles. But the collaborators must now be aware that the time of abstraction was over; if criminals were executed it would not be in the name of a class or an ideology, but "at the insistence of all the accused that we ourselves were for the past four years. . . ."

No defense of Pucheu, this, or of collaborators in general. But the CNE leadership, Eluard first of all, felt that Camus' irony made light of Pucheu's crimes in attributing them to lack of imagination. Eluard was known as a kind man but pitiless to those he felt were responsible for Nazi crimes. The majority of the board refused to allow Camus' article to be published as an editorial, although they agreed to accept it as an article, with a rejoinder which Eluard asked to attach to it. Morgan was asked to write another editorial representing the CNE's true position on the Pucheu execution. Morgan's contribution appeared in the left-hand column of the front page of the April 1944 issue of *Lettres Françaises*. (The front page headline that month was "Max Jacob assassiné.") Morgan's article, "Justice de la France," began:

> Pucheu sentenced to death, shot for collaboration with the enemy. One feeling dominates: Justice has been done to France. . . .

He pointed out that the CNE itself, along with other resistance groups, had specifically requested that de Gaulle's provisional government try and execute Pucheu, in the name of Jacques Decour, founder of *Lettres Françaises,* who had been shot by the Nazis in May 1942, and of others tortured by Pucheu's police and turned over to the Germans.

Camus' unsigned article, entitled "Tous ne s'arrange pas," appeared in the May 1944 issue of the periodical. (Other anonymous contributors to that issue were François Mauriac and Jean Paulhan, as well as Morgan and Elsa Triolet.) Beneath Camus' article was Eluard's disclaimer, equally anonymous:

> Faced with the article "Tout ne s'arrange pas" which appears elsewhere in this issue, several of our friends, in agreement with the general thesis of the author, nevertheless wish to state that this convenient lack of imagination of which he speaks seems to them, and particularly in the case of Pierre Pucheu, voluntary. . . .[17]

That the incident did not lead to an immediate break between Camus and the hard-liners of CNE is suggested by the fact that Camus remained a member of the committee until late in 1944, after the liberation of Paris, when he resigned because of the Communist-oriented policies of the group, and refused to write for the postwar *Lettres Fran-*

*çaises.*[18] But was there to be a final, more subtle conclusion to Camus' second falling out with the Communists?

For at the very moment that Camus was airing his differences with CNE in their clandestine meetings, an anonymous tract was circulated in Paris attacking existentialist writers as "pseudo-resistants." The four writers cited and thus exposed to the attention of the French police and the German occupying forces were Sartre, Camus, Lescure, and a poet named André Frenaud. At least one of the writers thus targeted had reason to believe that the tract was written and secretly distributed by the Communists, who used this tactic to expose and thus eliminate potentially troublesome opponents.[12]

# 24

---◆---

# THE MISUNDERSTANDING

> The fact that I am asked today to explain the deep intentions of *Le Malentendu* demonstrates sufficiently that the reception of this play wasn't the most flattering. I don't say that to complain, but for the truth of the matter. And the truth of the matter is that *Le Malentendu,* although seen by a rather large audience, was disavowed by the majority of this audience. In simple language, that is called a failure.
>
> *Le Figaro,* October 15, 1944

After the foregoing, it will be more difficult than ever to persuade the reader that during the same period in which Camus was helping to publish the underground edition of *Combat,* planning the first issues of daily *Combat* to appear as soon as Paris was liberated from the German occupation, he was also making his debut as a playwright in the Paris theater. For two of his plays were ready now. In the unsigned text Camus wrote to introduce Gallimard's publication of *Le Malentendu* and *Caligula* in a single volume in May 1944, their author linked both plays to the philosophy of the absurd already illustrated by *L'Etranger* and *Le Mythe de Sisyphe.* While not being "thesis plays" both works represented a "theater of the impossible." Camus wrote:

> Thanks to an impossible situation (*Le Malentendu*) or character (*Caligula*), they try to give life to apparently insoluble conflicts through which all thought must pass before producing the only valid solutions. This theater suggests, for example, that each of us bears in himself his part of illusion and misunderstanding which is destined to be killed. . . .

But were the plays also impossible productions? Was the misunderstanding to encompass the public's reaction to the intentions of their author? At first it seemed that way.

During the German occupation, as has already been said, the Paris theater carried on business as usual. Collaborators, the non-committed, but even ostensibly engaged resistance activists such as Sartre, began or pursued careers as producers, directors, playwrights, actors and actresses. All the great names and the lesser celebrities of the Paris stage were busy—Charles Dullin (a favorite of the press of that time), Jean-Louis Barrault (who played Hamlet at the Comédie Française and there put on Claudel's *Le Soulier de satin,* which disturbed Sartre and Beauvoir because Claudel was also the author of an ode to Marshal Pétain), Jean Cocteau, Raymond Rouleau; actors like Jean Marais and Serge Reggiani would make their first appearances now. Camus was in touch with some of the newest generation of theater people, such as actor-director Jean Vilar, a disciple of Dullin and friend of Sartre, who by the second postwar decade would be France's leading director of epic theater, in fact the only innovative director in what had become a theatrical wasteland. But when Camus met him in occupied Paris, Vilar was just beginning. They sat in a Saint-Germain-des-Prés café and Vilar said he would like to do *Caligula,* although he lacked the financial backing it would require.[1]

Barrault, then a member of the regular Comédie Française company, would have liked that troupe to do *Caligula* in a kind of experimental theater. He discussed it at Gallimard, but nothing was to come of that, either.[2] These discussions ran concurrently with Camus' beginnings at clandestine *Combat,* his first secret meetings, his contacts with the underground Comité National des Ecrivains.

Finally *Le Malentendu* was accepted for production not by a young director but by one of Paris' leading theaters of the time, the Théâtre des Mathurins, which was something of an institution in Paris' Madeleine district; this is where Camus had been taken in January 1943 by Janine Gallimard to see Maria Casarès in Synge's *Deirdre of the Sorrows.* Built at the turn of the century, the Mathurins had been a home of boulevard comedy, written by popular but shallow authors like Sacha Guitry, starring veteran actors like Raimu and Harry Baur. The style changed with the Pitoëffs, a Russian-born theater couple who brought leading representatives of the modern stage to Paris. (A plaque on the façade of the theater commemorates their fifteen-year reign.) They were succeeded by the inventive and apparently intelligent Marcel Herrand, a friend of Darius Milhaud and of Arthur Honegger, surrealists André Breton and Paul Eluard. At twenty Herrand had played in Apollinaire's *Les Mamelles de Tirésias,* was taken on by Copeau at the Vieux Colombier. He had met the Pitoëffs in Geneva, and at the Mathurins he co-starred in Cocteau's *Orphée* with Ludmilla Pitoëff. As a film actor he had roles in *Les Visiteurs du Soir* and *Les Enfants du Paradis.* Herrand and an associate, actor Jean Marchat, brought unknown classics (such as *Deirdre*) and plays by beginners to the attention of the French public. In the Parisian theater, owners or managers of theaters produce the plays which are presented in their theaters, assuming much or all of the financial risk, a system which often results in a certain homogeneity in choice, stability in casting, but also limits the number and the quality of productions.

In wartime Paris, a play with as small a cast, as simple a scenic requirement as *Le Malentendu,* would not be a great risk. Herrand, then fifty-two, had already discovered the potential in Maria Casarès, who was remarked at the examinations at the Paris acting academy by Jean Marchat. (When Maria began to play in *Deirdre,* she missed so many classes at the academy that she was expelled.) After *Deirdre* she was given the role of Hilda in a revival of Ibsen's *The Master Builder,* which opened in April 1943. She joined Herrand in the filming of Marcel Carné's *Les Enfants du Paradis* the same August, playing opposite Jean-Louis Barrault; and so her image is preserved for us on film to see her as she looked and might have spoken to Camus. That fall she would be on the stage again, alongside Marchat and Herrand in *Le Voyage de Thésée,* by Georges Neveux. Of her role in this play another debutant, young critic Claude Roy, wrote in René Tavernier's *Confluences:*

> That voice which always seems ready to crack, to break with emotion—That body which plays, trembles, vibrates, and always so harmonious, so pure . . . A great tragic actress. She is twenty years old.[3]

With veteran director Herrand as his guide, Camus set about in the first months of 1944 to make revisions in his script; rehearsals began in March. Maria Casarès was given the role of Martha, who with her mother would murder an unknown guest in their simple inn, a guest who in fact was Martha's brother Jan. Despite his age Herrand took the role of Jan (and directed the play). Sarah Oettly's son Paul played the old servant.

During the three months of rehearsals—then a quite normal span in the French theater—the playwright divided his time between the theater—and everything else. He was working, for example, on the essay which Jean Grenier had asked for, to be published in his anthology on existence; Camus completed the essay, called "Remarque sur la révolte," in March 1944, after which he returned to *La Peste,* working at night and "without pleasure."[4] He was corresponding with his new friend, Guy Dumur, an aspiring writer, also from North Africa and also tubercular; Dumur was then convalescing in the mountains. Camus had recently seen René Leynaud in Paris, and now (May 16) Leynaud was arrested; he would not leave German hands alive. Events which coincided with the Prix de la Pléiade couscous lunch with Sartre and Beauvoir, and with Gallimard's publication of *Le Malentendu* and *Caligula.*

Although Camus had not yet met André Gide, through his association with the Gallimards he had been introduced to Gide's intimate circle, and now he was invited to leave his grim hotel and to move into a sixth-floor studio connected to the Gide apartment at 1 bis, Rue Vaneau, in the Faubourg Saint-Germain district a few minutes from his Gallimard office. The studio had been the private quarters of Gide's young companion Marc Allegret, also of Gide's daughter Catherine. It adjoined the main apartment, then occupied by Maria van Rysselberghe, a sensible old woman—she was then sixty-eight—whom Gide called *la petite dame,* and whose delightful and quite frank journal on life with Gide, published as *Les Cahiers de la Petite Dame,* is a useful corrective to the mystifications of Gide's own journal; by Maria's daughter Elisabeth, mother of Gide's daughter Catherine; and by Elisabeth's husband Pierre Herbart, a writer of the Gide entourage then active in the anti-Nazi underground.[5] The studio Camus was to occupy was a high-ceilinged room with a loggia, and with a trapeze hanging from the middle of the ceiling. In his memoir on Gide, Camus would write that he had the trapeze removed, "being tired of watching intellectuals who visited me hanging from it." There was also a piano on which Gide used to play.[6]

Maria Casarès was a frail child of thirteen when the Spanish Civil War broke out. She asked immediately to be allowed to take part in the defense of Republican Spain, and with the approval of her father, who had been Minister of War and Prime Minister, she found volunteer work in a hospital. But she fainted there more than once, and when the war moved closer to Madrid her father sent Maria and her mother to France, where he joined them after Franco's victory. When the Germans came to France, Casares Quiroga took his wife and child to Bordeaux for the sea voyage to Britain. But there wasn't room on the ship for the women, so Maria's father was evacuated to Britain and they returned to occupied Paris. By the next year she was at the acting academy, encouraged by her mother, who loved the theater. She also had to learn French, of course, both for her acting and in order to pass her high school diploma (the *baccalauréat*). In 1942, when she began playing in *Deirdre of the Sorrows,* she was also working for her *baccalau-*

*réat de philosophie,* which she passed at the same time she left the academy. By now she needed no formal acting lessons, for Marchat and Herrand kept her busy acting on the stage.

Later she would not recall having met Albert Camus, then convalescent in Le Panelier, when Janine Gallimard took him backstage during his brief visit to Paris. But she was present at the concert performance of Picasso's *Le Désir attrapé par la queue* in the Leiris' apartment, where Camus had read out the stage directions. She had thought then that he was a fine actor. Next time she met him was at the Mathurins, when his play was being read by the cast.

She was not the only young member of the company. All of the actors and actresses were young, all were impressed with Herrand, who had a passion for discovering actors as well as authors. For Maria, certainly, the atmosphere seemed electric; team spirit was strong. A stagehand would tell her: "You were good today." Or even "Not too good." And in those gray years of the German occupation people were more likely to stick together, especially if they liked each other. Herrand, who was a sociable man and who may have been the "last dandy," lived in rooms above the theater which were a gathering place for painters, writers, and other creators, as well as people of the theater. Opening nights at the Mathurins drew the intellectual elite of Paris.[7]

Camus was entranced by the actress who had been chosen to play his Martha. ("Marthe," for what it is worth, was also the name Camus had given to the young lady in his first attempt at fiction, *La Mort heureuse,* and who had been intended to carry some of the burden of Simone Hié's sins.) Maria Casarès, he was convinced, was one of France's most promising tragediennes. He would soon be telling Jacqueline Bernard that Casarès "understood everything without having to be told," and that she had "everything." From now on, and until the last months of his life, in sickness and in health, Maria Casarès would never be very far from Albert Camus. At those times when they were separated, he would bridge the distance between them with a painstaking narration of what he was doing and thinking. But the link was less literal than spiritual, and it was not always to be a respite from the world and its troubles: Casarès was never the docile lady waiting by the fireside for the warrior to take rest on her shoulder. Perhaps she appealed to the dark side of Camus, to emotions which could be purged in private when *pudeur* and the code of the male would not let him manifest them in public; one could shout and sob, even weep, and talk about death. Casarès' excesses, her effusive presence on stage and off, compensated for the dull servitudes of his public life. She represented Camus' Spanish blood, later his concern not only for Spain's political plight but for its literature, its stage; she was his private way to remain in touch with the Mediterranean.

On June 5, less than three weeks from opening night, Camus introduced Maria to his friends at another fiesta staged by Sartre and Beauvoir, this one at the apartment of Charles Dullin and his Camille, Rue de La Tour d'Auvergne, an apartment garnished with flowers, ribbons, wreaths. There was a large circular drawing room, opening to a garden. The apartment was believed to have been the home of the actress Juliette Drouet, mistress of Victor Hugo. Here the Sartre crowd, and some of the *NRF* regulars, entertained each other with poetry, danced to phonograph records, from curfew to dawn. And this time Camus was here with Maria, who "wore a Rochas dress with violet and mauve stripes, and had combed her hair back; a slightly strident laugh revealed in starts her young white teeth—she was very beautiful."[8]

While this particular fiesta was taking place—in fact ninety minutes after midnight—American parachutists began to land near Utah Beach southeast of Cherbourg on the Cotentin Peninsula in Normandy. After intense Allied bombings the first troops dashed onto the beaches.

But if the Allied landings signified the beginning of the end for the German Army in France, the immediate consequences were a tighter occupation, stricter surveillance of the underground movements which represented a potential danger to the German rear. It was in mid-June that *Combat*'s Lyons printer André Bollier was tracked down. And now serious preparations were being made by Camus, Jacqueline Bernard, and their small task force, meeting secretly in one and then another Paris apartment, for the first daily issues to appear in liberated Paris.

At some undetermined time during this period, the young man who was about to attain quasi-celebrity with a first play on the Paris stage had to leave the intellectual Left Bank atmosphere of the Gide studio to hide out at the flat of an old friend from Algiers, Paul Raffi, on the Rue Chalgrin just off posh Avenue Foch, with a view of the Arch of Triumph. Raffi had made his presence known to Camus by calling on him at Gallimard, and they were seeing each other occasionally. But few knew of their association, so that Camus could live at Raffi's flat without anyone knowing about it. Raffi got to meet Maria Casarès for his pains.

On June 24, 1944, while the press was headlining the battle of Cherbourg (and a Soviet offensive in the Vitebsk region), the first public performance of *Le Malentendu* was held at the Théâtre des Mathurins. The play had been postponed from an earlier date because of restrictions on the use of electricity.

It was a stormy evening—inside the theater. No one who attended that opening night was likely to forget it. For Paris's intellectual elite refused to accept the intentional gloom of this play all in monotones, the inexorable progression of the action toward a tragic climax that even a naïve spectator could foresee, the purposeful artificiality of the symbols. With the best of intentions, Maria Casarès' friend and acting teacher, Dussane, confused by the atmosphere of the play, exhausted because of what she would later describe as the "extraordinary life" everybody was leading at the time, got up and walked out after the second act (which was already being drowned out by the hooting; and she later heard that the third act would be a battlefield). Dussane wondered whether some of the casting may have been responsible for the failure; and then everybody was so nervous at the time that "a rough edge in the contour of a play seemed intolerable to us. No one any longer possessed normal balance or the ability to understand, or to associate ideas." But Casarès was as usual: superb. "This woman whose charm is lauded at every new play, this sinuous, trembling, palpitating woman, who wore those full Grès or Alix dresses so well, this time appeared with hair harshly drawn back, abrupt gestures, closed face, as the wild and poor innkeeper of a lost corner of Europe." Not only did she bring life to the role, but she had to do battle with an unruly audience:

> Thus there was the revelation of a warrior Casarès (she still so young, and still seemingly so frail). No matter how loud the tumult, she, and she alone, dominated it. She imposed what she had to say, and the noise took up afterwards. But such circumstances—in which one had seen veteran actors weaken—call for an exceptional psychic power. Casarès held out victoriously, up to the last line. After which—but only then—with the curtain lowered, she allowed herself to melt into tears, out of exhaustion and distress.[3]

Only one critic made a public protest against the behavior of the first night audience, and he was a playwright himself, Henri-René Lenormand:

> The public at the opening night didn't want us to forget the immortal vulgarity of which it is sometimes capable. Its sneering laughter followed many lines of *Le Malentendu*. Is it too much to ask, of this public, that it wait until the curtain is lowered before demonstrating? To understand that, despite the realistic appearance of the play, it wasn't watching a crime story, but a tragedy? To perceive the element of sur-reality which transcends and ennobles our daily lives? To hold back for two hours its little sentimental needs? . . .
> But literate youth were present at this belligerent evening, and their bravos responded victoriously to the manifestations of Parisian conformity.

Lenormand predicted: "In twenty years *Le Malentendu* will perhaps be accepted in its present plenitude and splendor."

There was a feeling among Camus' friends that the hostility of the audience was due, at least in part, to the fact that Camus was known to be anti-Nazi, and perhaps an active participant in the resistance.[9] Maria Casarès certainly didn't understand the reaction of the audience, and she too wondered whether politics had something to do with it. But there was no further hostility of the sort during the other performances of the play during the German occupation of Paris.[7] It was said that Sartre had experienced the same hostility. In fact Sartre and Beauvoir attended that famous opening night, but they arrived with a prejudice against the play, which they had already read (and felt to be inferior to *Caligula*). So they were not surprised that in performance, and despite Casarès' talents, the play did not hold up. They didn't feel that the play's failure was a very serious matter, and Simone de Beauvoir noted rather curiously in her memoirs that "our friendship for Camus wasn't affected by it." Sartre and Beauvoir were irritated, nevertheless, at the satisfaction of the critics of the collaborationist press, who knew (she said) where Camus stood on the war. And so Sartre and Beauvoir also laughed, watching the critics march off. "Doubtless it was the last opening night about which they would be writing; from one day to the next they were going to be expelled from the press, from France, from the future: and they knew it. . . ."[8]

Surely both elements—the newness of the style, its awkwardness, and also suspicions that Albert Camus did not share the collaborationist ideology—must have been involved. But perhaps the politics were less important than Camus' friends were ready to believe. If "everybody" knew that Camus was pro-resistance, anti-collaboration, why hadn't he been arrested?

As for the play itself, even the young Gallimards were uncomfortable with what they saw on the Mathurins stage that evening. Michel, Pierre, and Janine had been watching rehearsals. They found the several references to a cup of tea quite awkward (the tea contained the poison that would be fatal to Martha's brother Jan). At the opening night, sure enough, there were snickers when Martha (played by poor Maria) mentioned the cup of tea. At the rear of the orchestra Gaston Gallimard and his wife Jeanne, Pierre, Michel, Janine Gallimard, and Jean Marchat applauded loyally when the audience booed. Yet this audience contained no more and no fewer collaborators than any other audience of the time.

Camus knew that the play was the issue; he was also somewhat pleased that he had provoked people; and, after all, he had met Maria.[6]

As for Maria, she was delighted with the play. She admired the "surrealism" of its sober tones. And she too observed that Camus was excited, almost stimulated, by the hostile audience, for after all he had wished to provoke.[7]

Perhaps it was now that Camus noted with serenity in his journal: "It took me ten years to conquer what seems to me priceless: a heart without bitterness." And there is the suggestion that his clandestine activity helped to protect him from exterior disturbances, even emotional ones:

> One can't be capable of involvement on every level. At least one can choose to live on the level where involvement is possible. To live what is honorable and that only. In certain cases this can lead to turning away from people, even (and especially) for a person who has a deep feeling for them.

After the liberation of Paris, Camus did not fall back on the political bias of his audience, but addressed himself to the artistic problems presented by his play. He realized to some extent that the play was *manquée*.

> Some awkward details, more serious longwinded passages, some uncertainty in the character of the son, all that can rightfully disturb the spectator. But in a certain sense, why not admit it, I felt that something in my language wasn't understood and that that was the fault of the public itself.

He was aware that the play took a pessimistic view of the human condition. "But that can be reconciled with a relative optimism concerning man." He knew that to put the language of tragedy into the mouths of contemporary characters was also to shock, but he felt that the public needed to get used to that. "Theater isn't a game." And then:

> Personally I received on the occasion of the staging of this play the greatest joy an author can receive: that of hearing his own language borne by the voice and the soul of a marvelous actress in the exact register one dreamed for it. This joy, that I owe to Maria Casarès, was quite sufficient for me.[10]

A reading of the collaborationist press after the stormy opening night seems to put down the idea that the Nazis and their friends knew that Camus was sympathetic to the resistance. (Indeed, a collaborator would be more likely to worry about a Casarès, whose father was a Spanish Republican refugee in England, or actress Hélène Vercors, who played Jan's wife, Maria, and whose husband was Pierre Bourdan of the Free French radio.) Certainly the German occupying forces' own newspaper, *Pariser Zeitung,* should have been particularly sensitive to playwrights suspected of plotting or working against the German war effort. Yet the *Pariser Zeitung*'s critic, one Albert Buesche, who in the July 2, 1944, issue of that paper's French-language weekly supplement had called Sartre's *Huis clos* "a theatrical event of the first order" despite some philosophical reservations, was more than kind to Camus' play. After noting weaknesses in the plot (e.g., why didn't Jan reveal his identity to his mother and sister?) Buesche decided that Camus must have wished to symbolize some of the fatality of the era. The critic did feel that Camus might have expressed himself more clearly, and that the performance had done a disservice to the text; Raymond Rouleau's staging of *Huis clos* had been superior. He didn't quite appreciate Maria Casarès, for example. She "certainly has talent in the role of the daughter . . . but she ended by assuming an artificial brutality which became insupportable." And Marcel Herrand, playing Jan, "was nonexistent. . . ."

> As for the play, nothing in its scenic quality or literary value will satisfy. It is nevertheless filled with profound thoughts, and that incites us to indulgence.

The *Pariser Zeitung* critic also observes that *Le Malentendu* brings the theater season to a close. He says nothing of the German occupation coming to a close, but that would happen in less than sixty days; the French supplement of the paper would be published for the last time with the August 13 issue. But the critic does see some changes coming:

> Camus' *Le Malentendu* is a pioneering work. The form and the idea are curiously juxtaposed, but the essential is clear. More than any other play, *Le Malentendu* touches the heart of the evil which surrounds us, and all of man's spiritual and moral existence. It seems to affirm that man of today cannot hope for a future unless he knows how to renew the very bases of his existence.[11]

*Comoedia,* the cultural weekly, published a front-page photograph of Maria Casarès and Marcel Herrand in the play. The paper's reviewer, one Roland Purnal, found the work *"extrêmement curieux,"* linked to Camus' revolt against the absurd. Yet Camus was too fine a writer, the critic went on, to be treated gently, so it must be said that the play is a failure. (But perhaps, concluded Purnal, it was still better than many successes.) And *La Gerbe,* an anti-Semitic literary and entertainment weekly which featured the Fascist polemicist Robert Brasillach, ran a review by André Castelot (later a popular historical writer of postwar France). Castelot, who had earlier suggested that Sartre's *Huis clos* be banned "not for mediocrity but for harmful ugliness," while recommending that playwrights be required to receive their right to create through a board of governors,[12] now mocked Camus' play, calling attention to lines which had provoked unintentional laughter; he decided that *Le Malentendu* was "Grand Guignol." (But he added that Herrand had staged the play to give a role to Maria Casarès, and that was the play's luck.)

*Le Malentendu* was given again on the very next night, June 25, and then ran from July 2 to 23, while allied forces were hammering their way across Normandy and south toward Paris. It was then withdrawn until after the liberation of the capital, after which it was performed from October 18 to 31.[13] During one period of electricity shortage, the cast played three times on one weekend day to compensate for canceled performances on other days.[7]

On July 11, 1944, Jacqueline Bernard, the essential link between the teams that were writing, editing, printing, and distributing the underground newspaper, went off to a meeting with an agent who in fact was an informer; she was trapped and arrested by the Gestapo. She had to think quickly. She had an appointment for that very evening to meet Camus near the Mathurins theater; he was to have introduced her to Maria Casarès, who was willing to join the *Combat* staff as a courier. Since Jacqueline Bernard would not be showing up, she hoped that her absence would suffice to alert her friends to her detention, and they would inform the others. For the ante had been raised now. Not only was their present underground activity at stake, and the men and women who carried it out at the risk of their lives, but the Combat movement was counting on having a decisive voice in postwar France. Shortly before her arrest a meeting had been held in Gide's studio to plan the layout of the first public issue of *Combat,* and the articles to appear in that issue had been assigned. (She had felt it unwise to meet at the home of one of their group—although Camus may actually have been staying at Paul Raffi's flat at the time—but she also enjoyed the idea that they were having a meeting *chez* Gide.)

During the interrogation at a Gestapo headquarters on the Rue de la Pompe following her arrest, she was given an opportunity to warn her comrades. The Germans discovered her address book with coded phone numbers—a rudimentary code, consisting simply of subtracting three digits from the first two numbers and adding to the second two— Paris telephone numbers then having three letters and four numbers. She feared that the Germans would discover the code. She would regularly phone Camus, for example, at the Gallimard office, and when asked who was calling would use the name on her false identity card. With the number of Gallimard, the Germans might discover who it was that a certain "Mademoiselle Abbesses" used to ask for at the Librairie Gallimard. . . .

So she offered to deliver a letter to one of her contacts to set up a meeting, at which meeting (so the Germans hoped) they could nab the rest of the group. She knew that what she was doing was harmless; the "contact" was in fact an occasional helper who had no present ties to the movement. But it allowed Jacqueline Bernard to slip inside the building alone, with her captors hidden outside, so that she could whisper a warning for Camus while delivering the useless letter.

The interrogators did not know that Jacqueline Bernard was Jewish. So she got off with a sentence of hard labor at the Ravensbrück concentration camp.[14]

When Camus learned that she had been arrested—or guessed that she had—he went off to the Gallimard apartment building on the Rue Saint-Lazare. (Janine Gallimard had run into Albert Ollivier in the street, and he had asked her to warn Camus not to return home, but by the time she found Camus he had already been alerted.) He had Janine watched from the balcony of her apartment while her husband Pierre and Pierre's cousin Michel rode off on bicycles in the direction of Camus' Rue Vaneau flat, the Gide studio, to remove some of his clothing. Janine was convinced that any minute she'd see German soldiers in the street below aiming rifles at them. The next day they left Paris on three bicycles—Pierre Gallimard, Janine, Michel, Camus—Janine riding with the men in turn, although Pierre and Michel didn't want her to ride with Camus because of the strain it might cause their sickly friend. They went to Verdelot, some fifty-five miles east of Paris on the banks of the Petit-Morin, where Gallimard editor and author Brice Parain had a home. One of Parain's relatives owned another house in the village, which was made available to the Gallimards and their fugitive.[6]

Meanwhile Camus had alerted fellow *Combat* conspirators Sartre and Beauvoir, and they too took precautions. In her memoirs Beauvoir describes their somewhat pathetic attempts to take protective cover: first by moving in for a few days with the Michel Leiris; then, by train and by bicycle, leaving Paris for the countryside, finding refuge in an inn doubling as a grocery store, where for three weeks they sat in the public rooms writing, among villagers playing cards, pool, or simply discussing things, receiving visits from the Leiris, from Jacques-Laurent Bost. And when they heard that the American troops were approaching Chartres, they got back on their bicycles and by side roads made their way to Paris. For part of that way, from Chantilly to Paris, they rode the train, but it was attacked by Allied bombers. Back in town, they quickly changed hotels—from the Louisiane to the Welcome ten yards away.[8]

At Verdelot the Gallimards and Camus lived a life that was in part vacation, in part deadly serious. The house that had been lent to them turned out to be in an advanced state of deterioration, even lacking windowpanes. There weren't enough beds for all of them, so Michel Gallimard took a room in a nearby hotel. They listened to the BBC broadcasts for news of the Allied advance, lunched at a local bistrot, dined at home. Janine and Albert discovered that they both liked a porridge of flour and milk, the *bouillie* which all French children know. Or they would all eat eggs. Daytimes they walked with the Parains, or swam in the Petit-Morin. They felt so relaxed that one day while they were standing outside a bistrot, leaning their bicycles against the wall prior to entering the restaurant for a meal, one of the Gallimards called out: "Camus!" oblivious of the German soldiers standing nearby who were examining identity papers of passers-by. And yet they had promised to call him nothing but Albert, which happened to be the given name on his false identity papers. Fortunately the Germans didn't know who Camus was, and they probably hadn't been listening.

But the news of the Allied advance, the imminent liberation of Paris, drew them back to the city. For the return trip they again rode three bicycles for the four of them, with the same seating arrangements. Peddling along, they saw planes diving and dropping bombs, Germans taking shelter in the woods along the road. They decided, "idiotically," that the bombs weren't meant for them.

Back in Paris, in the final days of the German occupation, Janine was soon planning another move of her own, for she and Pierre had decided to get a divorce. And she would marry Michel Gallimard, joining him in an apartment made available in the new building the Gallimards had purchased on the Rue de l'Université. She and Michel would go out evenings with Camus and Maria Casarès.[6] Meanwhile, Sartre and Beauvoir ran into Camus outdoors at the Café de Flore. Camus told them: All the resistance leaders agreed that Paris had to liberate itself. The subway had shut down, electricity cuts became more frequent, gas was cut, and there was practically no food left in the city. The Germans began to leave.[8]

♦

# 25

# LIBERATION

Paris fires all of its bullets in the August night. Against this immense backdrop of stones and fountains, all about this river whose waters are heavy with history, the barricades of freedom, one more time, have been raised. One more time, justice must be purchased with the blood of men.

*Combat,* August 24, 1944

History is made of little things. Had the young refugees not decided to abandon their rustic retreat at the precise moment they did, Albert Camus would not have been present at the liberation of the city from the German occupying forces, at which time he and his fellow editors of underground *Combat* suddenly and dramatically surfaced, offering a public which was demanding a new world at once a new newspaper and a new kind of journalism, suggesting to the long-suffering French that its freedom fighters might be capable of changing France. In the weeks and months that were to follow, Camus and his team represented for many the best hope for their liberated nation, a new political morality, a chance that the nightmare of their lost war would never be repeated.

Indeed, the bold masthead of *Combat* was one of the clearest, least ambiguous developments in that confused period.

By the time Chartres had fallen, much of Northern France was in Allied hands, and the United States Third Army had begun to surround the capital. The plan was to isolate Paris without entering the city, thereby obliging the Germans to evacuate and to surrender without bloodshed or destruction; of course French soldiers fighting with the Allies would be given the privilege of entering the city first to receive the German surrender. But it was also important for the resistance forces to feel that they were liberating their capital, recapturing official buildings, landmarks, and monuments, one after the other. . . . The result was confusion, if glorious confusion, with different factions (the Communists, the Gaullists) issuing different sets of marching orders. By the time the resistance was mobilized inside the city, the Germans were already on their way out, although they still had a large force in the area and could have put down an uprising at great cost to the insurgents. This call to the barricades inside Paris forced General Eisenhower to revise his plans, allowing General Leclerc's forces to move rapidly toward the center of the capital. The danger remained that the Germans would attempt to destroy the City of Light before the last of them retreated.

The battle which began on August 18, 1944, saw singular acts of individual initiative and bravery, largely unco-ordinated capture of the symbols of Paris and of Republican France, literally under the surprised gaze of the all but vanquished Germans, while a Swedish consul and the German commander tried to work out a less bloody evacuation, and the German failed to carry out Hitler's order to destroy the city. On August 21 the Comité Parisien de Libération issued a call to arms:

Parisians,
    The insurrection of the people of Paris has already liberated many of the capital's public buildings. . . .
    The fight continues. It must go on until the enemy is driven from the Paris region. . . .
    The population must prevent the movement of the enemy by all means.
    Cut down trees, dig anti-tank pits, set up barricades.
    The Allies will be greeted by a victorious people.

The insurrection was marked by sniping from windows and roofs, storming of public buildings, skirmishes among familiar landmarks, even in the narrow streets of Camus' Saint-Germain-des-Prés, until the entry of Leclerc's forces on August 25. Nearly 1,500 persons died during the battle, 901 of them members of the Forces Françaises de l'Intérieur (the FFI), 582 civilians.[1]

The atmosphere of the insurrection as seen from Left Bank Paris is recorded in the memoirs of Simone de Beauvoir. While the resistance partisans of Paris took back the Hôtel de Ville, police stations as well as public buildings, the FFI fought German convoys in the streets. From her hotel window Beauvoir could see the German swastika flag still flying from the Senate (Palais de Luxembourg). It was a time for rumors—for even the true version of events could only be learned from a phone call to a friend, from the cries of passers-by, bicycle riders. The men had rejoined their resistance groups; Sartre was in almost continual session with the theater movement at the Comédie Française. The women cooked meals for the FFI. Sartre and Beauvoir walked across Paris to meet Camus at *Combat,* but when they reached the Seine quays they found themselves in a no-man's-land, with bullets flying. They crossed the bridge bent over, its parapets serving as their protection. When they reached the Rue Réaumur newspaper building where *Combat* had set up its headquarters, they saw young men with machine guns guarding the entrance. The whole building was "an enormous disorder and an enormous gaiety." Camus asked Sartre to write a series of articles on the liberation of Paris, which, as published, is one of the best eyewitness accounts available.[2]

By decision of the Comité de la Presse Clandestine, the underground resistance was to take over the plants of the collaborationist press. Three underground movements and their newspapers were to occupy the large newspaper building on the Rue Réaumur which before the war had belonged to the *Intransigeant,* and during the German occupation was utilized to publish the German Army's *Pariser Zeitung: Défense de la France, Franc-Tireur,* and *Combat.* And "occupy" was the right word, for the resistance press moved in at the outbreak of the insurrection, while the Germans were still in Paris, and indeed still in possession of the buildings under a truce worked out between the liberators and the German commander. They began publishing virtually under the eyes (and the guns) of the last German troops in the city, sold their papers on the still dangerous streets.[3] The large building, which is still standing and now serves the successor to *Défense de la France,* the mass-circulation afternoon daily *France-Soir,* had presses in the basement, the three resistance papers on the upper floors. The three papers shared the composing room.

Pascal Pia, leaving his job at the Mouvements Unis de Résistance, was one of the first to arrive at the building, probably on Friday, August 18. He discovered a number of German uniforms in the offices, probably discarded by departing Germans who preferred to wear civilian clothes in their flight. Georges Altschuler began writing for *Combat* while he was still taking part in the liberation of Paris in an armed group; he witnessed the surrender of the German High Command, whose headquarters were a bank on the corner of the Avenue de l'Opéra and the Rue du 4 Septembre. The *Combat* staff discovered cases of grenades in their offices, presumably placed there to protect the *Pariser Zeitung.* Henri Cauquelin, who had been participating in the publication of underground *Combat* and whom Camus had summoned to the Rue Réaumur, dragged the cases up to the top floor terrace, ready to toss them at the German tanks if any of them (which could be seen further along the street) approached the building. Knowing that the Paris police who were resisting the Germans lacked ammunition, Altschuler and a chauffeur later transported the grenades to the prefecture on the Ile de la Cité, through German fire.[4]

Another recruit for daily *Combat* was a young resistance worker named Jean Bloch-Michel, who had served in an intelligence-gathering group before joining the Combat movement in Nice in 1942. He was arrested and tortured by the Gestapo, later wrote articles in underground *Combat* under the name "Villette." When he showed up at the Rue Réaumur, German soldiers were still standing at the front entrance of the newspaper plant, so he and fellow staffers walked around to the rear of the building, making their way in zigzags between the huge rolls of newsprint which seemed to be serving as barriers. Pia immediately asked him to handle the business side of the paper. "I don't have any experience with that," Bloch-Michel objected. "You'll do a better job than someone who does." The staff, which by this time included—in addition to Pia, Altschuler, Cauquelin, and Bloch-Michel—Albert Ollivier and Marcel Paute ("Gimont"), slept in their offices on piles of old newspapers for the first few days, living on rations the Germans had left behind in the building cafeteria.

Bloch-Michel was introduced to one of the paper's editors, "Brochard" (probably "Beauchard") a lean, pallid young man who seemed to have great charm. Neither of them was using true names yet; the first issues of public *Combat* were to be as anonymous as the underground paper had been.[5]

Camus himself, on the first visit or on one of his early visits to the Rue Réaumur, was caught in a roundup by the Germans, and had the design for the masthead in his possession (a Gaullist Cross of Lorraine cutting through the "C" of *Combat*), but he managed to get rid of it before he was searched.[6]

When they took over the *Pariser Zeitung* plant, the resistance editors discovered that they had inherited a supply of paper, and that was to last for a while. No one on the staff was paid right away. As the vendors of the paper came in with cash, it was thrown into wastebaskets, for no one could find keys for the office safes. Pia as publisher and Bloch-Michel as business manager worked out a salary scale, and then dug into the wastebaskets to pay their staff. "Beauchard," who had soon become Albert Camus, wrote editorials, Altschuler was editor for domestic political affairs, Marcel Paute for foreign affairs.

By Saturday, August 19, the *Combat* team was ready to publish the first public issue of the newspaper. But the printers union, Fédération du Livre, insisted on respecting the orders of de Gaulle's provisional government, represented in Paris by "Cérat." And "Cérat," the pseudonym of Alexandre Parodi, wished to postpone open publication of the resistance press, for fear of provoking the Germans to reoccupy the captured newspaper plants. Only after pressure was brought to bear on Parodi by the directors of the resistance press—Pia acting for *Combat*—did Parodi finally sign the authorization to publish. That was on the afternoon of Monday, August 21.

The first issue, then, dated and distributed on August 21 (but numbered "4th Year, No. 59," a tribute to the clandestine newspaper which had preceded it), was a large-format page, about 15½ by 17 inches, printed on the front and back of a single sheet. Following plans made earlier, it was sold by hawkers in the immediate neighborhood (as far south as the Rue de Rivoli, as far west as the Opéra); all copies had disappeared in an hour's time.[7] (The very first of them were simply tossed out of the windows to passing pedestrians.) Establishing a practice that would not vary, the front page carried an editorial running down the leftmost of the eight columns, unsigned (but written by Camus):

> Today, August 21, at the moment when we are appearing for the first time, the liberation of Paris is being completed. After fifty months of occupation, of struggle and of sacrifices, Paris reawakens to the sentiment of freedom despite the firing which suddenly breaks out on a street corner.

The editorialist warned that freedom must be won:

> It's by the fight against the invaders and the traitors that the French Forces of the Interior are reestablishing the Republic in our country.

The liberation of Paris was only one step in the direction of the liberation of France. After that there was another struggle coming, for liberated France must not be a France of Money. The Allies would have made possible the unshackling of the country, but it was for the French to win their freedom. So *"Le combat continue."*

On this same page there was another unsigned text entitled "De la Résistance à la Révolution," which was the slogan of the newspaper as well; it would appear daily under the masthead. This editorial has not been reprinted in Camus' published works, and one friend of Camus remembered only that he had "inspired" it,[8] but much of the language sounds like his. Pia certainly would have had a hand in writing it, as indeed Pia collaborated on several of the first editorials attributed to

Camus. But Camus read "De la Résistance à la Révolution" over the airwaves on Radio Liberté, in a dramatic voice and against the background of the resistance "Chant des Partisans,"[9] something he would not have done had he not been its author, or its chief author.

And to be sure that the text was heard, it was repeated on the following day. It began:

> It required five years of silent and stubborn fighting for a newspaper, born of the resistance spirit, published without interruption throughout the dangers of clandestinity, to be able to appear at last in broad daylight in a Paris liberated of its shame.

Certainly this language describes Camus' own spiritual journey:

> These years were not without their usefulness. The French, who entered them with the simple reflex of humiliated honor, complete them with a superior knowledge which henceforth requires them to place the highest value on intelligence, courage, and the truth of the human heart. And they know that these demands which seem so general create daily obligations for them on the moral and political level. To speak clearly, having only a faith in 1940, they have a politics, in the noble sense of the term, in 1944. Having started by resistance, they want to finish with revolution.

The writer promises that in the days to come, in acts as well as in words, *Combat* would define its Revolution. Meanwhile the newspaper was demanding the creation of a "people's and workers' democracy," a new Constitution guaranteeing freedom, structural reform, an end to trusts and the power of money, a foreign policy based on loyalty to all allies without exception. "In the present state of affairs, this is called a Revolution."

Thus was spelled out the political platform of postresistance *Combat*. At the time it certainly represented the thinking of a large part of left and center-left French men and women.

Paris remained a battlefield. Once the bulk of the German forces had withdrawn, parts of Paris were subjected to heavy aerial bombing at night, but the German ground forces were never to show themselves again.

The first issue of *Combat* on August 21 had headlined:

**THE INSURRECTION LEADS THE REPUBLIC
TO TRIUMPH IN PARIS—ALLIED TROOPS ARE
SIX KILOMETERS FROM THE CAPITAL**

Camus took time out to cross the city, perhaps in one of the chauffeured cars made available by the resistance, to visit Dr. Georges

Brouet, a leading specialist in tuberculosis, who was giving him fortnightly pneumothorax injections. Dr. Brouet's office was on the Rue
Théodore-de-Banville just off the Avenue de Wagram. While Camus
was in the doctor's office, they heard shooting outside and stepped out
to the balcony to observe what sounded like random firing. Camus
turned to the doctor and in what sounded to Brouet like melancholy
said: "You see, it's now that the difficulties are going to begin."[10]
Presumably Camus was referring to the different conceptions of the liberation struggle of Communists and non-Communists, manifested in the
orders and counterorders of insurrection on the streets of Paris.

Certainly Camus and his comrades on the newspaper acted as if
they had the truth on their side, and as if young France was with them.
The second issue listed the dailies that were authorized to reappear because of their clandestine activity or their "patriotic" attitude. These included the Communist *L'Humanité,* the Socialist *Le Populaire, Le
Figaro, Le Parisien Libéré,* and of course the wholly new press born of
the underground. As for those who collaborated with the enemy, *Combat* warned, there must be "neither forgetting nor indulgence."

Meanwhile fighting continued on the outskirts of the city. Camus
dispatched Altschuler on an assignment to locate the American troops
then advancing toward Paris, not only to report on their progress but to
urge them to come in to help in its liberation. Altschuler grabbed a bicycle and took Pierre Gallimard along as his photographer. They
crossed German lines easily enough but were pinned down by the
bombing around Versailles. Finally they met up with U.S. forces in the
Vallée de Chevreuse southwest of Paris. Gallimard took his pictures,
Altschuler interviewed an American tank officer, and they started back
to the city. At the Porte d'Orléans retreating Germans of the Afrika
Korps requisitioned their bicycles, so they had to walk back to the
newspaper.[4] The story appeared the next day, August 24, under the
headline

### TWO HOURS WITH MAJOR ALVIN P. UTTERBACK

Altschuler quoted Utterback: "We are coming." Actually neither Altschuler nor Camus—nor probably the major himself—would have
known that the Americans had agreed to hold back while French soldiers became the first to enter Paris.

"On the fourth day of the insurrection, after the first retreat of the
enemy," Camus wrote in the night of August 22 for the editorial to appear the next dawn, "after a day of false truce broken by the murder of
Frenchmen, the Parisian people will continue the combat and set up
barricades."

He went on to issue battle orders:

> The enemy entrenched in the city must not leave. The enemy in retreat which wants to enter the city must not be allowed to penetrate it. They shall not pass.

The writer explained: A people that wished to live doesn't wait for its freedom to be handed to it; it takes its freedom. Furthermore, he wrote, "Every German who doesn't leave Paris is one less bullet for Allied soldiers and our French comrades in the East." The fight which had begun on August 21 was a fight for "liberty or death."

By August 24 Camus' tone had become still more tense; surely his unsigned editorial of that date, "Le Sang de la liberté," was his most emphatic writing of those heroic days:

> Paris fires all of its bullets in the August night. . . .
> Time will testify that the men of France did not wish to kill, and that they entered with pure hands into a war they did not choose. . . .
> Yes, their reasons are immense. They have the dimensions of hope and the profundity of revolt. . . .

Once again the moral lesson was driven home:

> One cannot expect that men who fought during four years in silence and long days in the tumult of the sky and of guns, will agree to the return of the forces of resignation and of injustice in any form. . . .

On August 25, the last day of the battle for Paris, the editorial entitled "La Nuit de la vérité" (referring to the night of August 24–25) began:

> While the bullets of freedom still whistle in the city, the cannons of the liberation enter the gates of Paris, amidst shouts and flowers. On the most beautiful and hottest of August nights, the sky of Paris mixes with the eternal stars tracer bullets, the smoke of fires, and the multicolored rockets of the people's joy. . . .

It must have been an exhilarating moment, and surely the Camus of *Combat* was the poet of this exhilaration. The fighters in the insurrection, who were necessarily optimists, must have recognized themselves in the portrait of the resistance drawn by Camus and his colleagues in those first issues of *Combat:* battle-weary heroes, but also politically and socially conscious ones, aware of the shameful history of the occupation years, of the corrupt society which had made those years possible, determined to change their country so that no such events could occur again. One could hardly be a member of a resistance movement, a participant in the Free French government, without desiring change, and perhaps even believing change possible. Whatever one's politics, one could recognize oneself in the new paper's idealism. Simone de Beauvoir took note of Camus' admonition in *Combat:* "Politics is no longer dissociated from individuals. It is the direct speech of men to other men." Yes, she agreed. "To speak to men was the role of those of us who write."[11]

> Hard battles still lie ahead of us [Camus' August 25 editorial went on]. But peace will return to this disemboweled earth and to these hearts tortured by hope and memories. One cannot live forever by murder and violence. Happiness, tenderness, will have their moment. But this peace will not allow us to forget. And for some among us, the image of our brothers disfigured by shells, the great virile fraternity of these years, will never leave us.

The day's headline read:

### AFTER FOUR YEARS OF HOPE AND OF STRUGGLE
### FRENCH TROOPS
### ENTER THE LIBERATED CAPITAL

Other stories on that page announced that de Gaulle would be in Paris that very day, that Lyons and Bordeaux were liberated, that the Germans had installed Pétain and his cabinet in a castle refuge, that Sacha Guitry, Jérôme Carcopino, and other celebrities of occupied France had been arrested. A war correspondent reported the progress of Leclerc's armored column en route to Paris, a boxed message urged Parisians to fly flags for the liberation, while another message warned Parisians not to use gas for heating or cooking because of the dangers of fire and explosion.

Now *Combat* would take on more of the appearance of a peacetime newspaper. By August 27 the first staff list was published, noting that "Albert Camus, Henri Frédéric, Marcel Gimont, Albert Ollivier and Pascal Pia are now writing 'Combat' after having written it in clandestinity." (No one later recalled who "Henri Frédéric" was. Actually it was a disguise for Cauquelin, who became editorial secretary here as he had been at *Paris-Soir*.) Readers would have to wait some weeks to learn the hierarchy of the Comité de Direction, of which Pia was *directeur,* Camus editor in chief; the other members of the committee were Gimont (the pseudonym Marcel Paute would continue to employ) and Ollivier. The August 28 issue managed in its two pages, front and back, to publish some paragraphs of sports news. (The top item of the front page that day was the first of seven signed articles by Sartre on the liberation of Paris.) On August 29 an article reported the presence of Ernest Hemingway in Paris. On September 9 there was a report that Malraux was alive; the September 22 issue recorded his visit to the

*Combat* office on the previous day, a visit memorialized in a photograph often reprinted: a thin Camus in shirtsleeves and a dark necktie, staring in what seems to be shy admiration at a thin Malraux, in uniform and military beret, holding a cigarette in his mouth, returning Camus' stare.

By then Camus' sister-in-law, Christiane, was also back in Paris. She had come in on the second shipload of government personnel which sailed from Free French headquarters in Algiers, crossing the Strait of Gibraltar, then up the Atlantic coast to Cherbourg for the train journey to Paris. She phoned Camus at *Combat,* and he sent an automobile to pick her up and take her to the Gide studio on the Rue Vaneau, where he was living again; he joined her there. Later they walked out and along the Rue de l'Université, where a young man riding a bicycle stopped short when he saw Camus, and asked him for the latest news. Camus explained that a pocket of German resistance was being mopped up in the Paris region, but that the fighting was practically over. "Then I'll be going back to school," the young man on the bicycle said. And then: "Now that it's all over, can you tell me what your name is?" Camus told him. Turning pale, the youngster asked: "The author of *L'Etranger?*" He was visibly moved to discover that his underground comrade was the author he admired.[12]

The moral bias of Camus' *Combat,* or more accurately the *Combat* of Camus, Pia, Altschuler, Paute-Gimont, Ollivier, and their colleagues, was the newspaper's single distinguishing feature, making concrete the vague and often unexpressed hopes of the younger generation, certainly of most of the resisting younger generation. It guaranteed that there would not be a moral vacuum during the scramble for power that was taking place in the first months of liberated Paris. Camus and *Combat* were a new morality or they were nothing. Carried out to the letter, it was a morality which demanded a great deal of its followers, and the men and women of the newspaper had themselves chosen a Spartan existence, renouncing material gain, and in gaiety. Not everybody appreciated the moralism of *Combat.* Later Claude Bourdet—who couldn't begin to read the newspaper until his liberation from Buchenwald on April 18, 1945—would admire the style Camus had imposed on the paper while fearing that its moralism was accompanied by an "above the crowd" attitude that was not quite right, for the resistance movement had to dirty its hands, to enter the daily political battle.[13] *Combat* offered no political line as such, its editors preferring to remain on a higher plane than that, although their hearts were on the left. But they wished to be free to criticize the Socialists as well as the Gaullists or anyone else.[4]

On August 31, Camus wrote the first of a series of editorials whose subject was the press itself, "Critique de la nouvelle presse." He recalled the hope of the clandestine journalists that the resistance would be able to give postwar France an honest press, unlike the prewar model where "The appetite for money and the indifference to noble things" made some men powerful while serving to "abase the morality of everyone." That kind of press developed into the collaborationist press, the shame of the nation. Yet the liberated newspapers were failing to live up to this promise; many had simply taken up as before, appealing to "this shopgirl sensibility" (an expression he had long ago applied to *Paris-Soir*). He continued to examine the press, its responsibilities and its failures, in the following days.[14] As it happened, one of the new dailies which seemed to be lapsing into prewar sensational journalism was housed under the very same roof as his own *Combat*. For *Défense de la France,* born of the resistance, was soon to take the name *France-Soir* and become just the kind of newspaper Camus was objecting to; it would assume the profile and even the mass circulation of prewar *Paris-Soir*. *Défense de la France* even took on *Paris-Soir*'s former editor in chief, Pierre Lazareff, on his return to France in September (from the Office of War Information, the American propaganda organization, in London). Camus found that hard to accept, and when Lazareff invited Camus and Pia to drop in to his office to shake hands for old times' sake, they told him they would rather not. Camus had nothing against Lazareff, his old boss, but certainly resented his having been hired to make over a resistance paper into the image of hated *Paris-Soir*.[15]

Camus could have written his August 31 editorial using *Défense de la France/France-Soir* as his model.

Again, on December 1, Camus wrote: "Men who don't like the fact that the world is changing feel today that they have been cheated." And then he explained himself:

> The liberation of France for them only meant the return of traditional dinners, the motor car, and to *Paris-Soir*. Let freedom come quickly, so we can at last be mediocre and powerful at our ease!

Later, when the illustrated weekly *Match* was revived, the magazine of *Paris-Soir*'s Jean Prouvost, an article in *Combat* signed "Suétone" congratulated the government for allocating paper for a magazine filled with photographs of torture and unclad dancers, "a publication which is the honor of France."

Certainly *Combat* was a young man's paper; with few exceptions the faces were new ones. When a student then serving in the Army, Jean-Pierre Vivet, dropped in at *Combat* in September to meet Camus,

on the recommendation of a mutual acquaintance, and told Camus that
he had just written a thesis for his *diplôme d'études supérieures* comparing *L'Etranger* and *Le Mythe de Sisyphe* on the inspiration of
Sartre's analysis, Camus told him to come back when he was released
from the service. Vivet did and was taken on as a reporter.[16] Roger
Grenier, then twenty-five, had defended Camus in a resistance periodical called *Libertés,* published in the Rue Réaumur building, when the
Christian Democratic daily *L'Aube* had attacked Camus and Sartre.
Grenier was told that Camus would like to thank him. During their
meeting Camus asked Grenier if he would like to write theater criticism
for *Combat;* Grenier replied that he preferred being a reporter, and
some weeks later Camus offered him a job.[17] Shortly after Paris was liberated, Sartre's one-time student and friend Jacques-Laurent Bost ran
into Camus on the street and told him that he would love to be a war
correspondent. Camus hired him on the spot and sent him around the
different fronts while the war against Germany continued.[18]

It was at this time that Camus made his position clear with respect
to the Comité National des Ecrivains and *Lettres Françaises.* Both CNE
and its newspaper had performed as broad groupings of left-wing
Frenchmen—broad enough, as has been seen, to include Paulhan and
Mauriac. But now the Communist-front nature of CNE and the newspaper was evident to all but the most gullible of fellow travelers.

What actually happened is difficult to piece together now. Certainly
Camus would not have forgiven *Lettres Françaises* for its disclaimer of
his editorial contribution on the execution of Pierre Pucheu. In view of
his personal experience of the Communist movement he would have
been suspicious of the origins of the anonymous tract which in effect
identified him and others unwilling to be subservient to the Party line to
the Gestapo and collaborationist police.

All one can know now is that following a difference of opinion
with Claude Morgan, then a key figure both in CNE and *Lettres Françaises,* Camus told Jean Paulhan that he was resigning from CNE,
and asked that his decision be communicated to all members. He felt
that CNE did not allow objectivity and moral independence but insisted
on conformity to a line. The controversy left him bitter; he wondered
whether he should be participating in any form of public life.[19] And
when Morgan phoned Camus to ask if he would be willing to write for
*Lettres Françaises,* Camus refused.[20] *Lettres Françaises* pursued its career for another twenty-four years, until its editors Louis Aragon and
Pierre Daix disapproved the Soviet intervention in Czechoslovakia in
1968 and began to support dissidence in the Soviet bloc, after which
the Communists ceased to finance it, and it had to suspend publication.

——————◆——————

# 26

# FIRST COMBATS

. . . . We have chosen to accept human justice with its
terrible imperfections, careful only to correct it through a
desperately maintained honesty.

*Combat,* October 25, 1944

Camus' *Combat* could not have been indulgent to the collaborators who
represented not only misguided enthusiasm (as a man living in a world
designed for esthetics, Jean Paulhan, believed), but the opportunism
and the greed of prewar France, the struggle for power in Pétain's and
Laval's France, and whose words when transformed into policies led to
torture, the execution of hostages, death camps. With his fellow *Combat*
men and women dead (like Bollier and, soon, Leynaud) or still in
camps (like Jacqueline Bernard and Bourdet), Camus for all his high-
flying moral abstractions was closer to the firing lines than a Paulhan
could be—or a fine Catholic moralist with courage but little experience,
like François Mauriac. "Who would dare to speak here of pardon?"
Camus wrote in one of the first issues of daily *Combat* (on August 30,
1944):

> Since the spirit has at last understood that it could only conquer the
> sword by the sword, since it has taken up arms and achieved vic-
> tory, who would ask it to forget? It is not hate which will speak to-
> morrow, but justice itself, based on memory.[1]

It was a problem that troubled thinking Frenchmen during the first
months of liberated France, and the theme would be developed in a
number of editorials written by Camus. He went so far as to criticize
Church authorities who were collaborators or silent in the face of evil,

feeling that Christianity should reject without pardon "those who have proved that they were only Christians by profession." (September 16) Punishment of collaborators—*l'épuration,* it was called—he insisted was a necessity. "It is not a matter of purging a great deal, but of purging well." That meant to extend the purge beyond government circles, to banks, industry, other institutions, and to punish offenders in their financial or professional life (e.g., by banning Sacha Guitry from the stage). (October 18) He refused indulgence for Pétain. "French heads have fallen because of laws signed by him." For Pétain he demanded "the most pitiless and the most resolute of justices." (November 2)

Now François Mauriac, who occupied in conservative but patriotic *Le Figaro* the moral position that Camus occupied in *Combat,* and controlled roughly the same place on the newspaper page for his editorials, began to reply to Camus. Mauriac opposed what he felt were abuses of the *épuration,* which he attributed to the zeal of resistance movements. In a series of editorials in *Le Figaro* beginning in October 1944, to which Camus was to reply regularly in *Combat,* Mauriac spelled out this position of charity first. In one of these editorials, published at the top of the front page of *Le Figaro* on October 19, the elder writer asserted that Frenchmen favored national reconciliation, and recommended that collaborators be pardoned.

"We do not agree with Mr. François Mauriac," Camus replied in the next day's *Combat.* "We can say this without any difficulty because, every time that it was necessary, we have given our support to Mr. François Mauriac." If some persons were afraid, Camus said, that might be good for them. In an October 22 "Réponse à 'Combat'" Mauriac teased Camus for using the language of Christian theology to encourage the prosecution of collaborators. Camus retorted (on October 25): Even though we are not Christians—"precisely because we are not"—we have decided to deal with this problem.

> A Christian will think that human justice is always compensated by divine justice and that, in consequence, indulgence is preferable. . . . We have chosen to accept human justice with its terrible imperfections, careful only to correct it through a desperately maintained honesty.

"There is a kind of tacit contract between Mr. Mauriac and us: We supply each other reciprocally subjects for editorials," Camus observed in the December 5 *Combat,* adding with kindness that it was perhaps because their action was similar after all; open discussion of this kind was a good thing.

Finally in *Le Figaro*'s January 7–8 issue, under the heading "Le Mépris de la charité," Mauriac showed fangs. He criticized Camus, "our young master," for attacking a collaborationist author from on high—"from very high, from the height, I imagine, of his future work." Stung by this personal attack, Camus replied on January 11 that Mauriac had been "neither just nor charitable." Later Camus would admit: "On one side and the other silly things were said." But by then Mauriac had assumed a tone which made further dialogue impossible. (September 1, 1945)

Camus may not have been aware—there is no evidence that he ever became aware—of the intense personal animosity Mauriac held for him, expressed in Mauriac's comments to others. These others attributed it to jealousy. Camus represented a moral position, not a Christian one—and not Mauriac's—but a moral position all the same, and his record was not only as honorable as Mauriac's but he had his youth, and a public platform that even Mauriac with his *Figaro* front page did not have. Whatever the motives, Mauriac would seldom miss an opportunity to attack Camus.

Camus' own position on the death penalty for collaborationist crimes would evolve, as the fever of the liberation months subsided, and his lifelong abhorrence for capital punishment regained its priority.

Without necessarily wishing to stir up polemics, Camus seemed pleased to enter into a dialogue, but he did expect that both sides would show good faith. His obvious sincerity attracted not only the young men and women whose work at *Combat* represented their first jobs, but many veteran journalists too. Among the newcomers on the staff besides Vivet, Grenier, and Bost were Paul Bodin, Camus' Gallimard colleague Jacques Lemarchand, Alexandre Astruc, Maurice Nadeau, and there was help from Sartre, from Maurice Merleau-Ponty.

Camus had soon settled into a routine of his own. He would make handwritten notes for his editorials, then sit down beside a secretary to dictate his text—with no corrections after that.[2] But before he wrote the editorial there would be a meeting of the top staff, Pia included, and Camus encouraged the others to try their hand at editorials (even if their contributions were likely to reflect Camus' ideas and even his style, so close was this group). This interplay has made later identification of the authors of editorials and other articles difficult, when not impossible. Camus wrote some—but not all—of the columns signed "Suétone," for example. In addition to his writing he would also assign stories to others. But the layout was Pia's responsibility, later assisted by Roger Grenier.[3]

Not surprisingly, Camus objected to sensational crime stories, the kind that filled the pages of the "shopgirl" press. He once simply asked the staff not to cover a particularly bloody affair.[4] There was a quality of writing, a concision in style, rare in daily journalism. Thanks to this concern for language *Combat* became, in the word of Jean Daniel, "one of the best-written newspapers of the French press since the beginning of its existence."[5]

By December 1944, when he arrived in Paris, Edmond Charlot discovered that readers were literally grabbing *Combat* off the news-stands to read Camus' daily editorials; they were the talk of Paris.[6]

Everybody who counted was reading *Combat* every day, whatever else they read.

On October 4, 1944, *Combat* had published an unsigned article on Maria Casarès:

> . . . This little girl fleeing Franco Spain had a singular destiny, landing in an unknown capital, without speaking one word of French, and becoming by strenuous effort one of the most surprising stars of the Paris theater. . . .

A new play would soon allow her to "prove that she possesses the soul of a very great actress."

> She already has the flame, the intelligence, and the savage beauty. Some defects in diction and the very excesses of her passion will not prevent us from recognizing the authenticity of this deep cry that she has imposed on our stage. . . .

Nothing in the language or the style of that testimonial suggests that Camus was its author. Soon he had an opportunity to explain his intentions in writing *Le Malentendu,* not in the pages of *Combat* but in *Le Figaro.* For on October 18 the play opened for a new run at the Théâtre des Mathurins. The next day *Combat* reported not on the play—Camus was not to exploit his position on the newspaper—but on a benefit for families of Spaniards killed during the liberation of France, an occasion at which Maria Casarès had participated.

Soon after that another priority shipload of government personnel was to arrive from Algiers, as the provisional government shifted its ministries to liberated mainland soil. Francine Camus was on this ship, which sailed from Algiers on October 14. It was a long voyage, made even longer by a typhus case discovered on board. But before the end of the month his wife had joined Camus at the Gide studio on the Rue Vaneau.

A life that was already turbulent, divided between the Rue Réaumur newspaper plant in late afternoons and evenings and the later-night activity of Saint-Germain-des-Prés, with its cafés and clubs and Sartrian

fiestas (without benefit of curfew), now had to make room for a domestic side. He had to make choices, above all to choose between resumption of family life and the romantic idyll with Maria Casarès. The
break was stormy, and on both sides it was agreed that it should be
final.

A number of notations in his journal suggest Camus' state of mind
at this time. During the months of launching *Combat* he had not had
time for his personal writing—for completion of *La Peste,* for the major
essay on revolt. But he could dream of future writing. And so he entered some unconnected and unexpected schemes and thoughts in his
journal:

> Sunday, September 24, 1944. Letter
> Novel. "Night of love, of tears and of kisses. Bed soaked by
> tears, sweat, love. At the peak of all heartbreak."
>
> *
>
> Novel. A handsome creature. And he wins forgiveness for every-
> thing.
>
> *
>
> Those who love all women are those on the road toward ab-
> straction. They overtake this world, despite appearances. Because
> they turn away from the particular, from the individual case. The
> man who would flee all ideas and abstractions, the truly desperate
> man, is the man of a single woman. By stubborn desire for the single
> face which cannot satisfy everything.
>
> *
>
> December. This heart filled with tears and with night.

Maria Casarès was too proud to accept life as part of a triangle,
and that contributed to the completeness of the separation. His wife's
pregnancy would be the *coup de grâce;* even Camus could understand
that. But it could not palliate the effects of separation or cushion the
hurt. What did help was the richness of the public lives both were now
living, and Camus certainly returned to work (perhaps to play as well)
with a new intensity.

His home was an extension of his office, to the extent its dimensions allowed. So were the nights at Saint-Germain-des-Prés with his
*Combat* team and other friends. Then his office became an extension of
Saint-Germain-des-Prés. Persons soon to become landmarks of French
intellectual history would drop in: Malraux of course, and Sartre. There
would be "fabulous" evenings there, veritable debates, postmortem ses-
sions on the contents of the newspaper in the presence of many of these
persons.[2] Or at an editorial conference around the large unpainted

table spotted with inkstains and cigarette burns, a particularly well-written article might be read aloud by an admiring member of the staff.[7] In the camaraderie, the newspaper socialism of *Combat* in which the most important writing was still anonymous, Parisians in the know would try to guess from the style who had written a particular editorial—Camus, Ollivier (who later shared the job with Camus), or even Gide's Pierre Herbart.[8]

A note in the December 8, 1944, issue announced:

> In order to relieve our regular editorial writer, the editorial will be written, depending on the day, by two or three other editors of the newspaper. It will continue to express the common thought of the *Combat* team.

To certain sophisticates in the outside world, the inside combination came to be known as "Ocapia," for Ollivier, Camus, and Pia.[9]

On October 28, 1944, Camus wrote an editorial on the death of his friend René Leynaud; he had been killed earlier, but his body had only now been identified. Camus took the occasion to speak of the obligations of survivors, who did not do enough. "Let no one worry," he added, "we won't use him who never used anyone else."

> But here where we have always tried to avoid bitterness, he will forgive us for allowing it to return and to wonder whether the death of a man is not too high a price to pay for the right given back to other men to forget in their acts and their writings the value of the courage and the sacrifice of some Frenchmen during these four years.

For the war went on. From August 1944, when *Combat* was first published as a daily, the Western Allies and the Soviet armies would pursue their march toward Berlin. *Combat*'s editorials followed the war. Camus predicted that Hitler's end would be "theatrical and bloody" (September 20). His irrepressible interest in Spain manifested itself even before the end of the war with Nazi Germany. "Some readers ask why we are taking sides in the affair of Spain," he wrote on November 21. "It is because one must take sides in certain cases, and if France is today obliged to wage war against Fascism, it should do it totally or not at all."

He was convinced (as the Gaullists were) that France's Western Allies were wary of the French government born of the resistance. "Today France forms a whole," he insisted (on September 30).

> And one must take it as a whole, with General de Gaulle and with the Communists. . . . We are not forced to approve General de

Gaulle all the time, to share all the opinions of the Communist
Party. It can even happen that, on one point or another, we oppose
them energetically. But today there is only one France, which is
that of hope and danger. . . . If our American friends desire a
united and strong France, they don't contribute to that by dividing the country from outside.

Although Camus would later move away from the Gaullists of
*Combat* to join his leftist friends in their suspicion of the postwar political ambitions of this man on horseback, at this time he seemed very
much of a France-firster, and France meant de Gaulle. The Gaullist
government hadn't been elected by the people? And what about
Franco's, which the Allies recognized? American diplomacy, Camus
wrote on October 14, is in a paradoxical position, fighting Fascism,
maintaining official relations with the most dictatorial of regimes, Spain,
all the while refusing to recognize a government born of the struggle
against Hitler, de Gaulle's France. He warned that France and its government "can live very well without being recognized." (October 17)

And when de Gaulle went to Moscow, Camus wrote that if the
United States worried about Franco-Soviet friendship it had to be
remembered that the Americans shared responsibility for the defeat of
prewar collective security. "Today we must begin again at zero. The
Franco-Russian alliance is the first step." (December 18) Later (April
10, 1945), he expressed regret for France's traditional ignorance of the
U.S.S.R., where "an astonishing experiment is now taking place." Even
the moral tragedy of the German-Soviet pact of August 1939 could be
explained by the Munich pact which preceded it. Not being Communists, he added, we have more freedom to say that the Soviets, like the
Americans, created a new civilization. And "anti-Sovietism is a stupidity as dangerous as would be systematic hostility to England or to the
United States."

Clearly Camus was saying the right things at the right time, with
the ease and felicity of expression natural to the writer. It was as if he
had been born into this newspaper, as if the times had been created for
this newspaper and for Camus, rather than the opposite. He seemed
conscious, too, of the influence he had acquired. The November 22
issue of *Combat* contained his "Autocritique": "We are not certain that
we have always escaped the danger of letting it be thought that we
believed we have the monopoly of clearsightedness and the superiority
of those who are never wrong." But the writer promised that "we have
not forgotten the duty of reflection and of honesty which must be that
of all journalists." He concluded: "To tell all, we don't forget ourselves
in the effort of criticism which seems necessary to us at this time."

Camus had an opportunity to express more of a personal philoso-

phy in a periodical called *Résistance Ouvrière*. In an article published
in this weekly on December 14, 1944, he betrayed a left-socialist, syndicalist approach to the class struggle, but also the simple morality on
which his position was based. "Our workers must not, as they sometimes do, aspire to bourgeois life," a life which he defined as dim subur-
ban existence, cheap department store furniture, and Sunday movies.
But tomorrow the working class would lead France. "For the improvement in their lives to have a meaning, French workers must maintain a
clear consciousness of that nobility and that anguish." What he wanted,
in sum, was a noble working class, and he felt "that there are in man
more things to admire than to scorn."

He found his kind of worker right in the Rue Réaumur building,
for the printing trade (he had already learned this at *Paris-Soir*) was
composed of independently-left trade unionists who were often too intelligent to accept Communist Party marching orders, and creative
enough to go beyond the socialism of books. At the moment of liberation from German occupation some of these workers wished to set up a
workers' co-operative instead of the usual trade union; Camus told
them that he agreed with their scheme. But a minority of the printers
rejected the proposal, so the co-operative was never created. Soon the
workers' delegate responsible for presenting the point of view of labor
to management had discovered that Camus as a representative of the
latter could deal quickly and efficiently with their grievances (and used
their methods and vocabulary to do it). The printers had thrown themselves into the adventure of *Combat* as the editors had, sleeping and
eating on the job, not knowing at first how they would be paid. Daniel
Lenief, Camus' colleague of *Paris-Soir* days, now a member of the
*Combat* team, found that Camus was a good boss; he always said yes,
and his business manager Jean Bloch-Michel seconded him.[10]

In early December 1944 an old friend from Algiers turned up. Edmond
Charlot had been assigned to the Ministry of Information in Paris, after
having worked for the provisional government in Algiers. He began to
reorganize his publishing activity, using the unoccupied ground floor of
Camus' old Hôtel de la Minerve on the Rue de la Chaise. From there
he moved to a ground-floor shop on the Rue de Verneuil a short block
from the Gallimard building. (Camus lent him *Combat* funds so he
could buy what he thought was a lease but turned out to be an outright
purchase.) Charlot became another visitor to the *Combat* office in the
afternoons. The two Algerians would dine early, and then Camus would
return to the office to write his editorial. Camus put Charlot in touch
with a number of useful people, although he was necessarily less involved with the publishing house than he had been in the past.

Thanks to Charlot's intensive publishing program during the war in Algiers—where he had signed up many of the vital writers of his time and could get the paper (through his government connection) to print their books—he was soon a publisher to reckon with. After the ban on revival of *Nouvelle Revue Française* (because of its wartime publication) and the temporary eclipse of the house of Gallimard as a whole—Paulhan had become the official "liquidator" of *NRF* in a move he suspected was designed to exonerate the house for having carried on its book publishing—Charlot filled a vacuum. At Gide's suggestion he launched a substitute for *Nouvelle Revue Française* called *L'Arche,* whose editorial committee included Camus (at the outset), Gide, Robert Aron, Jean Amrouche. He was soon publishing as many books in Paris as Gallimard. By 1946 he was able to display a forty-eight-page catalogue which featured Henri Bosco's *Le Mas Théotime,* winner of a prestigious literary prize (the Prix Renaudot) in 1945, and Jules Roy's *La Vallée Heureuse,* winner of the same prize the next year. Camus' name appeared as director of his old series Poésie et Théâtre, Max-Pol Fouchet's as director of a series called Fontaine (which was also the name of his magazine); there was also a book called *Paris France* by Gertrude Stein. There were limited editions of García Lorca, of Gide's *Deux interviews imaginaires,* of the complete works of Lautréamont. There were Jane Austen, Henry James, Ignazio Silone, D. H. Lawrence, Alberto Moravia, Joseph Hergesheimer; importantly, there was Arthur Koestler's *The Yogi and the Commissar.* And of course the old team from Algiers: Roblès, Fréminville, Blanche Balain, Edmond Brua.[11]

The Gide studio now occupied by the reunited Camus couple became a meeting place of the postliberation intellectual elite, but also of the old Algiers crowd. When Robert Jaussaud called on them one day it was very cold, and they were burning every available combustible. Jaussaud had a government automobile and helped his friend transport a wooden stove lent by the poet René Char.[12] Then Robert Namia turned up, spent two weeks at the Rue Vaneau, where he was cold and hungry all the time. He slept in a tiny room in an iron bed and Camus told him: "You always dreamed of meeting Gide; now you're sleeping in his bed."[13] In *La Force des choses,* her memoir of that era, Simone de Beauvoir described that first free New Year's Eve, celebrated by Sartre and Beauvoir at the Camus', which meant at the Gide studio, with its trapeze and its piano. It was their opportunity to see something of Francine Camus, who had arrived from Algiers "very blond, very fresh, lovely in her blue-gray suit." Several of the other guests were unknown to the Sartre-Beauvoir couple. Camus pointed out one of them, who hadn't said a word all evening. "He was the model for *L'Etranger.*" Surely it was Pierre Galindo, who was given a job as Bloch-Michel's deputy at *Combat.* But Beauvoir felt that the evening lacked "intimacy." At about 2 A.M. Francine played Bach. No one drank much except Sartre, who was convinced that the party resembled those of the recent past, and soon was too far gone to notice how it didn't. Sartre was about to go to New York, sent by *Combat* on an invitation of the U. S. Government, which desired to make its own war efforts better known to Europeans. He would write news dispatches for *Le Figaro,* more reflective pieces for *Combat.* (Camus was distressed to discover that the rival paper got Sartre's report on the liveliness of American cities while *his* paper received a study of the economy of the Tennessee Valley Authority.)

Almost immediately after the liberation of Paris, Sartre began to execute a wartime dream: to publish a magazine of his own. Camus was too busy with *Combat* to participate in the adventure, and Malraux refused. The early board would include Raymond Aron, Michel Leiris, Maurice Merleau-Ponty, Albert Ollivier, Jean Paulhan (who in a sense represented the moral dowry of "liquidated" *Nouvelle Revue Française*). Thus began *Les Temps Modernes.*

But if Camus did not join Sartre's magazine, he was to remain intimately associated with the Sartre group, and not only with their partying. For at least another five years there was not only a social mix but something of a working relationship. Camus sent Sartre to the United States; he assigned a series of articles to Simone de Beauvoir when she traveled to Portugal. (Her reports were submitted under a pseudonym, but, according to her later recollection, publication ceased abruptly while Camus was out of Paris.) Sartre and Beauvoir shared Camus' views on the trials of collaborators, which she felt represented a *juste milieu* between pardons on one side and Communist severities on the other. Sartre was condescending about Camus in his lucid, non-drinking hours? So was Camus about Sartre.[14] But Camus gave jobs to all the Sartre people who asked for them, and when he was responsible for a series of books by new authors at Gallimard, he published as many of them as he could. Camus' newspaper of that early postwar period, in Beauvoir's own admission, was almost a house organ for their group. *"Combat* reported approvingly everything that came from our pens or from our mouths."

And soon their fabulous nights of drinking, occasionally interrupted by conversation, would assume sufficient importance in the lives of all the talented participants to be worthy of inclusion in the cultural history of France.

Camus could not, it should have been clear to him first of all, keep up that pace. Sharing the writing of editorials was a useful palliative but not the solution. Bloch-Michel, who had grown close to his new friend, found Camus' behavior increasingly strange, but, not being familiar with the history of Camus' illness, he did not identify the trouble. (He could not know—none of those around Camus at *Combat* or at Gallimard probably knew then—how much Camus had been affected by the sudden change in his personal life.) Finally he stalked in to Camus' office to demand: "What's going on?" Camus broke down, complained that he was overwhelmed with work. Bloch-Michel decided that he was both exhausted and ill.[15]

Whatever the causes, an immediate if temporary withdrawal from the paper was required. On January 18 *Combat* published a note from Camus:

> I thank the readers who have written to me to express their sympathy and I regret not being able to reply to them individually. The serious health reasons which have been keeping me away from *Combat* do not prevent me from maintaining my solidarity with it. My only wish is to return to the job as soon as possible. In any case, *Combat* is above all the work of a team.[16]

Pierre Herbart told Maria van Rysselberghe—Gide's *petite dame* —that Camus' doctor had ascribed his condition to overwork. Herbart, who took over part of the editorial writing, further warned his mother-in-law on January 28 that Camus' health was seriously compromised, and that he was not expected to live very long.[17] Certainly an exaggeration, but from a man who was close to Camus at home as well as at the office (as his next-door neighbor on the Rue Vaneau).

Camus tried to use this withdrawal for a return to his writing. He had done no significant work since leaving Le Panelier well over a year earlier. His journal was being filled with further notations for *La Peste,* that book he found so hard to write, and for another novel on justice, which would have dramatized much of his recently acquired political experience. One note dealing with "la grâce" admonished:

> We must serve justice because our condition is unjust, add to happiness and joy because this universe is unhappy. In the same way, we must not sentence to death because we have been given death sentences.

This question of the death penalty had followed him home, for it would require a more personal response than anything he had provided his polemical enemies up to now. The trial of the writer Robert Brasillach on charges of collaborating with the enemy had begun on January 19—this Brasillach whose pitiless attacks on anti-Nazis had been a black mark on intellectual Paris. Brasillach had been considered a brilliant and promising young critic as well as the man who said that Fascism was "the very poetry of the 20th century." And his Fascism had not only been intellectual; his anti-Semitic and pro-Nazi denunciations in the collaborationist newspaper *Je Suis Partout* became dangerous to his targets.[18] Brasillach was found guilty, sentenced to death by firing squad. French intellectuals, who happened to include many active collaborators who were not troubled for their collaboration (at least by the authorities), joined to request a pardon for Brasillach. In this appeal the most active of all was not a collaborator but the good soul François Mauriac, whose expense of energy was such that Brasillach asked his lawyer to see that everything he had written against Mauriac be omitted from future editions of his work.[19]

Mauriac probably didn't dare ask Camus for his support of the Brasillach pardon. That chore fell to Marcel Aymé, himself a contributor to *Je Suis Partout* and other periodicals published during the occupation.[18] Aymé wrote Camus on January 25, 1945, requesting that he sign the petition asking Charles de Gaulle to grant a pardon to Brasillach. It required of Camus a re-examination of his position on the punishment of those who had caused the arrest, torture, and death of his comrades.

He paced the floor, his family would remember, all that night,[20] and when he replied, favorably, to Brasillach's attorney (on January 27) he made it clear that he was signing the petition only in his personal capacity, not as editor in chief of *Combat*. He also warned Aymé that his motives for joining the request for clemency were not those of Aymé (who had compared Brasillach's case to that of a François Villon). Camus despised the writer and the man who had encouraged the beatings and mutilations of his friends, and Brasillach had never asked for clemency for resistance writers such as Jacques Decour of *Lettres Françaises*. No, if Camus opposed Brasillach's execution it was because he opposed the death penalty in all circumstances.

And once he took such a position he would be stuck with it. Later he would have to request clemency for Lucien Rebatet and other convicted collaborators of *Je Suis Partout*. He agreed that it was unjust to spare Rebatet when Brasillach had been executed, but so was it unjust to spare the politicians who had protected Rebatet.[21] *Combat* was to oppose the death penalty for Marshal Pétain (despite Camus' earlier demand for "pitiless justice"):

> First of all because one must resolve oneself to say what is true, that any death sentence is a denial of morality, and then because, in this particular case, it would give this vain old man the reputation of a martyr, according him a new status in the minds even of his enemies. (August 2, 1945)

The petition for Brasillach went to de Gaulle with fifty-nine signatures, Paul Valéry, Georges Duhamel, and Mauriac at the top of the list, but there were also the names of Paulhan, of Jacques Copeau, Jean Schlumberger, Jean Anouilh, Jean-Louis Barrault, Jean Cocteau, Jean Effel, Maurice de Vlaminck, Colette, Gabriel Marcel, Aymé, and of course Camus. Brasillach sent a letter of appreciation to the signers, with a particular bow to those he had opposed in the past (not many of whom had signed the petition). De Gaulle received Mauriac, received Brasillach's lawyer, read the file, and let the sentence stand. Brasillach was executed at the Fort de Montrouge near Paris on February 6, 1945, a month short of his thirty-sixth birthday.

# 27

---◆---

# ARMISTICE

We must serve justice because our condition is unjust, add to happiness and joy because this universe is unhappy. . . .

*Carnets*

Albert Camus' identification with *Combat* was such that even his temporary absence was bound to cause speculation about what had now become a national institution. "It seems that *Combat* has changed its orientation," Camus began a signed note—his first in nearly a month—in the February 9 *Combat*. He affirmed that the newspaper's line had not changed, for its editorial writers were as one person. And then he proceeded to spell out the policy of this person: nationalization of industry, economic democracy, but also a world economic order in which raw materials, markets, and currencies would be internationalized pending the establishment of a true world federation. Criticized for opposing de Gaulle's provisional government, Camus replied that it was the government which had retreated from this program.

And in truth the *Combat* team was still united, not yet reflecting the splintering into factions of the France beyond the Rue Réaumur. Later, but not yet, a Pia and an Ollivier would turn toward the Gaullists, the young Sartrians would move in another direction from Camus. But for the moment solidarity could be expressed in another way: After a period when various members of the staff signed editorials with their initials, now the editorials would be printed without any identification of their authors at all. One spoke for all, all for one.

And if Camus was first among equals when he was physically present and in proper physical condition, if Albert Ollivier was his most articulate stand-in (he would one day be responsible for the ideological control by the Gaullists of the country's incipient television network), the cement which held the paper together from day to day, in sickness and in health, was by all accounts Pascal Pia. He was the man behind the scenes, *Combat*'s *éminence grise,* as he had been at *Alger Républicain,* as, indeed, he had been for the early career of the writer Albert Camus. Pia seemed to need no public recognition, no praise, and the way he worked—putting the paper together from first line to last, reading every sentence, rewriting many of them—could only be admired, even by those who felt that he was leading a killing pace. If Camus, after the first weeks, spent less and less time at the paper, got more and more glory for his contribution, Pia's responsibility seemed to increase, and he was certainly the paper's forgotten man so far as the general public was concerned. The break between the two men, which would be consummated in the final days of this newspaper experiment, has been attributed to Pia's jealousy. But it should be evident that Pia consciously encouraged the reputation of the man of whom he was said to be jealous. Had Pia wished to, he could have written for *Combat,* and with a byline in bold type. As it was, the only thing anyone remembered seeing over his signature was a postscriptum to a movie critic's review, taking exception to the critic's opinion.[1]

Undoubtedly Pia felt a change in Camus, who had never refused to wear the mantle of success. He observed that Camus was too sure of himself, judging quickly, just as he thought and wrote quickly. Shortly before the first issues of *Combat* appeared he lunched with Camus at a Left Bank restaurant. Noticing a former editor of *Paris-Soir* at another table, Pia greeted him. Camus said that he felt the editor had been too subservient to *Paris-Soir*'s management. Pia told him that the editor in question had a wife who was mentally ill and a deficient child, which explained why he had been a meek employee. Camus blanched.[2] Later Camus' absolutist behavior—what Jean Grenier called his "African temperament"—was to be matched by Pia's own.

But that was later. Meanwhile Camus, Pia, and the others continued to labor at the production of a daily paper which remained the talk of Paris, symbolizing the hope of postwar France. Its intelligence too. Camus was spokesman for that intelligence, and that hope, in his talk to a Christian students group at Paris's La Mutualité hall on March 15, 1945. The Germans had denounced intelligence, he said, and the Vichy government had blamed the war and the defeat on intelligence. "The peasants had read too much Proust," Camus said mockingly. "And everybody knows that *Paris-Soir,* Fernandel, and old-timers' banquets were signs of intelligence. It appears that the mediocrity of elites of which France was dying had its origin in books."[3]

In one of his rare signed editorials of this period—one of only five attributed to him that month—Camus took up his pen in the April 3 *Combat* to regret that in a speech to the people of Paris de Gaulle (who in the absence of elections and a new Constitution continued to serve as chief of the provisional government) had celebrated its history but failed to mention the revolutions of 1830 and 1848, and of the Commune. "It is not possible . . . to lead this country to power while ignoring its revolutionary virtue," he warned. "It is a truth consecrated by four years of silent struggle and which should have become inscribed in the politics of this country. Our hope for tomorrow is the strength of new ideas and of rebellious courage." In a concluding remark which showed the distance Camus was able to take from de Gaulle he wrote: "If the voice of General de Gaulle, so often a solitary one, had been able to accord itself for an instant with that of the people who were hailing him, it is this hope that it would have expressed."

De Gaulle would continue to govern by consensus for another eight months, backed by all of the resistance veterans including the Communists, and when he withdrew (on January 20, 1946), it was because he could not get along with France's first postwar parliament.

At last Camus could return to Algiers again, to see his mother, the friends who had remained, the familiar streets and shores he hadn't been able to approach for nearly three years. He was not going on holiday, but on a self-imposed assignment, and he was to bring back a series of articles.

This trip left no traces in the recollection of friends. What we know of it comes from a then private diary, the journal of Gide's *petite dame,* for Camus would meet Gide in Algiers. Later Camus himself forgot that encounter, for in his evocation "Rencontres avec André Gide," written for a special homage to Gide in *Nouvelle Revue Française,* he would remember meeting the old writer for the first time at the Rue Vaneau apartment.

Maria van Rysselberghe's version is more entertaining, and certainly true. One day in April 1945 in Algiers, Gide asked her: "Try to describe Camus for me; I don't know anything about him." She tried, for she had been seeing Camus in Paris, but she found it difficult. "This person whose accent is so special has a physique which isn't special at all." Finally Gide asked her which of their friends Camus resembled and she said Jacques Rivière, the novelist and essayist but above all Paulhan's predecessor at *Nouvelle Revue Française,* who died in 1925 (at the age of thirty-nine). And the very next day, April 24, Gide was amused to receive a telephone call from Camus, who was in Algiers and requested an appointment for that day. Gide gave his confidante a copy of *Noces* which he had found in Jacques Heurgon's library—for he was staying at the Heurgon home—and remarked that he liked the way it was written; Camus had a sense of language. And then Camus arrived. His visit was "perfect," confirming Madame van Rysselberghe's feeling about him: ". . . no constraint, no misunderstanding, a very real and simple cordiality." Camus told them that he was on assignment, was leaving for the south the next day, and promised to call again when he returned to town. (But by then Gide and his *petite dame* had left for Paris.) [4]

Gide himself did not see fit to record his meetings with Camus in his own journal. The passing references in Gide's journal to the younger writer are not uncomplimentary, simply uninformative and non-committal. Camus' own admiration for Gide—he had told Heurgon in 1942 that he thought of him as an old friend[5]—had not been shaken by Gide's ambiguous position during the occupation, his failure to use his moral position in behalf of anti-Fascism. On the contrary: Camus defended Gide vigorously against Communist attacks. He felt that Gide's behavior had been honorable, while age excused his lack of involvement.

When Gide reached the Rue Vaneau, he was met at the door by Francine Camus and her sister Suzy. Francine had already called on Gide in Algeria before her departure for France, knowing that she would be living at his studio in Paris. She and her sister now went downstairs to bring up his baggage, and then offered him tea. Before it was ready Gide went into his own rooms for a quick change, returned in the proper attire for afternoon tea—Gidean *coquetterie*.[6]

On his departure for Algeria, Camus couldn't have known that he was to be on hand at a tragic moment in the history of French Algeria, during events which were to anticipate the outbreak of the insurrection less than a decade later. For the nationalist movement had been growing, and Messali Hadj's influence was at its zenith. In March 1945, at the first congress of the Association des Amis du Manifeste et de la Liberté —the "Manifeste" being what would now be considered a moderate statement of demands of Algeria's Moslem population written by Ferhat Abbas—Messali had been hailed as "the incontestable leader of the Algerian people." On April 25, the day after Camus' visit to Gide, the French sent Messali into exile. Nationalist fever reached new heights, as May Day demonstrations proved. Then on May 8, a day of celebration of the victory over Nazi Germany, there were bloody riots in two Algerian towns, Sétif and Guelma, followed by uprisings in rural areas. The repression was severe: some hundred European dead were avenged by thousands of Moslem dead.

Camus' eight articles, six of which were reprinted in his *Actuelles III* (*Chroniques algériennes*), were an attempt at a long view, written after a three-week trip covering 1,500 miles across Algerian territory, including the southern desert region. He asked for a suspension of judgment—at least hasty judgment—and proceeded (beginning with the issue of *Combat* of May 13) to deliver an over-all survey of the Algerian situation he might have written had there been no Sétif riots, no repression. He painted a grim picture of an Algeria suffering from famine; the language was reminiscent of his prewar inquiry on Kabylie in *Alger Républicain*. Not only were the official rations for the indigenous population lower than they were for Europeans, but the Arabs actually received even less than their allocations. He warned that the "Arabs"— he continued to use the term to refer to the Moslem population—no longer desired to be French citizens. He described the Blum-Viollette Bill, which attempted to grant voting privileges to a tiny minority of Moslems, and the way it had been allowed to die on the desks of the legislators of the 1930s. Today the world was changing, Algeria's Moslems could see what was happening in the rest of the world—the rest of the Arab world—and so assimilation as a policy was no longer desired. In a follow-up article he treated with sympathy the nationalist movement grouped around Ferhat Abbas, and in a final article he pleaded for the application of French democracy to Algeria. "It is the humble force of justice, and it alone," he concluded, "which must help us to reconquer Algeria and its inhabitants."

Who is this man, his enemies were quick to ask, who after only three weeks in Algeria claimed to know all the answers? *Combat* replied to that on May 25: Born and raised in Algeria, Camus had cared *only* about Algeria until the June 1940 armistice. Far from being indifferent to French deaths in Algeria (another point made by critics), Camus still had his entire family there, exposed to rebel action. "Therefore if he asked that one not reply to hatred by hatred but by justice, there is the likelihood that he did not do it lightly, but after reflection."

It was now that his friend Jaussaud, working for the government, accompanied Interior Minister Adrien Tixier on an inspection tour of Algeria. Tixier suggested to Jaussaud that Camus join the government to help deal with the Algerian problem. No specific title or task was mentioned. At that time, a number of changes were being discussed to transform the territory, bringing Algeria closer to France, perhaps by eliminating the middleman, the Governor General.

Jaussaud relayed the proposal to his friend, who said that he would be happy to work in Algeria among Algerians, preferably in the cultural area. He agreed to meet Tixier, but mainly as a matter of courtesy. They spoke of many things, none of them specific, and nothing would

come of the idea, Camus having brought the discussion to a close by
saying that he would think about it.[7] Camus told the story to Roger
Grenier, adding the detail that he refused an official appointment, having told the minister that he was a newspaperman not a politician.[8] In
fact, if Camus had no serious quarrel with the provisional government
which was then running France, and which included Communists and
Socialists as well as Gaullists, he had a visceral reaction against anything reminding him of the Government General of Algeria, his old
enemy. For him the Government General was the captive of local conservative forces, not representing the best of France. Once, when
Gabriel Audisio asked Camus to be interviewed in *Algeria,* a governmental publication, his first reaction was an outburst: "For those
skunks!" Then he softened and said to Audisio: "To make you happy,
all right." Audisio interpreted this as a token of reconciliation with the
French authorities of Algeria,[9] but Camus' later reactions to similar
proposals suggest that this was an optimistic judgment.

Camus would always believe that Algeria could be saved for
France by genuine reforms. He put his hopes in liberalized voting rights
for Moslems. When elections were held, the nationalists boycotted
them, a situation that could have been predicted by a careful reader of
Camus' own reports in *Combat* in May 1945. In fact only eighty thousand Moslems out of eight million were allowed to vote.

Now Jacqueline Bernard was back in France, after release from a
Nazi camp. Taking up her job at *Combat,* now published in broad daylight, she found the familiar atmosphere of camaraderie, and relations
with the printers that one would expect from a staff with the social commitments of the Combat movement. Camus' rapport with the workers
downstairs seemed ideal, although Pia was clearly in charge. The editors would meet in his office each afternoon between five and six. Pia
would divide up the news dispatches, suggest lead stories and the people
to write them, the space to be allotted to each. As before, it was very
much a collective creation, each contributing a point of view. There was
a continuing paper shortage, even a period of crisis when the paper had
to appear in a miniature format resembling that of the clandestine
monthly, which did not allow the staff much space for expansive
stories.[10]

Jacqueline Bernard's accounts of her confinement in a concentration camp clearly made an impression on Camus. He added her stories to others of a similarly horrible quality which he recorded in his
journal under the curious title "Creation corrigée." One of the anecdotes he recorded told of the French concierge of a Gestapo headquarters in Paris who each morning did the housecleaning among the
victims of German torture, explaining "I never pay attention to what

my tenants do." He would use that anecdote in speeches made during lecture tours abroad, to explain one aspect of France under German occupation. Another story of Nazi behavior he recorded told of a woman inmate of a camp who was released with a skin tattoo: "Served for one year in the SS camp of . . ."

"Deep disgust for all society," Camus confided to his journal at this time:

> Temptation to flee and to accept the decadence of one's era. Solitude makes me happy. But feeling also that decadence begins from the moment when one accepts. And one remains—so that man can remain on the heights where he belongs. . . . But nauseous disgust for this dispersion in others.

Asked to write a preface for a book about the resistance, Camus replied to its author that he had no objection to doing it save the press of time, but he didn't see what advantage it would be to have his endorsement. "Is it my resistance credentials?" he asked. "I risked far less than your hero . . . Is it to the writer that you are addressing yourself? But in that case it has always seemed to me that a book, especially a testimonial like this one, should be presented alone and without commentary." He promised to write a preface, nevertheless, if the author insisted. Instead, the book was published with this letter as the preface," a demonstration that even a word signed by Camus was considered useful support for a new book.[11]

In the first month of peace, a threat to *Combat*'s identity loomed up in the person of Henri Frenay, former national leader of the Combat movement. As Minister of Prisoners and Deportees (i.e., veterans of Nazi camps), Frenay sued the Communist Party's daily, *Humanité,* for libel after it had accused him of carrying out his responsibilities in a partisan manner. Frenay also wrote a series of articles about the dispute, which he wanted *Combat* to publish. Pia told him that he could not make such a decision by himself but would have to consult the other members of the staff. The next day Frenay got the reply: It was friendly but negative.[12] In fact the decision of the staff had been a consensus.[13]

Frenay was angered. "But I created *Combat*," he reminded its staff.[10] He had even invented and designed the title. Claude Bourdet, who had inherited the movement and the clandestine newspaper when Frenay left occupied France, agreed that the present staff did not have the right to deny Frenay space in the columns of *Combat*. It was decided to take the matter to arbitration, Frenay and Bourdet on one side, the Pia-Camus team on the other.[12]

Then Frenay became angry again when he discovered that the

paper's business manager, Jean Bloch-Michel, had registered the title in his own name.[10] The explanation was simple enough. In that informal, amateur atmosphere of the early days of daily *Combat,* the editors had learned that the title of the newspaper had to be legally registered. As no company existed in whose name they could register it, Bloch-Michel solved the problem by putting down his own name, attaching no importance to what he considered a bit of bureaucratic red tape. When a company was finally set up, its owners included Pia, Camus, Bloch-Michel, Altschuler, Paute, and Albert Ollivier.[14]

The arbitration was put in the hands of Louis Martin-Chauffier, both a resistance veteran and president of the Comité National des Journalistes. He decided that the title belonged to Frenay and Bourdet, although it had been perfectly proper for the paper's clandestine editors to carry on publication after the liberation; the postwar success of *Combat,* he added, was due to the present editorial team.

The decision, which was handed down the following winter, on February 24, 1946, concluded:

> That it is therefore incontestable that the present value of the title "Combat", of the clientele attached to this title, of the system of administration and distribution, comes, for the most part, from the effort, the labor, and the personal competence demonstrated since the liberation of France by the members of the Pia-Bloch-Michel group, and that a great part of the result of this effort would be compromised if the title were to be separated artificially from the enterprise set up to pursue the activity. . . .

Thus it was determined that the title of the newspaper was indivisible, belonging not only to Frenay and to Bourdet and to the present staff but to all who contributed to its publication during the years of underground activity. And since an agreement between the opposing parties could not be worked out, it was just and reasonable that the exclusive use of the title belong to those who ran the paper during the occupation years and who "have assumed and overcome the material risks inherent in the operation of a great daily." Should the present staff decide to liquidate the company, the former directors and all those involved in the wartime effort would become proprietors of the title.[15] Meanwhile a sum of money was to be turned over to Frenay and Bourdet as compensation. (The figure has been given as 1.5 million francs of the 15 million that *Combat* was then said to dispose of. If that is the correct figure it is a tidy sum, worth 171,300 francs of the mid-1970s, or some $35,000.)

Bourdet and Frenay used the settlement to publish a leftist weekly called *Octobre,* which lasted only six months, until the government cut off their paper supply became of their hostility to France's colonial war in Indochina. And Bourdet's association with Frenay represented a break with Camus which would not make things easier for Bourdet later on when he would have liked to have Camus' support.[16]

That no political differences separated Camus and Frenay is suggested by an editorial Camus wrote for *Combat* during Frenay's fight with the Communists. It was presumably because Frenay had been one of their "camarades de combat," Camus said, that his newspaper had abstained from praising or defending Frenay, and Frenay had always refused to ask for their support. "But in pushing our scruples too far, we would end up by lending ourselves to a lie and . . . betraying both friendship and truth." Faced with the demands of returning war prisoners, Frenay wished to be heard in his defense, and he was to be congratulated for having met demonstrators face to face. *Combat* asked that Frenay be heard in the name of the freedom for which the French had fought.

The arbitration would have another effect. The payments to the victors began at a time when *Combat*'s sales had begun to decline and its treasury was in jeopardy.

With the war over against Germany, Camus seized an opportunity to inspect the military occupation of that country. For the first time in his life he put on a military uniform, as a war correspondent should, to tour the sector then occupied by French troops, the Rhineland dukedoms of Baden and Württemberg, Catholic and agricultural. He traveled along roads that had been ravaged by war. "In peacetime I would already be uncomfortable here, having more taste for the countries of light," he wrote in *Combat*'s weekly supplement (a short-lived venture called *Edition Magazine*) on June 30, 1945. The Rhineland seemed prosperous compared to the war-torn regions of France he had crossed to get there. He compared the sickly children of France to the young Germans who seemed tanned and well fed, proving that Germany "has won the war biologically."

The reporter found the French occupation severe but orderly, "within the limits of justice as a victor can carry it out." He was billeted in a private home. "I was welcomed cordially, they came in to wish me a good night, I was told that war was not a good thing, and that peace was better, especially eternal peace." Every French soldier had a girl friend, which added to the stupefying impression of holidays which one could feel on the shores of Lake Constance. These were first images, but deeply impressive, disorienting. (The article was entitled "Images de l'Allemagne occupée.") And when the good grandfather who lodged the author of *Lettres à un ami allemand* spoke of Christ's eternal peace, Camus thought of the woman deported to Germany, prostituted to the SS troops, and then tattooed on the chest: "Served for two years in the SS camp of . . ." [He had added a year to the trials of the woman first mentioned in his journal.]

On his return Gide and his family, including *la petite dame,* had the Camus, still their guests and neighbors, to dinner with Malraux. Camus arrived late, she noted in her journal, back from Germany, his patience exhausted by the Army. She remembered nothing else of the evening's conversation, for "Camus has a mute voice and the glibness of Malraux jumbles the sounds."[4]

In his memoir on Gide, Camus would evoke those months of proximity to his boyhood master. No familiarity was involved, for Gide detested "that noisy promiscuity which takes the place of friendship in our world." And forty years of age separated the two men.

But Gide's smile was a welcoming smile. Sometimes he knocked at the double door which separated the Camus studio from the library of the main Gide apartment. He would be bringing back the Camus' cat Sarah, who had entered the Gide domain via the roof. At times Francine's piano playing drew him. He was with Camus to hear the news of the armistice which ended the war in Europe (as *la petite dame* also reported in her journal). Otherwise, Camus knew of Gide only his "steps" on the other side of the door, "rustlings, the little hustle and bustle of meditation or revery."

A different sort of armistice celebration, in fact "a very merry night," is reported by Simone de Beauvoir. There were Camus, the actress Loleh Bellon, the actor Michel Vitold, and "a ravishing Portuguese girl called Viola." When their Montparnasse bar shut for the night they walked to Simone de Beauvoir's hotel. Loleh Bellon was barefoot, repeated: "It's my birthday, I'm twenty." They bought bottles to take back to the rotunda-shaped room, the window open to the mild evening, and passers-by shouted friendly greetings. "Paris remained as intimate as a village; I felt a bond with all those unknowns who had shared my past and who were stirred as I was by our deliverance," she remembered.[17]

Soirées on the town or no, Camus was about to become a father. And not only that, but as he and Francine learned in June, they would have twins. The doctor prescribed rest, and in a more comfortable place than the Gide studio. They found such a place, a *maison de santé,* in a site just south of the city called Vallée aux Loups, in the hamlet of Aulnay. The rest home had been the residence of author-statesman François René Chateaubriand. It was a fine old house in a park whose trees had been planted by Chateaubriand himself. But the park had been converted into a vegetable garden, a wartime necessity. (Camus complained to the Michel Gallimards that they were living there on boiled vegetables.[18]) Chateaubriand had lived in the house from 1807 to 1818, to stay away from Paris after provoking Napoleon, and he began his *Mémoires d'outre-tombe* there; he would write that, of all the things that had escaped him, the Vallée aux Loups was the one he regretted. In July and August the Camus rented a house at Vincennes, where Francine would be joined by her mother in preparation for the birth.[6]

That Camus was aware of his responsibilities is suggested by a note he recorded in his journal and dated July 30, 1945:

> At thirty [he was actually going on thirty-two], a man should take himself in hand, know the exact reckoning of his defects and his qualities, know his limits, foresee his failings—to be what he is. And above all to accept them. . . . To settle into the natural but with one's mask. I have known sufficient things to be able to give up almost everything. There remains a prodigious effort, daily, stubborn. The need to be secret, without hope or bitterness. No longer to deny anything because everything can be affirmed. Superior to suffering.

He continued to set down thoughts and resolutions in his journal, and sometimes bitter reflections like this one: "Reputation. It is given to you by mediocre people and you share it with the mediocre or with rogues." He told himself that the meaning of his work was to do what the Christians had not done: "to help the damned."

In August, when they were living at the sparsely furnished villa in Vincennes, Camus was working on *La Peste* again, spending late afternoons and evenings at *Combat*. (He was seldom at the Gallimard office these days, having taken a leave of absence as of July 31, 1944, to devote himself to the newspaper.) The book was still not flowing, and he told the Michel Gallimards that he feared he would die of *La Peste*.[18] But there was brightness on the horizon. At long last *Caligula* was to be put on the stage. Rehearsals began on August 16, and the opening was scheduled for early autumn. Meanwhile Charlot had republished *Noces,* from his new offices in Paris as well as from Algiers. Soon Camus would return to a period of uninterrupted work on *La Peste,* withdrawing from regular activity at *Combat,* and already he was discussing the resumption of his editorial responsibilities at Gallimard, where he was asked to become editor of a series of books he would choose himself, a series for which he had suggested his preferred title, "Prométhée." (In fact it would be called "Espoir.") On September 1, he resumed active employee status at the publishing house.

One of his last chores at *Combat* was to deal once again with the thorny problem of resistance vs. collaboration. When Georges Bernanos returned to France after seven years in Brazil, his arrival had been reported on the front page of *Combat* (June 30, 1945) as something of a national event. Father Bruckberger had brought Bernanos and one of his sons to lunch with Camus and Malraux at the Michel Gallimards, who were now living the newly acquired Gallimard town house on the Rue de l'Université, on the attic floor above the Gallimard rotunda offices, with views over the large formal garden. Janine Gallimard remembered how Bernanos, with his handsome, harmonious features, gray hair and protruding blue eyes, had become animated, indignant, etc., while telling his own stories. But later when they drove Bernanos and Bruckberger to their country house in their Mercury convertible, Janine fell asleep, caressed by the summer breeze, while Bernanos went on talking.[18]

Camus asked Bernanos to write for *Combat,* and Bernanos agreed to deal with the Pétain trial. He sent in a weekly article, which was published. But then he wrote a touchy description of the behavior of French prisoners at the time of the armistice, which included kind words for collaborator Joseph Darnand (who had organized a collaborationist police force against the resistance movements). Camus turned the article down. He wrote to Bernanos on August 29 that what bothered him most were his remarks about French prisoners. As for Darnand: "I'm not going to deliver an indictment against this man or any man in the world, since I refuse the principle of all death sentences." But he couldn't consider Darnand's bravery an attenuating circumstance, for the Germans were also fine soldiers. He added that it was up to Bernanos to decide whether he wished to continue to write for *Combat*.[19]

The next day's *Combat* contained an editorial by Camus in a different vein. He protested the odious turn that the purge trials had taken, politics having been mixed in with the need for justice. And so a pacifist guilty only of writing literary articles in a collaborationist newspaper was sentenced to eight years at hard labor, when a man who had recruited for the pro-German Legion of French Volunteers received only five years. A society judges itself, Camus warned, if it cannot punish genuine criminals and sends pacifists to labor camps.

Earlier that same month Camus had been on the job when news came in of the atomic bomb dropped on Hiroshima. For Camus "mechanical civilization has just reached the last degree of savagery. It will be necessary to choose," he warned, "between collective suicide or the intelligent utilization of scientific conquests. It was indecent to celebrate a discovery in the service of destruction and organized murder.

Let us be understood. If the Japanese surrender after the destruction of Hiroshima and thanks to intimidation, we shall be delighted. But we refuse to draw from such grave news anything else but the decision to plead still more energetically in favor of a veritable international society. . . .

That Camus' withdrawal from *Combat* coincided with the end of the war may be only that, coincidence. In fact he was leaving a newspaper still in good health, with a competent staff, to return to his writing. Exhausted by the political arena? Surely. No longer in agreement with *Combat*'s policies? That has been said.[13] But he had been free to make his own policies, to write his own editorials.

It can be assumed that Camus was the author of a final editorial before this first departure from *Combat*, published on September 1, this written on his last evening in the office, and which summed up a year of experience in publishing that newspaper. *Combat*'s ambition had been to break with the past. Not, as some believed and others feared, to compete with Marx or Christ. "Neither Communists nor Christians, we simply wish to render dialogue possible. . . ."

On September 5 the Camus twins, Jean and Catherine, were born in a private hospital at Belvédère, outside Paris beyond the Porte de Saint-Cloud. From the hospital they were to go in a hired ambulance to Bougival, a pleasant west Paris suburb, where they were given the use of a house belonging to the Schoeller family (Guy Schoeller was a childhood friend of Michel Gallimard). Camus helped Francine get into the ambulance, loaded the baggage, and then climbed in himself, saying: "Let's go!" Francine reminded him that their babies were still inside the hospital, so he got out meekly to fetch them.[6]

# 28

---◆---

## SAINT-GERMAIN-DES-PRES

November–32 years old.
. . . None can say that he has attained man's limit. The
five years we have just lived through taught me that. . . .
It is up to each of us to exploit in himself man's greatest
chance, his final virtue. When the day comes that human
limits have a meaning, then the problem of God will be
posed. But not before, not before the possibility has been
lived to the full. There is only one goal for great deeds and
that is human fecundity. But first to achieve mastery of
oneself.

*Carnets*

It could be said that the play *Caligula* was a lifetime work, if one
remembers that it was one of Camus' earliest projects, one of the first to
be executed, at least in a first draft. And then, after its first production
in September 1945, it would be taken up again and again, significant
changes would be made between the published version of 1944 and that
of 1947, it would be revised for the performances at the Festival of Angers in 1957 and in Paris a year later. In successive versions, as students of Camus' work have demonstrated in a sizable and convincing
collection of papers, secondary characters have been transformed, but
the Emperor Caligula's deeds and his underlying character and motivations change little, and these are of course the principal features of a
play at once intriguing and repelling. One thing is proved by the presence of *Caligula* at virtually every step of Camus' writing life: its importance to him as a symbol (of absurd man, the absurd world).

Only a reading or a rereading of the play will clarify what has just
been said.

A young student actor, Gérard Philipe, had been chosen by theater director Jacques Hébertot to play the title role. While a student at Paris's acting academy Philipe had a brief but acclaimed part in Jean Giraudoux's *Sodome et Gomorrhe* at Hébertot's theater. "We remarked, as everyone did, the passage of an angel who was called Gérard Philipe," Simone de Beauvoir had noted in her diary.[1] Then he had been seen briefly at the Mathurins in March 1945 in a play called *Federigo,* by a young author, René Laporte, a play remarked especially for the starring role of Maria Casarès:

> What to say of Miss Maria Casarès, who, this time, attains a kind of perfection? [wrote the critic Philippe Hériat] She has everything: beauty filled with style, grace in the slightest movements, charm, an adorable bust; she has above all ardor, poetry, conviction, and when she wishes, variety.

There was no role in *Caligula* suitable for Maria Casarès, from whom Camus was now estranged. She continued her career elsewhere, after an inexplicable interruption: "Maria Casarès seems tired these days—or did she have a case of flu?" her friend and teacher wondered, after a performance of Casarès in *The Brothers Karamazov* in December.[2] In January her mother died, and to his despair Camus could only console her from afar.[3] (There was another regretted death that month, that of Uncle Gustave Acault, his benefactor in adolescence.)

Was Gérard Philipe, then a very young twenty-three, old enough to play Caligula? Camus had intended to take the part himself with the Théâtre de l'Equipe when he was twenty-five (so he later told a radio interviewer; the text of the interview appears in the Pléiade edition of his work). Hébertot had first chosen a much older trouper, born in 1888, who had begun playing at the Comédie Française as early as 1917, but that actor had fallen ill. Hébertot suggested: "Why not use Philipe and rejuvenate the part?" If they chose Philipe it was because the young man had shown that he had a dark side as well as an angelic one. In order to see him on the stage Camus attended the three-day examination held at the Odéon Theater as the final test for students at the acting academy. Camus confided to Michel and Janine Gallimard that Philipe had excited him.[4] He had also noticed another young actor (then nineteen), Michel Bouquet, went up to him, and asked if he too would play in *Caligula*. Bouquet explained that he had an acting job that fall; Camus relied that it didn't matter, he would like to have Bouquet play Scipion if only for thirty performances. Bouquet was impressed, liked Camus; they would become friends as well as associates in the theater.

The director this time would be Camus' near-relative Paul Oettly, son of Sarah Oettly of Le Panelier. During rehearsals, which began in mid-August, Oettly was clearly in charge, put the actors in place, ordered the sets, while Camus, who seemed to know nothing about directing technique or the mechanical side of staging, stood by to put in his word when the text was at issue.[5] The scenery was done by Louis Miquel, an old friend from Algiers; another old friend, Marie Viton, designed the costumes. Miquel felt that Camus, although remaining in the background, was the real director. He was particularly struck by Camus' singular insistence that the stage be bathed in light throughout the play.[6]

When *Caligula* opened on September 26, 1945, it was to mixed reviews. An example of the worst was that of Kleber Haedens, son of an artillery colonel, right-wing author, contributor to prewar and wartime collaborationist periodicals. In *L'Epoque,* Haedens wrote: "They are shadows who think, flat silhouettes . . . who seek to put together the scattered elements of a philosophy." But the play launched Philipe to stardom. "Thirty articles," Camus noted in his journal:

> The reason for the praise is as bad as that of the criticism. Scarcely one or two authentic or aroused voices. Fame! In the best of cases, a misunderstanding. But I won't assume the superior attitude of one who scorns it. It is also a sign of men, neither more nor less important than their indifference, friendship, or hatred. . . .

He would take this "misunderstanding" for a "liberation." His ambition, if he had one, was of another dimension.

In October the anthology which Jean Grenier had put together on *L'Existence* was published with Camus' "Remarque sur la révolte," an early draft of the first chapter of *L'Homme révolté* and an indication, more than an outline, of what the full book (published exactly six years later) would contain. The publication of the essay at the very moment when Grenier had left France for Egypt, to teach at Cairo and Alexandria universities for the next five years, served as stimulus for a new burst of note-taking for the book itself. The journal contains abundant evidence of this. And if the essay published in Grenier's anthology seemed somewhat abstract—more existentialist than political, it would be noted—Camus was also taking his distances from the postwar apologists for the Russian Revolution. Simone de Beauvoir records the first instance of dissension between Camus and the Sartre group. It happened in November 1945, when Camus was driving her home. He defended de Gaulle against Communist Party leader Maurice Thorez. Then, as he drove off, he shouted through the car window: "General de Gaulle still has a better-looking mug than Mr. Jacques Duclos." (Communist leader Duclos would soon be elected vice president of the French Parliament.)[7] In his journal he wondered by what right a Communist or a Christian could reproach him for pessimism; it wasn't *he* who felt that man was lost without God, or who showed the suspicion toward his fellows that the Marxists did. Christianity is pessimistic about man and optimistic about human destiny, Marxism pessimistic concerning destiny and human nature, optimistic about the march of history. "I shall say that, pessimistic as to the human condition, I am optimistic about man."

With their infant twins, the Camus continued to reside at Bougival. It was a large house, requiring a servant they couldn't afford, set on some two acres of land on the Rue du Chemin de Fer.[8] But what they really needed was a place in town, easier to heat, but also convenient for working. Camus was now back at Gallimard, working there as regularly as he had been working at *Combat* the previous hectic year. And the Schoeller house, in any case, was only a temporary arrangement. So the ever-reliable Gallimards came to the rescue again. They owned a building at 18 Rue Séguier, a narrow street deep in the old Left Bank, which had housed the offices of one of their subsidiaries which published large illustrated books. It had been the home of the eighteenth-century scholar and philosopher Henri-François d'Aguesseau. The old town house had extraordinarily high ceilings, tall windows, letting in cold drafts, and when the space had been converted into offices it made for curiously proportioned rooms. But for four years the Rue Séguier would be home for the Camus.

Pending transformation of the offices back to living space, when they had to evacuate the Bougival house in the middle of February the Camus took refuge at the Michel Gallimards', at the top of the Gallimard town house on the Rue de l'Université.[4]

Both the Rue Séguier apartment and the Gallimard building were close to the center of literary and intellectual social life of those days, the neighborhood known as Saint-Germain-des-Prés, which takes its name from the nine-century-old abbey church on a corner of the square, vestige of a medieval monastery. But Saint-Germain-des-Prés was already more than a church or a subway station. The name signified, as Montmartre had a long time ago, as Montparnasse had in the between-the-wars era, cultural Paris, what Greenwich Village had been to New York City, Bloomsbury, Chelsea to London, Schwabing to Munich. The publishers and the booksellers occupied the place first, helping to define the district, drawing the creators. The Sorbonne, within walking distance, the attractive Seine quays with their outdoor bookstalls, also helped.

Centuries earlier, the neighborhood had drawn the *Encyclopédistes,* Diderot, Voltaire, Rousseau to ancient Café Procope. Later Beaumarchais was a habitué (when his *Marriage of Figaro* opened at the nearby Odéon Theater), Théophile Gautier, Musset, George Sand, then Balzac, Zola, Huysmans, Maupassant. The Café de Flore, founded at the end of the Second Empire, had been frequented by Remy de Gourmont and Huysmans, and the right-wing group of Charles Maurras' *Action Française* had made it their headquarters. Apollinaire, who lived only a couple of blocks away, would meet friends there.

At first, writers and their friends had been drawn to Saint-Germain-des-Prés because it was *not* Montparnasse (lacking the attractions of Montparnasse, rents were cheaper, and so were the restaurants and the cafés). During World War II and the German occupation of Paris, Sartre and Beauvoir worked in the Flore as if in their own home; and it was the scene of early meetings of Sartre's retinue, of the café arguments with Camus, Koestler. There were also the Café des Deux-Magots next door (which would later advertise itself as the "rendezvous of the intellectual elite") and, across Boulevard Saint-Germain, the Brasserie Lipp, meeting place of successful writers—a favorite of Camus in the later years—as well as their publishers, film directors, politicians, and other celebrities.[9]

Of course it was the reputation of "existentialism" which made postwar Saint-Germain-des-Prés. For the public at large, those who read the popular press, the district signified cellar clubs where Juliette Gréco sang and Boris Vian, author, translator, and composer, played the trombone. (He himself would write a guide to that kind of Saint-German-des-Prés.)[10] The neighborhood received popular consecration, for example, in the sensational weekly *Samedi-Soir,* which once (on May 3, 1947) published a page-one photograph of Juliette Gréco and actor Roger Vadim "exchanging depressing thoughts at the entrance to an existentialist cellar." The article in *Samedi-Soir* made it clear that the life of the neighborhood was in these cellar clubs where "the existentialists, doubtless waiting for the atomic bomb which is dear to them, now drink, dance, love and sleep." At first they had been poor but now—so said the article—Sartre, Beauvoir, and Camus had made money on literature, so had another in the movies, a third in proletarian realism. . . . The Tabou Club on the Rue Dauphine was identified as the sanctuary of the new generation; a timetable informed readers of where the penniless existentialist was likely to be found at any particular moment of the day (e.g., at the Flore from 11 A.M. to 1 P.M., from 3 to 6, 6:30 to 8 P.M.; lunch would be taken at Les Assassins on the Rue Jacob; from 8 to midnight he or she would be at the Bar Vert on the same street, from midnight on at the Tabou). The existentialist worked each day from 6 to 6:30 P.M. in his or a friend's room, and on Sundays he switched from the Flore to the Deux-Magots.

A spoof—in fact written with the help of at least one habitué of the neighborhood—the *Samedi-Soir* article was also a fairly accurate description of the external décor of Saint-Germain-des-Prés immediately after the war, and above all an indication of what "existentialism" signified to the popular press and, one assumes, to the popular mind. The real Saint-Germain-des-Prés, at least to its working residents like the real Sartre and the real Camus, was certainly different. But it *was* a tumultuous time, a tumultuous place; sitting at outdoor or indoor café tables, and then in bistrots and in cellars, did represent a considerable part of every day and every life in those first postwar years. And Camus was part of it. Simone de Beauvoir's day-by-day record of the period (in *La Force des choses*) contains convincing descriptions of Camus' participation in the talking, the drinking, the dancing, the return to drinking. After the day at Gallimard, Camus would leave the office, perhaps asking his secretary, Suzanne Labiche, to join him. They would find Sartre and Beauvoir at a Saint-Germain-des-Prés café, go on to a bistrot for dinner, join friends at Le Tabou, or Le Méphisto on Boulevard Saint-Germain, the Cave St. Germain des Prés on the Rue Saint-Benoit just down from the Flore. They might watch Boris Vian and Juliette Gréco perform at the Rose Rouge. And then wind up the evening at an outdoor café on the Champs-Elysées for a final drink. During the course of the evening they would encounter an Arthur Koestler, a Manès Sperber, younger men such as Merleau-Ponty, Romain Gary, Jean-Pierre Vivet, Jean Cau. Sartre in his cups would begin to boast about how handsome he was, and often he'd become belligerent, especially when the others had to put him into a car so he could be taken home, or when someone else, Camus for instance, seemed a potential rival for a young lady he admired. At least once Camus walked into the Gallimard building with a black eye.[11] (Paul Flamand of Editions du Seuil, who had a lunch appointment with Camus one day during this period, saw him arrive with a black eye. Camus told him that Koestler had slammed a taxi door on him.)

Camus himself would turn pale, would be irritable, even belligerent, when he drank too much. Simone de Beauvoir was somewhere in the middle. She was obviously interested in Camus, while he confided to a friend that he stayed away from her because he feared she would talk too much in bed. Her caustic treatment of Camus in her memoirs has been ascribed to spite, just as Sartre was patently jealous of the younger man who could attract women even without the exploitation of his intellect and reputation. In fact, Beauvoir wasn't as caustic as all that in her memoirs; one finds tenderness there, as well.

A legend that circulated at the time had Camus saying to a respectable woman of letters: "We have, dear friend, spent a marvelous evening evoking high-minded subjects, but, you see, if a wench walked by
right now I'd drop you and follow her."[12]

One evening—it was while Sartre was visiting the United States
(from the middle of December 1945 to the following March)—Simone
de Beauvoir dined alone with Camus at the Brasserie Lipp, they went to
the Pont-Royal bar (down the street from the Gallimard building) until
closing time, after which he bought a bottle of champagne which they
took back to her room at the Hôtel La Louisiane, where they talked
until 3 A.M. Because she was a woman, therefore not quite the equal of
this feudal man (says Beauvoir in her memoirs), he was able to confide
in her. He read her passages from his journal, spoke of his personal
problems. He often returned to a theme which preoccupied him: One
day it had to be possible to write the truth. The truth, as she saw it, was
that in Camus the gap between his life and his writing was wider than in
many others. When they were out together, drinking, talking, laughing
late into the night, he was droll and cynical, wicked and naughty,
confessed his feelings, yielded to his impulses. He could sit on a curb-
stone in the snow at two in the morning and meditate on love: "You
have to choose: it lasts or it ignites; the drama is that it can't last and
ignite at the same time!" But in serious discussions he closed up, took
on airs, spoke noble phrases; pen in hand, he was a moralist she no
longer recognized. Camus himself knew, she concluded, that his public
image didn't coincide with his private truth.[7]

This was the mask which other intimates of Camus would identify
or have occasion to suffer from. "To settle in to the natural but with
one's mask," was the way he had put it in his own journal. But in the
case of Beauvoir, she was no longer willing to seek the motivations
behind the role-playing when it came time to record the wild years at
Saint-Germain-des-Prés.

Jean Daniel, a *pied noir* growing up at the time in the shadow of
Camus, found his hero "particularly handsome," a young Humphrey
Bogart with "a more Japanese mask and a more expansive zest for life."
When he called on Camus at Gallimard the older man asked him to
wait until he had completed an urgent letter to discourage an unknown
correspondent from committing suicide. "It's the tenth this week,"
Camus told Daniel (this meeting probably took place late in 1947, after
publication of *La Peste*). Daniel had heard that Camus was surrounded
by a court of young men, not homosexuals, but who would carry on
veritable scenes of jealousy. During the *Combat* period a young film
critic, after having broken several glasses and a bottle of whiskey in
a night club, climbed onto the bar to proclaim: "I'm going to speak to

you about an injustice worse than those we denounce in column after column of our daily for the intellectual elite; this injustice is alive and it is there before us—it's Camus; he has everything it takes to seduce, to be happy, to be famous, and in addition, he dares to have all the virtues! Against this injustice we can do nothing." At Le Tabou or Le Méphisto, Daniel knew there were some who might prefer Camus to Sartre, even while feeling that the older writer was more important, because Camus was "more handsome and liked himself more." (Dancing in the company of Jean Daniel one day, Camus described himself as *"un voluptueux puritain."*)

Meeting him at Gallimard, Daniel found Camus excessively polite. "A little later, please," he said gently whenever the office door was opened. He was still a provincial with a *pied noir* accent; he felt that Camus had not changed from Algiers. When Camus showed his visitor the small terrace outside the office, Daniel was surprised to hear the pride in Camus' voice as he said: "I'm one of the few people here to have a terrace."[13]

Camus wore loud Algerian-style suits, often topped with a trench coat. He drove about Saint-Germain-des-Prés in an old black Citroën. Friends would shout: "Ho! Albert!" He would not shout back, but merely waved his hand. To one observer he seemed to be playing his own part in an unfinished movie.[14]

His association with the Sartre crowd, more perhaps this personal association than anything he had said or written, would contribute to the popular and journalistic typing of Camus as an "existentialist," a typing he did not ask for and did not like. But it was one which would plague him all his life, particularly among non-readers, and abroad, and quite regularly in interviews in the foreign press. "No, I'm not an existentialist," he told an interviewer for *Les Nouvelles Littéraires* (November 15, 1945). "Sartre and I are always astonished to see our names associated. We are even thinking of publishing a little advertisement in which the undersigned affirm they have nothing in common and refuse to answer for the debts of the other." He and Sartre had published "all" their books before they met, and when they did meet it was to take note of their differences. Sartre was an existentialist, he explained, while the only book of ideas he himself had published, *Le Mythe de Sisyphe,* was directed against so-called existentialist philosophers. If neither he nor Sartre believed in God, neither did Jules Romains, Malraux, Stendhal, Sade, Alexandre Dumas, Montaigne, or Molière. . . . Were they all of the same school? On his own philosophy of the absurd he was more eloquent, and seemed to be throwing some light on his future projects and preoccupations.

To accept the absurdity of everything around us is a step, a necessary experience: It must not become an impasse. It provokes a revolt which can become productive. An analysis of the notion of revolt can help to discover notions capable of restoring a relative meaning to existence.

In an interview published a month later Camus spelled out his differences with existentialism, both the religious type of Kierkegaard and Jaspers and the atheist existentialism of Husserl, Heidegger, and Sartre.[15] And in a letter to the magazine *La Nef,* published in January 1946 (and in the Pléiade edition of his work), he took pains to deny what Henri Troyat had written in a review of *Caligula* in that magazine ("The whole play . . . is nothing more than an illustration of Sartre's existentialist principles."). Camus insisted: *Caligula* was written in 1938 before French existentialism had assumed its present atheistic form, *Le Mythe de Sisyphe* was written against existentialist philosophies, and he had insufficient confidence in reason to be able to enter into a philosophic system, which is why the manifesto by Sartre in the first issue of *Les Temps Modernes* seemed unacceptable to him. "Note that I don't have many illusions about what *Caligula* is worth," he concluded. "But it's still better to be criticized for what one really is."

"Against engaged literature. Man is not *only* a social being," he was writing in his journal. "At least his death belongs to him. We are made to live for others. But one really dies only for oneself."

For the first time, that Christmas, Camus went off with the Michel Gallimards to one of their favorite places, doing one of their favorite things: sailing off Cannes.[16] At Gallimard he was now busy preparing the series that would bear his name as editor, while continuing as a general reader and adviser for that house. Henceforth, and for the rest of his life (except for the one year of illness), whatever he might be writing or producing, he would have an office waiting for him at Gallimard —always the same one, with the terrace overlooking the Rue Sébastien-Bottin. Taking advantage of the secretarial service, then the private secretary he would have there, he would send all of his letters from Gallimard (most of them on Gallimard stationery, no matter what the subject). This is where even his personal friends would reach him by telephone, and much of the youngest generation of writers passed through his office for guidance, to show a manuscript, or for consolation. Soon there would be a routine: work at home in the morning, the office after lunch to read and dictate correspondence, to reply to telephone messages, to read submitted manuscripts, to receive visitors by appointment.[11]

Now the reading committee would meet in the large semicircular room with bay windows open to the formal gardens. Actually the office of the Gallimards, it was converted once a week into a conference room for the most prestigious group of men and women of letters in France, employees all of Gallimard, each with an assigned seat (in the lineup of chairs facing the windows, Camus was in the sixth chair from the right). When it was his turn to describe a manuscript of which he approved, he would speak briefly, precisely, leaning forward, perhaps remarking: "It's a very fine book." Michel Gallimard, who said nothing at these meetings, sat on the opposite side of the room, his back to the windows.[14]

When an editor was put in charge of a series, it signified that his name was in itself a drawing card. Camus could publish more or less what he wanted to, although there was an unwritten understanding that he would not insist on a book in the face of strong objections from the other editors.[17] Although directors of series usually received a percentage of the royalties on sales of each of the titles in the series, Camus waived his, drawing only his regular Gallimard salary and a special honorarium as *directeur de collection.*

With or without money, one could do little to alleviate conditions in the immediate postwar period, in that nation that had been stripped during years of enemy occupation, and whose recovery was proving difficult. In February, Camus reported to Jean Grenier that he had spent half the winter defending his children against the cold and getting food. Having children added to what was already a struggle for existence, although Camus was proving to be an attentive father if not a very adroit one. He never got used to the crying of babies, especially when he got home after a long day and a long night, but he was also softened by the sight of the infants, and would sing them to sleep with Spanish lullabies—or at least Spanish songs.[18]

Rationing was still in effect, and even to buy baby shoes required exhausting effort. One of those who were helping was Nicola Chiaromonte, who from New York sent the Camus packages of food, diapers, soap—even stockings for Francine. It may have been at this time that Jean Hytier, the Algiers professor who had been a member of the editorial board of *Rivages,* ran into Camus at Adrienne Monnier's bookshop on the Rue de l'Odéon (just opposite the bookshop of Monnier's friend Sylvia Beach, Shakespeare and Company). Camus was picking up food packages sent to French writers as a gift from the Argentine.[19]

There was a joke among Camus' friends that the first book in the series known as Hope (*Espoir*) was called *L'Asphyxie* (by Violette Leduc, a friend of Sartre and Beauvoir).[20] Indeed, gloom pervaded the early list of Espoir books, with Jacques-Laurent Bost's *Le Dernier des métiers,*

Colette Audry's *On joue perdant*. The volumes were printed in gray covers, distinguishing them from Gallimard's literary Collection Blanche, and also adding another grim touch. Each bore on the front cover (a soft paper cover, as were all original editions at Gallimard):

**Series**
**ESPOIR**
**NRF**
**Directed by**
**Albert Camus**

Although NRF was in fact a vestige—at the time the magazine was still under a cloud if not to say ban—the name continued to appear on all Gallimard publications. The back cover of books in the Espoir series each contained an unsigned text by Camus:

> We are living in nihilism. . . . We shall not get out of it by pretending to ignore the evil of our time or by deciding to deny it. The only hope is to name it, on the contrary, and to inventory it to discover the cure for the disease. . . . Let us thus recognize that this is a time for hope, even if it is a difficult hope. . . .

The series would contain both fiction and non-fiction. Camus would publish his friends, Bost, Bloch-Michel, Roger Grenier, a fellow *pied noir* Jean Sénac, a poet who would become a close comrade, René Char, an office colleague, Brice Parain. Later, apparently through Parain, Espoir published a posthumous work by Simone Weil, *L'Enracinement.** Camus was enthusiastic when he read it for the first time (in March 1948); he thought it was a revelation, and it certainly helped to crystallize his own views on non-violence and even anti-history.[20] In his presentation of this book, published in the monthly listing of new titles called *Bulletin de la NRF* in June 1949, Camus wrote that *L'Enracinement,* a report on the moral situation of France in 1940, was one of the most important works to appear since the war. He quoted two of Weil's phrases: "Official history consists in believing the murderers at their word," and "Who can admire Alexander with all his soul, if he doesn't have a base soul?" Imagine, added Camus, the solitude of such a spirit in between-the-wars France.

Espoir would be a small and short-lived series, as publishers' series go, but a number of works by Simone Weil would appear under the Espoir logo, including several published after Camus' death. Camus and Parain both dealt with the Weil heirs to discuss publishing problems.

But Camus not only looked for books for his own series. He read through manuscripts received at Gallimard from authors known or un-

---

* Published in English as *The Need for Roots.*

known. He brought in Violette Leduc, but he would also be associated with veteran authors such as Louis Guilloux, who had been published at the house long before Camus arrived in Paris. And when Guilloux completed *Le Jeu de patience,* he submitted it to the reading committee through his friend Camus.[21] Camus was favorably prejudiced toward anything or anyone coming from North Africa, and young writers had another priority. He replied personally to authors showing promise. At the outset he tried to reserve what he felt were the best of the new authors for his Espoir series,[11] but later he recognized that this was not necessarily a service to render to an author.[4] For it was not a highly successful series; apart from the works of Simone Weil, none of the books published in it enjoyed great critical or public favor.

At Gallimard the editor did not work as he might in some other French houses (and in all American publishing firms), following the book from the receipt of the manuscript to publication, which includes supervision of production, promotion, and advertising. Gallimard's prestigious readers were too removed from commercial considerations for that. But Camus did interest himself in the editorial problems a manuscript might present. A young Algerian writer, Marcel Moussy, when he submitted a first novel to Camus and received notice that it had been accepted for publication, then sat down with Camus for a detailed discussion of changes that could be made. Camus pointed out an error in the title of a tango of the 1945 era, hummed the tune to convince Moussy he was right. He also suggested that a French Algerian word might not be understood in France, and they found a substitute for it. And then suddenly, changing his tone at the close of the meeting, Camus looked Moussy in the eyes, told him in a grave voice: "Above all don't forget: You have to be ambitious."[22]

Perhaps this wouldn't be considered as much editing in the publishing worlds of New York or of London, but for Paris of the time, and for Gallimard, it represented more than usual dedication. Another young author discovered that Camus' suggestions were directed to what the author could do best, not what Camus himself would have done.[20]

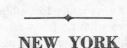

# 29

# NEW YORK

I loved New York, with that powerful love that at times
leaves you full of uncertainty and abhorrence: there are
times when one needs an exile.

"Pluies de New York"

"I am not displeased," Camus wrote to his aging Belcourt elementary
schoolteacher Louis Germain, "to abandon for a while this Parisian life
which wears down your nerves and dries up your heart."[1]

A representative figure of the French resistance, a young cultural
and social personality of eminence, Camus was a logical candidate for a
mission to the United States, particularly to its universities, under
French Government sponsorship. His tour was sponsored by the Cultural Relations Section of the French Ministry of Foreign Affairs; while
in the United States he would be on official business for the Provisional
Government of the French Republic (but with no particular obligations). Such trips were at once good public relations for the dispatching
government and a reward—a paid vacation—for eminent citizens.

Camus sailed from Le Havre on the *Oregon,* which was being operated by the French Line as a cargo and passenger liner. The fact that
it was a freighter came as a surprise to Camus, especially when he discovered that all its passengers could fit into a small dining room. Conditions were virtually those of wartime austerity (France was out of the
war but it had lost the war, and the armistice had been signed less than
a year ago). Camus shared a cabin with three other men, one of whom
was a doctor and a new friend.

Dr. Pierre Rubé, a psychiatrist by training, had been an army doctor at the outbreak of the war, assigned to a hospital train. He partici-

pated in the June 1940 débacle, and after unsuccessful attempts to get out of France, during which he joined an underground intelligence network in Montpellier, he managed to escape over the Pyrenees with a Spanish Republican guide. Arrested in Barcelona, he was interned in a camp for six months, then sent to North Africa, where he fought with the Leclerc division, following it to the battlefields of Normandy, Paris, Strasbourg, taking part in the liberation of the Dachau concentration camp. He returned to Paris sick at heart, the very sight of Nazi collaborators making him nauseated. A friend got him a mission to the United States to study psychiatric teamwork, a specialty which interested him. While applying for the necessary travel documents he met Camus, who was of course going through the same procedures. Rubé had just seen *Caligula* at the Hébertot theater, and he had been moved by it. He introduced himself and expressed his admiration for the play. It was snowing, and they had to go to the American Consulate for their visas. Camus offered to drive Rubé there in his black Citroën.

On board the *Oregon* they found not only accommodations but amusement facilities spare; there were no movies or other group entertainment. But Camus was in excellent humor, joking with everyone, flirting with the younger women. Rubé noticed one characteristic of his new friend, an aspect of Mediterranean man: He always took it for granted that he, and not a woman, would go through a door first.

They could take showers whenever they wanted to, but there was a French consular official sharing their tiny cabin who never did, and the Camus-Rubé team wondered how they could oblige him to bathe. Finally Rubé had an idea. He enlisted the help of their steward, with a tip, so the steward knocked at the door of their cabin the next morning to announce: "Monsieur the Consul, your shower is ready." The steward was carrying soap and a towel, and the strategy worked.[2]

When their ship docked in New York on March 25, 1946 (it had been anchored in the middle of the Hudson since the previous evening), foreign passengers were interrogated by Immigration inspectors. They were asked, among other things, whether they had ever been members of the Communist Party or had friends who had been members, and Camus apparently refused to reply to either question. Arriving passengers were questioned individually, and Rubé and the others in their group waited outside the examination room for Camus to come out, but he did not. An hour passed, then another half hour, and finally one of the group returned to find out what had happened. He was informed by an angry Camus that he had Communist friends but wouldn't name them. Finally the others went on to the French Cultural Services to tell the people there what had happened, and an emissary was sent to help get Camus out.[2]

Camus himself reported having been held up by Immigration inspectors, who seemed to have mysterious sources of information—but who later apologized for the delay.[3]

As it happened, the head of French Cultural Services in New York at the time was the anthropologist Claude Lévi-Strauss (who would remember nothing of the incident).[4] What seems certain is that *Conseiller culturel* Lévi-Strauss called in another man on a French cultural mission to the United States, architect Pierre-André Emery, knowing that he was a friend of Camus. Lévi-Strauss asked Emery to go to the pier to meet Camus. Did Lévi-Strauss do this after being informed by Rubé and the others that Camus was held up at Immigration? In any case, Emery went down to the pier. When Camus emerged he was in a nervous state, told his Algiers friend that he had been questioned because he was carded as a Communist.[5] Still another friend was at the pier to greet him: the anti-Fascist Italian émigré writer Nicola Chiaromonte, who had spent the war years (since escaping with Camus' help from occupied France via Algeria and Morocco) writing for American periodicals such as *The New Republic, The Nation,* and *Partisan Review.* He now had an American wife, and Camus would be seeing much of Nicola and Miriam in New York.[6] A free man at last, Camus discovered that he was tired, and an attack of flu was returning; it was on unsteady feet that he walked his first blocks of Manhattan.

On the day following his arrival a press conference was held for the American and French press in the large salon of the French Cultural Services on Fifth Avenue. The guest was introduced by Lévi-Strauss. He would quickly express surprise at the abstract nature of the questions he was being asked. "And yet they had told me that America likes concrete questions," he observed. For the time being, he said when asked about his philosophic position, his philosophy consisted of doubts and uncertainties. "I'm too young to have a 'system.'" He repeated, once again, his rejection of existentialism as a school à la mode and as a system.

Asked what he thought of the definition of the United States as the capital of materialistic civilization he replied: "Everywhere today man suffers from materialistic civilization. In poverty and hunger, European man is materialistic. Can it be otherwise?" He thought the real question was, Can man in his present plight act, nevertheless? He believed that the answer was yes. As for his own work, he explained (or so he was quoted), he had become a playwright by *accident biographique,* having had to earn his living as an actor (*sic*). His next work would be a novel about plague. To another question he replied that he had read American fiction from Dos Passos to Faulkner, and that he was certainly influenced by the interior technique of the American novel. "But I wonder whether this technique doesn't lead to an impoverishment of the means of literary expression. Besides, American novelists are freeing themselves from this formula." He knew little about the American stage, apart from the work of Eugene O'Neill.

He was questioned about his resistance activity and replied that he preferred to speak of his comrades, for others had done far more than he had.

He had read and reread Kafka, whose work seemed to him prophetic, one of the most significant of our time. And the reporter for the New York French-language newspaper *La Victoire,* who signed "P.," perhaps for editor Michel P. Pobers, contributed the thought that Camus himself was "our Kafka without dreams."[7]

Camus' arrival in the United States had been anticipated by a full-page article in the New York *Herald Tribune Weekly Book Review* on March 24, under the headline:

### BOLDEST WRITER IN FRANCE TODAY

In the article Justin O'Brien, of the Department of Romance Languages of Columbia University, informed American readers (who had not yet been able to read Camus unless they read French; *L'Etranger* would appear in an English translation only in April) that Camus was "one of the two or three most vivid young writers in France, and his arrival in America this month is awaited by many as one of the cultural events of the season." O'Brien went on: "Sartre has paved the way for him; Vercors has praised his young friend in New York, Chicago, and San Francisco; our little reviews are beginning to mention his name with something like reverence; Genêt [pen name of Janet Flanner] made some swash comments in 'The New Yorker' on his popular play now running in Paris." The article was certainly the most thorough introduction of Camus that would appear during his visit to New York.

On March 27, the third day of his stay in New York, Camus was to have a significant encounter in the person of A. J. Liebling, essayist-reporter for *The New Yorker*—significant especially for Liebling, who would never forget his young French friend, no more than he would forget anything about the France he loved. Abbott Joseph Liebling, born in New York in 1904, had spent a year at the Sorbonne and had covered the war from France, Great Britain, and North America from 1939 to 1944. He was awarded the French Legion of Honor, and three of his notable books were *The Road Back to Paris, Normandy Revisited,* and an anthology of resistance writing in French and English editions (*The Republic of Silence,* also published as *La République du silence*). Although *The New Yorker*'s "Talk of the Town" interview with Camus, which appeared in that magazine on

April 20, 1946, was unsigned, and the magazine's records contain no
indication of who wrote it,[8] in fact Liebling did, as he explained in the
last article he was ever to write, a review of the American edition of
Camus' journal, published in *The New Yorker* on February 8, 1964:

> When he first [*sic*] visited New York, shortly after the war,
> [Camus] was thirty-two, but I wrote that he reminded me of a
> character in the comic-strip "Harold Teen," an impression aided by
> his absurd suit, the product of a French tailor whose patterns
> evidently dated not only from before the war but from before the
> great crash of 1929. (His New York publisher, who was bringing
> out "The Stranger," hadn't offered him an advance on future work
> and he had already spent his advance on "The Stranger," so he was
> in no position to improve his wardrobe.)

Liebling found Camus, "who is thirty-two and dresses like a character in 'Harold Teen,' " in a hotel room on West Seventieth Street,[9] described him as having "a snub-nosed face that looks more Spanish than
French," noting Camus' ancestry (as Camus would have explained it to
Liebling: Spanish on his mother's side, Alsatian on his father's). "His
birth there gave him a distinctive chemistry, because the European
cities in French North Africa are as new and as ruthlessly commercial
as Birmingham or Detroit." The thing that bothered Camus about
France, the unidentified *New Yorker* interviewer remarked, was the
oversupply of historical and literary associations. "What the heart
craves, at certain moments, is places without poetry," he quotes
Camus.* "West Seventieth Street ought to suit him fine," "Talk of the
Town" concluded.

A student of journalism as well as a passionate admirer of things
French, Liebling was of course interested in the journalist Camus. The
interview opened with Camus' "idea for a daily newspaper which would
take a lot of the fun out of newspapering." Camus told him: "It would
be a critical newspaper, to be published one hour after the first editions
of the other papers, twice a day, morning and evening. It would evalu-
ate the probable element of truth in the other papers' main stories, with
due regard to editorial policies and the past performances of the correspondents. Once equipped with card-indexed dossiers on the correspondents, a critical newspaper could work very fast. After a few weeks
the whole tone of the press would conform more closely to reality. An
international service." The interviewer also reported that *Caligula* had
been acquired for New York production. Summing up Camus' work
and philosophy, and the symbol of Sisyphus condemned to pushing a
rock up a hill, "Talk of the Town" observed that "For a man arrived at

* In *Le Minotaure ou la Halte d'Oran:* "*Ce que le cœur demande à certains
moments . . . ce sont justement des lieux sans poésie.*"

such a grim conclusion, M. Camus seemed unduly cheerful, as did, in fact, M. Sartre when he was here some weeks ago." "Just because you have pessimistic thoughts, you don't have to *act* pessimistic," Camus is quoted. "One has to pass the time somehow. Look at Don Juan."

On March 28, Camus was to make his most important public appearance in the United States; in the company of two other writers born of the French resistance, he would speak at the McMillin Theater on the campus of Columbia University. The chairman of the sponsoring committee, Justin O'Brien, had discussed the meeting on the previous day with the guest speakers in what O'Brien later remembered as "Camus' room in one of those mothy hotels on upper Broadway." The other speakers would be Vercors, pseudonym of Jean Bruller, whose *Le Silence de la mer,* published in France by an underground printer, had already appeared in English, and Thimerais (Léon Motchane), not known in America because the essay he had published at the clandestine Editions de Minuit had not yet reached American shores. O'Brien later noted "the utter simplicity" of Camus' smile, "reminiscent of a Paris street urchin." Camus was the youngest of the group, and received an admiring glance from an attractive girl who rode up with them in the elevator. Then the moment they were in Camus' room "the athletic young man had stretched out on the bed with a few notes in front of him" and "easily dominated the group."

That is how it looked to O'Brien, but in fact Camus would spend the following whole day writing his talk, and when he confronted the crowd at the McMillin Theater he would experience a quiver of stage fright. For there were at least 1,200 persons in the hall that evening (no one could recall any meeting in French that had drawn an audience of more than three hundred in New York). And Camus—O'Brien's recollection again—clearly dominated that audience. "Making no distinctions between victors and vanquished in the war, he rapidly sketched a horridly debased conception of man that was, he said, the legacy of World War II. . . . When he told us that, as human beings of the twentieth century, we were all of us responsible for the war, and even for the horrors we had just been fighting . . . all of us in the huge hall were convinced, I think, of our common culpability. Then Camus . . . told us how we could contribute, even in the humblest way, to re-establishing the honesty and dignity of men."[10] The original French text of Camus' talk, entitled "The Human Crisis" (perhaps this is a re-translation of the subject of the evening's symposium, "The Crisis of Mankind") has not been found, but an English translation exists and has been published.[11]

Camus began by suggesting that he had not reached the proper age for lecturing, but he had been told that the important thing was not to express his personal views but to present elementary facts about France. He had chosen to speak not of literature or theater but of the spiritual experience of the men of his generation, of men "born just before or during the first great war, [who] reached adolescence during the world economic crisis, and were twenty the year Hitler took power. To complete their education they were then provided with the war in Spain, Munich, the war of 1939, the defeat, and four years of occupation and secret struggle." He illustrated the human crisis with four stories. In an apartment rented by the Gestapo a concierge proceeds to set the place in order, oblivious of two persons still bleeding and tightly bound. To the reproaches of one of the torture victims she replies: "I never pay attention to what my tenants do." (The story has already been remarked in Camus' journal.)

A German officer interrogates one of Camus' comrades in Lyons. In a previous session the prisoner's ears had been torn to shreds, and the German asks in a tone of affection or of solicitude: "How are your ears now?" In Greece, a woman is asked by a German officer to choose which of her three sons taken as hostage should be spared; she chooses the eldest because he has a family, thereby condemning the two others as the German officer intended. A group of deported women, among whom is a comrade of Camus, is repatriated to France via Switzerland. Seeing a funeral, they laugh hysterically: "So that is how the dead are treated *here*." (Also taken from his journal.)

These stories allow him to affirm that there is a human crisis, since the death or the torture of a human being can, in our world, be examined with indifference, with friendly or experimental interest, or without any response at all. He summed up what was wrong in "the single tendency described as the cult of efficiency and of abstraction." The problem was Hegel's "detestable principle" that man is made for history. Anything which serves history is considered good; acts are justified not as good or bad but by their effectiveness. Men of his generation were tempted into thinking nothing was true, or that historical fate is the only truth. Their revolt was to say no to the absurdity of the world, to abstractions, affirming nevertheless that there was something in us which rejected the offense and which could not be endlessly humiliated.

What must we do? Camus asked. "We must call things by their right names and realize that we kill millions of men each time we permit ourselves to think certain thoughts." We must rid the world of terror, put politics back in its rightful place, a secondary one, move from negation to positive values, to universalism. "There is in France and in Europe today a generation which takes the view that whoever puts his

trust in the human condition is a madman, while whoever despairs of
events is a coward. . . . Whenever one judges France or any other
country or question in terms of power, one aids and sustains a conception of man which logically leads to his mutilation. . . ."

One of O'Brien's students passed a note up to the stage to inform
the chairman that thieves had just stolen the evening's receipts, which
had been intended for French war orphans. After Camus finished his
talk O'Brien took the floor to observe that the "Crisis of Mankind" was
at their very door. Someone rose from the audience to suggest that on
their way out everyone pay his entrance fee a second time, and the two
girls whose cash box had been stolen set up the box again. The second
"take" amounted to more than the original one, an effect of Camus'
"persuasive words," thought O'Brien. One of the speakers told the incident to *Le Figaro,* providing an opportunity for a story about America's
gangsters and generous hearts.[10] Camus himself was enthralled by the
event, seeing it as the embodiment of American crime.[2]

The French-language weekly *La Victoire* of April 6 hailed the evening at Columbia as *"Une grande fête française,"* assuring its readers
that the meeting would occupy a place of its own in the annals of the
French colony of the United States. (The article contained some choice
lines from the original French of Camus' talk, all that seem to have survived.) Was there a question period after the talks? An employee of the
French Cultural Services recalled a question from the audience: "How
many Frenchmen were there in the resistance?" and Camus' quick
reply, a figure like 360,728, an ironic way to suggest that in such situations numbers didn't count.[12]

Camus did submit to a question-and-answer session at Columbia,
in any case, at the Maison Française. Camus had telephoned its director, Eugene Sheffer, at the suggestion of a former student of Sheffer's,
Peter Rhodes, onetime United Press correspondent and chief of the
Psychological Warfare Branch of the Office of War Information in
Paris, to say that he would like to meet American students. Sheffer set
up the meeting in the salon of the Maison Française, invited some fifty
Columbia undergraduates and a few of his fellow teachers. Camus
walked in, and his boyish grin put them all at ease at once. He asked his
listeners to sit on the floor, and then *he* proceeded to ask questions.
Camus said that he had visited several European capitals where men
would stare at women on the street, but it didn't seem to happen in
New York and he wanted to know why. The question was greeted by
embarrassed silence until a professor, Otis Fellows, broke in with:
"Monsieur Camus, in this country we believe that there is a time and a
place for everything." Camus stared at Fellows for a moment in

surprise and then broke into a hearty laugh, acknowledging that it was a very good answer indeed, but one which had never occurred to him.[13]

His friend Emery arranged for Camus to be received at the home of Dr. Ludwig Eidelberg and his wife Marthe, who as a young widow of French birth had met Eidelberg in 1938. He had been head of the Neurological Clinic in Vienna, had taught at the Viennese Psychoanalytical Institute, and was one of the psychoanalysts whose evacuation from Nazi-controlled Austria had been facilitated by British and American colleagues. He was practicing at Oxford when Marthe met him in Paris. After their marriage they moved to the United States, where Dr. Eidelberg developed a practice while teaching at the Psychoanalytic Institute. Later he would publish the first *Encyclopedia of Psychoanalysis;* he died in 1971.

The Eidelbergs were living in a small apartment on East Eighty-sixth Street with a view over Central Park's reservoir and toward the George Washington Bridge. There were fewer than a dozen guests for dinner. Mrs. Eidelberg realized that she was being an inadequate hostess, because she talked to Camus all evening long. Having been in exile for seven years, she felt uprooted, and here she was seated beside a fellow Frenchman, and a great writer and resistance hero in the bargain. Emery had found a copy of *Lettres à un ami allemand* in a secondhand bookshop, and Camus autographed it for her:

. . . because we have many common passions . . .

Emery had also brought along a phonograph record containing a text by Camus on the liberation of Paris, but it was read disappointingly by an effeminate male voice. Although quite taken with his hostess, Camus found time to speak with her husband, discussing psychoanalysis and *Caligula,* even displaying familiarity with a little-known paper on that Roman emperor written by a Viennese psychoanalyst. Camus told Mrs. Eidelberg that he found New York overpowering; when all the lights went on in the evening the city seemed to be on fire —a frightening experience for him.[14]

Some days later Marthe Eidelberg accompanied him to a cocktail party given in his honor at the Institut Français on East Sixtieth Street (now called French Institute-Alliance Française). While she knew that many of the French settled in the United States had been anti-Free French, partisans either of Pétain or of General Giraud, at the party everyone wished to shake hands with the guest of honor, for of course they had all been patriots. Whenever Mrs. Eidelberg noticed someone with a reputation as a notorious Vichyite, she would whisper to Camus: "He's a scoundrel!" They had a wonderful time.[15] Presumably this party was held in conjunction with a talk that Camus gave at the insti-

tute on "Le Théâtre à Paris aujourd'hui." Nothing remains of the talk
except the institute's log, which recorded that there were 294 persons in
the audience and the weather was fair; weather was always mentioned
in the log because it had an effect on attendance. The capacity of the
hall was about three hundred.[16] Camus also visited New York's Lycée
Français, where he chatted with students on their own level, answered
questions. He also talked with Pierre Brodet, then a teacher there, and
autographed a copy of *L'Etranger* for him.[17]

Early in his stay Camus was able to move out of the mothy hotel and
into a small duplex apartment in a twin-tower high-rise standing on
Central Park West between Sixty-second and Sixty-third streets, a
1930s streamline-style building called Century Apartments, and he got
it without having any rent to pay. His benefactor was a furrier named
Zaharo, believed to be of Polish extraction; his illiterate immigrant father had grown rich in furs. Apparently Zaharo had heard Camus speak
and was enthralled, and phoned Camus' hotel to tell him that he was
leaving town on business, begging him to take his apartment. At first
Camus refused, and Zaharo asked if he could telephone occasionally to
see if Camus would change his mind. Then Camus caught cold and
when Zaharo called again he accepted. Camus told his wife one story of
Zaharo's he remembered. Zaharo's father had become blind, and his
son would read to him. One day the son read Plato's account of the
death of Socrates and the father said: "From now on you will read me
this until the day I die," and the son complied.[18]
  The apartment was by no means an elegant one. It consisted of a
living room and a kitchen on one level, a small bedroom or two and a
bath upstairs. Camus would have an American breakfast at the corner
drugstore: orange juice, two eggs and bacon, toast and coffee.[19]

Soon Camus had created his own nucleus of friends and drinking or at
least walking companions in New York. He remained in close touch
with Pierre Rubé, and when he felt a fever rising—as happened occasionally—he would phone the doctor for reassurance. Rubé observed
that Camus liked or needed constant companionship, whether of men
or of women. They went together to cheap restaurants and cafeterias, to
a Harlem dance hall to listen to jazz. Clearly Camus was feeling very
alone in this city so unlike anything he had ever known. Rubé also observed that men a bit older than Camus, like himself, always felt fa-
therly toward Camus, and women felt motherly. Camus expressed astonishment at the beauty of American women, but also experienced
what he called their terrifying inaccessibility, and Rubé himself knew of
cases where Frenchmen had become impotent with American women,

for they confessed to him afterwards. It was in the Bowery, where the women were old and ravaged, that Camus relaxed noticeably.[2] Even Claude Lévi-Strauss, who saw very little of Camus during the latter's nearly three-month visit, once took Camus to dinner in Chinatown, then to a brassy cabaret in the Bowery specializing in women singers who were not young, "in general grotesque and of a repulsive aspect."[4] Was it then Lévi-Strauss who introduced Camus to Sammy's Bowery Follies (then a popular cabaret answering to this description)? The notion is pleasant.

One evening Pierre Rubé and Camus went to pick up A. J. Liebling at *The New Yorker*. Liebling took them to Little Italy to look into shopwindows displaying elegant bridal gowns, so incongruous on these grim streets. Liebling led them on from bar to bar, although Camus was careful about his drinking because of his ever fragile health. Their escort then showed them the Bowery, ushered them into bars to hear third-rate singers. Was it rather Liebling who introduced Camus to this scene which so fascinated him? By the end of the evening Liebling was quite drunk, but his two companions managed to get him into a taxi and gave the driver his home address.[2] Camus later told a Paris friend how he had loved Liebling at first sight.

One night, Camus would recall, they staged a drinking contest which Camus won (but that is inconsistent with Dr. Rubé's observation on his friend's cautious behavior). Liebling amused Camus with a story of how he had invented a boxer whom he reported on regularly in *The New Yorker*.[20] The Camus-Liebling friendship would be carried on under similarly rowdy circumstances during the American writer's visits to France. And in the last days of Liebling's life, in delirium, before he went into his final coma, he spoke only in French and was apparently addressing his friend Camus. But Camus had died by that time. In the spring of Liebling's final year, 1963, he traveled to North Africa in the hope of alleviating a deep depression that had settled over him; his wife saw it as a search for Camus.[21] Liebling once observed comically about his friend: "His energies were dissipated in creative writing and we lost a great journalist."[22]

One day Camus even asked Eugene Sheffer of the Maison Française to accompany him to Sammy's Bowery Follies; Sheffer remembered Camus saying that his curiosity had been aroused by advertising for the establishment. Was Sheffer then the witness to Camus' introduction to the *Walpurgisnacht* of lower Manhattan? Sheffer recalled an incredible show in which all of the actresses were so-called former burlesque queens now well along in middle age. As he watched these faded, overweight women go through their bumps and grinds, he felt it was both a hilarious and somewhat degrading performance, and he noticed that Camus got a great kick out of it.[13] What Camus *was* feeling, as he told his journal, was that here at last was the concrete.

Camus tried to put some order into the disorder of his impressions of this city which reminded him of Oran, impressions he was picking up in the ways we have just observed. He put much of what he saw and felt into long and funny letters to the Michel Gallimards, letters which he knew would also be read by his wife, who was then "camping" in their apartment at the top of the Gallimard town house on the Rue de l'Université. And then when he got home he borrowed the letters and made of them an essay he called "Pluies de New York"[23] published in the Pléiade edition of his work. (The chief source of the essay was the letter he wrote the Gallimards on April 20, and which he signed "Al Capone"; his letters to Michel and Janine usually bore comical salutations and occasionally comical signatures.) Since he wrote these impressions first of all for friends and family, they can be taken as the closest approximation to what he really felt at the time; since they are available in extant publications in both French and English, they need not be repeated, and only (for the sake of thoroughness) the reference to the Bowery Follies will be cited:

> I knew what was waiting for me, these nights on the Bowery, where at a few steps from those splendid shops with wedding dresses (not one of the wax brides was smiling), some 500 yards of such shops, live forgotten men, men who let themselves be poor in the city of bankers. It is the city's most sinister neighborhood, where one doesn't meet any women, where one man in three is drunk, and where in a curious café, seemingly out of a Western movie, one can see fat old actresses who sing of ruined lives and maternal love, stamping their feet at the refrain, and shaking spasmodically, to the roaring of the audience, the packets of shapeless flesh with which age had covered them. Another old woman plays the drums, and she resembles an owl, and some evenings one feels like knowing her life story, at one of those rare moments when geography disappears, and when solitude becomes a somewhat disordered truth.

And perhaps one might linger over this essay to savor the nice things Camus had to say about New York, about which he said he still knew nothing, although he had "powerful and fugitive emotions, an impatient nostalgia, instants of heartbreak." He loved the mornings and the nights of New York.

After the lecture at the French Institute on April 16, a young woman seated with her mother in the audience was introduced to Camus. Her name was Patricia Blake, she had completed her college program at

Smith (although she would not receive her diploma until June), and she was working for *Vogue* magazine, writing for the New York *Times Book Review*. She was nineteen years old and stunning. That, and the fact that she was intelligent and spoke good French, made her the most desirable possible companion for the tourist Albert Camus. He lost no time in making a date with her (for the very next day). Although she had to spend days at her job, they could have lunch together, and evenings they would go sightseeing, to meet friends, or just walking; she also accompanied him to his lectures. He had brought his draft of *La Peste,* and she typed part of it for him while he was in New York. There was also time for serious talking, and she allowed herself to be persuaded to change her politics: She had been sympathetic to Communism, and his description of the crimes of Stalinism made her feel differently about the Soviet Union. (Patricia Blake was later to become an authority on the Soviet Union and things Communist.) After Camus' return to France the relationship was pursued in correspondence and when Patrica Blake would visit France; for a while she lived in Paris when she was married to the composer Nicolas Nabokov.

She was also concerned for Camus, for she was observing a side of him that he managed to hide from his public: He ran a fever every day in New York. If he felt very ill he would ask her to leave him; that happened four or five times. (She felt that he was coughing up blood but she could not be certain of it.) His attitude toward the future seemed that of a man who did not expect to live a long time. He never explicitly told her that his illness could be fatal but she felt that it must be. She knew that he was seeing a doctor although she did not know who it was. (But she did accompany Camus on his outings with Pierre Rubé.)

His talk about life was cynical; it took on the form of black humor. He told deathbed jokes, e.g., the last words of the writer Alfred Jarry, while friends leaned over his hospital bed. Finally he said, "A toothpick," and died. And when Ingres was dying his wife called in a priest, although the painter had been an atheist all his life. The priest told him: "You will soon be in the face of God." Ingres: "Always in the face, never in profile." Camus was fascinated by funeral services in New York and asked Patricia Blake to buy him undertakers' journals, one of which was called *Sunnyside.*

She was to discover that he loved much New York lore: Chinatown, the Bowery, popular dance halls, garish and gawdy night clubs with floor shows. Although his understanding of spoken English was slight, he would ask his young companion to listen to conversations at adjoining restaurant tables and repeat them to him. (If he could not carry off a conversation in English, he could read the language, and would sometimes write her a few lines in English.) They would go to restaurants like Le Steak Pommes Frites or Larré's, went to the theater a great deal (while the Old Vic was visiting New York with Laurence Olivier, they saw Sheridan's *The Critic* and Sophocles' *Oedipus Rex* on the same bill). Camus didn't seem to care for music, so they attended no concerts, but they did go to the Chinese opera, which was then housed in the foundations of a lower Manhattan bridge, where Camus was fascinated by the stagehands who walked onto the stage during the performance to change the scenery. They would try different restaurants in Chinatown. (Patricia Blake would later write an article about Chinatown, and one of the first surveys of the American "death industry," about which she became interested through Camus, for *Life* magazine.) Then they would go to Grand Street, where he would look at the rows of shops displaying wedding dresses (which he presumably saw first with Liebling).

Camus liked the Central Park Zoo and was an indefatigable visitor; Blake may have seen it with him twenty times. They would walk across the park from the Century Apartments, often in the afternoon, occasionally in the evening. Camus enjoyed observing the monkeys.

She discovered that he had a phobia about going into stores, and she would walk in to make purchases for him. (This led to a misunderstanding: Once, when Pierre Rubé was walking downtown with Camus and Blake, they stopped at the window of a chocolate shop, perhaps on Fifty-seventh Street, and Rubé heard Camus ask the young woman to go inside to buy the chocolates he was pointing to. Rubé assumed that this was an example of Camus' sovereign attitude toward women,[2] when in fact it was an example of the phobia Blake had already witnessed.)

Camus was accompanied by his young admirer to meet people he had to see in New York, such as the writer Pierre de Lanux, who drove Camus to Fort Tryon Park for the view, and then to New Jersey, where they admired the East Orange Public Library and its large children's reading room until Camus noticed that the library's card index under "Philosophy" listed William James and no one else. They met publisher Jacques Schiffrin, who had been a friend of Gide (about whom Camus made a derisive remark which brought on laughter, but Blake didn't know whether or not Camus was joking about his lack of appreciation of Gide's talents). Camus had met the Thomist philosopher Etienne Gilson and they spent an evening with him. After dinner they went to a noisy night club where she fainted and Gilson seemed, to say the least, out of his element. She went with Camus to the NBC studios for an interview of Camus by George Day, beamed to France on April 27.[24]

Day had begun the interview by saying that he did not desire polite stereotyped phrases but wished Camus' impressions of "our country."

Camus replied that indeed he could give impressions but not judgments, because it was difficult to judge a nation which required six days to cross from coast to coast. As for details, they could have no significance in themselves. He noted that garbage collectors wore gloves, that brides in shopwindows look sad, while advertising is all smiles.

As for general judgments: Camus said that he had come to the United States as other Europeans had, with the vague hope that a formula or life style then being sought in Europe could be found there. He couldn't be definitive about what he had discovered. Were Americans interested in French culture? Yes, if the curiosity expressed by students in the universities, and if their theses and examination subjects were indicative. While the demands, problems, and confusions of American and French youth were similar, American young people did not seem ready to change things, probably because they lived in a more stable society, an advantage for them, although for Frenchmen who needed to feel less alone it could not seem an advantage. Was it a lack of dynamism? Certainly not, Camus told his interviewer and his French radio audience. He was impressed with the vigor and the sturdiness of young Americans, struck by the fact that there was no sign of ruse in their expressions, and when you come from Europe that was important.

What young Americans lacked most, Camus told Day, was passion in the sense he understood it, passion for justice, for example. The French may have this passion because recent events required it of them, and he agreed with Day finally that Americans could be as passionate for justice as the French. Day suggested that traditional Anglo-Saxon reserve explained the absence of visible excitement.[25]

The first out-of-town campus visit was to Vassar, on April 6, where he discovered a legion of long-legged starlets decorating the lawns. The college's *Vassar Miscellany News* of April 3 had described Camus' visit to the United States as "one of the cultural events of the season"—the phrase perhaps taken from Justin O'Brien in the *Herald Tribune*. Camus spoke on "Le Théâtre français d'aujourd'hui" at Avery Hall under the auspices of the Department of French and the French Club. When Sartre had been in New York, he had declined a visit to Vassar but said that Camus would come, so when she heard he was on his way Mrs. Maria Tastevin-Miller, then chairman of the Department of French, asked the French Consulate in New York to request Camus' appearance. He took a train to Poughkeepsie, and told Mrs. Tastevin-Miller that he was very impressed with the student body, especially with her French speakers; he spoke to the audience in French without an interpreter.[26] On April 15 he spoke on "La Crise de l'homme," this time at the New School for Social Research in Manhattan; on April 16 he made the capital acquaintance of Patricia Blake after his talk at the

Institut Français; and on April 29 he spoke at Pendleton Hall at Wellesley, where the subject was announced as "Littérature française d'aujourd'hui."[27]

At Bryn Mawr he stayed at the home of Germaine Brée, who happened to be a childhood friend of the Faures of Oran; later she would become an authority on Camus' writing. He spoke informally to the students, his general theme being how to cope with contemporary problems without embracing a metaphysics or a system.[28] Either at the same meeting or at another session with students at the college he discussed the war and its effect on French writers just beginning to be known in the United States. Someone asked why he had left the existentialist movement and he replied impatiently that he was not an existentialist. He described his divergences with Sartre, talked movingly about Dostoevsky. Someone asked him what he thought of Proust now, and he answered something like "not much." A member of the audience noticed that he smoked incessantly. Patrica Blake joined him for the day, and they traveled back to New York by train after a further talk given in a large auditorium in Philadelphia (whose sponsorship and audience have not been traced).[24]

Back in New York, he spoke at Brooklyn College. It was a special occasion: The school was inaugurating its second Journée Française. Before Camus' talk President Harry D. Gideonse made a brief speech on France, a student recited Paul Eluard's hymn to freedom. Camus gave the student audience his impressions of the American youth he had been meeting on various campuses, for this was to be the final stop on his tour of Eastern universities. He said that he thought youth was the same everywhere in the world. But he had expected to find American youth more passionate. Inertia is man's greatest temptation. It is not enough to do one's job; youth must be active in the world, for the world would be saved by this generation or it would not be saved. He described a "solidarity of misfortune": If we accept the power principle then we must struggle. Concerning European pessimism (life is tragedy) and American optimism (life is marvelous), he felt that a synthesis was necessary. "We must create, on the level of sensibility, the United States of the world that we are incapable of founding on the juridical level." He appealed for material help for French students, but also for exchanges of correspondence and then of persons.

After the talk he replied to questions. Once more he was asked if he was an existentialist. He said he was not, because existentialism claims to answer all questions, which is impossible for a single philosophy, and he wanted the freedom to say yes as well as no. The meeting ended with a piano solo of music by Debussy.[29]

He had time for a visit to Washington, D.C. Here, and along Riv-

erside Drive in Manhattan, from the top of the Hotel Plaza overlooking
Central Park, he was inspired to reveries by a peculiarly American
landscape, where crowds seemed not to spoil a certain softness and lack
of tension he found in this country.[30] He had two days on the beach at
Falmouth on Cape Cod, where he discovered lobster Newburg. He met
and talked with more people he admired and with whom he could
relate, such as Waldo Frank, who he felt was one of the rare superior
men he had met in the United States. He visited the Chiaromontes at
their West Eighth Street Greenwich Village apartment, met personalities
such as the writer and critic Lionel Abel there.[6] He was spotted at a
soirée at William Phillips', co-founder of *Partisan Review,* on West
Eleventh Street, in an apartment described as an informal salon, a
home away from home for New York's intellectuals;[31] perhaps Chiaromonte brought him there.

On the lighter side, he teamed up with Jacques Schoeller, the
brother of Guy, Michel Gallimard's friend. He had been an early employee of Gaston Gallimard at Publications Zed, producing trashy magazines such as *Detective,* and later set up an advertising agency for
Gallimard. During the war he escaped from a prison camp and from
North Africa went to Mexico, where he founded a radio station. He
knew New York well, and took Camus around on foot. They saw
Harlem, Coney Island, and Brooklyn, the West Side Highway, night
clubs, the old skating rink on Fifty-second Street where organ music accompanied the skaters' acrobatics. Schoeller found Camus naïve and
shy, with little experience of the wide world. His candor seemed almost
childlike, he was not entirely sure of himself. And whenever Camus
wasn't busy with Patricia Blake or with cultural obligations, he would
phone Schoeller; they would arrange to meet at the end of a reception
or other social encounter, and then go out on the town.[32]

On April 11 the firm of Alfred A. Knopf published *L'Etranger* in an
English translation by Stuart Gilbert. It was greeted in that day's New
York *Times* in a review by Charles Poore, who called *The Stranger* "a
novel of crime and punishment" which "should touch off in this country
a renewed burst of discussion about the young French writers who are
at the moment making more unusual literary news than the writers of
any other country." Despite what he felt to be the "Britannic" quality of
Gilbert's translation, the reviewer pronounced Camus' novel "brilliantly
told." The book and the author were naturals for Knopf, who had pio-
neered in modern European literature, and Alfred Knopf's wife and
best talent scout, Blanche, had met Camus in Paris almost a year
earlier, and would be meeting him there again and again on her trips to
the Continent.[33] Knopf threw a party for Camus on the old Astor Roof

above Times Square.³⁴ *The New Yorker*'s "Talk of the Town" interview
appeared shortly thereafter: the Sunday New York *Times Book Review*
had already published a report from John L. Brown in Paris identifying
Camus as an outstanding leader among writers who had emerged in
France since the war. Then in *The New Republic* of April 29
Chiaromonte reviewed the American edition of *L'Etranger* in the form
of a lengthy introduction to Camus the man and the writer; the novel
was described as "admirable."

Camus received consecration of sorts in the June 1 *Vogue,* which
published a somewhat coy full-page head portrait of him by the photographer Cecil Beaton, over a caption which described Camus
as a "slight, thirty-two-year-old Frenchman." If *Vogue* saw Camus as
slight, it may have been that in America he did seem slight; Beaton
himself was over six feet tall. Camus was extremely thin at the time,
often seemed tired and sickly. His clothes didn't fit him properly—they
were baggy, and this too would have contributed to the impression.²⁴
He was nevertheless taken by the ladies of *Vogue* for a young
Humphrey Bogart, an observation which delighted him.²³

Then the New York *Post* opened its magazine section on June 5
with a full-page interview by Dorothy Norman, who reported that "As
France's most talented young writer to emerge from the 'resistance' period, he has had a warm welcome from many in this country." She
noted his shudder when asked whether he was an existentialist. "You
can explain nothing by way of principles and ideologies," he declared.
He felt that "revolt" usually implied romantic revolt à la Byron or a
form of Marxism. "But revolt can be much more modest in its implications." He gave the example of the hero of *L'Etranger,* "a man who refuses to lie. . . . If a man dares to say what he truly feels, if he revolts
against having to lie, then society will destroy him in the end." The interviewer found Camus modest in his comments, including his impressions of New York, where once again he explained that he was moved
not by skyscrapers but by the Bowery. He preferred Melville and Henry
James to any twentieth-century writers. He dressed and spoke in a
relaxed way (tweed; no jargon). If he was struck by the fact that he
could wander around the United States without identity papers, the
American attitude to Negroes disturbed him. He had expressed his own
feelings, he noted, by seeing to it that the works of Richard Wright were
translated and published in Paris. He felt that Europe could offer something to America, a sense of disquiet.

Outlining his future, he described the completed cycle of books on
aburdity, and that to come on revolt. Finally there would be a novel,
essay, and play based on the concept "we are." What then? "Then," he
said with a smile, "there will be a fourth phase in which I shall write a

book about love." He had given up journalism in order to devote himself to writing, but it was not easy to support a wife and two children
that way in present-day France, especially when he refused to compromise or to popularize.

While in New York, Camus had one serious piece of work to do
for his friends at Gallimard. The French publisher had a contract with
Antoine de Saint-Exupéry signed in 1929 which gave it all rights to his
future work (at that time, and until a French law of 1957 barred such
agreements, publishers could obtain such an option on an author's future work), but when Saint-Exupéry came to the United States in 1938
he had signed a contact with an American publisher, Reynal & Hitchcock, for *Wind, Sand and Stars,* and during the occupation of France
had written and published with Reynal & Hitchcock *Flight to Arras* and
*The Little Prince.* Now Saint-Exupéry was dead, and Gallimard filed
suit in New York against the American house.[35] Gaston Gallimard's
brother Raymond, Michel's father, came to New York to follow the
proceedings, and was roundly attacked in the New York French-language weekly *La Victoire:*

> Is he coming to pursue the ridiculous and scandalous law suits
> against American publishers who committed the crime of helping
> French authors during the somber years of the occupation [of
> France] . . . while the *NRF* had Drieu La Rochelle as its
> Fuehrer? Is he coming, on the contrary, to put an end to a policy
> which discredits all of French publishing?

Saint-Exupéry's widow, then living in New York, had asked the
French-language press not to speak of the matter until the Gallimards
had arrived in New York, and now the press was anxious to know
more.[36] Camus served mainly as an intermediary, meeting the widow,
providing moral support to Raymond Gallimard. He was convinced of
the moral right of the Gallimards, of the low state of U.S. publishing,
especially of French writers during the war—or at least this was the argument he used to appease the Gallimards.[23] The suit ended without
bloodshed, with a court order providing some satisfaction to each side.

The American stage adaptation of *Caligula* was to be done by a
young producer named Harald Bromley, although the project would
never get off the ground. Nevertheless Camus was impressed by this
sympathetic and enterprising young man. When it was time for him to
fulfill his lecture commitment in French Canada at the end of May,
Bromley offered to drive him there, and even bought a secondhand car
for the trip.[2] They left New York on May 25 to drive up through the
Adirondacks, stopped at a mountain inn at what seemed a remote part
of that region (at Camp Downey, Clayburg, New York); for a brief

moment Camus imagined himself, in the face of the silence of nature, the simplicity of the lodgings, the remoteness, staying here forever —cutting ties with the world as he knew it.[30]

They arrived in Montreal on May 26. But this time Camus had really had enough, and he was anxious to return to France. He had even tried to change his Montreal lecture date, but the Canadians replied that you can postpone a lecture, you can't advance its date. He had no good things to say about this Canadian experience, although on the whole he was satisfied with his transatlantic trip. It had been useful to him; he had even discovered that he was not a bad public speaker. Physically he was in better shape than he had been for a long time; with hot baths and vitamins he had gained some weight. But it was time to go home now.[23]

He remembered to arrange for shipment to his family of a food parcel—in fact a crate weighing 176 pounds and containing six pounds of sugar, six pounds of coffee, three pounds of powdered eggs, six pounds of flour, four pounds of rice, six pounds of chocolate, thirty pounds of baby food, twenty-eight pounds of soap, and other products, not to speak of some $160 in purchases which accompanied him. On June 21, after ten days at sea, he was in Bordeaux, where his wife and the Michel Gallimards were waiting for him, and they drove back to Paris in Michel Gallimard's automobile.[3]

On shipboard his old travel sadness had settled in again. He had time to think about what was in store for him on his return.

> In 25 years I shall be 57 [he told his journal]. Thus 25 years to create my work and to find what I seek. Then, old age and death. I know what is most important for me. And I still find the way to yield to small temptations, to waste time in vain conversation or sterile strolling. I have mastered two or three things in me. But how far I am from that superiority which I need so badly.[30]

# PART III

---

# Fame

# 30

---

## NEITHER VICTIMS NOR EXECUTIONERS

> Thus we all know, without the shadow of a doubt, that the
> new order we are seeking cannot be merely national or
> even continental, and especially not western or eastern. It
> must be universal.
>
> "Ni Victimes ni Bourreaux"

Camus returned to Paris to discover that he had been given a Resistance Medal, the first of many decorations he would be offered or receive without his having asked for it; he would refuse them when he could. But this was an official act of government; a decree published in the *Journal Officiel* (of July 11, 1946). His was a somewhat higher distinction than the ordinary medal; he got the Rosette. In all 4,345 Rosettes were given out, in addition to 42,902 regular Resistance Medals.[1] Replying to the congratulations of his elementary school teacher Louis Germain, he made his position clear: "I didn't ask for it and I don't wear it. What I did was very little and it hasn't yet been given to friends who were killed at my side."[2]

But there was no doubt about it now: He was a celebrity, even if he fought off honors. The symbols of fame could assume diverse forms. While he was in the United States and Francine Camus was living with their infant twins at the Michel Gallimards', she advertised in the press for a helper. A young woman applied who was hired at once. But she was a curious helper. Janine Gallimard's own maid confided to her that the new recruit wasn't very experienced. And she was always asking questions about people who came to visit. Then when Camus returned, Alexandre Astruc, a young writer for *Combat* who would later be a successful film maker, was invited to dinner by the Camus' at the

Gallimard apartment. When Francine's maid served coffee, Astruc's face reddened. Later he phoned Janine to warn her that the maid was really a reporter. Informed by Janine, Francine stopped the helper/reporter on her way from the bedroom to the bathroom with the children's chamber pot. "You can't spend another five minutes here," she told the girl. "Can I at least empty the chamber pot?" And she confessed that she was free-lance but had planned to write a story for a weekly scandal sheet. Camus warned the papers not to print anything.[3] (Simone de Beauvoir used the incident in her roman à clef *Les Mandarins,* although she made Sartre the victim.)

The irony is that Camus was not yet a successful writer, not *materially* successful. If *L'Etranger* had begun to sell when Camus became known as the editor of *Combat,* and if *Caligula* on stage kept his name before the public, he was making little money from his writings or his job, found it hard to make ends meet, and was depending on the Gallimards even for shelter in the austerity economy of post-Liberation France. Worse, the work to come was coming hard. He had been writing *La Peste* for—how many years? He had had the book with him in Oran, in Le Panelier, Paris, New York; the history of France was being written faster than this elusive novel. A man as concerned with present achievement as he was knew that what counted was work in progress. In fact he would have another year of labor on *La Peste,* not a day of it seemingly joyous. "In all my life," he told his journal, "never such a feeling of failure. I am not even certain that I shall reach the end. At certain times, however . . ."

To young Patricia Blake, who would henceforth be the receiver of many confidences, for she was both intelligent and sympathetic to his artistic problems besides being sympathetic *tout court,* he reported these doubts. He was determined to complete the book even if he saw it as a failure—a *livre manqué*—but he was as sure that it could be published. He turned in circles, unable to write, at loose ends with respect to his career; he thought he might work better in the country.[4] Once more the Camus had the use of a house outside the city, at Saint-Loup-de-Naud near the cheese-producing center of Brie to the southeast, lent to them by the painter Clairin. Then they were put up at "Les Brefs," the home of Michel Gallimard's mother (Raymond's first wife, Yvonne) near Les Moutiers in the Vendée. In fact this was a small castle set in the center of a pine forest; Camus worked long days and still had time for horseback riding in the late summer evenings. But the house had no electricity, and one had to carry one's own gas lamp to bed.

During their stay he made a trip to Paris and returned with Michel Gallimard in Michel's light plane, which had been given to him by his father. (The following winter, when Michel offered to take Camus with him on a flight to Tunisia for a winter holiday, Camus' wife put her foot down. Finally it was Michel's illness—the discovery of his tuberculosis —which put an end to that project.)[5]

When Camus returned to Paris in September, he had a finished manuscript of his novel—but at first he dared not reread it.[4] *"La Peste* is a tract," he told his journal—in despair?

He made one more trip before the end of September. With his friend Jules Roy, who had been invited by the novelist Henri Bosco, a regular resident of the village, he traveled south to Lourmarin in Provence, which would become his last home and resting place. Accompanied by author and editor Jean Amrouche and Odile de Lalène (later Mrs. Odile Tweedie), they rode in a third-class coach train. Camus seemed to be taken with Lourmarin,[6] but apparently none of his friends knew that he had visited the place before. It was to his journal that he confided that this was the "First evening after so many years." He also noted the "immense silence, the cypress tree whose tip shudders at the depths of my fatigue. Solemn and austere country— despite its staggering beauty." There is also some confusion as to whether he met René Char at Avignon at this time. The Pléiade edition of Camus' work says that he did, but all the evidence suggests that the visit took place the following year.

Autumn in Paris is always a charge of electricity. It is called *la rentrée,* and derives its importance from the scope of the previous summer's exodus, when Paris's cultural and social life virtually disintegrates. (For a man of Saint-Germain-des-Prés to be in Paris anytime between July 1 and September 15 usually requires an explanation to friends.) This autumn 1946 was a particularly important *rentrée* for Camus. After his long absence in the United States, a long summer hiatus, he would now have to settle down to serious work. To put the final touches on *La Peste,* of course, but also to work on—to complete if possible—the essay on revolt. No sooner had he returned to France at the beginning of summer than he recorded in his journal a commencement for that essay: "The only really serious moral problem is murder. . . ."

It was almost a word-for-word repetition, not without irony, of the opening of *Le Mythe de Sisyphe,* except that "murder" would now replace "suicide," reflecting the shift of his concern from his personal relationship to the world to man's relationship to the world, to historical necessity, institutional murder (in the universe of Stalinism). Indeed, if these would not be the actual words of the opening of *L'Homme révolté,* they are a useful gloss on its introductory chapter.

On his return to Paris he looked in at *Combat,* and he could not have liked what he saw. For one thing, the unity of action of the resistance years had long since shattered into fragile splinters. The Communists were strong, and tugging hard in one direction; the Gaullists, now shaping up into an ideology, anti-Communist but rigorously nationalistic, in another. On the international scene the great powers were moving apart from their wartime coalition, and in France each seemed to exercise a lunar attraction, pulling one way (toward the United States) and the other (toward the U.S.S.R.). All of this fractioning was playing havoc with resistance ideals in general and in particular, even at the most idealistic, least partisan of resistance newspapers, *Combat*. Camus got an inkling of the problem when he ventured over to the Rue Réaumur to see his old friends. While Camus was in New York, Raymond Aron had joined the staff to write the editorials. An old friend of Sartre (he had brought Sartre's first manuscripts to Malraux and to Gallimard), already enjoying a distinguished teaching career, Aron had been editor in chief of *France Libre* in London during the war.

But not everybody was pleased with what they considered the turn to the right represented by Aron's presence on the paper. Already in May, Jacques-Laurent Bost told Sartre and Beauvoir "of the passion that Pia brings to bear to kill the paper in killing himself, of Ollivier whom everybody hates and who feels it, of Aron who is disliked because he understands *Combat* quite well and says so." (What Aron understood about *Combat* will be apparent in a moment.) Beauvoir, who reported this in her memoirs, also remarked that Camus himself on his return from New York seemed less friendly to the United States than Sartre had been, although his hostility to the U.S.S.R. was not lessened by the experience. In his absence, she said, Aron and Ollivier had favored the Socialist Party, whose majority was petit-bourgeois, and Camus did not disavow them. Soon after Camus' return he received Bost in his old office. Aron was just leaving, his parting words being, "I'm off to write my right-wing editorial." Camus expressed astonishment, and Bost told him what he thought of the present line of the paper. "If you're not happy, leave," Camus is supposed to have said. "That's what I'm going to do," Bost replied, and Camus called after him: "That's gratitude."[7] Beauvoir observes that if Camus had stopped writing for *Combat* it was, she heard, because of Aron's growing influence; he was purposely avoiding politics.[8]

Actually Aron had joined *Combat* long after Camus' withdrawal (for illness and in order to write), although it is true that on Camus' return his relations with Aron were not of the best. Aron mocked the presence of so many intellectuals on the staff, the uncertainty of its leadership; workers confided to him: "If only we had a boss"—for Pia wasn't interested in being one. There was a faithful readership but a pitifully small one, growing smaller all the time. Aron would joke: "We're read by everybody, of course, but everybody is 40,000 people."⁹ Then in May 1946, at the time of a national referendum at which voters were asked to approve a new French Constitution already adopted by the Constituent Assembly (supported by the Communists, opposed by de Gaulle because of its emphasis on government by parliament), there was agitation at *Combat* (so Bost reported to Beauvoir) because of the articles of Aron and Ollivier favoring a *non* vote; others on the paper favored a *oui* for the new Constitution. "It seems that they all stay on the newspaper because of the personal charm of Pia," noted Beauvoir, "whose anti-Communism makes one forget that he pretends to be a man of the left."⁸

Camus did not in fact return to *Combat* at this time. Not yet, despite the tone of the conversation with Bost; he was only morally one of the editors and directors of the newspaper in 1946. But he would contribute to the newspaper's survival, and incidentally organize some of his present political and moral thinking, in a series of articles published in *Combat* from November 19 to 30, 1946, under the general title "Ni Victimes ni Bourreaux" (Neither Victims nor Executioners). As preparation, Camus had the political ferment of post-Liberation Paris, the urgency of the late-night talks with Sartre, and now also with Koestler, who was a living witness to the crimes of Stalinism. He recorded a conversation with Koestler in his journal: "The end justifies the means only if the reciprocal exchange is reasonable." You can send a Saint-Exupéry on a fatal mission in order to save a regiment, but you cannot deport millions of persons and stamp out freedom for a future good.

Yet while writing "Ni Victimes ni Bourreaux" he was filled with uncertainty: "Déchirement" was the word he used in his journal. Meanwhile he participated in a discussion (on October 22) where he spelled out in a few phrases what would be the theme of *L'Homme révolté* and of all of his political philosophy until the end of his life. "It seems to me incontestable that we are living in a world of terror," he affirmed,

> to the extent that a man believes in the inevitability of progress,
> to the extent that he believes in inevitable historical logic . . . in
> relying on his absolute rationalism, one places historical values
> above the values that we are accustomed by education or by prej-
> udice to consider valid. Therefore if we rely on absolute rational-
> ism or on one or another idea of progress, we accept the principle
> that the end justifies the means. . . .²

Arthur Koestler—"a newcomer with a tumultuous personality," according to Beauvoir—entered their lives in October 1946 when he came to Paris for the staging of a play. In her memoirs Beauvoir describes this tumultuous personality in some detail and with concealed admiration, concealed because of his politics diametrically opposed to that of the Sartrians, but privately the relationship of Beauvoir and Koestler could not have been closer. Or is it because the character based on Koestler has a brief affair with the character based on Simone de Beauvoir in the latter's *Les Mandarins* that Saint-Germain-des-Prés believed that Beauvoir and Koestler were lovers? During the weeks he spent in Paris, in any event, Koestler became a fast friend and drinking partner of the Sartre-Camus group (*Les Mandarins* also reports a memorable evening of Russian gypsy music at a posh cabaret earlier described in her memoirs, *La Force des choses*). In his cups Koestler reproached not only Sartre but even Camus for being soft on the Soviet Union. Camus is quoted (by Beauvoir) as having confided to Sartre and to her: "What we have in common, you and I, is that individuals count most of all for us; we prefer the concrete to the abstract, people to doctrines; we place friendship above politics." The late hour and the alcohol contributed to the acceptance of that remark by Sartre and Beauvoir, for they continued to feel that they were separated from Camus only by nuances. "If we could write the truth!" she quotes Camus as saying—that theme dear to him.

They continued their drinking in a bistrot in the Halles neighborhood, weeped for humanity as they walked across a bridge over the Seine. "To think that in a few hours I'm going to talk about the writer's responsibility," Sartre remarked, referring to a lecture he was to give that day at the Sorbonne; Camus laughed.[8]

A more serious attempt to deal with the changing world was the meeting held at Koestler's suggestion in André Malraux's apartment in Boulogne-Billancourt just outside Paris on October 29. Koestler felt that, since the French League for Human Rights was under Communist influence, there should be a new organization, and it was up to intellectuals to create it. Malraux was of course present. (The meeting was being held in his home because that is where he worked, and Koestler felt it was important to bring him into the movement.) So was Malraux's longtime friend Manès Sperber. A Jewish refugee from Hitler's Germany and a Comintern emissary who broke with Stalin at the time of the Moscow purge trials, he had known Koestler in the 1930s. Sartre and Camus were also present. Koestler explained the purpose of their encounter, and Sperber carried on from there. Camus agreed with the project, Malraux was skeptical, and Sartre negative. Not to have Sartre was to condemn the project at the start, for Sartre's *Les Temps Modernes* had become an influential channel to opinion, while Malraux's reluctance also discouraged the others.[10]

In his own account of the meeting (where he was seated "between Piero della Francesca and Dubuffet"), Camus set forth in his journal the positions of each of the participants in this intellectual summit meeting. Koestler's desire to define a minimum political morality, to plan specific action. Malraux's unwillingness to believe they could reach the proletariat, and anyway, is the proletariat "the highest historical value?" Camus' attempt to keep the meeting on a philosophical plane. Sartre's "I cannot direct my values uniquely against the U.S.S.R." Koestler warned that as writers they would be traitors before history if they did not denounce what was to be denounced. And during all this time, Camus told his journal, "the impossibility of defining how much fear or truth enters into each person's remarks."

There would be no further meeting, no follow-up to the Koestler scheme.[11]

Soon after that the Boris Vians threw a party, and Maurice Merleau-Ponty was one of the guests. Camus arrived at eleven—Beauvoir is the reporter here—in ill humor. He attacked Merleau-Ponty for an article he had written against Koestler, "Le Yogi et le Prolétaire," of course referring to Koestler's *The Yogi and the Commissar.* Camus accused Merleau-Ponty of trying to justify the Moscow purge trials, and Sartre defended Merleau-Ponty. "Camus, visibly shaken, slammed the door." Sartre and Bost ran after him in the street, but he refused to return. The break was to last until March 1947. Commenting on Camus' behavior, Beauvoir attributes it to Camus' fear that his golden age was coming to a close, the triumphant years during which he was loved by everybody. He was drunk with success, convinced, after the success of *L'Etranger* and the victory of the resistance struggle, that anything he attempted would succeed.

She cited the portrait of the self-satisfied man that Camus himself would later inscribe in *La Chute:* "They found me charming, imagine that. You know what charm is? A manner of hearing others reply yes when one asks no specific question!"

She recalled, too, how at a concert where Camus had come accompanied by a young singer, he had said of the elegant Tout-Paris audience: "When I realize that tomorrow we could impose her on this public!" He advised Beauvoir, when embarrassed by a question at a lecture, to reply with another question; more than once, she said, students were disappointed by Camus' evasive replies. He leafed through books instead of reading them, refused to understand that history opposed his individualism, refused to put aside old dreams. His reaction to criticism or contradiction was a cry of ingratitude.[8] It is true that Simone de

Beauvoir published these observations in 1963, long after the final
break between Sartre and Camus (1952) and after Camus' death.

Other indications, including Camus' own attempts to make sense of
the changing world in the privacy of his journal, and his general self-
doubts, suggest that Beauvoir had not quite understood her onetime
friend. "Obvious that I must cease all creative activity as long as I don't
know," he was writing in his journal at that very moment:

> What made the success of my books is what makes them lies to me.
> In fact I am an average man + demands. The values that I must
> defend and illustrate today are average values. It requires such a
> spare talent that I doubt that I have it.

He attached considerable importance to the series of articles published in *Combat* that November, collectively entitled "Neither Victims
nor Executioners." He published them again in Jean Daniel's magazine
*Caliban* a year later, suggesting at once their timeless quality and the
urgency of the message. Then he published them a third time in the first
collection of his political essays, *Actuelles,* in 1950.

He set the stage in the opening article, "Le Siècle de la peur," published in *Combat* on November 19. In this age of terror, men like himself who refused both the Russian and the American way, who refused
a world where murder is legitimate, were men without a country. Men
who refused to kill or to be killed were automatically caught up in a
series of consequences, and it was the purpose of this series of articles
to discuss some of these consequences. He denied (in the second article) that he was advocating Utopia. He knew murder would go on, but
he refused to justify it. Socialists were forced to choose between the
Communist doctrine that the end justifies the means, that murder is legitimate, and the rejection of Marxism except as a critical tool. If they
accepted the latter, they were showing that our era spelled the end of
ideology, "absolute utopias which destroy themselves in history by the
price that they end up costing."

The end of ideology had brought on a world dominated by the
great powers. The alternative to bloodshed was a "relative Utopia," and
in the longer run a universal order, not through a war which thanks to
modern weapons could kill hundreds of millions, but through mutual
agreement. This meant not only an international political solution, but
an economic one as well, with the pooling of resources. Inside existing
nations men must strive for a new social contract; on the world level, an
international convention should abolish the death penalty. Camus saw
groups of individuals in each country working together not for Utopia
but for honest realism. He himself, he wrote in the concluding article,

believed that he had chosen. To combat silence and fear, to defend dialogue. "All that seems desirable to me at this time is that in the middle of a universe of murder, we decide to think about murder, and to choose." Then, he felt, the world would be divided between those who agreed to be murderers when necessary and those who refused with all their strength. In the years to come, on all continents, the struggle would continue, he affirmed, and if a person who was optimistic about the human condition was crazy, he who despaired was a coward.

There was to be no immediate support for his position, as he noted bitterly to a friend, but the attacks came—attacks which would take on more significance after republication of the series in *Caliban*. His onetime comrades of the Comité National des Ecrivains had been criticizing him in *Lettres Françaises,* and now Claude Morgan wondered who was working hardest for the reactionaries, Camus, Malraux, or Koestler.

He turned away from the political arena now, took up the manuscript of *La Peste*. Tired of looking at the manuscript, he was prepared to hand it in to his publisher if only not to have to read it one more time.[12] It went to the printer just two days after Christmas. He confessed his doubts about the book to Jean Grenier, who was now living in Egypt, too far away to be really helpful. Indeed, for the first time, a book by Camus would be published without Grenier having gone over it first.

In a journal entry a month before his thirty-third birthday this man who certain of his friends felt was too sure of himself observed that he had been losing his memory, that he would have to note more and more details in his journal, "even personal ones, so much the worse." He came down with flu.

At last the apartment on the Rue Séguier was ready for the Camus. And of course what struck them most in this old mansion transformed into offices and now transformed back into living quarters was a good deal of useless space. In town houses like this one the "noble" floors had high ceilings, and although the rooms that had been sliced out of the outsized halls were tiny, the ceilings remained absurdly high. Such space was difficult to heat, impossible to insulate. The Camus flat ran along one wing of the old house, its windows facing the courtyard (and, at the far extreme, the street). There were, to the right of the entrance, a dining room (but the Camus didn't even have a table at first; Camus warned Nicola Chiaromonte that if he came for dinner he'd eat standing up), then a drawing room (overlooking the Rue Séguier) which when it got a desk also served as Camus' office. To the left of the entrance, off a corridor, were the Camus' bedroom, the children's room, a tiny *cabinet de toilette,* tiny kitchen. The apartment is described fairly accurately in that capital story "Jonas" (in English, "The Artist at Work"), although Camus added a makeshift loggia in the story which the Rue Séguier didn't have.[5]

In those early months the material problems—of furnishing and heating the new apartment—heating it as one could in those early post-war years, with coal or wood for the individual stoves—of feeding and clothing the children and themselves—would occupy a considerable portion of the couple's time. If anyone said that Camus was without material problems, he need only visit the Rue Séguier, amidst squawling babies and in an atmosphere which is not betrayed in the comic descriptions of "Jonas." Apart from his evenings on the town with the Sartre crowd, the *Combat* crowd, his peers or young followers, Camus' life was frugal enough. He traveled second class on trains, for example, in the days when there were three classes. He continued to leave his royalties at Gallimard, drawing only what he needed, never knowing how much remained in his account.[13]

But in those times, and for many years to come, to have any kind of living quarters at all in Paris (when one was not born and raised in them) was a blessing. (He had tried to find a place to live not only for himself but for his first wife Simone and her husband, Dr. Cottenceau, and had to explain to his former mother-in-law that the rarest thing of all in Paris was an apartment.[14]

Solving the problem of that first winter, he packed off his wife and the babies to Algeria, where they could stay with the Faures in Oran. (They could not have remained with the Michel Gallimards in any case. When he took the routine medical tests for his marriage to Janine, Michel was informed that he had tuberculosis, and the doctors put him to bed for a year.[15])

With *La Peste* now in production, Camus could take time out for other projects. He gave a talk, later to be widely and carefully read for its hints of his Christianity—or lack of it—on the subject of "The Unbeliever and Christians" at Paris's Dominican monastery (which he felt worthy of publishing in part in *Actuelles*). Here he made it clear that he was speaking to Catholics as one "who does not share your convictions"; he didn't say that Christian truth was an illusion, he just couldn't share it. He confessed that when he had meditated on his polemic with Mauriac concerning the trials of Nazi collaborators, he decided finally that Mauriac had been right, which demonstrated the utility of a dialogue between believers and non-believers. But he blamed the Pope for silence in the face of Nazi terror; Christians must speak out. If not, Christians would live but Christianity would die.

Leaving the meeting at the Latour Maubourg monastery, he encountered an old friend whom he had recruited into the Combat movement. He noted in his journal that the man appeared reticent if friendly.
"You're a Marxist now," Camus began.

"Yes."

"So you will be a murderer."

"I've already been one."

"I too. But I don't want to any more."

"And you were my sponsor," the man said, referring to Camus'
help in finding him an assignment in a clandestine action group.

"Listen," he replied. "Here is the real problem: Whatever happens
I'll always defend you against the firing squad. *You* will be obliged to
agree to my being shot. Think about that."

"I'll think about it."

It was a difficult position to maintain Camus' "Unbearable solitude," he noted immediately after that, "in which I can't believe or resign myself to."

Henceforth he was going to feel alone a good deal, for he *was* to
maintain and to develop this position, increasingly misunderstood, attacked because he was misunderstood—or understood.

Soon he would demonstrate that he meant what he said about
agreeing with Mauriac. He wrote a letter (December 5) to the Minister
of Justice to ask for a pardon for editors of the collaborationist newspaper *Je Suis Partout*. He did not wish to make light of their crimes; he
felt they were guilty; but these men were waiting to be executed each
morning, and that seemed to him sufficient punishment. He had long
believed that justice was paramount, but now he realized its limitations,
and that the country also needed pity.[2] In his journal he suggested to
himself the publication of a collection of material on the earlier trial
and execution of Robert Brasillach.

He continued to be concerned about Franco Spain, wrote a preface
for an anthology on the Spanish cause, *L'Espagne libre.* "Doubtless I
have personal reasons for my choice. By blood Spain is my second
country." In a world without memory, it was good that some remained
faithful, rejecting trade with Spain—passing up imported Spanish oranges.[2]

To change the pace, he agreed to participate in an evening devoted
to the writing of French North Africans, sponsored by a group called
Club Maintenant, held in the curious little meeting room of the Sociétés
Savantes on the Rue Danton. The subject was the "North African Contribution to Modern Literature," with Gabriel Audisio as the billed
speaker, and the contributions of Camus, Amrouche, Armand Guibert,
Fréminville, Raoul Celly, and Jules Roy (in the order in which they

were listed on the flyer announcing the meeting). Audisio later remembered that he had felt that Camus should chair the meeting, but Camus had said, adopting the accent of the Algiers streets: "Come on, you're the chairman type. Why, you're really the father of all of us." (Audisio was then going on forty-seven, Camus had just turned thirty-three.)[16] Indeed, Audisio seemed to have a clearer notion of Camus' position in French letters than those who put together the meeting, or who reported it in the Algerian press, where Camus was treated as only one participant among many, and received less attention than one or two of the others.

December 11 was a cold night, but some one hundred persons attended the Club Maintenant affair. An account of the meeting in an Algiers magazine (which noted that Roblès was not present, being in Algeria at the time) reported that the speakers attempted to define the North African contribution to French literature. Yet one of the characteristics of the North African soul was *pudeur,* an unwillingness to deliver one's secrets, and the audience of mainland Frenchmen was also disconcerted by the unwillingness of the participants to be considered part of a group.[17] Each in turn addressed himself to the question: Is there an Algerian school? There was no agreement, so Audisio commented: "You have before you the wild beasts of Africa."[18] Another listener was moved to hear the Berber Amrouche state with modesty and pride: "We are not foreigners; our masters were French. . . . Our ambition is to compose classical works."

As for Camus, he confirmed that the North Africans owed their talent to the French culture they had received; their particular contribution was "both a sense of spareness, of reserve, and also the sense of friendship, of human brotherhood."[19]

Asked what it meant to feel Algerian, he replied by describing the horror of the Paris subway. When he was pushed further, asked why he wasn't replying in more detail to questions, he snapped: "Perhaps *pudeur,* sir." Audisio felt that the Parisians probably did not understand what he meant, but his Algerian colleagues did.[16]

Sometime during 1946 Camus wrote a short closet play summing up what he presently thought of his Saint-Germain-des-Prés friends, or giving dramatic form to the popular image of that group. His *L'Impromptu des philosophes* seemed to evoke Molière's *L'Impromptu de Versailles,* a one-act comedy in which the seventeenth-century author was replying to his critics (and there is more than a touch in it of Molière's *Le Bourgeois Gentilhomme*). Although various dates have been ascribed to Camus' playlet, the manuscript in the hands of the estate is dated 1946; certainly it could have been written in the period immediately following Camus' altercation with the Sartre group over Merleau-Ponty's attack on Koestler. While it may have been written as a spoof, to be read only at parties, Camus' corrections on the typescript suggest that the text mattered to him (but why did he sign it "Antoine Bailly"?).

One of the characters, Monsieur Néant (Nothingness), is an existentialist. There are also Monsieur Vigne, his daughter Sophie, and Sophie's suitor, Monsieur Melusin, as well as the director of the institution where Néant will be interned. When Melusin asks Vigne for the hand of his daughter, Vigne asks whether Melusin had slept with his own mother, and if he had slept with Sophie. If not, he should have, and should have given her a child; Vigne had been tutored in the modern way by mad Professor Néant, who believes that anguish is "the best thing in the world" and tells Melusin that he isn't Melusin at all but would be so only at the end of his life.[20]

# 31

## THE END OF CAMUS' *COMBAT*

> There are several ways to become rich in journalism. As
> for us, I don't have to say that, entering this daily poor, we
> are leaving it poor.
>
> "A Nos Lecteurs," *Combat*

Camus' doctor took a serious look at his patient's chest now, and decided that it was time to stop the pneumothorax injections he had been
undergoing regularly for the past four years. But he had to get away
from the damp Paris winter, too, from the unheated Rue Séguier (and
from Michel Gallimard and *his* infection). He was sent to Briançon,
over four hundred miles from Paris, 4,375 feet high into France's
Hautes-Alpes, a recommended site for the ill. But also a very remote
one; had he known that it would take sixteen hours to reach Briançon,
he would not have gone there. He was booked into a totally empty
Grand Hotel on January 17, 1947, with snow falling outside, no hot
water or electricity inside. The experience quickly confirmed his dislike
for mountains, and as soon as he arrived, he confessed to his friends, he
wished that he could be on his way out. But in this boring country, this
deserted resort hotel, he could not only rest, he could do that other
thing he came to do: get to work on his book. "The evening which
flows over these cold mountains ends by freezing the heart," he told his
journal. (This followed a draft paragraph for the first chapter of his
next major book, perhaps written during the long train ride.) "I could
never stand this hour of evening anywhere but in Provence or on the
Mediterranean beaches."

For it was time to begin serious work on the second panel of his triptych: the still-untitled "essay on revolt," notes for which had been accumulating for years. He worked. He was getting ten hours of sleep each night, and with country food and siestas after meals he gained weight. He rose each morning at nine, read (Hegel) and took notes until eleven, walked until twelve-thirty, after lunch napped until two-thirty, wrote letters or did other chores until four, when he returned to his writing table (from four to eight, and after dinner until ten-thirty). He read Montaigne in bed, and his journal notes show he was also reading George Orwell. But after a week of solitude he wondered, privately, whether he was up to this task "that I began with the maddest of ambitions." There was a "temptation to give it up." He thought that this long debate with a truth more powerful than himself needed a simpler heart, a greater intelligence. Yet he pursued it, worked through his three-week stay; he would leave Briançon in time to greet Francine, who was returning from Algeria with the twins on February 10.[1]

He noted other ideas in the mournfully peaceful atmosphere of the Alps: a title for the future, "Système," for a book that would be 1,500 pages long (probably the "Création corrigée" which would have dealt with the horror of the concentration camp era). He wanted to do a play about government by women.

Before leaving Paris he had had a serious talk with his former colleagues at *Combat*. Things had taken a turn for the worse on the newspaper. For one thing, the paper shortage had prevented the newspaper from attracting readers by a fuller presentation of news and comment—which of course was *Combat*'s chief appeal to its intelligent audience. It also reduced the number of copies printed and therefore available for sale. Estimates vary, but one key staff member believed that in the earliest post-Liberation months, with a circulation of 200,000-plus copies, *Combat* was the leading newspaper of Paris; certainly it led among serious papers. Then, after initial supplies of newsprint ran out, paper was allocated by calculating the total printing less the number of copies returned unsold, so that it was necessary to maintain sales at a high level in order to keep one's allotment. (The *Combat* people—or some of them—even believed that the man in charge of distributing paper, who published a daily of his own, manipulated the statistics on unsold copies by placing a few copies of *Combat* at the top of a large pile of his own paper's returned copies, since calculations were made by counting the stacks.)

As *Combat* printed fewer copies, fewer were sold. Then during the summer, sales declined because the readership of professors and teachers was on holiday. By 1947 sales had dropped under 100,000.[2] Maintaining circulation without compromising quality was an uphill struggle. Pierre Lazareff, who, as has been seen, had turned the resistance paper *Défense de la France* into a popular daily called *France-Soir,* was said to be confiding to friends with mock seriousness: "Everybody at *Combat* is delirious with joy because they sold seven more copies today."[3]

Camus' absence, and the growing split on the staff between supporters of de Gaulle and those who accepted his eminent role as repository of France's honor but who desired a return to parliamentary government *sans* man on horseback, had contributed to *Combat*'s lack of direction and declining influence. In the final months of the reign of the original team, when the newspaper reappeared on the stands after a month-long printers' strike, it was necessary to deny rumors that the staff was closing down the paper or selling out to a tycoon.

Before going off to Briançon, then, Camus had met with Pia, Bloch-Michel, Jacqueline Bernard, Georges Altschuler, and other members of the original team. He had been persuaded that his presence was required for the salvation of the paper. He promised to come back to help. It would mean leaving his Gallimard job, and the new Espoir series, at least momentarily, and he so informed the Gallimards. Then in further negotiations with his friends at the newspaper it was agreed that he could fulfill his obligation, putting his name and his personal stamp on the paper again, with no more than two hours' work each evening. He liked that idea, for it would symbolize the temporary nature of his intervention. He could remain at Gallimard and take the two hours from his personal writing, but in fact he hoped to continue his writing and to take them from his leisure time. He would try the new arrangement until March 15.[1]

Camus' commitment was a wholehearted one; at least one of his colleagues remembered it as a full-time return.[4] One of the problems henceforth would be to find the strength and the resolution to keep *Combat* independent, for tempting offers were coming in from political and financial groups, and such offers had been resisted until now. It was probably in the last weeks of 1946 or early in 1947 that one of the most significant offers was made. Diomède Catroux, nephew of General Georges Catroux (one of de Gaulle's most trusted emissaries), called on *Combat*'s business manager, Jean Bloch-Michel. Catroux himself had participated in the resistance, had worked for influential members of de Gaulle's cabinet; later he would be director of press and propaganda for the Gaullist Rassemblement du Peuple Français (RPF). The young Catroux explained to Bloch-Michel that General de Gaulle had great respect for *Combat*'s directing team. He suggested that *Combat* become the newspaper of the Gaullist movement, implied that the Gaullists would find the funds needed to keep the paper alive. Bloch-Michel replied that *Combat* was an independent newspaper, but that he was prepared to consult the other directors. He did. They agreed, perhaps with one notable dissent on the part of Albert Ollivier (whose editorials were permeated with the Gaullist mystique) not to follow up Catroux's proposal.[5]

The position of the directors on the Catroux offer was not, however, necessarily indicative of individual feelings about de Gaulle. For most wartime and postwar Gaullists, the General's nay-saying (to fellow Frenchmen, to France's allies) represented a show of strength, symbolized a return to greatness after the severe humiliation of defeat and enemy occupation. If Camus himself was neither pro nor anti-Gaullist—rather a lower-case socialist, favoring reform and social progress—the omnipresent Pia was a partisan of de Gaulle, but he at least never inserted his political views into the paper. Thanks to Pia, *Combat* had scooped the rest of the French press on de Gaulle's withdrawal from power in January 1946. De Gaulle had called a morning cabinet meeting; on the previous night Malraux phoned his friend Pia to give him the tip that de Gaulle was leaving office. To avoid allowing rival *Franc-Tireur* to steal the story (for its publisher Georges Altman could read the type in the composing room the two papers shared), *Combat* held the story for its second edition, and it was in the hands of each minister who went into the cabinet meeting the next morning.[4] But it was *after* de Gaulle left the government that the Gaullist movement really took off, sparked by Malraux and other ideologists, transmitted through the RPF; the movement would not die until de Gaulle came back to power after the quasi-coup of May 1958, after which it didn't so much die as become a party.

There was another opportunity for outside financing, this from what seemed a less compromising alliance with *La Voix du Nord,* a newspaper also born of the resistance, published in the northeast industrial city of Lille, and, like other regional newspapers highly successful, less vulnerable to competition than a Paris daily could be. Finally the offer of the paper's publisher was rejected, for the Lille daily conceived *Combat* as a money-maker, and that would require the kind of changes in format and content the staff did not want.[5] Then an old friend of Pierre Galindo from Oran, Marcel Chouraqui, told him that a group of Freemasons was prepared to offer financial support for the paper if Camus would continue to run it. Informed of this, Camus replied that the paper was not his, but a team effort.[6]

Even Raymond Aron tried to save the paper and talked to bankers about the possibility of their support for a paper under his direction. But each potential banker had his own political line, and Aron also knew that the staff would not have accepted his leadership, because he himself was politically committed.[7]

The problem was aggravated by inexperience. With professional management they might have been able to survive, as *Le Monde* had succeeded as an afternoon paper. Pessimistic, Pia believed that an intelligent newspaper could not last, and he felt that the best solution was to shut down. But his colleagues thought that if they accepted that solution everybody would be out of a job (and they would not incidentally owe considerable dismissal benefits to the staff).[8]

The break in relations between Pia and Camus took place about now, and there are as many explanations of why it happened as there are surviving witnesses. The most obvious one is jealousy, jealousy on the part of Pia. He had worked without a break from the very first public issue of *Combat* in August 1944, had seen Camus retire and return at will, make a temporary contribution of the series of essays "Neither Victims nor Executioners," and then (after beseeching on the part of staff members) return again in February 1947 as the white knight called in to rescue the kingdom. Pia resented this; he was overheard saying to Camus: "You're in our way."[9]

But this is the same Pia who had always chosen to remain in the background, friend or *éminence grise* to Malraux and to Camus and to others, calling the tune at *Alger Républicain* while giving Camus his first bylines, finding a place for his desperate young friend at *Paris-Soir,* maneuvering incessantly for the publication of *L'Etranger* and Camus' other early works; and without doubt if their wartime magazine had seen the light of day Pia would have been its silent editor, Camus one of its writer-stars. If jealousy was a factor in the break which would last as long as Camus lived, it represented a change in Pia.

Even on *Combat,* Pia had expressed admiration for Camus. He had soon told Altschuler how he had dispatched Camus, then a beginning reporter on *Alger Républicain,* to write about conditions in Kabylie, and when Camus submitted his articles not a line needed to be changed.

It would have been natural that, without being jealous of Camus, Pia would resent public acknowledgment of Camus' role on *Combat* when in fact every line of every day's paper—apart from the signed editorials—was Pia's responsibility. Camus was surrounded by admirers, many of them attractive women, and he clearly enjoyed that. As Camus stood out more, Pia seemed to recede further into the background.[10] Yet the younger Camus had *also* been a social lion, a culture star, something of a neophyte Don Juan, when Pia worked alongside him in complete harmony, and in Camus' home city, in 1938 and 1939. Whatever attraction-repulsion Camus exercised on Pia now would have existed earlier.

Was the chief reason for the split political? If Pia did not allow his Gaullist preference to show during day-to-day editing of the paper, the fact is that on his departure from *Combat* he would step into a job at a news agency, Agence Express, which shared a staff with the Gaullist weekly *Le Rassemblement,* in which Pia was associated with Ollivier. Yet a close observer of those last days felt that their differences could not have been political, for Pia believed in nothing. Except that the paper should be scuttled, and that was a direct challenge to Camus' feeling that it had to be kept alive in order to keep the staff working.

"He's come back as a savior," Pia quipped on Camus' return, and then he took his first vacation since the founding of *Combat,* saying as he left: "I'm exhausted." He sent a telegram to say that he would not return.

In truth, that multiple man Pascal Pia was too complex for there to have been a single reason for his break with Camus.[11] He himself attributed the cooling of relations to the argument concerning whether or not to close down the paper, hopelessly in deficit. This difference of opinion was aggravated by attacks against Pia within the staff to which Camus expressed no objection; Pia resented Camus' failure to defend him.[12] Indeed, one of their colleagues heard Pia refer to rumors that were being spread about him to the effect that he had received offers from the Gaullists prior to his leaving *Combat,* and he seemed to blame Camus for this. Jacqueline Bernard tried to reconcile Pia with Camus and the others, but he snapped: "Let's talk about something else."[8] Later other friends would try to bring the two together again, but Pia rejected all overtures. They lived in different worlds, Pia and Camus. Both were journalists who cared little for journalism in the end. They knew each other *on the job,* and when they were no longer working together they had no reason to see each other.[12]

Prior to his return to *Combat,* Camus graced its pages with his replies to an interview on American literature (published on January 17, 1947, while he was en route to his mountain retreat at Briançon). He dismissed current American writing as a *littérature de l'élémentaire* which was popular because American fiction employed a *technique de facilité.* Comparing Steinbeck to Melville, he felt that nineteenth-century grandeur had been replaced by magazine writing, where interior life was simply ignored; man was described, never explained. Worse, he felt that those who read American novels in French translation thought that these techniques contained underlying meaning which in fact they did not. "We read *Of Mice and Men* in the same spirit that we read *La Princesse de Clèves,*" he told the interviewer. "But the men in American novels, unlike the Prince de Clèves, are really elementary creatures." American techniques were useful when one was describing a man without an apparent interior life, and Camus admitted to having utilized these techniques. But to generalize such use would be an impoverishment, for nine tenths of what makes the richness of art and of life would thereby be lost. The American literature we read, with the exception of Faulkner and of one or two others who like Faulkner have no success in the United States, is useful as documentation but has little to do with art.

He attributed the low state of American writing to commercialization of literature, advertising, the possibility of earning a great deal of money from one's writing. Europeans would do the same, he thought, if they could choose between becoming a millionaire or remaining a great but undiscovered talent.

But he admitted that if there were great writers in America today they would not be known, just as Melville was ignored, Poe was discovered by Europe, and Faulkner gets small printings while *Forever Amber* sold millions of copies. He felt that if Hemingway's *The Sun Also Rises* was a fine book, the same author's *For Whom the Bell Tolls* was a child's tale, an MGM love story, compared to Malraux's *Man's Hope* (L'Espoir).

Was he then thoroughly hostile to American writing? No, because

> I discovered in America both the reasons for this literature and the promise that it will be outgrown, if it hasn't already been. And I feel a solidarity with some of these reasons (in my country, North Africa, one also lives in this brief and violent manner), as with this promise. America bursts with still unused forces and it hasn't finished astonishing the world.

He believed that one could help by encouraging not the vulgar books coming from the United States but its rigorous art. "Art is the only domain in which honesty and standards are sometimes rewarded."

Camus began writing again in *Combat* as soon as the printers' strike was over. Although he contributed only a couple of editorials each month, he was on the scene or available all the time, and that was what his friends hoped could save the paper. On March 22, 1947, after a number of priests were indicted for having helped the collaborationist police, and liberal opinion suggested that monasteries had been hotbeds of pro-Nazi collaboration, Camus took up his pen to deny collective responsibility, to affirm the historical fact of resistance within the Church. He knew that he would be criticized for defending the Catholics, but "Unbelievers like ourselves hate only hatred. . . ." On April 22 he dealt with Gaullism in a signed editorial entitled "Le Choix." "It appears that one must choose," he began. One had to be for the RPF or against it. He felt that such urgency had its comical side; was the house burning down? *Combat* hadn't been founded to be the organ of a party, he wrote, but to exercise free criticism. De Gaulle's RPF was only one movement among many, and should be treated "just like any other party." He felt both excommunication and adoration of the Gaullists to be equally childish attitudes.

But de Gaulle would not be insulted in this paper. "We, at least, have a memory." Just as de Gaulle's actions were criticized in *Combat,* the RPF would be judged according to its acts, not its still vague principles.

*Combat*'s leading Gaullist, Albert Ollivier, wished to reply to Camus' editorial, affirming that he was the only member of the staff to have made the choice of which Camus wrote. To save the newspaper, or so it is said, Camus refused to publish Ollivier's letter.[13]

In May he would write two more editorials in *Combat,* one to attack French racism as manifested against an alleged murderer of Malagasy origin, as well as hostility against Jews, and in Algeria by brutalities against Moslem nationalists. The other was a plea for renewal of the dialogue with the vanquished Germans.

After they had put the paper to bed each evening, the old team would have a drink with the printers.[8] They might go out as a group to the liveliest Saint-Germain-des-Prés club of the time, Le Méphisto, where the likes of Juliette Gréco would be. There was a piano in the club, on which jazz might be played by their friend René Leibowitz, composer, later orchestra leader, contributor of music to Sartre's *Temps Modernes* and author of a history of the opera. In the very last days of *Combat* they paid their night club bills from the newspaper's petty cash account, which led to stories that when Camus left *Combat* he took its treasury with him.[5] Sometimes, after Le Méphisto, Camus would bring the gang to his Rue Séguier apartment for a nightcap in the salon facing the street, several rooms removed from the sleeping twins.[14]

One day Claude Bourdet, armed with his moral claim to the paper, made a phone call to Jacqueline Bernard. "You're not going to scuttle *Combat,*" he said. "I've got a financial backer." She replied that she would have to consult her fellow directors. Bourdet argued that the paper did not belong to the staff, and they had no right to shut it down.[8] (After his return from the camps—he had been held by the Nazis successively in Neuengamme, Sachsenhausen, and Buchenwald, and was brought back from this last on a stretcher—he had been elected vice-president of the Consultative Assembly, and for a time served as director of the French Radio.)

Bourdet returned, not only with Combat founding officer Henri

Frenay, but with a financial angel, Henry Smadja. Born in Oran in 1897, Smadja had gone on to Tunisia, where he became a successful olive grower and a power in politics and the press; he was publisher of the Tunis daily *La Presse*. Although he was unknown in Paris, Bourdet discovered that he had impeccable resistance credentials: In Tunisia during the war he maintained liaison with offshore British submarines. Reduced to essentials, Smadja was offering, for 50 per cent of the shares of *Combat,* to take over its deficit (which Bourdet found to be 17 million francs, or some 1.3 million francs of the mid-1970s, about $260,000). He would print and manage the paper while leaving the writing and editorial policy to its staff. It seemed an irresistible offer: Without strings, Smadja would guarantee the survival of the best postwar legacy of the resistance press, while leaving the political line of the paper in the hands of a wartime leader of the resistance, Bourdet himself.[15]

Bourdet would later recall that when things began to look bad for *Combat* it was Pia's idea to turn over the paper to him. Camus, in Bourdet's recollection, had wanted to suspend operations. Bourdet began discussions with Pia, and then Bloch-Michel was brought in. Bourdet told Camus that he was morally obliged to take in Frenay and his comrades as partners. Camus replied, according to Bourdet, that he could not do that, for *Combat* had become something quite different from what it had been in wartime France. Camus is supposed to have added: "But we are giving you 100 per cent of the shares and you can do what you like; I don't even want to know what you do."

Altschuler and Paute would stay on; Bourdet convinced them that they were serving an institution.[4] Bourdet brought in Frenay and other Combat movement veterans including one Jacques Dhont. Later these new partners would ally themselves with Smadja against Bourdet; even Frenay, to the right of Bourdet politically, would turn against him on the colonial question. In the end, Bourdet would be forced out by the people he brought in, Smadja and the veterans.[16]

By a protocol dated June 2, 1947, five of the six shareholders of *Combat,* Camus, Pia, Jacqueline Bernard, Bloch-Michel, and Ollivier, turned over their shares to Claude Bourdet at their nominal face value —each had held a hundred such shares. It was understood that Bourdet was representing not only himself but a group of friends. Smadja's name would not appear in the agreement, which read in part:

> Finding themselves in the presence of financial difficulties, which prevent them from assuring the survival of the newspaper in its present state, and because of the problems faced by the press in general at this time, they [the present shareholders] felt that the most

qualified person to take their place at their head of this newspaper was Claude Bourdet.

Bourdet in turn declared that he wished to maintain the character given to the paper since the liberation by the retiring directors. He had the support of a group of Combat veterans associated as the Fédération des Amicales "Combat," whose president was Dhont, Bourdet being vice-president.[17]

Those members of the staff who desired to leave the paper had the benefit of what is called in French press legislation the *clause de conscience;* it allows a member of the staff of a newspaper whose ownership has changed to resign with an indemnity, rather than to serve a new publisher and a new policy.

One printing plant employee noticed that Camus was relieved when Bourdet and Smadja took over, since he hadn't been able to make of *Combat* the truly open forum he had wished it to be—undoubtedly an unrealistic hope. About a year later Camus wrote one of these printers about the failure of their hopes. "But we were disarmed," he explained, "because we were honest. This press that we wanted to see worthy and proud is now the shame of our unhappy nation. . . ."[18]

On June 3, 1947, Camus signed a two-column page-one editorial set off by a box, headed "A NOS LECTEURS." He announced that the political and business directors of the paper were withdrawing but the newspaper would continue. This required more explanation, which he proceeded to give. While *Combat* had enough readers to allow an enterprise without ambitions to survive, only a large-circulation newspaper could hope to balance its budget. Despite its present deficit operations *Combat*'s accumulated surplus from the better years might have allowed it a year's grace to reorganize and gain circulation but the printers' strike had wiped out this surplus.

> Of course it was impossible for us to ask for money from outside and even to receive it without asking. Proposals were not lacking, one can imagine (and among them many were both honorable and generous).

But the directors did not feel they could accept any such offer, given the paper's situation. For weeks, with reduced means, they had tried to carry on, and thus to save the staff from unemployment, but they could no longer continue. Since the title of the paper belonged not only to them but morally to all those who had written, printed, and distributed the underground *Combat,* they were now turning it over to veterans of that movement. "After agreement with the Federation of Combat Veterans, our comrade Claude Bourdet, one of the founders of the underground newspaper, arrested and deported in the exercise of his functions, and whose political views have always been close to those of our newspaper, has decided to take over the enterprise himself."

Camus wished it to be clear that the directing team was changing. "We offer sincere good wishes for the success of an enterprise which was so dear to us," he went on. "But just as our comrades who will produce the newspaper tomorrow must not have to accept the responsibilities we undertook, in the same way our departure releases us from any future obligation. . . ."

Bourdet would not fail to note the lukewarm quality of such an endorsement. He would attribute part of the blame for his future difficulties to Camus' failure to back him with more enthusiasm, if not to join him in the enterprise.[16]

Just below Camus' editorial, a second editorial, signed by Bourdet, explained that its former directors had been prepared to scuttle the paper and had asked for his help, he who had brought together the present staff. He listed those who would stay on, twenty-seven names in all, including Gimont, Altschuler, Roger Grenier [who would later join Pia at Agence Express and then go on to *France-Soir*],[19] Jean Sénard, Jean-Pierre Vivet, Maurice Nadeau, Jacques Lemarchand, Serge Karsky, Jules Roy, Henri Cauquelin, Daniel Lenief. The columns of the paper, assured Bourdet, remained open to Camus and the other former directors. "In taking up this task that I had to leave in the hands of Pascal Pia on March 25, 1944, thanks to the intervention of the Gestapo," he concluded, "I promise the readers of *Combat* to try not to disappoint them."

On the very last day the old gang met at the Rue Séguier, where Camus gave each of them a signed copy of *La Peste,* which was to be published the following week. Then they went to a couscous restaurant on the Rue Monsieur-le-Prince—probably the Hoggar. They were all of them quite sad; it had been a beautiful experiment, their *Combat.* They had tried to publish a decent daily newspaper; in a way it was amusing to think that Pia may have been right in saying that a high-quality newspaper could not survive. They were also aware that their own amateurism had been responsible to some extent, as well as the harsh facts of the business world. But there was no blame or bitterness. When they negotiated with Bourdet they had insisted that the entire staff including the business side should benefit from the *clause de conscience,* proof that they did not blame the business office for their failure.[8]

And Camus' departure triggered an avalanche of letters from every intellectual level, every walk of life, protesting the decision or expressing regret.[20] Bitterness too. Henri Cauquelin, his old friend from *Paris-Soir,* when he objected to Camus' withdrawal, was shocked to hear

Camus' reply that he had no time to waste, that he had a work to achieve.[21]

The further history of *Combat* would not concern Camus directly except for one incident, and in the resentment of Bourdet, who felt that as a fellow crusader, differing in politics but not in essential feelings from Camus, he should have had Camus' complete support when his back was to the wall. Later Bourdet would say that Camus and his team could have warned him that his contract with Smadja put him in a position of inferiority. He also felt that Camus' final editorial, "A Nos Lecteurs," was so unenthusiastic that many readers believed he was turning away from the paper, and that it was changing its policies. He wanted Camus to send in an occasional article, and in any case to write one to help launch the new regime; Camus failed to honor these wishes.

Bourdet complicated his position by voluntarily sharing his stock in the paper with Frenay and distributing other shares not only to Paute and to Altschuler but to members of the Combat veterans' association. This allowed Smadja to maneuver. Armed with 50 per cent of the stock to begin with, he needed only to win over Frenay or one or more of the Combat veterans. (Bourdet even heard that Smadja promised to make the president of the veterans' association director of the newspaper once they got rid of Bourdet.) Later, when Smadja did force Bourdet out with the help of Bourdet's onetime associates, Smadja made the delicious remark: "Mr. Bourdet, you surely have a great deal against me, but nevertheless I'll do something for you: I shall avenge you for the betrayal by your ignoble friends." (That is, the Combat veterans Bourdet had himself brought in as stockholders but who voted with Smadja against Bourdet.)[22]

Bourdet would also begin to feel that Smadja's entry into *Combat* was not so much philanthropy as a smart business move. If Smadja had to cope with the deficit, he obtained many advantages, too. The paper was printed in his plant, which was paid for the work. Smadja was also able to import modern printing equipment and to acquire a building at low cost thanks to the *Combat* connection. Then Smadja began to cut expenses, to fire staff. He became known as "La Peur du Salaire"— Fear of Wages, a play on words on the title of the novel *Le Salaire de la Peur* (The Wages of Fear). When Bourdet sought to stop Smadja, he was fired by a vote of the general assembly of shareholders, on February 27, 1950, the grounds for the firing including his excessively high salary and other pretexts. When the other editors refused to take Bourdet's place, Smadja himself took the title and was forced by court order to allow members of the staff to resign under the *clause de conscience*.[16] Bourdet himself went to court, got testimonials from Sartre, former

*Combat* staffers such as Bloch-Michel and Pierre Herbart; Camus himself told the court on March 20, 1950:

> Bourdet carried on the tradition of *Combat*. The present director [Smadja] has no moral right to run a newspaper which was published and consecrated by men whose outlook was different. . . .[17]

Bourdet won his case against Smadja, receiving an indemnity (of 300,000 1952 francs).[16] But *Combat* now belonged to Smadja; it would be published—under different editors—until 1974.

The incident involving Bourdet and Camus, or which should have involved them, remains obscure, in the absence of some of the key actors. At the worst period of his struggle with Smadja, Bourdet later recalled, and after many vain appeals to Camus for solidarity—an article or some other token of support—Bourdet had an opportunity in early 1950 to buy back all of Smadja's shares of the paper if he could find the capital. He found it, through a friend of Camus, but the backer required that the paper be run jointly by Bourdet and Camus. Bourdet consented at once, and asked Camus to agree; he even offered to become Camus' assistant on the reorganized paper, all power belonging to Camus. Camus refused. Bourdet knew that Camus' health was a factor. (Indeed, if the date is right, Camus was recovering in Southern France after a severe relapse of tuberculosis; his convalescence would last over a year.) But Bourdet also felt that Camus wished to have nothing to do with a newspaper which was no longer his.[23] Problems of health aside, that was true enough. Camus would not return halfway, where he would not have complete control of what was said and done in his name. It was not that he did not like Bourdet, but that he'd had enough of journalism.[24] In 1950 or in 1951, in any case, he could not have been an effective presence in anyone's newspaper plant.

But this is to simplify. Subsequent events were to demonstrate that there was a basic incompatibility between Camus and Bourdet.

On the lighter side, there is evidence that Smadja was also thinking of asking Camus to save the paper. He told this to Jean-Pierre Vivet, whom Camus had originally recruited to serve on the paper as a young man. Vivet replied to Smadja: "Don't forget that you owe him money." To which Smadja exclaimed: "You're not going to tell me that Camus is a man of money!"[25]

# 32

# BEST-SELLER

Sadness of success. Opposition is necessary. If everything was more difficult for me, as before, I should have more right to say what I say. It remains that I can help many people—while waiting.

*Carnets*

Evidently Camus still had the power to maintain his distances from someone or something which no longer interested him. What was done was done; he had withdrawn from *Combat* in spirit a long time earlier, and there is little reason to believe that he held any hope for the newspaper even during those final weeks when he had pitched in to try to save it. Nothing in his journal at that time, for example, can be taken as an allusion to the newspaper, while there was much concerning his present and future creative activity.

*La Peste* itself was now about to enter his past, although there would be some difficult months during which it became a best-seller and an almost too accessible symbol of recent history, all too easily evoked, and not for its artistry alone.

Publication of *La Peste*—officially on June 10, 1947—was preceded by the appearance of early fragments of the novel as "Archives de la peste" in the second issue of *Cahiers de la Pléiade,* an elegant annual edited by Jean Paulhan, as another substitute for the absent *NRF*. Its table of contents offered contributions by Gide, Henri Michaux, Roger Caillois, René Char, Maurice Blanchot, Marcel Arland, Malraux, Jacques Audiberti, Marcel Jouhandeau, Jean Giono—more evidence of *NRF* wish-fulfillment.[1] The extracts published as "Archives" contained a good deal more free-flowing irony than Camus was able to allow himself within the strict confines of his fiction. Then in June, just a week after Camus' farewell editorial in *Combat, La Peste* was published in a printing of 22,000 copies—high for that time, high for a serious novel, but an underestimate on the part of the Librairie Gallimard of the suitability of the book for its era.

For it was obviously what the public was waiting for, a book about their years of trial with no direct allusion to those years, nothing about defeat, Nazi occupation, atrocities; it was all in the allegory. The disaster which strikes the Algerian coastal city of Oran is plague, not war; the heroes are doctors and medical aides, not resistance fighters; the city is isolated not by the Wehrmacht but by quarantine. This is the way the book was read, in any case. Marcel Arland in his review of Camus' novel in the following number of *Cahiers de la Pléiade* (winter 1948) would even say: "Nevertheless, if for many reasons I like the latest book by Camus, *La Peste,* I am not certain that its ideology, however generous it may be, doesn't dissipate it, doesn't weaken it somewhat." (Arland had written the major and favorable review of *L'Etranger* in *Comoedia,* the cultural weekly published in Paris under the German occupation.)

Camus' previous books had been published during wartime austerity or in the scarcity of the immediate postwar. Now the newspapers had room to review again, and Camus was soon submerged with clippings.

He was less happy with the literary prize he was to receive on the very week of publication, the Prix des Critiques. It was voted on the third ballot—the final vote being seven for Camus, two for Paul Gadenne, one for Julien Blanc, one for Henri Thomas, one for Pierre Klossowski, and it was reported that Camus would have received it by unanimous vote if the jury had been able to read it sooner, but many of its members received their copies only two days before the vote.[2]

Then and later, the literary prize system was a triste affair, a matter of "you scratch my back and I'll scratch yours." Then and later it would be supported, even promoted, by the leading literary publishers of France. But not by Camus. He knew that the Prix des Critiques was given by a jury the majority of whose members were his colleagues at Gallimard (Paulhan among them). He was stung by the insinuations of one paper that the prize had gone to him because of Gallimard's intervention, and that otherwise it would have gone to a deserving beginner, stung all the more because he hadn't received the cash award that went with the honor—100,000 francs (some 7,580 francs in 1975, or about $1,500). He himself was going to resign from another jury, the one which gave the Prix de la Pléiade; composed of Gallimard people, it had voted its prize that year to Gallimard author Jean Genet.

But he would also say no to another token of recognition, one which was not controlled by Gallimard: the Legion of Honor.

*La Peste,* prize or no, had taken off. By fall it had sold nearly 100,000 copies, and Camus was joking to Michel and Janine Gallimard that henceforth he'd have to pick up everybody's restaurant checks, he was in debt up to his neck, and expected that his tax bill would be tripled, while Francine felt that it was the right time to buy clothes for the children. He expected that he'd soon be as poor as Job.[3] But he had a good reason to be pleased with sales: He had a better contract with his publisher than ever before, providing him a straight 15 per cent royalty on sales of the regular edition (a year earlier he received 12 per cent for *Lettres à un ami allemand;* prior to that, for his wartime books, he received 10 per cent to 10,000 copies, 12 per cent thereafter).

In a letter from Paris to *Partisan Review* in New York his friend Nicola Chiaromonte noted the success of Camus' novel "at a moment when book buying is a luxury." *La Peste* was "neither faultless nor written to please," Chiaromonte said, "but the general public have apparently found in it an answer to their yearning for ordinary humanness and good sense."[4]

In a listing of the best-selling books published in France in the ten years since World War II, *La Peste* was number seven, with 360,000 copies sold by 1955. Number one was Giovanni Guareschi's *The Little World of Don Camillo; The Little Prince* was number six, immediately preceding *La Peste.*[5]

Almost as soon as the novel was published, its author and his family left Paris for Le Panelier, site of his wartime exile. This time Madame Oettly put them up in the tall stone building in the yard of the fortified farm, a building called the dungeon. He took over a room on the topmost floor which he could use as an office, for he had returned to this quiet place to work. The journey down had been troublesome, with the expected problems of taking twenty-one-month-old children on a night train. The twins had soon come down with infant illnesses, and after a fortnight Francine's mother would show up from Oran. Country peace was disturbed once by a reporter for the weekly gossip sheet *Samedi-Soir,* who traveled all the way from Paris to interview the author of the new best-seller. Camus read the pile of favorable reviews, felt himself buried under a heap of flowers.

But Le Panelier hadn't changed, with the overcast skies, drizzly days: the melancholic landscape of his exile. He thought that he liked it, all the same, and he was here to rest, to gain some weight, and of course to work. "Marvelous day," begins a description of the countryside in his journal (June 17). But some days later he reread his notebooks and discovered that landscapes were disappearing from them little by little. "The modern cancer gnaws at me too."

He read (*Mémoires d'outre-tombe*), made notes for the essay on revolt, meditated on what he would do now, which direction to take. He thought that he would like to change his way of life, but didn't know how to do that except by traveling.[3]

For he had the leisure—part of the reward for the completion of a worrisome piece of work—to take a long view now, not only of his present way of life but of his future writing. In his journal he told himself that the step beyond the Absurd (his past work) and Revolt (his work in progress) was compassion: *l'amour et la poésie,* but he felt that demanded an innocence he no longer possessed. All he could do was to survey the road which led to it, and "let the time of the innocents arrive." He concluded: "See it, at least, before I die."

In Le Panelier he set down one more time the cycles, series as he called them, of his past, present, and future work, most of them in triptychs:

> 1st series—Absurd: *L'Etranger—Le Mythe de Sisyphe—Caligula* and *Le Malentendu.*
> 2nd—Revolt: *La Peste* (and appendices)—*L'Homme révolté*—Kaliayev.
> 3rd—Anguished love: The Stake—On Love—The Seductive One.
> 4th—Création corrigée or The System: major novel + major meditation + unactable play.

Later, in editing his manuscript journal for publication, Camus inserted another series between the second and third, containing "Le Jugement" and "Le Premier homme," giving the impression that he had planned them as early as mid-1947, when in fact they were both later conceptions; "Le Jugement" may have been *La Chute,* a tentative title for which was "Le Jugement dernier."

But if one assumes that all of the other titles found in this journal entry—written between June 17 and June 25, 1947—were actually entered into his notebooks at Le Panelier, then all of Camus' original works apart from *La Chute* and *Le Premier Homme* (and some stories) were already in his mind then, and more besides. (In the second series, "Kaliayev" would become *Les Justes,* whose central character was Ivan Kaliayev; henceforth his journal would be filled with notes and bits of dialogue for this play, completed and produced in Paris in 1949.)

On July 15 the Camus returned to Paris, and it may have been at this time that they joined Jules Roy in renting a house at Choisel in the Vallée de Chevreuse, a largely rural and wooded, hilly region not far from Versailles. They had discovered a charming old house with an untended garden, in a clearing at the edge of a woods, with room for all the Camus (and Camus' mother-in-law too). When the Camus returned to the Rue Séguier, Roy kept the house. Camus and Roy were now good friends as well as literary colleagues. Charlot had published Roy's *La Vallée heureuse,* a novel transposing his experiences as a pilot with the Free French; in Camus' review of the novel in Charlot's magazine *L'Arche* he placed the book "among those works of strength and reserve whose taste we have forgotten." (The book won the prestigious Prix Renaudot, as has already been remarked.)

His family safely sheltered, Camus joined Jean Grenier on a trip to Grenier's native Brittany, leaving Paris on August 4 in Camus' newly acquired black Citroën (the 11 CV of prewar French movies, the police and gangster car, for a while the Gestapo car, then the car of FFI combatants). But they drove slowly, sightseeing along the way, taking two days to do the 240 miles, visiting Combourg, site of Chateaubriand's castle (described in *Mémoires d'outre-tombe,* which Camus had just been reading); Saint-Malo, the old fortified port (not yet rebuilt after heavy wartime damage); finally Saint-Brieuc.[3] (At Combourg, Camus confessed to Grenier that he wished to acquire something of Chateaubriand's style, without forgetting Stendhal's.[6]

At Saint-Brieuc they called on Louis Guilloux, a childhood friend of Grenier, a fellow Gallimard author. The son of a shoemaker raised in modest-to-poor circumstances, a scholarship student, author of books about his and his fellows' harsh life influenced by populist socialism, Guilloux continued to live simply on the outskirts of Saint-Brieuc, working in a studio in his two-story house. With Guilloux they drove on to Tréguier to see the house where Ernest Renan was born, and the superb Breton cathedral and cloister there. Camus jotted down some of the things Grenier discussed with him, and made notes for a study of Grenier—"G. as a spirit opposed to Malraux," today's world as a dialogue between the two men.

Louis Guilloux also took Camus to the Saint-Michel Cemetery at Saint-Brieuc's edge, where, in a military section, Camus' father is buried. Guilloux walked with Camus to point out the regulation stone slab with his father's name on it, then moved off to leave Camus alone. What thoughts he had, Camus kept to himself. Only later would he say that he had been struck, in looking at the simple stone with the dates of birth and death of his father, by the early age at which Lucien Auguste Camus had died—by the fact that the son had already lived much longer than the father had.[7] He would go on from these thoughts to the search for his lost childhood which *Le Premier Homme* is.

Soon after that, when fellow *pied noir* Jean Daniel launched a magazine of his own, *Caliban,* each issue to contain the text of a little-known work, Camus suggested that he reprint Guilloux's novel of childhood poverty, *La Maison du peuple.* Daniel agreed, provided that Camus write a preface, and he did;[8] it began:

> Nearly all French writers who pretend to speak in the name of
> the proletariat today were born of comfortable or well to do pa-
> rents. This is not a fault; there is accident in birth, and I find this
> neither good nor bad. I only call the attention of sociologists to this
> anomaly and subject for study.

The preface is important because his insistence on the need of experience of poverty to write about the subject seemed a justification of his own work, past and future, as well as an attack on poverty in itself, for he was far from suggesting that it was good for art. "An excess of poverty shortens the memory, weakens the strength of friendship and loves," he would add. "Fifteen thousand francs a month, factory life, and Tristan has nothing more to say to Iseult."

Because he had been away in June and July he had to work in August, when nearly everyone else in publishing was on holiday. At the Gallimard office he was literally alone, and could report with humor to Michel and Janine that he bore all the weight of that enormous publishing empire on his shoulders, taking all the telephone calls, speaking for the business department, the literary department, the production department, the magazines published in the house, depending on who was calling, which phone he was answering. Evenings he returned to Choisel, where there was time for a swim. But when the twins came down with whooping cough and it was considered advisable for Camus, who had never had the disease, to live away from home, he went to stay with friends.[3] In September he traveled south to the Vaucluse, first to Avignon, once the capital of the French papacy, where René Char picked him up to take him to the Hôtel de l'Europe; there they met local friends of Char before driving on to the poet's home at L'Isle-sur-la-Sorgue.[9] "Large room opened to autumn," he noted in his journal. Here he was to get to know Char, whom he had only frequented as one writer among others in the corridors of Gallimard. The encounter was indeed a significant event. Camus would henceforth live with the image of that burly, sometimes stormy and sometimes silent hermit as a model for a man's life; doubtless he learned

some of his refusal of the world, his flight from crowds, and the futilities
of literary life as it was practiced at Saint-Germain-des-Prés from Char.
Much in the biography of this former rugby player now lyric poet
evoked his own, or what his could have been; one could be a virile hero
and a fine writer.[10]

In his journal he recorded an anecdote told him by Char. When
Char had left his resistance group in May 1944 to fly to North Africa,
he could see from the plane all along the Durance Valley the fires lit by
his fighters as a final salute to him.

Back in Paris in October, there is a curious journal entry. Camus is
visiting the Hôpital des Enfants-Malades, perhaps to see one of his own
children. The low-ceilinged, closed-in, overheated room, full of the
smells of fatty bouillon and bandages, caused him to faint.

He flew to Algiers in November (his journal speaks of "The airplane as
one of the elements of modern negation and abstraction."). But he
would soon decide that one must not return to places where one had
been young: The girls have become stout mothers, men have died. And
this city which had been a site of pleasures had become one in which he
paid respects—to his family, his old teacher, his professors, and places
—where he had gone to school, to college. . . .[3]

Privately, in Stockholm, the Swedish Academy discussed giving Camus
the Nobel Prize that fall; it was the first of several times his name would
be mentioned. Had the academy voted for Camus that year, at thirty-
four he would have been the youngest winner in the history of the
Nobel.[11]

He didn't win the Nobel that year, but he won a place in the private portrait gallery of "M. Saint-Clair," the pen name of Gide's *petite
dame,* Maria Van Rysselberghe. In her book called *Galerie privée* she
described exceptional people who had come her way.

> . . . The mouth frankly sensual opens willingly into a smile [she
> wrote of Camus], a smile tender but rebellious, and perhaps not
> free of flirtatiousness. But where does the feeling of firmness in his
> expression come from? Could it be from the tight manner of closing
> his mouth? This firmness which accommodates itself so well to po-
> liteness and is tempered by a deep concern for being fair.

Coming to the essential, she spoke of *"Le charme de Camus, qui est
grand,"* and which was composed

> of a kind of density in his presence, of a spontaneity never caught
> short. . . .
> A big man, of a bearing so natural that one cannot say anything

else about it. "He has," as Vauvenargues said, "that simple appearance which suits superior spirits so well."[12]

To help him deal with his augmented obligations, to ward off his admirers, those who would have made his work difficult and his life unbearable, he now had that strong-willed young woman as his secretary at Gallimard. If one wished to speak to Camus, one spoke first to Suzanne Labiche.

Mademoiselle Labiche had been another youthful victim of tuberculosis. She was sent to the Sanatorium des Etudiants at Saint-Hilaire-du-Touvet, in the southeast region of Isère; Max-Pol Fouchet had been there in the early 1930s. Once the acting treacher Béatrix Dussane came to lecture to the patients. Herself a descendant of the nineteenth-century comedy writer Eugène Labiche, Suzanne Labiche had an opportunity to meet Dussane, who said she would help her find a job when she returned to Paris. In 1946, when Suzanne Labiche got there, she did contact Dussane, who as a friend of Maria Casarès knew Camus. Camus was enlisted, found her a job with a philosophy professor, but that didn't last. She had wanted to be a teacher herself, but her illness ruled that out, although she managed to obtain a bachelor's degree in law at the sanatorium. Camus then found her a job in a bookshop, and there for the first time she actually met Camus when he came to lecture there. After his talk she introduced herself to him, and he said that she ought to have a better and less tiring job. Three days later he telephoned to offer her a job as his secretary.

She began by working half time for him and half in another office in the Gallimard building for Father Bruckberger, who was then editing a magazine called *Cheval de Troie*. (Camus shared credit for the translation of some poems by Joan Maragall i Gorina, a turn-of-the-century Catalan romantic, in the second issue of that magazine.) On Suzanne Labiche's arrival her first job was to type the final version of *La Peste*. Camus tested her for three months to see whether she could handle correspondence on her own, and when he left *Combat* to work regularly at Gallimard again, she began working for *him* regularly—and full-time. Excited by the prospect of this intimacy, she began to keep a private journal which he discovered and took away from her; when he gave it back he warned that if she continued to keep a journal she couldn't keep the job. He took a match and set it afire and she promised never again to do such a thing; periodically he would ask her about it; she kept the promise for the thirteen years she worked for him.[13]

She was an attractive girl, intensely devoted to Camus, who referred to her as "Labiche."[3] Soon she had developed means of warding off importune admirers, requests for appointments, interviews, speechmaking, article-writing, petition-signing, sponsorship of causes, and attendance at public or private functions. She kept in her drawer a series of model letters with variant refusals, e.g.:

> . . . Problems of health now place Mr. Albert Camus in the obligation, on his doctors' orders, of reducing his activity considerably. . . .
>
> I have established a rule never to accept any honorary title and not to collaborate with undertakings in which I cannot participate personally.
>
> Not being able to keep up with the abundance of my tasks, I have established the principle of no longer replying to any survey or interview and in general to refuse all new activities.
>
> I have adopted the principle of refusing all requests for prefaces. Indeed, if I agreed to do one, I would immediately receive twenty requests that I should be obliged to refuse.[13]

Among those he would later be turning down was Henry Kissinger, who tried several times to get Camus to write for *Confluence,* the Harvard international magazine of which he was then editor. Camus generally rebuffed his requests and managed to be absent during Kissinger's visits to Paris, but they finally have what Kissinger called a pleasant conversation in 1953 in Paris.[14] And among the prefaces Camus *did* agree to write in the early days of his fame was a short but strong introduction to a book on Nazi atrocities, *Laisser passer mon peuple,* by Jacques Méry, and another for the *Poésies posthumes* of his Lyons resistance comrade René Leynaud, the journalist-poet shot by the Nazis. (Both essays are reprinted in his collected works.)

Did success spoil Albert Camus? There are as many witnesses who say that it did as there are defenders of Camus. It is true that with the coming to France of American-style promotion in new media assuring broad dissemination, instant notoriety, the myth which would not die of Saint-Germain-des-Prés and its obvious vices, hidden virtues, Camus would henceforth be a good news story; his constant efforts to maintain privacy only whetted appetites. Certainly the consequences of fame would intrude on his private life, the life he intended on keeping private. "Labiche" could fend off the requests for formal encounters, interviews, etc., but Camus was also a night person, he liked to go out to dine, drink, and dance, and with this new fame he could no longer be anonymous in these sorties. More than once he played rough with a prying reporter.

Of course fame also gave him more bargaining power with his publishers. With more money he could live more comfortably, and he began to be treated with deference. A master of irony, Camus was well aware of the motives behind this treatment, but he enjoyed it anyway.

The paradox was that if it changed his behavior, being famous did not change his work, nor did it help to remove his doubts about himself.

Drawn increasingly into public life, he often had to choose among obligations. He had less time for old friends. While he gave priority to his fellow North Africans, to the young men around *Combat,* he had less time for them as well, and some of them felt snubbed. Suzanne Labiche believed that such persons were unfair in their refusal to comprehend how precious his time was.[13] On one hand a Jean Grenier— who was not in Paris and did not often meet Camus during these early years of success—saw him as lacking concern for personal advantage, ready to reply personally to most letters, especially to appeals for help; Grenier observed that Camus never locked his car, offering the explanation that "If someone steals, it means he's in need." But Grenier also felt that Camus had an accurate idea of what he was worth. Camus knew that his worth would have to be recognized by others and, because he had started out low on the ladder, he needed success more than some others did. When it came, it had a good influence on him, thought Grenier; Camus could be generous with his gifts. Yet Grenier also speaks of Camus' *"désir de grandeur . . . nostalgie de la noblesse. . . ."*[6]

As time went on, others close to him felt that Camus had begun to take himself too seriously, to ponder his phrases (and then the same phrases would appear in an article or a book); more than one of Camus' intimates was convinced that such "pomposity" was typical of the "North Africans"; fellow *pied noir* Jean Daniel showed similar signs. Each time Camus spoke he felt that his words would be repeated, so he became increasingly cautious about what he said, and even friends detected a new solemnity. At least one acquaintance found it difficult to contradict him, for he spoke with precision and left no opening for a reply.[15] For his part, Camus sensed that he was under surveillance; the intellectual class was waiting to see what his next work would be like, and without excessive sympathy. At the same time he was being consulted as a master, disciples sprouting up everywhere, when his own work hadn't yet ripened.[16]

The long-term effects of fame, the sincerity of his reactions, would become clear later on, in the aftermath of the Nobel Prize, for example. In the meantime Camus was putting out little hints, which friends might have taken as danger signals. There was the essay entitled "L'Enigme," dated 1950 and published in the collection called *L'Eté,* an evocation of facile literary success:

To make a reputation in literature it is no longer necessary to write books. It is sufficient to be known for having written one which the evening papers had talked about, and upon which one will sleep from now on.

And there would be the story "Jonas," published in *L'Exil et le Royaume,* which with *La Chute* would certainly be Camus' most significant autobiographical writing, comic to the outsider, heartrending to those who knew Camus.

Participation in public affairs did not come to an end with the end of the *Combat* adventure. What Camus actually felt about world politics during the early period of cold war can be gleaned from an article or editorial drafted at this time (but there is no record of its having been published anywhere), commenting on President Harry S Truman's call for the co-ordination of the efforts of free world nations against the threat from the Communist bloc. Earlier in 1947 Truman had enunciated what was to be called the Truman Doctrine, offering support to Mediterranean countries against the pressures of Soviet expansion. When Truman reiterated the policy for the Western Hemisphere, Camus saw the new statement as defining "a policy of blocs which risks opening the gates of war." War had to be resisted, for it would mean the occupation of Europe, or its destruction, by Soviet armies, and neither France nor Europe would ever recover from that. In this draft Camus went on to say that he did not believe that a policy of blocs would establish a balance of power: Armed peace was not peace. War or preparation for war destroyed the very ideals that each camp claimed to wish to preserve, and explained why true socialism did not exist in Russia, why political freedom had been set back in the United States. War was not inevitable, but to refuse war did not mean to renounce one's time. On the contrary, Camus favored a world society freed of the myths of sovereignty. He concluded with an appeal to Europeans and to all peoples for united action against war.[17]

When *Caliban* published Camus' "Ni Victimes ni Bourreaux" in the November 1947 issue, it was prefaced by Jean Daniel, who underlined its importance as a political statement.

This *Caliban* was a curious magazine, at least in appearance. It had been launched in February of that year as a pocket-format magazine (about the size of *Reader's Digest* but of pulp magazine quality); it was called a "weekly" temporarily being published bimonthly; in fact it would soon become a monthly (but often with no indication on the cover of which month). Although published with the trappings of sensationalism (the gawdy cover), its contents were often deadly serious, and Camus' writings were perfectly at home among contributions by other notable left-of-center intellectuals. So that it was no surprise that the reply to "Ni Victimes ni Bourreaux" by a leading spokesman for the other camp, Emmanuel d'Astier de la Vigerie, was also printed in *Caliban*. Baron d'Astier, a prewar rightist, had joined the underground resistance to the Nazi occupation, coming out of the war an ally not only of the Gaullists but of the Communists, who would support his daily newspaper *Libération* for all the years of the cold war and beyond (until d'Astier showed signs of independence, at which time the Communists allowed this deficit operation to collapse). D'Astier was an intimate both of Charles de Gaulle and of Joseph Stalin; for the former he had undertaken wartime missions (even to Washington) and served as Interior Minister in de Gaulle's postwar cabinet. But he would also be vice-president of the Soviet-sponsored World Peace Council and a winner of the Lenin Prize, awarded to foreigners having provided notable services to the Soviet cause.

D'Astier's reply to Camus, published in the April 1948 *Caliban*, was entitled "Arrachez la victime aux bourreaux" (Wrest the Victim from the Executioners). He began by observing that the motivations of resistance fighters had varied: the proud refused to accept defeat at the hands of the Nazis, the dignified stood with the oppressed; and then there were those with revolutionary motivations who perceived the links between Fascism and capitalism. He placed himself in the last group. Today there are three choices: Communist revolution, capitalism, the third force. D'Astier asserted that Camus realized that the third option inevitably served the second, creating a dilemma. But Camus refused to choose, preferring to save bodies. "You flee politics," wrote d'Astier, "and you take refuge in morality. What a long road traveled since La Peste!" If Camus considered peace an end in itself, d'Astier preferred to eliminate the causes of war. For not only the guillotine kills; so does hunger.

"I am a pacifist," affirmed d'Astier. "You are a pacifist." But Camus' proposed social movement for peace resembled a social movement against tuberculosis which might reject the means necessary to prevent the disease on the pretext that they were Draconian. He agreed that ends didn't justify means, but those wishing the ends must accept the "frightful necessity" of certain means; slaves must turn against masters. He found it shocking that Camus equated capitalism and Communism; in refusing to choose, in trying to "save bodies," Camus, a "lay saint," becomes the unwitting accomplice of capitalism.

Now more clearly than before the options remaining to post-Liberation Europe were being set forth frankly. The paradox was that in choosing

the moral road, far from the power blocs, Camus believed that he had
avoided the dangers of supporting the "American" position, say, in
order to register his firm refusal of the "Stalinist" one. But now he was
being told that by refusing to accept legal murder—that was the chief
argument of "Ni Victimes ni Bourreaux"—he was an accomplice of one
of the blocs. He replied quickly in the issue of *Caliban* dated June
15–July 15, in an article entitled "Où est la mystification?" (which he
would later republish in *Actuelles*). Here he denied that he was non-
violent; he believed that violence was inevitable, something the years of
Nazi occupation had taught him. But he believed too that any justification of violence had to be refused, whether from an absolutist state or a
totalitarian philosophy. D'Astier had asked why Camus had been on the
side of the resistance. "This is a question which has no meaning for a
certain number of people including myself," he replied. "I couldn't
imagine myself elsewhere, that is all." He had discovered that he hated
violence less than the institutions of violence. Those who resisted had
the right to protest the Greek Government's repression of Communists,
but without killing non-Communists, Camus admitted that he had not
learned about freedom in Marx, but "in poverty." He didn't wish to
fight either capitalism or socialism, but *liberalisme impérialiste* and
*marxisme*. Above all did he oppose war in this era of atomic bombs. As
for Marxism, Marx had been more modest than his present-day followers; he loved living men, not future generations (at the expense of
living men). Accused of unwitting or objective complicity with bourgeois society, Camus reminded d'Astier whose accomplice *he* was.

> Those who claim to know everything and to settle everything end
> up killing everything. The day comes when they have no other rule
> but murder, no other science than the poor scholastic arguments
> which occasionally serve to justify murder.

All the message of *L'Homme révolté* was here. And of course he
was working on *L'Homme révolté* at this time. On October 17, 1947,
his journal entry reads simply "Début," possibly of the first full draft of
the book (unless it was of the play *Les Justes,* whose theme was identical, another panel of the same triptych). "Write everything," he resolved, "as it comes," a remark which sounds as if he was referring to
the essay.

A few days earlier, on October 14, he had reminded himself: "No
time to lose." His journal was filled with notes on readings of the
French and German philosophers, Russian writers and revolutionary
philosophers, ideas for stories, novels (e.g., on "Justice"). In August he
had told the Michel Gallimards about an idea he had for a play that

would star Gérard Philipe and Maria Casarès; it could have been but didn't have to be *Les Justes*.[3]

Indeed, Maria Casarès, with whom he had been so close, now seemed so far away. And she was playing with Philipe in a controversial play by the young writer Henri Pichette, *Les Epiphanies* (it was denied use of one theater because of its allegedly shocking scenes). It had been rumored that Philipe was the lover of Casarès, and stories were told of Camus' reactions to that. When one friend asked him whether he had seen the Pichette play, he responded shortly: "Oh, you know, I don't live with my times." To another friend, one of his college classmates, Camus had harsh words for Philipe.[15]

Of course at that time Camus would not have wanted to see a play starring Maria Casarès, whatever he believed about her relationship to Gérard Philipe.

In fact she was not, not then, having such an affair. She had been seeing a number of men, had come close to marriage to two of them, breaking off at the last minute. Then, in the late spring of 1948—she remembered the date as June 6, the fourth anniversary of the longest day, and of the fiesta at the Dullins'—Camus ran into Maria Casarès on the street at Saint-Germain-des-Prés. She was on her way to the theater, he to see Gide. But she did not go to the theater, nor he to his appointment with Gide.[18]

## 33

DON QUIXOTE

We swallow lies all day long, thanks to a press which is the shame of this country. Any idea, any definition, which risks adding to this lie or to maintain it is unpardonable today. So that in defining a certain number of key words, in rendering them sufficiently clear today so that they can serve tomorrow, we are working for freedom and we are doing our job.

"La Démocratie, exercice de la modestie"

The dilemma for intellectuals in still-free Western Europe was worsening. If the claims of peace were ever more urgent as the nuclear threat grew, the dangers were so much more obviously growing in the East. Stalinism would soon reach an apotheosis of sorts in the coup against the democratic government of Czechoslovakia (February 1948); the Berlin blockade would begin in June; in July, Tito's Yugoslavia would be expelled from the Communist bloc. For the moment it still seemed feasible to offer a third way (neither the Soviet nor the American umbrella). Elements of the French left, including Socialists not in agreement with the position of the official Socialist Party (the SFIO), suggested a joint appeal on behalf of peace, and a neutral, socialist Europe. Sartre's friends, Merleau-Ponty included, André Breton, Combat's Claude Bourdet, the left-Catholic movement around Esprit, launched such an appeal in December 1947. The group might have gone on to plan concrete action. But according to one historian of that period, Simone de Beauvoir, Camus and Breton wished to emphasize a campaign to abolish the death penalty for political crimes. "Many of us," Beauvoir recalled later, believed that on the contrary political crimes were the *only* ones for which the death penalty was justified. The group broke up without further agreement.

Simone de Beauvoir speaks of other differences between the Sartre group and Camus, although politically they continued to share many opinions: Camus too disliked the Gaullist movement, over which he had broken off relations with Albert Ollivier. The Sartre-Camus association continued, if it was less intimate, less free than it had been. But on one notable evening that winter, and in the presence of Camus, Sartre and Beauvoir would break with that unreconstructed anti-Stalinist Arthur Koestler.

It started out with a friendly enough encounter. Simone de Beauvoir was working at the Café de Flore one morning in the fall of 1947. She accompanied Koestler and his wife to the Jeu de Paume museum of Impressionist paintings; Koestler remarked that the great painters, like Sartre and Koestler, had small heads. She found his vanity almost touching until he said: "How many copies did *La Peste* sell? Eighty thousand. Not bad." Then he reminded her that his own novel, *Darkness at Noon,* had sold two hundred thousand. Later, Koestler wished to repeat their wild evening at a Russian cabaret. The party included Koestler and his wife, Camus, Sartre, and Beauvoir. Koestler quickly made it clear to the cabaret's headwaiter that he had the honor of serving Camus, Sartre, and Koestler. He then plunged into his theme: no friendship without political agreement. All of them were drunk by now; Sartre was flirting with Koestler's attractive wife. Suddenly Koestler threw a glass at Sartre's head but it broke against the wall. The others got up, but Koestler wanted to stay. Sartre was staggering around on the sidewalk; finally Koestler decided he would also leave, and crawled up the stairs to the street on hands and legs. He wanted to start fighting with Sartre again. "Let's go! We're going home," Camus said in a friendly way, taking Koestler by the shoulder; he pulled away violently and hit Camus, who wanted to leap at him but the others prevented that.

Leaving Koestler in the hands of his wife, the others got into Camus' automobile. Himself well doused with vodka and champagne, Camus had tears in his eyes. "He was my friend! And he hit me!" He fell onto the steering wheel, abandoning the car to itself. Sobered by fright, Sartre and Beauvoir raised Camus' head.

On the days that followed they talked about that night more than once. Camus asked them in a puzzled voice: "Do you believe that we can continue to drink like that and still work?" Beauvoir felt that one could not, and she insists in her memoirs that such events were rare. They made sense at an earlier time when the friends refused to accept the fact that their war victory had been stolen from them; now they were able to live with that. Koestler, who favored the Gaullist solution, pretended that Sartre was also secretly supporting de Gaulle; that was the end of their relationship as far as Beauvoir was concerned.[1]

With other personalities of the non-Communist left that spring Sartre had founded a Rassemblement Démocratique Révolutionnaire (RDR), designed to rally intellectuals not tied to the Communists or any other party, and who believed that Europe could serve as a mediator between the two great powers. Sartre would be involved with the RDR for nearly two years (resigning in October 1949 after having fought what he considered pro-American tendencies in the movement). Camus would never join, but on several occasions he participated in its activity.

In January 1948, Camus provoked a minor explosion with an essay entitled "Les Meurtriers délicats," an early version of a chapter of *L'Homme révolté*,[2] published in the first issue of a new magazine, *La Table Ronde*. The essay contains the essence of his play, *Les Justes*, which he would begin writing the same month: Kaliayev, one of a group of young revolutionaries pledged to kill Grand Duke Serge by throwing a bomb into his carriage as it drove through the streets of Moscow in February 1905, decided not to throw the bomb because there were children in the carriage.

It was not the content of "Les Meurtriers délicats" which created the problem, although in microcosm all of the moral content of *L'Homme révolté* is found in it. It was the magazine itself, which in the same issue also published a controversial writer whose attitude during the Nazi occupation had been attacked; *La Table Ronde* also announced future contributions by controversial personalities, such as Henry de Montherlant. The magazine's editorial board included both Camus and his lifelong antagonist François Mauriac, as well as Raymond Aron, André Malraux, Jean Paulhan. Simone de Beauvoir would note that *La Table Ronde* "opened its columns in a fraternal way to ex-collaborators and their friends," and also remarked Camus' presence in that first issue and his absence from subsequent issues—because he had understood.[1]

The Comité National des Ecrivains at once decided to exclude Mauriac from membership; he had written the lead article in that first issue.[3] *La Table Ronde* had promised another article by Camus for the next issue, but no second article by Camus would appear. Camus' name was included on the editorial board in the second issue, but not thereafter (issue number three simply avoided publishing the names of board members).

Camus journeyed to Switzerland on January 19 to visit the Michel Gallimards, who were living at a hotel-sanatorium in Leysin. For Michel's year-long bed rest hadn't cured him of his tuberculosis; effective medicine was still not available. He would spend a total of eight months in Switzerland.⁴ Camus stayed with his friends for nearly three weeks, in a landscape of "Snow and clouds in the valley up to the peaks." Something also led him to enter this reflection in his journal now:

> I withdrew from the world not because I had enemies there, but because I had friends. Not because they did me an injustice as usually happens, but because they believed me better than I am. It's a lie I can't accept.

But had he withdrawn from the world? Perhaps, if the entry is to be taken literally, he was referring to the necessary distance he was taking with his literary world, and with his admirers, after the success of *La Peste*. But his political activity, his speeches and polemical articles, had by no means ceased.

The quiet of Leysin was to allow him to finish writing the script of *L'Etat de siège*—at least he thought that he had finished it—a play that Jean-Louis Barrault was to produce on a theme similar to that of *La Peste*. Barrault, who had been following Camus' work since his unsuccessful attempt to produce *Caligula* during the German occupation while he was a member of the Comédie Française, had long desired to do a play whose central theme would be plague. He had discussed an adaptation of Daniel Defoe's *A Journal of the Plague Year* with Antonin Artaud prior to the war, and after the war he took it up again. Then Camus' novel was published, and Barrault, who liked to work with a partner, asked Camus if he would collaborate on such a play.

Incredible as it may have appeared later, there was a misunderstanding at the outset of their project. Barrault, like Artaud, saw plague as a catalyst, a purifying disease. But why then contact the author of *La Peste,* whose plague was an absolute evil, symbolizing Fascism, the Nazi era, the occupation of France? In Barrault's opinion, the explanation was that neither he nor Camus realized the contradiction while they were working together on what was to become *L'Etat de siège*. Neither realized that they were about to produce a two-headed monster. Barrault attributed it to naïveté.⁵

But at the time things seemed to be going smoothly enough. After completing the draft in Switzerland, Camus went on to write the opening scenes of *Les Justes*. He also came to know Michel Gallimard's doctor, René Lehmann, whom he would see again on Lehmann's visits to

Paris. They would remain friends through the final years of Camus' life, and occasionally Camus would be examined by Lehmann.

But his main preoccupation now was Michel Gallimard. Camus found his friend in a state of almost perpetual gloom. His disease seemed to threaten all the things worth living for. Attempting to cheer him up, Camus reminded him that Goethe had said that only a stubborn man was capable of hope, which also meant that an idiot could accept anything. Camus confessed that few persons could have contemplated their disease with as much horror as he himself had back in his youth when he was first informed of its nature. And the horror explained much about the man that Camus had become.

This didn't mean that he was satisfied with the man he had become. Camus also evoked the new man described by Dostoevsky, who faced death with indifference. What justifies man is his love of life, but that didn't necessarily require orgies, boogie-woogie, or driving a car at ninety miles an hour.[4]

Francine had taken the children to Oran in January, and now Camus joined them there. And he was apparently still full of thoughts of the plague when he listened to his children learning to talk. Soon, he would report to Nicola Chiaromonte, he had taught them a play of his own making. He would ask: "Who is the plague?" and his boy, Jean, would reply: "It's Cathie." Then: "Who is cholera?" and this time Catherine would reply: "It's Jean." "Who is the victim?" their father would ask, and both children were to respond together: "It's papa!"

Leaving the children with Francine's mother, the Camus went on to Sidi Madani, where in a rugged site in the Gorges de la Chiffa south of Algiers an old hotel had been converted into an educational center for the official youth and sports administration, of which Camus' sister-in-law Christiane was the local director. When she had been asked to transform the educational center into a cultural hostel to which creative writers would be invited for stays of a fortnight or more, she had consulted with Camus about persons to invite. Now Camus himself was a guest, along with friends Francis Ponge, Brice Parain, Louis Guilloux, Emmanuel Roblès, writer and *Combat* contributor Henri Calet, and some Moslem authors, among them Mohammed Dib.

Each guest had his own room and was quite free; there were no formal seminars, although the guests might travel around the country to lecture, as Guilloux did.[6] Camus' only actual duty was to give a series of talks to local teachers.[7] Perfecting his Ping-Pong in what was in truth a magnificent resort hotel with excellent food, he decided that he was living something of the life of a sanatorium here.[4]

The Camus' spent a fortnight at Sidi Madani. Between Oran and

Algiers they visited deserted beaches. Once, when they stopped to swim in the March sun, they returned to find a window of their automobile broken and their clothing and personal effects stolen. They reported the incident to the gendarmes not in the expectation that they might recover their possessions but in order to be issued temporary identity papers, for theirs had been taken with everything else.

At Ténès, on the coast halfway between Oran and Algiers, standing at the foot of a mountain, Camus discovered a bay forming a perfect half circle. "As evening falls," he told his journal

> an anguished fullness soars over silent waters. Then one understands that if the Greeks conceived despair and tragedy, it is always *through* beauty and the oppressive quality of beauty. It is a tragedy which culminates, while the modern spirit built its despair from ugliness and mediocrity.
>
> Doubtless what Char means. For the Greeks, beauty is at the beginning. For a European it is a goal, rarely attained. I am not modern.

Of course he had to revisit Tipasa, accompanied by Louis Guilloux, who expressed disappointment that there was no Brittany mist over the ruins—only blue sky.[8] In Algiers, Camus visited his family, and then went to the hilltop town of Bouzaréah to call on the Roblès. Camus brought his papers with him and spent the day working on Act IV, Scene 1, of *Les Justes*. Then Roblès asked questions for an interview on Radio-Algérie and Camus replied in writing. When Roblès commented to him afterwards that it was good to hear the word *bonheur*—Camus had spoken of Algiers as a city of happiness—rather than the despair some had read into his writings, Camus took up the script again and added:

> It is true that the men of my generation have seen too many things to imagine that the world of today can retain the atmosphere of a children's book. They know that there are also prisons and mornings of execution. . . . But this is not despair. This is lucidity.[9]

Being up here at Bouzaréah in that magnificent site overlooking Cap Matifou revived his nostalgia for this city of sun and sea, although he hadn't waited until he got here to long for a return to his native soil. But from here the uncomfortable quarters on the Rue Séguier, and the life of postwar Paris in general, seemed even grimmer. From Paris, Camus had already let Roblès know how anxious he was to get back to Algeria. He had some money now, and could think of having a house in a desirable location overlooking his beloved Algiers bay, while pursuing his career in French letters. Roblès' wife had found such a house for him on the Bouzaréah crest, and had written Camus that winter for a decision. But that was when he had had to go to Leysin to see the Michel Gallimards; he had promised to reply on his return. So Roblès had to tell him that the villa they had found for him had been snapped up by somebody else. Now Roblès took him to see the villa he had missed, and Camus asked him to find another one like it.[10] He had also asked Charles Poncet if he thought that he could find a house for him in Tipasa; Poncet understood that his old friend was looking not for a permanent residence but an oasis to which he could repair when he wished to escape Paris. Poncet did ask friends in Tipasa to see what they could come up with, but nothing came of this.[11]

Later in 1948, Camus would tell Gabriel Audisio that if various factors which didn't depend on him had not prevented it, he would have settled in Algeria. He felt "surrounded" in Paris.[12]

So he contemplated his return to the French mainland without joy. He flew back from Oran, leaving his wife there with the children for another three weeks. But after takeoff the plane lost one of its four engines, and the pilot announced that they would have to return to La Sénia Airport for repairs. He began to experience the claustrophobia that often troubled him in enclosed spaces, and fainted.[4]

Back in Paris, the question was still on the table: how to get out of the Rue Séguier, where daily life, because it was taken as temporary, was never quite organized. Should he stay in Paris, go to North Africa, or go to Provence?[4]

Emmanuel Roblès had written a play called *Montserrat*, which dramatized the liberation struggle led by Simón Bolívar against the Spanish conquerors in Venezuela in 1812, although, as the author noted in a preface, the subject could have been transferred to ancient Rome, Spain under Philip II, occupied France, "etc." (Roblès happened to be a specialist in Spanish history.) The play opened in Paris at the Montparnasse Theater on April 23, and on the same day in Algiers; its success was immediate and considerable, for it would be translated into twenty-two languages. Camus wrote of it in *Combat*, praising it as "curious and strong," but adding: "It is not in the Americas that 'Montserrat' takes place, but somewhere in Mauritania, between the two deserts of sand and of the sea." ("Mauritania" was being used in the ancient Roman sense, to signify all of North Africa.)

Not long after Francine Camus' return the Camus were off again, this time to London and to Edinburgh, for another officially sponsored cultural visit. They arrived in England by train and Channel ferry on May 4, attended a reception in their honor at the French Institute, then a formal dinner at the French Embassy. Their Oran friend Jean-Paul de

Dadelsen was there and drove the Camus in his old car to the embassy; Camus told him to drop them off before they reached the embassy so that no one would see them arrive in such a vehicle.[13]

> I remember London as a city of gardens where the birds woke me up in the morning [he told his journal]. London is the contrary, and yet my memory is correct. Flower carts in the streets. The docks, prodigious.

At the National Gallery he found the Piero della Francesca and Velázquez paintings "marvelous."

They went to Oxford, staying at Magdalen College—"Silence of Oxford. What is the world doing here?" And to Glasgow, Edinburgh:

> Early morning on the coast of Scotland. Edinburgh: swans in the canals. The city encircling a false acropolis, mysterious and misty. The Athens of the North has nothing of the north. Chinese and Maltese in Princess Street. It's a port.

For *L'Etat de siège* to become an actable play, it was found that a considerable amount of additional work would have to be done, and the opening was scheduled for that autumn. In content, if not in spirit, the play Camus was writing for Barrault had little resemblance to *La Peste*. The scene was no longer Oran in Algeria but Cádiz in Spain. The plague would be represented by a man, a giant with a gift for irony, who has taken over the city, ruling it with the arbitrary cruelty of a Caligula. A student, Diego, revolts against fear, rallies the people of Cádiz against the Plague. The Plague offers to allow Diego and his fiancée to escape if he may continue his reign of terror undisturbed; Diego refuses and dies, but Cádiz is saved.

Camus took the script with him down to Provence, where he was to spend the summer working alongside René Char at L'Isle-sur-la-Sorgue. Char had helped him rent a large old country house in an isolated spot. The house had a name, "Palerme," a corruption, for it had been named for a Duke of Palerne whose family had since died out.[14] It had disadvantages which the romantics Char and Camus hadn't considered—isolation, the exposure to the intense heat of midsummer (when the Camus were to use it), its location at the edge of a canal, without a fence to keep the children away from the water's edge. Camus had found the isolation attractive, of course, and hadn't considered that his family might find it even more isolated than he did, for they would be spending more time there than he.[13]

Camus left Paris with Char in what was to be a memorable automobile ride. For the black Citroën was already tired, and a long journey down through France took on something of the stations of the cross.

The gas pump wasn't working, a problem Camus blamed on his Paris garage mechanic. By the time they got to their evening stop they were filthy; Camus was sure they resembled gangsters, and the hotel owner confirmed his opinion, for he told the pair with respect that they could sign the register with whatever names they liked, he wouldn't ask for their identity papers. The colossus Char wrote on his registry card that he was a manufacturer, Camus identified himself as a journalist. Was that all right? they asked the innkeeper? Anything at all—as long as you don't say Pierrot le Fou (the name of a gangster made famous in the popular press).[4]

Just before leaving Paris, Camus had read the long reply of Emmanuel d'Astier de la Vigerie to his defense of "Ni Victimes ni Bourreaux." He would have to reply to d'Astier once again, but he had forgotten to bring d'Astier's new attack with him, and asked Michel Gallimard to find it in his desk and send it on. D'Astier had published this second article, entitled "Ponce Pilate chez les bourreaux," in the fellow-traveling newspaper *Action;* this time Camus' reply would appear, for want of an appropriate medium, in the RDR monthly organ *La Gauche.*

D'Astier had taxed Camus with evoking his childhood poverty; Camus explained that he had been obliged to correct the record, the pro-Communist press having called him a "son of the bourgeoisie" so often that it was necessary, at least this once,

> that I remind you that most of you, Communist intellectuals, have
> no experience of the condition of the proletariat, and that you are
> ill-placed to treat us as dreamers ignorant of realities.

He conceded that he had not been as important in the resistance movement as d'Astier had been; he'd been only a simple private.

D'Astier had challenged him to explain what he meant by the justification of violence by the totalitarians; Camus pointed to the Nazi and Soviet concentration camps, and forced labor for political prisoners.

D'Astier had suggested that Camus send an open lettter to the American press protesting against the complicity of the United States in the execution of political prisoners by the right-wing Greek regime; Camus pointed out that d'Astier was ignorant of his true position, that he had discussed this very issue during his visit to Great Britain, and had taken up similar matters during his public lectures in the United States in 1946. He would hand d'Astier such a letter, nevertheless, if d'Astier for his part would protest the Soviet concentration camp system and forced labor practices, and if he would demand the uncondi-

tional release of Spanish Republicans still interned in Soviet camps.
(D'Astier never followed up the offer.)

In his conclusion Camus told d'Astier, and the French left through
d'Astier:

> My role . . . is not to transform the world, nor man. . . . But it is,
> perhaps, to serve in my way the several values without which a
> world, even transformed, is not worth living. . . .

Didn't the Marxists need a conscience? If they did not, no one
could do anything for them, and Europe would finish in a bloodbath.
Yet:

> If they need one, who will give it to them if not these few men
> who, without separating themselves from history, conscious of their
> limits, seek to formulate as they can the misfortune and the hope of
> Europe. Solitaries! you will say with scorn. Perhaps, for the mo-
> ment. But you would be quite alone without these solitaries.

Identifying himself with the liberal conscience, with the solitaries,
Camus was indeed mapping out a lonely course for himself and his
friends, who were unwilling to accept without protest abuses of freedom
and human decency whether in the Western or the Eastern bloc, and
this at a time when the Cold War was making nearly everyone else a
partisan of one bloc or the other.

Camus had one pleasure at L'Isle-sur-la-Sorgue: His mother had joined
him there. For himself he had chosen a quiet room at the top of this
house called Palerme, with a view of the Lubéron mountain chain. He
would spend hours at a time there, smoking, daydreaming, working,
too. Evenings, he would take long walks in the countryside in the company of an old dog.

But writing came with difficulty. The play he was doing for Barrault was making him suffer.[4] His journal became something of a fever
chart, recording his highs and lows, his readings, his observations of nature, things that Char or Char's friends said to him. A friend of Char:
"We shall die at forty of a bullet that we fired at our heart at twenty."

Another notation made at Palerme:

> The good fortune of my life is that I have met, loved (and dis-
> appointed) only exceptional beings. I knew virtue, dignity, ease,
> nobility, *in others*. Admirable—and painful—spectacle.

He mocked the young man he had been ten years earlier, who had
listed the books he would write. Still, he had mastered his art.

He told himself that one couldn't do something for someone without denying someone else; if you can't deny people you are sterilized. "In the end, to love a being is to kill all the others."

Writing block or no, he would now write a brief essay, "L'Exil d'Helène," which introduced the theme of the Mediterranean man's sense of proportion, the philosophical proposition with which he would conclude *L'Homme révolté*. He dedicated it to René Char, dated it August 30, 1948; it seems in retrospect another confirmation of the influence of Char on the essay on revolt to come.

Back in Paris, back at that crowded, disorganized, dark flat, he felt unhappier than ever with his living arrangements. He worked overtime on *L'Etat de siège;* he would tell Jean Grenier that he had been at it for five weeks, from 2 P.M. to 2 A.M. each day, in order to provide Barrault with a satisfactory text by the beginning of rehearsals. He not only worked on the script until the last minute, he continued to work on it after rehearsals had begun.[15] Now the cast had been chosen. The young challenger of the Plague, Diego, would be played by Barrault himself, and Maria Casarès would be his fiancée (saved by Diego's sacrifice). La Peste himself would be played by Pierre Bertin, the Plague's secretary by Barrault's wife Madeleine Renaud, Nada by Pierre Brasseur. In this all-star cast, the "bearer of the dead" was the mime Marcel Marceau.

To choose a title for the play, Camus and Barrault invented a game. One of them would say, "Get dressed, darling, we're going to see ————," and then decide what might fit the blank. One couldn't say, for example, "Get dressed, darling, we're going to see 'The Plague,'" nor could one say "The Black Tumor" or "The White Evil." But *L'Etat de siège* fit the blank perfectly.[5]

In that month of September 1948, Camus discovered another image of the Sisyphian labor of the individual against the terrible power of the blocs, in that lonely American Garry Davis. Rereading Don Quixote, Camus told Jean Grenier that he found in Davis "the style of a lean Sancho, with the madness of his master.[16] On September 12, Davis began his celebrated sit-in at the temporary headquarters of the United Nations at the Palais de Chaillot in Paris, renouncing his American citizenship to proclaim himself citizen of the world. Expelled from U.N. territory by the police, he was supported by a board of solidarity to which Camus, Breton, the left-Catholic philosopher Emmanuel Mounier, Richard Wright lent their names. On November 19, Davis created another scandal when he got up to deliver a speech at a United Nations meeting. Camus was standing by, held a press conference in a neighborhood café in support his gesture. On December 3 some three thou-

sand persons attended a rally at Paris's Salle Pleyel, another two thousand stood outside to listen to the proceedings through loudspeakers, as
Camus, Breton, Vercors, and Paulhan defended Garry Davis; on December 9 they took a still larger hall, the Vélodrome d'Hiver (popularly
known as the Vel' d'Hiv), where Davis appeared alongside Camus,
Breton, Paulhan.[17] (Camus was even hurt that Sartre refused to participate in the campaign, and insisted with pride that the Vel' d'Hiv meeting had drawn a crowd of twenty thousand. But Sartre agreed with the
Communists that the Garry Davis phenomenon was just hot air; the
United States was filled with eccentrics with simplistic slogans. What
was significant, Simone de Beauvoir noted in her memoirs, was that
Davis was being taken seriously in Europe by left-wing intellectuals.)[1]

"What are you doing here?" Camus asked himself at the opening
of his speech at the Salle Pleyel, and supplied his own answer: "What
we can."

"What's the use of it?" "What's the use of the UN?"

"Why doesn't Davis go to Soviet Russia?" went Camus' next rhe-
torical question. "Because they won't let him enter. Meanwhile he
addresses himself to the Soviet delegate as to the others."

Camus went on to say that Davis had abandoned many privileges
in giving up his American passport, so why, he asked himself, don't I
give up my French citizenship? Being French brings with it more bur-
dens than privileges; one doesn't give up one's country when it is in
trouble. Davis' gesture was spectacular? So did Socrates give permanent
spectacles on the market place.

"Don't you see that Davis serves American imperialism?" he asked
himself, and replied:

> In abandoning his American nationality, Davis disengages him-
> self from that imperialism as from others. This gives him the right
> to attack such imperialism, a right that it seems to me difficult to
> grant to those who wish to restrict all sovereignties except the Soviet
> one.

And Soviet imperialism? Camus observed that imperialisms were like
twins, they grew up together and couldn't do without each other. If the
objection is made that sovereignty is a reality, then so is cancer. To his
critics, he asked in turn a question: Were they so sure of the infallibility
of their political convictions or doctrine that they could reject without
consideration the warnings of those

> who tell them of the misfortune of millions of creatures, the cry of
> innocence, simple joys? . . . Are they so sure to be right that they
> will risk even the one chance in a thousand of increasing the danger
> of atomic war?[18]

*"Brilliant et incisif,"* *Le Monde*'s reporter characterized Camus' speech. When Davis himself was introduced, he was greeted with cheers, his words were frequently interrupted by applause. Reporting it, the Spanish syndicalist organ *Solidaridad Obrera* saw the meeting as of great pacifist significance, of potentially great impact. In *Esprit* one of the men who took part in the meeting, Emmanuel Mounier, praised Davis' futile gesture and suggested that Davis' supporters were not heroes, but were only doing their duty.

Friends would see in Camus' support of Garry Davis an echo of his own naïve idealism. Not that he believed that Davis could succeed, but Davis' crusade was an opportunity to communicate a message that was dear to Camus.[19] The veteran French anarchist Maurice Joyeux, who would later be allied with Camus in other left-idealist causes, insisted that when Davis camped in his sleeping bag on the steps of the Palais de Chaillot or in front of the Cherche-Midi prison, "his gesture was greeted by an immense enthusiasm by youth who had said no to war and yes to sentimental pacifism . . ." Anarchists of all kinds joined Davis, this former bomber pilot with the air of a boy scout, hoping that he would bring about a miracle. The anarchist newspaper *Le Libertaire* reported: "It's the first stage, a first step toward the human and universal liberation that we have always fought for, and we salute it," but, the newspaper added, "this pacifist tendency must evolve toward a clearly revolutionary position."[20]

Should Camus have been mocked and insulted for supporting Davis? In an open letter to his eternal opponent François Mauriac, published on December 25 in *Combat,* Camus in effect replied to all who were treating Davis' gestures (and the support of intellectuals like Camus for Davis) with irony:

> Some other writers and myself were asked to protect by our solidarity a man who had accomplished all by himself a courageous and meaningful act and had been rewarded by the mocking of a press which never lacks the opportunity, as you know, to bring honor to this country.

The job had been to defend Davis against the bureaucracy, to draw attention to his campaign, and for that Camus was being treated as an appeaser or a Fascist, attacked by Socialists and Gaullists. The anti-Soviets seemed to be saying that, since Davis could only propagate his ideas in the West, he would disarm the free world and contribute to the victory of Soviet imperialism. But the alternative seemed to be to support the U.S. and the Gaullists. "I believe that we still must try to save Europe and our country from a vast catastrophe," Camus went on, to conclude:

Neither Davis nor those who welcomed him claim to be bearing truth to the world. They know quite well that their path is elsewhere, and their true vocation. They have only uttered a cry of alarm. . . .

Mauriac replied to Camus in *La Table Ronde* (in February 1949), suggesting that *he* might be the *"incrédule."* Perhaps, Mauriac said, he had yielded to bitterness because, after rejecting the Son of Man, Camus had chosen to follow *un petit homme*. Mauriac remarked that every time he met Camus and dined with him all went well, but the next day Camus took his distances again; Mauriac suspected a conflict in generations. Henceforth, he promised, their dialogue would be polemical. And yet Camus was a natural Christian, said Mauriac—*anima naturliter christiana* in St. Augustine's phrase. Mauriac refused to be forced into the alternatives offered by Camus, refused to believe in the efficacy of a Garry Davis in the face of the problems of the world.

In a letter from Paris to the New York magazine *Partisan Review,* published in April 1949 Lionel Abel reported:

> . . . Then there was the comedy of the Gary Davis affair. This young man, as everybody knows, conceived the idea of turning in his passport and renouncing his American citizenship, laying claim to the title of first world citizen. . . . Camus, Breton and Bourdet came out flat-footedly for the action of Gary Davis as something presaging a new kind of intervention in politics by the individual. I read what they wrote of Gary Davis and said at the meeting, with much astonishment, for these are surely well informed and clever men, and how could they think the course of history would be influenced in any essential respect by this Orson gee Wellsian gesture of a politically naive young man? On the other hand, neither Camus nor Breton wanted Davis' gesture to be generalized into a mass surrender of citizenship, for when the young and impressionable poet Pichette, who had heard the speeches at the Pleyel Meeting, sent his own passport, French papers, and carte d'identité to *Combat* . . . Camus, Bourdet and Breton urged him to take back his papers, arguing that such behavior would be likely to harm the symbolic value of Gary Davis' act. . . .

Abel went on to criticize Camus in more general terms:

> Camus' political writings, from what I have seen, have become wordy, soft and vaguely noble . . . Of late he has taken to identifying the morally desirable and the politically effective. . . . Camus will only raise his voice for what is clearly good. . . .

# 34

---◆---

## EUROPE-AMERICA

It is not a matter of adding more hatred to the world and to choose between two societies, even though we know that American society represents the lesser evil. We don't have to choose evil, even the lesser. . . . We have only to give a form to the protest of men against that which crushes them, with the single goal of holding on to what can be held, and with the simple hope of being on hand one day, workers in a necessary reconstruction.

Manifesto of Groupes de Liaison Internationale

*L'Etat de siège* finally opened at the Marigny Theater on October 27, 1948, the Compagnie Madeleine Renaud-Jean-Louis Barrault directed by Barrault, with scenery and costumes by the painter Balthus, a friend of Artaud and one of France's best known moderns, and a score by Arthur Honegger. With an all-star cast and contributions from these notable artists nothing should have gone wrong. But everything did. The critics looked for life in this play and could find none. The action seemed academic, the characters unconvincing. In adapting his thinly disguised fable to the stylized theater of Barrault, in attempting to fit this square peg (the plague as totalitarian horror) into that round role (the beneficial plague of Artaud), a mélange was conceived which pleased no one at all. The difficult but highly influential critic of *Le Figaro,* Jean-Jacques Gautier, while acknowledging the poetry and the exceptional casting, confessed to feeling "indifferent" to the flowery language; no contact had been established between author and public. "Since I have been going to the theater," wrote René Barjavel, novelist and essayist, in *Carrefour,* "I believe that I have never suffered as much." *Le Monde*'s Robert Kemp found the play "caricatural," the allegory *"enfantin."* "What disappointment! Bitter grief! Heavy boredom. . . ." Even Camus' friend of Gallimard and of *Combat,* Jacques Lemarchand, had to attack the production in Camus' old newspaper, although he blamed the staging of Barrault, which was not quite right for contemporary authors.

Maria Casarès' friend Dussane also attributed the failure of the play to Camus' unnatural alliance with Barrault, Camus having simply been the librettist of Barrault's conception. Even Maria was miscast, having to play love scenes with a Barrault not meant for such roles.[1]

"On the opening night," Barrault himself later recalled, "the 'Parisians' found it hard to hide their joy at the idea that we had failed; I felt a physical pain whose scar I continue [in 1954] to bear." It was, Barrault says, his first failure, and he feared that Camus would be lost to this theater. There was a small group of persons favorable to the play, and Barrault wanted to keep it on his repertory program longer but could not afford to, with one hundred persons on his payroll.[2] Others believed that Barrault might have saved the play by keeping it in the repertory, since in any case he was not performing it every night but alternating it with other plays in the program, but after seventeen performances he cut his losses.[3] Several times Camus would express interest in reviving *L'Etat de siège,* modifying it, perhaps for an open-air theater (this was after his successful outdoor productions at the Angers Festival), but not with Barrault; they could no longer be comfortable working together; something had snapped.[4]

In his introduction to the American edition of the play Camus was careful to point out that *L'Etat de siège* "had without effort achieved critical unanimity"; few plays had received "such a complete cutting up." All the more regrettable because he had always felt that the play was "that of my writings which is most like me." He insisted that it was not an adaptation of his novel; it was more of a morality play, an allegory. "My avowed purpose was to tear the theater away from psychological speculations and to allow to be heard on our murmuring stages the great cries which bend or liberate masses of men today."

He had another score to settle. Writing in *Nouvelles Littéraires,* the Catholic philosopher and playwright Gabriel Marcel questioned the courage of placing the action in Spain rather than in Eastern Europe, where there was sufficient reason to despair. In *Combat,* Camus replied with an essay-letter, "Pourquoi l'Espagne." It was not Barrault but Camus himself who had decided to place the action in Spain; he took on himself Marcel's charge of opportunism and dishonesty. Today evil comes from the state, the police or the bureaucratic state. And why Spain? Because here, "For the first time, men of my age encountered injustice triumphant in history." He cited the recent sentencing to death of five opponents of the Franco regime, as well as other past and present examples of Franco's crimes. He blamed his own country for having co-operated with the Spanish dictator. He would never stop protesting, and if he attacked the Catholic Church in the play it was the Spanish Church which co-operated with the Franco criminals. Marcel, he wrote, was willing to be silent about Spain in order to combat the crimes of the Communist regimes, while he and his friends would be silent about nothing.

Indeed, he would be increasingly active in the cause of Republican Spain. Maria Casarès certainly had something to do with that, but not only Casarès. Camus had been contacted by José Ester Borrás, the secretary of the Spanish Federation of Political Prisoners (Federación Española de Deportados y Internados Políticos [FEDIP]), which with the anarchist trade union Confederación Nacional de Trabajo (CNT) —both of them émigré organizations based in France—had been campaigning for the release of Spanish Republicans who had been sent to the U.S.S.R. during the war and whom Stalin had locked into camps. Many had been children evacuated to save them from bombing raids; others were student pilots and sailors who had gone to the Soviet Union for training. When they wished to leave they were able to get permission to travel to Franco Spain—but not to a free country such as France. Camus had taken up their cause in his second reply to Emmanuel d'Astier de la Vigèrie, and now he became a frequent ally of the FEDIP and CNT, through such men as Ester, whom he would see regularly, and Fernando Gomez Pelaez, director of CNT's newspaper published in France, *Solidaridad Obrera*.

Soon Camus would draft an appeal for the creation of a committee of support for Spanish Republican émigrés, under FEDIP sponsorship, for which he promised to obtain the signatures of leading French intellectuals. When published in *Solidaridad Obrera* on August 20, 1949, Camus' appeal included the signatures of Gide, Mauriac, Sartre, Char, Ignazio Silone, Carlo Levi, Bourdet, Breton, Orwell and Pablo Casals.[5] The left-syndicalist but rigorously anti-Stalinist orientation of the émigrés naturally appealed to Camus; their struggle proved that one could fight for anti-Fascist principles without falling into the arms of the Stalinist totalitarians, that one could be a man of the left without being a Communist.

Meanwhile, on February 2, 1949, the government of the Spanish Republic in Exile admitted Camus to the Order of the Liberation (Orden de la Liberación). At a ceremony at the exile government headquarters on Avenue Foch, in the presence of the Spanish Republic's president and prime minister, the Grand Chancellor of the Order, exile Minister of Justice Fernando Valera, pointed out that while Camus did not like decorations he had accepted this one, which was an appeal not to vanity but to sacrifice. Valera thanked Camus for what he had done to help liberate Spain, and Camus in turn thanked "the only legal government of Spain." At no time did he confuse this honor with the kind that governments gave away so generously, he said. "The little I have been able to do, I have done as much for truth as for free Spain." And he would continue.[6]

On December 13, 1948, at the Salle Pleyel, Camus spoke at an international meeting of intellectuals for peace, sponsored by the RDR, sharing the platform with personalities such as Carlo Levi (the Italian anti-Fascist) and Richard Wright (for whom Simone de Beauvoir served as interpreter).[7] Camus' speech was a significant one, considered so by himself as well, for he caused it to be reproduced in his first collection of political writings, *Actuelles*. "We are in an era when men, moved by mediocre and ferocious ideologies, become used to being ashamed of everything," he began. The writer is made to feel responsible for the misery of the world. But he himself had no guilty conscience; he felt only gratitude and pride for his profession. He described the contemporary world of terror, affirmed that art was opposed to such a world. "In an era in which the conqueror, by the very logic of his attitude, becomes executioner and policeman, the artist is forced to be insubordinate." He went on: "In the face of contemporary political society, the only coherent attitude of the artist . . . is refusal without concession." So it is useless to demand justification and commitment of the artist; he is committed, even if against his will. "By his very function, the artist is witness to freedom. . . ." True artists are on the side of life, enemies of no one save the executioners.

He had to withdraw from the arena temporarily, at the end of December 1948, to fly to Algiers on an emergency call. His favorite aunt and benefactor, Antoinette Acault, Tante Gaby, was being operated on. He flew at night but couldn't sleep on the plane, watched the stars, then "the lights of the Balearics," as he told his journal, "like flowers in the sea." He spent all of the following day in the hospital alongside the old woman who didn't know how close she was to death. His mother was there too, but he saw that she was saved from anxiety by her goodness —and indifference. Leaving the hospital, he wanted to walk around his city, but the rain began to come down hard. He was alone in the street, felt that he was at the far reaches of the world. Next day he woke to sunshine.

He thought that he would have to stay at least ten days, through a second operation, and this time and for the first time since the war he could see his old home and his old friends at leisure. "The faces I recognize, after hesitation, and which have aged," he noted. "It is evening in Guermantes. But on the scale of a city where I lose myself."

One evening he met with Roblès, Edmond Brua, possibly with the Moslem writer El Boudali Safir, and other old acquaintances at the Brasserie des Facultés to see whether they could launch still another publishing venture connected with, and for the greater glory of, French-Algerian letters. By this time Emond Charlot's brilliant Paris-Algiers publishing operation was in trouble and soon it would expire of exhaustion. The idea was to combine the prewar *Rivages* with a company Brua himself had founded, Editions du Cactus; their printer friend Emmanuel Andréo would manufacture the books (and put up most of the capital thereby). Camus said he would give the series his adaptation of Pierre de Larivey's *Les Esprits.* Their first book—it would turn out to be their only book—was a lecture on García Lorca by Roblès, published that April in two thousand copies. The prospectus promised Camus' *Les Esprits,* texts by Mohammed Dib, Carlo Levi, Arturo Serrano Plaja, Safir, Brua, Audisio. . . . But soon after that Andréo fell ill; his death would be the *coup de grâce* of the new *Rivages,* whose chief significance would be to demonstrate Camus' continued wish to create bridges to his Algerian past.[8]

He visited his old Belcourt apartment. Once, sitting alone with his mother there, he was tempted to talk with her about his private life— and then decided not to. He wasn't sure that she would understand his situation, but he knew that she would understand him, because she loved him.

A strange malaise accompanied him throughout the city, all the time of his stay in it. His mother apart, he decided that he would return to Algeria as little as possible. Finally, reassured that his aunt had been given a new chance, he was able to leave.[9]

This new year, 1949, would be marked by another long voyage abroad in the interests of cultural exchange, this time to Latin America. And although he was not booked to sail until the end of June, beginning now —on the first of January—he began to plan for it, or rather for the period preceding it. His chief concern was to finish writing *Les Justes* and *L'Homme révolté;* the way to achieve that would be to withdraw from the world altogether between January and July. In February he spelled out his priorities until June, listing the play (*Les Justes,* then called "La Corde") first, then the long essay on revolt, finally three volumes collecting his literary, critical, and political essays. He thought he could do the play in February, the first draft of the essay (*L'Homme révolté*) in March and April, put the collections together in May, then revise the play and the essay in June. This incredible program was reinforced by the resolutions which followed it immediately in his journal:

> To rise early. Shower *before* breakfast.
> No cigarettes before noon.
> Obstinacy at work. It overcomes weaknesses.

He noted that all his books, from *Noces* through the play and the essay to come, represented efforts at depersonalization, though each in its own way. "After that I shall be able to speak in my name." He explained what he meant in greater detail to the Michel Gallimards: He wished to put behind him all the projects which had been lying on his desk for years, then to take the holiday represented by the voyage to Latin America, before launching the cycle of work which would lead him, or so he joked to his friends, to universal glory.

But there would never be a time when Camus could withdraw from all public activity, and the years of his brief life would be marked by repeated ideological combat. Whatever his reticences, he would always be involved in one or another cause, often, and preferably, behind the scenes, and whenever possible in the form of private and personal intervention as opposed to the kind of political action then in favor—rallies, petitions, manifestos. For as the value of his name at the bottom of a petition increased, he grew more wary of those who were anxious to use it. Fearing to be manipulated, he preferred to work alone, even at the risk of disappointing friends by withdrawing from their movements or refusing to participate in the first place.

There is a significant but largely forgotten exception to his rule, which Camus and his friends called Groupes de Liaison Internationale. Before returning to Europe from New York, Nicola Chiaromonte had conceived a scheme with his friends there to provide material aid as well as moral support to intellectuals of besieged Europe, to political exiles from the totalitarian states (whether Communist or Fascist). Sometime during the winter of 1947–48, or by spring at the latest, two of Chiaromonte's associates in these discussions, Mary McCarthy and Alfred Kazin, drew up a charter for what they had decided to call the Europe-America Groups. Their manifesto announced the setting up of a center for solidarity and support of European intellectuals isolated, as the American signers themselves were isolated, not only from the major blocs who between them divided up the world, but from each other. They saw hope in true internationalism, an equitable distribution of wealth, respect for the individual. Their goal was to combat the spirit of despair in Europe by material aid for those in need.

For the American signers, Stalinism was the number one enemy of Europe, but it wasn't the only enemy. They identified other forms of police state: Franco's in Spain, Tito's in Yugoslavia, opposed even what they called the authoritarianism of the Gaullist movement in France, that of the Christian Democrats in Italy—such characterizations, they pointed out, didn't come from the U. S. State Department. They refused to identify themselves with American Capitalism. They were not pacifists, but felt that it would be an error to see the struggle against world Communism strictly in military terms.

Concretely, they had begun to help persons and groups in France, Germany, and Italy, giving them, modestly enough, books, magazines, other sources of information; they hoped to extend their material aid in the future. The signers of this charter included Chiaromonte, Mary McCarthy, Alfred Kazin, William Barrett, Elizabeth Hardwick, Sidney Hook, Dwight Macdonald, Nicolas Nabokov, William Phillips and Philip Rahv, Isaac Rosenfeld, Delmore Schwartz, Saul Steinberg, Dorothy Thompson, Niccolò Tucci, Bertram D. Wolfe.

The signers themselves contributed money to the fund, but there was also an art auction which brought in about a thousand dollars, and further money was raised through admissions to meetings (e.g., a debate featuring Mary McCarthy and Sidney Hook on the presidential candidacy of Henry Wallace). Chiaromonte, who was traveling between the United States and Europe, was the channel for taking the money to Paris (where he had been in early 1947, then in the spring of 1948, and again in February 1949).[10] The American manifesto was published in the anti-Stalinist French left-wing monthly *Révolution Prolétarienne* in August 1948.

On the European side, with the material as well as the moral support offered by these left-wing, anti-Communist intellectuals of the United States, Camus and his friends had soon set up a parallel group in Paris. In addition to the funds available through Chiaromonte, they had another source of material support: office space and supplies of the Socialist labor unions. A veteran labor leader, Roger Lapeyre, who had met Camus at a meeting in support of the Spanish Republicans, offered to help set up a program of concrete assistance to victims of totalitarian regimes. (As it happened, the first two victims they would help were American Trotskyists, for whom lodgings and jobs were found so that they could remain in France.) Camus wrote a manifesto for the new organization—the Groupes de Liaison Internationale—in his office at Gallimard, assisted by Lapeyre. Its language was quite similar to that of the Europe-America Groups appeal:

We are a group of men who, in liaison with friends of America, Italy, Africa, and other countries, have decided to unite our efforts and our reflections in order to preserve some of our reasons for living.

These reasons are threatened today by many monstrous idols, but above all by totalitarian techniques. . . .

These reasons are especially threatened by Stalinist ideology. . . .

These reasons are threatened also, at a lesser degree it is true, by American worship of technology. This is not totalitarian, because it accepts the individual's neutrality. But in its own way it is total because, through films, press and radio, it has known how to make itself indispensable psychologically and to make itself loved. . . .

The Camus group would offer "concrete international friendship" with non-bureaucratic material aid, but would also operate an information service to make known the facts—to let Europe know about the existence of non-conforming Americans and Soviet dissidents, to help Americans distinguish between the Soviet leadership and its people.

In addition to Camus and Roger Lapeyre (who identified himself on the manifesto as Transportation labor inspector, a civil service function he held in addition to his union responsibilities), signers of the manifesto included Robert Jaussaud, Jean Bloch-Michel, and Michèle Halphen (née Boussoutrot, daughter of a World War I aviator and political figure)—all close to Camus. There were also the writer Gilbert Sigaux; an old anarchist proofreader Nicolas Lazarewitch; a surgeon, Daniel Martinet; and a teacher of left-syndicalist orientation, Gilbert Walusinski.[11] Indeed, the group's membership came largely from the movement inspired by the periodical *Révolution Prolétarienne,* revolutionary, labor-oriented, and keenly anti-Communist Party. Lapeyre's father had been what was known as a *syndicaliste révolutionnaire,* and Lapeyre had joined the movement at its inception in the 1920s. Like the Trotskyists, these hard-to-define left-labor ideologists were opposed to the milder, reformist Socialist Party, while they felt that the Communist Party had replaced capitalist bosses with Party bosses. After World War II the magazine was thrown open to all the fringe tendencies in the French labor movement—even to reformists. Camus himself would remain a friend, even a financial contributor, to *Révolution Proletarienne,* from now on and until his death, without actually subscribing to any particular tenets or organizational structure.[12]

They would meet regularly, this informal group of friends, at the Force Ouvrière (Socialist trade union) building, a converted town house at 78 Rue de l'Université, to pool their resources and their contacts to help the cases that were brought to their attention. Many of the political refugees they would be called on to help were Spanish Republicans. Jaussaud, who worked for the government, would make sure they got work permits, essential for anyone wishing to remain in France. Michèle Halphen would see that they got residence permits through her contacts at the préfecture. Sometimes, if the refugee was an intellectual, Camus might certify that he was hiring the person as his secretary, although Jaussaud warned him that no man could employ as many secretaries as all that. But Jaussaud was not really troubled by what they were doing, for they were all still enjoying the freewheeling atmosphere of post-Liberation France, where false papers could still be obtained in a good cause. If Jaussaud had any problems in this area, it was when he tried to get papers for refugees from the Soviet bloc; the Communists in his office were prepared to help Spanish Republicans but not anti-Communists.[13]

Although there is evidence that the Camus-Lapeyre Groupes de Liaison Internationale became active as early as August 1948, when the American manifesto was published in France, and when Camus, then in L'Isle-sur-la-Sorgue, asked Michel Gallimard to pass on a sum of money to a Spanish refugee in the name of an international organization of assistance to refugees and victims of totalitarianism,[14] the first issue of the group's newsletter would appear only in March 1949. An introduction to issue number one of *Bulletin d'Information des Groupes de Liaison Internationale* explained that the organization would undertake no major campaign, would attempt to offer information instead of arguments, aid and not ideology, in *un esprit de résistance.* The issue led off with an article by Dwight Macdonald from his magazine *Politics,* on the problem of pacifism with respect to the Soviet Union: If pacifism is still valid, it must not be naïve pacifism, Macdonald argued. The second article was by George Orwell, reprinted from the New York magazine *Commentary.* The third was a text by Claude Morgan of CNE and *Lettres Françaises,* found in the Soviet newspaper *Literaturnaya Gazeta,* consisting of a denunciation of non-Communist Frenchmen. There was also a partial text of the constitution of the Mongolian People's Republic of the U.S.S.R., demonstrating how it perverted democratic principles. This first issue of the group's bulletin was mimeographed; later it would appear in printed form, the theme remaining the crimes of Stalinism.[15]

Camus and the others would gather in a large office with Directoire decoration, but which could have used a new coat of paint, facing the garden of this imperfectly converted noble mansion—the Force Ouvrière building. Despite the promises of their manifesto, they would spend a good deal of time on strategy, in an attempt (and their infor-

mation bulletin was another medium for that) to bring influence to bear
on labor leaders and other makers of public opinion. The aid to refugees, to Lapeyre's mind, had been undertaken in an effort to prove that
the group was not simply a forum for abstract discussion. Soon, however, Camus was discouraged with the whole effort. The information
bulletin was being sent to some one hundred labor leaders, but the
influence of the group remained limited.

And there was another problem. Some of the participants seemed
to welcome the forum provided by the group's meetings; these discussions became for them the reason for being of the group. Nicolas
Lazarewitch, for example, was an anarchist in the tradition of Russia's
1905 revolution, who would make each meeting the occasion for end-
less talk. An eccentric who lived in a suburb in a hut with a goat,
Lazarewitch exasperated the others; Camus would have to bring meetings to an early close, saying they had no time to waste, while Lazarewitch pursued his monologue.[15] At one meeting the old anarchist told
Camus and Bloch-Michel that one day they would have to explain why
they felt no remorse about having participated in the wartime resistance, and thus in the capitalist war.[16] Another time Camus told the
group that Sartre agreed with its aims and would donate an evening's
proceeds from *Le Diable et le Bon Dieu* to its work, but that never
came about, perhaps because Lazarewitch didn't want them to accept
money from the likes of Sartre.[17]

At one of the meetings at the Rue de l'Université, a Swiss who had
lived in the Soviet Union and had been caught up in the purges of the
1930s, to find herself deported to Siberia, described her experiences.
Jacques Monod, scientist and future Nobel Prize winner, also attended
some meetings, and Camus was interested in his experiences as a Communist.

Camus' discouragement manifested itself by his refusal to undertake tasks suggested by participants, on the grounds that he had other
work to do. He confided to Walusinski that he was depressed by the fa-
naticism which he was hearing. The group carried on its activity after
Camus' departure for Latin America in the middle of 1949, and while
he was ill from the end of that year through the summer of 1950.
Camus urged Walusinski to see that the group pursued its work, and
hoped that on his return to active life after a long convalescence they
would find a new basis for their operations—presumably without the
troublemakers who had prevented its functioning. Camus did return,
but largely to preside over the dissolution of the group. It was Camus
who drew the logical conclusion, suggesting that the Groupes de Liaison Internationale be disbanded, and offering a motion to the effect that

there was a consensus to cease activity.[17] He had felt that a brutal but voluntary liquidation, avoiding artificial attempts to keep the group alive, was the best way to put an end to an experiment which had lived its time.[18]

"Incapable of raising a little finger for what we love," Camus quoted Lazarewitch in the account of the group's dissolution (in his journal). "No, we are not powerless. But we refuse to do even the little we can do. A meeting is too much if it's raining, if we had a scene at home, etc., etc. . . ."

But the people who had come together to work within the group would not lose touch with each other for all that. Camus, for his part, would always say yes when asked to help a political émigré.[18]

During the same period Camus helped launch a literary movement which would not live much longer than the Groupes de Liaison Internationale. He joined Char, Albert Béguin (who would be editor of the left-Catholic *Esprit* after Emmanuel Mounier), and writer Jean Vagne in the publication of monthly *Empédocle,* whose first issue in January 1949 published Camus' own "Le Meurtre et l'Absurde," presented as the introduction to his essay in progress (*L'Homme révolté*). Other contributions in that first issue were from Camus' friends Jean Grenier, Char, and Guilloux, and the same issue published Camus' speech to the RDR meeting of intellectuals (under the title "Le Temoin de la liberté"). Camus would continue to colonize the magazine with the works of himself and his friends; it did seem as if he finally had the magazine of his own which he had often talked about, and subsequent issues would contain material by Simone Weil, Bloch-Michel, Ponge, Parain—even a translation of Melville by André Belamich. *Empédocle* would last only until the summer of 1950, its best-known contribution being the work of a young writer outside the Camus circle, Julien Gracq, whose "La Littérature à l'estomac" was probably the most telling attack on the French literary prize system to appear in postwar France.

In January 1950, *Empédocle* published an analysis of Soviet criticism of French writers, which cited an attack on Camus in *Novy Mir* (back in August 1947) as a "propagandist of decadent individualism." The Soviet critic would go on to say that

> Albert Camus attracted the attention of European and American critics by the perseverance with which he repeats impassively, like a functionary, that existence is absurd. Camus made his entry into European literature in parodying the sinister croaking of Poe's allegorical raven. He fears that men will prefer heroic struggle and action to the ivory tower and vegetal life. . . .

There was more along these lines to condemn "the nihilistic sophistries" of Camus. But *Empédocle* would show that Sartre and Beauvoir were not being treated any differently by contemporary Soviet critics.

The attacks were not coming only from the Soviet camp. François Mauriac's son Claude, a dedicated Gaullist, launched a monthly magazine for *la jeunesse intellectuelle* in February 1949. And in the first issue of *Liberté de l'esprit,* alongside contributions by Malraux, Max-Pol Fouchet, Jean Amrouche, and Jean Lescure, a young (twenty-three-year-old) right-wing polemicist, Roger Nimier, delivered a diatribe against the writers of the left, in which he spoke derisively of Camus' noble sentiments. Camus opposed the death penalty, he observed, but hadn't expressed much indignation over the death of Brasillach. He criticized Camus' silence during the purging of intellectuals who had collaborated with the occupation regime. "The silence of Mr. Camus, in the universal silence, would not have been very remarkable," he observed, "if the same writer didn't speak out (with eloquence) in favor of negroes, Palestinians [which at that time probably meant Jews] or yellow men. . . ." Nimier feared that France might find itself in a war, but "we won't wage it with the shoulders of Mr. Sartre, nor with the lungs of Mr. Camus."

Speaking of Camus' lungs in a polemic was unfortunate—for the author of the polemic, who apparently did not know about Camus' tuberculosis. At least one of the writers who had made common cause with Mauriac's intellectual Gaullists decided not to accept that in silence. Jean Lescure, who had worked with Camus in the wartime intellectual resistance (on *Domaine Français* and *Lettres Françaises*), had agreed to write for *Liberté de l'esprit* because his good friend Malraux had sent Claude Mauriac to ask for his help. Now he drafted an open letter to the new periodical, pointing out that not so long ago Sartre's shoulders and Camus' lungs were adequate to their participation in the anti-Nazi resistance. And in the same issue of *Liberté de l'esprit* which published Lescure's letter, Nimier also published a disclaimer: He had not been aware of Camus' physical condition when he wrote the original article. But Camus never forgave him.[19]

On March 6 he flew to London for the opening of a new production of *Caligula.* The way he would tell it to intimate friends, little he did or saw on his short visit pleased him. He arrived in a deserted Sunday London, deep in snow, was given bad food in a Greek restaurant (as the guest of the director of the English production). But if the restaurant was disappointing and the Basil Street Hotel equally so, he wasn't sure what to make of the play. He liked neither the cast nor what the actors were expected to do, and was quietly horrified by the ballet that had been introduced. At that point he ducked out of the rehearsal for a shot of whiskey, but of course the hour wasn't right, the pubs weren't open, so he settled for coffee—and that kept him up half the night, the Greek food he was given again that evening keeping him up the other half. The formal opening on March 8 was attended by ambassadors and elegant ladies, and he shuddered at the thought that they would think the spectacle was representative of the Paris stage; he counted the hours until he could fly home (on the day after the opening).[9]

In Paris he had been discussing a project that was probably closer to his heart. Prior to going to London he had met with Gabriel Audisio, the actor Pierre Blanchar, and other North African friends to plan the production of a motion picture that would present Algeria as something other than the pseuo-Oriental picturesque land it usually turned out to be in movies. "We have to tell the story of a friendship," he explained to Blanchar, who would remember Camus at this meeting:

> His premature wrinkles betrayed an exceptional mobility of expression and as a consequence an evident ability to be affected. His "indifference," so often alleged, certainly concerned speculations of the spirit, not the lives of people and of his own. . . .

He also remarked "the color of his pupils, rare in our country: sea-green . . . giving him an exotic touch."

But how to tell the true story of Algeria in a movie? They didn't quite know how, but they were convinced that such a project would serve French Algeria—promoting tourist travel, for instance. On March 9, the day Camus returned from London, a letter was sent out to Algerian intellectuals over the signature of Camus, Blanchar, Audisio, Amrouche, and Raoul Celly asking for suggestions on how to put together such a film. The signers felt that commercial movies which pretended to show a true picture of Algeria would ruin the chance to produce "a sound and true motion picture of which the country we love can benefit as from a donation."

It was a curious idea as well as a naïve one, and of course nothing would come of it. Camus' old friend Brua shot it down in an article in an Algerian paper, in which he asked what Algerian problems might be covered by such a film. How could a collective project succeed, when a work of art must be personal? And how come to grips with all of Algeria in a single film when thirty books hadn't been able to do it? Brua feared that such a scheme would become known as "La Grande Illusion."[20]

Camus was involved in one other non-book project that winter, a radio treatment of the German occupation entitled "Les Silences de Paris," broadcast on April 30 on the official network. He put most of the dialogue into the mouth of a secondhand bookseller, who remembered the German occupation as a curious time. "But it was neither a good nor a bad time. It was the absence of time. Or a time without color and without date, a time when one wound up the alarm clock every night, but when the calendar was false."

There are sounds—this is radio—of automobile traffic in the flight from Paris in June 1940, passages from speeches by Pétain, by Churchill, comments of shoppers queuing for food (the words supplied by Camus), sounds of bombing raids. The bookseller listens to the BBC broadcasts from England. "But finally I always preferred these moments when in the emprisoned city I heard accomplice silences. . . ." Children in schoolyards, or beauty . . . "A pretty girl reconciles you with the world. . . ."[21]

Such efforts, or effortless work, and the occasional pieces that a man of letters was called on to produce—a preface for *Actuelles,* texts for Daniel's *Caliban,* for the Gallimard monthly bulletin for booksellers, interviews, letters to the editors, even an introduction to a showing of paintings by the late Abd el-Tif artist Richard Maguet—all served to delay completion of the major works he had hoped to produce before his departure for Latin America. "Finish by June 1," he admonished himself in his journal, referring (undoubtedly) to the play *Les Justes.* "Then travels. Private Journal. Force of life. Never to become sucked in."

# 35

◆

# RELAPSE

I think that I understand now *how* one kills oneself.

Carnets

It was time for Camus' second and final extended cultural tour abroad, this one to cover several key nations of Latin America, beginning at the end of June 1949, and lasting until late in August.

First he drove his family down to L'Isle-sur-la-Sorgue, where they were again renting the house called Palerme for the summer. He had soon fallen in with neighbor René Char again. (With Char he composed a letter to *Combat* to protest the death sentences handed down by a French military court in Algeria against Moslem soldiers who had surrendered to the Germans in 1940, this in the face of the evidence that there had been two million French prisoners of war. Camus would later make the rounds of government offices to find out what had happened to the convicted soldiers, and learned that the sentences had not been carried out.)[1]

The trip to Latin America could have been an opportunity for rest and recreation after a year of effort, but something went wrong at the start, and Camus himself didn't know what it was. His friend Robert Jaussaud, who was a guest of the Camus at Palerme, joined Albert and Francine for the automobile ride down to Marseilles, where Camus was to board the SS *Campana* for Rio de Janeiro. Jaussaud thought his friend was acting strangely, decided that he was depressed. Camus told him that he felt he was under an evil spell, that it had been a mistake to accept the trip. Jaussaud had never seen his friend in such a low state of morale.[2] Camus hoped that what he himself had diagnosed as depression would disappear once he was out on the high seas. He was somewhat ashamed of himself, to feel so weak and without courage. As the ship floated free of the dock he had to fight off tears.[3]

From the time of sailing he began to keep a journal of the trip, faithfully recording everything in it each evening. In the monotony of the long ocean voyage he couldn't get rid of his depression. "On two occasions, notion of suicide," he told his journal. "The second time, while looking at the sea, a frightful burning struck my temples. I think that I understand now *how* one kills oneself."[4]

After sailing through the Strait of Gibraltar the *Campana* followed the African coast south to Dakar, where Camus was able to set ashore and walk for a few hours across the city, returning to the ship at 2 A.M. When he woke up next morning they were already at sea. This was no luxury liner; his cabin was strict and spare, and he found that he enjoyed the cell-like bareness. But there was a swimming pool, and in the South Atlantic sun he could swim each morning after breakfast before sitting down to his writing. After lunch he stared at the sea, slept, and worked some more. But he felt certain that nothing he did or saw in the new countries he was soon to visit could cure him of his gloom.

The weather turned bad as the ship approached the coast of Brazil. It docked in Rio at dawn on July 15, but even before they had moored Camus was the target of local reporters and photographers; they had boarded the ship in the bay. There were the usual questions—and the usual denials—of affinity to existentialism. He was taken to lunch and to a reception (where he met black actors who wanted to stage *Caligula*). He dined with a Catholic poet who was also a successful businessman with a chauffeur-driven Chrysler, and who told him: "We are poor people, miserable. There is no luxury in Brazil." The juxtaposition of tropical indolence and U.S.-style development was a subject of constant curiosity to him.

After a literary lunch he realized once again how much he hated this kind of life, and he resolved that he would not be ensnared another time.

His French Government hosts had put him up at an American-style hotel which he didn't appreciate, so he was moved into an empty wing of the French Embassy, where he had a room with a balcony facing the bay. At last he could go off by himself. With a black actor he went to a Negro ball where they danced the samba. With the same escort, he was driven some twenty-five miles to a small village, pursued the journey several more miles along a rugged path climbing a mountain, continued on foot to the summit, then descended the other side, climbed another hill, crowded into a thatched cabin; they were here for a macumba, a ceremonial mélange of dance and song where local religious practices are fused with Roman Catholicism. He learned that

its purpose was to obtain the descent of God into each of the participants, and he was impressed sufficiently to devote pages and pages of
his travel journal to a minute description of that long night.

One of the dancers asked him to uncross his arms, for that gesture
was preventing the spirit from descending among them. Docile, he
dropped his arms. The dancing became more violent, young black girls
entered into a trance, fell to the ground:

> They are picked up, someone presses their forehead, and they are
> off again until they fall down. The summit is attained at the mo-
> ment when all begin shouting, with strange hoarse cries which
> sound like barking. I am told that this will continue until dawn,
> without variation. It is two in the morning. The heat, the dust, the
> cigar smoke and the human odors render the air unbreathable. I go
> out, staggering, literally to drink the fresh air. I love the night and
> the sky, more than the gods of man.[5]

He would rise early each morning, work on his travel journal,
lunch with one dignitary or another, tour in the afternoon, dine with
still another dignitary, visit something else at night. He never got to bed
before midnight, and then read *Don Quixote* before dropping off to
sleep.

On July 20 he gave his first formal lecture in Rio, left for Recife
and Bahia the next day for more encounters. He wasn't sure that these
people were really interested in what he had to say about European culture and European politics, and his physical condition was getting
worse instead of better. He began to wonder if the depression and
gloom weren't something more: a return of illness. Certainly the damp,
heavy climate was exhausting him, and might itself explain his physical
and psychological state. Whatever it was, he couldn't appreciate what
he was doing, couldn't concentrate on what he was seeing.

On his return from Bahia on July 25 he came down with what he
thought was flu and spent the next day in bed, unable even to write.
When he did get up, it was to give a talk on Nicolas de Chamfort, a favorite subject, for he had long admired the versatile eighteenth-century
writer for his life style and cynicism as well as his writing. (He had
written an introduction, published in 1944, to Chamfort's *Maximes,* in
which he took exception to Chamfort's observations that "superiority
always makes enemies" and "genius is necessarily solitary"; he also
felt that Chamfort's scorn for women was unjustified. But now *he* was
talking about Chamfort to an audience of ladies in feathered hats.) On
August 3 he left for a talk in São Paulo, where the rapidly growing metropolis surprised him, half New York, half Oran.

In an interview with a local newspaper, *Diario,* reprinted in the
Pléiade edition of his work, after expounding on war, peace, and po-

etry, he found himself confronted once more with the question of existentialism.

> It is a serious error to treat with such frivolity a philosophical research as serious as existentialism is. Its origins go back to Saint Augustine and its chief contribution to knowledge certainly resides in the impressive wealth of its method. Existentialism is above all a method. The similarities that one generally remarks between Sartre's work and my own come naturally from the chance or the misfortune that we have to live in the same era and in confrontation with common problems and concerns.

Disregarding his health, he went off on an exhausting excursion, driving for over twelve hours on incredibly bad roads through virgin forest, crossing three rivers on primitive ferries, arriving close to midnight at a town called Iguape, where Camus and his escorts were put up for the night in a local hospital called Heureux Souvenir. There was no water in the hospital, so he had to shave the next morning with bottled water they had brought with them. Next day they were to attend a festival, the chief feature of which was a procession. The head marchers carried a statue of Christ (who was believed to have arrived here on the waves). Pilgrims of all races and colors, classes and costumes were assembled, some having traveled five days to reach the site.

Camus would later describe this expedition, including details such as the Heureux Souvenir Hospital, in his story "La Pierre qui pousse," the principal use he would make of this South American adventure in his writings.

The return trip to São Paulo was of course as long and as arduous as the trip out. And on the following morning, Monday, he was on duty for a round table discussion with Brazilian philosophers, after which he was to lunch with the city's French colony. At two-thirty he spoke to the Alliance Française, at four he watched snake fighting, at eight he spoke again.

He was to leave for Chile the following day, but it was discovered when he arrived at Pôrto Alegre that nothing had been done back in Paris about getting him a visa. So he had to go instead to Montevideo, where he was put up in a closet-sized hotel room while waiting to go on to Chile via Argentina. Sunday, August 14, found him at the Buenos Aires airport, waiting for a plane.

Back in June, the Margarita Xirgu company had staged Le Malentendu in Buenos Aires. Although a critical success, the play had been banned as atheistic by the Peronist authorities. On his arrival in Brazil, Camus had made a statement in which he denounced Argentine censorship (but the press response in that dictator-ruled country can be imagined). He was sorry, he had said, that he would not be able to meet his good friends of that country, but his dignity as a free writer did not allow him to pass over in silence the despotic attitude of the Perón military dictatorship.[6] Now, with Camus on the scene, the French Embassy would have liked him to lecture in the country, and he said that he'd be quite willing to do that if he could criticize censorship in his talks. In that case, the embassy thought that he'd do better to talk elsewhere.[7] Outside Argentina it would be reported that censorship had prevented him from meeting the press during his brief stopover in Buenos Aires, and that must have been true. But he did manage to see some individuals, such as the writer Rafael Alberto. And the mix-up about his visa, the added complications of his travel, added to his general depressed state. He was homesick, or at least missed having a friend with him.

From August 14 to 18 he was in Chile, staying at the Hotel Crillon in Santiago. And here there was a pleasant surprise; this was the first country visited on the South American trip about which he was able to care. Standing between the high waves of the Pacific and the snow-capped Andes, Santiago was a city of almond trees in flower, orange trees silhouetted on the hilltops. (He didn't say so, to his journal or to friends, but wasn't he reminded of Algiers here?) Again the schedule was a rugged one.

On August 15 he spoke on contemporary French literature to the Instituto Chileno-Francés de Cultura, in the presence of the French Ambassador, who with the Instituto was host to the reception which followed. Next day he spoke at the Salón de Honor of the University of Chile, his subject "Le Temps des meurtriers," in which he described a world in which torture had become a necessity of state, human beings were expendable. He told a story of the German occupation of France, when German officers overheard young Frenchmen at another table discussing philosophy. One of the French youths had said that no idea was worth dying for. The Germans called him over and one of them put a pistol to his head, asking him to repeat what he had said, and he repeated it. The officer congratulated him, and concluded: "I think that I demonstrated your error. You've just shown that some ideas are worth dying for."

On walking back to his hotel with local admirers Camus and his party nearly got caught in street fighting, and had to hasten their steps. The police were putting down a student demonstration.

On August 17 he was back at the university, this time to talk about French moralists, focusing on "Un Moraliste de la Révolte: Chamfort," although the lecture was also billed as "Roman et Révolte," the title of a chapter of his work in progress *L'Homme révolté;* presumably he had brought along several set lectures and was scheduling and rescheduling them according to his audience (or his mood?). On the same day, in the basement of a French bookstore, Librería Francesa, he was guest of honor at a cocktail party; he had lunched that day with the Minister of Public Education.

He received an enthusiastic press in Chile. The first stories had predictably billed him as *"el número 2 del 'Existencialismo,'"* but soon his disclaimer had been published too: *"No soy ni seré existencialista."* One popular paper nevertheless ran the story alongside a photograph of a girl wearing nothing but a scarf labeled "Sartre." He had praise for Sartre, said he preferred *Le Mur* among Sartre's writings, compared him to Diderot. Asked about the United States, he put Faulkner at the top of his list of contemporary authors, said that Char was the greatest French poet since Rimbaud, but that he knew of no great contemporary French novelists. Before he left, he saw a performance of *Le Malentendu* (La Equivocación) performed by a local theater group.

On August 20 he was back in Rio de Janeiro, emptied by his exhausting schedule, his inability to sleep. He had been fighting total breakdown, hadn't been able to throw off the depression, any more than he could the mobs—or he felt they were mobs—who had sought to meet him. He was a celebrity here, he thought without pleasure, as Fernandel might be, or Marlene Dietrich, he who could never stand the company of more than four or five persons at a time. Nothing could be as fatiguing as to play a part one played badly, he decided. There was little he could say he liked in what he saw (apart from a few moments in a few places—such as in Chile), and yet two months had been taken from his life. He knew that he would return to France marked forever by the experience.[8] And he asked himself if his illness was not something more serious than influenza.[4]

He flew back to Paris, reported what he had seen and felt to Maria Casarès, then returned to Provence to pick up his family. They returned to Paris in a driving rain, and Camus, who in normal circumstances was master of his automobile, skidded off the road—but no one was hurt. When they reached Paris his wife realized that he was running a high fever.[7]

Almost immediately they were off again, this time for Le Chambon-sur-Lignon, where at isolated Le Panelier he remembered the harsh months of isolation during the German occupation, and the writing of *Le Malentendu.* Now he was putting the finishing touches on *Les Justes,* incorporating suggestions made by Jean Grenier, who had gotten him to change the title from "Les Innocents," which he felt might seem pejorative.[9]

His mood can be gathered from a journal entry:

> The only effort of my life, the rest having been given to me, and largely (except for wealth, to which I am indifferent): to live the life of a normal man. I didn't want to be a man of the abyss. This overwhelming effort was useless. Little by little, instead of succeeding more and more in my endeavor, I see the abyss approaching.

He could not shake off the depression (which was certainly illness; he was clearly in the early stages of the relapse of his tuberculosis from which he would suffer that winter and beyond). Le Panelier didn't restore his strength, and he returned to Paris, and to the apartment which always seemed about to burst, with foreboding. He worked without respite, nevertheless, not only on last revisions for *Les Justes* before it went into rehearsal, on *L'Homme révolté,* but on schemes for later work. He gave Maria Casarès a collection of his aphorisms, which he labeled "Fidèle à la terre," and which he preceded with a quotation from Hölderlin to be used also as the opening quotation for *L'Homme révolté* (it begins: "And openly I vowed my heart to the grave and suffering earth. . . .").

The aphorisms led off with one that had a particularly moving note; he had taken it from his journal:

> Kleist who twice burns his manuscripts . . . Piero della Francesca, blind at the close of his life . . . Ibsen amnesic at the end, and relearning the alphabet . . . Courage! Courage!

Once more his name came up in Stockholm in discussions of the year's Nobel Prize. At the suggestion of the Swedish Academy's Nobel Committee, the first formal report on Albert Camus was requested of the academy's French expert, Holger Ahlenius (who had previously been consulted on the candidacy of Gide). Faulkner was the favorite that year, but the academy failed to achieve unanimity, giving Faulkner only fifteen of its eighteen votes, so no prize was awarded at all.[10] Of course Camus was still far too young for the Nobel Prize, but he was nevertheless conscious of the march of time:

> He was born in 1828. He wrote *War and Peace* between 1863 and 1869. Between the ages of 35 and 41.

So he spoke in his journal of Tolstoy. Camus was about to celebrate his thirty-sixth birthday. Soon, with the formal declaration of his relapse, he would find another literary brother in pain: Melville at thirty-five, in the darkest period of his mental and physical anguish. He would tell Patricia Blake that his own future "leads into the sea"—was non-existent.

He was seriously ill now, or he had been ill right along, ill before he set
foot on the ship bound for South America, but without realizing it. Flu
and depression were in fact a new and major attack of tuberculosis.
There was still no cure for the disease; he still carried the tubercle
bacillus.[11] He dated the reflections in his journal on his *rechute* "End October 1949":

> After such a long certainty of being cured, this return should
> crush me. It does indeed crush me. But following an uninterrupted
> series of crushing events, it makes me laugh. In the end, I feel liber-
> ated. Madness is also liberation.

For this time it could seem even worse. His private life—his hectic
home, his inability to spend all the time he wanted with those he chose
—was already a torture equal to his disease (so he says in his journal,
where he likens *souffrance* to *douleur physique* in one of a series of
reflections on the mental anguish he felt now). He avoided society; his
physical appearance—he had even developed eczema—made him wish
to avoid even close friends. But one evening after going to the opera
with Jean Bloch-Michel he wanted to stay up half the night talking; he
was in a highly nervous state; it was clear that he never slept a full night
through.[12]

He had moved back to the Michel Gallimards' to find as much
peace as he could. At last the antibiotic streptomycin was available, although it had to be used with care because it could cause deafness; that
new drug and bed rest were the best a doctor could prescribe. There
was also para-aminosalicylic acid, known as PAS, which was a holdover
from pre-streptomycin days, but which could not cure the disease.[11]
Camus' journal contains an indication of his treatment at this time: 40
grams of streptomycin from November 6 to December 5, 360 grams of
PAS, another 20 grams of streptomycin from November 13 to January
2.

Streptomycin, although a giant step in the fight against TB, because
it actually killed the bacilli—something no previous drug could do—
was not as effective as isonicotinic acid hydrazide, known as isoniazid,
or INH, which would be available on an experimental basis only in
1951, becoming a regular prescription drug in France in May 1952; this
INH (under the name Rimifon) could effect a cure, with no further
need for collapse therapy, usually prescribed with PAS to avoid the
growth of bacilli resistant to INH. [11]

So he was in bed again. Two months of bed rest, the doctor had
said. He could read and write in bed, and some afternoons he would be
able to go as far as the Hébertot Theater, where Paul Oettly was directing rehearsals of *Les Justes,* scheduled to open in the middle of Decem-

ber. Maria Casarès was to play the young terrorist Dora, Serge Reggiani
would be Kaliayev, Michel Bouquet would be Fedorov.

He missed the dress rehearsal, and had his sister-in-law Christiane
phone to tell him how it went, but he apparently got out of bed to attend the formal opening. To Simone de Beauvoir, a member of that
first-night audience, Camus seemed exhausted, but she remarked the
warmth of his greeting of Sartre and herself, reminding her of the great
days of their friendship. They thought that the play itself was well acted
but the text seemed academic. Camus appeared to accept the congratulations and compliments with a smiling and "skeptical" simplicity.
When a woman rushed up to Camus to say, "I like this better than *Les
Mains sales*" (Sartre's play about Communist morality) and without
noticing that Sartre was standing by, Camus smiled to Sartre with an air
of complicity and quipped: "Two birds with one stone," for, as
Beauvoir knew, he never liked to be taken for a disciple of Sartre.[13]

On stage, Maria Casarès had been acting only for Camus, this desperately ill friend whose illness separated them when they should have
been together.[3] But the feeling got through to others too—to *Le
Figaro*'s Jean-Jacques Gautier, always so hard to please:

> You know her waist of miraculous slenderness, her narrow eyes
> drawn toward the temples, her tapered brows, her pointed chin, her
> bulging forehead, the shiny traces of tears on her cheeks. . . . She
> amazed the audience by her acting at once passionate and measured.

Otherwise Gautier was harsh toward the play. It was difficult to accu-
mulate more pessimism, more discouragement, more negation, difficult
to show more liking for nothingness. Gautier found only murder, execution, death, death, death, and without a saving tenderness.

> A play? No! An ideogram. Living creatures? No! . . .
> They call men who write such things master thinkers? *I* call
> them masters at killing themselves, zealots of suicide. . . .

The critics also divided on ideological lines, the Socialist *Le
Populaire* finding the work "powerful and moving" the Communist
*L'Humanité* discovering quite different and even opposing qualities:
". . . worse than cold—icy. Fabricated characters. Banal dialogue
. . . Unbelievable action."

Casarès' friend Dussane attributed the mixed reception to the fact
that the play was supremely uncomfortable, requiring that one think beyond slogans. The left rejected this terrorist who dared to discuss his
action, the right rejected the bomb-throwing idealist.[14] Six months after
the opening, *Le Justes* was still running, and Chiaromonte reported on
it to readers of New York's *Partisan Review:* "After all is said about
the weakness of *Les Justes* as a play, it remains a piece of literary work

that commands respect, and a stage production that is moving if not really dramatic." After citing the words of some spectators—"Five acts about whether or not one should kill little children"—Chiaromonte said:

> What made the Parisians applaud *Les Justes* and burst into tears at some of its scenes was not the debate about the Revolution which is present only in a few sketchy sentences, but the reminder of the Resistance which it obviously contains.

Chiaromonte agreed that Camus neglected the question of the ultimate validity of the terrorists' revolution, but insisted that Camus was aiming at "artful mobilization of the emotional power contained in the western concepts of the 'human' and of the 'individual.'" The language, he concluded, was that "of a recent convert from nihilism who would rediscover by himself, step by step, the elementary norms of humanity."

Camus would be elated when the *Manchester Guardian,* which he considered one of Europe's best newspapers, praised the play from a broader viewpoint than Parisians had demonstrated. He was particularly pleased with the *Guardian*'s conclusion: "But for the first time for a long time we hear again in this work, and in the theater, the authentic voice of God, without the help of God, in the hearts of some men."[3]

No cure was possible for him in Paris, despite the medication, whether in that railroad station of a flat on the Rue Séguier or at the Gallimards', where his room was a simple, bright space, lined on all four sides by bookshelves, connected to the drawing room, and with a view over the formal garden and pond. The doctor wanted him away, to a high and dry place. There was such a refuge, as it happened, at Cabris, a hilltop town above the Riviera coast, where there was even a choice of dwelling places: either a vast, isolated mansion, something of a Victorian Gothic castle with a splendid view but few amenities (built by a friend of Maria van Rysselberghe, later to be a writers' residence), or the more reasonable scale of the vacation house of Pierre and Elisabeth Herbart (she being the daughter of Maria van Rysselberghe), on the flank of a hill not far from the village center.[15]

To reach Cabris from Cannes on the seafront, one drove some ten miles in an uphill zigzag to the old town of Grasse, then turned west on a narrow road for the final three and a half miles. Lying at 1,800 feet over the Mediterranean back country, Cabris was a favorite residence of André Gide (with whom Elisabeth Herbart had had a daughter).

Camus took a year-long sick leave from Gallimard; the formality, a *congé de maladie,* entitled him to his full salary, part of which was reimbursed to his publisher by the social security administration. While

Francine was taking the twins—just past their fourth birthday—with
her mother to Oran, Camus went down to Cabris alone, to reconnoiter
the unfamiliar terrain. He stayed first in the rustic discomfort of an inn
called Le Chêvre d'Or at the crossroads entrance to Cabris. At once it
was clear that he could not stay at the Victorian castle—where he
would freeze, would need a staff of domestics. The Herbart house,
called Les Audides, was bright, sympathetic, and would be easier to
heat; one didn't have to be a millionaire to run it. Reached by a road
climbing from the center of the village, it was a simple two-level
Provençal-style structure with the customary tile roof, balcony views
toward the benign hills which separate Cabris from the sea. In fact it
was located on the flank of the last slope of the Alpes-Maritimes, facing
due south, surrounded by small terraced fields covered with olive and
cypress trees.

On the ground floor of the Herbart house there were the living
room, kitchen, a small bedroom, and a room which served as an office;
one flight up were three bedrooms (with a bathroom attached to the
easternmost, and that would be his room—with two wide bay windows
facing the hills to the south and the village of Cabris). Indeed, all three
bedrooms had a view of the village, on a promontory just off to the left,
and of that sweeping landscape speckled with olive groves.

> In the afternoon, the sun and light flood into my room, the sky
> blue and veiled, cries of children rising from the village, the song of
> the garden fountain . . . and the hours of Algiers come back to me.
> Twenty years . . .

So he confided to his journal. Which was to say, he was as happy
as he could be now, in Cabris, though far from persons and matters
which concerned him. He did try to follow the fate of his play up in
Paris. He had no illusions about its success; he was already certain that
*Les Justes* was no more successful than any of his works had been, although his work—singular—seemed for the moment to have public
support. He even kept in touch with casting problems; for a while he
considered the possibility of replacing Reggiani with Gérard Philipe. By
February 1950 they were filling only a third of the theater each evening,
and the thought that more work might be required to improve the play,
but that he could not do it properly from his Cabris exile, frustrated
him. He was anxious for the play to continue, for Maria's sake. But he
had come to a virtual break in relations with the theater's owner-direc-
tor Jacques Hébertot, who had made it known that he would not have
produced the play at all if he had thought Camus would not dedicate it
to him. Angrily, Camus told Hébertot (although he was offering to
revive *Caligula*) that he preferred not to have his plays on the stage

rather than be forced to do something he did not wish to do. The play as published by Gallimard would carry no dedication at all.

In February, Maria's father died, and the following two performances of the play were canceled. He wanted to fly back to Paris to be with her then, but he knew that he couldn't do that.

When Jean Daniel's *Caliban* published a scene from *Les Justes* but seemed to be concurring with some of the criticism which had already been heard against the work, Camus sent Daniel a letter subsequently published in *Caliban* (and reprinted by Camus in his *Actuelles II*). The problem posed by Daniel had been: Can you kill a prison guard, even though he might have children, so that you can escape from the prison? To Camus the problem had to be posed in another way: Is it also useful to kill the guard's children to liberate all of the inmates of the prison? There were limits. Children were a limit, but not the only one. You can kill the prison guard in the name of justice, but then you must also be ready to die. He felt that the present-day reply was rather: There are no limits; kill everyone in the name of justice for all, and at the same time ask for the Legion of Honor.

The revolutionary socialists of 1905 were not choir boys. And their demand for justice was on another level of seriousness from what is exhibited today, with a kind of obscenity, in books and the press. But it was because the love of justice burned in them that they could not resolve themselves to become repugnant executioners. They chose action and terror to serve justice, but they chose at the same time to die, to pay for a life by a life, so that justice remained alive. All of the essential message of *L'Homme révolté,* which he would be writing for another painful year and a half, is here.

Almost from the day he arrived in Cabris, Camus was at his worktable. Ten hours a day, he reported to friends. He was determined not to leave Cabris until he had finished. He would wake at eight, breakfast on eggs, toast, oat cereal, write from nine to eleven, handle correspondence until noon, then walk until lunch at one. He would rest until four, work until seven, and after dinner study Spanish with his wife until 9 P.M. bedtime (for reading).

A rugged routine, and yet he was equally determined to get well, to take himself in hand in order to be done with illness once and for all. He had the feeling that he had been drifting for the past year, had allowed himself to be dragged along; whatever had happened, the relapse included, had happened *to* him. Now he wished to regain the mastery of himself which he felt he had lost. To accomplish what remained for him to accomplish, even to continue to exist, he would have to climb a long and steep road, to rejuvenate a will as well as a body. He didn't know whether he would be successful, but he did know that failure would be terrible.

If he began showing signs of recovery early in his stay in this hill village, it was because (he decided) of the strict organization of his life, the Draconian rules he had imposed on himself. He had always lived insouciantly, so that it sufficed for a given time that he imposed self-discipline for recovery to appear miraculous. "Disciplined work until April," he urged himself on in a February 1950 journal note. "Then work in frenzy. Be silent. Listen. Let it overflow."

Of course he had to see a doctor regularly in Grasse, where he was X-rayed and weighed (he gained steadily). At the beginning he had to force himself to eat, but then his appetite returned and—importantly— he began to sleep well. The main thing was not to begin counting the days remaining of his exile, for only the time and the distance from Paris stood between him and happiness.

He enjoyed being alone in the hills, the late winter sun warming him. A rented piano was brought in for Francine, who he felt could become a fine concert pianist if she worked at it. His brother Lucien, himself recuperating fom an operation, came to spend a month with them. The Michel Gallimards drove down for a visit; Jaussaud came, Bloch-Michel, even Sartre. Camus discovered that each visit left him exhausted; in his convalescent routine the slightest variation was upsetting. But early in his stay, when Roger Martin du Gard was in Cabris to work on a film with Pierre Herbart, he saw a good deal of the old writer, whom he adored for his simplicity, the honesty of his thought and life style.

Through his letters he kept in touch with the outside world, even when necessary with his Gallimard authors (including the parents of Simone Weil, for the pursuit of the publication of her works in the Espoir series). He also kept in touch with the fate of his plays (*Caligula* was having a successful run now in Montevideo). His reading included Stendhal's *De l'Amour,* Rimbaud's letters, the *Journal* of Delacroix. He decided that Delacroix was right: Every day which is not noted is like a day which does not exist. For he was losing his memory —he blamed it on PAS—and felt that he would have to be a more precise journal keeper.

He corrected the proofs of his essay on Oran, *Le Minotaure,* which was to be published as a book under the imprint of Charlot (but by his successors in that firm). The first real work he had done on his arrival in Cabris was to compose a preface for *Actuelles I,* which would clear his thoughts for the major effort in *L'Homme révolté.* These *Actuelles* were political articles and essays, some of them written long before, editorials from *Combat* (including the "Ni Victimes ni Bourreaux" series),

his polemic with d'Astier de la Vigerie and with Gabriel Marcel, interviews and speeches. He found it difficult, at this remove, to find the
right tone for such a preface. And then, after a slow start, the phrases
began to flow. These were moments of grace he had not experienced in
a long time. He hoped that there would be more moments like this during the writing of *L'Homme révolté,* which was to follow.

## 36

### L'HOMME REVOLTE

May 27, 1950.
Solitary. And the fires of love light up the world. It's worth the pain to be born and to grow up. But must one live after that? All life then finds itself justified. But all survival?

*Carnets*

Slowly spring was on its way, and in that region of ever-generous nature the vegetation grew thicker still. Now the sky behind the cypress trees was crisply blue. The north wind, the mistral, gave the sky a clean skin, he wrote in his journal.

From everywhere the song of birds explodes, with a force, a jubilation, a joyous dissonance, an infinite ravishment. The day trickles and sparkles.

Rosemary flowered. "At the foot of the olive trees, wreaths of violets." When he returned from Cannes one day with his houseguest Jean Bloch-Michel, they drove up on the road from Pégomas, known locally as the *route de mimosa,* along slopes covered with the yellow flowers.

His work on *L'Homme révolté* moved forward. There were days when he felt that he might finish the book during his stay in Cabris, and he mapped out a program for the weeks to follow. His journal filled up with admonitions:

March 1
A month of absolute self-control—on all levels. Then begin over again—
. . . .
After having written everything, rethink the whole work. . . .

He hoped to finish at least the first draft of the book by April; he told Jean Grenier that he would then be asking for his help again.[1] He planned to finish the book by June 1950, then follow it through to publication that October.[2]

The prediction was nearly a year off.

What did he think he was doing, in this essay which was conceived nearly a decade earlier (when he began making notes in Le Panelier), for which he had been reading and note-taking ever since, even in Cabris in the winter and spring of 1950; indeed, he would be reading, taking notes, up to the final days of writing and rewriting—what was he trying to accomplish? Nothing less than to examine in depth and in history the theories and forms of revolt, in an attempt to discover why ideals are perverted—revolt becoming murder (Prometheus becoming Caesar)—and then to attempt to lay true paths to a necessary revolt against our common fate from which crime—even legitimated, state-sponsored crime—would be rigorously excluded.

To do that meant to achieve a grasp of all the philosophies of revolt, those that inspired the Russians, but also to follow the applications of the theories through history, down to recent times (for only then could they be relevant to the totalitarian era). He had begun reading and taking notes in wartime Le Panelier. Already his readings on Russian revolutionary philosophy and the terrorists were preparations for *L'Homme révolté* as well as for *Les Justes*. His notebooks were seeded with citations of Hegel, Bakunin, Lukács, Rosa Luxemburg, Aleksandr Blok, as well as reports of contemporary Stalinist terror. But also with Dostoevsky, Nietzsche, Gobineau, Simone Weil. He would read appropriate passages in Marx, Berdyaev, histories of European and of French socialism. Not surprisingly the writer would also be obliged to examine the forms that revolt took in art; not surprisingly he would apply the Mediterranean outlook to the conclusion. And no wonder that he would work on the project, from inception to publication, over a span of nine years, would be working intensely and at great expense of energy in the final years. At times he would slow to a halt, at times he would wonder if he could ever start again. Didn't artists sometimes stop suddenly, once for all?[3]

By the middle of February he felt that he was ready to begin rewriting the entire book. The work went slowly. He complained of interruptions: Even rain discouraged him, and yet he wanted his friends to visit, to reduce his feeling of isolation.

At the end of March, in the final days of this first stay at Cabris, he was far from having completed the book, but at least his health had improved. He now weighed 165 pounds, and felt that he had regained some of his past form. Still, he was aware that he was no longer a young man; his face told all. Before returning to Paris he had a final examination in Grasse. The doctor told him that his chest X-rays were excellent, but that he would have to live cautiously for a long time to come. It was suggested that he stay a while longer in the south, but he found that he could not remain away from Paris any longer. Certainly he would be returning to the city even more of a savage than he had been before; even the rehearsals that were going to be necessary for substitutions in the cast of *Les Justes* seemed an insurmountable hurdle. And he resolved to take the precautions that would be necessary to stay alive, something he owed not only to himself.

Still, walking in a light rain one day in Cabris, he made some resolutions which seemed to conflict with that vow. He decided that henceforth he would live from day to day. Instead of hibernating he would move outside himself, to take more of an interest in other people and other things. Even ill and unhappy, he felt that it was possible to live generously.

He had little time to try out a new life in Paris—whether a cautious or a day-to-day one. His doctor had to tell him that it wasn't over yet. He who had felt so isolated and forlorn in Cabris now had to return there; the order was another three months in the hills of Provence. Back in Cabris in the last week of April, his mood was expressed in a notation in his journal, on the suicide of a friend:

> Shaken because I loved him very much, of course, but also because I suddenly realized that I felt like doing what he did.

Once more he was separated from Paris, from those in Paris who mattered to him. Desperate, he told Maria Casarès that if he could not, in the months to come, return to a normal life—if the disease continued to threaten life as he knew it—then he could have a decision to make. He did not tell her what it was, but hastened to reassure her: He would try to live. Her brief visit to Cabris lightened the weight of his exile, but could not redeem it.[4]

For this second stay in Cabris the Herbart house was not available, but he found another house for rent (between Les Audides and the village). It rained the first ten days of his stay. But what was worse, in the early weeks of this new exile, was that he experienced a total writing block. He found it difficult now even to write a letter to close friends. He satisfied himself with reading and making notes, for that required no inspiration, could be carried out even in the darkest moments.

The constricted framework of his book—all this disciplined reading, directed research—moved him to think ahead to a time when there could again be *création en liberté*. In a reflective note in his journal he told himself that his work of the first two cycles had contained beings who did not lie, thus unreal beings. They were not of the world, and this was why he was not a novelist in the accepted sense, but rather an artist "who creates myths corresponding to his passion and to his anguish." It was also why the people who moved him were always people with the strength and exclusivity of these myths. This analysis of the Camus of the past, this implication for the future, were indeed an accurate critique and program for the protagonists of his future work.

But the chief thing now was to get these further weeks of exile behind him.

> What is insane about love is that one wishes to precipitate and
> to *lose* the days of waiting. Thus one desires to approach the end.
> So by one of its characteristics love coincides with death.

Late in June he had an opportunity for a quick trip to Paris to autograph press copies of *Actuelles,* the *service de presse* ritual which was the traditional and often the only form of promotion of a new book in France. It was also an opportunity to seek a cure for his tuberculosis in a new direction. There was an unorthodox doctor in Paris who promised—or attempted—cures by methods of his own, and certainly some of his patients (including some in Gallimard circles) swore by him. Dr. Jacques Ménétrier found himself in the presence of an exhausted, seemingly desperate man. Camus' regular doctors had assured him that he would survive, but that he would have a better chance living in the south, reducing his activity. If he had to do these things, then life had no meaning for him. He told Ménétrier that he was in an *impasse* in every area—material, domestic, his writing—he couldn't finish the book on which he had been working for so many years. Ménétrier knew a desperate man when he saw one.

A disciple of Alexis Carrel (he would be secretary-general of the Fondation Alexis Carrel), founder of his own Centre de Recherches Biologiques, Jacques Ménétrier treated diseases such as Camus' not with traditional medication but with methods of his own devising to build up the body's natural defenses. Essentially this consisted of minerals in suspension. It was a medicine of catalysts, regulators, compensators, in which the metals considered to be indispensable components of soil, vegetal, and animal matter are taken to be agents which bring about ionic changes in the human body. Ménétrier prescribed specific elements for specific diseases, e.g., manganese, copper, cobalt, zinc, silver, gold—separately or in combination. He had been treating many prominent patients in the field of arts and letters; before the end of his career he had written a dozen books about his theories of medicine, had treated "tens of thousands" of cases, claiming to have altered the body's disposition to disease, attacking artificial or premature aging.[5]

Camus joked with Michel and Janine Gallimard about the cocktails of manganese, iron, and copper that had been prescribed for him. But he would not dismiss any possibility of putting tuberculosis behind him once and for all.[6] His Swiss doctor friend René Lehmann had told him noncommittally: "Minerals can't hurt you." Camus wasn't fooled by Lehmann's reaction, and Lehmann knew that in any case Camus could fall back on Dr. Brouet, one of Paris's best specialists.[7]

Back in Cabris, then, he began the Ménétrier treatment at once, and as soon as an X-ray showed improvement (in early July) he was prepared to believe that the new method was responsible for it. In fact he did begin to feel better, and he would tell the Gallimards that Ménétrier was responsible.[6] Three months later when Ménétrier saw him again, he warned his patient that the treatment would require another couple of months. Camus seemed skeptical, but the fact was that he never again had a physical problem specifically related to his lungs, and he seemed to have a new taste for life. Ménétrier was even convinced that the final pages of *L'Homme révolté,* a hymn to life seemingly unrelated to the earlier sections of the book, were the work of a rejuvenated patient prepared to live once more.[8]

While in Paris, Camus also discussed his status at the Gallimard publishing house with Michel, whose special relationship made him Camus' "editor" or at least the principal liaison with the Gallimard company. Camus was distressed at the idea that he was still receiving a full salary, and requested that for the time being Gallimard send him only the half-pay reimbursed by social security. By October he would, he said, make a definitive decision about his relationship with the Librairie Gallimard; at the moment he planned not to continue to work for them.

One thing was definitely decided: He would not be returning to the Rue Séguier. That apartment was to be turned over to Michel Gallimard's sister Nicole, and after their summer out of town the Camus would look for another place. (Meanwhile he asked the Michel Gallimards to watch the advertisements in *Le Figaro Littéraire.*)

Waiting for the *miracle Ménétrier* to occur, he found that—despite the summer heat—he was working again. If he had genius, he thought, *L'Homme révolté* would be *quite* a book[6]

In August he pursued his convalescence in the Vosges Mountains, some 250 miles east of Paris, high above the Alsatian plain and the Rhine valley.[6] With Maria Casarès he had discovered a virtually deserted village known as Le Grand Valtin at an altitude of 2,800 feet, where a forlorn hotel among the fields and tall trees had the advantages of silence if not of modern comforts. (There was no running water, the toilet was in a separate and fragile privy largely open to the world.) When bored there was always the aging Citroën to take them to local centers of civilization, good restaurants. He found that he could work here too, and the fact that it was raining two days out of three and that the temperature was dismally low encouraged that. Rest came easy, for the electricity was cut off at ten each evening.

In his journal, the cycles into which he had divided his work assumed Greek names:

> I. Le Mythe de Sisyphe (absurde).—II. Le Mythe de Prométhée (révolte).—III. Le Mythe de Némésis.

Two events from the outside world troubled this summer of convalescence and writing. The first was an international one: the outbreak of the Korean War, with North Korea's invasion of the south on June 25, an incident that alarmed him but that he hoped would be contained. Artists like himself didn't make history, he asserted in reply to a letter from a group of Japanese writers who had solicited his views. "All we can do is to add to creation, as much as we can, while others work for destruction. It's this long, patient and secret effort which has really represented men's progress ever since they have had a history."[9]

The other event was personal, one which he considered vital: the publication of his political essays. It was one book of his that he hoped to see widely read. But this time public or at least press reaction seemed a "religious silence." He observed with bitterness that the only significant reactions were coming from abroad—from Switzerland first of all. (He saved among his personal papers one good review, but from a conservative critic: "Better than a literary event, a moment of the French conscience." And a late review which may have pleased him more, from the anarchist newspaper *Le Libertaire:* "For the nobility of his style and of his thought which contrast so completely with the constipated manner of Gide, Albert Camus has rapidly acquired a virile and a virilizing influence on the youth of our time. . . .")

He was reading Lenin—"digesting" Lenin—at Le Grand Valtin, although he assured his friends that it was not for his pleasure. And this month of isolation helped him gain ground, although there was still much to be done. "I'm in a hurry to finish with it, you know," he wrote to René Char on September 19. "I imagine stupidly that life will begin again after that."[9]

Back in Paris in September, he was also making notes for novels, plays; all through his career it seemed as if intensive effort on one book engendered ideas in all directions, and he wisely recorded them in his journal as they came to him. (A note on the Nazi treatment of imprisoned intellectuals which may have been for the mysterious, never-commenced work called "Le Système" or "Création corrigée" appeared in his journal now; it would turn up as an anecdote in *La Chute:* the prisoner is locked into a cramped cell to be spat upon full in the face by each passing guard.)

At last an apartment had been found, but the Camus could not move in at once. Meanwhile he was staying at a small hotel on the Rue de Beaujolais. Michel Gallimard's father was living next door in the graceful old Palais Royal residential quadrangle, just above the legendary apartment of the novelist Colette. Camus grew quite fond of this neighborhood too, and would use the Hôtel du Palais Royal as temporary quarters whenever he needed to get away from his private circle. "I am working and that saves everything," he wrote Char. "I also have the impression of improving physically and morally. . . . This year has been hard, very hard for me, on every level."[9]

Henceforth the family residence would be on the narrow Rue Madame, a five-minute walk south from Saint-Germain-des-Prés square, about ten minutes from Gallimard—which he would not abandon after all. In a rather ordinary street of undistinguished houses, the Camus apartment was in a six-story building (counting the ground floor); in French terms, it was a four-story building plus a service floor. Their apartment covered all of what is called the "noble" floor (it had the largest ironwork balcony on the street side). As *moyen-bourgeois* as could be, but it had ample space, at last, for children and relatives and visitors. From now on, as long as he lived (and later), it would be the home of his loyal and long-suffering wife, of their growing twins (who were just five when they moved in).

In November 1950 the Swedish Academy was able to be unanimous about a Nobel Prize: the 1949 prize, which had not been given the previous year, went to William Faulkner. In his journal Camus noted the American writer's responses to interview questions, in which Faulkner expressed skepticism about a young generation of writers who knew not how to speak of eternal verities—pride, honor, pain. Faulkner attributed comtemporary nihilism to fear: When men stopped being afraid, they would be able to write lasting works again. But when Camus was asked (by the *Harvard Advocate*) to write an appreciation of Faulkner—it came at the very moment he was revising *L'Homme révolté* for publication—he limited his reply to the brief confirmation of his opinion that Faulkner was America's greatest writer, the only contemporary who deserved a place alongside the nineteenth-century American masters, and who had created his own universe as Melville,

Dostoevsky, and Proust had; he thought *Sanctuary* and *Pylon* were
Faulkner's masterpieces.[9]

While Camus would henceforth eschew organized politics—the rallies
dear to the Sartre group, the Malraux form of engagement in parties
and governments, the traditional left's petitions and manifestos—he
would be increasingly involved in what he believed was a more effective
form of action (although, as he would discover, a thankless one). If his
name had any value, then he could use it at least as well in private, discreet, and confidential messages to those having the power of life and
death. He was increasingly concerned, for example, with the situation in
Greece, where the struggle between Communists and conservatives had
been accompanied by arbitrary arrests and imprisonment of left-wing
intellectuals. From 1950 until his death Camus would be corresponding
through private channels with Greek authorities, asking for clemency,
leniency (he did, in December of that year, participate in one more petition with Sartre, Breton, Mauriac, Le Corbusier, and other prominent
persons to demand the liberation of young Greek intellectuals from detention camps). Indeed, in the final year of his life, he would write a
letter to be delivered to the Greek prime minister personally—whom
Camus assured that no publicity would be given to his intervention—
pleading for fairness in dealing with Greek Communist Manolis Glezos,
a hero of the World War II resistance to the Germans.[1]

Camus found that his natural allies in many of these quiet efforts
were men and women of the non-Stalinist left: anarchists, revolutionary
syndicalists, conscientious objectors. Many of his subsequent inter-
ventions, in fact, were to rescue anarchists or conscientious objectors
from the consequences of their convictions. They in turn would recognize in *L'Homme révolté* the expression of their own philosophy: a
revolt generated by individual aspirations rather than Marxist doctrine,
and which need not lead inevitably to the firing squad or to the concentration camp universe of the Stalinists.[10] One key to *L'Homme révolté*
might be these private expressions of protest against the absurd and the
arbitrary of the twentieth-century police state, just as the book itself is
a key to the enigmatic Camus of the 1950s who served his conscience
and his sense of justice in this solitary way.

During the final stage of the writing of *L'Homme révolté,* from
January to July 1951, there was ample justification for alarm in the
world at large. The Chinese had intervened in the Korean War, beginning the previous November; in January the evacuation of Seoul was
ordered. War fever had gripped France, where there was talk among intellectuals of the likelihood of a Soviet invasion and occupation of their
country. Simone de Beauvoir claimed to have heard Francine Camus

say, as they left a Bartók concert together: "When the Russians enter Paris *I* am going to kill myself with my children." In a high school class, Beauvoir also noted, the students drew up a pact for collective suicide in the event of "red occupation."

In a conversation at the Balzar Café, next door to the Sorbonne, Camus asked Sartre whether he had thought about what he would do when the Russians arrived. He added—in Beauvoir's quote—"Don't stay!" Sartre asked Camus if he intended to leave; Camus replied that he would do what he had done during the German occupation. That the Sartre group did not quite dismiss Camus' advice as hysterical is demonstrated by Beauvoir herself, who confesses that in the days that followed that conversation she adopted Camus' argument. She felt that the Soviets wouldn't touch Sartre if he remained silent, but she knew that he would not be able to do that, and they all knew what Stalin did to disobedient intellectuals. Another writer friend begged Sartre, if he did stay on, never to confess. . . . But if Beauvoir wished Sartre to flee rather than live under a Soviet occupation of France, they rejected the idea of going to the United States, which both detested. The North Koreans may have started the war, but they also believed that General MacArthur had set a trap for them.

That spring there was a brief revival of the Camus-Sartre friendship during rehearsals of Sartre's play *Le Diable et le Bon Dieu,* for Maria Casarès had a leading part in it, and Camus would pick her up, stopping to have a drink with Sartre. On opening night Camus and Casarès joined the Sartre group at a supper club, but Beauvoir remarked that the warmth failed to kindle between them.[11]

Once more he fled the damp Paris winter for Cabris. On the drive down, stopping in Valence, he took up his journal to confess that at thirty-seven he was obliged to relearn, painfully, how to live alone. He would spend all of this February 1951 absorbed in uninterrupted work, as he reported to Char. "The complete solitude and the will to have done with it keep me at my desk ten hours a day." He hoped to complete the manuscript by March 15, but he wasn't sure that he was happy with the product of these exhausting efforts.[9] Then he would return to Paris to rework the entire book; the hope now was to turn it in to his publisher in May.[12]

It rained without respite in his Provençal retreat; when the weather was clear it was cold, but at least he could look out at the cypress trees across the valley, There were photographs of Maria Casarès and of the young Russian terrorist Kaliayev over his writing table.

But he was brain-tired now. He looked forward to this spring as deliverance, the most important spring of his life, which would see him freed of everything that had been stored inside him, which would liberate him, after years of tension, for the human warmth he craved. There were days when he was pleased because he felt that he was ahead of the schedule he had imposed upon himself, covering piles of the large manuscript sheets he was now using with his small writing. Whenever he had a package—perhaps thirty of these large sheets—he would mail them off to faithful Suzanne Labiche in his old office at Gallimard; when she had finished typing them, she would mail them back for corrections and revisions, and by that time he would have another package for her.[13]

In his journal he indulged in daydreams, notes for new projects. A reference to an essay on destiny; this is "Némésis," or "Le Mythe de Némésis." He planned his essay on the sea ("La Mer au plus près") for a book of essays to be called "La Fête" (perhaps *L'Eté*). He planned prefaces for the American editions of his plays and essays, a translation of Shakespeare's *Timon of Athens,* other works titled "L'Amour du lointain," "La voix éternelle." One thing was certain: After *L'Homme révolté* there would be "an aggressive, stubborn refusal of the system." No more chains for him. "Henceforth the aphorism."

Paradoxically, a note of gloom is heard from time to time, and right in the middle of these projects which imply the pursuit of a fruitful career in literature. "What I have sought for so long is finally appearing," he noted in Cabris. "To die becomes a consent." On February 5 he wrote: "To die without having settled anything. But who dies having settled everything, or else . . . ? Settle at least the peace of those one has loved. . . ."

What he had wished to do in *L'Homme révolté,* he wrote in his journal, was "to tell the truth without ceasing to be generous." And on March 7 he noted proudly that he had completed the first draft; thus the first two cycles of his work had come to a close. "37 years old. And now, can creation be free?"[14]

In her study of Camus' writing Germaine Brée demonstrated that most of the essays which he wrote after *Le Mythe de Sisyphe* were incorporated into *L'Homme révolté,* and with only minor changes, indicating that the book touched on different facets of the problem as they came to him. From 1943 on, almost all of his political writings and editorials—"Ni Victimes ni Bourreaux," for instance—led to this major work, and material which would appear in the book began to be published as early as 1945, with "Remarque sur la révolte."[15] In every way *L'Homme révolté* was a personal statement, despite its disguise as a treatise of political philosophy. It was a statement of Camus' intentions in literature as well as an exposition of his views on public affairs, it was a platform on which he could stand to support literary and political friends (such as Char) and to demonstrate the error of the ways of his enemies. And now at last this compendium was about to be given to the world. "I am still at work redoing certain parts of my book," he informed Char, who was now practically the work's godfather, although it would be dedicated to Jean Grenier. *"Finalement,"* this letter (dated June 26) continued,

> it is not without anguish that I shall deliver myself of it. I had wanted to be both true and useful. But that supposes a constant generosity. I felt myself quite alone during all the time I spent on this work.[9]

And then it was all over, on or about July 10, if we are to accept the date on a letter to Char: "Now we must wait." He saw Char the next day to review the manuscript with him, and on the day after that sent him a copy of the typescript with a letter:

> Here is the object of so much suffering. . . . May it be worthy, in its form, of what we believe together. It is with deep joy, in any case, DESPITE MY ANXIETY OF COURSE, that I turn it over to you.[9]

Now he took off some time to help his Spanish friends again, at a meeting sponsored by the Casa de Cataluña in the small Récamier Theater belonging to the Ligue Française de l'Enseignement, to commemorate the fifteenth anniversary of the July 19, 1936, outbreak of civil war in Spain. Other speakers at the meeting would be the Mexican writer Octavio Paz and the Spanish exile government minister Fernando Valera. (Camus authorized the reprinting of his speech in his anarchist-syndicalist friends' *Solidaridad Obrera* provided that they published the original French text, something they didn't usually do, but they did it this time.)[16] Camus told the audience that the Spanish uprising had in fact been the first battle of World War II, a war that was now over everywhere but in Spain. Yet the cause was not lost. Summing up without citing the long book he had just finished writing, he observed that Spain, France, and Italy knew the secret of an idea which was equally distant from bourgeois philosophies and Caesarian socialism. He stood with

> another race of men . . . who never sought life or liberty other than in the liberty and happiness of all, and who even in defeat find reasons to live and to love. These people, even vanquished, will never be alone.

Then he was off to join his family at Le Chambon-sur-Lignon, after driving Maria Casarès to Brive in the Périgord region. Before leaving Paris he saw Jean Grenier, on summer leave from Lille University. He was thinking, he told Grenier, of a third major essay to join *Le*

*Mythe de Sisyphe* and *L'Homme révolté*. It might be called "Le Mythe de Némésis," and it would treat Christianity and Hellenism (as his *diplôme,* written for Professor Poirier, had done), to demonstrate the transition from the latter to the former. "Personally," he told his old teacher, "I feel closer to Hellenism. And, within Christianity, closer to Catholicism than to Protestantism." And he felt distant from the Bible because of its *"antinaturalisme."* He thought that one had to revolt to obtain happiness on earth, and not only to abolish injustice, that "one must have a wisdom of life in the immediate and not in the far-off. . . ."[17]

En route to Chambon his never-faithful old Citroën, which he had baptized Desdémone, had a breakdown at remote Saint-Flour, in the Cantal district, seventy-five miles from his destination, so he stayed overnight in a local inn. And on the following day, less than five miles from Chambon, the car broke down again; he was exhausted by the time he arrived.[18]

This time the Camus were not staying at Le Panelier, but in the town of Chambon itself, not far from the center, up a hilly road called Chemin de Molle. They were renting the upper floor of a simple stucco-faced villa called Le Platane, set in the middle of a large garden backed with pine woods. His room overlooked a vast pine-dotted landscape, and he expected to spend a good deal of his stay there sleeping, thinking—or simply contemplating.

But first there was a final chore in connection with *L'Homme révolté:* correcting the proofs. He began working on them on July 30 and was still at it a week later. But he was also sleeping, sleeping as he had not slept in a long while. There was nothing to distract him from that, in this austere mountain country he disliked so much; even the people of this region failed to awake his interest. He read Sainte-Beuve, flirted with his daughter not quite six, looked for ways to fight off the depression which he knew always affected him each time he completed a book. He feared a vacuum, and worried that because he had been working so hard the vacuum might be all the greater. Walking in the garden after dinner, smoking and looking up at the sky, he suddenly felt dizzy, and fainted. Dragging himself to his feet, he managed to climb up to the house, to dash into his room and throw himself on the bed. He was soon as fresh as a daisy.

But the weather alone could have depressed anybody: rain and wind. He would rise early, walk to Le Panelier, three miles away, to pick up Paul Oettly, and together they would fish for trout. Or he would work on the proofs in the morning and take long walks in the afternoon. In or near Le Panelier, he would never forget to remember the long, hard year he had spent there during the occupation of France, when the young Camus of Algiers, man-about-town, cynical, more flashy than brilliant, had become the aspiring writer who knew how far he had to travel, and was humbled by that thought. He realized now that the retreat of Le Panelier of 1942–43 had been a necessary trial.

In a sense, Chambon might be a turning point this time as well. He was looking forward to the post-*Homme révolté* period, when creation in freedom would be possible again.

At the end of August his wife went on to Italy, and he drove to the southwest to join Maria Casarès, who had been at an Atlantic beach resort.[13]

There would be one more trip—an unexpected one—in November. His mother was to be operated on for a fracture. He flew to Algiers as soon as he got the news, arriving on November 19, when she was already in the hospital. By midnight he was in the room alongside her (his brother at the opposite side of the bed); listening to her light moaning, he felt as if she were their suffering daughter. The operation took place the next morning, and the surgeon assured him that it had been successful; she would be able to return home in a few days. He stayed on, depressed by the damp Algiers climate. He breathed with difficulty, although he was certain that physically he was in better shape than he had been for a long time; he had continued the Ménétrier treatment. He was also somewhat anxious about what he was going to do now that the big book was behind him. There were days when he wished he would not have to do or to write anything at all in the future—a kind of fear of his vocation, something he had never experienced before. Perhaps this anguish could be attributed to general exhaustion; he had been pushing himself far too long. Yet without this pushing, he also knew, he would be nothing and his work would be nothing. Thinking of the future sometimes made him dizzy.

Meanwhile he was glad that he had come to Algiers to be at his mother's side. His presence, he knew, was good for her.[13]

He made her laugh by telling her: "Imagine, I was invited to see the President of the Republic [then Vincent Auriol] and I didn't go." His mother replied: "You did the right thing, my son. They aren't our kind of people."[18]

Before returning to Paris he visited Tipasa again, so that the trip would bring him some beauty at least. He dined with old friends. He was aware of the contrast between these healthy people, who knew how to live and to die in simplicity, and the artifice of the Parisians. And before he left his old city the weather turned fine again. He rediscovered the Algiers of his childhood, the aroma of orange trees in the city's narrow lanes. But he did not think that he could ever live here again, not in the city itself in any case.[13]

While in Algiers, he was told by his friend Charles Poncet that their civil liberties lawyer friend Yves Dechezelles needed his help in defending a group of Moslem nationalists who were being tried in Blida because of their activities in Messali Hadj's Mouvement pour le Triomphe des Libertés Démocratiques (MTLD). He prepared an affidavit to be read in court in their defense.[2]

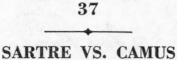

# 37

# SARTRE VS. CAMUS

Temps Modernes. They admit sin and refuse grace. . . .

*Carnets**

Even before the publication of *L'Homme révolté* the controversy had begun. A chapter of the book, entitled "Lautréamont et la banalité," was published in *Cahiers du Sud* early in 1951. In this chapter Camus had been severe with the author of *Chants de Maldoror* (1869), one of the precursors of surrealism, accusing him of conformity, intellectual servitude. The man who considered himself the spokesman for the surrealist movement, André Breton, replied to Camus in an angry article in the October 12, 1951, issue of *Arts,* then a newspaper-format cultural weekly which thrived on polemics. "One cannot protest enough," wrote Breton, "when writers enjoying public favor occupy themselves by attacking what is a thousand times greater than they."

Camus replied in the issue that followed, to say that Breton had not read him and that his arguments were purely emotional. Camus was not prepared to employ the tone which Breton's attack called for; all he had sought to do was to offer a new reading of Lautréamont. Then, in the November 16 *Arts,* there appeared a dialogue between Breton and Aimé Patri, in which Breton said that he esteemed Camus, feeling his voice to have been "the clearest and most honest" at the time of the liberation, and indeed up to the moment he had read Camus on Lautréamont. In a long letter—as long as the Breton-Patri dialogue—printed in *Arts* on November 23, Camus replied point by point, objecting that he was not obliged to admire the poets admired by Breton. He felt that

* Quoted in the Pléiade edition of Camus' work.

Breton would like to place all the blame for the present state of the world on the Marxists, whereas the nihilists had not all come from that camp. "I had taken the extravagances of the surrealists for what they were," he explained, "disordered cries that a young and legitimate revolt sends to the far corners of the earth. . . . The ferment of surrealism still seems useful to me, but in what it might become."

And he declared an end to the polemic. But Breton was back in the following issue. He had not wished to insult Camus, for he respected him, but he warned that conservatives had embraced Camus' notions of revolt. As for surrealism, he felt that it was no more dangerous than *L'Etranger*. By this time the storm created by the weekly back-and-forth led one of the editors of *Arts*, Louis Pauwels, to enter the ring. He admitted responsibility for having invited Breton to comment on Camus' essay, and did not believe that had been a frivolous thing to do. If he had been the cause for the break between Camus and Breton, it was a tribute to journalism.[1] Then the followers of Breton decided to reply to Camus collectively in a small book. Camus refused to participate in the rigged symposium or to authorize republication of his letters to *Arts*, on the grounds that he did not like the tone of the attack. The editor of the symposium felt that "scorn" and "immodesty" might also be involved.[2]

Thus the war between Camus and the surrealists.

*L'Homme révolté* was published on October 18, 1951. "To have delivered myself of this book," Camus wrote Char, "leaves me quite empty and in a state of 'aerial' depression." He told Char that if he had replied to Breton it was because his *affirmations gratuites* risked giving a false impression of the book.[3]

But now his essay was in everybody's hands, and not only in those of his friends. The author's unambiguous stand against Stalinism was bound to receive sympathy and approval from conservatives, from anti-Communists of all types: A critic in *Le Figaro Littéraire* found it not only Camus' most important book, but one of the great books of the present era. *Le Monde*'s philosophical critic said that no work of comparable value had appeared since the war. Also in *Le Monde*, Emile Henriot of the French Academy noted a contradiction in Camus' admiration of Saint-Just, one of the more extreme leaders of the French Revolution, and his disapproval of the beheading of Louis XVI: How would Camus have voted at the time of the French Revolution? But Henriot found the contradictions between heart and reason to Camus' credit. More worrisome was the praise in the right-wing extremist *Aspects de la France*, organ of Action Française, which suggested that the book showed a healthy return to nationalism and even to God. (If *Le*

*Mythe de Sisyphe* with its preaching of the absurd had been harmful to youth, *L'Homme révolté* showed that, like Charles Maurras, Camus was seeking order and duration.)

Enemies—or friendly enemies—said predictable things. Claude Mauriac saw in the book "an obscure and rather curious nostalgia for murder," and decided that Camus was providing ammunition to their common enemies. Max-Pol Fouchet objected to the insistence on *"mesure."* "Midnight can be the hour of crime," he warned. "Noon [*midi,* Camus' metaphor for the just measure of Mediterranean lands] risks being that of solar torpor." In *Combat,* Maurice Nadeau saw the book as filling a need, predicted that it would have an impact. "More than the coming to awareness of an era by a lucid and courageous spirit, it won't take long to see a reflection of the era on itself, the announcement of a turning-point after which certain problems will be posed differently." He too was skeptical of Camus' conclusions, particularly the idea that just measure was a Mediterranean racial trail. Later, Nadeau would recall that the book disappointed its public, more by its conclusions than its analyses. He felt that the author had chosen a public which was waiting for nothing other than this book to confirm its conservatism, its rejection of change. Camus furnished arguments to those who wished to do nothing, but with a good conscience.[4]

Of course—could Camus not have realized this?—by offering a demonstration of how revolutionary idealism degenerates into formulas, how formulas are transformed into police terror, Camus was clearly taking sides, objectively, in the Communist-anti-Communist war which was then the chief element of international affairs, not to speak of French domestic politics. But was that all he was doing? His critics simply dismissed as window dressing his genuine commitment to revolt (but to a clean revolt). Fortunately, the message did get through to at least part of the book's readership: the revolutionary syndicalists, the anarchists (in Spain as well as in France). The non-Communist left despised the Stalinists, and those who had become leading apologists for Stalinism, such as Sartre.[5]

In Algeria that November, at his mother's bedside, Camus realized that the polemics had made him angry—a function of his pride, and not the best kind of pride. But he had never been able to get used to literary mores or the frivolity of Paris. One of the reasons he lived at a distance from others, he confided to a friend, was precisely because he knew how incapable he was of taking certain things lightly. He knew that the irresponsibility of others could wound him.[6] At the very least, he confessed to Char, it made him physically nauseated.

He intended to abstain from further controversy in public print, or so he promised himself in his journal.[7] But several times he would infringe his own rule to write to editors or publishers of periodicals in which a misunderstanding or a misinterpretation of *L'Homme révolté* had appeared, e.g., to a Catholic magazine which had examined the religious conclusions of his essay, or to the anarchist *Le Libertaire,* to clarify what he had written about a Russian revolutionary.

Early in 1952 he let himself be interviewed by a friendly journalist, Pierre Berger, and after refusing to say which press articles impressed him most, adding that the personal mail he had received seemed to him more judicious than the response of reviewers, he explained how intellectuals could undo the harm they had done in sponsoring "the two forms of contemporary nihilism, bourgeois and revolutionary":

> 1. That they recognize this evil and denounce it; 2. That they not lie and learn to admit they don't know something; 3. That they refuse to dominate; 4. That they refuse, in any circumstances and whatever the pretext, all despotism, even a temporary one.[7]

Although he was now to move further away from active political life, to keep his distance from these intellectuals who were so ready to sell out to despotism, another emergency obliged him to make common cause with them. In Spain a group of labor leaders had been sentenced to death and a meeting was called in Paris (on February 22, 1952) by the French League for the Rights of Man. Of course Camus was ready to help. Not only would he make a speech, but he selected the speakers —leading intellectuals such as Sartre, Georges Altman, Louis Guilloux, Albert Béguin, and from Italy Ignazio Silone; René Char attended and sat in the audience. But Camus also felt that it would be useful for the Spanish Republican cause to have Breton present, despite the nastiness of his attack in *Arts*. He suggested that the Spanish organizers of the meeting—Fernando Gomez Pelaez of *Solidaridad Obrera,* the organ of the anarchist trade union federation CNT, and José Ester Borrás, secretary of the Spanish political prisoners federation FEDIP—go to see Breton but without telling him that Camus had sent them. For his part, Breton agreed to speak at the meeting even though Camus would be present. At that point Gomez told Breton that Camus had suggested his name, and Breton was so moved that he broke into tears. (Later Camus told the Spaniards that it was because he had never replied to Breton's angry words in kind that this near-reconciliation had been possible.) Camus and Breton sat on the platform together and were even seen chatting.[8]

But Camus had by no means returned to uncritical acceptance of the causes of the French or European left, and he had an early opportunity to demonstrate this. He had been a member of a Société Européenne de Culture, which was at once an austere and somewhat pretentious summit grouping of intellectuals and a loose and open-ended one. Its membership included Karl Barth, Sartre, Breton, Elizabeth Bowen, and Jean-Louis Barrault; Jean Grenier had gotten Camus to lend his name to it. The society was headquartered in Venice, run by a somewhat otherworldly person named Umberto Campagnolo. It met occasionally and published the proceedings of its meetings in an enormous but irregular magazine called *Comprendre*.

But to Camus' mind the Société Européenne de Culture had been too quick to encourage East-West dialogue as if it could be on a give-and-take basis, as if Soviet intellectuals were free to criticize their system as Western intellectuals were encouraged to criticize theirs. A manifesto published by the society had urged such a dialogue. On March 6, 1952, Camus wrote Campagnolo to explain that he had always felt that one should not belong to a group when one was not able to participate personally in its activities. "This rule is a bit puritannical," he conceded, "but finally beneficial for everyone, the group and the individual." If he had made an exception for the society because some of its members were his friends, now the society's activities were developing and he was confronted with texts of which he would not have approved. Campagnolo regretted Camus' decision, asking what specific differences Camus was referring to, and suggesting a meeting with Camus, Grenier, and Guilloux. From Cabris, where Camus was spending another early spring, far from the political arena (such was his intention), he spelled out his objections to the society's vague and wistful political pronouncements. "I do not believe in a dialogue which begins with silences." Each side must define itself. "To understand clearly what you are saying yes to in the two blocs, we must know to what you are saying no."

On the cultural level, why not say that one admires America's political freedoms but not its technical and often its moral conformity? Why not speak about Soviet repression as well as progress? True dialogue could not exist with lies or omissions; he found the society too indulgent to the Soviet forced labor camp system, while as a member he felt bound by these positions.[9] He would soon adopt a similar attitude to an organization which leaned the other way, the Congress for Cultural Freedom, refusing to participate in its activities or even to sign joint manifestos against Soviet violations of freedom.[10]

"The truth," he wrote Char on April 16, "is that I can't climb out of the hole in which I have been vegetating for months and where I suffocated particularly during these last weeks in Paris." So sensitive had he become to attacks on *L'Homme révolté* from the ill-intentioned that when *Observateur,* a left-wing weekly, called attention in passing to *"une remarquable étude"* of the book in the Communist magazine *La Nouvelle Critique* by Pierre Hervé, Camus wrote to *Observateur* (published by Claude Bourdet and Roger Stéphane) to question its characterization of Hervé's text, but misquoted the magazine, accusing it of calling the Communist review *"une belle étude."* He worried that the *Observateur* in trying to be objective had dropped all standards whatsoever. Stéphane replied that Camus had exaggerated *Observateur's* endorsement of the Hervé attack, and privately Bourdet was irritated by Camus' flash reaction, especially since Camus had said nothing about the *favorable* reception that *Observateur* had given to *L'Homme révolté* in two two-page installments the previous December; Bourdet had even attacked André Breton for criticizing the book.[11]

In August 1951 a chapter of *L'Homme révolté,* "Nietzsche et le nihilisme," had been published in Sartre's magazine *Les Temps Modernes.* The editorial board of that magazine met every two weeks, and at each meeting since the publication of Camus' essay in October the subject was brought up. Usually it was Simone de Beauvoir, in an attempt to give these editorial meetings a semblance of agenda, who would say: "Remember, we have to review Camus' book." All of the editors had read it, of course, but none was ready to write a review.[12] (There were some twenty persons in the *Temps Modernes* group, and among themselves they had already been saying that the book was based on secondhand material. Sartre felt that Camus was writing about things he hadn't understood, that he hadn't read Marx or Engels—while of course the *Temps Modernes* crowd had—yet had utilized résumés of the thoughts of the Communist philosophers.)[13]

Finally Sartre said: "It isn't necessarily better not to talk about the book. That's as insulting as to speak badly about it." He asked Francis Jeanson to review it. "He will be the harshest," Sartre added, "but at least he'll be polite."

Francis Jeanson was then twenty-nine years old. He had done preparatory work at the Sorbonne for the *agrégation de philosophie,* but for reasons of health—he too had tuberculosis—he had not been admitted to the examinations for the degree. After having fought with the Free French (Forces Françaises Libres) in North Africa, Alsace, and Germany, he had settled down to write. In 1947 he had written a small book on Sartre, and decided he'd better talk directly with him. He called on Sartre at the *Temps Modernes* office, where certain days and hours were set aside for receiving visitors, but was horrified to see the number of persons waiting for a chance to exchange a few words with the great man. So when his turn came he said: "I want to see you." Sartre replied, "Here I am." But he persuaded Sartre to walk into an adjoining room where he could ask him a couple of questions. Sartre made an appointment for another meeting, and then surprised Jeanson by writing a preface for the book. Jeanson published his first article in *Les Temps Modernes* in January 1948 and became manager of the magazine when Merleau-Ponty withdrew in 1951. Of an uncompromising nature, Jeanson would later be one of the few French intellectuals to follow up his ideological commitment to Algerian nationalism with dangerous engagement. He slipped out of France to spend the war (1957–62) working underground, published pro-rebellion books in Italy.

Jeanson had already read *L'Homme révolté,* of course. He had decided that Camus, like many others, was all too ready to settle the question of socialism without consulting the working class. And like Sartre, Jeanson was firmly opposed to anti-Communism, although he did not think of himself and Sartre as Communists.[12] In April, while Jeanson was working on the review of Camus' essay for *Temps Modernes,* Sartre and Beauvoir sat one day in a small café on the Place Saint-Sulpice. Camus was ridiculing some of the objections made to his book, and took it for granted that his friends liked it; Sartre was too embarrassed to reply. But shortly after that, in the Pont Royal bar near the Gallimard building which was an unofficial meeting place of the editors and writers of that house, Sartre warned Camus that the review in his magazine would be *réservé,* perhaps even severe; Camus seemed disagreeably surprised. According to Beauvoir, Jeanson's original text had indeed been harsh, although he had promised to be gentle, and Sartre managed to get him to attenuate some of the more brutal remarks, although there was no censorship on the magazine.[14]

In 1952 *Les Temps Modernes* was published in a smart design of black and red lettering on white covers; the name of its publisher, Sartre, appeared in red under the title. The contributors were in the main left-wing, "engaged" intellectuals, their subjects political philosophy, literature, and the arts. The May 1952 issue, which is of concern here, contained an article on the Korean War, a report on the situation of homosexuals in the United States. It also contained Francis Jeanson's long-awaited review, under the title "Albert Camus ou l'âme révoltée"—"or the revolted soul," in French a play on the book's title. The article covered twenty-one pages of the magazine.

Jeanson began with an ironic summary of the critical praise from which the book had benefited, an instant success which he claimed was unique. He cited right-wing critics: "a capital work," "one of the great books of recent years," "a turning point of Western thought." In Camus' place, Jeanson said, he'd be worried, and he understood that Camus *was* worried. But why is everyone so pleased with the book?

They like its style, but isn't that unkind to Camus, who himself warns against exclusive attention to style? Jeanson proceeded to analyze the book.

> Is Camus' hope really to halt the movement of the world by refusing every endeavor in the world? He blames the Stalinists (but also existentialism) for being totally captive of history; but they are not more so than he is, they are only captive in another way . . . If the revolt of Camus wishes to be deliberately static, it can only concern Camus himself. To the extent that it is meant to influence the movement of the world it must enter into the game, insert itself into the historical context, find its objectives there, its adversaries. . . .

He had a good word for Camus' "voice so human and charged with a genuine torment," but found it buried inside "this pseudo-philosophy of a pseudo-history of 'revolutions.' " He concluded:

> *L'Homme révolté* is first of all an aborted great book: hence, precisely, the myth to which it has given birth. We beg Camus not to yield to fascination, and to rediscover in himself that personal accent by which his work remains for us, despite everything, irreplaceable.

There is indisputable evidence that Jeanson's review in Sartre's magazine surprised, shocked, and pained Camus, no matter how inevitable it may seem to the observer removed from it in time. If in retrospect the split between Camus and the Sartrians also appears inevitable, somehow it was not so to Camus, who at the time took the event as a disappointed lover might; he was clearly reacting to an unexpected blow.

Should he reply? He felt so depressed about the Jeanson review that he found it difficult to work; he confessed to a friend that he had lost all appetite for life. And then when he had finally drafted a reply to Francis Jeanson he wasn't certain that he should send it at all.[6]

That June, he was writing an essay on Herman Melville for an anthology. He was also sending off a strong letter to the Director-General of UNESCO, Jaime Torres Bodet, who on May 30 had invited Camus to participate in an inquiry in the field of education and culture. Camus replied that he could not agree to collaborate with UNESCO as long as the question of Franco Spain's membership in that international organization remained on the agenda. If Spain's entry into the United Nations raised serious questions, including questions of decency, "its admission to UNESCO, like the admission of any totalitarian government, would in addition violate the most elementary logic." He regretted that he would have to publicize his letter as soon as Torres Bodet received it.

> I shall do it only in the hope that men more important than myself,
> and in a general manner free artists and intellectuals whoever they
> are, will share my opinion and will notify you directly that they too
> have decided to boycott an organization which has now publicly
> contradicted all of its past activity.

And the letter was released to the press.[15] Camus followed up with a
petition to UNESCO which he asked French intellectuals to sign, urging
that Spain not be admitted.[16]

And finally, on June 30,1952, he put the finishing touches on his
reply to *Les Temps Modernes* and mailed it out.

In July he wrote to Jean Gillibert, a young theater director with
whom Camus expected to be working:

> . . . My work, if you can call it that, still seems to be at its begin-
> nings. But it is also a constantly growing tension, and the question
> no longer seems to me to know if I shall ever to able to raise myself
> to the level of my artistic ambition (in the good sense of the word).
> It is only to know whether I can remain on the level of this tension.
> This is why *L'Homme révolté* is a test for me. The mediocrity of
> the reactions doesn't surprise me. For a long time I have known
> that in our era one is only judged by one's peers. But the futility, the
> adolescent stubbornness, the drumming of an interminable argu-
> ment, only represent, in a somewhat caricatural way, the heaviness
> to which, in my book, I try to oppose a counterweight. . . .[17]

After spending some days in Sorel, a village where Michel and Janine
Gallimard had bought a house not far from Diane de Poitier's castle of
Anet in the Eure-et-Loir district, some fifty miles from Paris, the
Camus went down to Le Panelier. This time they were put up in the
"dungeon" again, joined by Francine's mother. Camus felt emptied out,
dried out; unable to write, he went fishing.[18]

Francis Jeanson wasn't used to the spotlight, and after the publication
of his review of *L'Homme révolté* there was an uproar. The books he
had published until then, in addition to *Le problème moral et la pensée
de Sartre,* had titles such as *Signification humanine du rire, Montaigne
par lui-même,* and *La Phénoménologie.* And now he had an unexpected
and even an expensive notoriety: He subscribed to a press clipping
service, paying only for the articles mentioning his name, and all at
once there was a considerable pile of them. Then one day he had a
phone call from Simone de Beauvoir asking him to come around to see
Sartre. He found Sartre in an angry mood: He had just received Camus'
reply. He told Jeanson: "I'm going to answer him in any case. You can
if you want to."[12]

The August 1952 issue of *Les Temps Modernes* published Camus' letter, which filled seventeen pages of the magazine, then the reply to Camus by Sartre, which covered twenty pages, finally a new text by Jeanson, filling another thirty pages. Camus' reply began:

> I shall take as a pretext the article which, under an ironical title, your magazine has devoted to me to submit to your readers some remarks concerning the intellectual method and the attitude demonstrated by this article.

He added that the attitude interested him more than had the article itself, "whose weakness surprised me." He had considered it not a study of his book, but a symptom. He regretted that he would be as lengthy as Jeanson had been: "I shall only try to be clearer." Dismissing praise he had received from the rightist press, he nevertheless added: "If, finally, truth seemed to me on the right, I would be there." But he observed that the true right-wing press had criticized his book. After mocking Jeanson's suggestion that Camus' fine style was damaging to his thesis, he went on to defend his thesis, which he felt that Jeanson had distorted. Proceeding to the counterattack, he pointed out his critic's silence or derision concerning all revolutionary tradition that was not Marxist. Without naming him, he accused Jeanson of being a bourgeois Marxist. And, he added,

> I am beginning to be a little tired of seeing myself, and of seeing veteran militants who never walked away from the struggles of their times, receive without cease their lessons of efficacy from critics who never placed anything more than their armchair in the sense of history. . . .[19]

In his reply in the same issue of *Les Temps Modernes,* Sartre quickly assumed an equally personal tone.

> Our friendship was not an easy one, but I shall miss it. If you break it today, it is certainly because it had to break. Many things brought us together, few separated us. But these few were still too many: Friendship can also become totalitarian; one must agree on everything or fight. . . . Unfortunately you singled me out so deliberately and in so unpleasant a tone that I cannot remain silent without losing face. I shall therefore reply, without anger but, for the first time since we have known each other, without circumspection. A mixture of somber self-conceit and of vulnerability has always discouraged anyone from telling you whole truths. The result is that you have become the victim of a bleak immoderation which masks your internal difficulties and which you call, I believe, Mediterranean measure. Sooner or later someone would have told you; let it be me.

He reproached Camus for denying his own heroes:

> Where is Meursault, Camus? Where is Sisyphus? Where are these
> Trotskyists of the heart today, who preached permanent revolution?
> Murdered certainly, or in exile. A violent and ceremonial dicta-
> torship has taken possession of you, supported by an abstract bu-
> reaucracy, and pretends to rule according to moral law.

He wondered why one could not criticize Camus' work without calling
humanity into question, and observed that Camus' allusions to Jeanson's silence on the matter of Soviet forced labor were actually aimed at
Sartre, who had indeed attacked the camps and had never hesitated to
criticize the Communists. "How is it that it's me they hate and not
you?"

For Sartre, Camus had been and tomorrow could again be

> the admirable coming together of a person, an action, and a work.
> That was in 1945: One discovered Camus, the author of
> *L'Etranger.* . . . In you were summed up the conflicts of our time,
> and you surmounted them by your eagerness to live them. You
> were a *person*, the most complex and the richest. . . .

To Sartre, Camus had ignored the class struggle. More, he had
used police methods against his reviewer Jeanson. "Your morality
changed first into moralism, today it is only literature, tomorrow it will
perhaps be immorality."

The magazine, concluded Sartre, would remain open to Camus, but
Sartre would not reply, would not fight him; he hoped that silence
would lay their polemic to rest.

But in his reply Sartre had intentionally used the personal method
with whose use he had reproached Camus. To Camus' remark on
armchairs in the sense of history, there was Sartre's "In doing us the
honor of entering into this issue of *Les Temps Modernes,* you brought
with you a portable pedestal." He questioned Camus' credentials as
spokesman for *la misère:*

> Perhaps you were poor, but you aren't any longer; you are a bour-
> geois, like Jeanson and like me. . . . You are an attorney who
> says: "These are my brothers," because it's the word which has the
> best chance of making the jury cry.

He too attacked Camus' style, his "pomposity, which is natural to you,"
the *rouerie* in his outward calm, and of course his philosophical incom-
petence. Jeanson, whose reply followed (under the title "Pour tout vous
dire"), led off with two quotations in which Camus welcomed criticism,
and then addressed himself to a substantive response. In doing so, he
wrote, he felt that he was breaking a taboo, for one had not been al-

lowed to criticize Albert Camus, "the High Priest of Absolute Morality."

This August issue of *Les Temps Modernes* was of course a news event; large extracts were published in the press. Even the sensational weekly *Samedi-Soir,* whose front page on September 6 was taken up by pinup photographs, a story about the Duke and Duchess of Windsor, and a report on a murder, published a three-column headline on the second page:

### THE SARTRE-CAMUS BREAK IS CONSUMMATED

over a story which reviewed the history of their relationship from the time of Sartre's *Cahiers du Sud* essay on *L'Etranger* in 1943, and then cited passages of the *Temps Modernes* exchange. (Samedi-Soir concluded with regret that their common enemies would benefit from the controversy.) Of course everyone who counted in Paris had read it, and most had taken sides. It was generally felt at Saint-Germain-des-Prés that Camus had been hurt most by the exchange.[20] All of intellectual Paris joked about the attack on Camus, usually at Camus' expense, agreeing with Sartre that Camus had come to his task with insufficient philosophical background. (At least one of these intellectuals felt that Camus' essay represented an attack on Sartre by René Char using Camus as intermediary.[21]) Summing up the controversy in *Le Monde,* Pierre de Boisdeffre noted that Camus' "existentialism" had always been a misunderstanding; Sartre and Camus had always done what they would to keep their distance, although they had the same public. Yet their characters could not have been more unlike. Camus was a poet, Sartre a critic. Boisdeffre regretted that Camus had so often intervened in the press to defend his work.[22]

Back in Paris, Camus met Robert Gallimard, who had married Janine's sister Renée. Camus acted as if he expected everyone in the publishing house to be against him, and asked flatly: "What do you think of it?" He said that as a matter of friendship one had to choose. Robert felt that it was easy for his cousin Michel, having no connection with Sartre, to side with Camus, while *he* was a friend of Sartre. Finally he replied: "I'm sorry, but I can't take sides." Camus paused, and then said: "All right, I understand. But let's never talk about it." They remained friends, even close friends, and never did talk about it.[23] In another office in the same building, where several persons were working, Camus held out the copy of *Les Temps Modernes* and asked numbly: "Did you see this?" No one replied. Finally Dionys Mascolo said: "We'll talk about it later at L'Espérance." (That was a neighborhood bar they used to go to.) Camus turned on his heels and left. Years later one of the witnesses to the meeting, Robert Gallimard's wife

Renée, then Mascolo's secretary, remembered especially the pathos of that moment. All of them in the room had felt that Sartre was right, and none could find a word of consolation for Camus.[24]

Michel and Janine avoided asking Camus about the controversy, or commenting on it, so as not to aggravate the pain. Their friend's hurt was evident.[18]

Camus said nothing either. He saved his reflections for his journal.

> Temps Modernes. They admit sin and refuse grace—Thirst for Martyrdom. . . . Their only excuse is in this terrible era. Something in them, finally, aspires to servitude.[7]

# 38
♦
## JONAS

Each and everyone against me, to destroy me, demanding
their share without respite, without ever, ever offering me
a hand, coming to my aid, loving me finally for what I am
and so that I can remain as I am. . . .

Unpublished journal*

Camus' surprise at Sartre's counterattack may surprise. In retrospect,
the break seemed inevitable, and long in preparation. There were so
many premonitory signs, how could Camus not have realized what was
coming? For one friend of Camus, the break was a shock because no
one had expected it to go so far or so deep; after all, *Les Temps
Modernes* had published a section of *L'Homme révolté*.[1] Jean Bloch-
Michel would later wonder whether Simone de Beauvoir really felt, in
the early days of their friendship, what she reports in her memoirs that
she felt about Camus. For Camus, on his side, believed in their
friendship, and without reservations. According to Bloch-Michel,
Camus' greatest suffering in those years came from lost illusions about
the friendship of Sartre—and of Pascal Pia.

The most obvious motivation for the break was political. It would
be a serious mistake to overlook the fact that in 1952, the year of the
Camus-Sartre controversy, Sartre had formally declared himself on the
side of the Communists, and this at the height of Soviet terror in the
final months of Stalin's life. Sartre's commitment to the Communists
took the form of an essay, "Les Communistes et la Paix," the first section of which appeared in *Les Temps Modernes* in July 1952, after the
Jeanson review but a month before Camus' reply was printed along

* Quoted in the Pléiade edition of Camus' work.

with Sartre's *coup de grâce*. It is certain that Sartre's friends expected
this falling out; it should have happened even if Camus had never written *L'Homme révolté*. Perhaps it would not have been a clean break,
but they would have stopped seeing each other; it would have been in
part because they didn't like Camus' character, but the Algerian War
would have made the break definitive.[2]

Certainly at the beginning the friendship was sincere on Camus'
side. Simone de Beauvoir had said so: "*Combat* [in the early days of
Camus' editorship] reported approvingly everything that came from
our pens or from our mouths."[3] Camus welcomed the Sartrians in his
Gallimard collection Espoir.[4] And he surely believed, in his discussions
with the Sartre group, that in the end they would realize their errors.[5]

Yet one friend of both camps saw no true meeting of minds between Camus on one side and Sartre and his group on the other even at
the outset of the relationship. Their friendship had grown out of the
giddiness of the liberation era and couldn't last. Camus' true friends
were other North Africans, and René Char. On Sartre's side, he and his
friends had admired the black pessimism of *L'Etranger* and *Le Mythe
de Sisyphe,* but when they became aware of Camus' later realism and
optimism they lost interest.[1] In fact, one critic noted in retrospect, they
had always been separated, in thought and in writing, but it took the
spectacular break of 1952 for the blind to perceive this.[6]

A friend of Camus would see a certain degree of jealousy on
Sartre's part. Camus had been in the true resistance and Sartre had not.
(Camus privately laughed at the report that Sartre had "liberated" the
Comédie Française theater in the company of the playwright Armand
Salacrou.) Camus was a handsome lady's man; Sartre was equally inter-
ested in feminine conquests but did not have Camus' physical endow-
ment. . . .[7]

In her own summary of the break, Beauvoir saw its inevitability.
"In truth, if this friendship blew up brutally, it was because for a long
time very little of it had remained." The ideological opposition between
the two men had grown each year since 1945. Camus was an idealist, a
moralist, an anti-Communist. Since 1940 Sartre had wished to repu-
diate idealism, to live in history. Close to Marxism, he desired an alliance with the Communists. Camus fought for principles, which is what
got him involved with Garry Davis; while Sartre believed in socialism,
Camus defended bourgeois values. In a choice between the two blocs,
neutralism proving to be impossible, Sartre moved closer to the
U.S.S.R. Camus detested that country, and while he didn't like the
United States, either, Beauvoir felt that he was practically on their side.
"These differences were too serious not to shake a friendship." In addition to that, Beauvoir believed that Camus' character did not facilitate

compromises. She supposed that he realized the fragility of his own positions when he refused angrily to be contradicted. There had been a rapprochement at the time of *Le Diable et le Bon Dieu,* and it was true that they had published his essay on Nietzsche—but they had not really liked it.

And so this fragile return to friendship hadn't lasted. Camus was prepared to criticize Sartre's tolerance of authoritarian socialism at the first opportunity, and of course Sartre felt that Camus was wrong. Beauvoir rightly saw the connection between the publication of the first section of Sartre's "Les Communistes et la Paix" and Sartre's response to Camus, which appeared a month apart in *Les Temps Modernes.* "I had to undertake an act which would make me someone else," she quotes an unpublished note of Sartre concerning his essay on the Communists. "I had to accept the point of view of the U.S.S.R. totally," the note goes on, "and count only on myself to maintain mine." As for Beauvoir, the break did not affect her personally. "The Camus who had been dear to me for so long no longer existed."[8]

It is certain that Camus saw Sartre, the bourgeois Stalinist, as a figure of fun as well as a friend. Sartre had a comfortable background, he was never without the money he needed from early childhood, and even as an adult he could count on his mother to pay the taxes he owed, as he confessed in an autobiographical reminiscence.[9] It was almost as if he could afford to be more proletarian than the proletarians. While in New York, following Sartre's own trip, the ever-meticulous Camus had commented to a friend in a gentle mocking of Sartre: "It is good that foreigners become familiar with the sloppy intellectual side of France."[10] On his side, having come up from so low down, Camus couldn't afford to be sloppy, to have nicotine stains on his lips or his shirt. (A Camus couldn't afford to turn down a Nobel Prize, financially or morally; Sartre could.)

Sartre himself would later say that he had not been against Camus but against the form in which he had replied to Jeanson. He objected to the salutation of Camus' letter, addressed formally to the publisher of the magazine, to "Monsieur le directeur." (In fact, all of the letters that Camus wrote to the press, even to what he considered a friendly press, were addressed to "Monsieur le directeur" or to "Monsieur le rédacteur en chef.")

Like Simone de Beauvoir, Sartre had not been affected by the break:

> We were already seeing much less of each other and, in the most recent years, every time we met he bawled me out; I had done this, said that, wrote something which displeased him, and he bawled me out. It wasn't yet a breaking up but it had become less pleasant.

Camus had changed a lot. At the beginning he didn't yet know that
he was a great writer, he was a joker and we had fun together; he
had a spicy tongue, as I did, and we told a lot of dirty stories that
his wife and Simone de Beauvoir pretended to be shocked by. For
two or three years I really had good relations with him. You
couldn't go very far on the intellectual level because he frightened
easily; in fact he had a little Algiers roughneck side, very good-for-
nothing, very comical. He was probably the last to be a good friend
for me.[11]

Those who cared for Camus tried to console him. Malraux's friend
Manès Sperber told him that he was taking the matter too seriously;
*Les Temps Modernes* was marching toward Communism, so Camus
should not consider that he had been attacked personally. Camus didn't
agree, feeling that his own letter to the magazine had been confined to
the philosophical plane. Sartre's friendship had clearly been important,
he had shown warmth to Camus. Perhaps Camus had not expected a
favorable article, but he was unprepared for the violence of Jeanson's
review, and the attack on his *person*. And he was upset that a relative
nobody had written it, rather than Sartre himself.[12]

Jean Bloch-Michel also felt that the break, from Sartre's point of
view, had been tactical, for he wanted to become the philosopher of the
Communist Party, and that required that he take his distance.

But Camus would not be consoled. For years after the event he
would remain acutely affected, as if the hurt would not go away; until
the end of his life a scar would remain. His unpublished journal, or
what scraps of it have seen the light of day, is filled with bitter reflections—after the initial explosion of angry ones—on the *Temps Modernes* polemic. The best critics of *La Chute* recognized in that curious
monologue a further attempt to exorcise the trauma of the break with
Sartre.

There were attempts, for example, at reconciliation. Dr. Ménétrier,
who had treated Francis Jeanson's tuberculosis as well as Camus', told
Camus that Jeanson was prepared to apologize for the violence of his
attack; they could meet in the doctor's office. Camus snapped: "Meet
with that scoundrel? Never!"[13] The incident is equally revelatory as to
the impression Camus must have been giving others not party to the
controversy. If his doctor felt that reconciliation was necessary, it
means that Camus' pain must have been very evident. The irony is that
Jeanson had never met Camus. He had not participated in the Sartre-
Beauvoir "fiestas." Once, long after the *Temps Modernes* polemic, he
was seated in the Pont Royal bar with his wife and mentioned to her
that he thought he recognized a man but couldn't place him. She said:
"You're joking. It's Camus." Another time at a Gallimard cocktail

party he found himself standing back to back from Camus. They turned to look at each other for an instant, but nothing happened.[14]

Meanwhile large numbers of readers from all walks of life wrote to Camus to say that they supported him; many added that they did not understand or approve Sartre's attacks. Camus kept the letters carefully wrapped in a large package. "The core of the problem remains intact," Camus wrote to Roger Quilliot on October 31, 1952, "that at least is certain, and I feel that they offered nothing serious to oppose to my diagnosis." He concluded: "I therefore consider myself authorized to continue the same road, which I know, besides, is the road of many."[15]

Early in 1952, when the first wave of reviews of *L'Homme révolté* had come in, but some months before the Jeanson attack, Camus outlined for the first time the stories that would later be published in *L'Exil et le Royaume,* at this early stage called "Nouvelles de l'exil." One of them was to be "L'Artiste qui se retranche," to be published under the title "Jonas." With *La Chute,* "Jonas" is probably the most significant autobiographical writing that Camus would do in his maturity. Originally conceived as the story of a successful writer who sacrifices everything including his family for art, it became the story of a painter who is rather victim than victimizer, destroyed by the life of Paris which accompanies success. The editor of Camus' complete works placed "Jonas" in the framework of Camus' personal crisis, his inability to function, exemplified by the pathetic cry in his journal:

> Each and everyone against me, to destroy me, demanding their share without respite, without ever, ever offering me a hand, coming to my aid, loving me finally for what I am and so that I can remain as I am. They consider my energy without limit and that I should hand it out to them and help them live—But I put all my strength into the extenuating passion of creation, and for everything else I am the most deprived and needy of beings.

On a more down to earth level, "Jonas" is read in juxtaposition with a letter Camus wrote to the journalist Pierre Berger on February 15, 1953. Camus had broken an appointment with Berger, who reproached him for being difficult to deal with. "If you knew one quarter of my life and its obligations," Camus replied, "you would not have written a single line of your letter." And Camus proceeded to explain, "The 'haughty solitude' of which you complain, with many others who don't have your credentials, would be, after all, if it existed, a blessing for me." As a matter of fact—and he admits that he is the first person to blame for the life he is leading—he would need three lives and several hearts to do all the things he would like to do. He couldn't even see his friends as much as he would like to—"ask Char, who I love as a brother, how many times a month we see each other." He had no time to write articles, not even time to be ill.

> But the worst is that I no longer have the time, nor the interior leisure, to write my books, and I spend four years writing what, with freedom, would have taken two years. For several years now, my work hasn't freed me, it has enslaved me.

If he continued at all, it was because he preferred his work to everything, even to his freedom.

> It is true that I am trying to organize myself, to double my energies and my "presence" by a schedule, a daily time table, an increased efficiency. . . . Every letter brings on three more, every person ten, every book a hundred letters and twenty correspondents, during which time life continues, there is my work, those I love, and those who need me. Life continues, and as for me, some mornings, tired of the noise, discouraged in the face of the interminable work to be carried on, sick from the folly of the world which springs out of the newspapers as well, and convinced that I shall not suffice and that I shall disappoint everyone, I feel like simply sitting down and waiting for evening to come. I feel that way and sometimes I act that way.

Could Berger understand that? Camus realized that the situation was hard for others to bear; it was hard for him to bear. The bitterness in Berger's letter had saddened him, added "to all the reasons I have to flee this city and the life I lead here."[15]

It was certainly true that he was not writing. The only new work that would appear in 1952 was a translation of the very brief text of James Thurber's *The Last Flower*. "Jonas" itself was probably written during 1953, although it was not necessarily completed that year.

Before "Jonas," Camus sketched out what he called a *mimodrame* consisting of a series of pantomime scenes. It resembles the short story to come, except that here it is the wife and not the artist who dies, sacrificed to her husband's art; this conforms to Camus' first journal entry on the theme.

In the story itself, Gilbert Jonas "believed in his star." At thirty-five he was a successful painter. But he lived with his wife in a cramped apartment in an eighteenth-century building in an old neighborhood. Indeed, Jonas lived in the Camus apartment on the Rue Séguier:

> The rooms, particularly high-ceilinged, and equipped with superb windows, had certainly been designed, if one judged by their majestic proportions, for pomp and ceremony. But the require-

ments of urban crowding and of real estate had led successive
owners to partition these oversize rooms. . . .

Jonas' artistic success made him the target of invitations to lunch, to
dinner, of phone calls, impromptu visits—visits from other artists and
critics whose occupations left them free to call on Jonas during what
should have been working hours. Then the disciples arrived. In the
midst of this crowd he would try to paint, but his work was slowed
down. Fortunately his reputation grew as he worked less. He received
more mail, and he was too courteous to leave it unanswered.

> Some concerned Jonas' art, others—the most numerous—the per-
> sonality of the writer. . . . As his name began to appear in the pub-
> lic prints, he was solicited, as everybody was, for interviews to
> denounce very revolting injustices.

The crowds continued to grow. But now he was painting less, even
when alone, without knowing why that was so. "He thought about
painting, about his vocation, instead of painting." His reputation
declined, a long article said that his work was "at the same time over-
rated and out of date"; his gallery lowered his monthly stipend. Increasingly irritated by his visitors, fleeing acquaintances in public places, he
finally builds himself a narrow loggia, taking advantage of the high ceiling, to which he can retreat with his canvas. He will spend more and
more of his time in this makeshift loggia, nights too, but without painting. At last he asks his loyal friend Rateau (French for "rake," and
who plays the same role in Jonas' life that Char, French for "cart,"
plays in Camus') to hand him up an empty canvas. No longer taking
nourishment, exhausted, Jonas is placed under a doctor's care, but he
will live, the doctor assures his wife.

> In the other room, Rateau looked at the canvas, entirely blank, in
> the center of which Jonas had only written, in tiny letters, a word
> that they could decipher, although they couldn't tell whether it was
> *solitaire* or *solidaire*.

*Solidaire* he remained, despite the disappointments. He wrote an
essay on Oscar Wilde in prison, Wilde who henceforth would identify
with his fellow prisoners, turning his back on drawing rooms; Camus'
"L'Artiste en prison" is almost a metaphor for his present state of
mind. In the middle of November 1952 he received a visit from a left-
wing activist, Louis de Villefosse, who asked him to intervene in behalf
of a young naval officer, Henri Martin, sentenced to five years in prison
for having distributed tracts against the French Indochina War. The
campaign on Martin's behalf had been led by Communist sympathizers,
and once again Camus was cautious about lending his name to a propa-

Albert Camus and Michel Gallimard. Courtesy of Roger-Viollet.

Camus, Madeleine Renaud, and Jean-Louis Barrault at rehearsal for *L'Etat de siège,* 1948. Courtesy of Jean-Louis Barrault. Agence de Presse Bernand.

The trial of Philippe Pétain. Pierre Laval, standing, is speaking. Camus is in the second row (his face is next to Laval's). Pétain is seated in front, to the right, next to the gendarme. René Saint-Paul.

Pascal Pia with Camus.

Maria Casarès and Camus in 1948 at the Marigny during *L'Etat de siège*. Courtesy of Roger-Viollet.

Maria Casarès in *Dévotion à la Croix* in Angers. Courtesy Maria Casarès. Studio Bernard.

Camus. Courtesy of Micheline Rozan.

Camus and Jean Grenier. Courtesy of Roger-Viollet.

...cember 1957, Stockholm.
...ception for Camus at the Bonnier
...se, "Manilla," in Djurgården.
...t to right, Michel Gallimard,
...s. Jytte Bonnier, Camus, Danish
...lisher Otto Lindhardt. Courtesy
...ert Bonnier.

Albert Camus and Francine in Stockholm. Courtesy of Roger-Viollet.

Camus and his children in June 1957 (at the Angers Festival for the production of *Olmedo*.) Agence de Presse Bernand.

The car in which Camus was killed. Paris-Match/Lefebvre.

The grave of Camus in the cemetery at Lourmarin. Courtesy of Roger-Viollet.

ganda broadside. Villefosse had asked if he would contribute to a pamphlet to be written in co-operation with the *Temps Modernes* group; Camus' reaction was predictable. He said that he was willing to help, but in his own way. In fact he wrote an appeal for Georges Altman's left-of-center but anti-Communist *Franc-Tireur*. He led off with a settling of accounts: He had refused, he wrote in the opening lines (published in that daily in December, reprinted by Camus in *Actuelles II*), to contribute to a pamphlet in the company of the editors of *Les Temps Modernes*. "My reason is simple: Henceforth it is to compromise the values of freedom, among other values, to defend them together with *Les Temps Modernes* and with those who approve that magazine." Only when human life is in danger, as in the case of the Rosenbergs— whose pardon should be demanded by everyone—was it possible to accept such associations. Speaking to the case of the naval officer Martin, he defended the right of anyone, even in the military services, to be a Communist, and to oppose France's colonial war, which "costs dearly in blood and in suffering," and was "a heavy burden for the budget of his country as well as for his conscience." He had no illusions about the democratic bias of Communist leaders; what had contributed to the decline of Stalinism in the West was precisely "the strength of equity and the prestige of freedom." Martin's opposition had been political, his sentence was out of proportion to the act, and unjust.

The world had seen other violations of freedom, Camus went on, referring to the Slansky purge trial in Prague, eleven of whose defendants were executed while the Communists were going to Vienna (to a meeting of the World Peace Council) to talk about peace.[16] But it didn't matter that the Communists were exploiting the Henri Martin case, for a just cause was strong enough to withstand exploitation. Martin's cause should therefore be taken up by true defenders of freedom, not by those who apologize for Stalinist anti-Semitism (another allusion to the Prague trials) and the fake confessions of the purge courts.

And once more he spoke at a rally in behalf of Republican Spain, at Paris's Salle Wagram on November 30, in the company of Salvador de Madariaga, former Colombian president and newspaper publisher Eduardo Santos, and art critic Jean Cassou, under the sponsorship of Amis de l'Espagne Républicaine. Spain had been admitted to UNESCO after all, thanks in part to the French Government under conservative Prime Minister Antoine Pinay. Camus' talk contained invective against the Fascists, irony for the supporters of Franco Spain in the Western democracies. Not only would intellectuals refuse henceforth to collaborate with UNESCO, but they would combat it openly, to show up its false pretenses: "instead of a meeting place of intellectuals devoted to culture, it is an association of governments in the service of no matter what policy."[15]

It is at this time that Camus will show the first serious sign of his intention to become an active man of the theater, for theater and not books would dominate this last decade of his life. In the context of the stormy events of his writing career, the determination to return to a way of life in which he had found happiness in Algeria in the 1930s takes on particular significance. The theater could be a way out of the writing block; he had not done any work of consequence on a book for nearly a year and a half now, and he had no immediate plan for anything more than an occasional story, an occasional critical or political text. It could also be a way of removing himself from the literary-intellectual world of Paris which had grown so distasteful, and in the company of persons with whom he could sympathize, and who could sympathize with him.

The idea was to take over a small theater, where he could manage and direct a permanent acting troupe. For this first try, he had a met a young director (he was then twenty-seven), Jean Gillibert, who was then running the Groupe de Théâtre Antique de la Sorbonne. Camus introduced him to Marcel Herrand of the Mathurins Theater, who then hired Gillibert to help stage an outdoor theater festival in the Loire River valley town of Angers in the summer of 1952. It was agreed that Camus would try to rent the small Récamier Theater on the Left Bank, minutes from Saint-Germain-des-Prés, owned by a non-profit organization, the French non-religious teachers' association Ligue de l'Enseignement. Gillibert was to be Camus' assistant, and the company would of course include Maria Casarès, but also Pierre Blanchar's daughter Dominique, then a rising and surprising actress (who would stir Paris with her performance of Agnès in Molière's *L'Ecole des femmes,* playing opposite Louis Jouvet). A member of the old Théâtre de l'Equipe, Jean Negroni, would also join the company.[17]

But the theater was not available. It would be some time before Camus made another such proposal. He died in the month that a decision was to be taken which would have given him his own theater at last.

On December 1 he left for another winter visit to Algeria. This time he would go to places he had never seen: the famous oasis towns of the Sahara territories. In Algiers he learned that he would have to postpone his departure for the south for a few days because there had been signs of rebellion in the district, and travel was discouraged. He took the opportunity for another day trip to Tipasa, where he was relieved to discover that he felt the same emotion, the same nostalgia, that he had always felt here. It was what he had really gone looking for in Algeria, he would tell a friend. Not happiness—in fact it was more like sadness—but something that could move him. Of course it rained in Algiers, where he spent a week, seeing his mother and his brother.

He did something else during this week. On December 6 he drove along the Sahel crest running west of Algiers through the small agricultural villages where his mother's grandparents had settled. (His father's too, but he would never know that.) In a cemetery he even discovered —in an obscure corner—a moss-covered slab bearing their name. He found one of their living relatives too. The landscape pleased him, with its slopes and valleys set between the Mediterranean and the snow-covered Atlas peaks in the far distance. He discovered that he had a country of his own; it made him feel less alone.

Still, the severe depression he had been living with all that autumn had left its mark. He lingered on in Algiers, even hesitating to pursue his journey, although he knew that it was important for him to break out of his shell.

He did that at last, driving across the High Plains and the Sahara Atlas chain, fascinated by the monotonous landscape. On Sunday, December 14, he arrived in Laghouat, 270 miles south of Algiers, a large oasis town whose flat houses were surrounded by thick palm groves set against the red rock of the Sahara mountains. Laghouat fascinated him, especially the purity of the desert light, the variety of colors of the soil, the black tents of the nomads. He spent the next day wandering through the oasis; he was alone and knew no one here, and was quite pleased to be on his own this way. He probably decided here and now that Laghouat would be the scene of the first story, called "La Femme adultère," he had listed for his collection "Nouvelles de l'exil." It was cold in this place, and the wind quickly stirred up the desert sands. He discovered that he had developed a slight case of bronchitis, irritated by sand.

On December 16 he continued his solo drive 120 miles south to Ghardaïa, built up, beehive style, on the side of a mountain, taking on the appearance of a pyramid. This was the land of the curious Mzabites, Moslem heretics of the desert who developed their own architectural forms. Then the long drive back to Algiers on December 18. An exhausting trip but a healthy one for Camus, and Paris seemed even more enervating from here. He wished he could live far from all that, in Algeria for example—and with someone he loved. What he must do henceforth—it was a resolution—was to remove himself from everything that was harmful to him. He had a host of ideas for new writing, and he would force himself to concentrate on that.

He sailed from Oran to Marseilles, and from there he traveled along the coast to Nice to visit ailing Marcel Herrand, then on to Cannes to meet the Michel Gallimards.

With Michel and Janine he drove back to Paris early in that New Year of 1953. Certainly they would have taken the main Paris-Riviera highway. One imagines, too, that Camus sat in the front seat next to Michel, who was driving, that Janine was in the rear with her daughter, just as they would be seated seven years later, perhaps to the day, when Camus died on that highway.[18]

# PART IV

## Forty

# 39

# THE SEA

Those who love and are separated can live in suffering, but it is not despair; they know that love exists.

"La Mer au plus près"

Camus wrote a postscriptum to *L'Homme révolté* in the autumn of 1952 which his friends—Char certainly—urged him to publish. (It is undoubtedly the "Défense de 'L'Homme révolté'" included in the Pléiade edition of his work.) He hesitated, and then decided not to publish it,[1] although it is a dispassionate account of how he came to write the controversial book, how it was the product of lived experience and reflection, and why he concluded with the Greek concept of just measure, the contrary of excess.

Instead, he prepared a second volume of *Actuelles,* bringing together articles, prefaces, interviews, and polemical letters dealing with affairs of the world since 1948, the cut-off year for the first volume. Now, in January 1953, he wrote a brief preface for the new collection which summed up his hopes. The new world, true liberation, was not yet just around the corner, but nihilism was a thing of the past, and creation, always possible, now became more than ever necessary. A long section of *Actuelles II* looked backward, consisting as it did of letters written to defend or to explain his controversial book. But a final section, entitled "Création et Liberté," was an attempt to demonstrate the continuing need for art. "It's not enough to criticize one's times, one must also try to give them a form, and a future."

One of the texts in the new collection was a speech Camus delivered in May 1953 at the Labor Exchange in the industrial city of Saint-Etienne, where he had lost so many days in 1942 and 1943. A meeting

had been called there for "Défense des libertés" by a group of labor organizations, the French Christian and Socialist trade union federations,
the Spanish UGTE (émigré workers) and the CNT, and French
teachers' unions. In his Saint-Etienne speech Camus denounced threats
to freedom in Western societies as well as Eastern ones, pleaded for
freedom as the one good, the one heritage of the great revolutionary
conquests of two centuries. To choose freedom, he said, didn't signify
to follow Kravchenko's road from the Soviet regime to a bourgeois one;
to choose freedom was not to choose it against justice. On the contrary,
it was to join all those who suffered and struggled, to choose it *with* justice. "If someone takes away your bread, he suppresses your freedom at
the same time. But if someone seizes your freedom, rest assured, your
bread is threatened, because it no longer depends on you and on your
struggle, but on the pleasure of a master." He was making it clear to the
assembled union members that he would not advocate an abstract and
essentially intellectual freedom ignoring social justice.

In Laghouat, the desert oasis, Camus had written at least an outline of
what would be "La Femme adultère." Janine, the heroine, bored with a
boor of a husband who is clearly uncomfortable in this Arab territory
and goes to bed early, will commit her adultery with the mysterious
Sahara night. Camus was perhaps encouraged to proceed more quickly
with the story than he had planned by a fortuitous encounter with Noël
Schumann, who owned a bookshop and small publishing enterprise in
Algiers which he had founded in 1943 under the name Editions de
l'Empire. Schumann conceived a series of limited editions in which
prominent authors would write stories to be illustrated by equally well-
known artists. He told Camus that he needed about eighty pages (but
Camus was to give him only thirty-three). And when Camus told him
the story would be called "La Femme adultère" Schumann expressed a
timorous objection that it might be taken for something risqué. Camus
drew himself up to reply: "My dear friend, if it bears my name it will
be a very proper title." Schumann had to agree that a man with a reputation as a moralist could call a story as he liked. It was Camus' idea to
have the illustrations done by Pierre-Emile Clairin, a rather conventional figurative painter who had just illustrated a deluxe edition of
*Noces*.

That autumn Schumann came up to Paris to go over the proofs
with Camus. At the Gallimard office Suzanne Labiche told him that her
boss wasn't seeing anyone that day, November 7, 1953; it was his fortieth birthday. Finally Camus relented for the visitor from Algiers, and
Schumann spent three hours in his office. "It's not being forty that
bothers me," Camus said at one point, "but the impossibility of holding

up time." He spoke of Proust and the little cake which stirred his memory. "I go back to Tipasa and I find everything exactly the same, but it is not the same. You don't see things while you are living through them, and later, when you have sufficient experience to know what you have been looking at, it's too late."

While their book was being set in type by hand at a printshop just around the corner from the Rue Madame on the Rue du Vieux Colombier, Camus kept dropping in to correct proofs, and to rewrite, sometimes adding significant new material. The printer warned Schumann that it was going to cost him more if the author kept making changes. Indeed, during a holiday in the early summer of 1953 at Ermenonville (on the edge of a forest loved by Rousseau) Camus had read the story to Maria Casarès, who made some specific suggestions: The soldier seen at the beginning of the story was to be rendered more symbolic by reference to him later on. The husband was made slightly more sympathetic. And he rewrote the crucial last minutes of the story, when Janine holds herself open to the desert night.[1]

When it was finally ready, in the autumn of 1954, a prospectus announced that all copies of Schumann's edition were to be signed by both author and illustrator; the entire edition of three hundred copies was sold out in six weeks. Later, during a visit to Algiers, Camus was asked how much Schumann owed him for the story and he suggested 200,000 francs, which the publisher agreed was quite reasonable. He sat down to write out a check, but Camus told him to deliver the sum to his mother instead.[2]

For the Schumann edition Camus wrote a preface which would not be reprinted in subsequent publications of "La Femme adultère":

> In Laghouat I met the characters of this story. I am not certain, of course, that their day ended as I have told it. Doubtless they did not go forth to the desert. But *I* went, some hours after that, and during all that time their image pursued me and challenged what I saw. . . .

In Paris, on March 30, 1953, lunching with Jules Roy and Gabriel Audisio, Camus had suggested the holding of a congress of Algerian writers at Tipasa the following spring; the suggestion was never to be followed up.[3] If not this one, perhaps another? That autumn he would be approached by an old friend, Paul Raffi, who although he lived and worked in Paris had been appointed as a deputy for cultural affairs to Algiers' mayor, Jacques Chevallier, a childhood and lycée comrade. Raffi wanted Camus to stage a theater festival in Tipasa and Algiers. Camus talked to Chevallier and Raffi over lunch at the latter's home, and was tempted by the scheme. It was agreed that he would put together a program for such a "Festival d'Alger-Tipasa." When he did, it was not quite what Algiers thought it needed; it would have included such heavy fare as an adaptation Camus was anxious to do of Dostoevsky's novel *The Possessed* (Les Possédés); the French Algerians would have preferred more popular repertory. Meanwhile some of his friends urged Camus to refuse to co-operate with Algiers' liberal but essentially bourgeois administration; he replied that he would refuse not for political but for personal reasons. And yet he was so tired of solitude; he so wished to do something for his true country.[4]

His chief occupation during this year of 1953 would be in the theater all the same. His mimodrame, "La Vie d'artiste," the modified "Jonas" story, had now been published by the Oran cultural magazine *Simoun,* and he would have liked to see someone try it on the stage. In March he gave a copy to the Italian director Paolo Grassi while his Piccolo Teatro di Milano company was in Paris presenting three plays in Italian, suggesting to Grassi that it might be of interest to Grassi's school of mime. In fact the little skit would be performed, perhaps for the first time anywhere, by students of the Piccolo Teatro drama school in July 1959.[5]

More significantly, he was now unofficially in charge of the Angers theater festival (Festival d'Art Dramatique). Marcel Herrand, formerly co-director of the Mathurins Theater and now critically ill (he was soon to die of cancer), had staged the festival the previous year to great critical success. Herrand had been expected to run the festival again in 1953. But his meeting with Camus in Nice at the end of the previous December had in effect been a passing of the mantle; although Herrand would be billed as director of the 1953 festival, he died in the week preceding its opening. The plays were given in the courtyard of the city's thirteenth-century feudal castle built by Saint Louis, King Louis IX, on the banks of the Maine River; it was and is an imposing fortress with over half a mile of round towers. Spectators entered over a drawbridge spanning a moat to find themselves before a stage flanked by two fortress towers, the action taking place on three levels of ramparts. The festival was prepared in Paris, with early rehearsals at the Mathurins Theater (which would run these festivals over a period of a decade).

At last Camus' adaptation of Pierre de Larivey's sixteenth-century *Les Esprits,* which Camus had begun early in the war, was to be given a first performance. Maria Casarès would star in it, with Herrand's associate Jean Marchat, and Paul Oettly. But alongside Larivey's commedia dell'arte there would be the stark tragedy of Pedro Calderón's *Devotion to the Cross* (La Dévotion à la croix), again starring Casarès, with Serge Reggiani (who had played in the ill-fated *L'Etat de siège*), Jean

Marchat, and Paul Oettly. Calderón's play had been translated from the Spanish by Camus himself, with the important assistance of Casarès, just as she would collaborate in his translation of Lope de Vega's *The Knight from Olmedo* (Le Chevalier d'Olmedo) for a future festival.[1]

*La Dévotion* was presented on June 14, 18, and 20, 1953, *Les Esprits* on June 16 and 19, with as a curtain raiser a reading of poems by the Angers poet Joachim Du Bellay by Casarès, Reggiani, Oettly, and other actors. Camus' adaptations received national press attention, and locally the press would say that the Calderón work was so perfectly performed it could never again be played on an ordinary theater stage. Camus was praised for "faithful and vigilant work," equalled only by "modesty and kindness."[6] Later he would say of the Calderón play: "I like the rugged side of the Spanish writer; I was seduced by this style. To translate it I attempted to rediscover the music, the tempo of Calderón, to imitate it in a sense."[7] He told an interviewer that for the Larivey comedy he had taken extreme liberties with the text, making a prologue out of the play's lengthy exposition, in the interest of brevity.[8]

The experience had been an exhilarating one. Camus was back in Algiers at the vast Salle Pierre Bordes, except that he was not—he was directing professional actors, receiving national attention for the work, and before an audience which could exceed two thousand persons nightly. If he had been tempted by a full-scale return to the theater before, now he was convinced that this was the only possible salvation. Here were his friends—the actors, on occasion the directors—and he seemed to fear neither critics nor public.

One of his new friends was a young man—nine years his junior— who was now deputy director of the Mathurins. Robert Cérésol had been born on the Riviera of a Swiss father and a Jewish mother. When Mrs. Harry Baur, the widow of the famous prewar stage and film actor, had taken over the Mathurins from Herrand in 1950, she had brought Cérésol with her. But he was also a would-be writer, and Herrand had sent him to see Camus with an essay he was working on. "You're a philosopher," Camus told him. "I suppose I am." "I left philosophical terminology behind me a long time ago," Camus warned him. But something about Cérésol appealed to Camus; certainly it was the combination of Mediterranean birth, his ambitions, and his association with the theater Camus loved. At any rate they became fast friends from that day, spending many long evenings about town—dining, drinking, often simply walking the length and breadth of that city of inexhaustible resources. Cérésol was also, of course, an ideal companion for going to the theater. Camus felt that he could talk to Cérésol and be understood; equally importantly, that he didn't have to be on stage with the younger man. He could trust him.[9]

Another favorite companion of the time was an old friend from Equipe days, Raymond Sigaudès. Camus found *him* an excellent companion for watching Sunday matches of soccer at Paris's Parc des Princes stadium, especially when Le Racing was playing. Le Racing was the Racing Club de Paris, but through their nostalgia it was the old Racing Universitaire d'Alger. They would meet by prearrangement, Camus and Sigaudès, in seats they would reserve just to the right of the *tribune d'honneur*.[10]

Before the summer holidays, he would be summoned back to the political boxing ring on three occasions. In May, it was an errand of mercy, when an old colleague, writer and critic Victoria Ocampo, was arrested in Argentina. Camus asked a number of writers, including Mauriac, André Maurois, Roger Martin du Gard, and Paulhan to join him in signing a letter of protest to the Argentine ambassador in Paris, emphasizing Ocampo's contribution to literature through the magazine *Sur*.[11] In June, immediately after the opening performances at Angers, the workers of East Berlin had risen against the Communist regime, only to be put down brutally by Soviet forces. On June 30, Camus spoke at a protest rally at Paris's La Mutualité Hall. He said that he refused to share the satisfaction of the bourgeois press that a Stalinist crime was compensating for the execution that same week of the Rosenbergs in the United States. "But if I don't believe it is possible for the Berlin mutiny to allow us to forget the Rosenbergs, it seems to me still more horrid that men who claim to be of the left can attempt to hide the German victims in the shadow of the Rosenbergs." He felt that the Berlin riots were the most serious event since the liberation of France, and demanded, with the sponsors of the meeting, the dispatching to East Germany of an international trade union panel of inquiry.[12]

On July 14, during a demonstration by supporters of the Mouvement pour le Triomphe des Libertés Démocratiques, the Messali group, the Paris police stopped a parade of Moslem workers who were carrying banners demanding the liberation of Messali Hadj (then in French custody in a remote town in southwest France). The clash at the Place de la Nation ended with seven Moslems dead, forty-four wounded (and eighty-two injured policemen). Once more Camus sent off a "Monsieur le directeur" letter, this time to the newspaper *Le Monde,* to protest the filing of charges against those who had assaulted the police, when in fact the violence had been directed against the North Africans in "a racism which dares not say its name." He demanded an investigation to determine who had ordered the police to open fire, and who in the government had then carried on "this ancient conspiracy of silence and of cruelty which uproots Algerian workers, keeps them in miserable slums and makes them desperate to the point of violence, to kill them occasionally."[13] This admonition would not be heeded, nor would any other plea in behalf of Algerian Moslems in mainland France or in North Africa, and in a year the built-up pressures would become armed insurrection.

That summer of 1953 Francine Camus fell ill. Her illness was not immediately definable, except that it was nervous, and after a long and trying summer it would become worse instead of better. Henceforth Camus would be a helpless witness to his wife's trouble. He felt responsibility, he would have liked to do his duty. But it seemed as if he was not then or ever prepared to give up the way of life which could have been the primary cause or one of the principal causes of the trouble. He was both necessary and an irritant; about that he could do nothing.

He joined his family at Thonon-les-Bains, on the French side of Lake Leman (also called Lake of Geneva) near Evian-les-Bains and facing Lausanne. For his part he saw his stay in Thonon as an opportunity to work again, but of course work was not going to come easy, writing was not to flow. So he did what one does in a landscape of convalescence: He walked (it was also a landscape out of Rousseau). Twice he went swimming in the lake, despite standing orders from his doctor, only to discover that he hardly knew how to swim anymore, and that caused another sadness. But he could always read—Tolstoy's letters, for instance. The weather was poor, the atmosphere flat; it was the hope that those with fragile nerves would find all this soothing.

Here he completed the reading of the proofs of *Actuelles II*, at the last moment adding the speech he had recently delivered at Saint-Etienne. And here he worked over "La Femme adultère," incorporating suggestions made at Ermenonville.

Finally he attacked a work long in germination, the ode to the sea which was to be the final entry in his next book of miscellaneous essays, *L'Eté*. "La Mer au plus près" came out, he decided, as a curious piece of writing—but he was writing curious things these days. The log of an ocean voyage, it is of every ocean, and the voyage is life itself. It opens with a drumbeat:

> I grew up in the sea and poverty seemed a sumptuous thing to me, then I lost the sea, and all luxuries seemed gray, misery intolerable. Since then I have been waiting. I wait for returning vessels, the house in the waters, the bright day. . . .

Back at their Rue Madame apartment, he remained a witness to illness, tried to be of help when he was wanted or needed. He could not yet consider beginning a major piece of writing, but at least his notebook had begun to blossom with ideas. "The inventory is complete," he told his journal. "Commentary and polemic. Henceforth creation."[14] He spent his first days in Paris that fall clearing up his desk at Gallimard, organizing himself for what he hoped would be a fruitful year.

First, he would return to the theater, stimulated by Angers. His first thought was for the ambitious Dostoevsky play. But although he would begin serious work on the adaptation of *Les Possédés* now, in October 1953, it would be the hardest dramatic work for him to finish, the most difficult to see through to production. It would take nearly six years; several other adaptations of his would be produced before it; *Les Possédés* would be presented to the public only in the last year of his life.

But he began at once to go to the theater, seeing every play he could, already looking for actors for his *Possédés*. He had soon spotted one who could play Stavrogin, the key to the play (in his journal he was reminding himself: "The enigma of Stavrogin, the secret of Stavrogin, this is the unique theme of *Les Possédés*.")[12]

Each night, in bed, he worked on the play, cutting it into scenes. He realized, of course, that he had tackled a difficult work—first for the adapter and then for the public, more of a saga than a story, running 652 pages in the most compact French translation.

But one night—probably the night running from Saturday, October 17, to Sunday, October 18—he had insomnia, and rose at 4 A.M. to work on the outline of his next novel: so he confided to a friend. But which novel was that? Was it *La Chute?* It could have been, for he was living through the dark age which would be its subject. It could also have been the growing-up book, *Le Premier Homme*. Whichever it was, it represented the beginning of a future work, and he so desperately wanted to work again. But the atmosphere at the Rue Madame had grown still more oppressive.

He found himself going out of his way to avoid a polemic. The preface he had written for *Caliban,* Jean Daniel's magazine, to introduce the republication of Louis Guilloux's *La Maison du peuple,* had now appeared in book form. Its opening had been intentionally provocative:

> Almost all French writers who today pretend to speak in the name of the proletariat were born of comfortable or well to do parents. . . .

And it was predictably attacked in d'Astier's *Libération*. But that provocation was an old one, and now he was weary; he left the counterattack to friend Guilloux. Meanwhile *Actuelles II* was ready for release, and he signed his press copies. It received respectable reviews from the expected reviewers, nothing more. But *L'Homme révolté* was published in London, and to great praise. Camus read (and kept among his papers) a review in *The Cambridge Journal* by Richard Wollheim which placed *The Rebel* in the great tradition of Hobbes and Rousseau, Locke and Hegel. "In Camus the twentieth century finds a minor prophet not unworthy of his line," Wollheim wrote, "a Zephariah or a Zechiariah to set against the Isaiahs and the Jeremiahs of an earlier age— Schopenhauer and Herzen and Nietzsche." That should have pleased him, and yet it left him without feeling; the very thought of that book disgusted him now. But he took secret pleasure in the fact that André Breton, who had taxed him with false testimony in his treatment of the surrealists, was now asking him to be a character witness in a trial.[15]

For a new Belgian politico-literary magazine which had inaugurated its first issue with a crisp analysis of "Sartre et le parastalinisme," he offered the exclusive gift of a "calendar" consisting of twelve succinct and ironical anecdotes or commentaries on events of the day. Samples:

> Some ten French doctors, without any other information than the statement of a dictatorial government several thousand kilometers away, sign a declaration applauding the arrest of their Soviet colleagues, destined for a certain death.* Triumph of the scientific spirit.
>
> Then the same government decrees, without warning, the innocence of these same doctors. Their French colleagues publish no declaration. Power of the spirit of humility.
>
> To a beggar who shows himself to be obtrusive, the owner of a restaurant, to protect her lobster eaters, reproaches him softly: "Just put yourself," she says, "in the place of these ladies and gents."[16]

Camus would later tell an interviewer that he had not initiated the project of adapting William Faulkner's *Requiem for a Nun* to the stage, but that it had been suggested to him, and he had accepted it. Apparently Marcel Herrand had planned to produce it at the Mathurins shortly before his death, and Camus was asked to carry on. In fact Faulkner's *Requiem,* although published and advertised as a novel, was written largely in dramatic form, its characters speaking as actors.

Camus asked Michel Gallimard's sister, Nicole Lambert, who handled such matters, to contact Faulkner for permission to translate and stage *Requiem* in France. Faulkner apparently liked the idea but first wanted to have the approval of his friend Ruth Ford, the actress. The matter was passed on to Faulkner's agent, Harold Ober. And then

---

* Reference to the January 1953 "doctors' plot" in the final weeks of Stalin's life.

the whole question of authorizing a stage version got bogged down in the long-drawn-out efforts of Ruth Ford to produce an English-language stage version; in any case, there would be no reply from New York, and Nicole Lambert would try again in January 1954. Finally, Camus himself wrote to Faulkner in October of that year assuring him that he had a good cast lined up. Camus said that he would supervise the translation and, with Faulkner's permission, the direction; in any case he would take full responsibility for the production.[17]

Then his fortieth birthday on November 7 had found him melancholic and very much alone; Noël Schumann had been an unwitting witness to that. His wife continued to show distressing symptoms, Maria Casarès was off on a road tour, and he discovered that if he had many playmates he had few persons in whom he could or would confide. For his birthday his secretary Suzanne Labiche—now married and Suzanne Agnely—gave him a fine new note pad, he received a quatrain from a poet and a cigarette lighter which he felt was a waste because one of his fortieth-birthday resolutions was to give up smoking. That night he went to see a bad play (Giraudoux's *Pour Lucrèce*). Later he would remember this fortieth year—concluded with the writing of *L'Eté* (sent to press in December)—as "a sort of threshold in my work and in my life."[12] And as if that life were already over, a retrospective exhibition of his career, "Documents sur Albert Camus," opened on Boulevard Saint-Germain, consisting of photographs, sets for his plays, manuscript pages of two versions of "La Femme adultère" which he was said to be in the course of writing, a copy of the original edition of *L'Envers et l'Endroit,* articles from *Alger Républicain,* the first public issue of *Combat* of August 21, 1944, and critical articles from the New York *Times Book Review* and other foreign periodicals.[18] Not long after that, when he was ill and at home in bed, a friend of his Algerian days, Robert Jaussaud's wife Madeleine, came to visit. She told him that the next day would be her own fortieth birthday. He replied: "If you were hit by a car today the papers would say that a young woman was run over. If it happens tomorrow they'll make it: 'A fortyish woman. . . .' "[19]

A famous man he was at forty, but of the past or of the present? Henceforth his work would consist largely of translations and adaptations of other people's work, of occasional essays, none of them of book length. He would continue to polish those fine stories, each in its own way seeded with keys to himself, of *L'Exil et le Royaume.* And then he would surprise and delight his readers with a story which outgrew *L'Exil* to become a book in its own right, *La Chute.*

He would plan, and then begin to work on an ambitious project, his Tolstoyan novel perhaps, *Le Premier Homme.* Otherwise, the six remaining years of his life are a succession of scenes of frustration, melancholy, writer's block; as his fame and his influence grew, so did the need to shun his public and even his friends. Francine's illness, then the explosion of that inevitable colonial war in Algeria, would be followed by the irony of the Nobel Prize.

He told a friendly witness, Roger Quilliot, in July 1954, that he had not been able to do any work at all for the past six months, and began to enumerate the reasons: his wife's illness, his children's health . . . and then he stopped short.[12]

His refuge was company. Char was good but too often absent. There was his fellow night owl Cérésol. And then the men and women of political movements with which he could still sympathize, those of the far-out left, who on their own chosen terrain were often as lonely as he was. Typical, or symptomatic, was his special relationship with the group which was producing a tract-sized magazine, *Témoins,* in Switzerland. The publisher was Jean Paul Samson, a poet and a World War I deserter who lived in that country because he could not reside in France. He was a friend, and translator, of Silone. One could not be more of a loner than Samson, who lived in exile not only in Switzerland but in German-speaking Switzerland, and when he began publishing *Témoins* in Zurich in 1953 as an independent, anti-doctrinal and anarchistic review, he was certain to attract Camus' sympathy. The magazine's French editor was a left-wing labor unionist, Robert Proix, a proofreader by trade. He met Camus for the first time in the office of Suzanne Agnely when he was correcting proofs for her. Camus liked *Témoins* and set up a meeting in his library office at the Rue Madame with a number of left-anarchists and revolutionary syndicalists, Samson, and Pierre Monatte. Monatte had been a revolutionary trade unionist from before World War I, had resigned from the labor confederation in protest against its pro-war policy of the time. He was arrested in 1920 in connection with an alleged plot against national security, kept in pre-trial detention for a year before being acquitted. He joined the French Communist Party but was expelled in 1924, founded *Révolution Prolétarienne,* which, as has already been remarked, became a platform for left-wing labor leaders and socialists opposed to the Communist Party. (One contributor before World War II was Simone Weil, writing under a pseudonym.) Monatte lived in a small apartment outside the city limits on his salary as a proofreader until his death in 1960, at the age of seventy-nine.

Another participant at the meeting in Camus' home was Monatte's young disciple Gilbert Walusinski, who had already worked alongside Camus in the Groupes de Liaison Internationale. Camus took part in other meetings of the *Témoins* group, including one at the home of his old *Paris-Soir* colleague Rirette Maîtrejean, who had published *L'Anarchie* with Victor Serge, Russian émigré revolutionary socialist who had been banished from the U.S.S.R. by Stalin. On another occasion Proix arranged a meeting between Camus and Giovanna Berneri, widow of an Italian revolutionary whom Stalin had ordered killed in Spain in 1937.

Significantly, Camus allowed his friends of the *Témoins* group to use his name in a way that many magazine editors in France and elsewhere would have envied: He was listed as a "correspondent" along with Daniel Martinet, also of Groupes de Liaison Internationale, Proix, Walusinski. (In the very first issues he was identified as a member of the editorial board—*comité de lecture*—but he apparently felt that this implied more responsibility than he was assuming.) He followed up the promise of his name by giving *Témoins* a number of his brief political writings—his speech on the East Berlin uprising, for example, and later a speech on the Soviet repression of the Hungarian revolt. From time to time Walusinski would also ask Camus for a text for *Révolution Prolétarienne;* Camus gave him the Saint-Etienne speech, entitled "Le Pain et la Liberté."[20]

What Camus had in common with the left-socialists and anarchists of *Témoins,* and of *Révolution Prolétarienne,* in addition to a shared quality of outsider, was perhaps an underlying contempt for bourgeois society and its social injustice, and some instinctive but hardly organized plans for changing it. Observing Camus, Robert Proix decided that he was at heart a *libertaire*—an anarchist, but without knowing that he was; his place was *beyond* the extreme left, with the revolutionary syndicalists of the Monatte school.

Camus became a friend of Maurice Joyeux, who virtually ran a one-man anarchist movement connected with the newspaper *Le Libertaire* (and *Le Monde Libertaire*). Camus first met him when a contributor to *Le Libertaire,* Maurice Lemaître, suggested that a campaign be launched to bring back the writer Céline from exile after his wartime ideological collaboration with the Nazis. Writers were asked to sign a petition, and Camus signed—his first formal link to the Joyeux group. Later, at a meeting for Republican Spain in 1952, the Socialist Daniel Mayer would remark from the speakers' platform that "We have here a man who makes history—Joyeux—and a man who writes it—Camus," and the two met for the first time. Camus saw Joyeux as an admirable example of a workingman who acted according to Camus' principles. They would meet at public events such as the Spanish Republican meeting, exchange letters, and when Joyeux opened a bookshop in Montmartre called Le Château des Brouillards (from a Dorgelès novel) Camus would sometimes drop in to talk to him.[21] Joyeux felt that of all contemporary works it was Camus' *L'Homme révolté* which most closely defined the aspirations of the young students and workers who created France's essentially anarchistic revolt of May 1968.[22]

As for Camus, he defined his attitude concerning the *solidarité essentielle* between worker and artist in a letter on proletarian literature sent to a labor magazine on August 8, 1953 (published for the first tine after his death, and in *Révolution Prolétarienne*). "Tyrannies, like the democracies of money, know that in order to rule, they must separate work and culture. For work," he wrote, "economic oppression is more or less sufficient—"

> For the latter, corruption and derision do the job. The merchant society covers with gold and privileges its decorated amusers, calling them artists, and lures them to all the necessary compromises. . . .[23]

In another vein, Camus had begun to jot down his favorite words, on a sheet of paper which was later dated March 1951–December 1953:

> The world, pain, earth, mother, men, desert, honor, poverty [*la misère*], summer, sea.[24]

# 40

✦

# INSURRECTION

Is it possible to pretend to be a teacher of civilization when one introduces oneself with the Declaration of the Rights of Man in the left hand and, in the right hand, the bludgeon of repression?

Message (May 1954)

It was sufficient for Camus to satisfy himself that a literary prize—the Prix Algérien du Roman—was to be financed by his old enemy, the Government General of Algeria, to make him decide to withdraw from its jury. At first it had sounded like a good idea, and Camus had agreed to participate the previous November (just after his fortieth birthday). His "old repugnance" against membership in literary juries had been overcome by the possibility that was offered to serve Algeria. He also got Jules Roy to agree to join.

The idea for the prize had come from an occasional writer and civil servant, Jean Pomier, who headed a group called Association des Ecrivains Algériens, and published a magazine called *Afrique*. (He also happened to be chief of the public works division of the Algiers prefecture when young Albert Camus worked for the Cartes Grises et Permis de Conduire section of that division.) Pomier's own writers' group had already been giving a literary prize but to decreasing enthusiasm and at longer intervals between prizes, and the hope was that a more prestigious jury, centered in Paris, with the prize limited to novelists, would increase its impact. "To serve Algeria by means of this Prize," Pomier wrote in *Afrique*, "is to help its youth become established in the world, in the consideration of the world, and first of all in that of France. . . ." A loyal French Algerian and a civil servant himself,

Gabriel Audisio was enlisted to contact French Algerians settled in Paris, Camus among them. Hence Camus' acceptance, on November 12, 1953. But soon after that Audisio wrote Pomier to advise him that Camus wished to be absolutely certain that the origin of the funds, the 100,000 francs (some 3,000 francs of the mid-1970s, or about $615) to be given to the winner, would not tie the hands of the jury. Pomier hastened to assure Audisio that the money was by no means from a secret fund, but that it was automatically included in the Algerian legislature's annual budget.

Apparently Camus had not been aware that any official budget at all had been involved. From Algeria, Emmanuel Roblès dispatched a copy of Pomier's announcement of the award in *Afrique,* which made it clear that the Government General was backing the project. Camus fired off a letter to Pomier, dated February 26, 1954:

> . . . As I have just said to Audisio, the tie to the Government General and official personalities of Algeria is so clearly stated (and we are grateful for this clarity) that I cannot, to my great regret, continue to remain on the Prize jury. . . .

He had, he went on, always made it a rule to abstain from official Algerian programs.

> First of all, of course, I am far from always approving this official action. Then it happens that I was long the target, as an Algerian journalist, of pressure and intimidation from the Government General. Things came to such a point that if I left my country over fifteen years ago, it was because my attitude of independence caused me to be reduced to unemployment at the time.

He was not bitter, but he wanted to be clear. He had thought that the new literary prize would be given by writers who wished to help other writers, as he had always helped "men of my country" and would continue to do so.

With Camus, all of the jurors who mattered also withdrew.

The following issue of *Afrique* headlined:

### THE PRIZE ASSASSINATED

In the article which followed Pomier claimed that Camus should have realized from earlier correspondence that the prize came from an "administrative" subsidy. Now the prize had been assassinated, but who was the assassin? Who had convinced Camus to withdraw? Pomier did not say. But meanwhile he was bitter about Camus. "Deep inside Albert Camus, is there a man? I see coiled there only a mean and venomous resentment." Years later Pomier would publish at his own expense a book almost entirely devoted to the incident.[1]

With *L'Eté* at the beginning of spring 1954, Camus would publish his last collection of lyrical essays. The essays "belong to the essential vocation of Camus," Pierre de Boisdeffre wrote in *Combat;* "they reflect a face naturally turned toward the light." Boisdeffre suggested that *L'Eté* be read as one listens to Mozart or Vivaldi, with one's heart. Camus himself characterized the essays as *solaire* in the promotional description (the publisher's *prière d'insérer*), and likened them to the essays of *Noces*. Here were published together "Le Minotaure ou la Halte d'Oran," his early essay on that city already issued in a slim volume under the Charlot imprint; a brief homage to Algiers as if to establish a balance: "Petit guide pour des villes sans passé"; a true return to *Noces* with "Retour à Tipasa"; and the concluding "La Mer au plus près." But among the occasional pieces also included in this volume was the very personal "L'Enigme," dated 1950, in which the author describes the place of the writer in society in the age of instant reputations (in which a writer becomes famous without being read). Coming still closer to home, Camus pointed out that it was possible to write an essay about the Absurd without being desperate himself, just as one could write about incest without throwing oneself on one's sister; had Sophocles killed his father and dishonored his mother?

In mid-March Camus received an interviewer, Franck Jotterand, for the literary supplement of a Swiss newspaper, to talk about *L'Eté* and other things, including projects present and future. Jotterand had called on Camus at his Gallimard office, where of course he was shown the terrace. The visitor noticed hyacinth bulbs that were lying on the window ledge and that Camus told him belonged to his neighbor Jacques Lemarchand. "I am exasperated by this reputation of austerity and of virtue—of which I am quite unworthy—and that I am constantly being beaten over the head with by well-intentioned people." He hoped that the publication of *L'Eté* would help to erase the image. He felt that he had been typed: He no longer dared to use the expression "It's absurd" in ordinary conversation—and said that he was seeking to go beyond the concepts of *limite, mesure.*

Camus told the interviewer of his plan to bring *Les Possédés* to the stage. But more importantly, and for the first time in public, he mentioned his future novel on a young man growing up in Algeria, *Le Premier Homme*. "It's been a long time since I wrote a work of imagination," he explained, revealing that he was now writing short stories in the way of transition. As for *Le Premier Homme,* "I now have the title and the subject, but for everything else I always make changes along the way. . . . Its background will be those lands without a past of which I speak in *L'Eté,* lands of imagination, composed of a mixing of races." The interviewer asked whether the immigrants brought their traditions with them to Algeria. "In general they aren't very strong, they quickly disappear, not resisting the climate," he replied.

> Thus I imagine a "first man" who starts at zero, who can neither read nor write, who has neither morality nor religion.
> It will be, if you like, an education, but without an educator. It will be inscribed in contemporary history, between revolutions and wars.

Jotterand concluded by asking what Camus thought of the attitude that we are all guilty. "Many modern writers, like the atheistic existentialists, have suppressed God, but they kept the notion of original sin," replied Camus. "One has too often affirmed the innocence of creation. Today they want to shoulder us with the weight of our guilt. There is, I believe, an intermediary truth." He felt that men needed indulgence, and quoted Sancho Panza, appointed governor of an island: "Since we cannot render a simple justice, let us at least appeal to mercy." Camus smiled as he commented on this. "Try to talk about mercy today, in the streets of Paris. . . ."[2]

Instead of getting better, as seemed possible in the late spring, his wife suddenly appeared worse, and he did not know how to deal with her, or with his family drama. By July 1954 he was in the deepest of depressions himself. He no longer went out, except to his office, the rest of the time standing by, powerless and awkward witness. He knew that he needed to work, not only for himself but for everyone. But he could not, really he could not.

Talking to Roger Quilliot on July 13, he described his writing block, then (by his reckoning) in its sixth month;[3] the silence irritated and worried him. He wondered if his imagination was drying up. Yet he had projects: Again he described *Le Premier Homme* and *Les Possédés,* but also a "Don Juan" along lines suggested in *Le Mythe de Sisyphe.* He also hoped to write an essay on love. Two of the stories that would appear in *L'Exil et le Royaume* had already been composed (probably "La Femme adultère" and "Le Renégat").[4]

Sending René Char a copy of his preface to *L'Allemagne vue par les écrivains de la résistance française* by Konrad Bieber, to be published in Paris that year, he told Char that it was a poor piece, "because I no longer know how to write."[4]

So he grasped at chores that could give him the feeling that he was working. In April he recorded his reading of the complete text of

*L'Etranger* for a French radio series.[5] In June he was the subject of one of a series of radio broadcasts on Algerian writers, and on July 17 he appeared on the series to read texts in Cagayous dialect, in the framework of a program on the street language of Algiers.[6] He spent a month working on a scenario of *La Princesse de Clèves* for Robert Bresson which came out unsatisfactory, and since he had worked without a contract he had worked for nothing.[7] He accepted a high fee for a very brief piece to be published in an illustrated volume produced by the Walt Disney company, *The Living Desert,* together with other well-known writers such as Marcel Aymé and Louis Bromfield. The man who relayed the offer thought that he'd be thrown out of Camus' office for suggesting such a thing, but Camus apparently needed the money.

Once more, in October, he wrote Faulkner for permission to adapt *Requiem for a Nun* to the stage.

And the Swedish Academy again discussed the possibility of giving the Nobel Prize to Camus that autumn.[8]

The voyage about which less has been said than any other took place now, although it would provide the setting for his final novel published during his lifetime, *La Chute.* Indeed, it was the briefest of journeys: the visit to the Netherlands lasted only from October 4 to 7, 1954, train travel included, and of those four days less than two were spent in Amsterdam, where the judge-penitent hero of *La Chute,* Jean-Baptiste Clamence, delivers his monologue. It was Camus' only visit to the Netherlands. Did the country make such an impression on him? It did, if only because he traveled alone, and during the darkest years of his life, in the wake of the controversy over *L'Homme révolté* and of his domestic drama, events that would provide essential materials of this, his most personal work.

As usual, a trip abroad was a time for official receptions; he was on stage again, which he detested. But the hall in which he was to appear on October 5 in The Hague, that small country's small capital, was too small, so at the last minute the site was switched to a Protestant church. On the next day he walked around The Hague in the rain, visited that splendid jewel of a museum, the Mauritshuis, where he looked for Vermeer's portrait of a girl with turban (the *Young Girl with Pearl*) and the Rembrandts, which included *The Anatomy Lesson, Susan and the Elders,* and *David and Saul.* In the afternoon he took the train for the ride (less than an hour) to Amsterdam. He quickly found one of the flat glassed-in sightseeing boats which take tourists under the low bridges, along the central city canal system. That evening after dinner he walked in the lively streets of the old city, streets he found fascinating, but in a rain which never let up, and in a cold wind. That was the evening of October 6. He returned to France the next day.[9]

The importance of the setting of *La Chute,* the fact that it takes place in the sailors' red-light district and on the narrow tawdry street called Zeedijk (where as late as the mid-1970s two of the bars bore the names Saloon Mexico and City Café), may be inferred from the amount of time Camus devoted to visiting Amsterdam. As for the themes and the writing of *La Chute,* they will be discussed in due time.

In this year of Algeria's crisis Camus had been paying close attention to the consequences of the repression of the legitimate aspirations of North Africa's Moslems by a heavy-handed colonial administration. "Is it possible to pretend to be a teacher of civilization when one introduces oneself with the Declaration of the Rights of Man in the left hand and, in the right hand, the bludgeon of repression?" he asked, in a message of May 1954 to a Comité pour l'Amnistie aux Condamnés Politiques d'Outre-Mer. He warned that the colonialists represented a "formidable power." It had sufficed that Algeria's mayors banded together in a protest movement for the Blum-Viollette voting franchise bill to be withdrawn from the French Parliament without debate in the 1930s, he reminded his fellow countrymen. He drew the picture of a small group of wealthy men who dominated press and public authority in the North African territories; their most recent achievement had been the execution of three Tunisian nationalists (for whom Camus had vainly attempted to win pardons).[4]

In July, Camus offered another text, this for the first issue of *Libérons les condamnés d'outre-mer,* in which he cited a remark made to him shortly after World War II in Tlemcen by an Arab nationalist: "Our worst enemies are not the French colonialists. On the contrary they are Frenchmen like yourself. For the colonialists give us a revolting but true idea of France while you give us a deceptive idea, because a conciliatory one. You weaken us in our will to struggle. . . ."

French liberals preach fraternity, Camus added with irony, but while the Arab liberals are moved by these words, they are bludgeoned by the colonialists. Arab terrorism, he warned, was born of solitude, of the idea that no recourse existed, that the walls were too thick and had to be blown up. Liberals were not only responsible for the repression, but for Arab terrorism. It was too late for speeches on fraternity, time for positive acts such as amnesty—but not at the expense of silence on terrorism, whose origins must be explained while its consequences are denounced.[4]

On November 1, 1954, it was indeed too late for speeches. Armed action was launched in the early hours of that day in the name of a new

movement which represented the behind-the-scenes victory of younger
and more militant Algerian nationalists over moderates who continued
to seek reforms through negotiations. For Messali Hadj's MTLD
(Mouvement pour le Triomphe des Libertés Démocratiques) had
divided into factions; the most determined was composed of MTLD's
Organisation Spéciale, responsible for clandestine action, which evolved
during the summer of 1954 into a revolutionary committee for armed
insurrection. With the French having lost the battle of Dien Bien Phu in
Indochina that spring and Tunisia having been promised internal autonomy in July as a result of nationalist agitation in that country—
including guerrilla activity—the Algerian rebels set their attack for late
on Halloween night. The targets were army camps, police stations, local
officials—symbols of colonial power. The new Front de Libération Nationale (FLN) declared its intention to liquidate the colonial system,
but also "all the vestiges of reformism," the goal being Algerian independence.[10]

There was no immediate reaction on Camus' part. It is possible
that he was not immediately aware of the gravity of the uprising. He
had been preoccupied just then with a different sort of Algerian problem, an earthquake in Orléansville, a city of thirty thousand inhabitants
halfway between Algiers and Oran, which had claimed some 1,500 victims in September. Camus helped organize a fund-raising campaign, which included an autographing sale of books by North African
writers, held at the Paris outpost of the Government General on Avenue de l'Opéra, inaugurated by the wife of Prime Minister Pierre
Mendès France. Camus was joined by friends such as Emmanuel
Roblès, and of course by the French-Algerian representative Gabriel
Audisio. The press reported the acquisition by the Société des Auteurs
of the manuscript of *L'Etat de siège* for 15,000 francs (worth 450
francs of the mid-1970s, or under $100).[11]

He busied himself with projects for the theater. He met with the
Mathurins director, Mrs. Baur, and then with Jean Vilar, director of the
Théâtre National Populaire, and although he was horrified by Vilar's
lack of decisiveness and authority, he decided to send him a number of
plays, including *L'Etat de siège* and his Angers festival translation of
Calderón's *Dévotion à la Croix*. (Nothing would come of this.) He took
time out to watch the French Racing team lose to Monaco at the Parc
des Princes—and freeze.[12] Above all, he was preparing for a return to
another country of the sun, which had meant so much to him as a
young man.

He had not been back to Italy since that time—since 1937. He
thought that by returning to his real country, the Mediterranean, he
would also be able to find himself again. In escaping family crisis, but

also the new Algerian crisis, he might be able to regain the interior strength which was necessary to him if he was going to be able to write.

The occasion was an invitation from the Italian Cultural Association (Associazione Culturale Italiana), which had asked him to speak in Turin, Genoa, Milan, and Rome. Between speeches, and once he got to Rome, he would have ample time to arrange an itinerary of his own for the final fortnight of his trip.

He was actually pleased that he was going to be alone, to be able to wander as and where he wished. He was exhausted, but he slept badly in the sleeping car, although part of the reason was the excitement of seeing Italy once more. At 7 A.M. he decided that he must be in Italy at last, so he raised the window shade in his compartment—and burst out laughing: He was riding through a snowstorm. Heavy snowflakes were still coming down when the train pulled into the Turin station two hours later, and it would snow all that day. He went to the city's famous Egyptian museum to admire mummies, he froze as he walked through higher and higher snow to the house where Nietzsche wrote his last books in madness. But he was discouraged by the heavy skies, the blasts of snow, that greeted his return to the country of the sun. He liked Turin all the same, with its paving stones and graceful buildings, and of course the Italian friendliness.

He met the press on November 25, and then gave his first lecture the following day in an attractive eighteenth-century theater of the kind dear to Stendhal; it compensated for the stodgy luxury of the hotel where he had been put up. Then he experienced stage fright. He had gone back to his room for an hour's rest prior to his talk and spent it with teeth chattering as he worried about confronting his first Italian audience.

His talk in Turin, and in the three other cities, was entitled "L'Artiste et son temps" (*not* identical with an interview of that title published in the Pléiade edition of his works, nor with the similarly titled Nobel lecture). In the Italian talk Camus attempted a definition of art, based on reality and revolt against reality. It was neither refusal nor total consent, and in consequence it represented a heartbreak perpetually renewed. The point was neither to flee reality nor to submit to it, but to know precisely how much reality to bestow on a work so that it did not disappear into vapidity. For over a period of a century and a half writers had been able to live in happy irresponsibility, but this was no longer possible; we must know that we cannot escape the common misery, and our only justification as artists is to speak for those who cannot. The free artist is not a man of comfort nor of interior disorder but of imposed order. Camus' plea was for freedom of the artist; art is the enemy of all oppressions, artists and intellectuals were the first victims of modern tyrannies of right and left, and when modern tyranny sees the artist as a public enemy, it is justified in its fears.[13]

He was greeted in Genoa not by snow but by torrential rain, although the city was as he had remembered and loved it: fresh, bright and sparkling, opulent. Then in Rome, where he arrived to more gray skies, the weather finally improved. As soon as he had completed the official part of his visit, he checked out of the Grand Hotel, which seemed to him like all the world's department stores, and found a *pensione* facing the Villa Borghese, where he had a terrace view of the park. He spent his days wandering about the city under sunny skies, dined with writers he knew—Chiaromonte of course, Ignazio Silone, Guido Piovene, Alberto Moravia. Each night before bedtime he stood on his balcony looking out over the city. Of course he loved Rome, the people as well as their sky. And now at last he found himself transported back those twenty-seven years to prewar Italy, when he had discovered art and how art and life were one. What he liked most of all, he decided, were the hills of Rome—the Janiculum, the Palatine—and Rome's fountains.

He felt that with some luck he would find the strength to change his life now. It had to change, in one manner or another, for he could not face any more of the kind of misery he had been living with. He would not work in Italy, but he did expect to build up his will, which he would have to do in order to work again.[14]

Chiaromonte had a friend, the painter Francesco Grandjacquet, who possessed an automobile, so Chiaromonte got him to drive them south from Rome to Naples and Paestum. But when they arrived in Naples on December 7 Camus fell ill, and they could not pursue the trip. Confined to his room with the prospect of a relapse, he was irritable, unhappy. When he could go out again the friends wandered through poor neighborhoods such as Piazza Capuana, which reminded him of old Algiers.

After three nights in Naples they were able to pursue their journey south to the Greek temples of Paestum, on what was then still an attractively wild archaeological site with crows flying low over the deserted ruins. They drove out to the Amalfi coast but did not go as far as Sorrento; the unexpected extra days in Naples made that impossible. For Camus had to return to Paris (he did so on December 14).[15]

Back in Paris, Camus' doctor examined him thoroughly, found nothing serious about his condition, but put him on a diet. He soon felt quite healthy again, although now it was the diet which got him down.[7]

Early in January 1955 he settled down to write. On January 6 he wrote his young friend and would-be theater associate Gillibert: "I'm hiding out right now, and in odd places to try to work, to hold on to the little energy I have."[16] One of these "odd places" may have been a small flat on Boulevard Montmorency, which Jules Roy lent him, with a terrace view of Paris and with a maid. A couple of days later he completed the brief introduction to an American college edition of *L'Etranger*,* where he explained something of the book's intentions,[4] and then on January 11 he wrote to the critic Roland Barthes to take issue with Barthes' interpretation of *La Peste,* in particular the critic's remark that the novel *"fonde une morale antihistorique et une politique de solitude."* Camus replied that the book's obvious content was "the struggle of the European resistance against Nazism." He cited as evidence the fact that a long passage from *La Peste* was published in Jean Lescure's resistance anthology *Domaine Français.*

Comparing this book to *L'Etranger,* Camus told Barthes that it clearly marked the transition from *révolte solitaire* to recognition of community. Barthes had stressed the importance of the theme of separation in *La Peste?* Precisely, and the journalist Rambert, who incarnates that theme, renounces private grief to join the collective struggle. The book ends, furthermore, with the announcement and the acceptance of struggles to come.[4]

Early in this new year Camus was asked to help his anarchist friends. In the final stages of France's Indochina war (which ended with the Geneva Conference agreement of July 1954), Maurice Laisant, who was secretary for propaganda of an anarchist group, Forces Libres de la Paix, as well as an editor of *Le Monde Libertaire,* had published an anti-war poster using the format of official military draft posters. He was promptly indicted for subversion. At the trial, which took place in Paris during the first weeks of 1955, character witnesses were called on the defendent's behalf, first among them Maurice Joyeux's friend Albert Camus. Camus told the court:

> I met Laisant at a meeting where together we demanded the liberation of some men sentenced to death in a neighboring country. Since then I have seen him often and have been in a position to admire his will to fight against the disaster which threatens the human race. It seems impossible to me that one can condemn a man whose action identifies itself so thoroughly with the interests of all men. Too few men are fighting against a danger which each day grows more ominous for humanity.

Having completed his statement, Camus took his place in the courtroom in an audience composed largely of worker-militants, who (it was reported) surrounded him with affection. In his concluding remarks the defense attorney warned that the trial was a means of pursuing a war which had ended months before. But Laisant was not lucky; France was

* See Chapter Sixteen.

not yet out of its period of colonial wars. He was found guilty and re-
cieved a heavy fine.[17]

It was in another period of discouragement—he had even begun to feel
the strain at his office, where he detested the atmosphere, and commented to his friend Michel Gallimard that he expected soon to be
required to punch the clock—that he left one more time for Algiers,
flying from Paris on February 18, 1955. His mood hadn't changed
when he dropped in to talk to Noël Schumann at Editions de l'Empire.
Schumann remarked that he seemed anxious, but was unprepared for
the response. "If it were only that—" he began, and then exploded: "I
can't write anymore!" He seemed to blame himself. "I'm increasingly a
prisoner of my form. . . ."[18]

The war in Algeria? It was still far away; this was a period
resembling, at least for city people, the *drôle de guerre* in 1939–40 before the German offensive. He was staying at what was then the top-
class Hôtel Saint-George, where almost immediately he ran into petite
Dominique Blanchar. He took her to dinner and then out dancing with
some of his old friends, and then next day to Tipasa.[14]

On February 22 he met Edmond Brua at an outdoor table of a
Rue Michelet café to be interviewed for Brua's *Le Journal d'Alger*.
Camus told his old friend that on his first visit to Algiers in two years
he liked what he saw, despite the new high-rise buildings. If he could,
he would spend six months of every year at this source of his inspiration. (Brua called Algiers Camus' "Acropolis," where he had the revelation of another Mediterranean miracle.) They spoke of serious matters—with the apparent exception of the insurrection—but also of
sports. Camus remarked that the weekly newspaper of the Racing
Universitaire d'Alger (RUA) was the only periodical for which he
wrote regularly, and that next season he would be sending in regular reports on Paris soccer games. (Brua was also the editor in chief of *Le
Rua*.) He spoke of fellow North Africans in Paris, said he admired
Max-Pol Fouchet's literary columns in *Carrefour*, mentioned Jean
Sénac, the Algerian novelist and poet Yacine Kateb, and the non-North
African Jean Grenier. On February 24, *Le Journal d'Alger* published
this interview at the top of the large-format front page under the headline:

> Simple Encounter with Albert Camus who finds Algiers "more
> beautiful than ever"

On the day the paper came out Camus was in Orléansville to inspect the earthquake damage to that town and surrounding villages; he
returned to the capital in low spirits.

On Friday, February 25, the RUA and the soccer fans association, Allez-Rua, sponsored a reception for Camus at the Brasserie Le Quartier Latin, announced in the organization's weekly on February 23:

> All the Veterans and all the members of sections are invited to the apéritif which will be given for our comrade.

He was received with hurrahs, which lifted his morale somewhat, and he promised to watch them play next Sunday. He was accompanied by a member of the team in Camus' time who had gone on to become a famous soccer player in France. After remarks by other veterans of the team, "Bébert" got up to say how happy he was to be with them and in Algiers.[19]

The weather was fine, mornings sunny. He sunbathed at his open hotel room window and enjoyed the benefits of it all day. Once more he measured the difference between the way he felt in Algiers—a man—and the shadow he was in Paris. Something here stirred him. He was not working, but he felt that back in Paris he would be *able* to work now. Only the unresolved family drama prevented him from looking forward to his return.[14]

# 41

---

# L'EXPRESS

It is probably not a bad thing that a writer, both solitary and united [*solitaire et solidaire*] with his people, speaks frankly after reflection, and states that he will wage open battle in his articles, first of all for freedom.

"Sous le signe de la liberté"
(in *L'Express*)

One of the make-work projects Camus had accepted at this time when he was at loose ends, unable to pursue any substantial work of his own, was the adaptation of a curious Italian play, *Un Caso clinico,* by the novelist Dino Buzzati. The director Georges Vitaly had asked Camus to help him bring it to the French stage. In the context of Camus' own troubled existence of these months, his willingness to undertake the job is easy to understand. Buzzati's somewhat sinister play takes place in a hospital, where an Italian businessman is growing progressively worse, each time being tranferred to a lower floor of the hospital, which as he knows symbolizes his decline (for all the while he is lucid).[1]

Camus had flown back from Algiers on March 1, in time for final rehearsals of the play, which opened on March 12 at the Théâtre Bruyère to the kind of reception the promoters of such a dark comedy might have expected. "I have never, you hear me, never, seen such a horrible work," exclaimed *Le Figaro*'s Jean-Jacques Gautier, "as cruelly sadistical, as oppressing, as appalling, as abominable, as intolerable." Buzzati came to Paris for the opening, somewhat intimidated at the prospect of meeting the famous author who had adapted his play. But he was reassured by his rough appearance—more like a garage mechanic than an intellectual, he decided, and at the reception following the performance Camus danced without a break.[2]

Camus knew, as he confessed in a preface to the play, whose French title was *Un Cas intéressant,* that in the present state of theater culture the Buzzati work contained certain risks, but he had agreed with Vitaly that the risks were interesting ones. The play seemed a mixture of Tolstoy's *The Death of Ivan Ilyich* and of Jules Romains' black humor play *Knock;* to a friend Camus confided that it was of the "sinister" kind.[3]

On March 26, Camus gave a complete reading of *Caligula* to a young crowd at the Noctambules Theater; he began by reciting in a monotone, but by the final act he was playing out the parts, giving his listeners the impression that they were actually watching a performance.[4]

The left-Catholic monthly *Esprit* had reviewed Konrad Bieber's anthology on *L'Allemagne vue par les écrivains de la résistance française* without mentioning the preface contributed by Camus. When Jean Paul Samson's magazine *Témoins* published this preface in the Spring 1955 issue, Samson called attention to *Esprit*'s omission. Either it was involuntary or it was "one more example of the mental restriction which neo-Stalinist or new-left obedience has required of our Christian progressives." The editor of *Esprit,* Jean-Marie Domenach, fired back a letter to Samson, declared that the omission was indeed intentional, by respect, he said, for the prefacer as well as the subject. That Camus pursued his dispute with Sartre in *Les Temps Modernes* or in *La Nouvelle Nouvelle Revue Française* was proper, and *Esprit* would report such a development. But that Camus should use the occasion of a resistance memorial to commit a *"perfidie"* against his enemy seemed to Domenach scandalous. (Without mentioning Sartre, Camus in his preface to the Bieber volume had warned against intellectuals prepared to collaborate with a new enemy.)[5] With irony, Domenach observed that Camus implied that he would be a future partisan of resistance. "With past and future united in his hand," wrote Domenach, "he crushes all he detests, after having taken from them the very freedom to choose at the decisive moment, to be other than that which his hatred pretends that they are." While Domenach shared few of Sartre's views, he felt that Camus' preface was directed against his political position as well. As for Camus, why didn't he protest German rearmament, and "terror in North Africa"?

Camus replied not to Domenach but to Samson; his letter was printed together with Domenach's in the Summer 1955 *Témoins.* He protested that the essential problem of "our movement" today was this conflict between the free left and the progressive left, i.e., between the independent and the Communist-oriented left. And if he was not allowed to raise the issue without being accused of returning to ancient literary quarrels, then his only solution would be silence, which Domenach and his friends would also criticize. Sartre was not his enemy; they had had no literary quarrel; they had been adversaries on an issue which Camus felt of paramount importance to everyone, and Sartre had not been a loyal adversary. Furthermore, Bieber's book was not a solemn memorial to the resistance movement, which he should have respected; it was a university thesis, and Camus believed it was his duty to speak out in the name of their common past. "I don't see how an intellectual, today, can justify his privileges other than in the shared risks of the struggle for the liberation of work and culture." And Camus had replied to clarify an issue which continued to be obscured.

> I long hesitated to do this, tired of always having to correct the same erroneous statements, the same personal attacks, and the same interminable fallacies, as if our progressives, all together, possessed only a single damaged sword which they used in turn in battles without danger.

Separated by only a few months from the writing of the extraordinary monologue of *La Chute,* the basic elements of the exchange with Domenach are worth remembering.

On April 26, 1955, Camus flew to Athens, for the first leg of his first Greek tour. For, as he told an interviewer of an Athens daily newspaper on his arrival, this trip had been planned fifteen years earlier, and he even booked a steamer voyage for September 2, 1939. He spoke with enthusiasm of Greece as the source of Mediterranean civilization, again expounded on Mediterranean equilibrium: Fascism when it reached Italy hadn't shown the barbarity of German Fascism, Communism in Yugoslavia becomes bearable. He explained that the Mediterranean divided him from most of his fellow French writers, who had been nourished on German literature while he had been raised on Greek. Plato was more important to him than Hegel. But he admitted the influence of Pascal, Tolstoy, and Nietzsche. "This choice will seem strange to you, and I myself agree that they don't go together. To tell the truth I haven't managed to work out my own internal contradictions."

Of Greek writers he especially admired Kazantzakis, whose *Zorba* he preferred, as more "Greek" and colorful than his other works. He hoped one day to stage that author's *The Bee,* and had given the text to Jacques Hébertot, who had replied that he liked it but if he produced it he'd lose millions on it. Camus felt that the argument was crushing but he continued to have hopes because he knew Hébertot.

He insisted that *L'Homme révolté* had not been anti-revolutionary; he himself admired the pre-October Revolution terrorists. Of French writers he thought René Char was the best poet, although he admitted that he could be mistaken. Aragon had great talent although he disapproved of his political orientation and aesthetics. In Italy he placed Silone above all others, and saw nothing new coming out of the United States, Great Britain, or Germany. Why didn't he make movies? Because he didn't have the patience or the disposition to run after the money needed to produce a film. When the cinema became independent he'd consider it.[6]

On April 29 he carried out the official part of the trip, with a talk in the early evening at the Institut Français d'Athènes on "L'Avenir de la tragédie," which included a brief history of contemporary theater, centered on Copeau and the theories which interested Camus, as well as speculations on the likely renaissance of tragedy. He read from plays by Gide, Giraudoux, Montherlant, Claudel, in which he perceived signs of a return to true tragedy.[7]

From Athens he visited Mycenae, Mistra, Delphi, the north (including Salonika), the small island of Delos—which he loved—and Olympia. And he found himself exquisitely happy; he was sorry when it came time to return to France. "I found what I was looking for and more still," he wrote to Char on May 11. "I return standing up." Back in Paris on the sixteenth, he discovered a new Francine. It was as if his voyage had helped her, for she seemed cured. He set to work completing one of his major critical essays, an introduction to the complete works of his literary friend Martin du Gard, then seventy-four, and who had received the Nobel Prize in 1937.[8]

One more time Camus agreed to become a working newspaperman. The opportunity was offered to him by *L'Express,* a weekly of liberal tendency owned and edited by ambitious Jean-Jacques Servan-Schreiber, later the author of *The American Challenge,* a politician more American than French in style, and then an active supporter of Pierre Mendès France, who, in or out of office, himself represented a new style in French politics. On the subject of colonialism, for example, Mendès attacked France's Indochina policy head on, liquidated that war, then turned to the problem of French rule in Tunisia, which would be phased out; and he seemed to offer a similar reasonable approach to the Algerian situation. Mendès spoke the plain language Camus admired but had never heard in public places, while *L'Express* borrowed techniques from the American press (it would later copy the format of

*Time*) and also seemed to take a fresh approach to contemporary problems.

From the point of view of Servan-Schreiber and of his chief deputy,
Françoise Giroud, only a handful of intellectuals really counted in
France, and nearly all of them were contributing to *L'Express*. With
Mauriac, Sartre, Merleau-Ponty writing for the magazine, it seemed
logical that Camus would write for them as well. Why not ask him?[9] Servan-Schreiber walked over to the desk of one of his editors, Jean Daniel,
whom he knew to be a friend and admirer of Camus, and told him:
"We must do the impossible." Daniel, who welcomed the opportunity to
strengthen his personal ties to Camus, knew that Camus had avoided
collaboration on political publications, while he was quite willing to
write for a friend's magazine, and without payment—as he had for
Daniel's own *Caliban*. But Daniel told his boss he would do everything
he could to make it happen. Servan-Schreiber sent a wire, followed up
by a letter, to Camus during the Greek trip. Camus replied with an article comparing the reconstruction of devastated Orléansville and the excavation by French archaeologists of the ruins of Argos in Greece. He
concluded with a postscriptum appeal for the victims of the Greek city
of Volos, recently destroyed by earthquake. Reading it, Servan-
Schreiber commented to Daniel: "Who will be interested in that?"
Daniel told him: "If you don't publish it you won't get Camus." Of
course Servan-Schreiber published it, in the May 14, 1955, issue, and
wired Camus to say that it was a magnificent piece.

Back in Paris, Camus agreed with Daniel that Mendès France's
policies were impressive. He had been moved by a speech Mendès had
delivered at the time of the fall of his government, in which he said that
he had found children in Moroccan prisons. "Everything I can do to
bring Mendès France back to power I'll do," Camus promised.
(Mendès' government had fallen in February.) Daniel told him that
the best way to help Mendès would be to write for *L'Express*. Camus
was willing to try, but without being tied down.

Camus had met and spoken with Mendès France several times.
Once he even made the journey to Louviers in Normandy, the region
Mendès represented in parliament, for a private conversation about
French and Algerian problems. Mendès came away from these meetings
with the impression that Camus believed that the Algerian crisis
required a change in the French attitude in the direction of true fraternity and emancipation of a people who until then had been subjected to
intolerable segregation. To Mendès, Camus seemed vague about the
form these changes would take; he expected a true change in French
behavior both in France and on the scene in Algeria, although he probably did not consider total independence as one of the options. But at

that time Camus' views were far in advance of what the French Government was ready to accept.[10]

Certainly his motivations for agreeing to write for *L'Express* would have included nostalgia for the world of the press. He would also have been impressed by Servan-Schreiber's dynamism, in part a function of ingenuousness, but which had nevertheless attracted such persons as Daniel, Mauriac, and Pierre Viansson-Ponté (his editor in chief), not to speak of Mendès France. Servan-Schreiber ran his magazine as a team. The top staff ate together on airline platters, invited outsiders to these American-style cafeteria lunches, outsiders who might be the Cardinal of Paris, a leader of the Communist Party, or a contributor such as Camus. The magazine went to press on Wednesday, after which the editors would have a midnight supper on the upper floor of elegant Fouquet's on the Champs-Elysées. Camus might also attend these dinners on occasion.

*L'Express* became a daily newspaper in preparation for the national legislative elections, largely in the hope that Mendès France would be returned to power. It might have continued as a daily had the *Mendèsistes* won, but it was losing money, and Servan-Schreiber decided to cut losses by returning to weekly publication (in March 1956).[11]

The *Express* connection at the very start was the pretext for another polemic involving Camus. A brief item in Claude Bourdet's *France-Observateur* on May 12, 1955, on a page headed "La Vie des lettres" and in a paragraph titled "Water in their wine" began by noting that some surrealists had begun to write for conventional literary weeklies. With irony the anonymous writer commented:

> Literature is a large family to which, somewhat late, its prodigal sons have returned. On his side, Mr. Albert Camus, who should nevertheless have different ideas about the nature of the press than Mrs. Françoise Giroud, will write a literary column in *L'Express*.

On his return from Greece Camus fired off a reply to "Monsieur le rédacteur en chef" of *France-Observateur*. As Françoise Giroud was one of those responsible for *L'Express* and its style, he said, he had no difficulty in approving her conception of journalism, convinced that he was justified in writing for that magazine, and in total freedom. On the other hand, and for contrary reasons, he would not have written for *France-Observateur,* since he disagreed with its editors on the role and objectivity of a weekly magazine of opinion.

Camus' letter was published in the May 25 issue of *France-Observateur* together with a reply signed by Bourdet and his fellow editor

Gilles Martinet. They began by paying tribute to modern journalism, and to *L'Express,* agreeing that it was regrettable that Françoise Giroud's conception of journalism had been questioned in their magazine.[12] It was to her moral conceptions that they would address themselves. Quoting her, they noted that she believed in success, American-style, which they felt conflicted with Camus' position in *Combat* which emphasized the need to liberate the press from capital, and to give it a tone and a truth worthy of the best of its public, the caprices of a star not necessarily being more interesting than the misfortunes of peoples, the blood of armies, or the effort of a nation to find its truth. *This* was the different conception that *France-Observateur* had been talking about; it was strange to see the advocate of extreme journalistic austerity working for a magazine which seeks to "seduce."

*France-Observateur*'s editors called Camus' derogatory remarks about their own weekly "indecent" and "ridiculous." They reviewed the earlier polemic over their comment on Pierre Hervé's criticism of *L'Homme révolté,* and now reported Camus' reluctance to sign a protest against the arrest of Roger Stéphane. Camus had been willing to sign only with the reservation that he contested Stéphane's journalistic methods, which they assumed referred back to Stéphane's account of the Sartre-Camus polemic in *Les Temps Modernes.* Camus had felt that Stéphane was dishonest, instead of realizing that he simply believed that Sartre was right.

Camus' *réflexe égocentrique,* wrote Bourdet and Martinet, was a frequent occurrence. But it took on importance when Stéphane was put into jail.[13] They concluded with a round attack on Camus' "extraordinary mixture of pride and susceptibility"—doubtless common enough among writers—which is why they had not earlier reported his attitude on Stéphane. But this week he had exceeded the limit and they had to tell him so.

Camus replied in an article called "Le Vrai débat," which covered a whole page of *L'Express* on June 4. He mocked the final lines of the *France-Observateur* open letter. "We're in the lodge of the porter, who finds that the artist on the third floor is rather stuck up, and that this will not bring him good luck." He contested their version of the Stéphane affair. His reservations about that journalist had not prevented him from supporting Stéphane, for the reservations were expressed *privately.* As evidence he quoted from his letter to Gilles Martinet: "At your request, I join your demand for the release of Roger Stéphane. You may use this statement with the authorities on whom his release depends, without reservations."

Then Camus moved the debate to another plane. His attitude toward *France-Observateur* did not derive from the magazine's position on the Sartre-Camus polemic. But it was true that certain of the problems which underlay that debate, first of all *la décadence révolutionnaire,* were indeed still live issues and continued to divide Camus from the Bourdet group. Revolution in our time would regain its grandeur and efficacy only if it relinquished cynicism and opportunism, which meant refusal to collaborate with contemporary Communism. Whatever it would cost him in friendship or repose, Camus would continue his fight against both bourgeois and pseudorevolutionary reaction.

So in *France-Observateur,* Bourdet replied again (in the June 9 issue). This time he clarified the attack on Camus over the Stéphane affair. Camus had been asked to participate in a meeting to demand the release of Roger Stéphane, and he had replied with the promise to send a message. They had received Camus' message along with others, but could not use his because, in addition to the lines cited by Camus, he had added that his reservations about Stéphane did exist, and that his message should not be taken as approval of Stéphane or of his journalistic methods. Camus hadn't mentioned these lines in "Le Vrai débat," Bourdet said, probably because it would have sounded like a disavowal of the opposition to the French Indochina War (which had been opposed by *L'Express* as well as by Bourdet's magazine). But Camus' disclaimer had prevented them from making use of his letter, for they were not sending a confidential message to the judge but a public one, and in view of Camus' animosity, they could not have printed the first part of his message without the second part.

Bourdet went on to say that they had never asked Camus to write for them, except to contribute opinions along with others. Not that they felt his opinions were so far from their own, but they knew he preferred to express himself in his books. They were pleased that he was now writing political articles for *L'Express.* But, Bourdet added, Camus had aped French McCarthyites in accusing *France-Observateur* of being part of the pro-Communist left—an amusing charge, said Bourdet, since the Communists accused them of anti-Communism. The real problem was Camus' refusal to collaborate with the Communists, since it was possible to collaborate with them to fight the errors and crimes of bourgeois regimes while continuing to criticize Communist parties and regimes. At *L'Express,* Bourdet warned, Camus would also have to come to grips with politics, for *Mendèsisme* would have to consider the problem of its relationship to the French Communist Party—to work with it against the bourgeoisie. As for Camus:

> It is not forbidden to the writer to remain above the crowd, and he
> can, in solitude, accomplish his task for the good of all. But if he
> does join in, he must accept the rules, which are those of collective

action and the responsibilities they imply, and which include a certain sense of humor in the face of attack.

He concluded that Camus was now in the same camp as they, and would have battles to wage at their side.

In fact they would never again be in the same camp.

This nastiness aside, Camus began to write regularly for *L'Express*. At the time the weekly was published in tabloid newspaper format on newsprint, its front page devoted to headlines, a photograph, and a summary of contents. François Mauriac had a regular weekly column on the back page. The issue which introduced Camus—May 14, 1955 —printed three names on the front page, bordered in red:

**MENDES-FRANCE**
**MAURIAC**
**CAMUS**

That issue also contained Mendès' first articles, the first he had written since his departure from the government. Following the June 4 reply to *France-Observateur,* Camus' first articles of substance, on July 9 and 23, concerned Algeria. At last he had an opportunity to speak out, and in a major opinion-forming medium. He used the opportunity to denounce at the same time the terrorism of the Algerian rebels and the repression by colonial authorities, affirming his solidarity with all Algerians. He was closer, he said, to an Arab farmer or a Kabyle shepherd than to a shopkeeper of Northern France. Algeria was not inhabited by a million and a half colonialists: Only a small group of Frenchmen there were reactionary; French Algerians could not all be moved out of that territory to leave it to the Moslems. The solution, he suggested, was a conference to bring together the French Government, colonial authorites, and representatives of Arab nationalist movements. He spelled out what the conference could do. After dissolution of the present Algerian legislature, born of faked elections, an honest vote could elect true representatives of both the French and the Moslems who would sit down to work out a new community which would see Algeria as a member of a federation of French territories, each of which would have internal autonomy.

In anticipation of France's own forthcoming elections, the editors of *L'Express'* were in the process of retooling, to become a daily rather than a weekly. The need for writers would of course be greater, and Servan-Schreiber had remarked in the presence of Camus' old Algerian comrade Robert Namia—a member of the staff—that he wanted Camus to become part of the daily enterprise. Soon after that Namia met Camus in the street as Namia was getting off a bus and Camus was climbing out of a subway station. Camus told Namia that Servan-Schreiber had asked him to become director of the daily *Express;* he asked Namia what he thought of the idea, although Camus had already said no. Namia snapped: "You're an idiot. We need a left-wing rag." They walked up to the office together. A few hours later Servan-Schreiber summoned Namia to his office, where the latter also found Françoise Giroud, editor in chief Viansson-Ponté, and Camus. Camus addressed Namia: "We should do a morning *Le Monde,* with small headlines and a serious format; don't you agree?" Namia did not agree; he thought a sensational appearance was necessary in the midst of a political campaign. "And you couldn't compete with *Le Monde* by coming out a few hours earlier with the same format." Servan-Schreiber said: "Thanks, Robert," and Namia left. Later Namia heard that Camus had refused to take over the paper because of Namia's objection; Camus had said that he would do it if Namia agreed. Namia rushed through the building looking for Camus, found him in the composing room, demanded: "Why didn't you tell me that you were setting me up like that?"[14]

When in October *L'Express* became a daily, it continued to be published in tabloid format, but now got tabloid-style make-up as well: banner headlines, photographs of crime on the front page. The idea was to provide a popular platform for Mendès France (and of course for ambitious Servan-Schreiber). The October 8 issue announced that Camus had agreed to join the staff. He would write for the paper twice a week. In the same issue Camus published a credo entitled "Sous le signe de la liberté," explaining why he was entering the arena, why an intellectual *should,* despite his own work, the brevity of his life, his shortcomings. But, he wondered, when you disapprove of the death or even of the dishonoring of your adversary, when you are hurt by the inadequacies of right as well as left, how can you be in politics? When you oppose both the police state and the merchant state, when you see the two merging, when you realize that you can't oppose in the West what you applaud in the East, wishing to remain faithful to the working class while refusing either bourgeois or pseudo-revolutionary mystification, how do you participate? Is not silence better?

But dawn approaches, and with it a return of one's confidence. Of course it is easier to be silent. But an artist cannot be silent; how justify his privileges if he doesn't take part in the long struggle for the freedom of work and of culture?

> Not the license, violent and empty, to destroy everything, nor the derisory freedom to be hungry all alone in the crowded slum where one vegetates, but, no matter what kind of society one is speaking

of, the uncompromising freedom to demand unceasingly, at times to achieve: justice.

The first daily issue was dated October 13, 1955, and Camus' first column, called "Actuelles" (with a passport-sized photograph to accompany it) appeared in the October 15–16 weekend edition. In this and subsequent columns on October 18, 21, 25, 28, November 1 and 4, and then again in January 1956, Camus dealt with the Algerian crisis (these columns would be published together in *Actuelles III,* whose subtitle is *Chroniques algériennes*). His first column on a non-Algerian subject dealt with working conditions, which he feared were of less interest to the public than the breakup of the relationship of British Princess Margaret and Group Captain Townsend (November 8). On November 11 his column discussed the problems of the great powers, China, and nuclear weapons. But alongside it was an unsigned editorial entitled "Onze novembre," and this too was apparently written by Camus.[9] It is a bitter comment on the request by the Edgar Faure cabinet for a parliamentary vote of confidence on Armistice Day; the anonymous editorial writer noted that the war dead would refuse their confidence to this government which had killed them.

> This is why men who, according to the expression of Michelet, suffer today from France, will not take part in the official ceremonies and the intolerable rhetoric in which they are bathed. But neither will they remove themselves from the misfortune or the hope of their country. The hope is great as is the humiliation. Hope nevertheless remains for a strong and just France where neither labor nor intelligence will be degraded. It is this hope that we must meditate today in order to serve it tomorrow with resolution, against the men of misfortune.

In Algeria, on October 1, the first issue of *Communauté Algérienne* appeared, edited by Aziz Kessous, an Algerian Socialist who had been a member of Ferhat Abbas' Manifeste movement. The magazine's purpose was to facilitate the development of understanding between Europeans and Moslems, and in this spirit Camus had written Kessous a letter published in the first issue (and reprinted in *Actuelles III*). Camus began by saying that "I suffer from Algeria, at present, as others suffer from the lungs." Since the outbreak of new guerrilla action in a heretofore quiet part of the territory, he was close to despair. Even if the French Algerians could forget their victims of these massacres, and if the Arab masses could forget the repression, the two communities were now on opposing sides. And yet they—Kessous and Camus— were so much alike, of the same culture, sharing hopes, united in the love of their land as brothers; they knew that they were not each other's enemy. And they were "condemned to live together."

That was the crux of the problem:

> The French of Algeria, and I am thankful to you for having remembered that they are not all proprietors hungry for blood, have been in Algeria for over a century, and there are more than a million of them. This alone suffices to differentiate the Algerian problem from the problems posed in Tunisia and Morocco.

But at the same time there was no reason why nine million Moslems (whom Camus referred to collectively as Arabs) should live as forgotten men; the dream of a silent and submissive Moslem mass is as ridiculous as the idea that the French natives of Algeria could all be asked to leave.

Meanwhile in *L'Express,* Camus' columns continued to deal not only with Algeria but with other events which seemed urgent to the writer (Franco Spain was of course one of them). He would continue to write for the newspaper until the beginning of February. During all of this period he would go to the *Express* office on Mondays and Thursdays, spend time with the editors (who now included his old friend Jean Bloch-Michel). In the hierarchy he was closest to publisher Servan-Schreiber, he would of course see fellow *pied noir* Jean Daniel, and he even had a couple of comical brushes with fellow columnist Mauriac, whose jealousy of Camus was a subject of staff gossip.[15] Daniel observed that Camus was not a facile journalist: He would write out his text, revise it and type it, then revise it again; he was writing like a writer, not a reporter.[16]

The chief reason for Camus' withdrawal from *L'Express* was certainly the series of disappointments he experienced in January 1956: evidence of the rapid deterioration of the political atmosphere in Algeria (to be discussed in a subsequent chapter), the fact that Mendès France was not asked to form the next French Government despite the victory of the Front Républicain in the elections, but also a feeling that the Algerian line of *L'Express* was not the same as his own. (The publication had by then moved to the position that no solution was excluded for Algeria including independence, a position he could not accept.) From the management point of view, Camus did not slam the door when he left *L'Express;* he simply stopped sending in articles after a final, noncommittal homage to Mozart (published on February 2, 1956). He was asked to contribute another article and he didn't reply, but there was no formal letter of resignation. He would occasionally phone Servan-Schreiber or Viansson-Ponté or others on the staff to take issue with an

*Express* story, and it was understood that the door would always be open for his return. But did he say that he would never again write about Algeria in that publication? Sometime later, when he offered *L'Express* an article on Spain, Servan-Schreiber commented to one of his intimates: "We're going to get him back." But they did not.[11]

As for the newspaper itself: On March 1 the daily *Express* headlined its sudden decision to revert to weekly publication. It explained, in the first weekly issue on March 9, 1956, that with 150,000 copies printed each day the newspaper had been fourth in rank among Paris morning dailies, yet it could not have carried on without outside financial support, to which there would necessarily have been political strings.

In fact Camus never felt comfortable about *L'Express*. For one thing, as has already been observed, he did not like the daily format. (When he saw the first issue he told Servan-Schreiber and Françoise Giroud: "You have to start all over again.") He felt the paper was exploiting the victims of the Algerian War, although Daniel didn't agree with him on that; Daniel believed that public opinion had to be moved in some way. And then there was the French political scene. Camus had joined *L'Express* to bring Mendès France to power and what had they got? Guy Mollet, who Camus felt would bring no good to Algeria.[16]

Later, when Viansson-Ponté himself left *L'Express* (because it had adopted the *Time* format, which he felt would result in a superficial magazine), Camus offered him his moral support, remarking that he shared Viansson's disappointment with the magazine—which Camus himself no longer even read.[11]

At the end of July 1955, Camus drove to Italy's Adriatic coast with Maria Casarès. Using the popular beach resort of Rimini as their base, they spent the month of August visiting Siena and everywhere else they could find paintings by Piero della Francesca (but not Florence, because she was expecting to go there shortly with a traveling company of the Théâtre National Populaire). He had told friends that he was off on an incognito working trip, and indeed he probably completed the first draft of the stories for *L'Exil et le Royaume* that month and the next.

Just before that, he had taken his children to a mountain resort near Chamonix, where a chalet had been lent to them. Invited to join them on Sunday, René Lehmann, his friend and Michel Gallimard's doctor, came over from Lausanne to discover a troubled man. High mountains not only disagreed with him psychologically, they affected his breathing, and a recent bronchitis which would not go away added to his difficulties. It was agreed that he would go over to Lausanne for an X-ray.

The film showed the old TB scars with inevitable aftereffects: swelling of the pleura, and other permanent signs of the years of pneumothorax injections. It was the sclerosed tissue which reduced his breathing capacity. Disturbed, Lehmann suggested that a pleurectomy might be advisable to try to restore a certain flexibility to the lungs. But after Camus' departure Lehmann wrote him to express regret for what he had said, for in fact—considering the age of the scars—there was little chance that a pleurectomy would help him. Back in Paris, Camus went to see Dr. Brouet, who found no basic change in his patient's condition, agreed that the sclerosis and swelling were worrisome, but felt that Camus would have to resign himself to that. Camus didn't bring up the subject of an operation but Brouet did, rejecting that and other eventual remedies. There was nothing to do but wait. Lehmann privately felt then and later that an accurate prognosis was impossible. The rapidity of functional deterioration depended on many things: the patient's life style, his smoking, the early treatment of bronchitis, avoiding heavy physical effort. Camus was taking better care of his health now, knowing how much he still had to say.[17]

William Faulkner arrived in Paris in late September 1955, and Gallimard threw one of the large garden parties for which it was known, drawing a crowd of some four hundred of France's literary elite. The guest of honor duly shook hands with all those who were introduced to him; "claustrophobic and withdrawn," as Faulkner's biographer described him, he also shook Camus' hand, but nothing more than that transpired. "A shy man himself sometimes, Camus sadly withdrew."[18] Faulkner had now signed the agreement for Camus' adaptation of *Requiem for a Nun,* and at this time Camus was having a rough translation made of it.

In fact the only public appearances that fall in which Camus seemed to take an interest were events involving Spain (or Spanish America, for he would deliver a speech on December 7 in honor of Eduardo Santos, exiled publisher of Colombia's *El Tiempo* and a friend of Republican Spain). On the morning of October 23 a commemoration of the three hundred and fiftieth anniversary of the publication of *Don Quixote* was held in the Richelieu amphitheater of the Sorbonne under Camus' chairmanship, and with the participation of the rector of the University of Paris and other personalities; the meeting's sponsors included Pablo Casals and Salvador de Madariaga. The event was actually organized by Camus' old friends at *Solidaridad Obrera,* the organ of the anarchist labor union federation CNT (the paper was eventually banned by the de Gaulle government to avoid giving offense to General Franco).[19]

In his talk Camus saluted *Don Quixote* as an ironic and ambiguous work, whose hero refused the easy victories and realities of his century.

> But it is important to note that these refusals are not passive. Don Quixote fights and never resigns himself. . . . A refusal which is the contrary of a renouncement, an honor which bends the knee before the humble, a charity which takes arms.

Speaking of the Spanish knight's failure in his century, the mockery he had suffered, Camus seemed to be speaking from personal experience. The irony, he said, is that the anniversary of the book had brought together, in the catacombs of exile, the true faithful of Don Quixote's religion:

> Those who, like myself, have always shared this faith, and who indeed have no other religion, also know that it is a hope as well as a certainty. The certainty that with a certain degree of stubbornness, defeat becomes victory. . . .
>
> But for that one must carry on to the end. Don Quixote, as in the dream of the Spanish philosopher, must descend into hell to open the gates for the most miserable. . . .[20]

# 42

# THE FALL

> But in an era of bad faith, the man who does not want to renounce separating true from false is condemned to a certain kind of exile.
>
> Letter to Jean Gillibert, February 1956

Of all Camus' works, least is known of the conception and the sources of *La Chute,* and *La Chute* may be his most probing, his most personal creation, as well as a key to Camus' darkest years. Part of the answer will be found in the still unpublished journals of that period, certainly. But the mystery will remain concerning the sudden explosion of the work: Conceived as a short story, as one of the *nouvelles* of *L'Exil et le Royaume,* it grew quickly, almost before Camus had time to talk or to write about it to friends, into the short novel it became. *La Chute* had not existed the previous autumn, hadn't been mentioned to friends or family, and then as if by spontaneous combustion it was finished or about to be finished at the beginning of February 1956, the manuscript ready for the printer in the middle of March. In this way did it race ahead of the other stories of *L'Exil,* which would not be ready for publication until the following autumn.

Jean-Baptiste Clamence—and he admits that this is not his real name—had been a well-known lawyer in Paris. "I had a specialty: 'noble causes.'" He had even refused the Legion of Honor, and with a discreet dignity in which he found his real reward. He loved to help blind people cross streets; he knew how to be familiar, silent, nonchalant, serious. His popularity was considerable. "I wasn't bad looking, I showed myself to be at once a tireless dancer and a discreet scholar, I managed to love at the same time—which is not easy—women and justice, I practiced sports and the fine arts." He was modest in the bargain, if vain in secret.

As for women: "First you have to know that I always succeeded, and without great effort, with women," Clamence will say. "I don't mean that I succeeded in making them happy, nor even in making myself happy through them. No, succeeded—just that." His looks helped him, and he was sensual. "Even for an adventure of ten minutes I should have renounced father and mother, ready to regret it bitterly later on." He had principles, of course, such as that the wives of friends were sacred. "It's only that I ceased, quite sincerely, some days before, to be friends with the husbands." Society bored him, women never. "How often, standing on the sidewalk, in the middle of a passionate conversation with friends, I lost the thread of the argument someone was making because a pretty wench, at the same instant, was crossing the street." He had no trouble with his overture, being a lawyer, and having been an apprentice actor as well.

But Clamence's womanizing created problems. Men resented the time he spent with women. He thought that he was liked by everybody, when in fact he was the object of harsh judgments. When lucidity returned, he received all the wounds at once.

Up to this point, intimates of the Camus of the postwar years would have had no trouble recognizing this self-mocking self-portrait.

Then one evening this man successful in all ways, walking across the Pont des Arts between the Institut de France and the Louvre, was surprised by a mysterious burst of laughter. For, when he had crossed the river a couple of years before that, he had learned that he would do nothing to save a woman from drowning. This time all his confidence in himself is shattered. He becomes his own prosecutor, and the prosecutor of his peers, abandoning family, home, career, to wind up in a tawdry bar in Amsterdam's honky-tonk district, setting himself up as a judge-penitent. He will tell his story in an uninterrupted monologue (to an imagined visitor from France who has stumbled into the bar).

The bluntness of this self-criticism, or this criticism of others in the guise of self-criticism, the shock of the theme, the setting of the action on the dark side of Amsterdam, were likely to disconcert Camus' regular public. Critics and the academic community compared the new novel to Dostoevsky's *Notes from Underground;* Camus was then living with Dostoevsky's *Possessed,* of course, and with the Dostoevskian *Requiem for a Nun.* But someone knowing Camus as a human being as well as an author of books could look at *La Chute* in another way. At the end of a long period of writing block, of substituting for his true vocation the miscellaneous article, the adaptation, Camus had at last found a medium in which he could work. If he could not write because of his condition, perhaps he could write *about* his condition.

For the most convincing keys to the shock of *La Chute* were autobiographical. The refusal to help a woman in distress was too clear a metaphor for Camus' personal situation to be overlooked by his friends. No more surprising were the echos of the controversy over *L'Homme révolté,* which had affected Camus so deeply and for so long. Camus' unpublished notebooks, as evidenced by the selections from them which have been published, betray his pessimistic view of his contemporaries born of the long-drawn-out polemic. In November 1954, for example, Camus wrote in his journal: "Existentialism: When they accuse themselves one can be sure that it is in order to crush others: judge-penitents."[1]

In publishing an early table of contents of *L'Exil et le Royaume,* at that time still "Nouvelles de l'exil," Camus' Pléiade editor noted that two of the planned stories, "L'Intellectuel et le geôlier" and "Nouvelles de la folie," were never to be written. Either could have been an early title for an early conception of *La Chute* (and of course the anecdote of the intellectual who is spat upon regularly by his jailers is contained in *La Chute*). Camus' journal in 1953 also contains this note:

> *Le Pilori.* We must blame him. We must blame his ugly manner of appearing to be honest while not being so. In the first person— Incapable of loving. He tries to, etc.

Again: "What a man accepts with the most difficulty is to be judged."[1]

Camus had other titles for the work in progress: "Le Jugement dernier" appears on the manuscript of the first version. Or *Un Héros de notre temps* (A Hero of Our Time), as he told *Le Monde* in August 1956. His journal in 1954 also gave the title *Un Puritain de notre temps* (A Puritan of Our Time).[1] On one of the versions of *La Chute,* Camus had attached an epigraph of Mikhail Lermontov, whose *A Hero of Our Time* was published in 1840. Camus quotes Lermontov about that novel: ". . . indeed a portrait, but not that of a man: It is the assembling of the defects of our generation in all the fullness of their development."

When the book was contracted for with Gallimard on February 8, 1956—when it had outgrown the dimensions of *nouvelle* to become a book in its own right—Camus gave its title as "L'Ordre du jour."[2] Camus had his friend Jean Bloch-Michel read and comment on the manuscript, and Bloch-Michel urged him to add what is now the final paragraph, for otherwise he felt the ending sounded too much like that of *L'Etranger.* And then on Sunday, Camus telephoned to ask for a title for the book, which he said was then being called "A Hero of Our Time." They spent a whole day thinking up titles; it became a joke.[3] At one point Camus thought of "Le Cri," but the announcement of a film of that name by Antoninini eliminated that one.[4] Finally it was Martin du Gard who came up with the title that would be used, as Camus would tell Bloch-Michel some days later.[3]

Camus provided the most succinct explanation of all for the novel in a *prière d'insérer* which he initialed:

> The man who speaks in *La Chute* delivers himself of a calculated confession. Exiled in Amsterdam in a city of canals and cold light, where he plays the hermit and the prophet, this former attorney waits for willing listeners in a shady bar.
>
> He has a modern heart, which means that he can't stand being judged. Thus he hastens to try himself but he does it so as better to judge others. The mirror into which he looks will finally be held out to others.
>
> Where does the confession begin, where the accusation? Is the man who speaks in this book putting himself on trial, or his era? Is he a particular case, or the man of the day? A sole truth, in any case, in this studied play of mirrors: pain, and what it promises.

As he wrote new pages of the book on the large glossy sheets which were his favorite writing paper, he would hand them to Suzanne Agnely for typing. She remarked that the book was being written in fragments; he would rewrite certain pages several times, or give her paragraphs (*béquets* in French printer's jargon) to be inserted. While creating, he might drop in at his Gallimard office at any time of day with new manuscript sheets, and even wait while they were being typed so that he could correct and revise in his office.

Sometimes he would ask his secretary what she thought of the manuscript he was giving her. She would reply frankly, and he seemed to be taking her suggestions seriously. She wondered why he had chosen Amsterdam as the scene of the story, for she herself felt it to be an attractive city. But he told her that he had found Amsterdam ugly, and to be there was punishment: appropriate surroundings for his judge-penitent. As for personal experience, she thought that she remembered that Camus told her, one night when he was quite drunk, that he had seen a suicide on the Pont des Arts and had felt remorse about not having saved the victim. But she also observed that the changes he was giving her regularly went in the direction of making *La Chute* less personal and more universal.[5]

He told Maria Casarès that the book was not a confession, but "the spirit of the times, and even the confused spirit of the times." She didn't feel that he was writing about himself, and yet he was working on it at a time when he had severe feelings of guilt, which occasionally manifested themselves in claustrophobia. Thus he would begin to suffocate in the street, tearing off his necktie as he walked in the door.[6]

Certainly the book was consciously spotted with references to the author that his friends would be quick to recognize. The turning down of the Legion of Honor, the refusal to lock his apartment or his automobile, his indifference to material possessions. Some claimed to recognize the night club dancer in a singer at Le Champo, just as they remembered when Camus got into a fistfight at the same cellar club.

More significantly (perhaps), the novel was quickly seen as a time bomb, a long-delayed reply to Sartre's August 1952 *Temps Modernes* attack (and of course Jeanson's in the same and an earlier issue). An American scholar, Warren Tucker, would later cite chapter and verse. No more than his hero, Camus could not accept a defeat. He chose to reply through art. He did it by exposing himself, thereby removing himself from the judgment of others. "I am like they, of course, we're in the same soup. Nevertheless I have an advantage, that of knowing it, which gives me the right to speak." Tucker compared specific accusations of Sartre and Jeanson with Clamence's self-accusations. Sartre and Jeanson say that Camus paid too much attention to style? Clamence will mock his own style, "the exactitude of my tone, the accuracy of my emotion . . ." Other examples:

> Sartre: "My God! Camus, how *serious* you are, and to use one of your words, how frivolous!"
> Clamence: "Without a doubt I gave the impression, at times, of taking life seriously. But very quickly the frivolity of that very seriousness showed itself to me."

> Jeanson: "You also had the tone of the Solitary, his arrogance and his haughtiness."
> Clamence: "In solitude, especially when tired, what do you expect, one easily takes oneself for a prophet."

Jeanson saw Camus as "that great voice soaring over factions," and Clamence sees himself "soaring by thought above this whole continent, which is in my power without knowing it." Sartre reminded Camus that he had been close to exemplary in 1945, and Clamence uses the word. Sartre accuses Camus of being a judge and Clamence admits that when threatened he became a judge. Sartre said that Camus needed someone to accuse, and "if it's not you, it will therefore be the universe," to which Clamence replies that everyone needs to be innocent at any price, even if "one must accuse humankind and the sky."[7] A similar analysis by French scholar André Abbou turned up additional parallels—Sartre accusing, Clamence admitting to be a bourgeois;

Sartre accusing, Clamence admitting that he utilized guilt by association
—"*l'amalgame comme défense.*" And so on.[8]

Between the writing of *La Chute* and its publication—more accurately,
between the early and final versions of the book—another decisive
event was taking place in Camus' life, and one hestitates to say in his
"public life," for it would inflict another personal wound before it was
over.

For a long time he had sought a way to intervene in the rapidly deteriorating Algerian situation, but he didn't know how or where. From
early youth he had been in the avant-garde of the French Algerian community in his belief in, active support of, emancipation of the Moslem
population—voting rights, but also economic and social equality, and
of course he had broken with the Communist Party because he would
not temper his pro-Moslem position. He did not think that Moslem
emancipation need necessarily signify the displacement of the French
(European) population of Algeria which had known no other home.
His family was of Algerian soil, and so were the families of his French
Algerian friends.

His friends were keeping him informed of the situation down there,
and when once again he had a platform from which he could be of
some influence, the column in *L'Express,* he asked old comrades such
as Charles Poncet to provide him with information on new developments. Poncet was a member of the European liberal minority, composed of men and women from the ranks of left-wing movements of the
1930s and 1940s, whose *pied noir* commitment (to remain in Algeria)
was tempered by the knowledge that Algeria would have to be transformed to accommodate the justified demands of its Moslem population. (Later official French policy would be to "integrate" the Moslems,
to grant them the same rights as French Algerians, but by then Algeria
was already lost.)

The liberals were soon creating forums for their activity—organizations, publications—although they were conscious of the fact that
they represented an infinite minority of the vocal French population of
the territory. They looked for Moslem moderates who would share their
hope that a new deal could be worked out without an escalation of violence. One minor medium for collaboration between the two communities was a theater group which evolved into an Association des Amis du
Théâtre d'Expression Arabe, whose members included Camus' old
friend Louis Miquel, and on the Moslem side Amar Ouzegane, his
nephew by marriage Mohammed Lebjaoui, and Boualem Moussaoui
(all in fact, although presumably without the knowledge of their French
counterparts, members of the FLN insurrectionary movement).

At one meeting of the Amis du Théâtre d'Expression Arabe, in a back room of the Café de la Marsa, owned by the Ouzegane family, probably after a discussion of blueprints for an Arab theater that Miquel and fellow architect Roland Simounet were working on for the Marine district, Lebjaoui took the floor to suggest that in the present crisis, with war at their doorstep, it might be time to talk about more pressing things than theater. They were working together in an atmosphere of friendship; why not take advantage of their close ties to find ways to bring the two communities together? At further meetings, usually held at Simounet's office, plans for more concrete activity were discussed. They decided to ask Camus, on his next visit to Algiers, to take a leading role in getting their movement off the ground, and to write its manifesto. But this was the moment of the French election campaign and Camus' involvement with the Mendès France candidacy through *L'Express*. "Between my personal work, which I want to pursue in spite of everything"—he would be writing *La Chute* now—"publishing, journalism, with all the obligations which it carries with it, I am constantly late with everything," Camus wrote Poncet on December 7. "Besides, I'm going to continue a little while longer, because this is the only way I have found to deal with the serious crisis from which I was suffering; then I'll go back to a more reasonable existence."

He added that he did not believe that Mendès would be able to solve everything alone; Camus discerned his limits, "and then I'm not a man of parties or elections." But he did see a chance that Mendès would be able to put France on its feet economically and morally, and he was the only one who could impose a program for Algeria which would respect everyone's rights. Camus promised to help his liberal friends, but not to come to Algeria before January 1956. He thought that the extra time would allow a new government to act, and to allow Camus and his friends to develop their own plans.[9]

After the elections, held at the beginning of January 1956, Poncet and his friends suggested that Camus make a speech in Algeria. He replied that he preferred to participate in a broader debate, with participation of both communities, and in any case he did not wish to be the sole speaker on the program. It was decided to invite representatives of the different religions represented in Algeria. The mayor was to rent them a hall in the Hôtel de Ville. Camus was kept informed of the plans, and he passed on his own suggestions. Finally he agreed that he would indeed launch his liberal friends' movement with a speech. Since there was no hope of obtaining authorization for a public meeting in the feverish atmosphere of Algiers, it was decided to call it a private one, with admission by invitation only. The date was set for January 22, 1956.[10]

Before that, in an *Express* column of November 1 commemorating
the FLN uprising just one year earlier, Camus had suggested that both
parties to the war agree, simultaneously, not to harm civilian popula-
tions. "This agreement will not modify any situation for the moment,"
he insisted. "It will be aimed only at removing from the conflict its
inexpiable character and to preserve, in the future, innocent lives." He
developed the idea in subsequent columns. "We must at last cry truce,
for all," he pleaded in a column entitled "Trêve pour les civils" on January 10. "Truce until it is time for solutions, truce to the massacre of
civilians, on one side and the other!" By this time his own role in the
Algerian crisis seemed to have been cut out: He could concentrate on
the effort to spare civilians, pending a settlement of the war. ("This
truce achieved, the rest is likely to follow," he added hopefully in a
follow-up column on January 17.)

So he would carry this message to the battlefront, to Algiers itself,
in the hopes of obtaining a hearing for men of reason on either side.

He flew to Algiers on January 18, where he was met at the airport
by Poncet and Miquel; his friends remarked that this time his habitual
banter was lacking. He had already received threatening letters from
Algeria—*poulets* in the French slang—and he was determined to be
cautious.[9] Worried that he might be kidnaped by extremists to prevent
him from speaking at their meeting, his friends wanted him to stay with
Poncet rather than at the Hôtel Saint-George. But on the first night
Camus returned to his hotel and phoned Poncet from there. On the
other hand, he later requested the protection of two or three bodyguards for the day of the meeting—chosen from among his childhood
friends of Belcourt.[10]

He found himself in the midst of feverish premeeting preparations
on the part of his French and Moslem friends. One meeting was held in
the Kasbah's Mahieddine Theater (in fact a rehearsal hall), with
Ouzegane present (probably on January 19). It was here that Camus
asked Emmanuel Roblès to be in the chair for the January 22 meeting.[11]
One participant at the Mahieddine meeting remembered that Camus
seemed ill at ease in that basement room; it seemed to him to suggest a
gathering of conspirators. When Camus remarked here: "We can't approve the crimes of either side," a young Moslem who seemed about
fifteen—he would later be killed in the war—got up to say that Arab attacks were justified by their liberation struggle. Camus replied severely
that ends did not justify means.[12]

Then it was the turn of the Comité des Libéraux d'Algérie to meet,
in a borrowed hall on Rue Drouillet. Camus refused to have any formal
connection with this group because its membership included Communists, but Roblès, who was an editor of the committee's organ, *Espoir-*

*Algérie,* persuaded him to attend anyway; Camus remained in the rear of the hall. Some Moslem nationalists took the floor, and Roblès observed that Camus seemed disturbed by their frank remarks. Camus and Roblès left the hall together to drive with André Rosfelder, a writer, later an engineer in San Diego, California, to Poncet's home. Camus spoke in a pessimistic vein and said that he felt the war was going to become even more atrocious. It was clear to Roblès that Camus still believed that the Moslems would be willing to live in a French federation, as Puerto Rico under U.S. authority. Roblès said firmly: "It's too late for Puerto Rico."[11] Another participant at the Liberals' meeting (he remembered it as a clandestine gathering) heard one of the Moslem speakers warn that if no agreement were reached to grant Algeria its independence, terrorism would be extended. Camus, standing at the back of the room in a trench coat, replied: "Then I wonder what I'm doing here." He walked out, and that ended the meeting.[13]

On January 21 a dozen persons met at the Baghdad Restaurant to eat couscous, to the surprise of the other patrons of the establishment—Moslems all—for in the tense atmosphere of the city French Algerians no longer came there. The diners were the nucleus of the future Comité pour une Trêve Civile. Poncet brought along Camus' college classmate Yves Dechezelles, now attorney for Messali Hadj and other Algerian nationalists of his tendency. But the Moslems present were all clearly pro-FLN, and Camus seemed upset when he realized that this was the case, although he said nothing to his friends.[14] (In fact Amar Ouzegane had a violent argument with Dechezelles, who he felt was attempting to influence Camus in favor of the Messali movement to the disadvantage of the FLN.)[15] After the dinner a preparatory meeting was held with representatives of the French and Algerian communities and the major religious groups; with some young actors from the Mahieddine troupe there were about fifty persons present in all. (Note that this may have been the meeting already described as having taken place on January 19, for it was here that Roblès was selected to be chairman of the January 22 meeting, which he was to learn on the twentieth.)[14]

In the end Mayor Chevallier had withdrawn his offer of space in City Hall for the January 22 meeting. So it was switched to the Cercle du Progrès, a building owned by Moslem organizations on the old Place du Gouvernement, and snugly located at the edge of the Basse Kasbah. (Here it was that the child Albert Camus had descended from his tram to complete the daily trip to the lycée on foot, and here he would find his favorite ice-cream vendor in the late afternoon.)

Two preparatory meetings were held at the Cercle du Progrès. At the first of these, Roblès was called to the telephone by an old friend, then head of the French political police, Renseignements Généraux. "How did you know I was here?" Roblès asked his friend. "I know everything," the officer replied snappily. He requested an urgent meeting at a café.

Roblès brought Roland Simounet along as a witness; his officer friend arrived alone. He said: "It isn't nice that you didn't invite me to your meeting next Sunday." Roblès gave him a puzzled look, so the policeman went on: "Fortunately I have invitations," and he extracted a few from a pocket. Roblès, who had ordered the printing of the invitations, and from a printer of whom he was sure, noticed at once that there was something strange about the cards the man from RG had handed him. If the type was the same, the row of dots designed for the name of the invited guest was not. "Would these cards have fooled you?" the officer asked. "Not me, but they'd certainly fool the people collecting them at the door."

The officer warned that the right-wing extremists—known as *ultras* —would stop at nothing to sabotage the meeting. It would be rough, not a simple bit of heckling. But he said that Roblès and his friends would have to arrange for their own means of protection. So Roblès immediately had new invitation cards made, and he signed each one. Then in a rubber eraser he carved a rough seal in the shape of a three-leaf clover and stamped each card to make it forgery-proof. When Camus arrived at the Cercle du Progrès, they told him what happened, and it was then that he enlisted his old Belcourt friends as bodyguards.[11]

It might be useful to stay the unfolding of events here, and to look at the preparations for the January 22 civil truce appeal from the point of view of the Moslem sponsors of the meeting. For they were all, secretly, leaders of the rebel organization known as Front de Libération Nationale (FLN). They were men in responsible and risky positions in the clandestine movement, men who would later be prominent in independent Algeria. In the order they appeared in the list of sponsors published with Camus' January 22 speech, they were:

> Amar Ouzegane
> Mouloud Amranne (or Amrane)
> Boualem Moussaoui
> Mohamed Lebjaoui

Ouzegane, a member of the FLN's underground brain trust, would later be a cabinet minister; Amranne would be attached to his cabinet; Moussaoui would become the new Algerian republic's ambassador to Paris; Lebjaoui, the first chief of the FLN's Fédération de France, would serve as an adviser to the first independent government.

The French Algerian members of the Comité pour une Trêve Civile en Algérie were Jean de Maisonseul, Roland Simounet, Charles Poncet, Emmanuel Roblès, Maurice Perrin, and Louis Miquel.

From the point of view of the Moslem members, this civil truce committee was an FLN front. It was conceived by Ouzegane, who at the time was believed by the French to be apolitical; all remembered his exclusion from the Communist Party, while none of course could know that he had written the draft program of the insurrectionary army. His idea was to create front organizations, even for illusory goals such as civil truce, so that French Algerians would realize what Moslems already knew—that no such remedy would work now, violence being the only salvation for those seeking justice. So the FLN never had any illusions about the success of the proposal for a civil truce. On the other hand, the rebels hoped to make a large number of French Algerians neutral—and a minority revolutionary. The FLN went so far as to publish a communiqué disavowing Camus' civil truce initiative, so that a fence-sitting Moslem who had not yet declared himself for the insurrection nevertheless refused to participate in the appeal.[15]

Lebjaoui, who was later caught by the French and spent five years in prison, eventually wrote a book in which he recorded the Byzantine intrigues leading up to Camus' civil truce appeal. He described one of the preparatory meetings—at which "Camus seemed to us both tense and determined, resolved, but anxious, precise in his judgments, but uncertain as to solutions,—and still very far, especially, from the realities of the moment." For Camus the war was criminal and stupid. He hoped to obtain the agreement of the French Government, the FLN, and Messali Hadj's movement—which Camus wrongly considered to be of equal importance—for the civil truce scheme. In coming to Algeria he also hoped to make contact with the nationalists, without daring to hope that he would actually be able to meet representatives of the FLN!

After the European extremists printed their fake invitation cards, a second and very restricted meeting was held at the Cercle du Progrès, so reports Lebjaoui, to take a closer look at the situation. (This may have been on Saturday night, January 21.) Those present included Ouzegane, Amranne, Lebjaoui, Camus and two or three friends, including Maisonseul. Camus confirmed that the situation was risky, for a high French official he knew personally had said that his own life might be in jeopardy (from the *ultras*) because of his support of the Front Républicain alongside Mendès France in the recent French legislative elections. Camus even wondered whether the meeting should not be called off. The Moslems advised against that and promised that the security of the Cercle du Progrès could be guaranteed.

In Lebjaoui's later account of the events, it was then that he took
Camus aside and, after asking him to keep the secret, revealed that he
belonged to the FLN. Camus gasped. But immediately afterward he
showed his satisfaction: At last a member of the FLN to talk to. Lebjaoui went on to explain that the FLN was bound neither to Moscow
nor to Cairo, and was prepared to consider French Algerians full-
fledged citizens of independent Algeria—but for the moment it was the
Moslems who were not. Lebjaoui insisted that the FLN was ready to respect the rules of civil truce if the French Government would. "In that
case," Camus exclaimed, "perhaps we've won!" But the Moslem tempered his enthusiasm by repeating his conviction that the French would
not accept. If the FLN agreed to a civil truce and the French did not,
Camus promised to proclaim that fact everywhere in France.

Lebjaoui then assumed personal responsibility for the security of
the meeting on Sunday. The Moslems had heard that Camus might be
abducted, so Lebjaoui suggested that they put him up in safer quarters.
But after thinking about it Camus felt that this might be considered running away. In leaving, Camus embraced Lebjaoui and said: "From now
on, Lebjaoui, I want you to consider me like a brother."[16]

For Amar Ouzegane, once Camus' superior in the Communist
Party, the civil truce proposal was a tactical operation quite in conformity with the Plateforme de la Soumman, the Algerian Army of National
Liberation program which he had drafted, and which had analyzed tac-
tics with respect to the French in Algeria, liberals included. But the
FLN had to keep its role in the civil truce appeal secret. If Ouzegane
had refused the chairmanship of the committee and had declined to
speak in public on January 22, it was to safeguard the committee's impact. The progress of planning for the Sunday meeting was being
discussed nightly by the FLN militants at the Ouzeganes' Café de la
Marsa over a Spanish card game, la ronda, after which they would go
to Ouzegane's home for a working session. The political advisory group
which discussed the civil truce appeal was a virtual brain trust of the
Algerian revolution. But if one of its members, Abane Ramdame, was
surprised at the importance Ouzegane attached to the civil truce,
Ouzegane saw it as a psychological warfare operation. They didn't necessarily want the truce appeal to fail, but they knew that it would.[17]

On the Sunday of the meeting the Moslems met Camus during the afternoon. He seemed troubled; he had heard reports that there would be a
mass counterdemonstration by the European ultras, and he wondered if
the meeting should not be canceled after all. Lebjaoui replied that the
extremists would indeed demonstrate, but that if the meeting were can-

celed it would discourage all those trying to bring the two sides together; a threat from the *ultras* would suffice to give them their victory. Camus agreed. "I shall speak, at any cost. These hot-headed Algérois who would like to make me retreat better realize that I'm an Algerian myself with a head as hot as theirs."

There was another problem: Camus insisted on having a Moslem representative on the platform. But the FLN leaders could not risk sitting up there, and thereby become targets for the police. And neutral Moslem leaders unaware of the role of the FLN in the meeting feared that the FLN would consider them pro-French if they shared the platform with these French Algerians. There was a seat for Ferhat Abbas, but he arrived late (he too was unaware that the FLN was secretly backing the meeting). Finally they saw Dr. Abdelaziz Khaldi, an advocate of a "third force" neither French nor FLN, and brought him to the platform. (Later on when he was "sentenced" to death by the FLN he was saved by Lebjaoui, who merely issued him a warning.)[18]

Camus had also wanted the presence of his old friend Sheikh El Okbi, whom he had defended in *Alger Républicain* against the charge of having the Grand Mufti assassinated. Roblès arranged to meet him, escorted by two young Arabs who picked him up and took him to El Okbi's home after great precautions. Clearly they were under nationalist discipline, Roblès decided, and by now he had begun to suspect that the FLN was involved in the organization of the civil truce appeal; before the meeting was over many of the other French Algerians connected with the civil truce committee would feel the same way.

Roblès found the old man in bed with a fever. But when El Okbi heard that Camus wanted him, he promised to come, and indeed he would be carried into the meeting on a stretcher. Camus went to the rear of the hall to greet him, and leaned over the stretcher so they could embrace.[11]

Starting at 2 P.M. on Sunday everyone was at his post. By three the main hall and the small adjoining rooms were jammed, the crowd half French Algerian, half Moslem—something that had not been seen in Algeria for a voluntary endeavor in a long time. One man without an invitation insisted so strongly on being let in that Roblès was called down to the gate. The man said: "I am Camus' brother." It was the first time that Roblès had met Lucien Camus.[11]

Just as testimony varies as to the size of the crowd (Poncet put it at 3,000, *Le Monde*'s correspondent at 1,200, with 1,000 anti-meeting demonstrators in the parade across town to the Place du Gouvernement), there are varying estimates as the size of the protective force put in place by the FLN. The significant point was that the Moslems were on their home territory here. If Bab el Oued, the mixed-European working class district, began only on the other side of the square, on this side *they* were in control. The Kasbah was at their back. Only shortly before, a liberal French politician had been chased out of a room in City Hall despite the fact that the meeting was being chaired by a police commissioner. But it would be different at the Cercle du Progrès. When the first cries were heard from the *ultras* outside on the square—"Camus to the wall!" "Mendès to the wall!" and "Down with the Jews," Camus left the hall to inspect protective forces and also to note that the vast Place du Gouvernement was occupied by thousands of Moslems who had descended from the Kasbah to contain the opposition demonstrators—a human sea.[15] (Having good relations with the Prefect of Algiers, Jean de Maisonseul had told him about the civil truce meeting and was promised that the prefect would personally take responsibility for security on the square.)[19]

Impressed by the protective forces, Camus asked Ouzegane: "Are your friends armed?" Ouzegane replied ingenuously: "I don't know, but if they are, they have orders to use their arms only in an emergency." Indeed, in addition to the "human sea" outside the square, there were guards posted around the building, a double row of guards on the stairway winding up to the meeting room, and boxing champions in the hall itself. The organization of the protective service was in the hands of the chief of armed and political action of the FLN for the city of Algiers, who carried a machine gun concealed under his raincoat, which raincoat also covered the FLN colors embroidered on his jacket. Now Camus was quite certain that he was in the hands of the FLN.[20]

So the meeting could begin. Roblès took the chair. A member of a Catholic order, Les Pères Blancs, represented that church, a pastor attended for the Protestants; Dr. Khaldi ostensibly spoke for the Moslems, although there was no official representative of that group, just as no Jewish representative attended. When at last Ferhat Abbas entered the hall, he climbed to the platform while Camus was speaking. Interrupted by the applause for Abbas, Camus turned to greet him. They embraced for a long moment—an emotional one for the audience.

Camus' speech repeated the proposal he had already been making through the columns of *L'Express*. He believed that it was still possible, "today, on a specific point, to join together first of all, then to save human lives, and thus to prepare a more favorable climate for reasonable discussion." But this required that *"le mouvement arabe"* and the French, without entering into contact with each other or committing themselves beyond this, declare simultaneously that the civilian population will be respected and protected. In this way innocent lives would be saved, but it would also offer hope of future understanding.

During Camus' speech angry shouts were coming from the square outside. Camus would have heard the cry "Camus to the stake." Poncet saw his friend "pale and on edge," struggling to keep his sangfroid, glancing with despair at the large windows facing the angry mob. Down below, although the speakers and their audience could not see them, some of the *ultras* were raising their arms in Fascist salutes.[11] The extremists, who seemed prepared to break through the cordon of gendarmes, also began to throw stones at the large windows, breaking a few. Word came that the police might be overcome by the *ultras,* which would mean open confrontation between FLN militants and right-wing French extremists, all this to protect Camus. He began to read his text more rapidly. Although an exchange of views had been planned—at Camus' insistence—as soon as he finished talking he murmured something to Roblès, who proposed that the meeting be adjourned.[21] There was not even time to circulate the brief text of support of the civil truce appeal among the audience, and only a few dozen signatures were obtained. The text of Camus' talk was published in Algiers, with the printer's name purposely rendered illegible to avoid reprisals—so tense was the climate.[10] (Camus would reprint the text of his speech in *Actuelles III.*)

The crowd got out safely, walking past the bonfire that the *ultras* had lit in front of the bronze statue of the Duke of Orléans on horseback. Roblès accompanied Camus to the Saint-George, and later phoned Poncet to tell him how worried Camus had been that his action for concord and fraternity might have become the occasion for a tragic clash between the communities.[14]

The next day *Le Journal d'Alger,* for which Edmond Brua worked, and which was owned by a wealthy French Algerian inspired by liberal Mayor Jacques Chevallier, was the only newspaper in the territory to publish Camus' appeal in its entirety. An extremist friend of Brua who met him on the street commented: "If we had known what Camus was going to say we wouldn't have opposed the meeting as we did."[22]

Before leaving Algiers, Camus called on Governor General Jacques Soustelle, who said that he would be willing to discuss the possibility of a civil truce, but that in no case would it cover those who were civilians by day and guerrillas by night.[14] Another version has it that Soustelle tried to convince Camus, during a long evening's discussion, that the civil truce idea was impractical because one side, at least, would never comply with it.[23] Later Camus phoned Brua to thank him for printing his talk in full, for, he said, Soustelle had read it in *Le Journal d'Alger.*[22]

Camus was driven to Maison Blanche Airport for his return flight to France with Roblès and Rosfelder at either side of him in the rear seat of an automobile. Roblès was armed and believed that Rosfelder was too, but Camus wasn't aware of this. They were protected up ahead and at the rear by friends in other automobiles, but the one behind them got lost en route.[11]

Back in Paris, Camus wrote Poncet that he felt he understood the Arabs better now. "And what I understand reinforces my decision to sacrifice everything to the truce." He feared that he had disappointed his Arab and his French friends; was it because he stuck so close to the truce theme in his speech, or because the meeting was limited in its objectives? He felt that he had been right but desired his friend's opinion. "One is more alone in Paris than in Algiers, despite appearances."[9]

In Algiers the civil truce committee remained active. A draft convention for a truce was drawn up by a small committee. (Camus gave a copy to Dechezelles to submit to Messali Hadj.) Then on February 6 the new Premier, Guy Mollet, arrived in Algiers, but under a barrage of tomatoes tossed by *ultras* he withdrew his appointment of a liberal Governor General and substituted a hard-liner, Robert Lacoste. On February 12, Mollet received Camus' friends, who defined themselves as the only group uniting Frenchmen and Moslems in brotherhood. But Mollet did not seem to be listening. He took the truce proposal away with him, saying that he needed time to think about it. He also promised that he would call the liberals in later, and requested that they keep the meeting confidential. Finally, he asked them to maintain contact with the FLN, to which they replied that they had no such contacts. (In fact Ouzegane and Moussaoui were in the room as part of their delegation.)

Time passed. So the liberal group decided, in the absence of a reply from Mollet or his proconsul Lacoste, to send a delegation to Paris to meet the Premier again. Miquel and Khaldi agreed to go, and traveled to Paris carrying a draft letter to Mollet which Camus accepted with a few changes. They obtained an appointment with a member of the Premier's staff through Robert Namia, and the official promised to arrange a meeting with Mollet. Then *Le Monde* reported, erroneously, that the delegates of the truce committee had already met Mollet. Apparently Khaldi was responsible for the false report—but he had nothing to do with the FLN and had come with no instructions to sabotage the mission. Camus was dismayed; not only was the report untrue but it spoke of a "truce" rather than a "civil truce," and this in the context of dispatches reporting new acts of terrorism in Algeria. Camus insisted on a correction of the newspaper story, and drafted a letter to *Le Monde* with the help of Miquel and Lebjaoui (who had meanwhile arrived in France). The newspaper printed the denial over Miquel's signature.

But the delegation would never see Mollet. Finally Miquel could waste no more time in Paris waiting to be summoned by the Premier, and he returned to Algiers. The civil truce movement would die out altogether after Maisonseul's arrest in May, and in the deteriorating political climate—the beginning of true civil war—in Algeria.[24]

By that time Camus had himself withdrawn once more from the political arena. The tomato incident had seen to that. Power would henceforth be in the streets of Algiers; what could he do? He told Jean Daniel that he would no longer write about Algeria in *L'Express* or elsewhere,[25] but of course he had already withdrawn from that magazine weeks earlier.

A letter he wrote on February 10 to Jean Gillibert already contained a hint of this withdrawal, but with signs that he had not yet given up all hope.

> There is a solitude that one must accept, against which I balked for years, because everything that separates horrifies me, against which I balk still, but which is inevitable, if one has a minimum of standards. One would like to be loved, recognized, for what one is, and by everyone. But that is an adolescent desire. Sooner or later one must get old, agree to be judged, or sentenced, and to receive gifts of love (desire, tenderness, friendship, solidarity) as unmerited. Morality is of no help. Only, truth . . . that is the uninterrupted seeking of it, the decision to tell it when one sees it, on every level, and to live it, gives a meaning, a direction, to one's march. But in an era of bad faith, the man who does not want to renounce separating true from false is condemned to a certain kind of exile. At least he knows that this exile presupposes a reunion, present and future, the only valid one, that it is our duty to serve. . . . I returned from Algeria rather desperate. What is happening confirmed my conviction. For me it is a personal misfortune. But we must hold out, everything can't be compromised.[26]

In March, Emmanuel Roblès was in Paris, on personal business, but also on a mission for the Comité des Libéraux (to make contact with the French Socialist Party in the person of *pied noir* Claude de Fréminville). He saw Camus, and afterwards noted a remark by Camus that struck him particularly. "If a terrorist throws a grenade in the Belcourt market where my mother shops, and if he kills her," Camus told him, "I would be responsible if, to defend justice, I defended terrorism. I love justice but I also love my mother."[27]

# 43

◆

## REQUIEM FOR A NUN

The more I produce the less I am certain. On the road
along which the artist walks, night falls ever more densely.
Finally he dies blind. . . .

Letter to René Char*

When she received her copy of *La Chute,* Simone de Beauvoir opened
it with curiosity. She had been angered by Camus' public statements on
Algeria, in which statements she detected a *pied noir* bias, but she had
also been moved when she learned to what extent certain attacks on
*L'Homme révolté* had made him suffer. She also knew that Camus had
been having some painful moments in his private life, and that he had
been shaken. Now in *La Chute* she rediscovered the Camus she had
met during the war. At last he had achieved his long-desired goal, to
"fill the gap between his truth and his personality." The Camus who
was generally so stiff and formal nowadays was heartrending in the simplicity with which he offered himself up to public view in this book. But
then she decided that his sincerity stopped short. He began to disguise
his defeats in conventional anecdotes; from penitent he became judge,
removing all the sting from his confession in placing it too explicitly in
the service of his resentments.[1]

For when *La Chute* appeared at last in May 1956 (it had gone to
the printer on March 19), the reactions were to be nearly as curious as
the book itself. The French literary world saw it more as a confession
than as an account of the times. It did not strike most people, as it had
Beauvoir and presumably Sartre, as a revelation about his private life,

* Quoted in the Pléiade edition of Camus' work.

for very few people knew anything about that, even in the world of letters. What moved readers was Camus' return to a questioning, a pessimism which seemed the contrary of the affirmations of *L'Homme révolté*. At least one careful reader would later discover a parallel between *La Chute* and Sartre's autobiographical *Les Mots,* believing that the former had probably influenced the latter.

Camus himself had suffered a fall. After *L'Homme révolté,* which disappointed many of his friends, there had been (what they felt was) his silence on Algeria, the ambiguities of his politics. It was a fine book, but also a troubled and searching one—Dostoevskian, surely.[2] Jean Daniel, who had feared that Camus was becoming a starchy classic, with more dryness than mystery, was reassured.[3]

In the first version of a study on Camus, *La Mer et les Prisons,* Camus' editor Roger Quilliot had predicted that henceforth the subjective and confidential character of Camus' work would be strengthened, with less emphasis on moral and abstract questions. When Camus sent a copy of the new novel to Quilliot, he dedicated it: "To Roger Quilliot, to show that his prophecy was right."[4]

Later, when the scholars got to work on it, they would find a great deal more than that in *La Chute*. Christianity (the hero's name is of course an allusion to John the Baptist, "the voice of one crying in the wilderness") and Dostoevsky as well. When Conor Cruise O'Brien pointed out in *The Spectator* that the novel had Christian overtones, Camus confirmed, in a letter to his British publisher, that this approach was justified.[5]

The book was also a popular success. Sales reached 500 to 1,000 copies a day a month after publication. And he was now getting better terms than ever from his publisher: a 15 per cent royalty and a two-thirds share of subsidiary rights, which included translations into foreign languages, rather than the usual fifty-fifty split.[6]

He took the time now to settle a personal problem. His presence at the Rue Madame apartment had not always been a good thing either for him or for his wife, and he had often found temporary lodgings elsewhere. What he really needed, for his work as well as his independence, was a place of his own, and that he now found on the Rue de Chanaleilles, a narrow street connecting the Rues Vaneau and Barbet de Jouy—once more within a ten-minute walk of the Gallimard building. He rented a small apartment from the Comte de Tocqueville, great-nephew of Alexis de Tocqueville, on the third floor of a town house on that quiet street. But most importantly, his great friend René Char lived in the same building.[7] Char of course divided his time between the Rue de Chanaleilles and his retreat at L'Isle-sur-la-Sorgue, with the latter receiving the lion's share of his attention. He may even have been absent when Camus moved into the new flat, for the Pléiade edition of Camus' work quotes from two letters in May, letters which say something of Camus' admiration for Char, and of Camus' own state of mind at the time:

> Before I met you, I did without poetry. Nothing of what was published concerned me. For the past two years, on the contrary, I have an empty spot inside me, a hollowness which I can only fill in reading you, but then to the brim. (May 16)
> The question is only to know what life, at least in what it contains that is worth adoring, is to become. That alone suffices to make one suffer. But if we are unhappy, at least we are not deprived of truth. That I would not know all alone. Simply, I know it with you. (May 18)

The Rue de Chanaleilles apartment consisted of two moderately sized rooms off an entrance hall, one used as a living room, the other as a bedroom (but it was here that Camus would install the stand-up desk he used for writing); both rooms faced the little street. (Char's apartment was identical in size but with a different arrangement of room space.) The apartment came furnished, but he quickly began to add things that he liked: heavy Louis XIII (or Spanish) wood furniture, Romanesque statues also of wood. He found an old Italian screen with a monkey motif. Soon the apartment would be decorated with portraits of Dostoevsky and of Nietzsche; there would be books piled here, there, and everywhere, but nevertheless giving the impression of some order. (Yet a later visitor had the impression that Camus had just moved in, for nothing seemed in place; there were paintings on the floor propped against the walls, etc.) In addition to writing at his stand-up desk he could work at the large living-room table piled high with books. And he used the little kitchen, making his own porridge and eggs in the morning, bought himself a laundry iron, a boiler for clothes, and other equipment a housekeeper requires. Soon he had a routine, writing in the mornings, going off to Gallimard or to rehearsals in the afternoon while a cleaning woman worked in the apartment.[8]

Leaving the new apartment, turning left, and left again at the end of the street, he was only a couple of hundred feet from 1 bis, Rue Vaneau, Gide's home, and his own for a while. (A plaque commemorates Gide's occupancy.) Behind Camus' building is the Cité Vaneau, where his old polemical enemy Emmanuel d'Astier de la Vigerie lived. (In that literary neighborhood par excellence, it would be only too easy to note other correspondences, e.g., just opposite the Camus-Char house, Antoine de Saint-Exupéry had lived in the 1930s. On the way to the Gallimard building, he would pass the Rue de Bellechasse residence of the Daudets, site of a famous literary salon which Bernanos had frequented—and so on.)

The pleasure of having a place of his own was interrupted almost immediately by news from Algeria, where the good Jean de Maisonseul, Camus' friend from early youth, had been arrested by the French security police.

Maisonseul had of course been involved in the January civil truce meeting, and he was a member of the committee set up to promote its purposes. His private view was that even if a civil truce lasted only a few days it would have the effect of tacit recognition of the FLN rebels by the French, which could then lead to negotiations. But the diehard colonial administrators knew that too, which was an excellent reason to attempt to frame one of the liberals on a treason charge. Otherwise, Maisonseul's views and activities were similar to those of his fellow liberal French Algerians, all of whom sought a peaceful way out of the crisis, giving satisfaction to Moslem demands while allowing French Algerians to remain in the only country which they had ever known.

What had actually happened—but Camus did not know it then—was that Maisonseul was temporarily in possession of a letter from a young woman who on departure from Algiers for Morocco, and almost as an afterthought, had asked him to deliver it to a young Algerian lawyer. (It contained information on Moroccans who sympathized with the Algerian independence movement.) Busy with the plan for the reconstruction of earthquake-torn Orléansville, Maisonseul had not had time to deliver the letter immediately, and instead took it to his office, where he slipped it into a book lying on his desk. When he looked for the letter some days later he couldn't find it. Walking into his office on May 25, he found that the French security police, the DST, had arrived ahead of him. They searched the room in his presence, and as if by miracle found the letter where he had not placed it (at the bottom of a dusty drawer), and also spotted the file on the civil truce project. Maisonseul assumed that someone in his office had found the letter and arranged for the search, and he was also sure that he had been chosen as a victim (the new Governor General Lacoste had made it clear that he didn't want to wage war on two fronts—against Moslem terrorists *and* French liberals). So Maisonseul risked a long prison sentence for endangering national security.[9]

Camus was also to fight on two fronts. He quickly composed a letter to Premier Mollet, sent a wire of protest to Lacoste, and at the same time a strong letter to *Le Monde* (dated May 28, published in the newspaper on May 30). In this letter, once again addressed to a *Mon-*

*sieur le Directeur,* Camus said that he had remained silent on Algeria "so as not to add to French misfortune and because, finally, I approved nothing of what was being said on the right or the left." But he could not remain silent in the face of "such stupid and brutal initiatives"— which happened to be damaging to French interests in Algeria. He had known Maisonseul for twenty years (actually it was closer to twenty-five). Maisonseul had never been involved in politics; his only passions were architecture and painting. He had been responsible for the recon-struction of Orléansville—building Algeria while others were destroying it. Only recently he had been involved in the civil truce appeal, which was in no way a negotiation, only a humanitarian proposal, and no one had called it criminal. A press dispatch had spoken of an "organi-zation" in connection with Maisonseul's arrest. That could only be the civil truce committee. Maisonseul was also reportedly a member of the liberal group in Algiers, but was that a crime? Did the extremists now rule Algeria? Then let Guy Mollet say so. Camus warned that he would make use of all of his possibilities to alert public opinion and to demand Maisonseul's release, after which there would have to be reparation.

In a postscriptum he added that the latest reports said that Maison-seul had been accused only of imprudent conduct, and that the charges would not be so serious. But, Camus observed, the damage had already been done on the radio and on the front pages.

Nothing happened. Camus wrote a second appeal for Maisonseul, this one published as a column under the bold black headline: GOU-VERNEZ! in the June 3–4 issue of *Le Monde.* Camus quoted Governor General Lacoste, who said that he hadn't been told in advance about the arrest and that local authorities were "grieved and surprised." In that case, why was Maisonseul still in jail, not even allowed to see his attorney? In other words, neither the mainland French Government nor the Government General governed in Algeria. If there was a plot, it was therefore against national authority and the French future in Algeria, for if liberals were enemies, then France was saying it would not in-clude *la justice généreuse* among its weapons. It was not enough for the government to regret Maisonseul's arrest; it had to release him from ar-bitrary detention, repair the injustice. Meanwhile, noted Camus, France was delivering arms to Egypt and to Syria which would be used against French soldiers sooner or later. Who was the traitor, Maisonseul or those who sold arms to the Arab states?

> The prolonged detention of Jean de Maisonseul is a scandal of arbi-trary behavior for which the government, and it alone henceforth, must be held responsible. For the last time, before appealing directly to public opinion, and persuading it to protest by every pos-sible means, I ask the government to release Jean de Maisonseul without delay, and to grant him public reparation.

The story, as Maisonseul heard it later, was that the Premier's office had phoned Camus to ask that he cease his campaign. Camus refused to take the call, but had Suzanne Agnely reply that he would stop writing articles when Maisonseul was released or Camus himself was arrested. (Charles Poncet, who visited Camus in early June while on a business trip to Paris, was told by Camus that because of Maisonseul's arrest he had broken off relations with the French Government, and that if Maisonseul were not released he would organize a demonstration with his friends of *Révolution Prolétarienne*.) The public prosecutor of Algiers was summoned to the Ministry of Justice in Paris and the day after his return Maisonseul was released on parole. His case was transferred to Paris, where Camus engaged a well-known attorney to defend his friend, but Maisonseul would have to wait until General de Gaulle's return to power for a *non-lieu* (no ground for prosecution) to be handed down, and his reintegration into the civil service took some additional months.

Later, on Algerian independence, Maisonseul (whose great-grandfather, a marquis, commanded the port of Algiers under Napoleon III) was appointed curator of the Musée National des Beaux-Arts in Algiers, after which he directed the Institut d'Urbanisme of the University of Algiers until 1975, when he returned to France.

René Char was back in Paris, and Camus could talk to him, could confide in him, for Char was at once intense in his art and a regular fellow, with all of the rough-tough aspect of a Galindo or a RUA player, and yet a man who shared the literary life of Saint-Germain-des-Prés (and his aversion to it). Char could also understand how Camus felt about French Algeria, and about those on the "female left" as well as on the right who were threatening its existence. For example, Char remarked to Camus at this time that the young intellectual generation reminded him of suppositories, and no one need be surprised that they did what all suppositories do: melt.[10]

At last Camus had a script for his adaptation of *Requiem for a Nun,* Faulkner's strange tale of expiation visited on a Southern couple in the person of a black prostitute who is also their angel, representing the author's own gloss on his early novel *Sanctuary*. He had turned over a copy of the original Faulkner novel to friend Louis Guilloux, who had worked up a rough translation of it, what the French call a *"monstre,"* so that Camus could revise and adapt from that for the Paris stage. Camus and Guilloux had undertaken this quite independently of the translation of Faulkner's novel which Gallimard had commissioned from Maurice-Edgar Coindreau, a celebrated translator of American fiction and then a professor at Princeton. A great deal has been said about Camus' adaptation, much of it in an attempt to clarify the origins of the major changes he made for the stage. For if Camus' stage version was different from the original Faulkner novel, so was an English-language stage version made under Faulkner's supervision, and some of the differences were similar. Did Camus have access to this English-language stage version, did those responsible for that version use Camus', or were the similarities coincidental?

Ruth Ford, Faulkner's actress friend, had adapted the novel for the stage, and it was presented as a play at the Royal Court Theatre in London in November 1957 and in New York in January 1959. It has been said that Ford used Camus' Paris adaptation in making her own. In fact the best evidence is that Camus—in all innocence—possessed a copy of the Ford adaptation when he did his.[11] He did receive a copy of the Ford version,[12] and he would have considered it logical to use revisions that Faulkner and his friend had themselves thought necessary in the interest of creating a more playable play. But Camus certainly went beyond these changes, even if he had them and used them, tightening the dialogue to create speech his actors could be comfortable with, developing characters, even rewriting scenes—for example, tempering what he felt to be the preachy quality of the final scene in the prison. He hesitated to use "Nun" in the title, but Coindreau convinced him that the term implied religiosity without necessarily implying orthodoxy, whereas "Saint," for example, would not have been appropriate. Camus explained what he had done to the original novel in his introduction to the Gallimard edition of Coindreau's translation in 1957. In sum, he had wished to retain Faulkner's style, but without destroying its theatrical possibilities.

For Camus was particularly anxious to have an actable play now. For the first time in his career he was not only writing or adapting a play for the Paris stage, but he was to direct it as well. He would choose the actors, put them through their paces; he would be responsible for the total effect, and he took the job seriously, as he made it clear in his unhappy complaints to Maria Casarès after the first reading of the play on June 18, 1956.

In the role of Gowan Stevens, there would be Michel Auclair, star of the cinema and the classic stage. But in this first play with whose casting he was concerned since the inception of his wife's illness, he could not associate the name of Maria Casarès with his own; a new actress had to be found.[13]

With Mrs. Harry Baur's associate, his bistrot and café companion Robert Cérésol, Camus had been going to the theater a good deal that spring, seeking an actress to play Temple Drake, the principal feminine role in Faulkner's work. He collected theater programs so that he would have a list of candidates for future casting. The friends not only saw all of the popular boulevard plays, but did an earnest survey of the Comédie Française classic productions. Sometimes they would drop in on rehearsals.

One day in May, on her return from the theater (she was playing at the Atelier in Chekhov's *The Seagull*), Catherine Sellers found a note from her mother saying that Monsieur Albert Camus had telephoned to talk to her about a part. She returned the call and they made an appointment to meet at Brasserie Lipp. Then twenty-nine, Sellers was by no means a star, and she knew that he was a famous writer, but she had a feeling at once that he was treating her as an equal, and that set her at ease in the first minutes of their meeting. He asked her if she would be willing to play the leading part in *Requiem,* and gave her a copy of the script. If she liked it, it was hers; there would be no audition.

But she was off on a tour of Algeria. She promised to read the play and to give him her decision on her return. It was a positive one; the first rehearsal was scheduled for August 10.

Catherine Sellers had been born in Paris of North African Jewish parents. During the Nazi occupation her father had been sent to the Auschwitz concentration camp, where he died. But he had first managed to get his wife and young daughter out of France, to Algeria, where they spent the remainder of the war in relative safety. Catherine was to obtain a degree in English literature, specializing in the Elizabethan theater, but she decided that she preferred to participate in theater rather than talk about it. She married an Englishman and lived for a year with him in *Wuthering Heights* country. Back in France, and alone, she got her first part in García Lorca's *Blood Wedding* in 1952, then played in Bernanos' *Dialogues des Carmelites* before Camus saw her in *The Seagull*.[14]

In Catherine Sellers, Camus would be discovering something new: a person of the theater who was articulate, who knew and cared about the history and literature of the stage (its texts), someone with whom one could discuss repertory. She could be his actress, but she could also be his helper in theatrical enterprises. She could read the plays he would choose for his theater-to-be; more, she could listen to him talk about his writing. Of course he could have found other partners capable of holding their own in a dialogue, but why look further? Catherine was a ravishing young woman, svelte and clear-eyed, and (of course) a fellow Mediterranean.

Meanwhile Camus had settled down in earnest to complete the stories for *L'Exil et le Royaume*. But he was being interrupted continually by a stream of visitors from Algeria, each of whom was anxious to keep him informed of developments in the rapidly deteriorating situation; in a relatively brief period he had seen a dozen such friendly emissaries.[10] He was getting ready to leave for Palerme, that refuge at L'Isle-sur-la-Sorgue, but before leaving there was yet another cause to take up, that of the workers of Poland, who had risen in protest against their conditions, to be met by bloody repression on the part of the Communist authorities. "The regime is not a normal one in which a worker must choose between misery and death," wrote Camus in a front-page protest in the daily *Franc-Tireur* on July 13. (He also signed a petition on behalf of the workers arrested after the uprising.) By that time he was already in L'Isle-sur-la-Sorgue, having left Paris in a state of total nervous exhaustion, as he confided to a friend.[15]

He had nevertheless promised himself a busy month in Provence. He had to work out the stage directions of *Requiem* first of all, for that August 10 deadline was inexorable. But he also hoped, at long last, to get started on the ambitious novel that had been occupying his mind (and his journal) for so long, *Le Premier Homme*.[10] Soon after his arrival he had completed revising the text of his adaptation of *Requiem* that Gallimard was to publish in September, simultaneously with the play's opening at the Mathurins.[16]

He also polished his short stories so that they were in shape for publication—although he continued to have doubts that they were precisely as he would have liked them to be.[17] The original plan had been to publish *L'Exil et le Royaume* in September, but with *La Chute* still selling so briskly, and the literary prize season drawing attention away from everything except prize candidates through autumn, he thought that December would be a better month for publication.[16] But before Gallimard could send the stories to the printer, he had called them back again, and he took a final look at them in October when *Requiem* was out of his hands. Did he also work on *Le Premier Homme* now? No, he was not quite ready for that, and he would again promise himself to begin in October.[10] Otherwise, he was sharing the heat and the isolation of L'Isle-sur-la-Sorgue this summer with his mother; in early August he put her on a plane for the flight back to Algiers.

Camus managed to spend a month each year (at least a month), during school holidays, with his children. He was conscious of his role as a father, and of his twins' need of a father. As is often the case, he had excellent rapport with his daughter. He felt that Catherine shared his vitality; he remarked that her handwriting resembled his, as well as her way of thinking. And of course the rapport was less good with his son, perhaps because he expected more from Jean. Camus felt that Jean was gifted and he didn't want to see the gift wasted; that made him seem severe. And Jean would grow to look more and more like his father, adopting his attitudes—his *pudeur* and his irony, his responses (and failures to respond). Jean even had a little raincoat like his father's familiar one, for their outings together. Jean was a frail child, but in the end it was Catherine rather than Jean who gave the Camus cause for concern, when a mysterious attack was diagnosed as rheumatoid arthritis. (An old fear of hospitals came through then; Camus refused to allow Catherine to be taken away from home for tests; they had to be carried out at the Rue Madame.)

Camus and his wife took pains to minimize the celebrity of Albert Camus the writer, but their father's fame gradually filtered through. Once, when Camus was angry at his son over a domestic incident and ordered him from the dinner table and to bed, Jean walked off mumbling: "Good night, minor writer of no importance."[12]

Rehearsals began on schedule on August 10, and now, for the first time, Camus was in full charge of a theater. He showed himself to be a pragmatic director, without a theory of theater. His new heroine remarked the importance of body movement on his stage. At the time, there were two kinds of theater in France: what she felt was the talky kind, and the deep psychology of the Russians. Camus put the two together and added the body. Later she would decide that what the younger directors were doing in the Paris theater of the 1970s Camus had been doing then. Eschewing abstract concepts, he would leap onto the stage—never using the stairs available for that purpose—to demonstrate what he meant by acting the part himself, and always with gusto. If he respected the text, what really distinguished him from other directors she had known was that he respected his actors as well.[14]

He was an energetic theater man, trying to get everything done at once as if the play were to open the next day. In fact he was soon running the rehearsals ten hours a day, after which he stayed on to work with the stage machinery, for that aspect of the stage was quite a new experience for him. There was a standard numbering system for the positioning of spotlights, but he didn't know it then. On his side, he felt he was spending half of his nights waiting for blown rheostats to be replaced.

He took a room at the modest Hôtel Havre-Tronchet across the street from the theater so as to be closer to the job, for toward the end they were rehearsing well into the night. (Officially, the hours were 1 P.M. to 1 A.M.; to get any of his attention at all, Suzanne Agnely would bring his mail to the theater and stand by for instructions.) After hours and hours of such work he'd still be leaping up onto the stage to show the troupe what he meant, commenting: "You see, I'm still lively." He felt that the theater was a place for muscle not brain. A play, he said, was "a story of nobility told by bodies." "Just walk across the stage reciting your lines," he'd tell an actor, "and the feeling will follow." But he would change a line if he saw that an actor was having trouble with it.[18] "No psychology," he warned Catherine Sellers. He didn't seem to mind that he had cast the small, dark actress as Temple Drake, or a stocky, shortish man to play a lanky American type; to mind would have been to accept the kind of realism to which he was indifferent. He observed to Catherine that Temple was a ball of wool which unraveled all through the play and then at the end you discover that it is still intact.[14]

Often he'd curse that small Mathurins stage, which didn't allow him to do what he wanted, demanded constant compromises. He was disappointed in some of his actors. In the final weeks he was getting no more than four hours sleep a night; the actors seemed ready, but was that matchbox of a theater?[10] So unsure was he of the production that he asked Cérésol to promise to let it run for a hundred performances whatever the public response might be. Before the official opening night on September 22, 1956, the cast went through four complete dress rehearsals, for a total of seventy rehearsals in all, and that without Camus losing the respect of his actors.

The result was—tremendous, beyond anything he could have imagined. The first night audience seemed to be holding its breath—he himself could feel the emotion rising in the theater—for an outburst of enthusiasm at the final curtain. (Night after night there would be the same reaction—tears followed by cheers.)[10] So it had to be a financial success. There were 497 seats in the theater, and during the early weeks many spectators sat on the floor; they were selling 530 tickets nightly, had to hire an extra cashier for the box office; in the end *Requiem for a Nun* would be remembered as one of the greatest triumphs of the Baur-Cérésol era at the Mathurins. The play would run two seasons with full houses every night of the week, and it could have gone on beyond its closing on January 12, 1958, had Camus not wanted his actors to go on tour where they could earn more money.[19] Just after the New Year, on January 4, 1957, Camus received a cable from William Faulkner: "As the New Year begins I send you greetings and appreciation for your collaboration in my work." Camus would later say that *Requiem* had been his *baccalauréat, Les Possédés* his *agrégation;* the next play to follow, had he lived to stage it, would have been his doctorate.[14]

Moreover, it was a critical triumph. For once a dramatic work of Camus' in Paris would get a good press without reservations. Difficult Jean-Jacques Gautier in *Le Figaro* began his review: "At last a really interesting evening." He praised Camus' adaptation and his direction, which he found *discrète* and *sobre;* he liked the cast, particularly *la jeune et authentique tragédienne* Catherine Sellers. "She is extraordinary." "Staggering," exclaimed the Express critic. "A revelation?" began critic Morvan Lebesque. "Better: an event." Even *France-Observateur* was positive, praising Camus as writer and man of the theater, cheering Catherine Sellers, who "takes her place henceforth in the very first rank of her generation." Camus had also admired that new voice, all the while hearing Maria Casarès', for whom the play had been intended. He knew that he would like to do more directing, but realized with bitterness that he would have to carry on without Maria.

The personal effect of these weeks of strain could have been predicted. Camus collapsed, attacked by flu, suddenly depressed and alone after the intense and promiscuous activity of seventy rehearsals. He should have been happy at the success of his first theatrical endeavor in Paris, but instead he was mortally sad, detached, weak-kneed as a horse after a race, empty. Even Maria couldn't help him, for she was outside the country—touring the Soviet Union with a French repertory company. Despite his lethargy he took up the stories of *L'Exil et le Royaume* one more time—for the last time—before finally giving them up to his publisher in early October. (They went to the typesetters on November 26.)

He took part in a protest for another anti-regime Spaniard, and on October 30 spoke at a meeting in honor of the Spanish Republican statesman and historian Salvador de Madariaga on his seventieth birthday, sponsored by a committee of émigré friends of various political tendencies, as well as by an international committee including the Colombian Eduardo Santos, political scientist André Siegfried, and Jules Romains. A "very Spanish speech," Camus' Spanish admirers would say,[20] in its strong support of a liberalism which refused to be intimidated by apologists for totalitarianism; Camus was of course defining himself in describing Madariaga.[21]

The speech included another theme: "the heroic and earth-shaking insurrection of the students and workers of Hungary." For that tragic development was now forcing itself on Camus' attention, despite his psychological state, putting another obstacle on the path of his retreat.

It was on October 23 that the Hungarian people added a date to history by rising up against their Communist regime and Soviet occupying army. When Camus spoke for Madariaga, the Soviet counterattack which crushed Hungarian resistance had not yet been launched. The insurrection had created a new government; true workers' and revolutionary councils were being set up to run local affairs throughout that country once believed lost to totalitarian rule. But then the Soviet tanks began to move early in November.

On November 8, before the Soviet offensive had crushed the insurrectionary regime, Camus received a telegram from a Hungarian émigré writers' group containing the text of an appeal that had been broadcast over the Hungarian insurgents' radio and had been intercepted in Munich:

> Poets, writers, scientists of the entire world. Hungarian writers are calling you. Listen to our appeal. We are fighting on the barricades for freedom of our country, for that of Europe, and for human dignity. We shall die. But let our sacrifice not be in vain. At the final hour, in the name of an assassinated nation, we address ourselves to you, Camus, Malraux, Mauriac, Russell, Jaspers, Einaudi, T. S. Eliot, Koestler, Madariaga, Jiménez, Kazantzakis, Lagerkvist, Laxness, Hesse and all other combatants of the spirit. . . . Take action . . .

Camus immediately responded with an appeal of his own, for the publication of which he addressed himself to his preferred liberal-left daily, George Altman's *Franc-Tireur*. That paper had published the Hungarian writers' appeal on November 9, following it on November 10 with Camus'. Because he had been named in the broadcast, and although he had never felt as powerless as he had in these recent tragic days, he wished to reply personally. International society, which after years of waiting had finally found the strength to intervene in the Middle East, was allowing Hungary to be assassinated, just as it had allowed the Spanish Republic to be crushed twenty years earlier, and that had brought on World War II. This time Camus was inviting all those named in the radio appeal to sign a message to the United Nations requesting that the General Assembly debate the genocide of which Hungary was now the victim. And if the U.N. refused, the signatories pledged not only to boycott the U.N. and its cultural organizations, but to denounce their failure to do so at every possible occasion. Camus also asked every European writer to collect signatures of intellectuals to forward to the U.N. Secretariat.[21]

Two days later *Franc-Tireur* published the first signatures to be received from France: René Char, Pierre Emmanuel, Jules Roy, and Manès Sperber, and from Italy Guido Piovene and Ignazio Silone. On November 23, Camus sent a message to a meeting of French students to protest the Soviet intervention. "Remember what we have just lived through," he wrote, "in order to remain faithful to freedom, to its rights as to its duties, and so that you never accept, never, that someone, no matter how great a man, no matter how strong a party, will think for you and dictate your behavior."[21]

The Hungarian affair would have repercussions in France (and elsewhere) for another year at least, and he would find himself involved in many of the public activities designed to prevent the issue from being forgotten, and above all to seek to protect Hungarians who were being punished for their revolt.

Despite his many expressions of intent to withdraw from that arena, Camus was also still very involved with Algeria, but now more discreetly. When Charles Poncet informed him of the arrest of a friend as a Communist, a widower with four children who was not actually a Communist himself although he had many Communists in his family, Camus promised to help, not with an article this time, because he had abandoned public activities, but in a private manner. Indeed he did intervene privately, and thanks in part to his intervention, the man was released shortly thereafter.

He also offered a more dangerous kind of assistance. Mohamed Lebjaoui was now in Paris, as the clandestine chief of the FLN on the French mainland. Camus met him for lunch at the Hoggar, where they ordered couscous, which Lebjaoui knew that Camus loved. During the talk that followed Lebjaoui remarked with satisfaction that Camus had come a long way in a year. He had a better understanding of what the Algerians were seeking. Lebjaoui was convinced that, if the FLN had managed to maintain good relations with Camus, his intelligence and his love for Algeria would have brought him even closer to the Front. But Lebjaoui himself would soon be arrested, to be kept in prison until the independence of Algeria. As they left the restaurant, Lebjaoui remembered, Camus pressed his arm and gave him his address, saying: "My house is yours. You can hide out there whenever you want to."[22]

---
◆

# 44

# THE NOBEL PRIZE

This sterility, this sudden insensibility affect me deeply.

Letter to René Char*

Despite his continued preoccupation with Algeria, his constant inter-ventions, the pain caused by each new report of deterioration of the French-Algerian link, Camus was taxed then and later with his silence on Algeria. One reason for this may have been his own professions of intent to be silent, so that his enemies took him at his word rather than examining his acts, and the results of his acts. His own notes contain various attempts to justify a posture of silence. "I have decided to re-main silent concerning Algeria," read one of these notes (dated Feb-ruary 1957), "so as to add neither to its unhappiness nor to the stupidities written about it." The draft of a letter? A letter never sent? In any case, he went on: "My position has not varied on this matter and if I am able to understand and to admire the liberation fighter, I have only disgust for the killer of women and children."[1] For this Al-gerian independence struggle, if it involved few major battles between opposing armies—the nature of guerrilla warfare was such that the Army of National Liberation avoided the sort of confrontation it could not win because of the enemy's superior firepower—remained a war of isolated incidents, surprise attacks, above all of bombs in public places.

The evidence is that Camus never withdrew from the Algerian cri-sis. It tore him apart; his anxiety grew as the war did; he would not be cured of it during the remaining thirty-six months of his life. If he was silent with respect to the press, he acted where he could, where he could be discreetly useful, when he was asked, often on his own.

* Quoted in the Pléiade edition of Camus' work.

At the request of the Italian magazine *Tempo Presente,* Camus had replied to some general questions about the role of the intellectual in today's world. The brief question-and-answer text was reprinted in *Tempo Presente*'s sister magazine in London, *Encounter,* in April 1957.² A reader of the British magazine wrote in to ask Camus to explain himself regarding "the French campaign in Algeria." Camus' reply appeared in *Encounter* that June. In it he said that he favored the proclamation of the end of colonial status for Algeria, a round-table conference with all sides represented, with discussion of the possibility of an autonomous, federated nation modeled on Switzerland, which would preserve the freedoms of both peoples living in that country. But he could not, he said, go further than that. He could not enlist in the Arab guerrillas, nor could he approve of terrorism, which happened to strike more Arab civilians than French. He could not protest French repression and not Arab terrorism.

That this blanket opposition to killing for a cause was not just a convenient tactic for the circumstances—a tactic allowing him to remain above the crowd, as his critics had charged and would again charge—should be clear to readers familiar with Camus' life to this point. His horror of the death penalty, shared by his unknown father, became, in the period of Stalinist terror, the horror of organized, "legitimate" murder expressed in *L'Homme révolté* and *Les Justes.* Indeed, in early 1957, he was writing an essay against capital punishment. Malraux's friend Manès Sperber had conceived the idea of a volume which would bring together Arthur Koestler's essay *Reflections on Hanging,* which had already been published in London (first by the Sunday *Observer*), with an essay by Camus.³ Camus agreed, and was deep into it by the end of February, reading up on the gory history of beheadings, on the legal system which justified them. Once more he found that writing was coming with difficulty, however, and this writing was particularly distasteful.⁴ "Strange, this sort of monotonous ravage from which I have been suffering for months," he would write to Char (on March 3).¹

Sperber also commissioned Jean Bloch-Michel, who was now one of Camus' closest friends in Paris, to write a lengthy introduction and study of the French system. In his introduction Bloch-Michel would point out that Koestler's text had been written after the launching of a national campaign for the abolition of the death penalty in the United Kingdom, which campaign had resulted in parliamentary debate and a vote to abolish the death penalty (tempered by reservations in the House of Lords). Camus' text, "Réflexions sur la guillotine," had been written in a different context, he added—one of indifference. In the book as published (under the title *Réflexions sur la peine capitale*),

Koestler's essay covered some ninety-two pages, Camus' under sixty; Bloch-Michel appended his study of the death penalty in France and an analysis of experience in other countries. Simultaneously with book publication, Camus' contribution appeared in installments in the June and July issues of *NRF*.

Meanwhile there had been other demands for his attention—involving Spain of course, but now Hungary, too. On March 15, Camus spoke at the Salle Wagram in Paris in another protest against Soviet occupation and repression in Hungary. "What Spain was for us twenty years ago," he said, "Hungary will be today."

> I regret in this respect to have to play Cassandra again, and to disappoint the new hopes of some of my indefatigable colleagues, but no evolution is possible in a totalitarian society. Terror doesn't evolve, except toward worse, the scaffold doesn't become liberal, the gallows is not tolerant. Nowhere in the world has one seen a party or a man disposing of absolute power not utilizing it absolutely.[1]

Finally *L'Exil et le Royaume* was a book. In his signed *prière d'insérer* Camus noted that each of the six stories dealt with the theme of exile, each in its own way, from interior monologue to realistic narrative, and that they had been written together, although reworked and revised separately—supreme understatement. As for the kingdom of the title:

> it coincides with a certain kind of free and naked life that we must rediscover, to be born again. Exile, in its way, shows us the way, on the sole condition that we are able to refuse at one and the same time servitude and possession.[1]

The book was published to a mixed, mild reception. No one thought that Camus was offering his best work here, but a perceptive critic could see something of what the stories signified to the total body of his work. "All the previous books of Camus *push to the extreme* a certain direction of thought," wrote Gaëtan Picon. "Here we are brought back to the half-way zone, to confusion, to the discreet mixture of ordinary existence. . . ."[5]

On the other hand, arch-rival François Mauriac was ready to pounce when Camus raised a moral issue, as he had done in "Réflexions sur la guillotine." Mauriac still had his column in *L'Express,* written in the form of a diary, and a July 5 entry read:

> I have always thought and believed what Albert Camus writes in N.R.F. against the death penalty. So why the uneasiness I feel in reading it?

Mauriac refused the right of the white race, Christians or their heirs, to be for or against—after the Spanish Civil War and the Nazi massacre of Jews. "Discussing the death penalty, I fear, dispenses good souls from dealing with more burning problems," was Mauriac's cruel swipe at the younger writer. "Abolish the death penalty when torture is re-established. A bit of logic, if you please, Camus!"[6]

Camus' friends at the weekly *Demain* headlined their counterattack on Mauriac: "François Mauriac's sin."[7]

For the month of June 1957, Camus had once more agreed to direct plays at the Festival d'Angers for the Théâtre des Mathurins. He told Maria Casarès that it was sheer *baraka*—Arabic for "divine favor," but that the *baraka* also meant seventy rehearsals. . . .[4] For this year's festival he had selected two plays: his own *Caligula* and Lope de Vega's *The Knight from Olmedo* (Le Chevalier d'Olmedo), this latter in his own translation. He had gone over it line by line with Maria Casarès, and he was to spend the final weeks of that winter of 1957 polishing it, adding words when necessary, or rewriting in the interests of producing a spoken text suitable for the modern audience. April would be devoted to preparations for the staging, and May to rehearsals. (The plan— once more—was to begin *Le Premier Homme* after all this was over, i.e., in July.)

In April, meanwhile, he was being asked to involve himself again, and this time by the government. Under pressure from the liberal community alarmed by the growing use of police and army terror in Algeria, Premier Mollet decided to set up a non-partisan commission which would investigate charges of abuse of civil rights, torture, and other brutalities; leading personalities, intellectuals, and jurists were asked to join the commission. Camus was one of those invited.

He said no. In a letter to Mollet on April 25, he pointed out that the powers of the planned Commission de Sauvegarde des Droits et des Libertés Individuelles en Algérie had not been spelled out, which signified that the members of the commission were being asked to accept their jobs before they knew what they were to do. He could not go along with that. He could accept only if the members of the commission received investigatory powers, and were empowered to operate in total independence—including of the government. Otherwise, he feared, the commission would be torn apart by differences of opinion, adding to the general confusion rather than remedying it, and "none of those who suffer today from the divisions and weaknesses of our country will be able to envisage lightly prospects of this kind."[8]

Nor would anyone complain that Camus was seeking a way out of commitment by avoiding membership in this commission. Mendès France privately felt that Camus was quite right to keep his distance, for the commission had been designed to camouflage the truth.[9]

On the other hand, in the same month of April, when Camus heard a report that Mouloud Mammeri, a Moslem member of the Comité des Libéraux in Algiers, had disappeared, he immediately contacted Emmanuel Roblès to find out what had happened, and what he could do to help. What had happened was that Mammeri, author and university professor, had been sought for questioning by police after an article he wrote (but did not sign) in the Liberals' organ *Espoir-Algérie*. Mammeri was already suspect—among other things, his brother was in the rebel camp. But he was no longer in danger, for in truth he had already slipped out of the country to Morocco, where he needed no help from Camus.[10]

On another occasion Roblès came to Paris to tell Camus that a Moslem friend had beseeched his help in the cause of his brother, then eighteen, who had shot a French Algerian *ultra* and had been sentenced to death although his victim had not died. At that time de Gaulle was back in power, and Camus had an appointment with him. He opened a desk drawer to show Roblès a pile of letters. "Look at all this I have to give to de Gaulle. Give me your file." Camus later told Roblès that the young Moslem had every chance of a pardon, and in fact he was subsequently pardoned.[11] Camus' files contained many exchanges of correspondence with the French Government before and during the de Gaulle regime, asking for mercy for individual Moslems or groups.[12] He was a mainstay of his friend, the civil rights lawyer Yves Dechezelles, who forwarded case after case for his intervention, Camus' only return request being that his role remain confidential.

His time was now divided between mornings at work at the Rue de Chanaleilles apartment, afternoons at Gallimard—where he still enjoyed the use of a telephone, a mailing address, and above all a loyal secretary. His responsibilities to that house were reduced now. He had some assistant readers to examine manuscripts, although he duly attended meetings of the Reading Committee, in the rotunda of the Rue de l'Université town house facing the garden.[13]

His office often served as a refuge, especially from domestic concerns. "It's my island," he told a friend. "But it's a pity that it's inhabited by Fridays."[4] For he was not always happy here; he would often say that he planned to quit, a dream that seemed close to realization in the final months of his life. At least once his sedition encountered similarly subversive thoughts on the part of Gaston's nephew Michel Gallimard, who also considered starting a publishing venture of his own; perhaps the two might have done it together.[14]

Meanwhile he would enjoy teasing the Gallimards about money—about being exploited—while professing indifference to the actual size of his printings. In fact he would leave most of his earnings in the company, as did Malraux and other successful authors, so that it was popularly said that these famous writers were the publisher's bankers. At the moment of his death, Camus had a large balance in his royalty account. His life style did cost him money: He always took the check at lunches, and he was an easy touch for loans. His salary at Gallimard, like those of the other editors, was a modest one, and alone could not have allowed him such generosity. But he never wanted more, and on their side the Gallimards felt that since he was getting ever-higher royalties from the sale of his books he didn't need a higher salary. He himself would tell them that he didn't want to talk about salary, he wanted to be free to take the long leaves of absence he would always take.[15]

Early in June, two weeks before the Festival d'Angers began, he drove down to that town in his black Citroën with the actor Jean-Pierre Jorris, Dominique Blanchar, and Suzanne Agnely. They had begun rehearsing the plays in Paris, and now they continued on the castle ramparts. *Le Chevalier d'Olmedo* was scheduled for June 21, 23, 26, and 29; *Caligula* for June 22, 25, 27, and 30—always at 9:30 P.M., when night had set in. For the Lope de Vega play the stars were Michel Herbault in the title role, the knight who is murdered by his treacherous rival, Don Rodrigo, played by Jorris; Jean-Pierre Marielle; and Dominique Blanchar. Michel Auclair played Caligula, Jorris Hélicon.

From the outset there had been problems. Camus was losing patience with the Mathurins theater, which ran the festival. The sets weren't ready on time, and rehearsals took place in the noise and commotion of carpenters sawing and electricians hammering. The extras weren't available until forty-eight hours before the first public performance, so that the actors had to rehearse until 3 A.M., although they had been reciting the same lines for nearly two months. The first performance was marred by rain, and Jorris was wounded on the foot by a sword, another actor on the wrist, a third by a dagger handle, despite the fact that Camus had brought in a *maître d'armes* to direct the fighting scenes. From then on they used gloves, furnished by a police motorcycle brigade.

And then—a more publicized incident—Camus wasn't getting along with his Caligula, Michel Auclair. He had actually wanted Jean-Pierre Jorris for the part, but the producers insisted on having an actor who was better known, and so it had to be Auclair. There seemed to be a conflict of personality between Camus and Auclair, which Cérésol, a romantic, attributed to a clash of temperaments, Mediterranean vs. Slav. Auclair was a star and did not yield easily to Camus' direction. He was remembered as having said privately: "Let him do his writing and not mix with directing."[16]

The first performance was inconvenienced by rain, but it worked. Jacques Lemarchand wrote in *Le Figaro Littéraire* that the production

> plays on all the surfaces and attitudes of the admirable castle and has made of this sumptuous story a tapestry gilded, black and fair, red, filled with those burlesque details which are appreciated on the fringes of an epic.

*Caligula* was a less popular work. It drew an audience of the same size, but with a higher proportion of students in it, and it was clear that the majority of spectactors were disoriented, having expected another classic in the grand manner—the usual fare of summer festivals—and not a painful philosophical work. A Paris critic would remark that Auclair was "heavier" than the 1945 Caligula, Gérard Philipe. The adolescent had ripened, but the work had acquired humanity.[17] Of course it was not only the actors who had changed; so had the play. Camus had lightened Caligula's speeches, developed Hélicon's, increasing the ambiguity of Caligula's attitude (Camus' editor was reminded of *La Chute*). The new version, which would be used (with further modifications) in a Paris production early the following year, was also the basis for a new edition of the play in book form.

In Paris there was more Algerian business to attend to. Yves Dechezelles and his aide Gisèle Halimi asked his support for a Moslem accused of killing a prominent French Algerian. Camus agreed to help. (Defending a Moslem accused of an act of terrorism was itself a brave act in the Algiers of that time, when the escalation of urban guerrilla activity had been met by the French Army's attempted cleanup, known as the Battle of Algiers: Dechezelles and one of his character witnesses, Maurice Clavel, were able to slip out of the city despite threats to their lives only because the *ultras* were busy hazing a university dean who was being expelled that day.)[18]

In July, again in September, Dechezelles appealed to his old friend. He reported the execution by guillotine of three Moslem militants at Barberousse Prison, the same Barberousse where Camus' father had watched a similar execution; he asked Camus for a statement which would help prevent further executions of would-be terrorists who had not actually carried out an act of terrorism. Camus wrote to President Coty to ask for a more liberal policy on pardons, and an aide to the President replied that procedures were being re-examined. He wrote to Coty again in October, and received a reply to the effect that his plea would be taken into consideration.[12]

For a summer respite he went off to Cordes, a medieval strong-point of the Cathari sect, now a peaceful village, fifteen miles from Albi, not far from Toulouse, in southwest France. He had seen Cordes before, and had been taken with the site, with the old houses climbing a small hill, the fortress gates and round towers, the steep and narrow cobblestone lanes. He had even attended an open-air performance there of Calderón's *L'Alcalde de Zalamea,* invited by Claire Targuebayre, who had once been manager of Charlot's bookshop in Algiers. Later Camus would give her a brief preface in praise of Cordes for a book she had written as a guide to the old village. It was a preface in the poetic vein:

> The traveler who, from the terrace of Cordes, watches the summer night, knows that he has no need to go further and that if he wishes, the beauty here, day after day, will protect him from solitude.[19]

With a friend, Claire Targuebayre had restored an old Gothic manor to become the Hôtel du Grand Ecuyer. Camus was one of her first clients, and the *chambre rouge* there now bears his name.[20] In that summer of 1957 he held what was virtually a theatrical conference at Cordes. With Maria Casarès, *"l'unique,"* he invited Jean-Pierre Jorris, who had just left the Comédie Française, to come down to discuss theater projects. They also picked up Catherine Sellers in a nearby town. Camus told them all that he was working on his adaptation of *Les Possédés* (but in fact he confided to other friends that he had done very little during his stay in Cordes; he had mainly relaxed, and he needed to do that; he felt good, and was sleeping more or less normally for the first time in years).[14]

With Jorris he discussed a Paris production of *Caligula.* Camus definitely wanted the young actor for the title role this time. They all walked together on the ramparts, sat on the old wall where the setting sun could be seen longest, when the rest of the town was already in shadow. Camus also took them to an old chapel some miles out of town, got the key from the mayor in order to show them a statue of Christ that was inside; clearly he had been there before. In a matter of fact tone he commented: *"I* find that beautiful." Then abruptly: "We're not going to remain in ecstasy here much longer, but look at it."[21]

This time he was definitely determined to strike out on his own. He was anxious to take over and manage his own theater where he would have total autonomy, and he hoped to convince Michel Gallimard to join him in the venture.[14]

After a spell in Paris he was off again, this time to the Michel Gallimards' house at Sorel, with his twins. But still not working, and with a new element of disquiet in his tone. "We resemble each other considerably," he wrote to René Char on September 17, "and I know that it happens that one wishes to disappear, to become nothing, in other words." And then: "I have accomplished nothing this summer, and yet I was counting on it. And this sterility, this sudden insensibility affect me deeply."[22]

As if a gong were sounding to set off this confession of sterility, Camus received the Nobel Prize. It was largely the doing of the Swedish Academy, for Camus had not been the candidate of any significant outside groups, it generally being assumed that the award was meant for a finished work, a full career. Camus was not quite forty-four years old, and France had been represented by nine candidates that year. Malraux, for example, had been suggested by literary organizations both in France and in Sweden, had been widely mentioned in speculation about the prize, and he had even been received by Sweden's king and was widely fêted when he visited Stockholm to lecture on Rembrandt. The Nobel Committee's choice of Camus, youngest laureate after Kipling (who had been forty-three when he won the prize in 1907), provoked a certain amount of astonishment, just as it had two decades earlier when Martin du Gard had been chosen over his elder and master Gide, who had had to wait another ten years for his Nobel. Other candidates for the 1957 prize were Boris Pasternak, Saint-John Perse, and Samuel Beckett, all of whom would receive it later, and a Finn, Väinö Linna.[23]

Did Camus expect the prize? Surely someday, but now? When his American publisher, Blanche Knopf, visited him in Paris after having been in Stockholm that August, she told him that she had heard his name mentioned in connection with the award. "We both laughed—it seemed impossible to use," she recalled later.[24]

In a chest at the Rue de Chanaleilles apartment Camus had saved a clipping from a Marseilles periodical, *Massalia* (of November 18, 1954), in which he or someone for him (possibly its author) had marked in red a literary letter from Paris by a critic, Renée Willy. Commenting on that year's Nobel award to Ernest Hemingway, the writer noted that Camus' name had been mentioned, but that his youth had probably made the jury hesitate. "Yet how his work, lofty and pure, should have deserved such recognition!" After much praise of Camus' work and its growing influence in France and abroad, Renée Willy concluded:

> The Nobel Prize should not only represent the crowning of a career. It would be nobler if it facilitated the access to total independence of an artist whose work is both a guarantee and a promise.

On October 16, 1957, Patricia Blake was seated at a table with Camus in the upstairs room of a restaurant on the Rue des Fossés St. Bernard (possibly it was Chez Marius, popular then and later for seafood), when a young waiter came up to tell Camus—who was obviously known here—that he had won the Nobel Prize. He became pale, seemed upset, repeated over and over that it should have gone to Malraux.[25]

For Camus realized immediately what was happening to him, and even before—or at least as soon as his most violent critics would. He was not writing, he was not sure of his past, his present, or his future, and this was the moment chosen to subject him to the torture of public exposure and solemnities. "I'm castrated!" he would complain later to a friend.[26] Janine Gallimard remembered him pacing back and forth in the Michel Gallimards' bedroom, moving like a caged lion, seemingly stunned, both pleased and appalled; here too he repeated again and again that Malraux should have gotten the prize.[14]

"Serves him right," was the smug remark of his enemies.[27] The cruelest comment may have been the one in the weekly *Arts,* which published on its front page a caricature of Camus in cowboy clothes and with pistols drawn, alongside the headline:

## IN AWARDING ITS PRIZE TO CAMUS
## THE NOBEL CROWNS A FINISHED WORK

The author of the article, *Arts* editor Jacques Laurent, right-wing polemicist and popular novelist, observed that Malraux would have shocked the Swedish Academy. But "the academicians proved by their decision that they considered Camus to be finished. . . ."

For conservative Frenchmen, Camus was not a conservative; he was a dangerous radical; he was not only *not* hesitant about Algeria, but he was a dangerous friend of the rebels. This came out in the attack of the right-wing weekly *Carrefour,* which observed that the Nobel Prize was usually awarded after consultation with the foreign minister of the country concerned, but that this time the Swedish Academy had clearly favored a liberal on the Algerian question rather than a partisan of keeping Algeria French. "What a strange and new form of interference in our internal affairs."

On the other side of the political spectrum, Roger Stéphane in *France-Observateur* said more or less what Jacques Laurent had said:

> One wonders whether Camus is not on the decline and if, thinking they were honoring a young writer, the Swedish Academy was not consecrating a precocious sclerosis.

Stéphane, who had been the target of Camus' scorn, now had his revenge. He saw Camus as beneath Malraux and Sartre; Camus was a
tame Sartre; *La Peste* was appreciated by readers of Anatole France
and of Franz Kafka both. And why hadn't Camus been speaking out on
Algeria? He wanted to hold onto his credit? "But what is he saving it
for?"

Pascal Pia in *Paris-Presse* said that his old comrade was no longer
*un homme révolté* but a "lay saint" in the service of a superannuated
humanism. He added that Camus was sure to please the Swedes, who
when their neighbors the Finns or the Norwegians were invaded showed
that their "obstinate love of peace always wins out over any other feeling." And in Camus' old newspaper *Combat* the critic Alain Bosquet
also noted that small countries admire *"parfaits petits penseurs polis."*

On the Communist side, of course, Camus could have expected
nothing better than what he received from the Party daily *L'Humanité:*
"He is the 'philosopher' of the myth of abstract freedom. He is the
writer of illusions." Later, when Camus was in Stockholm to receive the
prize, the organ of the Union of Czechoslovak Writers, *Literarni
Novini,* would write that in giving the award to Camus the Swedish
Academy had joined the camp of the cold war.

In Sweden, too, the press was negative from the outset, more concerned with Camus as a political person than as a literary one. *Dagens
Nyheter,* the influential Stockholm daily, in the person of its literary editor, Olof Lagercrantz, wrote that the choice of Camus was inexplicable;
Malraux and especially Sartre would have been better.[28]

A reception was held for Camus at Gallimard on October 17.
Camus arrived early to speak to reporters, wearing an elegant navy-blue
suit with pin stripes, a dark blue tie, and a white shirt. He was asked
how he learned about the award. "With much surprise and good
humor," was his reply. His name had been mentioned on several occasions, but he hadn't believed it could happen. "I thought, indeed, that
the Nobel Prize should crown an accomplished work or, at least, one
further advanced than mine," he was quoted as saying. "I wish to say
that if I had taken part in the voting, I should have chosen André
Malraux, for whom I have much admiration and friendship, and who
was one of the masters of my youth." Asked what he was doing, he
mentioned the adaptation of *Les Possédés,* was also quoted to the effect
that he was abandoning the theater to devote himself to his new novel,
whose tentative title was *Le Premier Homme,* and which he called a
*roman d'éducation.*

Then the salon was invaded by a tidal wave of photographers and
radio reporters. He posed over and over again, sometimes with the actress Madeleine Renaud, who had come to congratulate him and who

was mistaken for his wife. He shook hands several times with the Swedish Ambassador at the request of photographers.[29] More guests arrived, the party spilled over into the garden. The ambassador delivered a brief, formal speech, and the Gallimards served aquavit for the occasion.[30]

As for Malraux, whatever he thought of the award to Camus, he did not hesitate to congratulate the winner and to acknowledge what Camus had said about him on receiving the notification. "Your reply honors both of us," were his words.[31]

PART V

———————◆———————

# The Road Back

# 45

◆

# STOCKHOLM

I believe in justice, but I shall defend my mother above
justice.

Stockholm, December 12, 1957

After the party, panic. (It was the word used by Camus to describe his
condition to Nicola Chiaromonte.) He had not needed the critics of extreme right and left to tell him how unworthy he was, what a mistake it
had been to give the Nobel Prize to a man who could no longer write.
For months to come he would be ill because of it. How ill he seemed
depended on the degree of intimacy of the observer, for he could keep
up a front. He would go to Stockholm, for example, and he would participate in all the ceremonies required of him, write and deliver the
speeches, grant interviews; he would act the Nobel laureate.

For of course there was a good press too. The New York *Times*
had published the story of the prize on its front page (on October 18,
1957), duly noting the amount of the award ($42,000, which the
French press reported as 18,776,593.80 French francs). The *Times*
reported that the Swedish Academy had cited Camus as the world's
foremost literary antagonist of totalitarianism, had said he was selected
because of "his important literary production, which with clear-sighted
earnestness illuminated the problems of the human conscience in our
times." Then came a quote from the academy's permanent secretary Dr.
Anders Osterling, which Camus might not have endorsed. "Camus has
left nihilism far behind him and his existentialism can reasonably be
called a form of humanism," said Osterling. An editorial in the October
19 New York *Times* observed that Camus had outgrown existentialism
and "the philosophy that human life was absurd and futile . . . His is

one of the few literary voices that has emerged from the chaos of the post-war world with the balanced, sober outlook of humanism." It was pointed out in *Le Monde* that Camus was the ninth Frenchman to receive the prize. The poet Sully Prudhomme had been the first, when the prize was given for the first time in 1901, and other winners had been Romain Rolland, Anatole France, Henri Bergson, in addition to Martin du Gard, Gide, and Mauriac.

Martin du Gard, called on to speak of his young colleague and friend, provided this description for a literary weekly:

> The amused irony of the eye and of the smile might for an instant mislead. But, if the conversation develops, the secret depth is not long in appearing: a sensibility held in check but constantly excited . . . an underlying melancholy, which seems untouchable; and in contact with reality (of which nothing escapes him), a permanent state of bitterness in revolt, against which, for moral hygiene, he attempts to struggle without cease.[1]

Called on for a comment, even Mauriac had to provide one (which with the statement he made on news of Camus' fatal accident were the only kind words he would ever say about Camus): "This young man is one of the most listened-to masters of the young generation. He furnishes a reply to the questions it poses. In a way he is its conscience."[2]

No less important to him would be the November 1957 article in *Révolution Prolétarienne,* which set out to show that this Nobel Prize winner was not the haughty public figure that some critics were making him out to be; the harshest of the attacks are summarized, including those that suggested he had chosen "a facile socialism, that which creates no risks and earns dividends."

> Camus is a man of life, thus of contradictions, susceptible of error and of weakness. . . . What we know of Camus is his solidarity . . . toward the militants of Spain, Bulgaria, Hungary. Not only at the occasion of meetings or of manifestos . . . but when there are no other witnesses than anonymous ones. . . .
> . . . Others besides ourselves know this. The old rebels and aliens of the United States . . . the students of Montevideo, who publish him in their mimeographed bulletin, the young workers of Prague or of Warsaw. And this unknown person from Barcelona who sent Camus a postcard with this simple word: "Gracias."

The article, unsigned, was entitled "Albert Camus, Un Copain [A Pal]."

William Faulkner wired Camus, in French: *On salue l'âme qui constamment se cherche et se demande.*[3] And at the Théâtre des

Mathurins, where *Requiem for a Nun* with Catherine Sellers was continuing its successful career, Mrs. Baur and Cérésol put up new posters announcing that the play had been written by *two* Nobel Prize winners.

Everyone who had ever met Camus—French Algerians, Frenchmen, foreign friends—wrote him now, and he tried to reply to all. (Suzanne Agnely had to hire an extra typist for four months to help with correspondence and the telephone.) Camus wired his mother that he had never missed her as he did then, and she had a neighbor read her the telegram.[4] When Armand Guibert congratulated him and added that he was jealous that Camus still had a mother who could be proud of him, Camus wrote back:

> Yes, in this moment when the excess of honors embarrassed me, I was helped by a thought which was always a consolation for me. I turned toward Algiers. There is to be found what I love most in all the world and I waited, in order to know what I should think about what was happening to me, to know that my mother was happy about it. . . .[5]

And he wrote to his grade schoolteacher, Louis Germain, the severe *instituteur* who had wrested him from Belcourt:

> My first thought, after my mother, was for you. Without you, without that affectionate hand that you held out to the small child I was . . . nothing of all this would have happened. . . .[6]

He gave an interview, featured as "La seule interview du Prix Nobel 1957," to Bloch-Michel at *Demain* (published on October 24). On Algeria:

> My role in Algeria never was and never will be to divide. . . . I share the fate of all those, French or Arab, who suffer. . . . But I can't all by myself rebuild what so many men are trying to destroy. I did what I could. I shall try once more when there will once again be a chance to aid in the reconstruction of an Algeria delivered of all the hatreds and all the racisms. . . .

He evoked Richard Hilary's remark before dying in World War II, that we were fighting a lie in the name of a half-truth. Today it was a quarter-truth. "It happens that the quarter-truth that Western society contains is called freedom. And freedom is the road, and the only road, toward perfectibility. . . ."[6]

And he lent himself to all the necessary ceremony, although not more. Ambassador Ragnar Kumlin gave a lunch and then a more formal dinner at the Swedish Embassy. Camus asked his old Oran comrade André Belamich to accompany him for moral support, as symbolic representative of Camus' Algerian friends; Belamich had to rent a tuxedo and Camus lent him the appropriate socks. Jacqueline Bernard invited all the old *Combat* team to her home, and Camus improvised a speech that he said he would give at Stockholm.[7] He received from the Swedish Academy a detailed list of what he was to wear for each ceremony and event during his stay in Stockholm in December; the word "decorations" was used, and although he had always refused to wear any medals, he decided that he would like to display the one he had been given by the Spanish Republican exiles. André Benichou's wife found and purchased one, but in the end he would not wear it.[8] His wife bought him the Resistance medal he was also entitled to, but he refused to wear that either.[9]

When it was time to prepare for the trip, Suzanne Agnely accompanied him to the clothing store Cor de Chasse on Rue de Buci to rent formal attire for the Stockholm ceremonies. (When he returned from Stockholm he had a tuxedo made for him, because everyone said that he looked like Humphrey Bogart in the rented one, and he enjoyed that idea. He was to wear it at theatrical first nights.)[10] For the false shirt-front, Robert Cérésol lent him a set of diamonds which Cérésol had himself borrowed from a jeweler friend.

Camus dined with Cérésol at a small café on the Quai Voltaire, showed Cérésol the scrap of paper on which Malraux had scribbled his acknowledgment of Camus' respectful words. Yet Cérésol found his friend in a depressed mood, seemingly terrified by what was happening to him. The critics would be lying in wait for him now; he would no longer be able to write. He seemed feverish, talked about his tuberculosis. Holding up his fists, he said: "I'm going to die of pulmonary sclerosis with two little lungs like this."

He even wanted Cérésol to accompany him to Stockholm.[11] (He did not say the same thing to Maria Casarès; he avoided talking about the prize to her, knowing that she couldn't be with him when he received it.)

His friends would soon begin to notice the change in him. He seemed to take himself more seriously. He found that he had to keep people—even old friends—at arm's length. But he simply had to do that if he wished to continue his own work.[12] He wasn't snubbing friends, he hadn't "gone Hollywood"; nothing had really changed, not even his opinion of himself, because he always had been confident of himself, of his true worth. His retreat was rather a function of anxiety. And he himself wondered whether success would change him. He said to Bloch-Michel more or less what he had said to Cérésol: "It isn't pleasant to think that when I write now I'll have people looking over my shoulder."[13]

While bracing himself for the Stockholm ordeal, he tended to current business as he could. That included political action, of course. Now he could write to President Coty, who had wired congratulations after the Nobel announcement, and to other political leaders, with more authority. But he was also going to be asked to intervene more regularly. There was more to do for Hungary. The writers Tibor Dery (Hungary's best-known novelist, a friend of the Socialist revolution, then sixty-two), Tibor Tardos, Gyula Hay, and Zoltan Zalk, intellectual leaders of the popular insurrection, were on trial in Budapest, so Camus joined fellow Nobel laureates Martin du Gard and Mauriac in a telegraphic appeal (drawn up by René Tavernier) to Hungary's Prime Minister Janos Kadar on October 29.[14] The writers were sentenced to prison nevertheless, so at the end of November, Camus wrote to the minister in charge at the Hungarian Legation in Paris asking to be received on behalf of himself and T. S. Eliot, Ignazio Silone, and Karl Jaspers. The minister refused but sent a young attaché to see Camus at the Gallimard office (on December 6), where Louis de Villefosse joined Camus for the encounter. The attaché said that he could not accept the appeal since his minister believed that the Dery affair concerned only Hungarians. Camus attempted to demonstrate that he was wrong, and added pointedly that discreet contacts of this kind were better than the usual methods of petitions and publicity; still, they would not hesitate to use other methods if they had to. Then Camus had to leave for Stockholm, and Villefosse tried vainly to get a reply from the legation by phone; on Camus' return he pursued the campaign by letter, also in vain.[15]

He sent a message to the Hungarian Writers Association Abroad, which had asked for his participation in a meeting in London to commemorate the Hungarian writers' appeal broadcast during the insurrection a year before:

> As harsh as may be the idea of the solitude in which we have allowed the Hungarian combatants to die, and in which we allow the survivors to live, the regrouping that has taken place in Europe for this cause nevertheless gives a degree of meaning to this desperate struggle. . . .[16]

Intervening for Algerian Moslems accused of terrorism was complicated by the support given to these same defendants by what he considered to be a neo-Stalinist left. The dilemma arose during the prosecution of Ben Saddok, accused of the killing of a prominent Moslem not committed to the rebellion (who had been vice-president of the Algerian Assembly). The defense attorney wrote to Camus to say that his client had carried out a political act, and that he was appealing to Camus as author of "Réflexions sur la guillotine" despite the attorney's connection with political causes that Camus opposed. Yves Dechezelles seconded the appeal. Camus agreed to make a plea for Ben Saddok if the defense attorney guaranteed that no publicity would be given to the letter he would address to the court.

> I have been refusing for the past two years . . . and I shall continue to refuse until I see the possibility of useful action, any public manifestation susceptible of being exploited politically to add to the misfortune of my country. In particular, I wish in no case to give a good conscience, by statements bearing no personal risk to me, to the stupid fanatic who in Algiers might fire into a crowd where my mother and all my loved ones would be. . . .

He even drafted a letter for the court in support of Ben Saddok, which his editor quotes as if it had actually been sent, but he apparently left it in draft prior to his departure for Stockholm. On his return he told the defense attorney that he had intended to be of use to the defense, but he had just learned that *France-Observateur* had already publicized his misgivings and conditions, and to his disadvantage. Yet it was not so much political differences as methodology which separated Camus from Ben Saddok's attorney, and now he had been discouraged once and for all. Henceforth both attacks and private contacts from the extreme left would be met by silence.[17]

One bit of professional business had to be dealt with before his departure for Stockholm. *Caligula* was going to be seen on the Paris stage again. But Camus did not want Michel Auclair, with whom he had had difficulties in Angers the previous June, in the starring role; he wanted Jean-Pierre Jorris. The Mathurins directors did not think Jorris was right for the part. So Camus took the play elsewhere,[1] to Elvire Popesco and Hubert de Malet, who were about to open a pocket-sized Nouveau Théâtre in the building of their large and famous Théâtre de Paris. Once more Camus made changes in his text, significant ones; e.g., Jorris felt that Caligula's murder was actually a suicide, and Camus confirmed that by modifying the text. Rehearsals began in that freshly painted white box of a theater, with its cherry-red furnishings, in December.[18]

The Camus party that was to travel to Sweden included, in addition to Camus and his wife, the Michel Gallimards (and the Claude Gallimards). And when the Knopfs heard the news of the Nobel award, Blanche had said to her husband: "Let's go to Stockholm for the ceremonies," and he had replied: "Let's." He flew from New York to Stockholm, while his wife stopped in Paris to join the Camus party, and then she learned that they were going to make the long trip by train.[19]

Another member of the group was Carl-Gustaf Bjurström, son of a Swedish pastor, who had grown up in Paris, where he was a translator as well as a scout for Camus' Swedish and Danish publishers, Bonniers and Gyldendal (as well as Pantheon Books in the United States). He had translated two of Camus' shorter works for a Swedish literary magazine published by Bonniers (*BLM*), in fact had spent a summer writing a study of Camus and trying to meet him (but Suzanne Agnely kept him away). Now the Bonnier house asked Bjurström, who was then thirty-eight, to travel to Stockholm to be available to the Swedish publisher and to the Camus party. (The Bonniers had published *L'Etranger* as early as 1946 in a series called Panache, edited by Georg Svensson, who would now be on hand to greet Camus in Stockholm.)

Bjurström had already written to Camus to inform him that the Danish house of Gyldendal would like him to stop in Copenhagen en route, but Camus had felt that out of courtesy to the Swedish Academy he should go to that country first. Then when it was decided to travel by train (because of Camus' reservations about flying), they had to stop in Copenhagen anyway, so a brief reception was arranged there. (In fact Bjurström had been responsible for Gyldendal's being Camus' publisher. His work had previously been translated by another firm, but it had later abandoned general publishing to devote itself to educational publishing. When *La Chute* appeared Bjurström sent it to Gyldendal, whose editors weren't all that certain they could sell such a strange book, but their scout warned them: "You're crazy, it's a short book easy to translate, and one day he'll get the Nobel Prize!")

The Nord Express left Paris in the late evening of December 7, a Saturday night. As it pulled out of the Gare du Nord, it was discovered that Blanche Knopf's maid (from her Paris *pied à terre*), with whom she was busy talking, was still on board; she had to get off at the Belgian border. Bjurström, excessively shy, tried not to get in anybody's way, wishing to be discreet among all these important people, spent part of the trip talking to Blanche Knopf. But Camus came into his compartment to talk, anxious to know whom he would be meeting in Sweden, so Bjurström attempted to describe the Swedish literary scene, particularly the work of Pär Lagerkvist and Eyvind Johnson.[20] Two reporters for *Paris-Match* were also on the train and took pictures during the trip, which upset Camus at first, but he ended by liking them.[21]

Otto B. Lindhardt, then a very young publishing manager of Denmark's traditional house of Gyldendal, gave a small party for the group in Copenhagen with a few influential authors and critics. After that the group boarded another train for a second overnight trip (with the train riding a ferry part of the way). They arrived in Stockholm at eight on a freezing Monday morning (December 9) and checked into the luxury-class Grand Hotel on the water's edge, facing the Royal Palace and the Old Town.

At 11:30 A.M., Camus was at the French Embassy for his first meeting with the Swedish press. He was accompanied by a young officer of the Swedish Foreign Ministry, Hans Colliander, who had just returned from a two-year assignment in France. He knew Camus' work and the Algerian problem, and so he was selected to assist the Camus party (a Foreign Ministry aide is assigned regularly to Nobel Prize visitors). It would not be a simple job, because of the hostility of the local press already mentioned, but the government hoped to keep the atmosphere as unheated as possible.

The negative press began to manifest itself even before the Camus party pulled into the Stockholm station. Colliander, who met them there, showed Camus a headline from *Dagens Nyheter* reporting an interview with him in Copenhagen—which Camus denied had taken place. Colliander translated the headline and the opening paragraph for Camus so that he would be prepared for the worst. The substance was: Why had this man who had aways spoken out remained silent on Algeria? In the subsequent questioning of Camus the newspaper people often overlooked the fact that he was a writer, not a politician. And although he was not able to reverse the tide, the criticism gradually tapered off.[22]

Camus opened the press conference at the embassy by asking permission to remain standing, for he did not like to sit down while speaking. Asked at once about the writer's commitment, he quipped that it was not a voluntary one, but a *service militaire obligatoire*. He felt that the artist could not separate himself from his time while maintaining his originality, and he didn't know whether a writer formed his century or the century the writer. It happened that he sometimes wished to be *solitaire* but always felt the need to be *solidaire*.

Why had he left *Combat*? After three years of operation the newspaper required capital, but capital doesn't come without servitude. He refused both and withdrew from journalism.

On Algeria, he felt that a Franco-Moslem community was possible, and that it was infinitely preferable to any form of separation. He thought that this community could be based on a federal system—not territorial federalism, Swiss-style, since the different population groups in Algeria were not separated but intermingled—but a "personal federalism" by which he meant that each community, Arab, French, Berber, would be represented on the basis of equality in a legislative assembly which remained to be defined.

When he was able to speak of literature he mentioned Jean Grenier, his best friend since the age of seventeen. *All* the young Algerian writers were his friends, and that meant the Arabs as well as the French. He helped them get published, he shared their feelings about the crisis, which was as painful for them as for himself. Roblès and Roy were mentioned, but also Feraoun, Dib, and Mammeri. He was close to many Frenchmen—to Simone Weil for example, for one can feel as close to a dead person as to a living one. And to Char, a "brother" as well as the poet whose work was the best since Apollinaire.

On his fictional characters, he could not identify any one of them as his spokesman. Those for whom he had most affection were not necessarily those who resembled him most, but those he would most like to resemble. An author's work is chronological. *Le Mythe de Sisyphe,* written from 1938 to 1941, could not be the same book as *L'Homme révolté,* written between 1947 and 1951; not only circumstances but the man had changed. The heart of an artist is a battlefield, his books being successive images of that battle.

Was he writing a new novel? He didn't want to talk about *Le Premier Homme*—out of superstition. As it would be a novel of a traditional type and he wasn't sure that he was a traditional writer, the undertaking frightened him a little. "It's also the novel of my maturity, if you like. In consequence, I attach more sentimental value to it than to other books; therefore, I'd prefer to leave it in a happy obscurity."

He explained that his campaign against the death penalty had opened no debate, for people felt that it was not essential compared to worse horrors, an argument with which he disagreed. Was he an optimist? No one in the room could be an optimist in the sense of Ernest Renan on the progress of science. But he did not believe that because the world risked destruction one should not try to live in dignity. So "I am an ineradicable optimist." He was a *solitaire* independent of parties and believed that, after twenty years during which he refused no opportunity to take a stand on major issues, freedom remained the highest and surest of goals. Freedom permitted bettering of conditions, while tyranny did not. As for his religion: He was not about to convert. He was long considered to be associated with atheism and materialism, through his own fault. But he recognized that there was a part of mystery in man. He had written with warmth of the person of Christ and he had only respect and veneration for his teachings as well, although he did not believe in the Resurrection. He feared that in some so-called left circles a confession of ignorance, of a limit to man's knowledge, respect for the sacred, appeared as weaknesses. If so, he assumed these weaknesses. Communist philosophers called him reactionary, reactionaries said he was a Communist, atheists that he was a Christian, while Christians deplored his atheism. He would continue to be as he was and could be. Sartre? He had excellent relations with Sartre, the best relations being those in which people do not see each other. Each had a respectable position, but *parfaitement opposées*.[23]

Next day, December 10, was the day of the official bestowal of the prizes. The French Embassy had asked Bjurström to translate Camus' acceptance speech into Swedish, and immediately; but it was available only on the day of the ceremony because Camus had not wanted to show it earlier. So Bjurström dropped everything else and set to work, and later while dressing for the formal ceremony he had to reread the typed text while an embassy employee stood by to take it back. Stockholm was plunged in wintry cold that day, with night setting in during the afternoon. By 3 P.M. the vicinity of the old Concert Hall was unapproachable. That box-like building with its pastel blue façade (at that time somewhat soot-stained), in the downtown business district on Sveavägen and Kungsgatan, was the traditional site of the Nobel awards, with its slender gilt-tipped pillars and rose-tinted tapestries hanging from the balconies, and bright yellow dahlias decorating the stage. It was the big event of the year; crowds stood out of doors to watch the dignitaries arrive. Prizewinners and members of the Swedish Academy sat on the stage, while King Gustavus VI and his queen and other members of the royal family were in the front row of the orchestra ensconced in blue armchairs, and just behind them sat the families of the laureates, the diplomatic corps, the Swedish establishment.

The traditional ceremony began with homage to the founder of the prize, Alfred Nobel, chemist, inventor, and manufacturer of explosives, by the secretary-general of the Nobel Foundation; tributes to the winners in their own languages; the diplomas, medals, and checks were handed out by the King himself. Each winner left the stage to shake hands with the King, who spoke to him, smiling and holding his hand; there was applause, and then the next winner descended from the stage. Occasionally there was a music interval (Camus got Maurice Ravel's *Pavane pour une infante défunte*). The secretary of the Swedish Academy, Anders Osterling, presented Camus; Bjurström winced when the speaker described Camus as an existentialist. The King appeared to speak longer to Camus than to any of the other laureates, and the audience seemed pleased. (*Le Monde*'s correspondent would report back that Camus had conquered Stockholm, and noted also that Mrs. Camus had been called the Nobel pinup number one in five-column headlines.)[24]

Bjurström rushed out of the hall, taking the fur stole of Claude Gallimard's wife Simone to keep warm—for the men were all wearing tails and no overcoats—to grab a taxi, having been advised that there would be a mad scramble for transportation to the City Hall for the formal banquet, again in the presence of the royal family. Here in the Golden Hall, with its gold mosaic decoration, Camus delivered his short and formal acceptance speech.[6] After the banquet the guests moved to the larger Blue Hall, where they were joined by Stockholm's students, the girls in formal gowns, the young men in blue uniforms with white-lined capes. Camus joined in the dancing; Blanche Knopf remembered him "cha-cha-chaing with the best of them all night."[25] Clearly he was enjoying it all. At the City Hall an old woman Bjurström knew asked him to have Camus sign her program, but shy Bjurström dared not do that, so she simply walked up to Camus and he signed it.

Camus liked Stockholm's dry cold. The women did not appreciate it as much; they wore two pairs of stockings and woolen underwear, and were dismayed to discover that taxis never got close enough to their destinations; they would always have to walk the extra distance in the snow and then suffocate in heated interiors.[21]

On Thursday, December 12, at 5:30 P.M., Camus met students at Stockholm University for an informal question and answer session, and this too turned political; there was only one literary question, and that silly (about Françoise Sagan). Tension was high, but the Foreign Ministry aide Colliander, seated next to Francine Camus, could not intervene—nor could the head of the university.[22] There were questions on conscientious objectors, on Hungary, and it was Camus himself who introduced the subject of Algeria. Asked about freedom of speech for journalists and writers, he confirmed that censorship existed in Algeria, but insisted on the "total and consoling freedom of the mainland French press."

It was then that a young Moslem—*Le Monde* would call him a representative of the FLN—asked why Camus intervened so readily in Eastern Europe but never in Algeria. From that point the dialogue became confused, turned into a monologue in which the Moslem youth offered slogans, accusations, insults, prevented Camus from speaking. Camus waited for silence before replying, then said sharply: "I have never spoken to an Arab or to one of your militants as you have just spoken to me in public." He went on: "You are for democracy in Algeria, so be democratic right now and let me speak. Let me finish my sentences, because often sentences take on their full meaning only at the end. . . ."[26]

Colliander observed that Camus was upset. His face was pale; his patience had reached its limit.[22] Camus reminded his audience that he had been the only French journalist obliged to leave Algeria for having defended the Moslems, that he favored a fully democratic regime there, that he had spoken out regularly until it had become obvious that the statements of an intellectual could only aggravate the terror. But he assured the Algerian militant that some of his comrades were alive today thanks to actions of which the young man was not aware, and Camus was sorry to have to speak about that. "I have always denounced terrorism," he went on:

> I must also denounce a terrorism which is exercised blindly, in the streets of Algiers for example, and which some day could strike my mother or my family. I believe in justice, but I shall defend my mother above justice.[27]

*Le Monde* reported applause for that. Bjurström noted that the Algerian Moslem had come to the meeting with his own clique; he would return to the rear of the room to confer with them after each exchange. Camus seemed calm, even melancholy, while the Gallimards (also present) appeared nervous. Camus later told Bjurström that he sympathized with the Arab who had been baiting him, and in his letter to *Le Monde*, written principally to deny that he had said the French Government had committed only minor faults in dealing with Algeria, Camus added that he had felt closer to that young Algerian than to many Frenchmen who spoke of Algeria without knowing it. "He knew what he was talking about and and his expression was not one of hate but of despair and misfortune. I share that misfortune. . . ."

The meeting ended soon after Camus' remark about justice and his mother. As they got into their car Camus' wife began to cry, and Camus showed that he was not very satisfied with the incident.[22]

Nothing else would be that bad. Next morning was St. Lucia, and the Camus were served breakfast by a group of young maidens wearing nightgowns and crowns of lighted candles, part of a tradition evoking the shortest day of the year (in each home the youngest daughter is supposed to wake up first and with candles in her hair serve breakfast to the rest of the family).[20] On Friday the Bonniers gave a lunch for Camus at Stallmästaregården, an eighteenth-century stagecoach inn in the northern part of Stockholm facing a wooded lakeshore. There would also be a reception in the Bonnier residence, called Manilla, on the Stockholm island of Djurgården.[28] On Friday afternoon there was a colloquium at the French Embassy with Swedish intellectuals interested in French culture; as the Swedish guests were shy, shy Bjurström broke the ice with a question of his own about the differences between fiction and playwriting, and Camus spoke of his adaptation of *Les Possédés*. A reception at the embassy followed. The editors of *Dagens Nyheter* requested a private interview with Camus for that day, but as they had been hostile Camus was advised against it; he finally agreed to see them on Sunday, and that day didn't suit the reporters.[20] There was also a St. Lucia reception at City Hall during which Camus was to crown the tall blond maiden representing the saint. There was confusion backstage; Lucia was nervous. When Camus realized what was happening he took charge, became the director, told everyone where to stand, and from then on things went smoothly.[22]

Saturday, December 14, was the day of the Nobel lecture at Uppsala, forty miles to the north, on the campus of Sweden's oldest university. As this was Colliander's home town, he was in a better position to oversee things here without actually intervening. He phoned the head of the students' union, told him how things had been going in Stockholm, and requested some questions be prepared on literary subjects. At the railroad station on their arrival Colliander said to Camus: "This is my town and I hope everything will go well." Camus: "What have you done now? I hope you haven't intervened. I can face it." During the ninety-minute meeting with students only literary questions were asked. Afterwards Colliander said: "You see, there were no political questions." Camus: "I saw that." (Smiling.)

In the sober brick University House facing Uppsala's famous cathedral, the party moved into the large auditorium, the Aula, used for the bestowal of doctoral degrees. On that wide stage—a rotunda, resembling the sanctuary of a church, amidst gilt flowers on columns and ceilings—Camus delivered his lecture, which he called "L'Artiste et son temps," *not,* as has already been noted, the same as his 1954 Italian lecture of that title, nor the same as the interview published in *Actuelles II*. It was a wide-ranging speculation on the necessary involvement of the artist in affairs of the world, with a sharp critique of the dangers— the subordination of art to the state, socialist realism.[6]

That night, back in Stockholm, the Camus party went to the theater (to see a Strindberg play); on Sunday they were taken on an excursion and lunched at the Saltsjöbadens Grand Hotel.

They left for Paris on Sunday. On his return Camus would receive a letter from the Association des Algériens en Suède, regretting the incident at the students' meeting. The Algerian who had been shouting at him there represented no one but himself, and the association could certify that he was a member neither of their group nor of any Algerian nationalist group.

A few months later when Bjurström ran into Camus, Camus said he had just heard from a Swedish bank asking what he wanted them to do with his funds. He had deposited his check there in December and said that he had totally forgotten about it.[20]

# 46

## SILENCE

In the impossibility of joining either of the extremes, faced with the progressive disappearance of that third camp in which it was still possible to keep a cool head, doubting also my certainties and my knowledge, persuaded, finally, that the true cause of our madness resides in the mores and the functioning of our intellectual and political society, I have decided not to participate any longer in the unceasing polemics which have had no other result than to harden the uncompromising positions in presence and to divide a little further a France already poisoned by hatreds and clans.

Foreword, *Actuelles III*

The only persons Camus would see henceforth would be friends, those in whom he felt confidence, for whom he had sympathy. The Spanish Republicans always, of course. They fêted him on January 22, and he let them know the singular nature of his appearance: "Even though I have decided to make a rather long retreat, I wanted in any case to accept your invitation." First because these were men of his blood and he could refuse them nothing, and also because *they* had supported *him* in difficult times. In his speech of thanks, published as "Ce que je dois à l'Espagne" ("What I Owe to Spain"), he described the torments of the writer attacked on his right and his left, forced to continue his road while displeasing everyone. He had tried to do the right thing, to respect his profession, to participate, to sign when he was asked to sign. If he had been able to survive it was thanks to friends—friends of Israel, whose country was being threatened in the name of anti-colonialism, but whose right to exist had to be defended; those of South America, and of course those of Republican Spain. He would use his reputation —the prestige of the Nobel Prize—in their service.[1]

This curious speech, half apology for silence, half a promise of commitment, reflected his state of mind in the post-Nobel period. And then he made another public appearance, to meet his favorite left-revolutionary trade unionists, the proofreaders, at the Paris Labor Exchange, where two hundred workers had been assembled by the Cercle d'Études de Correcteurs. Asked for a rule of behavior, he replied: "I refuse energetically to be considered a guide to the working class. . . . It is really too easy to decide from an office what the wage-earner should do."[2]

But his public friends—the Spanish exiles, the revolutionary syndicalists —would not know how ill he was, how much he required rest. Some of his private friends knew, or would learn. Emmanuel Roblès was up from Algiers, staying at the French P.E.N. Club on the Rue Pierre Charron when Camus returned from Stockholm, and they were to meet in that last week of 1957 for lunch. But Camus didn't show up, and knowing that he had always been punctual, Roblès telephoned Suzanne Agnely, who said that he had left the office sometime earlier. When Camus finally arrived his voice was strained as if he were choking on something. He explained that when he had gone out to look for a taxi on Boulevard Saint-Germain he had begun to suffocate, finally managed to ask a passer-by to put him into a cab; he gave the driver his doctor's address and arrived in time for oxygen treatment. He told Roblès how ridiculous it felt to be so helpless, adding that it was not the first time such an incident had occurred.[3]

Or Suzanne Agnely would have to walk him home, at those times when even to go out on the street seemed to terrify him. He was afraid that he would be approached, would be surrounded—now that he was a celebrity. He began to see a psychiatrist as well as his regular doctor. His secretary urged him to visit a specialist on respiratory ailments, and this man told him that he was half-asphyxiated, his brain insufficiently irrigated; from that time on he visited a therapist regularly for exercises in breathing.

He described his condition as "diminished." He couldn't ride the subway because of his claustrophobia. When he flew, his secretary warned the airline that he wished to remain incognito—and that he might become ill suddenly.[4]

But he reassured René Char in a letter dated January 1, 1958: "I am improving. Don't be alarmed. . . . With the support of my doctor, I am going to take the measures necessary to regain repose and joyful wisdom."[5]

Still, his incapacity would last a good part of 1958, until he began to work in earnest on *Le Premier Homme,* which cured him,[4] or was a sign of his cure.

Meanwhile there was other work he could do, not all of it make-work. He wrote a preface for the American edition of his plays. More significantly, he worked on an introduction to a collection of his writings on Algeria—writings from the time of the inquiry on Kabyle poverty in *Alger Républicain,* and the *Combat* series, to the articles in *L'Express* and beyond; the book would be published late that spring. And in mid-January *Requiem for a Nun* ended its triumphal Paris run and was to begin an equally triumphal road tour. Camus had followed it as closely as he could during the recent difficult months, intervening when necessary, not forgetting his role as the play's director. Indeed, when one of the actors was ill—the man who played the Governor— Camus had actually taken over his part. He put on a false mustache but it tickled his nose, and he didn't wear it on the second night. He tried dark glasses but they prevented him from reading, and he had to glance at his lines because he didn't know them by heart. He was good on the first night, he began to tremble on the second, and was worse on the third. He confessed to Robert Cérésol that he couldn't have gone through with it a fourth time.

At the hundredth performance, following a stage tradition, the whole theater had been turned into a party which lasted until 6 A.M., with musicians playing in the theater and lobby; everybody got drunk.[6]

But that had been last year. Now he had a new play on the boards, the revived *Caligula* with Jean-Pierre Jorris. It had good but not great notices. In *Le Monde,* for instance, Robert Kemp thought that in the years since the original production *Caligula* had faded a little, not through its own fault but because of its imitators. And Jorris was not Gérard Philipe. Jorris himself felt that he was presenting a cooler Caligula than Philipe's romantic figure, and he also thought that his interpretation corresponded to Camus' changing attitude toward the play. Or else Camus was simply intrigued by what Jorris was able to do with the part. The play lasted a respectable minimum of performances.[7]

During this period of writing block, on one of their walks across Paris in the early hours of the morning, Camus told Cérésol about a theory of Brice Parain, which suggested a period of silence to allow one to write more and better later on. Camus also saw the theory as an expression of his own inability to create here and now.[8] Catherine Sellers, another constant companion, tried to convince him that he was indeed able to work, and that he *was* producing. She drew up a list of all the articles he had written and the plays he had adapted since she met him. But he told her that those were minor things, insignificant compared to his real work. She pointed out that Dostoevsky hadn't produced his important writing at Camus' age, that many other creators had suffered long periods during which they could not work. By doing even more work in theater, he began to feel that he was accomplishing something (at least), and theater seemed a more valid substitute for his "real work" than the miscellaneous pieces he had been turning out.

He began several projects in this area. One was a translation of *Timon of Athens,* that curiously imperfect play of Shakespeare, but whose central character, the Athenian betrayed by his friends who turns to extreme misanthropy, projects an unambiguous image. (He began by scribbling his own French version into the margins of a bilingual edition.) He also planned a play on Julie de Lespinasse, that eighteenth-century companion of the leading authors of her day, which would air his theory of a double love (loving two women at the same time, a theory which had already attracted him at the end of the 1930s in the work and the life of Eugène Dabit).

But then he would shut himself up in his apartment, as if in hiding. He said that when he felt ill he was like an animal which had to go off by itself. He often used that expression: *bête malade*. And if he was tempted by the notion of suicide, he rejected it in practice as *indigne*, unworthy.[9]

One of his oldest friends from the Algerian years remembered phoning him at about this time. Without saying hello or anything Camus snapped: "You called to ask for money?" There was no humor in his voice; he was clearly a man up against the wall.[10]

Examples of the kind of pressure he was under from family and friends on the Algerian issue can be seen in some of the approaches made to Camus at this time. One was a letter from someone close to his family, warning him to beware of undertaking another mission to Algeria. The last time he was there, this person reminded him, he had almost been the victim of a plot against him: French Algerians wished to murder him because they believed he wanted to give Algeria to the Arabs, while the French wanted nothing more than to stay in the territory without chasing the Arabs out. The letter went on:

> Mendès that ignoble Jew wants to SELL US OUT. Beware of him don't listen to him. He sold everything we had and would like to use you sympathetic as you are to make you his scapegoat. Beware of that snake my son.[11]

From another side came a longtime writer friend from Algeria, who marched into Gallimard one day and asked excitedly to see Camus. Suzanne Agnely said that he wasn't in, but just then Camus came out of his office to talk to his secretary. The visitor and Camus argued violently in front of her. He was demanding to know why Camus didn't join the Moslems' liberation movement. Camus said that he refused violence and murder. The visitor reminded him that he had accepted it during the Nazi occupation. Camus paled. He dismissed his visitor, but then told his secretary: "It's true that I wasn't shocked by resistance to the Nazis, because I was French and my country was occupied. I should accept the Algerian resistance too, but I'm French. . . ."[4]

Raymond Sigaudès, his comrade since amateur theater days, his Sunday companion at Parc des Princes soccer matches, but also a Communist Party member since 1943, made it a point to call on him at Gallimard shortly before the Nobel Prize. Sigaudès urged his friend to declare himself for Algerian independence, but Camus said that he could not. "It's because you are afraid that if you speak out you won't get the Nobel Prize!" Sigaudès cried. Camus seemed upset by the remark, and they would not meet again. Later Sigaudès regretted what he had said, but he would never have an opportunity to tell his friend so.[12]

At least one of the old Belcourt comrades felt that if Camus had lived all the while among his left-wing friends of Algeria he would have been more ready to understand what the Moslems were likely to accept. But living in Paris, Camus may have felt more of a duty to defend the interests of the *pieds noirs* against the unanimous hostility of the French left.[13] Most of Camus' friends realized that the fear of blind terrorism, the bomb in a public place which could kill his mother, was the very real motivation for his opposition to the FLN.[14]

Would Charles de Gaulle save French Algeria? There was more and more talk of a Gaullist comeback, as successive French cabinets showed themselves powerless to come to grips with the Algerian dilemma, let alone to bring the guerrilla war to a close. A strong movement existed—both public and clandestine—to bring de Gaulle to power, legally if possible, but not so legally that it would place de Gaulle in the position of accepting the rules of the game set forth in the Fourth Republic's Constitution he scorned. De Gaulle lived in Colombey-les-Deux-Eglises, some distance east of Paris, but he would come to Paris every Wednesday to receive visitors—who might include ambassadors, other foreign visitors such as Adlai Stevenson, even the Governor General of Algeria, who in principle answered to the French Government. Many of these visitors urged him to return to power, lamented the present state of government in France. Some were actually involved in a plot to bring him back to the captaincy of the state, or to convince him to accept it. By March 1958 the urgings became more pressing, as the danger of internationalization of the war became greater (i.e., interference on the part of the United Nations or of France's traditional allies). Each visitor would come away with a different view of what de Gaulle intended to do. Two visitors in March, for example, left convinced, one, that he would grant independence to Algeria, the other, that he would maintain the territory under French control.[15]

It was in this context that Camus paid a call on de Gaulle, on Wednesday, March 5, 1958, at 11:30 A.M. De Gaulle kept no notes of these Wednesday meetings and no one else did it for him, so there is no official record of what transpired.[16] It was such a discreet contact, in fact, that even a fellow Parisian Algerian who shared Camus' preoccupations, Jules Roy, wasn't told about it, and later in his fictional version of the events of May 1958 which brought de Gaulle back to government, *Le Tonnerre et les Anges,* he had de Gaulle reflect to himself: "Ah, if only I had talked to Camus . . ."[17] Camus' wife remembered only that Camus asked de Gaulle if he intended to return to power, and de Gaulle replied that he would do so only if by legal means, which he felt were excluded.[18]

By March 20, Camus thought that he had pulled out of the worst of his breakdown. "I've just gone through a long and bad period of depression," he confessed to Roger Quilliot, "complicated by respiratory difficulties, and during which I wasn't able to work. Just recently I've begun to catch my breath, which is the right word for it."[5] And he was off to Algeria once again. This time as the successful native son; inevitably there would be more ceremony attached to this visit, despite the atmosphere of urban warfare. Avoiding air travel, he had taken a ship from Marseilles. He was met at the Algiers harbor by brother Lucien, wearing the uniform of the territorial reserve (in which he served several days each week, for the maintenance of order).[19] There would be a reception at the University of Algiers. The hearty congratulations of friends. The significant silences of a visit to his mother in Belcourt.

He had a long talk with Mouloud Feraoun, a Kabyle novelist and essayist, born into a poor family of Haute Kabylie, now a schoolmaster. As Camus had described the poverty of Kabylie in *Alger Républicain,* Feraoun had done it in his book *Fils de pauvre* (1950), and he was certainly ripe for friendship with Albert Camus, although they would never have the time or the opportunity to become close. Feraoun, while hardly an extremist in his nationalism, was the target of French *ultras.* He would die at age fifty under the guns of the right-wing extremist Or-

ganisation Armée Secrète, specialists in counterterrorism, on March 15,
1962, leaving a journal which ends on that day. Feraoun had entered
into a letter friendship with Camus in 1951 after the publication of his
first book, and the 1958 encounter may have been their first real meeting. Camus took the time to visit Feraoun's classes, and posed for photographs with his children in the school gardens. Then they visited a
neighboring shantytown inhabited by poor Moslems, and talked about
the war. Feraoun remembered this remark of Camus that day:

> When two of our brothers engage in a fight without mercy, it is
> criminal madness to excite one or the other of them. Between wis-
> dom reduced to silence and madness which shouts itself hoarse, I
> prefer the virtues of silence. Yes, when speech manages to dispose
> without remorse of the existence of others, to remain silent is not a
> negative attitude.[20]

In his *Journal* entry of April 11, Feraoun noted: "We spent two
hours chatting quite simply and quite frankly." He felt as much at ease
with Camus as he did with his friend Roblès. "He has the same fraternal warmth which cares nothing for effects and forms." The Kabyle
writer felt that Camus' position on Algeria was, as he had imagined,
quite human. He pitied those who suffered, knowing that pity had no
power over evil.[5]

On his return to Paris, and sometime later, Camus wrote Feraoun:
"I have come to hope for a more genuine future, I mean one in which
we shall be separated neither by injustice nor by justice."[20]

While he was still in Algeria the son of Emmanuel Roblès died by
his own gun. Camus rushed to Roblès' home, telephoned to the
newspapers—since he had friends on all of them—to request that they
not publish a story, since Roblès' wife was out of town and they did not
want her to hear about her son's death from the press. Camus spent
that night with Roblès.[21]

There was even time, in that spring sun of the bay of Algiers, to
work, or at least to think about future projects. Once more he took up
that difficult, dense adaptation of Dostoevsky's *Les Possédés*. He decided that he would have to revise it thoroughly, thinking that the job
could be completed before summer. For his writing block continued to
turn his thoughts to the theater; he was more than ever determined to
have a theater of his own, his own production company.

He believed that he had found the right partner at last, in the person of a young theatrical agent in Paris, Micheline Rozan, and as soon
as he returned he would begin to negotiate seriously with all those who
could help him acquire and hold onto a theater. He had been making
other personal decisions: He now was sure that he should have a house

of his own in the South of France, both a family house and a writing house; that was another item for the spring agenda. He also expected that he would be needing another bachelor's flat in Paris, troubles having arisen with the landlord at Rue de Chanaleilles. He asked Micheline Rozan to help him find one, and in her usual business-like fashion she drew up a questionnaire for him; all he had to do was to circle preferred choices or cross out undesirable ones. His preferred Paris neighborhoods, in the order he numbered them for Rozan, were the Faubourg Saint-Germain (where he was then living), the Place Vendôme (perhaps because that would put him halfway between Gallimard and the theater district), Saint-Germain-des-Prés (of course), the pleasantly isolated Ile Saint-Louis (for its beauty, but for no discernible practical reason), Montparnasse, the Opéra (close to the theaters), the Luxembourg Gardens area, Jardin des Plantes, Passy. He struck out the Marais (whose renovation as a bohemian residential district had not yet begun), Parc Monceau, Montmartre. A ceiling was set of 3 to 6 million francs for the purchase of an apartment (some 30,000 to 40,000 francs monthly rent if that was obtainable). But he also realized that if he had to set up an apartment, buy a house, and invest in a theater, his resources would hardly suffice.[22]

He sailed back to France on April 12, was in Cannes at the apartment of the Gallimards on the sixteenth, in Nice the next day for the performance of Catherine Sellers in the *Requiem for a Nun* traveling company (and visiting the sickbed of Roger Martin du Gard there), then back to Cannes, where the Gallimards had left him their boat, a twenty-five-foot racing craft they called *Aya,* manned by two Breton sailors. He wrote mornings in a room facing the harbor, spent afternoons sailing, and he began to feel better.[23]

On May 9, Jean de Maisonseul was in Paris for the opening of an exhibition of his paintings at a small gallery on the Rue Bonaparte. Camus had supplied a preface for the invitation card:

> For the past twenty years, at over a thousand kilometers from Paris, where all is learned but all is forgotten, an artist works in solitude . . . without ever showing what he has been doing. . . .

Of course Camus' name was an additional attraction, and he was present at the *vernissage,* quickly surrounded by newspaper reporters. But Maisonseul was surprised at Camus' disdainful attitude toward the reporters. Seeing that he had distressed his friend, Camus confided to him: "You see, Jean, how I've learned to act a part."[24]

Soon after his trip there Algiers exploded. It was a mutiny, and an organized one, of French military officers, allied to colonialists, rich *pieds noirs,* and modest *ultras,* convinced that the Fourth Republic was giving Algeria away. But they were also convinced that Algeria could be saved for France, even at the cost of liberalized treatment of Moslems, and Moslems were brought into the mutiny, demonstrating for the news cameras alongside French Algerians in favor of a fraternal *Algérie fran-çaise.* The mutiny—or coup—of May 1958 was a strange conspiracy with no single leader, a coup not by Charles de Gaulle but *for* de Gaulle. The resulting disorder caused panic in Paris, the rapid disintegration of the Fourth Republic, thrusting of power into the hands of the providential hero. De Gaulle would begin as Premier under the old rules, to have time to draw up a new Constitution and a new (Fifth) Republic, whose powerful President he would become.

What did Camus think about May 13? His collection of articles on Algeria had already been sent to the printer when it happened, but there was time for a brief note placed before the foreword:

> . . . Great changes are taking place in the mind of Algerians and these changes allow immense hopes as well as fears. But the facts themselves have not changed and tomorrow it will still be necessary to take them into account in order to achieve the only acceptable future: that in which France, basing its action on its own free-doms, will know how to render justice, without discrimination ei-ther in one direction or the other, to all the communities of Algeria.

*Actuelles III,* subtitled *Chroniques algériennes,* was certainly not a way to be silent on Algeria. The material in it was written as late as that year, 1958, contained a clear statement of the author's position, e.g., his endorsement of the Moslem grievances, his disappointment with the refusal of the French to deal with these grievances. Where he differed from French liberals of mainland France was in his own refusal to consider the possibility of the departure of the French-European population from the territory of Algeria; the French Algerians were indigenous, as were the Moslems. The book seemed to lead to an impasse; certainly it made no impact; few in those feverish days seemed to be concerned with step-by-step, reasonable solutions. (De Gaulle himself would at first seem to be supporting an *Algérie française*—which is why the *mutins* and the *ultras* demanded that he return to power—only to become the architect of Algerian independence once he was in a position to bring it about.)

To one friend, Guy Dumur, who was having lunch at the Michel Gallimard apartment on the day de Gaulle returned to government, Camus seemed convinced that *le Général* could indeed save Algeria. Camus had not had lunch with Dumur and the Gallimards, but he had been in the apartment. He invited Dumur to talk to him afterwards;

Dumur came away from their meeting with the feeling that Camus had not been realistic about the significance of the FLN rebellion.[25] A still older friend, Charles Poncet, also discovered that Camus had believed in the "sincerity" of the events of May, i.e., that there had been true fraternity that day between French Algerians and Moslems on the vast, marble-floored Forum in front of the Government General. When Poncet explained to him how the French Army had organized the demonstration by sending trucks out to the countryside to round up Moslems, Camus was saddened, and murmured: "If that's what is happening, it's all over."[13]

Perhaps he might have become a useful asset for the Gaullists. Once they asked him, indirectly, if he would join the government to take a high position in the cultural field, but he refused.[18] His friends had the impression that he had met with de Gaulle several times to seek pardons for Algerians.[25] There is no record of any meeting except the somewhat formal public lunch later that year at the Prime Minister's residence, the Hôtel Matignon. Camus would not have gone at all because he disliked all such official occasions, but his wife, who was anxious to meet de Gaulle, had obliged him to accept. He had asked Suzanne Agnely to find out if it was to be a large gathering, and was assured that it would be a small one. But when the Camus arrived to find a dozen other guests, he was furious at his wife for having dragged him there. De Gaulle asked questions of each guest in turn. Camus asked an aide of de Gaulle what the government would do if there were an electoral majority in favor of integration (of Moslems and French Algerians) and the man replied: "The Algerians want economic improvement, not integration," to which Camus and his wife together exclaimed: "They want their dignity!" Camus spoke of the art of governing; there was talk of Tolstoy's *War and Peace*.

Soon after that Camus would confide to a friend: If the Fourth Republic had been the government of torture in Algeria, the Fifth was a shaky monarchy. France, he added, seemed to have a nostalgia for kings.[18]

But Camus' first bit of private business that May concerned the theater, and Micheline Rozan. At the age of twenty-three she had begun to work in public relations at the Théâtre National Populaire, during the heroic era of that repertory company, when Gérard Philipe was its star. She had been close to Maria Casarès. Then she went to work for the French branch of the American theatrical agency MCA, where she handled director Peter Brook, Jeanne Moreau, Jean-Paul Belmondo, and other French stars, as well as MCA's American authors such as Arthur Miller and Tennessee Williams. Through Maria Casarès she had met Camus, who after the Nobel Prize needed an agent to handle the foreign performances of his works. Soon she was helping him with domestic theater problems, too, and in the first months of their relationship she became associated with his attempts to find a stage for his adaptation of *Les Possédés*.

That would not be easy. One of their first ideas was actually an old idea, that of taking over the small Récamier, the theater he had first tried to rent from the Ligue de l'Enseignement as early as 1952. Now he drafted a formal proposal with Micheline Rozan, which would have made him president of a company operating the Récamier for a trial period of two years, with complete freedom to choose repertory and cast.[22]

While waiting for the Ligue to reply he was off to Greece. The Michel Gallimards had arranged to rent a boat moored in Piraeus, the harbor of Athens. They flew to Athens with Janine's daughter Anne and their favorite cruising partners, the artist Mario Prassinos and his wife Io, and their child Catherine. (Prassinos designed the bound editions, often considered first editions, of Camus' work.) Camus picked up Maria Casarès and took her to Rhodes, where they joined the others on their boat.

Before the trip both Camus and Michel Gallimard had expressed misgivings about going off at a time of crisis in France; certainly the press would criticize Camus for leaving. The situation was such that Michel had been afraid to leave Anne alone in Paris, which is why she was brought along.

But they had soon put such thoughts behind them. Their boat, called *Fantasia*, was a converted naval vedette, and had an English couple on board who served as crew. The Englishwoman did the cooking, with predictable reactions from her passengers. Her chicken dishes were particularly inedible and they threw their portions overboard as discreetly as they could. By the third day they got up the courage to tell the captain that his wife's chicken was not what they preferred. In compensation, he was a cautious navigator.

On one island they discovered Father Bruckberger, wearing a checkered cowboy shirt, in the company of a dowager, watching the boats sail in.

Prassinos did a book of pencil sketches during the voyage, to which Camus added a text in ink, a lyrical saga full of poetic repetition, a satirical log of their days on board. He described himself, for example, as chaste Saint Albert.

Camus was struck by one site: Sigri, at the western tip of the island of Mytilene (also called Lesbos, Sappho's island), a ruggedly moun-

tainous landscape of vineyards and olive trees. He promised himself
that he would come back here.[23]

On the other hand, their brief landing on the Turkish coast was to
prove less of a success. They attempted to walk around the village of
Marmaris, but they were followed everywhere by a growing crowd of
curious villagers; finally they fled back to the isolation of the *Fantasia*.[26]

Their idyll was interrupted by a French reality. In Paris at a press
conference on June 24, André Malraux, whom de Gaulle had immediately brought into his cabinet, declared that no act of torture had taken
place in Algeria since de Gaulle's visit there. (On June 4 de Gaulle had
delivered his ambiguous "I understood you!" to French Algerians who
mobbed the Forum to cheer him.) Malraux went on to say: "In the
name of the French government I hereby invite the three French writers
on whom the Nobel Prize had bestowed particular authority, and who
have already studied these problems, to form a commission which will
visit Algeria. I am in a position to assure them that they will receive
proper credentials from General de Gaulle."

But Martin du Gard was critically ill, would die in two months'
time; Mauriac was skeptical. As for Camus, he abhorred just this sort
of collective endeavor. He replied as soon as he could—from Athens on
July 1—asking his secretary to inform the press that he would give his
response when he had more information about the project.

Malraux's biographer reported that Camus did not wish to take
part in a campaign alongside partisans of the FLN; Malraux even
beseeched Camus to become a sort of permanent ambassador of the
French conscience in Algiers, in the name of de Gaulle, but Camus
demurred.[27] The charitable thing would be to add that Malraux's improvised invitation, like most of his other political initiatives of that period, was more ardent than practical; he had not bothered to make sure
that the Nobel Prize authors would accept before launching his appeal.[28]

The Ligue de l'Enseignement turned down the Camus-Rozan proposal
during his absence, and now he had to choose between Jacques Hébertot, owner of a theater called by his name (where *Les Justes* had been
produced), and Jean-Louis Barrault, who could offer space but no
financing. But the Greek islands had given Camus new strength, and he
would now take personal charge of negotiations.[29] On July 17 he met
with Hébertot, who told him that he would be interested in *Les
Possédés* and in Camus only with outside backing. Meanwhile the
Sarah Bernhardt Theater became available starting that October, but
Camus felt that his cast would not be ready by then; he had Catherine

Sellers and Dominique Blanchar particularly in mind. (Nor would he himself be ready, and that theater was far too big for his purposes.) Then Barrault, who indicated that he himself would produce the play at the smaller Palais Royal Theater, changed his mind. Instead he would join Camus as a partner if they could get the Récamier, and once again Camus pleaded with the Ligue. But this time *he* had to withdraw, for it was discovered that the small size of the Récamier, the cost of the production, and the conditions set by the Ligue for use of the theater made it impossible to produce a play of the dimensions of *Les Possédés* there.

These details are not important. What they—and further details to be presented here—are meant to show is that the stage would occupy a considerable share of Camus' days, and many of his nights, for the remaining months of his life. Finally *Les Possédés* would be put on at a boulevard theater—hardly the ideal site, but it was the fourteenth theater they had tried—as a co-production, financed by the theater's owners in part, in part by Camus and his friends and associates, including Micheline Rozan, who borrowed money to be able to do it. Camus and Michel Gallimard had each put up two million francs, in addition to which Camus lent the production four million; a part of Camus' investment came from Seven Arts Productions in the United States, which received in return an option on American performance rights to Camus' plays, and from MCA's French company. The investors would not get their money back.[22]

There were also two acts of piety to perform: to write a preface to a new edition of Jean Grenier's *Les Iles,* that book which had so affected the lycée student Albert Camus, and to issue a statement on the death of Martin du Gard. A discreet statement, for Martin du Gard "believed that a writer owed his public his work, and not his person," and practiced discretion concerning his private life:

> The last conversation that I had with him, in Nice in May, and during which he spoke a good deal about death, also contained several allusions to the necessity, for an artist, of reserve and secrecy. . . .

In tribute, Camus affirmed that "the very existence of this incomparable man helped us to live. . . ."[30]

At the end of August he joined Francine and the children at a house he had found for rent at Cabrières d'Avignon, not far from L'Isle-sur-la-Sorgue. It was a modest house, its main usefulness being as a base for exploration of the region to look for a house to *buy,* for that was definitely in the cards now. They were excited by one house in the Alpilles hills near Saint-Rémy-de-Provence, isolated and with a slope all to itself, and they saw others they could not agree on. But nothing was settled when it was time for Francine to return to her teaching job in Paris in September.[18]

The rest would happen quickly. Camus and his wife had already visited a house with a real estate agent in the market town of Cavaillon, Jean Cornut, a friend of friends of René Char. In fact they were tempted by an old country house, the kind called a *mas* in Provence, but they hesitated too long, and someone else got it. Shortly after that Cornut learned that Dr. Olivier Monod, the noted Paris surgeon, was selling a house in the village of Lourmarin. When Cornut looked it over he decided it was just what Camus wanted. Camus seconded the motion, and by invoking the Nobel Prize of his buyer, Cornut got the owners to promise a forty-eight-hour option so Camus could phone his wife to hurry down to look at it.[31] When she did, she immediately regretted the more isolated country places they had seen; this one was smack in the middle of a street of village houses. But her husband, tired of looking at houses (they had visited fifteen), warned her: "It's this or nothing." Confronted with an argument like that, she could only acquiesce.[18]

During his second visit, possibly on September 24, 1958, Camus asked that an effort be made to reduce the purchase price. Dr. Monod's daughter, then fifteen, promptly agreed to take 700,000 francs off the original purchase price, so that the final price was 9.3 million francs (some 220,000 francs of 1975, or about $45,000).

They signed the purchase agreement, handing over a portion of the price of the house, at a smaller house which the Monods also possessed in Lourmarin, on October 18. Camus also promised that he would take good care of the olive trees on the property.[32]

# 47

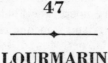

## LOURMARIN

The theater offers me the community I need. . . .

"Gros plan"

Unlike so many other Provençal sites Lourmarin was not overrun by progress, or by tourists. It remained a village surrounded by vineyards, the vineyards sheltered by the benign hills of the Luberon chain. Avignon, the capital of its Vaucluse Department, is thirty-five miles to the west and north, Aix-en-Provence, the art and university town, twenty-three miles to the east and south. René Char's L'Isle-sur-la-Sorgue is little more than twenty miles distant. With a population of some six hundred year-round inhabitants, Lourmarin seems to be on a side track; what summer residents there were then lived discreetly, and there was no apparent mushroom growth. Not even local inhabitants realized how many of the old houses actually belonged to outsiders.

The village faces an old castle across a field; the castle, with surviving medieval and Renaissance wings, owes its present use to a fatal automobile accident. It had been restored by Robert Laurent-Vibert, the adopted son of a wealthy manufacturer. A brilliant scholar, professor of history and author, Laurent-Vibert had discovered the Lourmarin castle in ruins, restored it, willed it to the Académie des Sciences, Agriculture et Belles-Lettres of Aix-en Provence. Then in the spring of 1925, after a voyage to the United States and while he was planning an archaeological expedition to a Roman site he had discovered in Syria, Laurent-Vibert was returning to Lyons from Lourmarin, accompanied by a friend (a Paris publisher named Georges Crès), driving rapidly as he liked to do, when the car skidded, turned over, throwing both passengers onto the road. Laurent-Vibert died, his friend survived.[1] Under his will the Aix academy established the Fondation de Lourmarin Laurent-Vibert, which opened the castle as a summer home for artists and writers—such as Jean Grenier at the end of the 1920s—who live among curiously sculptured Renaissance fireplaces and heavy oak furniture, use a serpentine staircase in carved stone, old porcelain.

The town of Lourmarin has Protestant and Catholic churches. Once the Protestants were in the majority, but, thanks to the Catholic rule that children of mixed marriages must be raised in the Church, the latter community is now the larger. A wall separated the two cults in the local cemetery, although the segregation is disappearing.

The Olivier Monods had long been associated with Lourmarin. Though a practicing doctor in Paris—his specialty happened to be lung surgery—Dr. Monod was elected mayor of Lourmarin. The Monods had discovered the village in 1938, and acquired the house they would later sell to the Camus in 1949. They had transformed the old structure somewhat: It had been the home of a local farmer and dignitary, and they made a maid's room out of a pigsty, a shower out of a wine-press. Then they decided to move a short distance out of the village proper, and so put up the house for sale.

It was a disparate structure, with small components on varying levels, each roofed with Provençal-style reddish-brown tiles. Medieval-seeming on the village side, its contours conformed to the winding lane (then called the Rue de l'Eglise, now the Rue Albert Camus) which starts at a stone fountain where the water gushes from a bronze lion's head. Facing the fields on the other side, the house seemed to be perched atop a platform, this platform actually a terrace on which it rested; the terrace was enclosed by a stone balustrade; from here there was a sweeping view of the Durance valley, the castle just opposite, and (to the left) the cypress trees marking the site of the village cemetery. The garden contained fig trees, rosebushes, rosemary. By the time the Camus moved in, it was largely abandoned; Camus told his gardener that he wanted it put in order, the grass trimmed, but with "nothing fancy." Facing the garden on a lower level was a stable where the Camus would keep a small donkey which Pierre Blanchar shipped them from Algeria. Above it was a garage where Camus would keep his faithful old Citroën.

Of course the Camus quickly made changes of their own. Camus decorated a small patio with a stone fountain and bench, set a sun motif into the wall above the door (which opened to a Ping-Pong room also containing a punching bag). He made an office of the large upstairs room which the Monods had called the Chambre du Doge, for it had been used by an amateur theatrical company in which their children played, and one of the plays had been *The Merchant of Venice*. Before their time, the room had been used for the raising of silkworms.[2]

The house would give Camus an opportunity to do more of the kind of shopping he liked, for old furniture in dim junk and antique shops. He told Robert Cérésol: "I'm ashamed to pay 150,000 francs for an old wardrobe when there is so much misery in the world." But when Jacqueline Bernard ran into him in Paris and he told her that he had been making the rounds of the shops looking for a Louis XVI bed for his daughter, and other pieces, she teased him: "Didn't you once say that you'd be content with a simple hotel room?" He laughed. "I said that I'd be willing to die in a hotel room, not to live in one."

For Camus, of course, Lourmarin was first of all Grenier's Lourmarin. Some of the first essays Camus had read by his teacher evoked this site, and Camus had been here, as we have suggested, before World War II, as well as shortly after the war. "I put my footsteps in yours," he would tell Grenier. It was not Char's L'Isle-sur-la-Sorgue, but then there had been nothing suitable to purchase there, and even with winding roads one could drive to Char's place in half an hour.

In Paris, rehearsals were under way for a second road tour of *Requiem for a Nun,* and soon after he returned from signing the papers for the acquisition of the Lourmarin house, *Les Possédés* was ready to go into rehearsal. Although he had been cutting and cutting—his first version was 268 typewritten pages in length and would have required five hours of playing—he still had twenty-eight actors and eight scenes.[3] (His earliest adaptation of the novel, which he dated 1953, contained sixty-five scenes.[4]) The stars would include Pierre Blanchar (as Stepan Verkhovensky), Pierre Vaneck (as Stavrogin), Michel Bouquet as Verkhovensky's son, Catherine Sellers as Maria Timopheievna Lebyatkin.

She was to discover that Camus' directing was now more polished, more elaborate, than it had been for *Requiem*. The cutting of the Dostoesvky novel into scenes was already an act of direction, and he had incorporated material from Stavrogin's Confession and from Dostoevsky's journal, kept during the writing of the novel. Camus emphasized the violence and even the madness of his characters, and felt that his actors were a bit too tame.[4] He respected the text and demanded respect for it, but beyond that left much of the interpretation to the actors themselves.[5]

They began with a reading of the play, seated around a table. Then veteran actor Blanchar discovered Camus' innovation: a second reading, this time in motion. "Move as you feel like, Camus would say, "or sit down when you feel the need to sit. Do what the text inspires you to do." And he watched, waiting for the characters to spring out of his actors; he believed the resulting interpretation had to be the true one, and rejected the idea of imposing his own. In one instance, when an actor had a choice of two roles and Camus preferred him in one of them, the actor said he himself preferred the other, and Camus accepted the choice. Never did he suggest the tone to take, the gesture or expression. He directed by convincing explanations. Seated near Camus in the empty theater when he wasn't needed on the stage, Blanchar observed the tension in his friend's expression and breathing, because he did want his actors to get it right. He would scribble little notes for individual actors, referring to the original text of the novel in support of a suggestion. Or he would have folk music played before rehearsals, and during breaks, to set the mood. When he was told that the play would go over better with the audience if two scenes were omitted, a childbirth and a murder, he refused to allow the cuts, preferring to sacrifice his interests rather than betray Dostoevsky.[6]

During this time of public silence and private activity, Algeria was not the only political problem on his mind. The war had put increased pressure on young men of draft age who did not wish to serve, but there was no law in France to protect them, not even a precedent for conscientious objection to military service. Now he would lend his pen and his name, with discretion, to the pacifists who had initiated a campaign to allow young men to choose alternate service to their country. He did this among the left-revolutionary militants with whom he preferred to work.

Old Louis Lecoin had been a lifelong pacifist, anarchist, crusader for liberal causes. He had spent twelve years in French prisons, calculating that only Louis Blanqui, a leader of the 1848 revolution, had served more time in prison because of his beliefs. In 1927 he campaigned for the release of Sacco and Vanzetti, and was locked up when he mingled with delegates to a Paris convention of the American Legion and began to shout: "Vivent Sacco et Vanzetti!" In 1936 he founded a Comité pour l'Espagne Libre, which became Solidarité Internationale Antifasciste, whose newspaper was regularly confiscated and prosecuted. As an active pacifist he was interned in the south Sahara during World War II.

In January 1958 he founded the periodical Liberté to campaign for conscientious objectors. Camus at once joined the sponsoring committee of a new Comité de Secours aux Objecteurs de Conscience, with André Breton, Jean Cocteau, Jean Giono, and others. Because those who refused to serve in the draft were then liable to long terms of imprisonment, Camus helped Lecoin draft a letter on behalf of the new committee, which was submitted to the government on October 15,

1958. The letter contained a request that, while a law was being considered which would give legal status to conscientious objection, those already in prison for refusing to be drafted should be released after having served a period equal to their military obligation. Camus also put his hand to the draft legislation which the committee submitted to the government. He would follow that up in March 1959 with a letter to President de Gaulle, also in behalf of the Comité de Secours. "We know that everything cannot be done at once and we understand the need for patience," he wrote. But some thirty sincere conscientious objectors were then in prison for over twenty-seven months, and time, which passed more slowly for them than for other people, made patience difficult.

De Gaulle replied that he would look into the matter, but more patience was needed. Camus had only nine more months to live. Lecoin, at seventy-four, with a heart disease, began a hunger strike, and by threatening to pursue it he contributed to the passing of a law in December 1963 which accorded special status to conscientious objectors, establishing a form of civil service, although Lecoin still hoped that in the future a bill would be passed which would eliminate the punishment factor, in the sense of the draft statute submitted by Camus.[7]

On November 12, 1958, there was activity of another sort. Making an exception to his refusal to take part in ceremony involving Algeria, he accepted an invitation to be the guest of honor at a dinner of French Algerians residing in France, members of a group called L'Algérienne. It was a true *pied noir* affair, and an *"Algérie française"* occasion; the guests included civil servants, businessmen, but also artists and writers. Pierre Blanchar was there, as was the prefect of the Paris police, Maurice Papon, formerly assigned to Algeria. The president of l'Algérienne, a retired colonel, noted in his introduction to Camus that his appeal for a civil truce had not been listened to in January 1956, but that it was an early example of the policy of fraternity in which de Gaulle's government was now engaged. Camus spoke *"entre Algériens,"* in a relaxed manner, letting his own *pied noir* accent show through.

> I owe to Algeria not only my lessons of happiness but . . . of suffering and misfortune. . . . These lessons have become a bit burdensome in recent times—

But he saw reasons for hope as well. The writers of Algeria had been doing their duty, he said, and for a long time. He didn't know what the Algeria of tomorrow would be like, how it would be created, what it would cost in blood and unhappiness. "But what I can say is that tomorrow's Algeria, we Algerian writers created it yesterday."[8]

These things he could do—but he could not write. He confided to Nicola Chiaromonte that he was able to work only when obliged to do a preface or other piece of occasional writing. He had tried, of course, but in vain. He was living in a kind of interior inertia, waiting for an interior revolution to occur.

And as the year drew to a close, he remarked to Robert Mallet, a fellow editor at Gallimard (who noted it in his journal at the date of December 5, 1958), that he felt that both sides in the Algerian conflict would have to be reasonable for there to be a basis for understanding. When Mallet suggested that Camus could help bring that about, he replied:

> I don't think so. I am suspect to the nationalists of both sides. I am blamed by one side for not being sufficiently . . . patriotic. For the other side I'm too much so. . . . What too many Arabs don't understand is that I love [Algeria] as a Frenchman who loves Arabs, and wants them to be at home in Algeria, without himself having to feel a stranger there because of that.[9]

His private interventions for Algerians indicted or convicted would continue, all during this last year of his life. The first one of the new year, as it happened, would be for an old friend. Amar Ouzegane, once a Communist Party secretary in Algiers (and Camus' superior and accuser), later a member of the FLN's underground brain trust, a member of the Civil Truce Committee, had been arrested as a dangerous rebel. He was brought to trial a full year later, in January 1959, and Camus sent a message to the Tribunal Permanent des Forces Armées in Algeria:

> I the undersigned, Albert Camus, certify that Mr. Amar Ouzegane participated at my side in the creation of a committee which, in February 1956, tried to organize a truce destined to spare the lives of French and Moslem civilians of Algeria, and that he did everything that it was in his power to do for the success of this enterprise of a purely humanitarian purpose.

It didn't help much, unless Ouzegane risked a death sentence, for he got eight years, and was freed only after the cease-fire in April 1962. After that he went on—but this has already been said in these pages—to become a cabinet minister in the independent Algerian government.[10]

Camus sent constant urgent appeals to de Gaulle, to de Gaulle's close adviser and minister Malraux,[11] and then to the new Commission de Sauvegarde when it was finally established. This group, in which he had refused to participate, he literally bombarded with requests for clemency, submitting lists of names, receiving from the commission status reports on the cases to which he had called their attention, i.e., lists of Moslems for whom Camus had intervened and who were to be liberated from jail. On at least one occasion Malraux told Camus that he had personally given de Gaulle some documents received from Camus appealing for pardons in death sentences.[12]

Malraux attended the opening of *Les Possédés* at Paris's Théâtre Antoine at the end of January 1959. Three hours before the opening the minister's chief aide had phoned Suzanne Agnely to ask that a box be set aside for him; she felt from the aide's remarks on that and on a later occasion that Malraux wanted to do something for Camus, to make amends in a sense. . . .[13] Whatever the motive, Malraux was on hand, and the popular afternoon daily *France-Soir* put his picture on the front page with a headline:

### AT THE OPENING OF "LES POSSEDES" AT THE THEATER ANTOINE, THE STAR WAS (IN THE AUDIENCE) ANDRE MALRAUX

The paper's gossip columnist noted, also on the front page, that the play ran three hours and forty minutes, so that at the first intermission everyone hurried to the buffet where a glass of whiskey cost 700 francs but vodka only 250 francs. Georges Pompidou, former aide to de Gaulle and later to succeed him as President of France, shared Malraux's box; Prefect Papon was also present, as were Louis Aragon and Elsa Triolet; Bouquet, Blanchar, Vaneck, and Catherine Sellers got most of the applause.

*Les Possédés* had a respectable press but a comparatively short run, and, as has been said, it would not make the investment back. The production was costly, the theater was not quite right for it: In Paris different kinds of plays went to different theaters, and this work was too serious for the boulevard audiences which the Théâtre Antoine generally attracted, although both Sartre and Tennessee Williams had been produced there. In October 1959 the play would leave for a four-month tour of the French provinces, Switzerland, Belgium and Luxembourg, North Africa and Portugal.

Being involved in theater again of course made Camus happy.[14] He told his new friend and neighbor Olivier Monod that Dostoevsky's play was dearer to him than any of his previous work, perhaps because it had cost him so much effort.[15] There may have been another reason. For now more than ever the political content of the play would have appealed to him. In essence, *The Possessed* recorded the stirrings of new Russia, but through reckless and irresponsible spokesmen. The novel offered a series of tableaux of the best of czarist Russia and the most questionable of the liberal views. From the beginning Dostoevsky's novel had been taken as an exposé of nihilism, but also as an attack on liberal-left apologists for what Dostoevsky construed as nihilism. Because of this political content the Soviet Union treated *Les Possédés* as right-wing propaganda, "socially obnoxious and detrimental to the cause of socialism," and it was regularly attacked by Communist critics after the October Revolution. One of Dostoevsky's readers, the late Marc Slonim, would write that Dostoevsky himself saw his novel as an attack on "the demonic nature of revolutionary forces"; he had wanted to mock the "beautiful souls" of the useless liberals, to demonstrate that the progressive humanists of nineteenth-century Russia were responsible for the socialist leanings of the following generation. The character Peter Verkhovensky, "who deals with human beings with utter cynicism," says Slonim, "and is always plotting, intriguing, thriving on scandals, is a typical Communist politician of the Stalin era."[16]

Camus may not have seen all of this in Dostoevsky's novel, but he certainly saw the opportunity to deal with an irresponsible form of revolutionary agitation. Until the final days of his life, in any case, he would keep close watch over his cherished work. Even at times and in places where he could not be present to meet with the cast, he would communicate with them by notes or letters to individual actors, sometimes containing suggestions, often simply words of encouragement.[4] One such note, marked "Prayer of the absent one," read:

> The play should begin with fireworks, continue as a flame-thrower, end in flames. So don't forget, firemen go through all red lights.[17]

By the time it closed in July 1959 *Les Possédés* had a net deficit of 11,212,000 francs. The director of the theater wrote to Malraux, now Minister of Culture in Premier Michel Debré's cabinet, to plead for a reimbursement of taxes (over 8 million francs) to help meet the deficit. Malraux's office replied that nothing could be done except to reimburse taxes on the first thirty performances, for a total of some 1.5 million francs.[14]

But the government was nevertheless to be the prime source of financing in the scheme drawn up by Camus and Micheline Rozan for a new theatrical company. France had a long tradition of government support for the stage. The Comédie Française, the Théâtre National Populaire, and other Parisian and provincial repertory companies were largely state-financed. The hope was that the government—with Malraux in a position to influence if not to direct decisions—would commit itself to a regular subsidy to meet the expected operating deficit of Camus' projected theater, a deficit estimated at some 40 million francs (about

900,000 francs of the mid-1970s, or about $180,000) per year. Camus discussed this face to face with Malraux. But, as would soon become apparent, for all his brilliance as an innovator Malraux was incapable of making the government machinery work for him. Instead of finding ways to make the necessary funds available to Camus, Malraux put the matter into the hands of his bureaucrats, and they would follow bureaucratic procedures. Later on, after Camus' death, theatrical subsidies of this kind became more common, but Camus' scheme arrived too early in Malraux's reign.

The negotiations would go on from the time of the opening of *Les Possédés* in January 1959 until Camus' death nearly a year later, and there is convincing evidence that they would have produced a concrete result early in the new year, 1960, had Camus lived.[14]

On March 18, 1959, Camus wrote to René Char about his feeling of depression, "against which it becomes so difficult, so exhausting to struggle when youth fades away, and with it, the strength of insolence and of indifference. Yes, I am tired right now, I admit it."[18]

Immediately after that there was another trial. He was called to Algeria, where his mother was operated on for obstruction of the bowels, after a strangulated hernia. He had been worried, because she was now seventy-seven years old, but everything went well. While in Algeria he was invited, as the favorite son, the Nobel Prize winner, to visit his birthplace, Mondovi (a site he wished to see if only to help him construct the autobiographical novel he was soon to begin). But at the last minute he had to wire his excuses; he was due back in Paris for the filming of a television program.[19]

The program was "Gros plan"—literally Close-Up, a series conceived by the producer-director Pierre Cardinal (who happened to be the scion of a French Algerian family), in which a well-known person would speak directly to the camera, and alone, on the theory that the television screen was designed for monologue. Cardinal had launched the series with the actor Michel Simon, the actress Michèle Morgan. One of his subjects, in 1956, had been Maria Casarès, and it was at that time that he met Camus. (He had noticed him earlier at the home of one of Algiers' wealthiest families, privately shocked that Camus seemed so much at ease in high society, but that was Cardinal's reaction against his own milieu.)

For the "Gros plan" on Camus, Cardinal began working with his subject the previous October; they would spend hours at a time planning the program. The idea was that Camus would talk about the theater, his monologue to be interrupted occasionally by excerpts of *Les Possédés* filmed with the original cast at the Théâtre Antoine. Camus would write out his text in Cardinal's presence and read it to him. (When Cardinal offered to take the scraps of paper on which Camus was writing and to have them typed, Camus insisted on having them done himself, saying that he wished to keep his drafts because he sold them to an American; that, too, shocked Cardinal.) They did three separate versions before they had what they wanted. Camus seemed to be afraid of television, wasn't sure how to approach it. He feared that his text would be too literary; Cardinal said that on the contrary it should be, for television was meant for that.

The actors had been filmed earlier. Cardinal had to meet with Gérard Philipe, who represented the actors' union in negotiations for the use of the cast, for the actors were not to be paid. When Philipe demanded that union conditions be respected, Camus replied: "My actors will play for me anyhow."[20] (In fact the actors *were* dissatisfied. They had been told that if they agreed to perform without pay for "Gros plan" it would help keep the play going; Camus seemed uncomfortable in the role of employer.[4])

Camus went before the cameras for four days in April, and Cardinal never forgot an incident that took place during the filming. At one point he called out to his cameraman: "Albert, go that way . . . Hurry up," using the familiar *"tu"* form to address him. Thinking that it was he who had been addressed, Camus snapped: "Call me Mister, if you please!" When Camus understood what had happened he apologized, and some days later he made overtures of friendship. But they would never really become close.[20]

What came out of "Gros plan" perhaps looked good on French television of the 1950s; television then had no experience with spontaneous dialogue, and—worried about stage fright—Camus had memorized his lines. The result seemed stiff and awkward to some viewers, while the fact that Camus was reciting a text written out in advance was obvious. But it is a significant text, being Camus' credo of theater, and if it doesn't have to be watched it is a helpful tool to the understanding of Camus' happiness as a director.[21]

In a talk with Robert Mallet shortly before the filming of "Gros plan," Camus had confessed that he was poor at improvisation, that his interviews betrayed preparation. "I like . . . to take the precaution of being clear." He winced when Mallet spoke of his *beau style*. "I prefer that people say: the style that suits a writer. . . . I'm convinced that a good writer is one who expresses himself as he is, as he feels, without more negligence than artifice. That's why I don't prefer disorderly people to mannered ones." He summed up: "I have only one certitude: my need to be moved in order to write well."[9]

Those who knew Camus as a man of the theater found a confirmation of what they already sensed in "Gros plan," which was first broadcast on French television on May 12, 1959. Why did he work in the theater? The reply, he feared, would seem of a "discouraging banality. Quite simply because a theater stage is one of the places of the world where I am happy." On the stage he escaped what "bothers me in my work as a writer," the senseless demands on his time, for "everybody respects work for the theater."

And it was true. All of those who worked with him knew that. Because of the jealousies prevalent in literary circles he had few true friends there, and didn't really like most of his fellow writers of Saint-Germain-des-Prés. He would escape into what he called *"la grande fraternité du théâtre,"* would work, eat, drink, and spend his evenings with his cast; while the play was running he would go to the theater late to stay on for supper or drinks with his actors and actresses. More, when he wrote and staged a play he felt that he was not alone to confront the critics: He had a *company* with him. In literature he had to wear a mask (and a tie), and assume a stuffy attitude; in the theater he was free. For the Festival d'Angers, for example, rehearsals had been held in the Bois de Boulogne Pré Catelan outdoor theater and he had brought his young children along, something that had practically never happened at Gallimard.

When his secretary arrived at the theater where he was working, carrying correspondence and messages concerned with his literary career, he would laugh and say: "I've got a show to put on." He might seem to have the same attitude when he was working at Gallimard and theater people showed up, but it was *not* the same attitude; he would have preferred to give up literature for the theater.

Still, he was quite aware in lucid moments that his "real work" was to write books, and in solitude.[13]

In May 1959 he was finally able to get away to the new house in Lourmarin. He arrived to bright sunshine, got to work settling in, soon had a routine: working on the house mornings, sitting at his desk afternoons, in the evening reading next to the fireplace. His wife and daughter came to stay for some days. He himself felt that he was getting better, and he found that he liked the life of the monastery. He signed letters to friends "Frère Albert O.D.," i.e., Order of the Dominicans.

Soon he had developed a routine in the village as well. He walked a lot. He enjoyed talking to the local people. One of his new friends was César Marius Reynaud, the village blacksmith, whose family had been smiths since the sixteenth century. Reynaud did some work for Camus at the new house, and told him stories of the Lourmarin of earlier times.[22] The villagers noticed that the newcomer favored no clan; he was friendly with everybody. The first time the owner of the garage called him *Maître,* a respectful term for a writer, he said he didn't like that. The garageman asked when he was going to be elected to the French Academy, and he replied: "Don't talk to me about that. I hate people who sit around doing nothing."[23]

The local people would occasionally run into another resident writer, Henri Bosco, the Avignon-born novelist and poet who was then seventy-one, but Bosco always seemed distant and haughty compared to Camus. (Bosco died in 1976, and was buried in Lourmarin's cemetery.) In a local café one day when he was with the Lourmarin soccer team—which he had begun to help finance—Camus was told that someone was on the telephone from Paris and he replied: "Let him call back later. I'm with friends." And when he was in Lourmarin on a Sunday he would watch the games played by the local Jeunesse Sportive.

He had a housekeeper who would cook for him, but he would take some of his meals at the old Hôtel Ollier and restaurant only a few steps from his house. The hotel had been in the same family for a century. A homely building, it had conventional tables and chairs designed for hard use, checkered tablecloths. Artists in residence at the nearby castle would draw sketches and paint watercolors into the guest book given to owner Paulette Ollier by Edy-Legrand, and which this painter had decorated. Two of Edy-Legrand's paintings are among the landscapes hung in the main dining room.

Even when he dined alone in the small private room to the right of the entrance hall to avoid mixing with patrons of the regular restaurant, Madame Ollier would walk through the restaurant shouting in the direction of the kitchen: "One cutlet for Mr. Camus," so he was hardly incognito in Lourmarin.[15]

And then he had a singular gardener, Franck Creac'h. A self-described *marginal,* living on the fringe of society, he had come to Provence as a way of demobilizing himself during the war. He was a declared conscientious objector and anarchist. Creac'h had restored a cluster of old cottages in an alley just down the street from the Camus house. A Breton born in Paris, self-taught, he was the son of a man who wrote a successful historical novel about Breton seamen. Like Camus, he was in touch with the Louis Lecoin movement. So that Camus had a man on the scene with whom he could talk about some of the things that interested him.[24] Later Creac'h would recall vignettes of Camus at Lourmarin. Such as when he was deep in conversation with his blacksmith friends and a stranger approached. Camus would say: "Excuse me, sir, you see, I'm very busy with these gentlemen." To the village pastor Camus had said: "You believers, you're the chosen, which is why I shall always be on the side of the others." The pastor's wife replied: "Men are quite often disappointing, only God is not." To which Camus after a moment's silence asked: "Are you quite certain of that?"

Of course Camus would often visit the castle, and took his guests to visit. He signed the guest book on one of his first visits in May:

> To know that one can, day after day, rush off to a rendezvous with
> a fragment of builded earth, as if it were a living creature.
> Gratitude, then, to this tranquil site!
>
> Boris Pasternak

He had soon decided that the castle would make an excellent site for a theater festival, and certainly if he had not died prematurely he would have been appointed to the board of directors of the foundation which supervised the operations of the castle, the next time a place became vacant.[25] Catherine Sellers had heard that there was a legend that all the benefactors of Lourmarin died violent deaths.[4]

When a stranger walked into the local book and magazine shop to ask for a book autographed by Camus, the vendor would write the purchaser's name on a slip of paper. When Camus dropped in to pick up his Paris newspaper and Disque Bleu cigarettes, he would sign the book.[26]

He was in Lourmarin in May to write, but did he? Probably not then; he would tell a friend on his return to Paris that "I think it's all over. It's not coming anymore." But he was still thinking about the theater. He would have watched the broadcast of "Gros plan" in a café in Lourmarin. He wrote his friend Jean Gillibert to say that he was interested in the Festival of Mers-el-Kébir (near Oran), where there was to be a special Don Juan year, with the plays of Molière, Tirso de Molina, Pushkin, Lope de Vega, Corneille, and perhaps Mozart's opera. Apparently he had been given a choice of productions, or an opportunity to direct them all, for he told Gillibert: "I couldn't do everything, that's clear." But he did want Gillibert to investigate the technical facilities at the site of the festival.[27]

His new Swedish friend Carl-Gustav Bjurström, who knew nothing of his plans for a theater of his own but did admire his stage adaptations, had done a translation of Strindberg's *A Dream Play* which he thought that Camus might like to adapt for the stage. Camus told him that he felt less close to this play than to other works of Strindberg such as *The Ghost Sonata,* but thought that they might work together on other plays.[28]

He had begun his Lourmarin month by communicating with one of Malraux's aides, the writer Pierre Moinot, to try to expedite Micheline

Rozan's negotiations with the government's cultural authorities for the theater subsidy. He left Lourmarin to be in Paris in time for a public discussion of *Les Possédés* after a matinée performance on May 30 (the hall had been fully booked by the early part of the month).[14] It was apparently during this encounter with his public, which was lively and even heated, that a member of the audience taxed Camus with contradicting himself and he retorted: "I demand the right to evolve!"[4]

It was time to make a concrete plan for the theater which Camus would manage, with government support, and he sat down with Micheline Rozan to draft a memorandum to all concerned. They called it "Propositions théoriques pour un nouveau théâtre," which in five typed pages explained Camus' conception of a repertory company designed to encourage the contemporary theater in three ways: by presenting examples of masterpieces from Greek tragedy, the Spanish Golden Age, the Elizabethan stage, classic and preclassic France; by inviting authors who did not usually write for the theater to try their hands at plays; and by exploring what was already available. The emphasis would be on good writing; productions would emphasize *text*. No fewer than three plays would be staged in alternance, for 210 annual performances in all. At least one of them would be a new play, although all three would be new if they could be found. The director, Camus, that is, would be in complete charge, would form his own team. There would be a core troupe, and a theater of some seven hundred seats, having a stage which could handle an *Othello* as well as a *Paquebot "Tenacity."* They now estimated that their annual deficit would be some 17.1 million francs, plus the cost of three productions (30 million francs) and dress rehearsals (3,150,000 francs), a total of 50,250,000 francs for which a government grant would be necessary each year. Rather than call it a *théâtre d'essai,* Camus preferred the title Nouveau Théâtre, which prevented nothing and allowed everything. He initialed the proposal and dated it June 25, 1959.

Now it was up to the government, and the evidence is that total confusion prevailed there. The hope was to open the Camus-Rozan Nouveau Théâtre in September 1960, but discussions dragged on. The government offered several empty theaters—the Sarah Bernhardt was mentioned again, the Palais Royal, even the Opéra-Comique. The owner of a small private theater was prepared to go along with Camus' conceptions but warned that if Camus took over the management there would be the problem of a large existing deficit.

Part of the problem was certainly the bureaucracy under Malraux. It was wasting his time, Camus felt; if to achieve something he would have to haunt the corridors of government offices all year long, he was not able to do that.[29] Finally in the closing days of 1959, with tacit agreement of Malraux, Camus and Rozan were in a position to make a detailed offer to the Théâtre de l'Athénée. Camus would sign a three-year agreement with the owners of that theater, would have freedom to choose the repertory, cast, to handle press and promotion, with first plays to open in September 1960.[30] (The plays would have included *The Good Woman of Setzuan* by Bertolt Brecht, the permanent troupe would have included Casarès and Sellers.[14] Catherine Sellers had a list of fifty plays he wanted to do, including *Timon of Athens,* John Ford's *'Tis Pity She's a Whore,* John Webster's *The White Devil,* Molière's *Dom Juan,* Eugene O'Neill's *Strange Interlude,* Dylan Thomas' *Under Milk Wood,* Pirandello's *As You Desire Me.*)

Malraux actually set aside some 100 million francs, realizing that a theater for new talent was one of the serious lacks in his over-all cultural program, and he was to have met Camus in the first week of January 1960 to put finishing touches on the project.[31] Had it not worked out after all, Camus was ready to associate himself with his old partners at the Mathurins Theater.[32]

## 48

# FINAL WEEKS

> In the brief time that is given to him, he warms and illumi-
> nates without turning from his mortal road. Sown by the
> wind, harvested by the wind, ephemeral seed and never-
> theless creative sun, such is man, through the centuries,
> proud to live a single instant.
>
> To René Char, December 19, 1959*

When they were working together on the television close-up "Gros plan," Camus told Pierre Cardinal that he thought that his novel *La Chute* was in the spirit of Cardinal's television series: a man alone, confessing. Why not make a television film of the book? Camus thought that the right actor for the part would be a Jules Berry type, Berry being a prewar actor, already dead, who had played cynical roles (such as the devil). Then Camus suggested himself for the part of Jean-Baptiste Clamence. Cardinal was surprised, for he felt that the Berry style was out of character for Camus.

But they began to talk seriously about the project. Camus had already read the entire novel on tape for his own recorder.[1] They would do *La Chute* as a ninety-minute film, all in monologue; Clamence's audience would be the television viewer. They decided to travel together to Amsterdam early in January 1960, on Camus' return from Lourmarin, to look for locations for the filming. Meanwhile they began marking up a copy of the novel, and Cardinal received the green light from his studio to make the trip to the Netherlands with Camus.

They often met in the late evening, after the performance of *Les Possédés* at the Théâtre Antoine. Cardinal would leave his automobile

---

* Quoted in the Pléiade edition of Camus' work.

parked near the theater on the Boulevard Strasbourg, to accompany
Camus all the way across Paris to his apartment—Camus still loved to
walk through Paris at night—and then Camus would insist on accom-
paning Cardinal back again to the theater to pick up his car. Once,
crossing a bridge over the Seine—it may have been the Pont Royal—
Camus said: "That was the bridge in *La Chute.*" Another time, he asked
Cardinal abruptly: "Which do you prefer, *La Chute* or *L'Etranger?*"
When Cardinal hesitated, Camus went on: "I'm tired of being *only* the
author of *L'Etranger.*"

Camus had an ear which stuck out, and which he felt was not pho-
togenic. He said that he would have an operation on it before they
began filming.

During their meetings Camus often expressed the desire to withdraw from the world of letters. He had begun as an actor, he wanted to
return to the stage, to do nothing else for a few years. Cardinal felt that
all during this period—the period of the creation of "Gros plan," of the
planning for the television film of *La Chute*—he was in the company of
a man traumatized by the Nobel Prize, by Algeria, by the literary
milieu. He recalled that in "Gros plan" Camus had remarked that in intellectual society "I always have the impression that I have to ask for-
giveness for something." By tacit accord they did not discuss Algeria.
Cardinal was ardently pro-independence, Camus too conventional in his
approach, in Cardinal's view, for there to be a meeting of minds. And
he observed that Camus never laughed, never relaxed, sat upright instead of comfortably against the back of a chair, even in his own home.
Everything he said was cut and dry, definitive. Of course Cardinal knew
that it was a trying time for Camus, with both his mother and his
daughter ill. But Cardinal was surprised, after saying that a book or a
person had "soul," to hear Camus snap back: "The soul doesn't exist!"
as if protesting the religious implication of Cardinal's innocent remark.[2]

On July 7 he took a morning train to Venice, where *Les Possédés*
with its Paris cast was to participate in the Festival del Teatro at the
Fenice Theater on July 9, 10, and 11. He arrived that night, and met
the Italian press the next afternoon, in the company of his actors. The
immediate problem, in sweltering heat, was to adapt his production to
the venerable Fenice opera stage, which he felt would be ideal for Goldoni, or for Marivaux or Molière, but not quite for this play. He had to
install equipment to allow quick changes of scenery. He explained to an
interviewer that with over twenty scenes, if it took thirty seconds to
change each one, that would seem too long to the audience.

He also talked about the novel he was soon to begin writing. He
had been working on *Le Premier Homme* for a year, he was reported as

saying, and he had another year to go. He had thought of calling the book "Adam." It would be a simple story which would begin with the beginning of this century, telling about a family and a man who found himself alive in this era. "Nothing complicated. Works that have the best chance of surviving are those which avoid eccentricity, exceptionality." The interviewer suggested that every one of us is the first man, the Adam of his own story. Camus: Exactly. And so his book would be vast in scope. Not a *roman-fleuve,* but a long novel, as must be the story of a man whose life was not unworthy, who could not remove himself from the vital problems of our time.[3]

In a review of the opening performance the local critic noted that the rapid scene changes had gone off as planned, and although the play lasted three and a half hours it was given a warm reception; he said he was not referring to the torrid temperature inside the theater. The audience even applauded before the end of scenes; after the play the author was acclaimed but preferred to stay hidden in the wings.[4] On Saturday night the French Ambassador, Gaston Palewski, was present and all the balconies were decorated with flowers; it was this evening that "exceptionally" the play would really begin on time, 9 P.M.[5] Camus was back in Paris on the night of July 13.

He spent the rest of that month in Paris, swimming mornings, working afternoons. A frequent companion now was a ravishing young woman associated with neither his literary life nor his theater, and so a companion of relaxed moments. He had met her for the first time two years earlier at the Café de Flore; she had been sitting alone when Camus spotted her and sent a young man who was having a drink with him to ask if she would join them. And in this final year of his life his new friend would accompany him on trips, would listen to him read the first pages of his novel; she would often be close to him during the final weeks of his life. At least one friend saw in Camus' interest in this lively, healthy creature an attempt to hold onto his own youth.

Michel Bouquet was also seeing Camus that summer. Bouquet ran into him at Les Petits Pavés, an attractive Saint-Germain-des-Prés restaurant run by a *pied noir* promoter, and as Bouquet was also at loose ends that month he saw Camus a good deal in the evenings, making appointments from one meeting to the next. Besides Les Petits Pavés, another favorite meeting place was the Catalan on the Rue des Grands Augustins, where there were flamenco singers and dancers (it was on Picasso's old street and he had liked the place too).[6]

Camus may have worked on adaptations of plays that August in Lourmarin; one of the plays may have been *Othello* (he was making revisions on a typed manuscript of a translation by someone else).[7] *Le Premier Homme?* He must have been working on that, too, although he wrote to Char on August 16: "I've been here a week and am waiting in vain to accomplish the slightest activity."[8] Perhaps the early pages of the novel began to come to him in the second half of that month. At the end of August, Catherine Sellers joined Camus, Francine, and the Camus children at Lourmarin.[9]

Back in Paris in September for further rehearsals of *Les Possédés,* for there had been replacements for some of the actors—Jean-Pierre Jorris taking Michel Bouquet's part, for example—he was tempted by still another bit of theater work, one that might have helped him get through the long months before the opening of his own theater. He had read a novel by the popular Catholic writer Michel de Saint-Pierre called *Les Ecrivains.* When Saint-Pierre was adapting the book for the stage in 1959, Camus asked Mrs. Baur—her Mathurins was to do the play—if he could have the part of the book's hero, Alexandre Damville.[10]

It was an odd idea—or perhaps it was not. Saint-Pierre's Damville was a grand old man of French letters, and a misanthrope, clearly out of tune with his times. He liked his women modest and "submissive," in work and in love. He separated human beings into creators and impotents, opposed the social life demanded of a writer, the requirement that he take a stand on everything. "People look for me, they telephone, they ring at my door, they write me," complains Damville in the novel. "You have no idea of the zeal people show in order to torture a writer." He opposed religion, had refused the Legion of Honor (twice), official voyages, galas, meetings with royalty. Damville felt that the best writers always kept away from politics and its turmoil. "Alexandre Damville, it's me," Camus told Michel de Saint-Pierre.

Cérésol brought a copy of the playscript to the Rue de Chanaleilles apartment late one night. He was surprised that Camus would be attracted to the work of a Catholic writer like Saint-Pierre (the story line involves an attempt to make a good Christian out of Damville), but Camus obviously liked the idea of the conflict of generations which is also treated in the novel. But he was less happy with the tone of the script, felt that he couldn't play comedy.[11] In the end he told Saint-Pierre that he had to give up the idea. "I'd have too much stage fright."[12]

His Gallimard colleague Mallet was getting ready for a long voyage. "You're lucky to be going away," Camus told him. (Mallet noted the date of their talk as September 28.) "Life in Paris is an inferno," Camus went on. "You agitate yourself, you overwork yourself. You don't move forward. After a certain time they make a public figure of you. You no longer have the right to a private life. . . ."

He didn't even have time to develop his projects for the theater,

Camus told Mallet, and he needed the theater, for he could relax there. It wasn't true of fiction, which isolated its author. "The novel demands a continual tension, the theater allows breaks in rhythm."

He didn't want to talk about his novel in progress. "I still don't know what it will become. It doesn't satisfy me. I destroyed pages and pages of it. It's moving slowly."

He added: "It's because they don't let me work that I'm exasperated." He stood up, held out his hand as if it point to an invisible antagonist. "I still have my word to say!"[13]

He had what must have been a painful encounter in this last autumn of his life. After five years in Switzerland undergoing a cure, Simone Hié was about to return to France. Camus asked her former husband, Dr. Cottenceau, what the Swiss doctors had advised. When he heard that they hoped she could lead a normal life now, Camus arranged to meet this ravaged woman. He thought of giving her work as a reader, for she had good literary judgment. They would talk about it again, he promised, early in the new year.[14]

His last piece of theater business would be to see the *Possédés* road tour off safely. He traveled with them to the cathedral town of Rheims for the opening, and then returned to Paris determined to begin writing.

But he was still being drawn into the Algerian drama, and now there was some hope there, or so he thought. On September 14, de Gaulle affirmed the right of Algerians to self-determination, and Camus confided to Nicola Chiaromonte that he approved the statement; it opened the road to a settlement. He told Edmond Brua that he hoped to be in Algeria that winter to find out as much as he could about the situation, and promised that if he did speak out it would be in Brua's newspaper (the one which, alone of Algeria's press, had published his civil truce appeal).[15] To Jean Bloch-Michel—and it would be the last time the two friends met—who asked if now, with de Gaulle's declaration on the future of Algeria, was not the moment for Camus to break his silence, he replied: "Yes. If there is a referendum on the Algerian question I'll campaign against independence in the Algerian press." He still believed that French and Moslem Algerians could coexist in that territory.

During their last meeting together in Paris, Camus walked along a Seine quay with Maisonseul, who reproached him for a lack of understanding of what was happening in Algeria, of seeing it from afar, spending only a week there every six months to see his mother while living at the palatial Saint-George Hotel. Maisonseul wanted his friend to stay at least a month, and offered his apartment. Camus promised to

come. (The plan was a very precise one. His brother Lucien was planning to take a week's leave from his job at the Algiers Social Security
Administration so that they could go together to visit Camus' birthplace
in Mondovi to provide firsthand material for the early pages of *Le Premier Homme.*) He also spoke to Maisonseul about his novel in progress, saying that at the age of twenty he had drawn up a program of
work of which he had accomplished only a quarter, and that his true
work remained to be done.[16]

And he began *Le Premier Homme* in earnest. Back in Paris, his
time was divided between discussions of the Nouveau Théâtre and preparing for a long stay at Lourmarin. For he was not able to work in
Paris. ("I want to leave Paris where I suffocate more and more," he
wrote Char[17].) He celebrated his last birthday, on November 7, with
lunch in a bistrot on the Rue du Cherche-Midi with Catherine Sellers.

He stayed around to catch the *Possédés* company at nearby Fontainebleau on November 12, then began packing.

The myth begins here. Because these were Camus' last hours in Paris,
the things his friends later remembered took on augmented significance.
In an interview of Emmanuel Berl, the essayist and novelist, published
after Berl's own death, Berl said of a last meeting with Camus in Paris
that November (Berl was then sixty-seven):

> I had just finished lunching with him and said: "Above all be care-
> ful. I don't like that highway business." So he said to me: "Don't
> worry, I hate speed and don't like automobiles," and he took out of
> his pocket the round-trip rail ticket that he had bought to go to
> Lourmarin. . . .[18]

A round-trip ticket about which much would be said and written.

During a final meeting with Roblès over lunch at the Brasserie
Lipp, Camus reproached his friend for not writing any longer for the
theater. Roblès replied that he was wrong, *"justement"* he had a subject, and he explained the plot of *Plaidoyer pour un rebel,* based on the
true story of a French electrical worker who had planted a bomb as a
pro-Moslem independence act, but then returned to the site to stop the
timing device when he realized that fellow French Algerians would be
killed. He was arrested, tried, and guillotined. Roblès saw the case as
tragedy, with the hero trapped: The Europeans were against him, but
so were the Arabs, because he sacrificed their cause to save lives; the
courts were against him too, for an act of terrorism was punishable
once it had commenced. Camus told his friend that he planned to have
his own theater, and that if it worked out, he would like to stage the
play.[19]

Now, in a final goodbye to Maria Casarès, he blurted out: "Could you imagine a time when we might be separated?" Then he broke down and sobbed. *"I* can't," he said, when he could speak again. She didn't understand his question nor his reaction, and later took it as a premonition.[20]

From Lourmarin, on November 14, he told Micheline Rozan that he did not know exactly when he would return to Paris. The plan was to complete a first draft of *Le Premier Homme,* and he had a long way to go. He gave himself eight months before returning to the theater (that is, he would have to begin rehearsals in July if the Nouveau Théâtre were to open in September). He would be lonely in Lourmarin in late fall and winter, but that was the only way to get any work done. If he absolutely had to make an appearance in Paris for the good of their theater project, then he would come, but otherwise he would stay at least through December.

But even from Lourmarin he was still being tempted by what might be considered frivolity if his psychological condition is not taken into account. As the agent of Peter Brook (through MCA), Rozan had been trying to put together a project for a motion picture version of *Moderato cantabile,* a novel by Marguerite Duras published the previous year. She wanted Brook to direct it, while another MCA client, Jeanne Moreau, would play the heroine. And she felt that Camus could take the male lead opposite Moreau, for the character of the man was not unlike Camus' own.[21] In that novel the heroine Anne, wife of a manufacturer, mother of a small boy, is a Madame Bovary living an impossible love with a silent man named Chauvin.

Jeanne Moreau and the would-be producer had gone to a private showing of "Gros plan" to see how Camus might look on the screen; presumably they were satisfied with the choice.[2] (They liked Camus not because of his acting but because of his personality.)[22] When Rozan suggested the project to Camus he was tempted—that was his "whore" side, thought Maria Casarès with affection, when he asked her to read the scenario.[20]

Finally the hands of the clock made the decision for him. If he had eight months to write a first draft of *Le Premier Homme,* he could not spare a month to make a movie. But he was certainly more interested in acting in that movie than in any other obligations he had, and if Brook could wait a year, Camus promised to take the part; his regret, he assured them all, was sincere.[21] But the film was to be made without him, with Jean-Paul Belmondo assuming the part Camus would have played.

Now he settled down to what he would call a monastic life, assuring the solitude necessary for the act of writing. Walks in the village, talks with the blacksmith, with his anarchist gardener, and other local people, lonely meals at the Hôtel Ollier. After only a week in Lourmarin he was able to report to a friend in Paris that he was pleased with his progress; life had begun to enter the manuscript.[23] By the end of the month he allowed himself an escape to a big city—another meeting with the cast of *Les Possédés* during their performance in Marseilles. He drove there in his black Citroën (which he kept garaged in Lourmarin now, for use only while he was in residence there). The actors were tired after six weeks on the road and probably played badly, for Camus was unhappy with them. As usual he scribbled little *billets* for each of them; comparing their notes later on, they remarked that all of the comments were negative. Jean-Pierre Jorris felt that Camus was doing his work in order to be doing something; he didn't believe that Camus' discontent was due only to their performance; Jorris assumed that Algeria was on his mind. Camus dined with the cast at a restaurant on Marseilles' Vieux Port, drove back to Lourmarin the same night.[24]

Robert Cérésol joined Camus in Lourmarin now. There was snow on the ground, roads were icy. More snow fell during the fortnight they were there; the temperature dropped to under 25° F. (−5° C.), mighty cold for the South of France. During the day Camus wrote, and in the evening the friends walked to what he called a twilight stone, a table built of three large slabs. They sat on it and contemplated the landscape. Camus observed that night is sad in the south.

They cooked their own evening meals. Camus whipped omelettes, Cérésol broiled steaks in the immense fireplace.

Some days they drove around in Camus' old car. Reading the local paper, they would discover the names of people they knew who had been in motor accidents. Both felt that death in a car was *une mort imbecile*. Once Camus said: "Hey, —— [a mutual friend] died in an accident." It wasn't true, but it was in tune with their black humor. (Later, when Fausto Coppi, the Italian bicycle champion, died in an accident on January 2, the day before Camus was to depart for Paris, he lamented with his housekeeper, telling her: "Famous people are particularly stricken by destiny these days."[25])

Cérésol sat down to work out a program for Camus at the Mathurins, which was the alternative plan for Camus, should the Athénée Theater not be available after all. Camus would have been *directeur artistique,* while the theater would continue to be operated by the owner, Mrs. Baur, with Cérésol. Camus told Cérésol that he had Boris Pasternak's only play, obtained from Pasternak's sister, and he wanted to stage that. He also mentioned his desire to write a play (for three characters) based on the life of Julie de Lespinasse.

On his last day in Lourmarin, Cérésol remarked that Camus had placed a batch of manuscript pages on his night table. He picked them up and discovered that they had been dedicated to him. There were six detached sheets of aphorisms on buff paper, with the title "Pour Némésis," a reference to the long-planned book-length essay. Cérésol saw them as notes for what Camus called "my return to pre-Socratism," i.e., intuitive poetry, a fusion between poetry and philosophy.

Later, too, Cérésol would remember conversations about aging, about death. Camus said that a Catholic had once told him that death was moral and he had been indignant, for death was not moral. It was not that he wished to live to be as old as Methuselah, he said. But he was placed on earth to live, not to die. One didn't ask to be brought into the world; it was unthinkable to have to leave it.

Camus had also given Cérésol some good personal news. Gallimard would publish his philosophical essay, "Le Déchirement," subtitled "Essai d'un psychanalyse de l'abstrait," which Cérésol had begun in the early 1950s, and which had been the original reason for his meeting Camus. Camus would write a preface for it, and they would meet on January 6 in the office of Gaston Gallimard to arrange details.

Before Cérésol left, Camus suggested that he return around January 1 to go back to Paris with him, he was so lonely. He felt like getting back to mix with crowds—to eat oysters.[11]

He did get away immediately after that, but to the little Grand Duchy of Luxembourg, where the Michel Gallimards joined him again for a performance of Les Possédés. They were received at the ducal palace by Grand Duchess Charlotte. Then back again to Provence, for a talk to foreign students at Aix (on December 14), at the invitation of the Institut d'Etudes Françaises pour Etudiants Etrangers. Aix was a major center for foreign students in France; thirty-eight nationalities were then represented at its university.

It would be Camus' last public appearance, his last opportunity to speak. According to Professor François Meyer, who was chairman of the meeting held in the Salle de Cours of the ancient and charming Hôtel de Maynier d'Oppède, Camus introduced himself as a writer, which he said was a "man's trade" and not a "gift of grace." Asked what happens at the moment of creation, he replied: much time, patience, and vain effort, days in which he wrote nothing, merely moving from the desk to the window and back again. And sometimes it was not a matter of days but of months. It took him three years to write L'Etranger, which had taken off only when he discovered what his technique would be. Which of his books did he prefer? "The next one!" Asked to explain it, he called it "Forty years of the life of a man," autobiography—but also life in his century.

He was asked all of the lofty questions, about his goals, dreams, even his faith. He said that the Christian God was not for him, that he felt no spiritual need to look for Him. His religion was based on man. Was Camus a "left-wing intellectual"? After thinking about that one he replied that he was not sure that he was an intellectual and as for the rest, "I'm for the left, despite myself and despite it." What about women in the intellectual world? He didn't wish to repeat a cliché about the eternal feminine. He felt that women were sensitive witnesses, there to remind men that intellectual activity was not all, but that man's true destiny was in fraternity, tenderness, "and in bearing witness for the honor of the spirit."[26]

He sent what was called a "final interview" by mail to the American magazine *Venture,* dated December 20, 1959, concerned with his art.[27] In fact he would send out at least one more, dating it December 29, and this probably was his "last message": a political one, for an anarchist periodical in Buenos Aires, which published it in its January–February 1960 issue. It was a pessimistic statement, a pox on the major powers; power renders mad those who possess it, the great powers coexist out of fear. He believed in a united Europe, supported by Latin America and later, when the nationalist "virus" had lost its strength, by Asia and Africa. What about space flight and other scientific achievements? Should the money rather be spent on the ground to feed the undernourished? Science went ahead for good and for evil, but the least he could say was that one oughtn't boast about achievements which were technically magnificent but politically abject.

What can we do to help bring about a world less miserable and more free? Give when one can. And not hate if one can.[28]

There were also the traditional holiday greetings, the acts of friendship and of duty. He wrote to Jean Grenier on December 28, remarking that he worked well in solitude, and said that he would henceforth divide his time between Lourmarin and Paris. He wrote to his mother (her neighborhood baker read the letter to her): "I'll come to pick you up soon, and you will spend all summer in France with us."[29] He was furious at an attack by François Mauriac on Maria Casarès' interpretation of Lady Macbeth, and told her that he would hurry back to Paris to be with her. She urged him not to give up his work on her account.[20]

In fact the work *was* going well now. He was writing *Le Premier Homme* on large-format manuscript pages (he now even used sheets with his name printed at the top). By January 2 he had 145 of these long pages filled with his tiny script; he had probably written eighty thousand words in all. During the Christmas holidays he explained to his wife that the book was quite autobiographical now but would be less so later; the young hero would be broken up into two persons. He called the book his *éducation sentimentale,* its chief purpose being to reveal his Algeria to mainland France. The title of the book, his wife understood, signified that all men are the first man, but also that the French Algerian is without a past, the product of a melting pot.[30] The unfinished manuscript left by Camus takes his young hero to the age of fourteen; he was about to begin a chapter or section called "L'Adolescent." One reader noted a new element in Camus' writing: For the first time he was using a Faulknerian lyricism, with repetition of words (although of course there is no way to know how much of this would have been retained in the final draft). What is clear is that Camus was following the details of his own early life closely, while attempting to give epic form, some universality, to the Algerian saga. And personal themes, incidents peculiar to Camus' own life are very strong in the partial draft he left.[31]

Undoubtedly, he would have let the first draft settle, assuming that he had finished it by July 1960, while he attacked a first season of his Nouveau Théâtre, from September 1960 through the following spring, and then he would have returned to the book in the summer of 1961 to write a second and perhaps final version.

Camus' wife and their twins arrived for the Christmas holidays. (The children were now fourteen, and Francine was teaching at André Benichou's Paris school.) During these year-end holidays his wife decided that Camus was talking and acting in a more morbid way than was usual for him. He confessed that he felt bizarre—was he going crazy? They had a large chest in the attic and in a moment of black humor he had his daughter climb into it to see how one looked in a coffin. He told his wife that if he died he wanted to be buried right here at Lourmarin. No national funeral, he added—but not necessarily a third-class one, either.[30]

The Michel Gallimards had also taken a Christmas vacation to coincide with the school holidays of Janine's daughter Anne, but they had gone down to Cannes in their Facel Vega, sailing the *Aya* off Cannes. Perhaps Michel asked Camus to join them there and he replied: Why not come to Lourmarin instead? So the Gallimards spent the New Year at Lourmarin with the Camus.

Camus, who had been buying old furniture and art objects in the shops of Avignon and the surrounding region, gave Janine Gallimard an antique silver cigarette box, with a note of New Year greetings which ended:

> And let's finish it as we began it—together.

They wandered around the village. Camus introduced the Gallimards to his blacksmith friend. And when it was time for Francine and the children to return to Paris, Michel and Janine suggested that Camus drive back with them rather than take the train. He agreed.

They all lunched together at the Hôtel Ollier on Saturday, January 2, and then Francine and the twins were taken to Avignon to board the train for Paris. For the drive to Avignon they used both cars; Camus' children wanted to ride in the sporty Facel Vega. Anne Gallimard joined the Camus in the old Citroën. She told them that for her eighteenth birthday, to be celebrated the following week, she was going to get an automobile from her parents. Camus spent the whole time they were in the car together advising her to be a prudent driver.[30]

In preparation for their own trip the Gallimards, accompanied by Camus, filled up the tank of the Facel Vega at the local Renault-Shell garage. Owner Henri Baumas, who had been holding onto a copy of L'Etranger waiting for Camus' next visit, brought it out to the car to ask for an autograph. Camus told him: "You shouldn't have bought it, I'd have given you as many as you want." He signed:

> To Mr. Baumas, who contributes to my returning frequently to beautiful Lourmarin. . . .[32]

Franck Creac'h was puttering around in the garden on the morning of their departure, and looked up to see Camus and the Gallimards taking an early walk. Camus was some thirty yards behind the others, looking morose. Creac'h interpreted that as his sadness at leaving Lourmarin—or at the idea of returning to Paris by car.[33]

# 49

## VILLEBLEVIN

Hope, naturally, meant to be shot down at a street corner,
while you're running, and by a stray bullet.

*L'Etranger*

On Sunday morning, January 3, 1960, Camus left Lourmarin with the
Michel Gallimards, Janine's daughter Anne, and their dog, a Skye terrier, in the Gallimards' automobile for the drive to Paris some 470
miles to the north. Several stops were planned on what had been conceived
as a leisurely two-day drive; it would also be something of a gastronomic
one. They had lunch quickly at Orange, which is only a half hour north
of Avignon (for they had gotten a late start). The route was the traditional one in the days before France possessed a Paris-Riviera toll expressway: the highway National 7 from Avignon to Lyons, then the
central National 6 through Burgundy: Mâcon, Chalon, Saulieu, through
Avallon, Auxerre, and Sens, the National 5 from Sens (via Fon-
tainbleau) to Paris. For the first night they left the main road just before Mâcon, to stop at the village of Thoissey, where they knew a fine
small inn called the Chapon Fin, with sixteen rooms and a restaurant
which rated two stars in the Michelin Guide, signifying "Excellent cui-
sine, worth a detour." At that point they had covered about two hundred miles of their journey.[1]

They had reserved the rooms in advance, for the roads and inns
were crowded with vacationers returning after the year-end holidays;
the restaurant was filled to capacity. The *patronne* of the inn, Madame
Paul Blanc, who with her husband had been running the Chapon Fin
for nearly twenty-five years, had received them with the courtesy due to
such distinguished guests, but because of the crowd she hadn't had time

to ask them to sign the *livre d'or*. She would, however, hold onto the police registration card filled out by Camus, which is probably the last signature he wrote.[2]

The Thoissey dinner was a celebration: It was Anne's eighteenth birthday, and they toasted her with due cheer. (Madame Blanc remarked that her clients were enjoying their dinner and seemed quite relaxed.) They had been talking about Camus' theater projects, and Camus had convinced Michel Gallimard to allow Anne to work with him after she received her *baccalauréat* degree (at the completion of secondary school studies). Michel didn't want to see her on the stage, so Camus promised that she would be learning one of the other theater trades. (On their excursions as a foursome Anne—until that day little Anne, whom Camus called Anuschka—would share a room with singleton Camus, but chastely; he would wake her by singing: "Open your pretty eyes. . . .")

After a late breakfast, on Monday morning, January 4, they were off again. Madame Blanc remembered that it was about 10 A.M.; a friend of Michel Gallimard would later say it had been nine. They would cover 190 miles before lunch.

During the ride north Michel raised the question of life insurance, which he would like to have had. It was not something every Frenchman thought of in those days. Camus suggested that with their lungs full of holes it might be difficult for either of them to obtain insurance. Michel, who often thought about dying, talked a lot about it too; he had taken care to draft a generous will for his wife. Camus expressed distaste for the idea that an author's heirs would be living on his copyrights. They ended that lugubrious conversation with humor. Michel said that he wanted to die before Janine did because he could not live without her; she said that she'd like to go on living with or without Michel. Michel and Camus agreed that if they both died they wanted to be embalmed and kept in Janine's living room so she'd talk to them every day. She said: *"Quelle horreur!"* She detested the idea of corpses, and said that in that case she'd move out of the apartment.

They were going to arrive in Paris sooner than Camus had announced, because he had an appointment with a friend there. They agreed that their excuse would be that Anne had to get back to Paris to see a dentist. Camus commented wryly that he felt he had made all of his women happy, even the ones he loved simultaneously.

They were not driving fast. Michel Gallimard had a reputation for fast driving, and the Facel Vega was something of a sports car, but the back seats weren't very comfortable; the women were sitting there, and they had to curl up their feet because there was no place for them under the front seats, so both Janine and Anne would remind Michel to slow down on occasion. Camus didn't like fast driving, except perhaps his own, and when he saw Michel speeding up he would say: "Hey, little friend, who's in a hurry?" Michel Gallimard never tried to drive the Paris-Riviera road in one day, afraid of tiring himself; going down to Cannes from Paris, he would often make the traditional stop at Avallon.

Before France built its north-south expressway the town of Sens was a major relay on the Paris-Riviera route, site of one of the country's great Gothic cathedrals, with a hotel-restaurant practically next door to it which was popular with travelers. The Hôtel de Paris et de la Poste was another Michelin two-star restaurant. Like many famous highway inns of the time it was set squarely on the main street of the town (which was also the national highway). Camus had been there before, and the owner greeted him at the entrance to the restaurant (he had never met the Gallimards), escorted the party to a table in the Burgundy-style dining room, with its large stone fireplace and embroidered red tablecloths, paneled walls and ceilings. They ordered a house specialty, *boudin noir aux pommes de reinette,* blood sausage with apples as a vegetable, and a simple bottle of Fleurie, a Beaujolais, which was a frugal choice for four French men and women.[3]

From Sens north toward Paris the old National 5 passes through a succession of villages. It is divided into three lanes, one in each direction, the center lane for passing. Usually trees line the road at a varying distance from the road surface. The land is flat. The houses seem to have no regional character; it is highway landscape, with service stations, signs announcing hotels, restaurants, cafés.

Pont-sur-Yonne is an old village of charm, but the automobile passenger scarcely sees it; the outskirts of the village crossed by the road is typical highway landscape too. Then comes Petit-Villeblevin, a hamlet consisting of a few scattered, separated houses. Trees line the road on either side here too, for there is no village street as such.

At the time of the accident—Michel Gallimard at the wheel, Camus seated at his right (without seat belts; they were not a common accessory then)—they were not moving at what the Gallimards would have considered excessive speed. Michel usually drove more slowly when he had someone to talk to, and they were talking in the car. Janine, in the rear with Anne, was aware of nothing untoward, heard no exclamation or other comment of her husband.[4] She felt as if she were suddenly on a curve (the road was a straight line now) and that something had collapsed—like the gearbox beneath them. Then she was sitting or lying in a field, in a state of shock. She was discovered calling for her dog Floc.

As the accident was reconstructed by police and the press, the Gallimard car had swerved off the road—whose surface was slightly damp

from January drizzle—smashed into one of the tall plane trees lining
the highway, then wrapped around a second tree some forty feet further
on. Camus was thrown backward against the rear window, thrust
through, his skull fractured, neck broken; he died instantly. It took two
hours to disengage his body. Michel Gallimard was found on the
ground, bleeding profusely, and was removed quickly to a local hospital. Janine was near her husband, in shock; leash in hand, she was indeed calling for her dog. Anne, splattered with mud, was in a field
sixty-five feet from the car. Neither woman appeared seriously hurt, but
they were also taken to the hospital.

The accident seemed to have been caused by a blowout or a broken axle; experts were puzzled by its happening on a long stretch of
straight road, a road thirty feet wide, and with little traffic at that time.
Newspaper photographs showed the asphalt surface, cut over a distance
of about 160 feet. Debris was scattered over a radius of 500 feet. Photographs of the twisted wreck of the Facel Vega showed the front
fenders and the dashboard projected thirty feet ahead, the motor and
radiator grille on the opposite side of the road at a distance of forty
feet; one wheel lay on the road surface. The dashboard clock was
stopped at 1:54 P.M. or 1:55, generally taken as the precise moment of
the accident. But accounts varied as to whether the speedometer needle
was stuck at 145 kilometers per hour (about 90 mph) or read zero.

A motorist from the nearby village of Villeblevin (which unlike
Petit-Villeblevin lay off the national highway), who had been waiting
on a side road, about to turn onto the highway, said that she had seen
the Facel Vega zigzag in the middle of the road and then crash into a
tree, to bounce off and come to rest against the second tree. A witness
in another vehicle was quoted as saying that he had been passed at 150
kilometers an hour—a bit over 90 mph; a truck driver (the same witness?) who had been passed by the Gallimard car said he had seen it
"waltz" and then "It was like an explosion."

A doctor from the next village to the north, Villeneuve-la-Guyard
—his name was given as Marcel Camus—reported the cause of the
death of his namesake as fracture of the skull and spinal column, and
crushing of the thorax; death had been instantaneous. "He didn't
suffer," he commented. A reporter described the expression on Albert
Camus' face as a look of horror. The eyes were open; there was no visible wound. When the body was at last ready to be moved, it was taken
by the gendarmes, the national highway police, to the town hall of
Villeblevin, a short distance from the scene of the accident, a few hundred yards east of National 5.[5] The author's black leather briefcase was
extracted from the muddy soil; later it would be found to contain his
passport, personal photographs, the manuscript of *Le Premier Homme,*

his journal, and some books (including Nietzsche's *Le Gai Savoir* and a school edition of *Othello* in a French translation by Jules Derocquigny).[6]

The town hall of Villeblevin had a curiously inelegant façade composed of disparate elements: stone blocks, imitation rustic stone, stucco, brick, imitation marble; it had been built in the nineteenth century. The village was mentioned in manuscripts as early as the ninth century; in 1214 the lord of Chaumont, also called sire of Villeblevin, had saved the life of Philippe Auguste at the battle of Bouvines. One of his descendants emancipated the inhabitants of the town in the thirteenth century. During World War I there was a military hospital in Villeblevin, and each year the inhabitants flower the graves of the fifty-three soldiers who died in it. Some were Moslems, and their tombs bear Arabic inscriptions. In 1960, as it is at the present writing, Villeblevin was a peaceful village, growing imperceptibly despite the proximity of Paris and the mushrooming of secondary residences.[7]

Camus' body was first taken to a small room on the Rue de la Mortellerie (which later became the village's catechism class), then was carried into the main room of the homely town hall, a somewhat ordinary room about fifteen feet wide and twenty-five feet deep, with its official photograph of President of the Republic Charles de Gaulle on the wall; here council meetings were held and marriages performed. They had put Camus on a cot, covered by a large sheet. Later in the afternoon a hastily arranged bouquet of ordinary flowers was placed on the body, and the walls of the plain room were draped in black cloth. The pendulum clock had been stopped.

At the hospital at Montereau, some twelve miles north of the scene of the accident, Janine and Anne had been placed in a ward. Michel was found to be in more serious condition, his spleen reportedly ruptured by the steering column. In the ambulance he had seemed stunned, asked Janine: "Was I driving?" He had to be brought out of shock before he could be operated on. Their friend Guy Schoeller brought Michel's father Raymond and his uncle Gaston Gallimard to Montereau, and then took them home with Anne;[8] Janine stayed by her husband's side. She was told only that Camus had been taken to another hospital because there was no room for him in this one. Michel Gallimard showed no improvement, and was transferred to a private hospital in Paris, where he died on January 10 during an operation for a brain hemorrhage. Then it was discovered that Janine had more than a bruise on her face: One of the bones in her neck had been broken, and she would wear a collar for four months.[9]

The *gendarmerie* quickly discovered the importance of the dead

passenger in the Facel Vega: Newspapermen who had been driving
past stopped to take pictures, identified Camus, and told them who he
was. The government in Paris was informed within the hour. Georges
Loubet, who as *directeur de cabinet* was André Malraux's chief deputy at the Ministry of Cultural Affairs, called in the *chef adjoint de cabinet* Paul Maillot, and instructed him—as a man of authority—to go to
the scene of the accident to take charge in the name of the government.
Before he left he was called into Malraux's office. "Camus refused all
religious ceremony," Malraux told him, "so if anyone suggests any kind
of ritual, such as blessing of the body, you must oppose it." It was the
only instruction Maillot was to receive. He sped south to Villeblevin,
where he became the highest ranking official on the spot. But when he
arrived the body had already been moved to the town hall council
chamber and the death certificate was being filled out. Noticing the
presence of loiterers, he instructed the gendarmes to watch for souvenir
hunters. He feared dispersal of Camus' personal papers and manuscripts. The Mayor of Villeblevin showed him the baggage found in the
car, which had broken open, and Camus' mud-caked briefcase. They
decided to lock everything up in the mayor's office. Maillot stayed on
until 10 P.M., then left to visit Michel Gallimard at the Montereau hospital. But before leaving Villeblevin he said a few formal words on behalf of the government: "I bow before the body. . . ."[10]

No one had been able to reach the widow. On that Monday she
had returned to her teaching job at the Cours Marcel Proust on the Rue
des Ecoles, founded and operated by her Oran friend André Benichou,
he who had employed Albert Camus in his improvised and quasi-
clandestine school for Jewish pupils during the racial ban under the
Vichy occupation government. Francine Camus had phoned André
Benichou's wife Madeleine to say that she was back from Lourmarin,
was putting her own children in school, and would be reporting for
work at the Rue des Ecoles. Then she said: "I'm worried." Madeleine
Benichou asked why. "Because I couldn't find Albert's beautiful leather
valise at the station." It had been checked through, to lighten the load
in the Facel Vega.

At about 4 P.M. the Benichous' son Pierre, who was a reporter on
a weekly paper, phoned home to tell his mother that Camus had been in
an accident. "Serious?" "Very serious. . . ." Finally he told her, and
she screamed into the phone. Then Madame Benichou tried to reach
Francine's sister Suzy without success, and phoned her husband at the
school. For reasons she herself could not understand later, she begged
her husband not to tell Francine—to let her go home first. Madeleine
Benichou sent her maid out to buy *France-Soir* and was reassured that
there was no headline.

Francine Camus was alone when she returned to the Rue Madame apartment. There were reporters in the hallway. None dared blurt out what had happened. "You're back from a trip?" one finally ventured. She brushed past, mumbled that her husband hadn't returned yet.[11]

The first news that Suzanne Agnely had of the accident was a telephone call at her office from the journalist Pierre Berger, who seemed to be sobbing. He had just seen the brief flash on the Agence France Presse wire:

**ATTENTION FLASH FLASH**
**THE WRITER ALBERT CAMUS KILLED**
**IN AN AUTOMOBILE ACCIDENT**
**IN THE YONNE NEAR SENS**

She walked into the rotunda office of the Gallimards; they were all there. No one had tried to call Francine, so Suzanne Agnely walked back to her own office and phoned her from there. Francine had just gotten in, she said, and it was obvious that she knew nothing.

"Wait for me," Suzanne Agnely told her. "Don't open the door to anyone until I get there."

"Albert is dead," Francine said.

"Don't open for anybody. I'm on my way."[12]

As Madame Camus remembered that phone call, Agnely said that there had been an accident. "Is he still alive?" she had asked. After a pause came the answer: "No."[6]

When Camus' secretary put the phone down after speaking to Madame Camus, the telephone rang. It was Malraux's secretary at Gallimard (who worked there to take care of Malraux's publishing interests). He told her that Malraux had ordered his aide Maillot to go to Villeblevin, and wanted her to bring Camus' widow there. A motorcycle escort would be waiting for them at Fontainebleau. Suzanne Agnely's husband quickly rented a car. When they arrived at the Rue Madame, Francine Camus was still in a daze. She told them that she had been aware of the reporters downstairs, had even heard the concierge say: "Poor Madame Camus"; worried about her children, who should have been home from school, she had rushed upstairs without asking any questions.[12] She took more time than she wanted to get ready to leave; she had to arrange for someone to take care of Jean and Catherine.

Sirens accompanied them on the road south from Fontainebleau; it was almost 10 P.M. when they arrived on the town hall square. Paul Maillot took Camus' secretary aside and asked her to go through Camus' possessions; she interpreted that as Malraux's desire to protect the public figure that Camus was. Jean Bloch-Michel came with her to examine the contents of Camus' pockets and his wallet, as well as the black briefcase. But Bloch-Michel felt that they had no right to read any of the manuscripts, and they were turned over to Camus' widow. Now other friends had begun to arrive. Emmanuel Roblès and Jean Grenier convinced Suzanne Agnely that she should return to Paris, where she would be needed; they would stay with the body.[12] The Benichous had also wished to be with Francine at Villeblevin, but when they arrived Madeleine didn't want to raise the sheet to look at their friend; she felt that he was "secret" and that she would be violating this secrecy by looking at him now. Walking through the town hall, standing in front of that building, she felt as if she were living a scene from *L'Etranger*.[13]

Emmanuel Roblès remembered raising the sheet to look at his comrade for the last time. "Under the light of a naked bulb, he had the expression of a very tired sleeper. . . ." But there was a long scratch across his forehead, like a line drawn across a page to strike it out.[14]

The first persons on hand to watch over the body were members of the humble village's town council. They would give way as members of the family and friends of the deceased arrived. When the crowd became dense, a gendarme was stationed at the door to screen visitors. The mayor asked the schoolmasters, Charles and Virginie Peugnet, who taught and lived in the building (the usual arrangement in French villages), to keep order and to take care of Madame Camus and other members of the family. The Peugnets invited Madame Camus, then her sister Suzy and Suzy's husband when they arrived, to rest in their living room whenever they wished. The other visitors remained in the council room with the body or in the entrance hall separating the two rooms; there was considerable movement back and forth. Suzanne Agnely and her husband talked to the Peugnets about the teaching profession, and asked whether her pupils knew Camus' work. They replied that the children from ten to fourteen read extracts of his work and were familiar with his career. Later Virginie Peugnet showed Francine Camus the classroom, feeling that it would help her relax, and they too talked about teaching. At midnight Francine Camus had to return to Paris to be with her children, accompanied by Madeleine Benichou, who spent the night at the Rue Madame, but her sister and sister's husband would stay with the body. After 2 A.M. the Peugnets retired upstairs, leaving a gendarme captain and one of his men to keep guard.[15]

The next morning the Peugnets posted themselves in the kitchen, which also opened onto the entrance corridor. Madame Peugnet was moved by the sight of Jean Grenier, who wept openly as the body was being prepared for removal.[16] At dawn a bugle summoned villagers to the ceremony, and the flag over the town hall was placed at half-mast. Local schoolchildren formed a double row as the hearse containing an empty coffin drove up from Sens. Madame Camus arrived from Paris at nine-thirty wearing a white scarf over her head. The body was in the coffin and ready to leave an hour later, and the prefect of the Yonne Department and his *sous-prefect* stationed in Sens were both present for the simple ceremony, along with Gaëtan Picon, writer and critic, attached to Malraux's ministry and representing him. Malraux had already issued a statement: "For over twenty years the work of Albert Camus was inseparable from the obsession with justice. We salute one of those through whom France remains present in the hearts of men."

Four strong men carried out the simple oak coffin; it was raining now; the gendarmes at attention gave a military salute as the coffin was placed in the hearse.[17] The villagers huddled behind the gendarmes; to some of Camus' friends they seemed at once sad and proud that this event had taken place on their doorstep.[18] The widow and children were put on the express train for Avignon, where they arrived that evening; by 8:30 P.M. they were at Lourmarin, and the hearse was there before midnight.

Seven years later the village fountain across the square from the town hall, a massive stone block with a stone knob, was decorated with a bas-relief (in stone) of Camus' head, and an inscription from *Le Mythe de Sisyphe* (also carved in stone):

The struggle toward the summits itself suffices to fill a man's heart.

On another façade of the fountain there is a bronze plaque:

> The General Council of
> the Yonne in homage to
> the writer Albert Camus
> whose body lay in vigil
> at the Villeblevin town hall
> on the night of January 4 to 5 1960

In Algiers reporters arrived at Camus' mother's apartment late on January 4, but when they realized that she knew nothing, they stammered that they were looking for someone else. Friends finally announced the news to her, and her son Lucien took her to his home in the center of the city.[19] She survived Albert only a little over nine months, died in her Belcourt apartment in September 1960.

Although French radio employees were striking, the strike committee agreed to interrupt the program of recorded music to broadcast a five-minute tribute to Camus.[20] Headlines greeted the news of the accident around the world. It was a front-page story in the New York *Times* on January 5, and the same day the newspaper published an editorial which began:

There is grim philosophical irony in the fact that Albert Camus should have died in a senseless automobile accident, victim of a chance mishap. For the central theme of his thought was the proper response of the thinking man to the plight that is posed by the gift of life. . . .

The editorial concluded:

There can be no surprise that our era responded to Camus' message. . . . The terrible slaughter of two world wars, the unprecedented menace of the hydrogen bomb, these are part of the modern setting which made Camus' austere philosophy comprehensible and assured his memory such immortality as mere man can give.[21]

At the performance scheduled at Tourcoing in northern France by the road company of *Les Possédés,* Pierre Blanchar asked for a minute of silence. For another three days, actors in the company would be receiving notes from Camus mailed from Lourmarin, wishing them strength, assuring them that they were not forgotten. Other theaters canceled rehearsals or performances, or observed a moment of silence.[22]

The town of Lourmarin circulated the printed notices that were always handed out on the death of one of the inhabitants. The funeral was scheduled for 11:30 A.M. on Wednesday, January 6, the villagers to meet at the Camus home. In Lourmarin funerals usually bring out one or another opposing faction, but there were no oppositions here. Freethinker Franck Creac'h would carry the coffin along with a devout Catholic whom he detested, and the young men of the village, the soccer players, would add their strength. The coffin had been lying in the Camus home, watched over not only by the widow but by Lucien, her husband's brother, by René Char, Jean Grenier, Emmanuel Roblès, Jules Roy, Louis Guilloux, and by that other old comrade Robert Jaussaud. With Lucien Camus and Jaussaud the widow had decided on a simple gravestone with nothing more than Camus' name and his dates of birth and death.

They carried the coffin not to a church, as usually happened, but directly to Lourmarin's tiny cemetery on the edge of the village, facing the castle and the houses of the village, including that of the Camus. When a non-believer dies, the bell is tolled not in the Catholic or the Protestant church, but in the clock tower dominating the village. It was a sunny winter day, and the procession of villagers in their Sunday clothes was augmented by the reporters down from Paris, by others from the regional press; but not all of Camus' personal friends had had time to get there. The cortège was headed by Madame Camus, assisted by her brother-in-law and by Char. Gabriel Audisio represented both the Société des Gens de Lettres and the *délégué général* of French Algeria in Paris. The Gaston Gallimards were present, and so was the Prefect of the Vaucluse.

Although the cemetery was still divided into two sections, Catholic and Protestant, the distinctions were falling into disuse, and a new annex to the cemetery had no such divisions at all—reflecting the evolution in thinking. It was agreed by the widow and Camus' friends, Char included, that Camus would be buried in the Catholic section—or what used to be called that. Francine Camus dropped a red rose onto the coffin. The mayor, Denis Sambuc, made a brief speech, noting that Camus, one of the great writers of his time, had in a few months made himself loved by all Lourmarin. He concluded: "Sleep in peace in this earth that you loved, among my fellow citizens who adopted you." They would never fail to flower his grave, he promised.

There were wreaths bearing ribbons: "To a friend of Hungary— Les Hongrois en exil," "Théâtre National Populaire," "Congrès pour la Liberté de la Culture," "Université d'Aix en Provence . . ."[23]

Later, Pierre-André Emery decided to put an absinthe plant from Camus' beloved Tipasa on his grave, but it grew too well in the climate of Provence, theatening to smother the other vegetation; finally it had to be removed.[24] The visitor who enters the cemetery today, walking past the sign whose accent slants the wrong way (*CIMETIÉRE*), will find a tomb of great simplicity, nothing more than a mound covered with a thick growth of rosemary; the stone bearing the name and dates seems centuries old. From time to time a passer-by drops a crucifix on the tomb—often a simple one taken from a rosary, but at least once it was a large stone cross, perhaps from the ruin of an old tomb.[25]

# 50

◆

# AFTERWORD

The time a lunatic society was willing to give him he
devoted to loving life in his own way, which was simple
and strong.

Preface for Richard Maguet*

Simone de Beauvoir was alone at Sartre's apartment on the Rue
Bonaparte when the telephone rang. It was her friend the journalist
Claude Lanzmann, to tell her about the accident at Villeblevin. She replaced the receiver and discovered that her throat was dry, her mouth
trembling, and she told herself that she was not going to cry; Camus no
longer meant anything to her. Sartre was also affected, and all that evening they talked about Camus with Jacques-Laurent Bost. For the first
time in a long time she had to take a pill, but still she couldn't sleep.
She got up to walk the streets of Paris in the January cold and drizzle.

Waking the next morning, she thought: "He can't see this morning." Far from having left the world, by the violence of the event
Camus had become its center, and she saw it only through his dead
eyes. She saw her own death in his. On the streets people were reading
the papers, indifferent to the large headline and to the photograph
which blinded her. She thought of the torture it would be for the
woman who loved Camus, to see his photograph offered up to everybody.[1]

It is often said that Sartre's eulogy of Camus, published in Jean
Daniel's *France-Observateur* on January 7, was the most moving of all.
Camus had been silent, momentarily, torn by contradictions that had to
be respected, he wrote. But he was one of those rare men who would

* Quoted by Gabriel Audisio.

decide slowly and remain faithful to the decision; his choice would show that he had evolved as the world had. They had broken up, Sartre and Camus, but what was breaking up? Another manner of living together, and which didn't prevent Sartre from thinking of him, wondering what he was thinking of the book or the newspaper which Sartre was reading.

> He represented in this century, and against History, the present-day heir of that long line of moralists whose works constitute what is perhaps most original in French letters. His stubborn humanism, strict and pure, austere and sensual, delivered uncertain combat against the massive and deformed events of the day. But inversely, by the unexpectedness of his refusals, he reaffirmed, at the heart of our era, against the Machiavelians, against the golden calf of realism, the existence of the moral act.

Soon there would be public manifestations as well. Notable ones were the meeting that January in Franco Spain, attended by some five hundred artists, writers, and students of Madrid; another in February, which filled an auditorium in the University of Warsaw in Communist Poland. And on the first anniversary of his death the Spanish Republicans would organize a memorial service, requesting that visitors place flowers under a large portrait hung at their exile government headquarters in Paris.[2]

It was obvious that the press, not to speak of Saint-Germain-des-Prés, would continue to talk about the circumstances of the fatal accident. One common reaction was to blame Michel Gallimard, who drove too fast or (said his critics) kept his car or his tires in poor condition, and then the make of car was blamed.

Everyone had his own story of Camus' abhorrence of speed on the road. In his homage to his former student, Jean Grenier would later remind readers that Camus disliked fast driving, used the train to go to Avignon to avoid the Paris-Riviera drive, and would tell the man who picked him up in the old Citroën not to drive too fast.[3] When Camus had driven Maria Casarès and Michel Bouquet to Auvers-sur-Oise years before to see Vincent Van Gogh's room, Maria Casarès had urged him to hurry, perhaps to get back to the theater, for he was driving slowly; Camus had replied: "I know nothing more stupid than to die in an automobile accident."[4] Roblès was quoted: "Whenever I stepped on the gas, he stopped me by saying: 'You'll end up a legless cripple.'"[5]

It was true that Camus teased Michel Gallimard about his fast driving, and it was also true that he drove with him, even on the Paris-Riviera road (as in the January 1953 return to Paris discussed in an earlier chapter).

Press reports spoke of worn tires or unequally inflated tires; the rear left tire had reportedly blown out at about ninety miles an hour, and (so the story went) the driver had braked when he shouldn't have.[6] Others reported that the tires were 40 per cent worn, to which Michel Gallimard's friends replied that they hadn't done 6,200 miles.[7]

It was then that an old friend of Michel Gallimard decided to enter into the battle. René Etiemble, who had been Michel's private tutor, ran into Louis Aragon in the Gallimard lobby, and discovered that Aragon, who was having some doubts about the Communist Party, seemed also to wish to make amends for past attacks on Etiemble in *Lettres Françaises*. All right, Etiemble told him, what I want is space in your newspaper to publish the facts about the accident. Aragon promised him all the space he needed.[8]

Etiemble's article appeared in the January 21, 1960, *Lettres Françaises,* on the front page. By that time Michel Gallimard was already dead. He wished to reply, Etiemble wrote, to insinuations and calumnies of press and radio which had made out Michel Gallimard to be a murderer; one radio report had said he would probably be indicted for *homicide par imprudence*. The reports spoke of worn tires, excessive speed; because he was an ill man, it was rumored that he might have had a *malaise*. He had allegedly been driving ninety miles an hour on a wet road, traveling from Lourmarin to Sens non-stop. Etiemble demanded proof of the charges, or excuses. After having been Gallimard's tutor, he went on, he had been his friend for thirty years, spent several months with him each year on vacations, worked with him at Gallimard.

The tires were not old. Michel Gallimard kept an extra set, said Etiemble, in case they showed wear. Etiemble then made a case for big cars, and their speed. "Besides, from the moment that we manufacture and import sports cars, can you demand that the purchasers of these machines sit patiently from Paris to Cannes behind a long line of small vehicles?"

He quoted Michel Gallimard, who would explain that his type of automobile allowed him to pass others on the road with safety. Speed is relative to the size of the car and the competence of the driver; Gallimard had driven over six hundred thousand miles. Camus didn't like anyone to drive him. "Except with Michel. With him I'm never afraid," so Etiemble quoted Camus. Etiemble had driven a great deal with Gallimard, even experienced a blowout with no alarm. Fatigue, *malaise?* From the time Gallimard had a tubercular kidney removed he had been in excellent health. Etiemble went on to describe the itinerary from Lourmarin, observed that they had left Thoissey at nine, arriving for lunch at twelve-thirty at Sens, doing the 306 kilometers in three and a half hours, for an average speed of 52 miles per hour. Nor had Gallimard overeaten. He would have one main meal a day, drink two glasses of wine. He had been relaxed, joking with Camus; when the car went out of control his wife and stepdaughter had seen him struggling against destiny. Then why the calumnies?

> Because it's a seductive image, the rich kid who kills the poor kid? Because in this affair it was necessary at any cost, for Camus' glory, to have a victim and an executioner?

He concluded by attacking the attempts to make a demigod of Camus by dishonoring Michel Gallimard.

Privately Etiemble would suggest that the fault lay with the automobile itself, a Facel Vega HK 500.[9] He set to work compiling a file of evidence which he hoped would serve in a suit against the manufacturer, but the Gallimards shied from the publicity. Etiemble's thesis was that the left rear wheel had blocked, something that had already happened on two previous occasions, that Michel Gallimard had been alarmed about that and confided his fears to Etiemble, and that when the car was returned to Gallimard after a repair the car dealer's driver commented: "This car is a tomb"; Etiemble hoped to get the man to testify at the trial.[10] Facel Vegas were not manufactured after 1965.

In Paris a search was made to find a paper by which Camus was to have appointed René Char as his literary executor, but it was not found in the examination of Camus' effects at the Rue de Chanaleilles carried out in Char's absence by Camus' secretary, with Bloch-Michel on hand as a witness. Only personal letters were returned to their writers; all of Camus' manuscripts went to the family, which already had the private journal and the manuscript of *Le Premier Homme*. The decision as to their final disposition was in their hands.

*Les Possédés* pursued its road tour. On February 16, 1960, *Caligula* opened in New York, directed by Sidney Lumet. Camus had planned to attend the opening; in fact he hoped to watch rehearsals, too. The New York *Times'* drama critic, Brooks Atkinson, said it had been produced with a kind of ruthless grandeur, "able" actors gave a "spectacular performance." But "In view of the modest content of the drama, it seems in the end to have been overproduced." Atkinson concluded that there would be "more enduring monuments to [Camus'] memory than this withdrawn and repetitious drama of horrors."[11] Nor would Atkinson be happy with a Los Angeles production in April of the same year: "The Circle Players have just concluded the gruesome experience of acting Albert Camus' 'Caligula,' an intellectual script that did not reform Hollywood very much."[12]

A cultural complex called the Centre Albert Camus, designed by Louis Miquel and Roland Simounet, was built in Orléansville, Algeria, with funds collected by French schoolchildren after the earthquake there. It contained a theater that could be open-air or covered, designed after discussions between the architects, Jean de Maisonseul (who was in charge of the urban plan of the reconstructed city) and Camus himself. It was inaugurated on the first anniversary of Camus' death.[13] The principal street of Mondovi, near Camus' birthplace, was named Rue Albert Camus prior to Algerian independence, and despite fears that the Moslem victors would quickly change it again, the name was kept, at least until 1975. A year after Camus' death his friend Edmond Brua, traveling in the region, found himself in the vicinity of Mondovi and had a friend drive him there. On the way they came upon a fatal accident: a smashed automobile, a soldier lying in a ditch below a farmhouse. Brua approached and saw that the dead man looked like Camus, so much so that he was shaken. He took out his camera, but at that instant a French officer walked up and threatened to confiscate it, although he showed his press card. Later, when the Mayor of Mondovi took him to the farm where Camus was born, Brua discovered that the body of the soldier had been lying just outside the window of the house the mayor pointed out as having been Camus' birthplace, but by then the corpse had been removed.

The mayor told Brua that the Ferme St. Paul was soon to be torn down because of its deteriorated condition.[14]

Also in Algeria, in April 1961, a group of Camus' friends, including Pierre-André Emery, Louis Miquel, Edmond Brua, Jean-Pierre Faure, and Marcelle Bonnet-Blanchet, attended the raising of a stone memorial to Camus at Tipasa. It had been a Phoenician tombstone, the height of a man, found among Tipasa's ruins, removed to Algiers to be engraved by Louis Benisti (because he could not work at the site, which sometimes came under guerrilla fire). Camus' name was mutilated at a later date, but it can still be read (the slab was still standing in 1975).[15] The inscription:

> Here I understand what
> they call glory:
> the right to love
> without limits. Albert Camus

# APPRECIATION

When one attempts to write the biography of a man who is no longer available to be questioned, one must depend on everyone else: contemporaries who knew him, the scholars who began to collect material earlier. I spoke, or corresponded with, hundreds of such witnesses, when I wasn't talking to them over the telephone, that modern instrument of research which seems to have no place in the wood-paneled study of which I spoke in my foreword. Some of the material I have utilized was gathered not without difficulty, often with devotion and stubborn persistence, by men and women who willingly shared it with me.

But it would be a supplementary labor for the reader to be confronted here with a list of sources running some pages in length. Those who contributed specific knowledge to this study are duly cited in the Notes. Let this also be my thanks to them, and if I have forgotten anyone I should not be pardoned.

Of course it will not always be clear from the Notes how much of their time some of these good people made available to this project—long days of submitting to interviews, sometimes over a period of weeks or even months, especially when the interviewee was a prime source, such as members of the Camus family, Michel Gallimard's widow Janine, Camus' private secretary Suzanne Agnely, friends such as Jean Bloch-Michel or Emmanuel Roblès. Some of my sources carried out research of their own on my behalf (such as the late Gabriel Audisio, the late Edmond Brua, and Pierre-André Emery), interviewed others on my behalf, or made available a lifetime of souvenirs (as did Blanche Balain, Jean de Maisonseul, or Charles Poncet).

Many of these willing sources had not always been on Camus' side (I am thinking of Yves Bourgeois, who wrote for me a memoir of the Algiers years, and Pascal Pia, Claude Bourdet, Amar Ouzegane,

Francis Jeanson, or Jacques-Laurent Bost), and yet they were as generous with their time and their information as anyone else.

In writing about a still-controversial figure, it was not always possible for me to satisfy myself that I had all the facts, or the true version of events previously told in different and conflicting ways. I am certain that I corrected errors, but I must have committed new errors. Let the reader with pertinent information contribute to later biographies or a revision of this one by calling attention to them.

Rather than list hundreds of names in order of importance or in alphabetical or any other order, as I say, I have simply acknowledged them in the Notes. And instead of dozens and dozens of thank-yous, let there be just this one heartfelt expression of thanks.

# METHODS

I have not cited specific editions or page numbers for Camus' own writings, including the posthumous publications, to allow the reader to consult either the originals or the edition that is most conveniently available. The writer himself has used the two-volume Pléiade edition of Camus' works, the Gallimard editions of the posthumous works published in the series Cahiers Albert Camus, as well as the Gallimard edition of the notebooks (*Carnets*).

For all other writings by Camus, including speeches, newspaper articles, manifestos, and appeals, an attempt has been made to cite the original publication rather than a subsequent reprinting, so that the reader will discover occasional variations in texts and new dating of some material.

# NOTES

## Notes for Chapter One

1. Interview by Franck Jotterand in *La Gazette de Lausanne,* March 27–28, 1954.

2. Jean Grenier, *Albert Camus* (Paris, 1968).

3. Jean Sarocchi, *Le Thème de la recherche du Père dans l'øeuvre d'Albert Camus.* Thesis presented at the University of Paris-Sorbonne, June 1975. Cf. also preface to *Cahiers Albert Camus 2* (Paris, 1973), for a résumé and quotations from the unfinished novel, and Jean Grenier, op. cit.

4. Interview by Aldo Camerino in *Il Gazzettino* (Venice), July 9, 1959.

5. I am indebted to the record officers of the Service Central de l'Etat Civil in Nantes, who not only dug out data going back almost two centuries but worked out a family tree to render them more comprehensible.

6. Prior to the French Revolution vital statistics were in the hands of local parishes, so that no official record exists of the parentage of Claude and Marie-Thérèse Camus.

7. The second largest town of the island, Ciudadela was once its civil and religious capital. It remained the latter after the British rulers arrived, and boasts the island's impressive cathedral. David Farragut, American naval hero and admiral, was the grandson of a Ciudadela sailor.

8. Information on Camus' maternal antecedents is contained in documents in the possession of the family, and in the oral recollections of Albert Camus' brother Lucien and of his aunt Antoinette Acault (née Sintes). Note that the French spelling of this family name takes the grave accent, Sintès. While visiting Algeria in December 1952, Albert Camus drove through the Sahel villages where his Minorcan ancestors had settled, discovered the family name on an old tombstone, but found only one of their descendants to talk to.

9. From Emile Camus, the son of Lucien Auguste's older brother Jean Baptiste Emile, born in 1876 in Ouled Fayet.

## Notes for Chapter Two

1. Information on Lucien Auguste Camus comes from his son Lucien, Albert's older brother; from Antoinette Acault, Albert's maternal aunt; and from Lucien Auguste Camus' military papers.

2. Or 1 meter 80. As an adult Albert Camus was 1 meter 78 in height, or almost as tall, the two centimeters' difference representing less than an inch.

3. Lucien Auguste Camus has been described as a vineyard worker, but vineyard technician would be a more accurate term. There were Moslems to work in the fields.

4. Marcel Moussy, *Simoun* (Oran), July 1960, special issue on "Camus l'Algérien."

5. Camus uses this story in *Le Premier Homme*. Sarocchi, op. cit.

6. Lucien Auguste Camus' *Livret Militaire,* his basic military document, which recorded his changes of address.

7. According to Albert Camus' friend Edmond Brua, who as an editor of *Le Journal d' Alger* visited Mondovi shortly after the death of Albert Camus and inspected the black clothbound ledger in which births were recorded. Cf. *Le Journal d' Alger,* June 26–27, 1960.

8. To Albert Camus' friend Emmanuel Roblès, who took photographs. By then screened porches had been added to the houses by the Moslem occupants, to allow their women to take the air out of the view of strangers.

9. Albert's brother Lucien Camus believes that Catherine and the children had been sent back to Algiers early because the climate of the Mondovi region didn't suit them, and the infant Albert had eye trouble.

10. No copy of the telegram survives, but his widow possessed official notification papers from the Algiers Hôtel de Ville dated three and a half years later "informing" her of the death. "It was a glorious death because this soldier bravely gave his life to his country."

11. The card is in his handwriting.

12. The widow also kept several small shell fragments, each the size of a wisdom tooth, in a box, all her life long.

13. From her sister Antoinette Acault. She might, for example, say "coucous" for "couscous" (a popular North African dish). Catherine and her mother spoke French to each other; no Spanish was ever used in the household.

14. According to her son Lucien, she learned to sign the name "Camus" in order to acknowledge receipt of her widow's pension.

15. Lucien Camus; Louis Guilloux.

16. Interview with Gabriel d'Aubarède, *Les Nouvelles Littéraires,* March 10, 1951, as quoted in *Essais* (Pléiade edition of Camus' works). Albert's brother Lucien in conversations with the author insisted that if the Camus children were poor they were not paupers, they had never been *"dans la misère."*

17. In his polemic with Emmanuel d'Astier de la Vigerie published in *Ac-*

*tuelles I:* "So often the sheet in which you replied to me and those which try to compete with it in lying, have called me a son of the bourgeoisie, that I must, *at least this once,* remind you that most of you, Communist intellectuals, have no experience of the condition of the proletariat, and that you are ill-placed to treat us as dreamers ignorant of realities."

18. Lucien Camus.

19. Reprinted in *Cahiers Albert Camus 1* (Paris, 1971). As an early draft of material developed in *La Mort heureuse,* this manuscript may be dated 1934 or earlier. The same material is used in *l'Envers et l'Endroit,* an early version of which, "Les Voix du quartier pauvre," is available in a manuscript dated December 1934, in *Cahiers Albert Camus 2,* op. cit.

20. Preface to *l'Envers et l'Endroit.*

21. Antoinette Acault.

22. Etienne would have been thirty-five in 1930, according to the age he announced to a reporter at the time his nephew won the Nobel Prize: *La Presse Libre* (Algiers), October 18, 1957.

23. The factual basis for this scene was confirmed by Lucien Camus to Jean Sarocchi, editor of the posthumous *La Mort heureuse.*

24. *La Presse Libre* (Algiers), October 18, 1957. Etienne Sintes died in 1960.

25. Lucien Camus. She would tell Lucien: "Albert always tells the truth. You always tell lies."

26. Antoinette Acault.

27. "We were happy with my mother," Lucien Camus said of this period.

28. Camus never witnessed an execution. Carl A. Viggiani, "Notes pour le futur biographe d'Albert Camus," *Revue des Lettres Modernes* (Paris), Nos. 170–78, 1968.

29. Sarocchi, op. cit.

30. Lucien Camus.

31. Sarocchi, op. cit.


## Notes for Chapter Three

1. For basic information on Belcourt, I am indebted to Emmanuel Roblès, Camus' longtime friend and the novelist of Algiers, as well as to Camus' elementary school companions Louis Pagès and Yves Doyon. Others who shared their recollections of the neighborhood include Robert Recagno, Ernest Diaz, Gilbert Ferrero, Sauveur Terracciano, and of course Albert's brother Lucien. A. J. Liebling, who knew Algiers well, described the approach from the sea as follows: "The French Alger that had almost wholly replaced the Corsairs' Al-jezair on the seaward side of the great hill rising from the shore looked as viable as Sydney or San Francisco. Of the buildings in the foreground, on the first tier above the docks, only the Great Mosque and the Mosque of the Fish Market dated from before the conquest. The others, sheltering the big banks and shipping companies, were of the period of Napoleon the Little, and had colonnades like those of the Rue

de Rivoli. On the next tier above were the then best shopping street, the Rue d'Isly, and, leading up from it, the Rue Michelet, with its university and its turn-of-the-century apartment houses. Above that, the buildings were newer and finer as the city swung south and west and climbed toward the golf links, but atop the oldest quarter of the city—the northeastern—the Casbah, with its cubical whitewashed houses, persisted, a combination slum and reminder. The Casbah housed the Moslems, who were the city's under-proletariat. . . ." *The New Yorker,* February 8, 1964 ("The Camus Notebooks").

2. Unless otherwise indicated, I have used throughout this book the names of streets and neighborhoods employed by the French during their administration of Algeria. Visitors to independent Algeria will find that many of these names have changed. Belcourt is called Sidi M'Hamed; the Rue de Lyon has become Mohamed Belouizdad, Rue Michelet Didouche Mourad. The Rue de l'Union, close to the Camus-Sintes apartment, is now Mohamed Bouguerfa. The Rue Alfred de Musset is one of the few Belcourt streets which has not been renamed as of this writing.

3. *La Presse Libre,* Algiers, October 18, 1957.

4. Later in the university he would maintain the same discretion. Some friends never realized that he was from a poor family. Yves and Myriam Dechezelles. One of Camus' closest friends of the 1930s, Jean de Maisonseul, had never been near Camus' Belcourt home; he assumed that it may have been a painful memory to his friend. Later in Paris, Camus could speak with nostalgia of his childhood poverty. Suzanne Agnely.

5. Lucien Camus. Camus told interviewer Carl Viggiani that he had been fascinated by Robin Hood. Viggiani, op. cit.

6. Louis Pagès.

7. From Albert Camus' birth certificate.

8. Sauveur Terracciano, with additional explanations from Louis Pagès and Yves Doyon. It is said that Camus spoke Cagayous. Actually, as he points out in a note for "L'Eté à Alger" in *Noces,* Cagayous is a literary reconstruction of the mixture of French, Maltese, Spanish, and Arabic used on the Algiers streets.

9. Yves Doyon. Mr. Doyon, a career officer in security and defense, also drew a detailed map of Camus' Belcourt neighborhood for the author. Doyon's father, an officer at the front in World War I, had returned badly wounded, so that Yves Doyon, like the Camus children, was a *pupille de la nation.*

10. Louis Pagès; Lucien Camus; Yves Doyon.

11. Lucien Camus. Camus' older brother would begin working at the age of fifteen, in 1925. At seventeen his mother got him a job at his father's old firm, Jules Ricôme, where he returned after his tour of obligatory military service. By that time he had married and moved out of Belcourt to central Algiers. When he returned from World War II, where he served with the French First Army in Tunisia and Italy, landing with U.S. forces in Provence, the Ricôme company had gone out of business.

12. Jean Sarocchi. Camus told Viggiani of Louis Germain: "He was severe, but warm. I loved and feared him." Viggiani, op. cit.

13. Quoted by Viggiani, op. cit. Another book read in the elementary school which left an impression on young Albert was apparently called *Les Enfants de la mer*. Little else is known about it except that at some point in the story children shout: "To the sea! To the sea!" The memory of that phrase was to remain with the adult Camus. Also Viggiani, op. cit.

14. Jean Sarocchi.

15. Robert Jaussaud.

16. "Arrachez la victime aux bourreaux," from *Caliban* (Paris), in *Actuelles I*.

## Notes for Chapter Four

1. Or the Lycée Bugeaud, so named to commemorate the popular marshal who governed the territory during the colonial wars. It is now (since Algerian independence) the Lycée de l'Emir Abd el-Kader, to commemorate the leader who resisted Bugeaud. The schoolmate who shared a tram with Albert Camus was Gilbert Ferrero.

2. For information on the geography of Algiers, I have used obvious sources such as a pre-independence *Guide Bleu*, the Larousse encyclopedias, etc. Extra detail comes from *Un Jour, je m'en souviens* . . . , a memoir by Max-Pol Fouchet (Paris, 1968), from Fouchet's conversations with the author, and from the recollections of Ferrero, Ernest Diaz, and other lycée students.

3. Although it has been said that some students looked down on Camus because of his Belcourt origins, this is considered unlikely by a former teacher of the lycée, Yves Bourgeois, who observed that the half-boarders were generally sons of small tradesmen and lower-ranking civil servants, while boarding students were from lower-middle-class families in the back country.

4. Gilbert Ferrero.

5. From a former teacher, Jean Domerc. From 7:15 A.M. to 7 P.M., Camus told Carl A. Viggiani: Viggiani, op. cit. Camus may have been including the travel time.

6. Viggiani, op. cit. In *Le Premier Homme*, Jacques Cormery works as a sorting clerk at the Quincaillerie de l'Agha (near Belcourt), later for a ship's broker, Jean Sarocchi.

7. Quoted in a talk by Jacques Heurgon which he kindly made available.

8. Yves Doyon.

9. *Le Rua*, April 15, 1953. In other words a lycée student following an academic program "belonged" on a University of Algiers team. Robert Jaussaud, a contemporary, remembered that the team would also practice daily after lunch in the lycée yard. He also observed that the soccer fields were not smooth playing greens but rugged terrain with jagged rocks.

10. Charles Poncet, "Camus à Alger," in *Simoun* (Oran), No. 32.

11. I am indebted to Dr. Louis Lataillade, a RUA comrade of Camus, for providing these articles from *Le Rua,* which he copied for me during a chance encounter with his friend Robert Fougère, who owns a collection of the newspaper. Camus told Carl Viggiani that his illness began in December 1930. Viggiani, op. cit.

12. Quoted in *Le Figaro Littéraire* (Paris), October 26, 1957.

13. Madame Jean Grenier; also Jean Grenier, *Albert Camus* (Paris, 1968). Yves Bourgeois, who began teaching at the same lycée five years later, confirmed that even in his time lycée teachers did not generally call on ill students (although they encouraged other students to do so). Grenier's visit showed his interest in Camus and of course his own kindness.

14. Antoinette Acault. Camus would later tell Viggiani that he had been hospitalized only for the (relatively brief) pneumothorax operation. Viggiani, op. cit. According to his aunt Antoinette, he spent only a day or two in Mustapha Hospital. Yet he told Viggiani that he read the Stoic philosopher Epictetus in the hospital, which had helped him endure.

15. Camus himself said to Viggiani that his tuberculosis was brought on by "Excess of sports. Exhaustion. Too much exposure to sun." Viggiani, op. cit. According to Robert Jaussaud, Camus experienced his first attack of hemoptysis while running along the Rue Michelet to catch a tram at the Agha stop which would take him to a stadium.

16. Lucien Camus.

17. Dr. Georges Brouet, a tuberculosis specialist who treated Camus from the time of his arrival in Paris just before the Liberation. Camus told Viggiani that he was indeed afraid that he would die, and that he had read similar fears on the face of the doctor after his hemoptysis. Viggiani, op. cit.

18. Max-Pol Fouchet. Years later Camus would also tell his friend Jean Bloch-Michel that tuberculosis is a metaphysical disease, because one doesn't know that one is ill.

## Notes for Chapter Five

1. Information on Acault comes from Pierre-André Emery, Jean de Maisonseul, Louis Miquel, Lucien Camus, Louis Benisti, and from previously cited works of Jean Grenier (*Albert Camus*) and Max-Pol Fouchet (*Un jour, je m'en souviens . . .*), and of course from Acault's widow, Antoinette Acault née Sintes.

2. "Rencontres avec André Gide," *Nouvelle Revue Française,* November 1951, reprinted in *Essais.*

3. Antoinette Acault. I am indebted to Blanche Balain, who had earlier interviewed Madame Acault and facilitated my meeting with her, and who later returned for an even more thorough interrogation at my request.

4. Jean de Maisonseul.

5. Max-Pol Fouchet, op. cit.

6. There is a hint in his unpublished novel that Albert/Jacques had become

a dandy, mocked by his schoolmates for his fancy attire, even before he came under Gustave Acault's wing. Sarocchi, op. cit.

7. Viggiani, op. cit.

8. So says Jean Grenier in *Albert Camus*.

9. André de Richaud, *La Douleur* (Paris, 1930). Richaud's father was killed in World War I and he was raised by his maternal grandfather in Provence. The story takes place in the Vaucluse near the Sorgue River, which region will be important in Camus' later life. It may be argued that Camus found in this love story of a forty-year-old widow an echo of his mother's affair with the fishmonger, although the latter may have occurred after Camus' discovery of *La Douleur*. A more significant connection may be the one between Richaud and Grenier, who in 1929 were both resident fellows at the Fondation Laurent-Vibert in the Lourmarin castle. When Grenier arrived in Algiers in 1930, he had just left there.

10. Jean Grenier, *Albert Camus*. Didier later became a Jesuit priest and would die in 1957 in an automobile accident.

11. Lucien Camus.

12. See the notes in *Cahiers Albert Camus 2*, in which the four essays from *Sud* are reprinted, together with other writings of young Camus.

13. Max Jacob, *Lettres à un ami* (Pully-Lausanne, Switzerland, 1951). Camus wrote to Grenier on August 25, 1932, referring to his correspondence with Jacob. The anecdotal material about Jacob is from Jeanine Warnod, *Le Figaro*, July 5, 1976. Further information from Madame Jean Grenier.

14. Grenier, *Albert Camus*. Note that *Nouvelle Revue Française* was running sections of Grenier's *Les Iles* during this period. An essay by Grenier on Lourmarin had appeared in the May 1930 issue.

15. Amar Ouzegane; Yves Bourgeois. The latter had heard that Camus may have actually met Emir Khaled.

16. André Belamich.

17. Who is "S.C."? The casual answer would be Simone Camus, but Camus did not marry her until June 1934 and would not have begun to call her Camus before that. Another "S.C." was Camus' friend and doctor Stacha Cviklinski, whose name he spells Cviklinsky.

18. Jean Grenier discusses in his *Albert Camus* this difference between the philosophy expressed in *Les Iles* and Camus' own work.

## Notes for Chapter Six

1. For evocations of Simone Hié I am indebted to her second husband, Dr. Léon Cottenceau, to Max-Pol Fouchet, Myriam Dechezelles (née Salama), Louis Miquel, Jean de Maisonseul.

2. From Fouchet, op. cit., and directly from its author. Years later, not long before Camus' death, as Fouchet recalls in his book, the former friends met again in Paris and discovered that they could talk with nostalgia about their youth. Fouchet pursued a literary career, took part in the anti-

Nazi resistance in Algeria, and published anti-collaborationist writers in his literary magazine *Fontaine.*

3. In addition to the sources already cited I am indebted for background to Louis Benisti, Yves Bourgeois (who felt that Simone Hié was more victim than vamp), Myriam Dechezelles, Marguerite Dobrenn, Pierre-André Emery, Robert Namia, Mr. and Mrs. Louis Nallard.

4. From an interview with Antoinette Acault by Blanche Balain.

5. Jean de Maisonseul.

6. Lucien Camus.

7. Max-Pol Fouchet, op. cit. There was no entrance or tuition fee at the university, although students purchased their own books. Professor René Poirier.

8. René Poirier; also Myriam Dechezelles and Liliane Dulong (née Choucroun), fellow students of Camus. The university certificates are in the possession of the Camus family. Camus told Carl Viggiani, op. cit., that he read *The Golden Bough,* by James George Frazer, while working for the *certificat de morale et sociologie.*

9. Yves and Myriam Dechezelles.

10. Henri Chemouilli, *Une Diaspora méconnue: Les Juifs d'Algérie* (Paris, 1976).

11. René Poirier. He felt then and later that Camus, whose dissertation on Plotinus and St. Augustine he would supervise, was more of an artist than a philosopher, and Poirier's job was to produce philosophers. Cf. Poirier, *Annales d'esthétique* (Athens, 1969): "Camus is certainly much more of a writer and an artist than a thinker in the narrow sense, and the passion he has always had for the theater perhaps allows us to understand this."

12. Viggiani, op. cit. Although Camus would study Greek at the university, he told Viggiani that he had read the classics in French translations.

13. René Poirier.

14. Yves Dechezelles. Pierre Cardinal, producer of the "Gros plan" television program on Camus and the theater (1959), had a similar experience when Camus thought that Cardinal was addressing him with *tu,* and there are other examples of his careful attention to abuse of the familiar form.

15. Jean de Maisonseul.

16. Yves Dechezelles.

17. *La Table Ronde* (Paris), February 1960.

18. Sabine Dupeyré née Coulombel.

19. Dr. Louis Lataillade, one of the editors of *Alger-Etudiant,* was kind enough to supply me with these articles, representing Camus' first journalism. For accounts of the artist milieu in which Camus moved, Jean de Maisonseul, Paul Raffi.

20. Jean de Maisonseul, Louis Benisti. Benisti had his first one-man show at Edmond Charlot's Vraies Richesses bookshop. Late in life he took up painting.

21. Jean de Maisonseul. Maisonseul told the author that it was this image which convinced him that Camus would become a writer.

22. In *Alger-Etudiant* of April 19, 1934. It should be noted that the Pléiade edition suggests that Camus wrote about art in the daily *Echo d'Alger*. There is no evidence of this. Certainly there are no signed articles in *Echo d'Alger*, and it seems unlikely that a young man not a staff member of the newspaper would be asked to write anonymous or pseudonymous reviews. The Pléiade assumes that a draft of a review of the work of Boucherle was written for *Echo d'Alger*, possibly because the *Alger-Etudiant* articles were not availa- ble. The false attribution has unfortunately been repeated in subsequent scholarly work on Camus, just as the *Alger-Etudiant* article on Maguet has been wrongly attributed to another publication.

23. André Hambourg. He would go on to an international career. Damboise would do the bust of Camus placed in Paris's Théâtre de l'Odéon after his death. Maguet, a friend of Camus, was killed while serving in the French Army in 1940. Camus wrote an introduction to a posthumous exhibition of this work.

24. Yves Bourgeois.

25. Jean de Maisonseul. The trousseau and rent receipts courtesy of Dr. Léon Cottenceau.

26. Madame Jean Grenier. The Parc d'Hydra house, in the vicinity of an eighteenth-century castle, was in the township of Birmandreïs about three miles from the university.

27. Antoinette Acault.

28. Dr. Léon Cottenceau.

29. Charles Poncet, Lucien Camus.

30. Quoted in *Cahiers Albert Camus 2*.

31. Max-Pol Fouchet, op. cit.

32. Private conversations. The final anecdote is from Jeanne Delais, *L'Ami de chaque matin* (Paris, 1969).

33. Yves Bourgeois.

## Notes for Chapter Seven

1. Jeanne Delais, op. cit.

2. Jean Daniel, *Le Temps qui reste* (Paris, 1973). During the Popular Front era *Nouvelle Revue Française* moved heavily into politics, provid- ing a platform both for Malraux and Trotsky, but the brilliant cast of char- acters on the covers of successive issues of the monthly magazine also in- cluded the intellectual leaders of the opposing camp, such as Drieu la Rochelle, Robert Brasillach, Marcel Jouhandeau, as well as major figures with other axes to grind (e.g. Antonin Artaud, whose manifesto, "Le Théâtre de la cruauté," appeared in *NRF* in October 1932). Or a special issue of *NRF* might be devoted entirely to a classic author such as Goethe, Stendhal, or even Faulkner.

3. Louis Pagès.

4. Charles Poncet, "Camus à Alger," in *Simoun* (Oran) 32, 1960.

5. Jacques Heurgon, from his student Geneviève Journau.

6. Myriam Dechezelles.

7. Published in *Essai sur l'esprit d'orthodoxie* (Paris, 1938). The same volume contains, in "l'Age des orthodoxies," dated April 1936, a warning against intellectual Communist fronts promoted by a party "which wages a reign of terror on intellectuals." The volume also contains a letter replying to readers who disapproved his essay on orthodoxy in the August 1936 *Nouvelle Revue Française:* "but I am stupefied that you accept certain beliefs with closed eyes and that you don't ask yourself certain questions." Finally, the same volume reprints a letter to Malraux criticizing his subordination to Communist Party orthodoxy.

8. Marcelle Bonnet-Blanchet; Mr. and Mrs. Edmond Brua. In fact the section was called Cartes Grises et Permis de Conduire, in the Division des Travaux Publics, whose chief was a sometime writer, Jean Pomier. See Pomier's *Chronique d'Alger 1910–1957* (Paris, 1972). A letter of application for a job at the prefecture exists somewhere in the depths of the Archives de France d'Outre-Mer in Aix-en-Provence, but at this writing it has not been located.

9. Charles Poncet.

10. Yves Bourgeois.

11. Marguerite Dobrenn.

12. Private conversations.

13. *Livret individuel* issued by the Ministère de la Guerre.

14. Jacques Heurgon.

15. André Abbou, in *Revue des lettres modernes* (Paris) Nos. 238–44 (1970).

16. Close readers of these *Carnets* will have remarked that there is a certain inversion of entries in the early pages. In fact the original manuscript of the first notebook was cut up and reassembled, with loose sheets inserted, possibly because it contained intimate reflections of a kind that Camus later decided did not belong in his journal. As a consequence the first notebook of *Carnets I,* to September 1937, is an inaccurate chronological aide.

17. For further detail and a summary of political events of this period, see Georges Lefranc, *Histoire du Front Populaire* (Paris, 1974).

18. Marcel Bataillon.

19. Roger Stéphane, *Fin d'une jeunesse* (Paris, 1954).

20. Emile Scotto-Lavina.

21. Robert Namia.

22. André Malraux, through the courtesy of Sophie L. de Vilmorin. Malraux informed the author that his first meeting with Camus took place in Paris in 1940 during a screening of his film on Spain, *L'Espoir,* when their mutual friend Pascal Pia introduced them.

23. Jean Grenier, *Albert Camus.* Clearly Camus was not living at the Parc d'Hydra villa if he was about to take a tram. This may have been during the time of Simone's stay in the Balearics in mid-1935.

24. Edmond Brua.

25. Paul Raffi; Marguerite Dobrenn. In letters to Grenier on August 8, 17, and 21, 1935, Camus refers to his relapse. He told Grenier that he had returned from Bougie by train, which according to Paul Raffi is the expression one might use, even though the actual means of transportation was a bus.

26. Jean Grenier, *Albert Camus*. Grenier dated this letter 1934; the original text bears no year. But Grenier in his book also placed the decision to join the Party after the staging of *Le Temps du mépris* and the planned production of *Révolte dans les Asturies*, i.e., after spring 1936. The fact that Camus' letter was actually written in August 1935 is clear from the context (the forthcoming trip to the Balearics), supported by dated letters of Fréminville and the testimony of others. See Chapter 8.

## Notes for Chapter Eight

1. From private conversations. As already indicated, the cut-up and reassembled first notebook covers the period May 1935–September 1937.

2. Louis Pagès. He is the nephew of Madame André Raffi. Camus never mentioned his Communist Party affiliation to his friend and first publisher, Edmond Charlot, who would be associated with his political as well as his literary activities. Edmond Charlot.

3. Roger Stéphane, op. cit.

4. Yves Bourgeois, Paul Raffi.

5. René Poirier. Camus would later tell Monsignor Léon Etienne Duval, then Bishop of Constantine, later Cardinal-Archbishop of Algiers, that from the time he discovered St. Augustine while writing his dissertation, he maintained a special "fidelity" to St. Augustine, who remained the "bishop" of North African writers whether believers or non-believers. Camus saw in this saint the artist with all the strengths and weaknesses of the "African" Camus felt himself to be. Cardinal-Archbishop Duval.

6. Paul Archambault, in *Recherches Augustiniennes* (VI), 1969, argues that in at least one section of the dissertation Camus simply incorporated the work of previous writers. See a commentary on this by Raymond Gay-Crosier in *Revue des Lettres Modernes* (Paris), Nos. 315–322 (1972).

7. Solange (Madame Louis) Benisti.

8. Elie Mignot. At the time Mr. Mignot was interviewed he was still an official of the French Communist Party, attached to Central Committee headquarters in Paris, and responsible for Arab and French colonial affairs. Amar Ouzegane, then secretary of the Party, in a conversation with the author said that in 1935 there were some hundred members in Algiers but five hundred in all Algeria.

9. Emile Padula.

10. Elie Mignot.

11. Jeanne Delais, op. cit.

12. Marguerite Dobrenn and Paul Raffi. Amar Ouzegane said that on his return to Algeria, Claude de Fréminville joined the Plateau Saulière cell.

13. Louis Miquel.

14. Louis Pagès. While no specific date can be attributed to Camus' Collège du Travail activity, Camus had written Jean Grenier in August 1935 that he could not stay away from Algiers long because he was teaching a course. But this could be a reference to the private class of lycée students he was teaching.

15. Yves Bourgeois. When the author tracked down Mr. Bourgeois, who was generally believed to have died or left France, and had never had an opportunity to discuss his association with Camus before, he wrote out his souvenirs in a memoir which he graciously put at the author's disposal, and subsequently responded to a number of questionnaires during the preparation and writing of this book.

16. Charles Poncet. For information on the Théâtre du Travail, particularly *Le Temps du mépris,* I have also drawn on the recollections of Louis Miquel, Pierre-André Emery, Yves Bourgeois, Louis Pagès, André Belamich. Apparently no one saved a copy of Camus' adaptation of the Malraux novel.

17. Yves Bourgeois.

18. Louis Miquel; Louis Pagès; André Belamich; Marguerite Dobrenn.

19. Charles Poncet, op. cit.; Pierre-André Emery. There were two performances, with total receipts of three thousand francs, according to Camus' open letter of April 13, 1936 (on *Révolte dans les Asturies*). Since the regular contribution per spectactor was one franc, this suggests that there had been 1,500 persons paying one franc at each performance, but it is likely that many of the contributions were considerably higher (one franc was the equivalent of 1.07 francs today, or less than U.S. 25 cents). So that anyone who attempted to estimate the size of the audience on the basis of receipts would be misled.

20. Quotations from the Algerian press are from Jacqueline Lévi-Valensi, "L'Engagement Culturel," in *Revue des Lettres Modernes* (Paris), Nos. 315–22 (1972).

21. Charles Poncet, op. cit. During this period Poncet was not a student but a full-time employee of the Schiaffino shipping company. Camus told him of his theater project the first time they met, at the Belcourt Amsterdam-Pleyel meeting. Poncet was not then a Communist.

22. Jacqueline Lévi-Valensi, op. cit.

23. Because of the inversion of pages of the early *Carnets* already referred to, it is not possible to say with any certainty that the outlines found between January and February 1936 entries really belong there, especially since the outline for *La Mort heureuse* refers to the Central European trip he made the following summer. But a text recognizable as an early formulation of a theme used in *Noces* is clearly dated January 1936. (Note also that Camus revised his original journal when preparing the typescript for publication as *Carnets,* which makes it unwise to depend on *Carnets* for a true dating of Camus' life and work.)

24. Jeanne Delais, op. cit.

25. Robert Namia.

26. The late Jeanne Sicard's recollections are summarized in the Pléiade edition of Camus' plays. Yves Bourgeois has provided additional detail.

27. To Liliane Dulong née Choucroun.

28. Jacqueline Lévi-Valensi, op. cit. The same author discovered that *Révolte dans les Asturies* follows closely an article entitled "Oviedo, la honte du gouvernement espagnol," by André Ribard, published in *Monde* (the magazine of Henri Barbusse) in November 1934—a special issue on Spain. Specific details, such as the dynamiting of the wall, are taken from this article. Material for the play was also drawn from other texts in the same issue of *Monde*.

29. Marguerite Dobrenn.

30. *La Lutte Sociale*, April 15–30, 1936.

31. Yves Bourgeois.

32. In *Simoun* (Oran), No. 31, 1960.

33. Edmond Charlot.


## Notes for Chapter Nine

1. Pierre-André Emery; Charles Poncet, op. cit.

2. Jean de Maisonseul.

3. Marguerite Dobrenn.

4. Camus would later tell Jean Grenier that a special commission of the Government General had deliberated at length on his case, finally issuing a definitive refusal of the medical certificate required for the *agrégation*. According to Jacques Heurgon, Camus' request for a medical certificate was twice rejected.

5. The foregoing and most of the running account of the trip through Central Europe are from Yves Bourgeois; there is supplementary material from Marguerite Dobrenn, and from others including Dr. Léon Cottenceau and Liliane Dulong (née Choucroun). I have used not only Bourgeois' material, but often his own words in following the travelers, for they are necessarily livelier than mine would have been. But I have added dates and other details for which Bourgeois is of course not responsible.

6. From private conversations with friends.

7. It is interesting to speculate whether Camus visited Franz Kafka's grave in Prague. He had certainly read *The Trial*, published by Gallimard in 1933 with a preface by Bernard Groethuysen. But Bourgeois told the author that the Jewish cemetery they visited had no twentieth-century tombs, and he has no recollection of searching for Kafka's grave or even discussing that author.


## Notes for Chapter Ten

1. Antoinette Acault.

2. Jean Grenier, *Albert Camus*, op. cit.

3. Marguerite Dobrenn.

4. Charles Poncet; also Poncet, op. cit.

5. Yves Bourgeois.

6. Pierre-André Emery; Robert Namia.

7. Edmond Charlot.

8. Pierre-André Emery; Louis Miquel; Yves Bourgeois.

9. Emmanuel Roblès.

10. Christiane Davila (née Galindo); Marguerite Dobrenn; Robert Jaussaud.

11. Jeanne Delais, op. cit. Claude de Fréminville did not contribute to the furnishing of the Maison Fichu at this time, as the source suggests, but he redecorated the villa when he took it over from his friends.

12. *L'Algérie Ouvrière* (Algiers), December 21, 1936, quoted in Jacqueline Lévi-Valensi, op. cit.

13. Marcel Chouraqui; Marguerite Dobrenn.

14. Liliane Dulong (née Choucroun).

15. Carl A. Viggiani, op. cit.

16. Pierre-André Emery.

17. Jeanne Delais, op. cit.

18. Documents of the Maison de la Culture are in the possession of Emile Scotto-Lavina.

19. Lucienne Jean-Darroy, *L'Echo d'Alger* (Algiers), February 10, 1937.

20. Anne de Vaucher-Gravili, "Claude Aveline et Albert Camus," in *Annali della Facoltà di Lingue e Letterature Straniere di Ca' Foscari* (Venice), September 1976.

21. Catherine Lerouvre, "Amour de la vie" in *Simoun* (Oran), No. 31, July 1960. Lerouvre dates the episode 1936 but says that Camus was already working at *Alger Républicain,* so it may actually have taken place in 1938–39.

22. Jacqueline Lévi-Valensi, op. cit.

23. Charles Poncet.

24. Liliane Dulong (née Choucroun).

25. Louis Benisti.

26. Louis Miquel.

27. Pierre-André Emery.

28. Louis Miquel; Mr. and Mrs. Robert Jaussaud.


## Notes for Chapter Eleven

1. Edmond Charlot.

2. Reprinted in the Pléiade edition of Camus' work.

3. Charles Poncet, op. cit.

4. Liliane Dulong (née Choucroun).

5. Louis Benisti.

6. Jacques Heurgon and Marguerite Dobrenn, the chief sources on the summer of 1937.

7. Liliane Dulong; Marguerite Dobrenn; Jacques Heurgon; Jeanne Delais, op. cit.

8. Camus' *Carnets* contain a partial outline and other material for *La Mort heureuse* dated August 1937, but because Camus cut up the original notebook in which he wrote these notes, other parts of the outline are printed forty pages earlier in the French original edition. Or was there an earlier version of this novel? A note Camus wrote from Embrun to Christiane Galindo suggests that he had thrown out such a manuscript.

9. Jean Varille, who in 1961 succeeded his father as director of the Fondation Laurent-Vibert, which owns the château and sponsors the fellowships. Varille remembers that Camus was a guest of his father. Grenier's essay "Cum apparuerit . . ." appeared in *Nouvelle Revue Française* in May 1930 before publication as a small book.

10. Jacques Heurgon; Liliane Dulong. Camus told Carl Viggiani that he had been appointed as a Latin teacher. Viggiani, op. cit. At the time Camus was invited to teach at Sidi-bel-Abbès, Jeanne Sicard was appointed to a school at Tlemcen, forty miles away. She taught for one day, went to the headmaster to say she had been offered a good job in the theater, and departed. Marguerite Dobrenn.

11. After World War II in *Combat,* Camus had occasion to describe Sidi-bel-Abbès as a reactionary bastion where there were wall inscriptions such as "Vive Hitler" and "Vive Franco." August 4, 1945.

## Notes for Chapter Twelve

1. Jean Grenier, *Albert Camus,* op. cit.

2. Max-Pol Fouchet, op. cit.

3. Speech to the Syndicat des Correcteurs, in *A Albert Camus, ses amis du livre* (Paris, 1962).

4. Viggiani, op. cit.

5. Charles Poncet, op. cit.

6. Jean de Maisonseul.

7. Louis Miquel.

8. Pierre-André Emery.

9. Amar Ouzegane. In early 1938 after a conflict with Robert Deloche, he resigned from his position as national secretary and editor in chief of *La Lutte Sociale,* while remaining a member of the Political Bureau. After the Communist Party was banned, he participated in its underground activities and was expelled from the municipal council for refusing to condemn the Stalin-Hitler pact of August 1939. Arrested in July 1940, he was interned, tried for spreading anti-Nazi propaganda in the camp, acquitted after eight months in a military prison, released on April 27, 1943, nearly six months after the American landing. He became third secretary, then first secretary (1944) of the PCA, led a campaign for amnesty of rebels after the May 1945 insurrection and massacre. Elected a deputy from Algiers (in the Moslem electoral college) with over eighty thousand votes, he was chosen as *secrétaire de bureau* of the Constituent Assembly in Paris in 1946. At the

Third PCA Congress he was demoted because of dissension with the mainland Party; by 1948 he was in open rebellion against the Communists and was expelled. In 1950 he participated in political activity with Moslem religious leaders, and joined the Front de Libération Nationale in January 1955, becoming a member of its national brain trust. He wrote the draft war program adopted in August 1956 by the underground fighters of the FLN.

10. Amar Ouzegane.

11. Emile Padula. Also Mohamed Lebjaoui, *Vérités sur la Révolution Algérienne* (Paris, 1970).

12. Yves Dechezelles. Also Mohamed Harbi, *Aux Origines du Front de Libération Nationale: la scission du P.P.A.-M.T.L.D.* (Paris, 1975).

13. Georges Lefranc, op. cit.

14. Jean Chaintron.

15. Robert Namia.

16. Jean Chaintron. After his departure from Algiers, "Barthel"-Chaintron was sent by the Party to serve in the International Brigade during the Spanish Civil War. During the Nazi occupation of France he was a leader of the Communist resistance in the South of France. Arrested and sentenced to death, he was saved by an appeal by the French Catholic Church to Pétain, and his sentence was commuted to life imprisonment. He escaped, took charge of the maquis in the Limousin region, became prefect of the Haute-Vienne at the Liberation of France. (Some of Camus' friends, and presumably Camus himself, only learned "Barthel"'s true name when they saw post-Liberation photographs of the new prefect.) He entered into dissidence with the Party after the twentieth congress of the Soviet Communist Party, when he expressed the view that the French Party also required de-Stalinization, and he was excluded.

17. Elie Mignot.

18. André Abbou.

19. Amar Ouzegane. He felt that the Party had not turned against ENA, but that ENA went against the Communists, notably by taking under its wing a dissident Communist movement, the Parti National Révolutionnaire, which had expelled its Communist founder.

20. Jean Grenier.

21. Essentially from Charles-Robert Ageron, *Histoire de l'Algérie contemporaine* (Paris, 1974); Edouard Bonnefous, *Histoire politique de la Troisième Republique* (Paris, 1965); J. Droz, *Socialisme et syndicalisme de 1914 à 1939* (Paris, n.d.); Charles-André Julien, "Léon Blum et les Pays d'Outre-Mer" in *Léon Blum chef de gouvernement* (Paris, 1967); Jules Moch, *Le Front Populaire, grand espérance* (Paris, 1971). Moslems were not then French citizens, although individuals could apply for French citizenship. At the time of the introduction of the Blum-Viollette bill the Communists had opposed it, but had agreed to a modified version, according to Jean Chaintron. When Camus published his petition in favor of the Blum-Viollette bill, described in Chapter 10, it was in line with Party policy.

22. Marguerite Dobrenn.

23. Emile Padula.

24. Maurice Girard.

25. Paul Raffi.

26. Amar Ouzegane. His exclusion, referred to in note 9 above, was attributed to his "national-deviationist" views. For an indication of Party opposition to the independence of colonial territories at that time, see the speech of Party chief Maurice Thorez to the Ninth Communist Party Congress in December 1937, published in Jean-Paul Brunet, *L'Enfance du Parti communiste* (Paris, 1972).

27. Jeanne Delais, op. cit.

28. Jacqueline Lévi-Valensi, op. cit. A witness recalls that Camus remarked to Prédhumeau during the altercation: "People like you, in my Party, are thrown out," or words to that effect, suggesting that the quarrel was political and that Prédhumeau was not a Party member. Charles Poncet. Prédhumeau called himself a follower of Bukharin or Zinoviev, notable Communist deviationists. Yves Bourgeois.

29. Raymond Sigaudès.

30. Yves Bourgeois.

## Notes for Chapter Thirteen

1. The second school notebook, published as Cahier II in *Carnets,* begins on September 22, 1937. The original manuscript is intact, which means that nothing recorded in it at the time is missing, whereas Cahier I in its stripped and reassembled form suggests self-censorship at a time when this journal was more of a record of intimate feelings, and precisely when these feelings may have concerned the wreck of Camus' first marriage. (See Note 16 of Chapter 7.)

2. Louis Miquel.

3. Max-Pol Fouchet, op. cit.

4. Gabriel Audisio, *L'Opéra fabuleux* (Paris, 1970).

5. Gabriel Audisio.

6. Quoted but incorrectly dated in the Pléiade edition of Camus' work.

7. Jean Coulomb. While Coulomb remembered that it was Paul Seltzer who introduced Camus to him, Seltzer said that he did not know Camus before Camus began to work at the institute, and that it must have been Jean Grenier or someone else who introduced Camus. (Coulomb also knew Professor René Poirier, according to Madame Jean Grenier.)

8. Jacques Heurgon; Liliane Dulong (née Choucroun).

9. Quoted in the Pléiade edition of Camus' work.

10. Jean Coulomb; Paul Seltzer. Coulomb left Algeria to pursue a distinguished career which would include the direction of the Institut du Physique du Globe, the Centre National de la Recherche Scientifique, the Centre National d'Etudes Spatiales, and the French Academy of Sciences.

11. Paul Seltzer. Dr. Seltzer has kept a manuscript page on which Camus explained how the averages were obtained.

12. Pascal Pia.

13. Reproduced in the Pléiade edition of Camus' plays.

14. Emmanuel Roblès.
15. Manuscript memoir by Blanche Balain, read and approved by Camus.
16. Charles Poncet, op. cit.
17. Jacques Heurgon.
18. Marguerite Dobrenn.
19. *L'Echo d'Alger* (Algiers), March 2, 1938. From Raymond Sigaudès, who furnished similar documentation on other Equipe plays. Mercier also failed to identify the young lady in "a charming costume of a Botticelli youth" in the Gide play; that was also Sicard.
20. *BT2* (*Bibliothèque de Travail*) (Cannes), June 1976. Special issue on Camus prepared by Blanche Balain.
21. Jacques Heurgon.
22. Christiane Davila (née Galindo). Madame Davila did not recall whether Camus had just talked to Heurgon or to Grenier. Undoubtedly Grenier had also been consulted, but he left Algiers at the end of the 1937–38 school year (July). He taught at the Lycée Michelet in Vanves the following year, then after a brief tour of military service was appointed professor at the University of Lille. From 1945 to 1950 he taught in Cairo and Alexandria, returned to Lille until his appointment to the Sorbonne in 1962.
23. It is conceivable that Camus rewrote all or part of *La Mort heureuse* during the summer of 1938 before showing it to Heurgon and Grenier, and that what he submitted to his mentors was a revised version (Fall 1938). In this case, the decision to abandon the novel was made late that year. A draft of the opening of *L'Etranger,* which of course would replace *La Mort heureuse* as Camus' first novel, is found in his journal just before an entry dated December 1938.
24. Edmond Charlot. But he did later tell Charlot about *L'Etranger* and even offered to let Charlot publish it.
25. Jean-Pierre Faure for most of the foregoing.
26. Paul Schmidt.
27. Christiane Davila (née Galindo), who possesses a telegram from Camus dated March 25, 1938. The date is important because the recollections of those responsible for publishing *Alger Républicain* and for hiring Camus place the date of his engagement in late summer or early fall 1938, just prior to the first issue of the daily paper in October.
28. Liliane Dulong (née Choucroun).

## Notes for Chapter Fourteen

1. Edmond Charlot.
2. Gabriel Audisio. Also Gabriel Audisio, "Souvenirs d'Albert Camus," in *Alger-Revue* (Algiers), Spring 1960.
3. Max-Pol Fouchet, op. cit. Fouchet published *Fontaine,* successor to the literary magazine *Mithra.*
4. Marguerite Dobrenn.
5. Emmanuel Roblès.
6. Emmanuel Roblès, "Visages d'Albert Camus," in *Simoun* (Oran), July

1960. According to Charles Poncet, Roblès had attended a meeting at the Maison de la Culture, where Poncet saw him as "a stout member of the air corps, talkative, and already quite self-assured." As he was looking for a publisher, Poncet introduced him to Charlot. Poncet, op. cit.

7. Christiane Davila (née Galindo).

8. Marcelle Bonnet-Blanchet.

9. Madame Albert Camus; Louis Benisti; Marcelle Bonnet-Blanchet.

10. Private conversation.

11. Madame Albert Camus; Christiane Faure.

12. Christiane Faure.

13. Christiane Davila; Mr. and Mrs. Robert Jaussaud.

14. Essentially from Pierre Galindo, Christiane Davila, Mr. and Mrs. Jaussaud. Descriptions of young Galindo from Emmanuel Roblès, Charles Poncet, Christiane Faure, André Belamich.

15. Jacques Heurgon.

16. Pascal Pia.

17. Camus so informed Christiane Davila by telegram on March 25, 1938. See Chapter 13.

18. Blanche Balain; Liliane Dulong (née Choucroun).

19. André Vandegans, *La Jeunesse littéraire d'André Malraux* (Paris, 1964). Also Francis Ponge.

20. Francis Ponge.

21. There are conflicting versions of what the poster depicted. The present author has chosen the artist's recollection of it. Jean-Pierre Faure remembered it as based on François Rude's nineteenth-century sculpture *La Marseillaise,* which adorns Paris's Arch of Triumph.

22. Jean-Pierre Faure.

## Notes for Chapter Fifteen

1. Pascal Pia.

2. Jean-Pierre Faure.

3. Laurent Preziosi.

4. Quoted in the Pléiade edition of Camus' work, which reprints the reviews of Silone, et al.

5. Jean-Pierre Faure. According to Pascal Pia there were two Moslem employees, probably hired through the Moslem board members of the paper. One had a desk job because he was deaf. The other was an older man, a former cadi—local religious authority—who Pia thought may have been a police informer.

6. Marguerite Dobrenn.

7. Georges Lefranc, op. cit. For an analysis of Camus' coverage of social problems in *Alger Républicain:* Jacqueline Lévi-Valensi, "La Condition sociale en Algérie," in *Revue des Lettres Modernes* (Paris), Nos. 315–22 (1972). Note that Camus had seven bylined articles in the first month of the paper's publication, October 1938; eight in November, eight in December,

eight in January, nine in February, etc. Camus' articles and editorials, with the exception of his reviews and essays on cultural matters, are published in *Cahiers Albert Camus 3* (*Fragments d'un Combat, 1938–1940*), edited by Lévi-Valensi and André Abbou (Paris, 1978).

8. Christiane Davila (née Galindo).

9. Jean Lacouture, *Malraux, une vie dans le siècle* (Paris, 1973).

10. Jacques Heurgon.

11. Edmond Charlot; Marguerite Dobrenn; Blanche Balain.

12. In an attempt to identify unsigned contributions by Camus, Professor Abbou watched particularly for Camus' humanistic and moral ethic, his political views, but also the constant references to abuse of language on the part of the government. In this way Abbou attributes to Camus unsigned reports on trials of members of Messali Hadj's PPA in December 1938 to January 1939, and of two members of a leftist relief group who had defended an Algerian Moslem who, after escaping authorities (after a minor conviction), had been tied to the tail of his guard's horse for a sixty-mile march. The affair was symbolic of arbitrary justice practiced in the southern territories, and Camus would use the image much later in his story "L'Hôte," whose victim walks only three kilometers (or less than two miles). André Abbou, "Combat pour la justice," in *Revue des Lettres Modernes* (Paris), Nos. 315–22 (1972).

13. Essentially from Abbou, "Combat pour la justice," op. cit.

14. In *Vérités sur la Révolution Algérienne* (Paris, 1970). But doubt is thrown on this "revelation" by Lévi-Valensi and Abbou in *Cahiers Albert Camus 3*, op. cit.

15. Amar Ouzegane.

16. Emmanuel Roblès.

17. Pascal Pia, "D'Alger Républicain à Combat," in *Magazine Littéraire* (Paris), September 1972.

18. Edmond Brua.

19. Charles Poncet, op. cit.

20. André Veillard in *La Revue Algérienne* (Algiers), April–May 1939.

21. Emmanuel Roblès, "Jeunesse d'Albert Camus," in *Hommage à Albert Camus* (Paris, 1967).

22. Robert Namia.

## Notes for Chapter Sixteen

1. Jacques Heurgon.

2. Madame Albert Camus.

3. Blanche Balain.

4. Edmond Charlot.

5. Christiane Davila (née Galindo).

6. Emmanuel Roblès.

7. Benisti placed the conversation in Oran in December 1941, when in fact *L'Etranger* had been completed months earlier. As noted, Camus had writ-

ten "Today, Mother died" in his journal in autumn 1938, but he did not then mention Meursault's going to the movies. Galliero had a run-down, odoriferous studio in the Kasbah in Algiers, where he slept on a cot. When visiting Oran he slept at the Camus-Faure apartment on a mattress placed on the floor. Christiane Faure. There is a mildly enthusiastic review of Galliero's gouaches painted while he was in the army, by Paul Raffi in *La Revue Algérienne,* February 1939.

8. Christiane Davila; Pierre Galindo.

9. Christiane Faure.

10. *Livret individuel* (military passbook); Madame Albert Camus.

11. Pierre-André Emery; Robert Jaussaud.

12. Pascal Pia; also Pia, op. cit.

13. Jean-Pierre Faure. He returned from Tunisia after a year as a prisoner of war in July 1941.

14. Jean-Pierre Faure; Pascal Pia.

15. Emmanuel Roblès, in "Jeunesse d'Albert Camus," op. cit.

16. Pierre-André Emery.

17. André Abbou, "Variations du discours polémique," in *Revue des Lettres Modernes* (Paris), Nos. 315–22 (1972).

18. Charles Poncet, op. cit.

19. Louis Miquel.

20. Gabriel Audisio.

21. Pascal Pia.

22. Jean-Pierre Faure. According to Jacques Régnier, who took over some of Faure's functions on his departure, police entered the *Soir Républicain* plant at 2 A.M. one morning while the presses were rolling, shoved staff members out of the way, and rendered the machinery inoperable with iron bars. But Pia had no recollection of this, and assumed the event occurred after the closing of the newspaper and Pia's return to France. Nor did Pia have any recollection of the Governor General's meeting with members of the board. According to Régnier, the police regularly interfered with operations of the paper by confiscating copies at newsstands, from street hawkers, even in the plant. But as soon as the police left the staff and employees would run off another issue, distributed under the counter.

23. Liliane Dulong (née Choucroun).

24. A second essay published in *La Tunisie Française* in 1941 (May 24), "Comme un feu d'étoupes," also opens with a reference (to the Borgia popes) entered in the journal in November 1939, i.e., during the height of Camus' resistance not to Vichy—which did not yet exist—but to the French war effort. In 1941, when these essays appeared in Tunisia, the colony was ruled by the Vichy regime. Read in this context, this essay also appears to be a reflection of the Camus of 1939–40 rather than of the 1943–44 resistance.

25. Madame Emmanuel Andréo; Madame Henri Karcher (née Gilberte Andréo); Christiane Davila. It is also said that the Government General would have been happy to "buy" Camus at that time or earlier by letting

him work for a government-sponsored propaganda magazine, or by purchasing a large number of copies of his book *Noces*.


## Notes for Chapter Seventeen

1. Pascal Pia.
2. Christiane Davila (née Galindo).
3. Jacques Régnier; Pascal Pia.
4. Henri Cauquelin; *A Albert Camus, ses amis du livre* (Paris, 1962).
5. Pascal Pia; Enrico Terracini.
6. Enrico Terracini; Madame Albert Camus.
7. Henri Cauquelin.
8. Madame Janine Gallimard (née Janine Thomasset).
9. Essentially from Janine Gallimard, Henri Cauquelin, Pascal Pia; also Rirette Maîtrejean, Daniel Lenief, et al., in *A Albert Camus, ses amis du livre,* op. cit.
10. Henri Cauquelin.
11. Daniel Lenief, in *A Albert Camus, ses amis du livre,* op. cit. But Charles Poncet remembered the final two lines this way:
    She died at the Trinity,
      That is Fatality.
Poncet, op. cit.
12. Georges Altschuler, "Albert Camus journaliste", in *L'Ecole et la Vie* (Paris), February 6, 1960.
13. Pierre Salama; Janine Gallimard.
14. Pierre Salama.
15. Madame Emmanuel Andréo; Marcel Paute.
16. Liliane Dulong (née Choucroun).
17. Adalbert de Segonzac.
18. Quoted in the Pléiade edition of Camus' work; also Raymond Sigaudès; Emile Scotto-Lavina.
19. Dr. Léon Cottenceau.
20. Madame Albert Camus; *A Albert Camus, ses amis du livre,* op. cit.
21. Madame Albert Camus.
22. Philippe Boegner, *Oui, patron . . .* (Paris, 1976); Robert Aron, *Histoire de Vichy* (Paris, 1954).


## Notes for Chapter Eighteen

1. Madame Albert Camus; Christiane Faure.
2. Laurent Preziosi.
3. Edmond Charlot.
4. Emmanuel Roblès. Camus took up the series Poésie et Théâtre again after the war. The last book published in it was Roblès' successful play *Montserrat,* translated and staged all over the world.

5. Pierre-André Emery. It has also been said that the play was submitted for approval but was rejected by the authorities.

6. Charles Poncet.

7. Louis Benisti. One of the young ladies involved in the plan of which Benisti speaks, Françoise Moeurer, had been entrusted by Charlot with Théâtre de l'Equipe records as well as his own papers and manuscripts of Camus. But during the Vichy period Miss Moeurer's mother, fearing a search, burned them all. Edmond Charlot.

8. Pierre Galindo. Camus later said that he had been in touch with groups in Algiers and Oran preparing the Allied landings but that their activity at the time was imperceptible. Christiane Faure.

9. Charles Poncet. In late 1941 or early 1942, Camus expressed admiration for the solid resistance of Soviet troops. "You see, it shows that the Soviet regime is accepted by the people."

10. Robert Namia. After his successful escape to the U.S., Pacciardi was editor of anti-Fascist émigré publications, returned to Italy as a newspaper editor, was Vice-Premier in the government, and Minister of Defense.

11. Enrico Terracini; Miriam Chiaromonte. Or else Terracini took him to the Maison Fichu and he met Camus there.

12. Madame Albert Camus.

13. Nicola Chiaromonte, "Albert Camus," in *Dissent* (New York), Summer 1960.

14. Christiane Faure.

15. Robert Namia. Namia later worked as editor in chief in the press bureau of the Allied Psychological Warfare Branch, was attached to the French army campaigning in Italy and the South of France, then Germany. He would be associated with Claude Bourdet's *Combat,* Emmanuel d'Astier de la Vigerie's *Liberation, L'Express, Jeune Afrique, Révolution Africaine* (Algiers), and *Nouvel Observateur.*

16. Jean Paulhan archives (Madame Jacqueline Paulhan); Pascal Pia.

17. Madeleine Benichou; Madame Albert Camus; Christiane Faure. Later, after Camus' departure from Oran and the American landing, Benichou founded a private school called Cours Descartes which took in non-Jews as well as Jews, and grew to a postwar institution of 1,300 pupils. Christiane Faure herself gave free private lessons to prepare Jewish pupils for the *baccalauréat,* while her sister Suzy taught in a Jewish school.

18. Camus told Viggiani that he had taught French, philosophy, literature (*lettres*), history, geography. Viggiani, op. cit.

19. Quoted in the Pléiade edition of Camus' work.

20. Edmond Brua.

21. Emmanuel Roblès. He would later use the typhus epidemic in *Les Hauteurs de la ville,* published by Charlot in Paris in 1948, and winner of that year's Prix Fémina.

22. Christiane Faure. Camus seems to have made an exception for André Benichou, an astute man and a philosopher, admirer of Proust (about which he was writing a book never published). Camus had the Benichous read a

"rolled-up manuscript" of *L'Etranger*, and according to Madeleine Benichou, Camus had André Benichou read sections of *La Peste* in Oran. Later in Paris, Camus would discuss *L'Homme révolté* with Benichou as he was writing it, and Benichou was asked to suggest changes. Benichou died in 1964.

23. Marcelle Bonnet-Blanchet.

## Notes for Chapter Nineteen

1. *Les Nouvelles littéraires* (Paris), November 15, 1945.

2. Simone de Beauvoir, *La Force de l'âge* (Paris, 1960). Here the author describes what intellectuals considered permissible activity under the occupation, and her own work for Radio Paris. See also Pascal Ory, *Les Collaborateurs* (Paris, 1977).

3. Quoted in *Cahiers André Gide 6* ("Les Cahiers de la Petite Dame") (Paris, 1975).

4. Ory, op. cit.

5. Essentially from *Cahiers André Gide 6*, op. cit.; *Jean Paulhan le souterrain* (Colloque de Cerisy) (Paris, 1976); *La Nouvelle Revue Française* (Paris), May 1, 1969 (special issue on Paulhan); Claude Martin, ed., *La Nouvelle Revue Française 1940–1943* (Lyon, 1975); Lacouture, op. cit. Note that *La Nouvelle Revue Française* was revived in 1953 as *La Nouvelle Nouvelle Revue Française*, the extra "Nouvelle" eventually disappearing.

6. Edmond Charlot.

7. Emmanuel Roblès.

8. Christiane Davila (née Galindo).

9. Essentially from Madame Albert Camus, Pascal Pia, Janine Gallimard, the Paulhan archives (Madame Jacqueline Paulhan); Jean-Claude Zylberstein; *Jean Paulhan le souterrain*, op. cit. Heller's rank was actually *Sonderführer* (Z), the Z standing for *Zugführer*. He told the author that, starting in the early months of 1941, the *Propaganda-Staffel* ceased to exercise censorship against books, having worked out an agreement with the French publishers' association for a kind of self-censorship. Heller's role became that of an observer, giving advice, and his "accord" for the publication of questionable titles was an informal one. A friend of the Gallimard house and an admirer of Paulhan, Heller kept Nazi authorities from interfering with the publication of a book by an Aragon, or the performing of a play by a Sartre. Heller now feels that he was helped along by ignorance, as well as by respect for the products of French culture. For the question of reorganizing *NRF: Cahiers André Gide 6;* Martin, op. cit. and Gerhard Heller.

10. Editions Gallimard. Actually copies were ready earlier, for Camus received one by June 17. The book was probably printed in mid-May.

11. Ory, op. cit.

12. José Corti.

13. Beauvoir, *La Force de l'âge*.

## Notes for Chapter Twenty

1. Madame Albert Camus; Christiane Faure; Madeleine Benichou; Liliane Dulong (née Choucroun).
2. Jacques Heurgon.
3. Madame Albert Camus; Emmanuel Roblès.
4. Francis Ponge.
5. Francis Ponge; Roger Darcissac. Cf. Roger de Raïssac, *Le Chambon-sur-Lignon* (Colmar-Ingersheim, 1974).
6. Jacques Heurgon; Louis Joxe.
7. Madame Albert Camus; Emmanuel Roblès.
8. Guitton later wrote that while a prisoner of war in December 1943 he received a card with a short note from Camus to tell him how much he liked *Le Portrait*. Guitton didn't know Camus, and was surprised that the author of *L'Etranger*, which was circulating in the camp, could admire the priest he portrayed in the book. Guitton, "Extraits d'un journal," in *La Table Ronde* (Paris), February 1960. Guitton was later elected to the French Academy. Jean Grenier reviewed Guitton's *Le Portrait* in the Paris *Comoedia* on June 27, 1942, one of his many contributions to that weekly.
9. Blanche Balain.

## Notes for Chapter Twenty-one

1. Pascal Pia; Henri Frenay, *La Nuit finira* (Paris, 1973).
2. The Paulhan archives (Madame Jacqueline Paulhan); Editions Gallimard.
3. Francis Ponge.
4. Roger de Raïssac, op. cit.; Pasteur Edouard Theis; Madame Andrée Trocmé; Roger Darcissac; André Chouraqui. Chouraqui would later be a deputy mayor of Jerusalem.
5. Roger Darcissac.
6. Jean Blanzat, "Première rencontre," in *Hommage à Albert Camus*.
7. Janine Gallimard; Dussane (Béatrix Coulond-Dussan), *Maria Casarès* (Paris, 1953).
8. Father Raymond-Léopold Bruckberger.
9. Madame Albert Camus.
10. In the Poésie/Gallimard edition of *Le Parti pris des choses* (Paris, 1966).
11. The Paulhan archives (Madame Jacqueline Paulhan); *La Nouvelle Revue Française* (Paris), May 1, 1969: special issue on Paulhan.
12. Armand Guibert, "Limpide et ravagé," in *La Table Ronde* (Paris), February 1960.
13. Gabriel Audisio.
14. Louis Aragon; René Tavernier; Father Bruckberger.
15. Guy Dumur.

16. Beauvoir, *La Force de l'âge*.
17. Blanche Balain.
18. Quotations from letters to Ponge were published in the Pléiade edition of Camus' work.
19. Pascal Pia.

## Notes for Chapter Twenty-two

1. Beauvoir, *La Force de l'âge*. Malraux later remarked: "*I* was in front of the Gestapo while Sartre, in Paris, let his plays be produced with authorization of the German censors." Lacouture, op. cit.
2. The Paulhan archives (Madame Jacqueline Paulhan); Jean-Claude Zylberstein; *La Nouvelle Revue Française*, May 1, 1969.
3. Jean Lescure.
4. The Paulhan archives (Madame Jacqueline Paulhan).
5. Pascal Pia.
6. In the 1970s Bruckberger pursued an unorthodox career by defending traditional liturgy against Vatican reforms, and was disavowed by the Maître Général of the Dominican order for "inadmissible attacks against the Pope and the bishops of France." *Le Monde* (Paris), October 26, 1976.
7. Quotations from letters to Ponge from the Pléiade edition of Camus' work.
8. Louis Miquel.
9. Maria Casarès.
10. Gabriel Audisio; Edmond Charlot.
11. Jean-Claude Zylberstein; Guy Dumur.
12. Janine Gallimard.
13. Guy Dumur.
14. René Etiemble, "D'une amitié," in *Hommage à Albert Camus*.
15. Gabriel Audisio.
16. Shortly after this, Picasso invited all his "actors" to his studio on nearby Rue des Grandes-Augustins, where they were photographed by Brassaï. Brassaï, *Conversations avec Picasso*, Paris, 1964.

## Notes for Chapter Twenty-three

1. Frenay, *La Nuit finira*, op. cit.
2. Pascal Pia.
3. Jacqueline Bernard.
4. Henri Cauquelin.
5. Claude Bourdet; also Bourdet in *France-Observateur* (Paris), January 17, 1960; Father Bruckberger; Jacqueline Bernard.
6. Flavien Monod; Sylvère Monod; *La Revue Noire* (Paris), March 1944.
7. The attribution of the additional articles was made by Norman Stokle in *Le Combat d'Albert Camus* (Quebec, 1970). But Jacqueline Bernard be-

lieves that, considering the conditions under which the articles were written
and the sharing of work, it is not possible to say who wrote what.

8. Georges Altschuler; Maurice Leroy, in *A Albert Camus, ses amis du
livre,* op. cit.

9. In the possession of the Camus family.

10. Janine Gallimard.

11. André Malraux.

12. Jean Lescure.

13. Lacouture, op. cit.

14. Dionys Mascolo.

15. Francis Ponge.

16. Beauvoir, *La Force de l'âge,* op. cit.

17. Jean Lescure; Claude Morgan.

18. The Paulhan archives (Madame Jacqueline Paulhan); Claude Morgan.
Morgan himself parted company with his Communist friends after the
Soviet crushing of the Hungarian uprising in 1956.

## Notes for Chapter Twenty-four

1. Guy Dumur.

2. Jean-Louis Barrault.

3. Dussane, op. cit.

4. Letter to Ponge quoted in the Pléiade edition of Camus' work.

5. "Les Cahiers de la Petite Dame," 1937–1945, in *Cahiers André Gide 6.*

6. Janine Gallimard.

7. Maria Casarès.

8. Beauvoir, *La Force de l'âge.*

9. Guy Dumur. See also Dussane, op. cit.: "Finally it is whispered—or
guessed—that Camus plays an important part in the resistance, and that is
enough to assure that a good third of the first night audience would be hostile to him in advance."

10. *Le Figaro* (Paris), October 15, 1944. Later Camus would make extensive revisions of *Le Malentendu;* the text we read today is this revised version.

11. *Pariser Zeitung* (Paris), July 16, 1944.

12. Ory, op. cit.; Marc Beigbeder, *Le Théâtre en France depuis la libération* (Paris, 1959).

13. From the French Société des Auteurs et Compositeurs Dramatiques,
which records performances of the play for which the audience paid admission. Actually, according to advertisements in *Combat,* the play was performed through November 6. For historical accuracy, it should be added
that there may have been a free performance on June 23, a *répétition
générale* for an invited audience, and it would have been at this performance that the audience hooted. This seems to be confirmed by an advertisement in at least one daily newspaper of the time, *Le Nouveau Temps,*

which announced the play for June 23 and then ran an advertisement on June 24 for the *première à bureaux ouverts*—the box office opening. Previous writings on Camus have set the date of the opening in May, June, July, and even in August, so that it is worth the attempt to pin it down.

14. Jacqueline Bernard.

## Notes for Chapter Twenty-five

1. Robert Aron, *Histoire de la libération de la France* (Paris, 1959).
2. Beauvoir, *La Force de l'âge.*
3. Pascal Pia; Jacqueline Bernard.
4. Georges Altschuler; Henri Cauquelin.
5. Jean Bloch-Michel; Jacqueline Bernard; Pascal Pia.
6. Madame Albert Camus.
7. Pascal Pia.
8. Jean Daniel, "Le Combat pour 'Combat,' " in *Camus* (Collection Génies et Réalités) (Paris, 1964).
9. Preserved on a recording available in the album "Presence d'Albert Camus" (Adès).
10. Dr. Georges Brouet.
11. Simone de Beauvoir, *La Force des choses* (Paris, 1963).
12. Christiane Faure.
13. Claude Bourdet.
14. The editorials of August 31, September 8, and November 22 are reprinted in the Pléiade edition of Camus' work, together with a selection of other articles and editorials written by Camus for *Combat* and cited in this chapter.
15. Jacqueline Bernard. Another version of the story is that Lazareff invited Camus to see him and Camus kept him waiting all day. Jean-Pierre Vivet.
16. Jean-Pierre Vivet. Vivet went on to become a writer and editor, then publisher of the French book trade journal *Le Bulletin du Livre.*
17. Roger Grenier. After *Combat,* Grenier went to Agence Express with Pia, then to *France-Soir,* later becoming a novelist and Gallimard editor.
18. Jacques-Laurent Bost.
19. The Paulhan archives (Madame Jacqueline Paulhan).
20. Claude Morgan. The reason Camus gave was that he would not write for a newspaper that depended in part on advertising revenue. *Combat* itself would have refused advertising if the idealists had had their way, but everyone rapidly realized the impracticality of that line of behavior. Jean Bloch-Michel.

## Notes for Chapter Twenty-six

1. Published in the Pléiade edition of Camus' work. Jean Paulhan objected to the blacklisting of authors who had collaborated with the occupation authorities, and almost resigned from CNE because of this. He later published

an open letter to resistance leaders (*Lettre aux directeurs de la Résistance*) in which he argued that the collaborators had been sincere in their own way.

2. Georges Altschuler.

3. Roger Grenier.

4. Henri Cauquelin.

5. Daniel, "Le Combat pour 'Combat,'" op. cit.

6. Edmond Charlot.

7. From a talk by Camus. Madame Albert Camus.

8. Jean Bloch-Michel; Daniel, *Le Temps qui reste.*

9. Georgette Elgey, *La République des illusions* (Paris, 1965). But none of the original *Combat* team recalled this expression, not even the surviving member of "Ocapia," Pascal Pia.

10. Pierre Blin, Georges Roy, Daniel Lenief in *A Albert Camus, ses amis du livre.*

11. Edmond Charlot; Jean-Claude Zylberstein; Blanche Balain.

12. Robert Jaussaud.

13. Robert Namia.

14. Pierre-André Emery.

15. Jean Bloch-Michel.

16. No interruption in Camus' contributions to *Combat* is suggested by the bibliography in the Pléiade edition, but it is likely, as Roger Grenier testifies, that not all of the columns signed "Suétone" were written by Camus, certainly not at this time.

17. "Les Cahiers de la Petite Dame," in *Cahiers André Gide 6.*

18. Ory, op. cit.

19. Jacques Isorni, *Le Procès de Robert Brasillach* (Paris, 1946).

20. Christiane Faure.

21. Madame Albert Camus.


## Notes for Chapter Twenty-seven

1. Georges Altschuler; Jean Bloch-Michel; Roger Grenier.

2. Pascal Pia.

3. Reprinted in the Pléiade edition of Camus' work.

4. "Les Cahiers de la Petite Dame," in *Cahiers André Gide 6.*

5. Jacques Heurgon.

6. Madame Albert Camus.

7. Robert Jaussaud.

8. Roger Grenier.

9. Gabriel Audisio. See the October 1948 issue of *Algeria.*

10. Jacqueline Bernard.

11. Preface to *Le Combat silencieux,* by André Salvat, reprinted in the Pléiade edition of Camus' work.

12. Frenay, op. cit.

13. Georges Altschuler.

14. Jean Bloch-Michel.

15. *Claude Bourdet contre Henry Smadja, Plaidoirie de M*e *Boissarie*, December 20, 1950.
16. Claude Bourdet.
17. Beauvoir, *La Force des choses*.
18. Janine Gallimard.
19. *Bulletin de la Société des Amis de Georges Bernanos* (Paris), March 1962. In *Alger Républicain* on July 4, 1939, Camus had defended Bernanos' right to be a monarchist.

## Notes for Chapter Twenty-eight

1. Beauvoir, *La Force de l'âge*.
2. Dussane, op. cit.
3. Maria Casarès.
4. Janine Gallimard.
5. Michel Bouquet.
6. Louis Miquel.
7. Beauvoir, *La Force des choses*.
8. Guy Schoeller; Jacques Schoeller.
9. Herbert R. Lottman, "Splendors and Miseries of the Literary Café," in *Saturday Review* (New York), March 13, 1965.
10. Herbert R. Lottman, "After Bloomsbury and Greenwich Village, St. Germain des Prés," in New York *Times Book Review* (New York), June 4, 1967.
11. Suzanne Agnely (née Labiche).
12. Guillaume Hanoteau, *L'Age d'or de St. Germain des Prés* (Paris, 1965).
13. Daniel, *Le Temps qui reste*.
14. Dominique Aury, "Deux places vides," in *Hommage à Albert Camus*.
15. Extracts from both interviews appear in the Pléiade edition of Camus' work.
16. Gabriel Audisio.
17. Dionys Mascolo.
18. Madame Albert Camus.
19. Jean Hytier.
20. Guy Dumur.
21. Roger Grenier.
22. Marcel Moussy, "Rencontres," in *Simoun* (Oran), No. 31.

## Notes for Chapter Twenty-nine

1. Quoted in the Pléiade edition of Camus' work.
2. Dr. Pierre Rubé.
3. Madame Albert Camus.
4. Claude Lévi-Strauss.
5. Pierre-André Emery.

6. Miriam Chiaromonte.

7. *La Victoire* (New York), March 30, 1946. After May 11 this weekly merged with *France-Amérique*.

8. Raymond Sokolov.

9. In this article in the April 20 *New Yorker,* Liebling spoke of Camus' "first five days in America," suggesting that the interview took place on March 29 or 30, not at their first meeting on March 27. This is consistent with the recollection of Professor Pierre Guédenet, then deputy cultural *conseiller* of the French Embassy, who had asked Liebling to be a sponsor of the March 28 Columbia University evening. Liebling was introduced to Camus prior to that meeting. Then, when Liebling told Guédenet that he would like to see Camus again, Guédenet set up a meeting at his apartment on Gramercy Park. Professor Pierre Guédenet. The interview took place at the West Seventieth Street hotel. Which hotel? Most probably it was the Embassy, at Broadway and Seventieth Street. Nearby the Sherman Square Hotel and the Ansonia were popular with artists and writers, but there is no reason to believe that Camus stayed in either of these.

10. Justin O'Brien, "Albert Camus, Militant," in *The Columbia University Forum Anthology,* ed. by Peter Spackman and Lee Ambrose (New York, 1968), also published in O'Brien, *The French Literary Horizon* (New Brunswick, N.J., 1967): an abridged version in French appeared in *Hommage à Albert Camus.*

11. In *Twice a Year* (New York), Fall–Winter 1946–47, and in *Revue des Lettres Modernes* (Paris), Nos. 315–322, 1972.

12. Anne Minor-Gavronsky.

13. Eugene Sheffer.

14. Marthe Eidelberg; Pierre-André Emery.

15. Marthe Eidelberg.

16. Jean Vallier, director, French Institute.

17. Pierre Brodet.

18. Madame Albert Camus.

19. Patricia Blake; Janine Gallimard.

20. Jean Daniel.

21. Mrs. A. J. Liebling (Jean Stafford).

22. A. J. Liebling, *The Press* (New York, 1961).

23. Janine Gallimard.

24. Patricia Blake.

25. Partial recording, courtesy of Patricia Blake.

26. Maria Tastevin-Miller. Mrs. Tastevin-Miller remembers the subject of the talk as "The Crisis of Mankind" (La Crise de l'homme), so perhaps Camus did not follow the original program.

27. *Wellesley News,* April 25, 1946; Professor George Stambolian; Germaine Brée. Pierre-André Emery recalls that Camus was the victim of heckling at the New School when he said that the October [Russian] Revolution cost too much in human lives.

28. Patricia Blake; Germaine Brée.

29. *France-Amérique* (New York), May 19, 1946. Files of the French-American press were consulted at the French Cultural Services, New York.

30. This and other personal observations by Camus were recorded in his notebooks, published as *Journaux de voyage* (Paris, 1978).

31. In Susan Edminston and Linda D. Cirino, *Literary New York* (Boston, 1976).

32. Jacques Schoeller.

33. Blanche Knopf, "Albert Camus in the Sun," in *Atlantic Monthly* (Boston), February 1961.

34. Alfred A. Knopf.

35. *Publishers' Weekly* (New York), April 13, 1946.

36. *La Victoire* (New York), April 13, 1946.

## Notes for Chapter Thirty

1. Commission Nationale de la Médaille de la Résistance.

2. Quoted in the Pléiade edition of Camus' work.

3. Janine Gallimard. Also told by Alexandre Astruc, *La Tête la première* (Paris, 1975), and in Jean Grenier, *Albert Camus.*

4. Patricia Blake.

5. Madame Albert Camus.

6. Jules Roy.

7. Beauvoir, *La Force des choses.* The incident is confirmed by Jacques-Laurent Bost.

8. Beauvoir, *La Force des choses.*

9. Raymond Aron.

10. Manès Sperber.

11. In his biography of Malraux, Lacouture reports the meeting at Malraux's apartment somewhat differently, as an initiative of Malraux to attract progressive writers to the Gaullists. Lacouture based his account on a talk with Koestler, who adds Beauvoir to the group assembled at Malraux's apartment. The Lacouture account puts Camus in opposition to Malraux, Camus bringing up the proletariat, Malraux snapping: "What's that?" irritating Camus, angering Sartre, ending the scheme. Lacouture, op. cit. But Lacouture assured this writer that Sperber's would be the more accurate report of the meeting, and Sperber's has been used for the account presented here.

12. To Nicola Chiaromonte.

13. Jean Grenier, *Albert Camus,* op. cit.; Suzanne Agnely; Janine Gallimard.

14. Dr. Léon Cottenceau.

15. Janine Gallimard.

16. Gabriel Audisio.

17. *Forge* (Algiers), February–March 1947 (G. A. Astre). This and other reports of the meeting were kindly provided by Gabriel Audisio.

18. *Les Nouvelles Littéraires* (Paris), December 19, 1946; *France Vivante* (Rennes) January 4, 1947.
19. *Alger-Soir* (Algiers), December 17, 1946.
20. Madame Albert Camus; Christiane Faure. There is no record of the play ever having been performed.

## Notes for Chapter Thirty-one

1. Janine Gallimard.
2. Georges Altschuler. But Jean Bloch-Michel remembered that *Franc-Tireur* and *Libération,* not to speak of *Le Parisien Libéré,* had higher morning sales. He said that the drop in circulation began in 1945.
3. Pierre Galindo.
4. Georges Altschuler.
5. Jean Bloch-Michel.
6. Marcel Chouraqui.
7. Raymond Aron.
8. Jacqueline Bernard.
9. Pierre Galindo (a remark Pia denies having made).
10. Bloch-Michel, Altschuler, and other members of the *Combat* staff; also Francis Ponge. Altschuler observed that Camus and Pia received the same salary at *Combat,* which in 1944 would have been 18,000 francs monthly—some 4,800 francs in 1975, or about 960 dollars.
11. Roger Grenier; Jean Bloch-Michel.
12. Pascal Pia. Pia would later work for right-wing periodicals taking him still further from Camus, and his public comments on Camus would be extremely negative, as will be seen in connection with Camus' Nobel prize. Camus admitted in his talk on journalism to the Syndicat des Correcteurs a decade later that he had never been satisfied with newspaper work. He had disliked the necessity of writing quickly without being able to reread what he wrote, and he hated polemics. *A Albert Camus, ses amis du livre.*
13. According to the editor of the Pléiade edition of Camus' work.
14. Madame Albert Camus.
15. Claude Bourdet. Smadja paid 30,000 francs, about 2,300 francs of the mid-1970s, or under 500 dollars, for his 50 per cent share of *Combat.*
16. Claude Bourdet.
17. *Claude Bourdet contre Henry Smadja,* op. cit.
18. *A Albert Camus, ses amis du livre,* op. cit.
19. Roger Grenier.
20. Christiane Faure.
21. Henri Cauquelin.
22. Of his 300 original shares—Smadja was given an equal number—Bourdet had given 12 to Paute, 12 to Altschuler, 12 to his lawyer and friend André Haas, then in September 1947 12 each to Frenay, Dhont, and two other members of the veterans' association. Later, when he gave Frenay an additional 102 shares for a total of 114, the lineup was: Smadja 300, Bour-

det-Haas-Paute-Altschuler 150, Frenay and the three other Combat veterans 150.

23. Claude Bourdet. There were in fact two potential financial backers of a Camus-Bourdet *Combat;* the intermediary was Camus' friend Jean Daniel. Jean Daniel.

24. Jean Daniel.

25. As told by Vivet to Jean Bloch-Michel. Vivet himself didn't remember details of the dialogue but said it was "probably true." Perhaps the money Smadja owed Camus was the indemnity owed to those who left the paper under the *clause de conscience.*

## Notes for Chapter Thirty-two

1. Paulhan had asked Camus how he felt about the presence of Jouhandeau in *Cahiers de la Pléiade,* Jouhandeau being in discredit because of his wartime attitudes. Paulhan said that he himself was hesitating, but felt that France should get all its voices back. There is no record of Camus' reply. Jean-Claude Zylberstein.

2. *Le Monde* (Paris), June 14, 1947.

3. Janine Gallimard.

4. *Partisan Review* (New York), September 1948. Chiaromonte noted that both the Communists and their adversaries interpreted *La Peste* as directed against Communism. In fact contemporary opinion seemed to be that Camus was referring to the war and Nazi occupation of France. Camus himself autographed a copy of *La Peste* to his old amateur theater comrade Raymond Sigaudès "a souvenir of the happy times before the plague." Sartre and Beauvoir not only interpreted the story in the same way, they felt that assimilating the Nazi occupation to natural disaster was a way of fleeing history and its real problems; Beauvoir felt it was all too easy to agree with Camus. *La Force des choses.*

5. *Les Nouvelles Littéraires* (Paris), April 7, 1955. Camus kept a copy of this article in a chest in his Rue de Chanaleilles apartment.

6. Grenier, *Albert Camus.*

7. Louis Guilloux.

8. Daniel, *Le Temps qui reste.*

9. René Char, in *La Posterité du soleil* (Geneva, 1965).

10. Jean Bloch-Michel. Because of uncertain memories and the lack of adequate documentation it is not clear whether Camus' first visit to Char in mid-September 1947 included a stay in Avignon with Francine, or whether that trip took place at a later date.

11. Kjell Strömberg, in *Albert Camus—Winston Churchill* (Nobel Prize Library), New York, 1971.

12. M. Saint-Clair, *Galerie Privée* (Paris, 1947).

13. Suzanne Agnely (née Labiche).

14. Madame Albert Camus.

15. Conversations with Camus' friends.

16. Dionys Mascolo, "Sur deux amis morts," in *Hommage à Albert Camus*.
17. Reprinted in the Pléiade edition of Camus' work.
18. Maria Casarès.

## Notes for Chapter Thirty-three

1. Beauvoir, *La Force des choses*.
2. The version published in *La Table Ronde* is reprinted in the Pléiade edition of Camus' work.
3. *Combat* (Paris), January 30, 1948.
4. Janine Gallimard.
5. Jean-Louis Barrault.
6. Christiane Faure.
7. Charles Poncet.
8. Madame Albert Camus.
9. Emmanuel Roblès, "Visages d'Albert Camus," in *Simoun* (Oran), No. 31, July 1960.
10. Emmanuel Roblès.
11. Charles Poncet.
12. *Algeria* (Algiers), October 1948.
13. Madame Albert Camus; Christiane Faure.
14. René Char in *La Posterité du soleil*.
15. Maria Casarès.
16. Grenier, *Albert Camus*.
17. *Combat* (Paris), December 9, 1948; Beauvoir, *La Force des choses*.
18. Reprinted in the Pléiade edition of Camus' work from *La Patrie mondiale* of December 1948. Cf. *Le Monde* (Paris), December 5–6, 1948.
19. Jean Bloch-Michel.
20. Maurice Joyeux, *L'Anarchie et la révolte de la jeunnesse* (Tournai, 1970).

## Notes for Chapter Thirty-four

1. Dussane, op. cit.
2. Jean-Louis Barrault in *Cahiers de la Compagnie Madeleine Renaud-Jean-Louis Barrault*, reprinted in *La Table Ronde* (Paris), February 1960.
3. Maria Casarès. Camus told Jean Grenier that there had been twenty-three performances.
4. Jean-Louis Barrault.
5. Fernando Gomez Pelaez.
6. Albert Camus, *España Libre* (Mexico City, 1966).
7. Beauvoir, *La Force des choses*.
8. Edmond Brua; Emmanuel Roblès.
9. Maria Casarès.
10. Mary McCarthy; Miriam Chiaromonte.

11. Copies of the American and French manifestos were furnished by Roger Lapeyre.

12. Roger Lapeyre; Gilbert Walusinski.

13. Robert Jaussaud.

14. Janine Gallimard.

15. Roger Lapeyre.

16. Jean Bloch-Michel.

17. Gilbert Walusinski.

18. Daniel Martinet, in *Témoins* (Zurich), May 1960.

19. *Liberté de l'esprit* (Paris), February and April 1949; Jean Lescure; Suzanne Agnely. Nimier died in an automobile accident in September 1962.

20. Gabriel Audisio; Pierre Blanchar, "Albert Camus, artisan de théâtre," in *Simoun* (Oran), No. 31, July 1960; *La Dépêche de Constantine* (Constantine), March 24, 1949.

21. Madame Albert Camus; Anna Otten, ed., *Les Meilleures pièces radiophoniques françaises* (New York, 1968).

## Notes for Chapter Thirty-five

1. Emile Véran.

2. Robert Jaussaud.

3. Maria Casarès.

4. Camus, *Journaux de voyage,* op. cit.

5. Albert Camus, "Une Macumba au Brésil," in *Livres de France* (Paris), November 1951.

6. *Solidaridad Obrera* (Paris), August 13, 1949.

7. Madame Albert Camus.

8. For most of the foregoing: Maria Casarès.

9. Grenier, *Albert Camus.*

10. Strömberg, op. cit.; Joseph Blotner, *Faulkner* (New York, 1974).

11. Dr. Georges Brouet.

12. Jean Bloch-Michel.

13. Beauvoir, *La Force des choses,* op. cit.

14. Dussane, op. cit.

15. The chief sources for the Cabris period are Maria Casarès and Janine Gallimard.

## Notes for Chapter Thirty-six

1. Madame Albert Camus.

2. Charles Poncet.

3. The chief sources for the writing of *L'Homme révolté* in Cabris were Maria Casarès and Janine Gallimard.

4. Maria Casarès.

5. Dr. Jacques Ménétrier. For a succinct account of his system: Jacques

Ménétrier, *La Médecine en mutation* (Tournai, 1970). In 1977, Dr. Ménétrier's first novel began appearing in installments in *La Nouvelle Revue Française*.

6. Janine Gallimard.

7. Dr. René Lehmann. Dr. Georges Brouet said that Camus never told him about the Ménétrier treatment.

8. Dr. Jacques Ménétrier.

9. Quoted in the Pléiade edition of Camus' work.

10. Joyeux, op. cit. The principal exception to the rule of discretion was of course the Spanish Republican cause. Even in the final weeks of writing *L'Homme révolté,* Camus spoke at a public meeting for Les Amis de l'Espagne Républicaine. Camus, *España Libre.*

11. Beauvoir, *La Force des choses.*

12. Charles Poncet.

13. Maria Casarès.

14. Camus' journal as published ends after one more entry in March 1951. Although he continued to keep the journal all his life, his heirs have chosen not to publish any further volumes of it, since it becomes increasingly personal with what is called Cahier VII, covering the period following the publication of *L'Homme révolté,* the break with Sartre, and the genesis of *La Chute.*

15. Germaine Brée, *Camus,* (New Brunswick, N.J., 1972).

16. *Solidaridad Obrera* (Paris), August 4, 1951. It is reprinted in the Pléiade edition of Camus' work from a 1954 republication.

17. Grenier, *Albert Camus.*

18. Marcelle Bonnet-Blanchet.

## Notes for Chapter Thirty-seven

1. *Arts* (Paris), December 21, 1951.

2. "La Révolte en question," *Le Soleil Noir-Positions* (Paris, 1952).

3. Quoted in the Pléiade edition of Camus' work. When Guy Dumur in *Combat* called attention to the surrealist symposium, René Char wrote Dumur to point out that the contributors to the symposium of good faith had been fooled by the falsely friendly attitude of its sponsors. *Combat* (Paris), March 3, 1952.

4. Maurice Nadeau, *Le Roman français depuis la guerre* (Paris, 1963).

5. Maurice Joyeux. See also Joyeux, op. cit.

6. Maria Casarès.

7. Quoted in the Pléiade edition of Camus' work.

8. Fernando Gomez Pelaez; also Camus, *España Libre.* Camus' speech is published in the Pléiade edition, but not identified as such, reprinted from *Esprit* (Paris) of April 1952.

9. *Comprendre* (Venice), July 1952.

10. Nicolas Nabokov.

11. *Observateur* (Paris), April 24, 1952, June 5, 1952; Claude Bourdet. In

his December 1951 articles Bourdet had said that *L'Homme révolté* was only the first step, for he believed that a truly scientific Marxism living up to Camus' moral standards could exist.

12. Francis Jeanson.

13. Jacques-Laurent Bost.

14. Beauvoir, *La Force des choses.*

15. *Le Monde* (Paris), June 21, 1952. This letter is the source of the often repeated error that Camus "resigned" from UNESCO.

16. Madame Albert Camus.

17. *Revue d'Histoire du Théâtre* (Paris), October–December 1960.

18. Janine Gallimard.

19. Camus' letter is published in full in the Pléiade edition of his work with a footnote indicating that Sartre had invited him to reply to Jeanson.

20. See, for example, Daniel, *Le Temps qui reste.* But Daniel, who was of course an admirer of Camus, said that in rereading the polemic in the 1970s he was no longer certain that Sartre's victory was total. For a curious interpretation of the split, see Conor Cruise O'Brien's *Camus* (London, 1970), in which the author finds that the quarrel was deformed to Camus' *advantage* because of the general intellectual climate of the time, i.e., the discrediting of intellectuals who refused to be anti-Communist. According to O'Brien these efforts were secretly encouraged by the U. S. Government.

21. Jean Lescure.

22. *Le Monde* (Paris), September 24, 1952.

23. Robert Gallimard.

24. Renée Gallimard (née Thomasset). Mascolo and another Gallimard editor, Robert Anthelme, both former Communists, could not sympathize with Camus' anti-Communism even if they opposed Sartre's pro-Stalinism, in addition to which they felt that Camus was then too infatuated with his own success. Dionys Mascolo.

## Notes for Chapter Thirty-eight

1. Guy Dumur.

2. Jacques-Laurent Bost.

3. Beauvoir, *La Force des choses.*

4. Editions Gallimard.

5. Francis Jeanson. Camus felt that every time Sartre took a political stand he was wrong, while he himself never wanted to be a "political" writer. Georges Altschuler.

6. Nadeau, op. cit.

7. Janine Gallimard.

8. Beauvoir, *La Force des choses.* On its publication in 1954 Beauvoir's novel *Les Mandarins* was often taken to include an only slightly disguised portrait of Camus, and of the Camus-Sartre split, although in *La Force des choses* she denied that the novel had been a *roman à clef*—a genre she said she detests. She insisted that Camus was not "Henri Perron," Sartre was not

"Robert Dubreuilh," nor she "Anne." Nevertheless her "Perron" is a journalist and acclaimed author who has written *the* novel of the occupation, his wife plays the piano and sings, he is a woman chaser (he even likes "Anne"), and he publishes a left-of-center but anti-Party newspaper called *L'Espoir.* "Perron"'s original relationship to "Dubreuilh"'s political group is not very different from Camus' to Sartre's RDR.

9. Apart from his autobiographical *Les Mots,* Sartre commented on his family situation in *Situations X—politique et autobiographie* (Paris, 1976).

10. Pierre-André Emery.

11. Sartre, *Situations X.*

12. Manès Sperber.

13. Dr. Jacques Ménétrier.

14. Francis Jeanson.

15. Quoted in the Pléiade edition of Camus' work.

16. Camus had been asked by the Congress for Cultural Freedom to sign an appeal with Jacques Maritain, Karl Jaspers, Julian Huxley, Ignazio Silone, John Dos Passos, François Mauriac, et al., which denounced the Prague trial and the World Peace Congress, but he objected to the tactic of linking the two events, and preferred an appeal not sponsored by any organization. (Family papers, courtesy of Madame Albert Camus.) While remaining aloof from organizational initiatives, he was prepared to act in cases of individual distress, e.g., in the Henri Martin case discussed in this chapter. Later Czeslaw Milosz would say that Camus was one of the few Western intellectuals to offer a helping hand when he left Stalinist Poland in 1951. Others considered him something of a leper or a sinner against the "future," while Camus' friendship helped Milosz survive in the labyrinthe of the West. *Preuves* (Paris), April 1960.

17. *Revue d'Histoire du Théâtre* (Paris), October–December 1960.

18. Maria Casarès; Janine Gallimard.

## Notes for Chapter Thirty-nine

1. Maria Casarès.

2. Noël Schumann.

3. Gabriel Audisio.

4. Paul Raffi; Pierre-André Emery.

5. *Sipario* (Milan), October 1960.

6. *Le Courrier de l'Ouest* (Angers), June 22, 1953.

7. *Gazette de Lausanne* (Lausanne), March 27–28, 1954.

8. *Le Courrier de l'Ouest* (Angers), June 16, 1953.

9. Suzanne Agnely; Robert Cérésol.

10. Raymond Sigaudès.

11. Madame Albert Camus.

12. Quoted in the Pléiade edition of Camus' work.

13. *Le Monde* (Paris), July 19–20, 1953. Background in *Le Monde* of July 16.

14. Quoted in the Pléiade edition of Camus' work, where it is dated October 1953.

15. For most of the foregoing: Maria Casarès.

16. *Démenti* (Liège), October 15, 1953.

17. Barbara Izard and Clara Hieronymus, *Requiem for a Nun: On Stage and Off* (Nashville, Tenn., 1970); Blotner, op. cit. The Pléiade edition of Camus' work contains an interview with Camus and supplementary information on how he came to adapt the Faulkner novel.

18. *Combat* (Paris), November 28, 1953.

19. Madeleine Jaussaud.

20. Gilbert Walusinski; Robert Proix. See also *Témoins* (Zurich), especially Robert Proix, "Albert Camus, tel que je l'ai connu," Spring 1963.

21. Maurice Joyeux.

22. Joyeux, op. cit.

23. *Révolution Prolétarienne* (Paris), February 1960.

24. Jean-Claude Brisville, *Camus* (Paris, 1959).


## Notes for Chapter Forty

1. Gabriel Audisio; Edmond Brua. For the texts of Camus' letters and other documents see Jean Pomier, *Chronique d'Alger (1910–1957) ou le temps des Algérianistes* (Paris, 1972).

2. *Gazette de Lausanne* (Lausanne), March 27–28, 1954.

3. See Chapter 39.

4. Quoted in the Pléiade edition of Camus' work.

5. Preserved in the Adès album, "Presence d'Albert Camus."

6. Gabriel Audisio.

7. Janine Gallimard.

8. Strömberg, op. cit.

9. Maria Casarès.

10. Ageron, op. cit.

11. *Combat* (Paris), September 25–26, 1954.

12. Maria Casarès. The popular weekly *Journal du Dimanche* (Paris) reported on November 28, presumably as a result of the talk with Mrs. Baur, that Camus would replace Jean Marchat (who was occupied at the Comédie Française) as a director, to do his first Paris productions, starting with a play whose title would be announced later, and then with a revival of *Le Malentendu*.

13. *Quaderni ACI* 16 (Turin, Associazione Culturale Italiana).

14. Essentially from Maria Casarès.

15. Francesco Grandjacquet; Miriam Chiaromonte.

16. *Revue d'Histoire du Théâtre*.

17. *Le Monde Libertaire* (Paris), February 1955.

18. Noël Schumann.
19. *L'Echo d'Alger* (Algiers), February 26, 1955.

## Notes for Chapter Forty-one

1. See Buzzati's remarks quoted in the Pléiade edition of Camus' work.
2. Quoted from *Corriere d'Informazione* (Milan), January 5, 1960, in the Pléiade edition of Camus' work.
3. Maria Casarès.
4. *L'Express* (Paris), April 2, 1955.
5. Published in the Pléiade edition of Camus' work. In his Bieber preface Camus praised René Char's poetry as "the greatest work born of the Resistance."
6. *To Vima* (Athens), April 28, 1955 (by L. Karapanayotis).
7. Text of the lecture published in the Pléiade edition of Camus' work.
8. Madame Albert Camus; Janine Gallimard; Miriam Chiaromonte.
9. Françoise Giroud.
10. Jean Daniel; Pierre Mendès France. According to Jean Bloch-Michel it was when Camus met Mendès and was "charmed" by him that he agreed to write for *L'Express*.
11. Pierre Viansson-Ponté.
12. According to the Pléiade edition of Camus' work, Maurice Nadeau wrote Camus to say that he had been responsible for the May 12 item, and to express regrets for the incident.
13. Stéphane was indicted for writing articles alleged to give information to the enemy during the French Indochina War (the articles compared public statements of French officials with what they were saying privately). He was arrested and jailed in March 1955, released in April. The investigation continued but he was never brought to trial. Claude Bourdet. (See *France-Observateur* (Paris), March 3, March 31, and April 28, 1955).
14. Robert Namia.
15. Jean Bloch-Michel. But Françoise Giroud said that Mauriac changed his attitude toward Camus when he learned about his working class origins, which she said happened during the *Express* period.
16. Jean Daniel.
17. Dr. René Lehmann. Dr. Georges Brouet also felt that, so far as his tuberculosis was concerned, Camus could have lived another twenty years beyond 1960 had he taken certain precautions, despite the lung damage and scars.
18. Blotner, op. cit.
19. Fernando Gomez Pelaez.
20. *Le Monde Libertaire* (Paris), November 1955.

## Notes for Chapter Forty-two

1. Quoted in the Pléiade edition of Camus' work.
2. Editions Gallimard.

3. Jean Bloch-Michel.

4. Christiane Faure.

5. Suzanne Agnely.

6. Maria Casarès.

7. Warren Tucker, *"La Chute:* Voie du salut terrestre" (in French) in *The French Review* (Chapel Hill, N.C.), April 1970.

8. André Abbou, "Les Structures superficielles du discours dans *La Chute,"* in *Revue des Lettres Modernes* (Paris), Nos. 238–44, 1970.

9. Yves Courrières, *Le Temps des léopards* (Paris, 1969).

10. Essentially from Charles Poncet and Louis Miquel.

11. Emmanuel Roblès.

12. Pierre-André Emery.

13. Laurent Preziosi.

14. Charles Poncet.

15. Amar Ouzegane.

16. Mohamed Lebjaoui, *Vérités sur la Révolution Algérienne* (Paris, 1970). Before the civil truce meeting Camus was approached by Yves Doyon, his Belcourt elementary school classmate who was then an intelligence officer. Doyon felt that Camus had been tricked by his former friends Ouzegane and Lebjaoui, who, unknown to Camus, were FLN members. Doyon said he warned Camus that the two Moslems were anti-French, but he felt that Camus did not want to believe him. Yves Doyon.

17. Amar Ouzegane. See also Ouzegane, *Le Meilleur combat* (Paris, 1962).

18. Lebjaoui, op. cit.

19. Jean de Maisonseul. Ouzegane also believed that it was thanks to the FLN that Camus could read his civil truce speech on the radio, but Maisonseul doubts the FLN had a role in that.

20. Amar Ouzegane. Lebjaoui said that 1,200 FLN militants were stationed inside or near the hall, many armed but with orders to avoid incidents. Lebjaoui, op. cit.

21. Charles Poncet; Lebjaoui, op. cit.

22. Edmond Brua.

23. Gabriel Audisio.

24. Charles Poncet; Louis Miquel; Amar Ouzegane; Lebjaoui, op. cit. A different account of the dénouement is recalled by Yves Dechezelles, who had taken the draft civil truce convention to Messali at his remote exile residence at Belle-Ile-en-Mer, and returned to tell Camus that Messali had approved the draft with reservations (Messali felt that violence of Frenchmen and Moslems could not be equated because of the massive means available to the French, while the guerrillas had to improvise). But when Dechezelles called on Camus at Gallimard Camus told him, he said, *"Mon pauvre ami,* there is no point revising the text. The FLN representative just left this office after telling me they are withdrawing their agreement." Dechezelles believed that it was from this moment that Camus became bitter; feeling unsure of himself, he would not engage himself more deeply.

25. Daniel, *Le Temps qui reste.*

26. *Revue d'Histoire du Théâtre*

27. Cited in the Pléiade edition of Camus' work, confirmed to the author by Roblès.

## Notes for Chapter Forty-three

1. Beauvoir, *La Force des choses*. Francis Jeanson did not read *La Chute* when it was first published, for he would have praised it; he felt it to be remarkable. But he also believed that it was a way for Camus to say: "We're all like that." It was a *mea culpa* at the expense of others, an attempt at salvation through confession, while bringing everyone else into the guilt. Jeanson.

2. Guy Dumur.

3. Daniel, *Le Temps qui reste*.

4. Roger Quilliot, *La Mer et les Prisons* (revised edition: Paris, 1970).

5. For a summary of the scholarly work on *La Chute: Revue des Lettres Modernes* (Paris), Nos. 238–44, 1970. Cf. O'Brien, op. cit.

6. Editions Gallimard.

7. Did Camus obtain the apartment through Char? Robert Cérésol of the Mathurins Theater, who was a frequent companion of Camus at that time—he and Suzanne Agnely helped him pack his belongings into two suitcases to move from the Palais Royal hotel to the new apartment—said that it was he who found the apartment through a rental agent. In that case the fact that Char lived in the building would be coincidence.

8. Suzanne Agnely; Jean Bloch-Michel; Catherine Sellers; Maria Casarès; Pierre Cardinal; Robert Cérésol.

9. Jean de Maisonseul; Louis Miquel.

10. Maria Casarès.

11. A chronological account of the negotiations and correspondence, and a comparison of the different versions of *Requiem*, is given in Izard & Hieronymus, op. cit. The authors, natives of Mississippi then involved in university theater in Nashville, Tennessee, carried out a detailed investigation of the various productions of the play.

12. Christiane Faure.

13. Robert Cérésol; Izard & Hieronymus, op. cit.

14. Catherine Sellers.

15. Charles Poncet.

16. Janine Gallimard.

17. The scruples Camus then felt about his stories come through in a letter to Char which his editor dates July 21, 1956:

> The more I produce and the less I am certain. On the road along which the artist walks, night falls ever more densely. Finally he dies blind. My only faith is that light dwells within him, that he cannot see it but that it shines all the same. But how to be certain . . . ?

Quoted in the Pléiade edition of Camus' work.

18. Robert Cérésol; Catherine Sellers; Suzanne Agnely.

19. Robert Cérésol.

20. Fernando Gomez Pelaez.

21. Published in the Pléiade edition of Camus' work.

22. Lebjaoui, op. cit. But Amar Ouzegane, who also revealed his FLN connection to Camus, remembered that Camus offered to hide *one* FLN militant, a particular person who had been a member of the Civil Truce Committee. Ouzegane lived in clandestinity from April 1956 to January 1958, then was held in prison until April 1962, so that he had no further contact with Camus, and was not available, for example, at the time that Lebjaoui says Camus made the offer.

## Notes for Chapter Forty-four

1. Quoted in the Pléiade edition of Camus' work.

2. And in the French magazine *Demain,* whose editor in chief was Jean Bloch-Michel. The French text from this magazine is published in the Pléiade edition of Camus' work.

3. Manès Sperber.

4. Maria Casarès.

5. In *Mercure de France* (Paris), May 1957.

6. *L'Express* (Paris), July 12, 1957.

7. *Demain* (Paris), July 17, 1957.

8. Published in the Pléiade edition of Camus' work.

9. Pierre Mendès France.

10. Emmanuel Roblès. Long after Camus' death, in a television interview, Mammeri, who apparently prefers the spelling Mamri, observed that as great as Camus was, he had not been able to escape his condition. He was a *pied noir* and could not, despite intellectual effort, be other than the son of poor whites. He added that he was not disturbed by the absence of Moslems in Camus' work; that was part of his sincerity. "Albert Camus," film by Cécile Clairval, shown on France's Second Channel in May 1974. (Mammeri does not mention and may not have known about Camus' desire to help him in 1957.)

11. Emmanuel Roblès.

12. Madame Albert Camus.

13. Suzanne Agnely.

14. Janine Gallimard.

15. Editions Gallimard.

16. Jean-Pierre Jorris; Jean Bloch-Michel; Robert Cérésol.

17. Georges Lerminier in *Le Parisien* (Paris), June 24, 1957.

18. Yves Dechezelles.

19. Claire Targuebayre, *Cordes,* published in the illustrated Sites de France series by Edouard Privat (Toulouse, 1954).

20. Claire Targuebayre.

21. Jean-Pierre Jorris.

22. Quoted from Pléiade edition of Camus' work, and from Quilliot, op. cit.

23. Strömberg, op. cit.

24. Blanche Knopf, "Albert Camus in the Sun," in *Atlantic Monthly* (Boston), February 1961.

25. Patricia Blake.

26. Pierre Cardinal.

27. Daniel, *Le Temps qui reste.*

28. Ambassador Hans Colliander; see also Kjell Strömberg, introduction to *La Peste* (Nobel edition by Rombaldi: Paris, n.d.).

29. *La Presse Libre* (Algiers), October 18, 1957. *Le Monde* of October 19 quoted Camus: "I heard the news as everyone else did, last night, before it was official. But I didn't dare believe it. Besides, for me it was an unexpected award: My work is unfinished, and I should have liked to see them honor André Malraux, who has always been my master."

30. Apparently Camus was sounded out prior to the Swedish Academy's vote, or the announcement of it, by a discreet visit to his office at Gallimard: Would he accept the prize, would he bring his wife to Stockholm? If so, this would have been an unofficial and totally unorthodox procedure, perhaps by cultural attaché Kjell Strömberg, acting on behalf of an uncle who was a member of the Academy. But Strömberg never mentioned it to his ambassador, nor did he record it in his memoirs. Ambassador Ragnar Kumlin. Yet Suzanne Agnely remembered such a visit. Camus later told Louis Miquel that he had spent the first night (October 16–17) asking himself if he would accept the prize. If he accepted, while thinking that Malraux deserved it more than he did, it was because he realized it had been given to him because of the Algerian drama.

31. Madame Sophie L. de Vilmorin. Malraux told Manès Sperber that the press campaign against Camus was ignoble, a conspiracy of "failures, homosexuals, etc." and Sperber let Camus know what Malraux had said. Manès Sperber.

### Notes for Chapter Forty-five

1. *Le Figaro Littéraire* (Paris), October, 26, 1957.

2. *Le Monde* (Paris), October 19, 1957.

3. Blotner, op. cit.

4. Charles Poncet.

5. Guibert, op. cit.

6. Published in the Pléiade edition of Camus' work.

7. André Belamich; Roger Grenier.

8. Madeleine Benichou.

9. Christiane Faure.

10. Suzanne Agnely.

11. Robert Cérésol.

12. Robert Jaussaud.

13. Jean Bloch-Michel.

14. *The Times* (London), October 31, 1957; Madame Albert Camus.

15. Madame Albert Camus. Dery received a nine-year prison sentence but was amnestied in 1960. He died in 1977.

16. *Le Monde* (Paris), November 6, 1957. He would also write a preface for *La Vérité sur l'affaire Nagy* (Paris, 1958), published in English a year later as *The Truth About the Nagy Affair*.

17. Madame Albert Camus. The fact that Camus' draft message to the court was not sent was later confirmed to Suzanne Agnely. Defense witnesses at the trial privately criticized Camus' absence, several citing his views on the stand, not without malice, according to Beauvoir, *La Force des choses*, op. cit.

18. Jean-Pierre Jorris.

19. An expert amateur, Alfred Knopf took a photograph of Camus one sunny morning outside the Grand Hotel, which he would later publish in a souvenir album, *Sixty Photographs* (New York, 1975), commemorating his sixtieth anniversary as a publisher.

20. Carl-Gustaf Bjurström, who kept a log of the trip in the form of letters to his wife. Bjurström's recollections and letters are used throughout this report of the Stockholm trip.

21. Janine Gallimard.

22. Ambassador Hans Colliander.

23. "Presence d'Albert Camus" record album.

24. Essentially from *Le Monde* (Paris), December 12, 1957, dispatch by Dominique Birmann; and from Carl-Gustaf Bjurström.

25. Blanche Knopf, op. cit. *Le Malentendu* was presented on Swedish television that night.

26. *Le Monde* (Paris), December 14, 1957 (Dominique Birmann).

27. Ibid. In his letter of December 17 to *Le Monde*, Camus approved this text of his remarks.

28. Georg Svensson.

## Notes for Chapter Forty-six

1. In *Preuves* (Paris), March 1958, reprinted in the Pléiade edition of Camus' work.

2. Raymond Guilloré, "Albert Camus et nous," in *Révolution Prolétarienne* (Paris), February 1960.

3. Emmanuel Roblès.

4. Suzanne Agnely.

5. Quoted in the Pléiade edition of Camus' work.

6. Robert Cérésol.

7. Jean-Pierre Jorris.

8. In his 1944 essay-review of Parain's "Sur une philosophie de l'expression," reprinted in the Pléiade edition of Camus' work, Camus wrote: "The miracle consists in returning to the words of everybody, but in adding the necessary honesty in order to diminish lying and hatred. In fact this is a path

toward silence, a relative silence, since absolute silence is impossible." He quoted Parain: "Language is only a means to draw us toward its contrary which is silence and which is God." (From Parain's *Recherches sur la nature et les fonctions de langage,* Paris, 1943.)

9. Catherine Sellers.

10. Madeleine Jaussaud.

11. The name of the writer of the letter is in the author's possession.

12. Raymond Sigaudès.

13. Charles Poncet.

14. Charles Poncet; Yves Dechezelles.

15. Merry and Serge Bromberger, *Les 13 Complots du 13 Mai* (Paris, 1959).

16. Institut Charles de Gaulle.

17. Jules Roy.

18. Madame Albert Camus.

19. Lucien Camus.

20. Mouloud Feraoun, "Au-Dessus des Haines," in *Simoun* (Oran), No. 31, July 1960. Jean Bloch-Michel got in touch with Feraoun through Camus. Later Feraoun sent an article to *Preuves,* of which Bloch-Michel was an editor, asking for anonymity, because in the situation in Algeria one remained silent or died. Three days after Bloch-Michel received it Feraoun had been murdered by the Secret Army, known as the OAS. Bloch-Michel nevertheless published the article without his signature. Jean Bloch-Michel.

21. Emmanuel Roblès.

22. Micheline Rozan.

23. Janine Gallimard.

24. Jean de Maisonseul.

25. Guy Dumur.

26. Maria Casarès.

27. Lacouture, op. cit. He also reported that in April 1958, prior to de Gaulle's return to power, Camus had refused to join Malraux, Martin du Gard, Mauriac, and Sartre in a petition to President Coty protesting the government's seizure of a book describing the army's torture methods in Algeria, and demanding a governmental declaration on torture.

28. Manès Sperber.

29. During Camus' trip to Greece, Micheline Rozan issued a press release in his name to say that by friendly agreement the producer-director Diego Fabbri would not produce in Paris his own adaptation of *Les Possédés,* already staged in Italy, Germany, and Latin America.

30. Published in the Pléiade edition of Camus' work.

31. Jean Cornut.

32. Dr. and Mrs. Olivier Monod.

## Notes for Chapter Forty-seven

1. *Robert Laurent-Vibert: In Memoriam* (Lyons, 1971). According to Dr. Olivier Monod, the brother of Jean Varille (administrator of the Fondation) had also died in an automobile accident on the Lourmarin-Lyons road.

2. Dr. and Mrs. Olivier Monod; Franck Creac'h; Fondation Laurent-Vibert; Henri Meynard; personal observation.

3. According to the Pléiade edition of Camus' work.

4. Catherine Sellers.

5. Michel Bouquet.

6. Pierre Blanchar, "Albert Camus, artisan de théâtre," in *Simoun* (Oran), No. 31, July 1960.

7. Louis Lecoin, *Le Cours d'une vie* (Paris, 1965). Other documents courtesy of Franck Creac'h, Lourmarin. Camus told Creac'h that, while not a conscientious objector himself, he believed them to be courageous individuals whom it was intolerable to keep in prison. According to Pierre Martin, who met Camus in Algeria while Martin was on a voluntary work project of the Service Civil International, Camus was interested in their pacifist activities and asked for further information on conscientious objection. (Martin had been in prison for that crime.) Then, when Martin's friend Lecoin began to publish *Liberté*, he asked Martin to join him for that task, and Martin in turn asked Camus to join Lecoin's sponsoring committee.

8. Gabriel Audisio; press release "Informations culturelles" of the French Algerian representation in Paris; *L'Echo d'Alger* (Algiers), November 13, 1958; "Presence d'Albert Camus" record album.

9. Robert Mallet, "Présent à la vie, étranger à la mort," in *Hommage à Albert Camus*.

10. Amar Ouzegane.

11. Lacouture, op. cit.

12. Madame Albert Camus.

13. Suzanne Agnely.

14. Micheline Rozan.

15. Dr. Olivier Monod.

16. "Afterword" by Marc Slonim to Fyodor Dostoevsky, *The Possessed* (tr. by Andrew R. MacAndrews), New American Library ed. (New York, 1962).

17. Reproduced in *Paris-Match* (Paris), January 16, 1960.

18. Quoted in the Pléiade edition of Camus' work.

19. Janine Gallimard; Edmond Brua.

20. Pierre Cardinal.

21. Micheline Rozan. The text is published in the Pléiade edition of Camus' work.

22. Roger Reynaud.

23. Henri Baumas.

24. Franck Creac'h.

25. Juliette Lisle, curator of the castle; Jean Varille, administrator of the Lourmarin Foundation and president of the Association des Amis de Lourmarin.

26. *Paris-Presse l'Intransigeant* (Paris), January 7, 1960.

27. *Revue d'Histoire du Théâtre*, op. cit.

28. Carl-Gustaf Bjurström.

29. The author of this book spoke to a key figure in these negotiations on

the government side, who remarked that Camus was interested in theater mainly as a place to meet girls. If this was his attitude in 1959, Camus' frustrating experience with Malraux's aides can be understood.

30. After Camus' death a program of the Athénée Theater contained a note to the effect that the 1960–61 season was to have opened *"sur un spectacle par Albert Camus."*

31. Georges Elgozy. The state of Camus' feelings may be gleaned from the report of his friend Bloch-Michel to readers of *Partisan Review* (New York) in the fall 1959 issue. While Malraux had undertaken to reorganize the state-subsidized national theaters, Bloch-Michel wrote, on experimental theaters "it must be confessed that the Minister has done nothing, even if he had talked a little. He has 'given' the Théâtre Récamier to Vilar for experimental plays; he has promised one to Camus. Of course it is odd that Vilar should be given a theater when he already has one, while Camus is merely promised one, though he had none." But Vilar had already arranged to take over the Récamier; Malraux could only confirm the decision. As for Camus, "this promise is likely not to be kept for some time: first a theater must be found, and besides, the subsidies allocated for the two 'théâtres d'essai' are so minimal that Camus will hesitate to commit himself, even if a theater is found for him." According to Camus' secretary, Suzanne Agnely, on January 4, 1960, the day of Camus' death, she had received a phone call from Malraux's secretary at Gallimard informing her that Malraux wished to offer Camus the direction of the Comédie Française (then in the throes of what the press called a leadership crisis). But Malraux later denied to this author that he intended to offer Camus anything other than the experimental theater proposed by Camus.

32. Micheline Rozan. She worked at MCA's French company until its dissolution in 1962, and then became an associate of theater director Peter Brook, who used Paris as a basis for theatrical activities. During her association with Camus she was also in touch with American (and other) theater and film producers on his behalf, e.g., with William Wyler, who once hoped to do a movie version of *La Peste;* Sidney Lumet, who wanted *La Chute* for American television, Laurence Olivier to be the star; Lillian Hellman, who discussed the possibility of adapting Camus' *Les Possédés* for the American stage.

## Notes for Chapter Forty-eight

1. Extracts are available in the "Presence d'Albert Camus" album.
2. Pierre Cardinal.
3. *Il Gazzettino* (Venice), July 9, 1959 (interview by Aldo Camerino).
4. *Il Gazzettino* (Venice), July 10, 1959 (review by Alberto Bertolini).
5. *Il Gazzettino* (Venice), July 11, 1959.
6. Michel Bouquet.
7. Christiane Faure. It is not known whose rough translation he was using.

8. Quoted in the Pléiade edition. But Camus would have been in Lourmarin for two weeks when he wrote the letter, according to Catherine Sellers' correspondence with him.

9. Catherine Sellers.

10. Michel de Saint-Pierre.

11. Robert Cérésol.

12. Michel de Saint-Pierre. The play was staged at the Mathurins on September 21, 1959, with Louis Ducreux in the role of Damville.

13. Mallet, op. cit.

14. Dr. Léon Cottenceau.

15. Edmond Brua.

16. Jean Bloch-Michel; Jean de Maisonseul.

17. Quoted in the Pléiade edition of Camus' work.

18. *Nouvel Observateur* (Paris), October 11, 1976. Other friends would report premonitions of the accident. André Chouraqui had just commented to friends about Camus' work: "He's at the end of the road; he's dead." Then, seeing an actress with whom he thought Camus was involved on the street with another man, he said to himself: "She's finishing him off." When he heard about the accident he felt as if he had killed Camus. Suzanne Agnely decided that Camus himself had a premonition because prior to his final trip to Lourmarin he organized his papers as if he were not going to return.

19. Roblès transposed the action to Indonesia, and when Camus read the play in Lourmarin he was afraid that the "Indonesians" were favored over the "Dutch," throwing off the balance required by tragedy. The play was later produced in France, Belgium, the United States, and Great Britain.

20. Maria Casarès.

21. Micheline Rozan.

22. Dionys Mascolo.

23. Confidential conversation.

24. Jean-Pierre Jorris. According to Morvan Lebesque, in *Camus par lui-même* (Paris, 1963), a local photographer caught Camus in the Marseilles theater: While the audience is laughing, Camus is watching his actors anxiously.

25. *Le Méridional* (Marseilles), January 6, 1960.

26. *La Semaine à Aix* (Aix-en-Provence), January 7, 1961.

27. Published in an extract in the Pléiade edition of his work.

28. From the French version in *Liberté* (Paris), May 1, 1960.

29. Jean Grenier, *Albert Camus; France-Soir* (Paris), January 6, 1960.

30. Madame Albert Camus.

31. Sarocchi, op.cit.

32. Henri Baumas.

33. Franck Creac'h.

## Notes for Chapter Forty-nine

1. The chief source of information for the automobile trip is Janine Gallimard.

2. Madame Paul Blanc, Au Chapon Fin, Thoissey.

3. M. Sandré, Hôtel de Paris et de la Poste, Sens.

4. It was reported that her husband exclaimed: "Merde!" as if the wheel was not responding.

5. Among sources used, or compared, for the reconstruction of the accident: *Le Figaro* (Paris), January 5 and 6, 1960; *Paris-Presse l'Intransigeant* (Paris), January 6, 1960; *Paris-Jour (Paris)*, January 5, 1960; *France-Soir* (Paris), January 7, 1960; *L'Aurore* (Paris), January 6, 1960.

6. Madame Albert Camus. The typescript translation of *Othello,* the first three acts of which were revised in Camus' handwriting, was found in the valise he had checked through to Paris by rail.

7. For most of the description of Villeblevin and of the events of January 4–5 there: Madame Virginie Peugnet, the village teacher.

8. Guy Schoeller.

9. Janine Gallimard.

10. Paul Maillot.

11. Madeleine Benichou. *France-Soir* reporter Helène Karsenty wrote that she went to the Rue Madame apartment just before 5 P.M. Madame Camus asked why she wanted to see her, and the reporter didn't have the heart to tell her why she was there, instead said she was writing a story on contemporary authors. Francine Camus was taking off her hat as she spoke, the children were in the next room listening to them. As the reporter left she heard the phone ring, then a cry: *"Mon petit! Mon petit!"* and a body falling. Francine Camus had fainted, the children were calling: *"Maman! Maman!"* According to this account, Malraux phoned Gaston Gallimard at about 3:15 P.M., and he told Michel's father Raymond. *France-Soir* (Paris), January 6, 1960.

12. Suzanne Agnely.

13. Madeleine Benichou.

14. Emmanuel Roblès, "Visages d'Albert Camus," in *Simoun* (Oran), No. 31, July 1960.

15. Virginie Peugnet; Madame Albert Camus.

16. Virginie Peugnet.

17. From press reports, e.g., *Paris-Jour* (Paris), January 5, 1960; *Paris-Presse l'Intransigeant* (Paris), January 6, 1960.

18. Mallet, op. cit.

19. *France-Soir* (Paris), January 6, 1960; *Paris-Presse l'Intransigeant* (Paris), January 7, 1960.

20. *Le Monde* (Paris), January 6, 1960.

21. Charles F. Masterson of the National Safety Council (U.S.) wrote a letter to the editor of the New York *Times* that day, printed in the January 10 issue, to say that the proper response of the thinking man to accidents such as Camus' was to prevent accidents, and asked for contributions to the work of his organization.

22. Lebesque, op. cit.; Jean-Louis Barrault; *France-Soir* (Paris), January 6, 1960.

23. Essentially from Madame Albert Camus; Franck Creac'h, and press

reports, including *Le Monde* (Paris), January 7, 1960; *Le Figaro* (Paris), January 7, 1960; *Paris-Presse l'Intransigeant* (Paris), January 7, 1960.

24. Pierre-André Emery. Another story has it that it was killed by frost—or smothered by rosemary.

25. Madame Albert Camus; Franck Creac'h.

## Notes for Chapter Fifty

1. Beauvoir, *La Force des choses*. Coincidentally, Claude Lanzmann was working for the same newspaper as Pierre Benichou; he was phoning Beauvoir while Benichou was calling his mother, Francine Camus' friend. See Chapter 49.

2. *Le Monde* (Paris) January 19, 1960; February 23, 1960; January 5, 1961.

3. Grenier, *Albert Camus*.

4. Michel Bouquet.

5. In *Le Figaro* (Paris), January 7, 1960.

6. *L'Aurore* (Paris), January 6, 1960.

7. *France-Soir* (Paris), January 7, 1960.

8. René Etiemble.

9. The characteristics of this French automobile as given: 335 CV, with a 5,907 cc motor and a maximum speed of 130 mph (205 kph). It was a two-door sedan with separated seats in front, selling at the time for 3,850,000 francs. It was reportedly a little over a year old and had gone 29,700 km. *L'Aurore* (Paris), January 6, 1960; *France-Soir* (Paris), January 7, 1960. The garage handbook says the HK series was manufactured in 1959, and the *cyclindrée* of 5 liters 907 corresponded to 34 fiscal horse-power (the French official terminology).

10. René Etiemble; Janine Gallimard. The court's finding, in the suit of the Camus heirs against the driver of the automobile, was that Michel Gallimard had been driving too fast, given the condition and pressure of the tires. No fault was attributed to the manufacturer. (*Jugement, Tribunal de Sens,* April 4, 1963.)

11. New York *Times* (New York), February 17, 1960.

12. New York *Times* (New York), April 23, 1960.

13. Jean de Maisonseul.

14. Edmond Brua.

15. Louis Benisti; Jean de Maisonseul.

# INDEX

740 INDEX